Max-Planck-Institut für ausländisches
öffentliches Recht und Völkerrecht

Beiträge zum ausländischen öffentlichen Recht und Völkerrecht

Begründet von Viktor Bruns

Herausgegeben von
Armin von Bogdandy · Rüdiger Wolfrum

Band 189

Eyal Benvenisti · Chaim Gans · Sari Hanafi (eds.)

Israel and the Palestinian Refugees

Springer
the language of science

ISSN 0172-4770
ISBN 978-3-540-68160-1 Springer Berlin · Heidelberg · New York

Bibliografische Information Der Deutschen Bibliothek

Die Deutsche Bibliothek verzeichnet diese Publikation in der Deutschen Nationalbibliografie; detaillierte bibliografische Daten sind im Internet über <http://dnb.ddb.de> abrufbar.

Printed in Germany

Satz: Reproduktionsfertige Vorlagen vom Autor
Druck- und Bindearbeiten: Strauss Offsetdruck, Mörlenbach
SPIN: 11948438 64/3153 – 5 4 3 2 1 0 – Gedruckt auf säurefreiem Papier

Introduction

This edited book offers diverse perspectives on the Palestinian refugee problem and the possible ways to facilitate its resolution. The book contains contributions of Israeli, Palestinian and other scholars, and its main goal is to initiate an informed dialogue that will bridge the "knowledge gap" between the different camps. The book is the culmination of a joint effort to assist people to realize how people on the other side envision the problem and the possible ways to resolve it, and to gain a comparative perspective on refugee problems and their resolution efforts in other parts of the world. The contributors come from diverse disciplines and backgrounds and their various contributions provide a comprehensive picture of the various aspects of the problem and of the possible means of its resolution.

The Palestinian refugees problem is perhaps the most acute challenge to a peaceful settlement of the Israeli-Palestinian conflict. It is a challenge that scholars must address in a calm and detached manner, but at the same time a deeply emotional matter that even the most sophisticated scholars find difficult to engage without compromising their academic integrity. Despite these difficulties, we undertook the task of convening a meeting where the papers were presented and of the publication of this book because we think the contributions in this book provide perspectives that contribute to the initiation of a constructive dialogue among the relevant communities.

Some of us found some of the contributions contained in this book severely biased and even offensive. We faced the tough choice between giving up the goal of publication and publishing a book that contains what some of us consider to be serious flaws that the authors refused to correct or address. Our ultimate decision was to publish the book, despite those flaws, because our initial goal remained valid: we think that it is important for people on all sides to realize the ways others conceive of the problem, discuss it, analyze it, however flawed we may think of these ways. In this sense, this book is not only an academic enterprise but also in itself evidence that calls for further academic analysis. Needless to say, each of the contributors is responsible solely for her or his contribution, and the editors are not responsible for any of the contributions.

It is a sign of hope that despite the wide gaps in approaches, the interaction between the Israeli and the Palestinian participants was always respectful and friendly. The discussions held during a workshop hosted by the Max Planck Institute for Comparative Public Law and International Law in Heidelberg in July 2003 proved that more discussions, rather than less, are necessary for any progress can be made.

The editors thank the Max Planck Institute for Comparative Public Law and International Law in Heidelberg and in particular its Directors, Professors Jochen Abr. Frowein, Rüdiger Wolfrum and Armin von Bogdandy, for hosting the workshop in July 2003 and for the generous financial support required for the convening of the workshop and the editorial process of this book. We also thank Drs. Ebrahim Afsah, Volker Röben and Thomas Straub for their crucial support in organizing the workshop and preparing the book for publication. Eyal Benvenisti and Chaim Gans thank the Cegla Center for Interdisciplinary Research of the Law and the Minerva Center for Human Rights, both at Tel Aviv University, for supporting the study of the Palestinian refugees problem and the workshop.

Two of the participants in this dialogue have tragically passed away after our workshop. Arthur C. Helton, an American lawyer and internationally-renowned human rights activist, died August 19, 2003 in the bombing of the U.N. headquarters in Baghdad, Iraq. Shelly Fried, an Israeli historian, died December 13, 2004 of an illness. For both of them the study of the Palestinian problem and its resolution was not only an academic exercise but also, and much more significantly, a moral calling. We dedicate this book to their memory.

Eyal Benvenisti, Chaim Gans and Sari Hanafi

Table of Contents

History, Geography, and Sociology

The Sociology of Return: Palestinian Social Capital, Transnational Kinships and the Refugee Repatriation Process

Sari Hanafi *

> "The refugee should be considered for what it is, namely, nothing less than a limit-concept that at once brings a radical crisis to the principles of the nation-state and clears the way for a renewal of categories that can no longer be delayed."[1]

I. Introduction[2]

The experience of repatriating refugees throughout the world bears evidence to the dearth of available aid packages from governments and international organisations.[3] This is why social capital seems to play an

---

* Although Sari Hanafi is the director of Palestinian Diaspora and Refugee Centre, Shaml, this work reflects only his views. He expresses his gratitude to Ann Lesch for her editing of this chapter. He thanks the many researchers who critiqued the first draft, including Roula El Rifai, Pamela Scholey, Riina Isotalo, Cedric Parizot and Nadim Rouhana.

1 G. Agamben, "We Refugees", <http://www.egs.edu/faculty/agamben/agamben-we-refugees.html>, 1997, 21-22.

2 A preliminary and short version of this research was published in Ann Lesch/Ian Lustick (eds), *Exile & Return. Predicaments of Palestinians and Jews*, 2005, 57-84.

3 Many repatriation and returnee reintegration programmes, especially in Africa, are not being properly funded by the international community. At the 1990 Executive Committee, Sweden noted: "because of the lack of contributions, ongoing repatriation programs were being hampered or even halted" (UNHCR, summary record of the 456th meeting, United Nations General As-

important role in supporting returnees, especially at the beginning of their return;[4] even though the experience of African refugees, for example, shows that refugees are able in some situations to take matters into their own hands and organise repatriation.

This article shall thus examine the social capital from which Palestinian returnees might benefit should they eventually be allowed to return to their homes. To that end, an analysis of attendant economic and social transnational kinship networks is required. A socioeconomic and anthropological survey using open-ended questionnaires, structured and semi-structured interviews, alongside quantitative and qualitative data also forms the basis of such an inquiry. The requisite analysis herein, therefore, emphasises the different types of networks to which individuals have access, granting particular attention to an understanding of the processes by which inclusion in (or exclusion from) them is sustained. One must always bear in mind that there are more subjective questions as well, such as those pertaining to perceptions of trust and normative reciprocity.

The survey referred to above was conducted by the Palestinian Diaspora and Refugee Centre, Shaml, between January and October 2003. A total of 560 open questionnaires were completed, not only by refugees living outside Palestine, but also by people in the Palestinian territories and Israel.[5] Given the conceptual complexity of the research and the multidisciplinary nature of the team, this process involved numerous drafts, tests, and discussions, as well as compromises. Other surveys,

---

sembly, Executive committee of the high commissioner's programme, 24 October 1990).

[4] The idea of social capital has enjoyed a remarkable rise to prominence in both the theoretical and applied social science literature over the last decade. While lively debate has accompanied that journey, thereby helping to advance our thinking while clarifying areas of agreement and disagreement, much still remains to be done. I am not using the term "social capital" in the same way that R. Putnam does. As D. Cohen and L. Prusak in their book *In Good Company: How Social Capital Makes Organizations Work*, 2001, 9, have commented, not everything of value should be called "capital." There is a deep danger of skewing our consideration of social phenomenon and goods toward the economic. In this study, we are mainly interested in the family contribution and in the degree of relevance of the familial and ethnic entrepreneurship.

[5] All percentages mentioned in this article come from Shaml's survey, unless otherwise stated. The Shaml survey was funded by the IDRC. The author thanks those who participated in the fieldwork, particularly Shereen Araj. The survey in Israel was conducted in cooperation with Mada Centre in Haifa.

like Birzeit University's Survey of households,[6] Fafo[7] surveys in Jordan and Lebanon, as well as the Palestinian Centre for Policy and Survey Research (PSR)[8] were used for comparison purposes.

My contribution in this field seeks to clearly identify some of the patterns of return and transnationalism; as I have chosen to highlight the social and economic kinship between Palestinians inside and outside the Palestinian territories, as well as the mode of entrepreneurship in the Palestinian territories. Unlike other studies on the absorption of refugees, which focus only on the contribution of the state and the international community in facilitating return, I remain keenly focused on examining sociological factors, such as social capital, in so far as they may encourage return or adaptation to a new economic environment. This study focuses on the structural factors that influence the decision to return, such as economic and social kinship networks, entrepreneurship and migration culture; as opposed to emotionally based attitudes, which merely express the subject's political position, while neglecting any actual intention to return.[9] Although some emotionally based attitudes are taken into consideration in this article, one must note, at the outset, that such positions were not given much weight in the final analysis due to their inferior analytical prowess.

---

[6] This survey encompassed 2,254 Palestinian households in nineteen communities in the Palestinian Territories in the summer of 1999. R. Giacaman/P. Johnson (eds), *Inside Palestinian Households. Initial Analysis of a Community-based Household Survey, Vol. 1*, 2002.

[7] Fafo is the Norwegian Institute for Applied Social Science. The Fafo survey is about the living conditions of Palestinian refugees in Lebanon and Jordan. In Lebanon it covers a sample of 4,000 households in refugee camps and relatively homogenous refugee areas (O.F. Ugland (ed.), *Difficult Past, Uncertain Future. Living Conditions Among Palestinian Refugees in Camps and Gatherings in Lebanon*, FAFO Report 409, 2003). In Jordan, the survey employed two methods; a survey of stratified probability sample of about 3,100 households selected from 12 camps, and 13 focus groups. The primary purpose of the focus group discussions was to learn how camp-dwellers perceive economic hardship, unemployment, and work opportunities (M. Khawaja/A. Tiltnes (eds), *On the Margins: Migration and Living Conditions of Palestinian Camp Refugees in Jordan*, 2002).

[8] PSR's survey was conducted between 16 January and 5 February 2003 targeting 1,498 Palestinian refugee households distributed among 150 localities in the West Bank and Gaza Strip.

[9] Here much criticism can be levelled at many surveys conducted in Palestinian Territories that have relied on emotionally-based questions.

Instead, my study attempts to rationally address the following questions. What pattern of return will take place? What will be the profile of returnees? Will there be a literal mass of refugees rushing in simultaneously, or a trickle of fragmented groups? What is the motivation for return: pure nationalism and the desire to stabilise identity(ies) after the experience of exile, or something extending beyond that? In case of an Israeli acceptance of the principle of the right of return, would return be voluntary or coerced? What constitutes return "in safety and dignity?" Should refugees be required to return if they cannot go back to their areas of origin, but must settle in another part of the country?

To answer the foregoing questions I posit that two equally applicable approaches must be taken into account. The *development approach*, on the one hand, deals with the study of all returnees who may chose to come home (or to a Palestinian political entity) and who are able to support themselves financially, either independently or through the help of one's extended family; this approach assumes that there is minimal intervention from a public authority (e.g. indirect absorption). This category would include Palestinian refugees who fall within the framework of family reunification, as well as refugees and displaced persons who are able to integrate easily due to their socioeconomic profile; and finally those who can be considered economic migrants. The second approach, which can be referred to as the *democratic approach*, concerns the refugee population at large. It focuses on the study of refugees who come home under an economic and social plan of absorption in their place of return, regardless of whether these refugees come from refugee camps or from cities and wealthy countries like the Gulf States. In both approaches, return includes those who are legally defined as refugees, including those with fragile status (bearing only travel documents), diasporic refugees (bearing passports of a host country), as well as economic migrants.

A wide spectrum of factors affecting the possibilities and potentialities of return, including the role of kin networks, refugee dispersion patterns, and pre- and post-return economic and social profiles must be considered. Other factors, including the desires of individual refugees to return to the (or *a*) homeland, and the ways in which return will be implemented (be it immediate or over an extended period of time) also play a part in analysing the sociology of return. Thus, Palestinian return migration can only bear fruit if one considers the perspectives offered by network analysis.

1. Assumptions

For the purposes of this study, four assumptions are key to understanding the Palestinian sociology of return. The first assumption is that *economic action is embedded in social structure*. For this reason alone it is necessary to study social networks. What is then this embeddedness? How do we understand the economic behaviour of Palestinian returnees and local entrepreneurs, at present and in the cases of return or in the intensification of transnational movement?

The second assumption concerns the privilege of family over friendship ties. As already mentioned, the present inquiry shall attempt to identify the different levels of social structures into which the individual – subject of intended (return) migration – is inserted (friendship, extended family, village ties, national ties). It must be stressed, however, that as regards the decision to migrate given the system of support for the future absorption of Palestinian refugees, one must consider the nuclear and the extended family as a major component. Therefore, one of the objectives of our fieldwork was to identify the relative strength of different types of family ties: strong, weak or torn.

The third assumption deals with a *pattern of return that is not just definitive but also transnational*. This assumption asserts that the refugees/returnees would maintain their social, economic, and political lives in both the country of return and the country in which they lived; where such refugees might even be citizens of both countries.

The last assumption of this research is political. The project of maintaining two, ethnically homogeneous nation-states remains popular with the majority of both Palestinians and Israelis, but this also requires *maintaining a system of apartheid in which the question of Jewish hegemony in the Israeli State will not be challenged any time soon*. What is still at issue is the type of nation-states that Israelis and Palestinians will develop. If Israel accepts the Palestinian right of return, this will make the return of the Palestinian refugees subject to sociological and economic considerations; if not, quotas and refugee profiles will tremendously influence the choices made by refugees concerning their future place of residence.

2. Factors Influencing the Movement of Refugees

Many factors influence a refugee's decision whether to return. Understanding the likely patterns and pressures regarding Palestinian return cannot be achieved by focusing on macro-processes of globalisation or the operation of global markets according to neo-classical principles, but, rather, must be achieved by a sociological understanding of the political, social, and cultural attributes of the Palestinian people.

In this next section, one need only focus on elements related to the economic sociology of Palestinian refugees (and Palestinians abroad in general), both in the host country and in the country of return (the Palestinian territories or Israel). Focusing on these elements, however, does not mean that they are the only important factors. For instance, geographical factors influence refugees' decisions too. Here it is worth noting the importance of Salman Abu-Sitta's work[10] in opening the debate concerning geographic absorption in Israel. His efforts demonstrate that, after dividing Israel into three demographic areas (A, B and C), 68 per cent of Israeli Jews are now concentrated in 8 per cent of Israel and that the areas in and around the former Palestinian villages remain empty and could absorb returning refugees. For him, this empty rural area also corresponds to the original location of many rural refugees of the majority of Palestinian refugees. However, it is important to ask if after 55 years these refugees can still be considered peasants. The majority of them have become residents of big cities; it is thus pertinent to ask if they should accept to be resettled in their villages of origin. Those who became urban refugees were stripped of their ecological and sociological relationships. They may no longer identify with the land upon which they were working, which is what happened with Algerian refugees after independence. Moreover, according to the 2003 PSR survey in the Palestinian territories, the former dwellings of half of these refugees have been destroyed; more importantly, 40 per cent declared themselves unwilling to return, if a family home no longer exists.

The ability to absorb refugees geographically is not a decisive factor in return scenarios. Irish-Americans did not return to Ireland following the end of British colonialism, few Armenians returned to Armenia after its independence, and only a small number of Lebanese returned to their country of origin following the end of the civil war. In all these

---

[10] S. Abu-Sitta, *The End of the Palestinian-Israeli Conflict. From Refugees to Citizens at Home*, 2001.

cases, there was not only ample capacity, but also the political will for re-absorption.

Another important factor, which demands attention, but which is out of the scope of this study, is the comparison between the social welfare systems in the host countries and that of the return areas. For instance, in comparison to Israel, the Palestinian territories and Jordan have inadequate health, social welfare, and educational services. This would surely be a factor in encouraging Palestinians to return to Israel, rather than to the Palestinian territories.[11]

Finally, the possibility of the return of Palestinian refugees is still closely connected with three elements: first, the right of return; second, the urban situation of the refugee camps; and, finally, the position of the Arab host countries. These three elements condition the degree to which the applicability of the right of return may be realised. It is also worth mentioning that many studies show that refugees have low expectations as to whether a political solution would allow most refugees to return. A PSR survey in 2003 found that half accepted the idea that, once a Palestinian state is established, the refugee issue will be postponed to an indefinite future.

II. Social Capital: The Density of Transnational Social Kinship Ties

Because the extended family network has been an important safety net for migrants, one must consider bonding, a form of social capital that ties together family members who are similar in terms of their demographic characteristics. Essentially, transnational kinship networks are affected by the occupation and national borders that structure, extend, and deepen the rupture of Palestinian society. This article, therefore, questions many aspects of the Palestinian sociology of networks: how should the strength of a tie be measured? Do close relationships link people who are similar to each other? Do weaker ties link more dissimilar people? Indeed, some forms of social capital can be used to hinder rather than help a return migrant, e.g. when group membership norms

---

[11] The Public Health Institute of Birzeit University is currently examining this issue.

confer obligations to share rather than accumulate wealth or when they deny members access to services.[12]

Connectedness between different members is based on the large spectrum of choices acted upon by individuals and families. The measurement of this feeling of connection is certainly subjective, but the Shaml survey chose a set of structural factors that may shape and ultimately limit these choices. The border predicament, the frequency of visits, phone calls, and the use of cyberspace are indicators of the (non)connectedness of the family network. Indeed, they all shape relations among family members and thus influence the decision to return.

1. Transnationality

The Shaml survey confirmed that a certain degree of transnationality exists among Palestinians (especially among those in the Palestinian territories, as compared to those in Israel proper). This suggests that there will be a transnational pattern of return migration in the future, much more than a definitive return, and that the kinship network can be used to facilitate this movement.

Among those living in the Palestinian territories, 40 per cent of their close relatives[13] live abroad and only a quarter of those are able to visit Palestine/Israel. In contrast, among Palestinians in Israel, only 15 per cent of close relatives live abroad of whom 13 per cent can travel to Palestine/Israel. When we broaden the picture to include second degree relatives,[14] 76 per cent of Palestinians living in the territories have second degree relatives abroad, half of whom are able to visit Palestine/Israel; more than 79 per cent of them are refugees. Social and economic ties are accordingly diminished for some, as only 15 per cent have received aid from their relatives abroad; a mere 8 per cent for those who live in Israel. There are also very few economic projects between the Palestinians abroad and those in Israel. The survey found that those who have property in the Palestinian territories tend to meet more often. It seems that the possession of property encourages Palestinians

---

[12] A. Portes, "Social Capital: Its Origins and Applications in Contemporary Sociology", *Annual Review of Sociology* 24 (1998), 1 et seq.

[13] Close relatives are defined as parents, spouses, children, or siblings.

[14] Second degree relatives are defined as matrimonial and patrimonial aunts and uncles and their families.

abroad to maintain contact with their families there, at least in order to discuss the use and the future of the property.

Relations with more distant relatives are very weak. A third said they had no ties whatsoever with them, and only 25 per cent said they had some ties. Moreover, the overwhelming majority said they have no economic ties. This is not unusual for such a society, but it means that the importance of ties inside the *hamula* (clan) is fading, possibly because of the quick urbanisation of Palestinian society.

The place of birth plays a major role in the degree of connection to the people who still live there. For example, 79 per cent of those born in Jordan retained ties with their close relatives in Jordan, even though they no longer lived there. For those who returned to the Palestinian territories, however, their relations with Jordan diminish with time. This may to a large extent be due to the fact that they are unable to cross the border to visit each other.[15]

Transnationality may also be expressed by an interest in owning property in the host countries. When asked what they intend to do with property in the host country when they return, the overwhelming majority of the refugees living outside the Palestinian territories stated that they would keep their property and rent it. In other words, refugees do not want to sever all their ties with their countries of refuge. Nonetheless, the duration of the exodus – now more than 55 years – and the impact of the borders have hindered the maintenance of ties between relatives.

Solidarity and Connectedness: geographical considerations and gender based hierarchies suggest that Palestinians in the territories retain more transnational kinship than those living in Israel.

The hypothesis that the closest ties are with family members and not with friends is confirmed by the fact that, when asked about their clos-

---

15 Shaml survey is confirmed by PBCS survey in West Bank and Gaza Strip, which was carried out from 29 April 1995 to 23 July 1995. In this survey, 15,735 households, or 97.2 per cent eligible were successfully interviewed. Of the Palestinians living in the OPT, 91.9 per cent are born in the territories, 3.8 per cent in Israel and 4.3 per cent in other countries. About 60 per cent of households in the West Bank have close relatives living abroad, compared to about 53 per cent of the Gaza Strip households. Most relatives abroad live in Jordan (49.2 per cent). 43 per cent have an Israeli identity card. About 6 per cent of those currently living in the OPT have changed their residence since 1987. Of these, 5.1 per cent came from abroad, while about 0.9 per cent changed their districts of residence (PCBS, <http:// www.pcbs.org/>).

est ties, only 5 per cent of Palestinians living on the West Bank mentioned friends and 8 per cent mentioned both family and friends. Men were more likely than women to declare that their best social ties are with their family. There was also a difference amongst the age groups: young people rank their relations with their siblings higher than with cousins and friends. However, *returnees give the most importance to their relations with friends*; most probably because these returnees do not have family in the Palestinian territories or because their long absence has diminished such ties.

Visits with Relatives: Palestinian men interviewed in Palestine/Israel have on average lost contact with a third of their close relatives; they meet mainly every two years. In contrast, women lost less contact: 29 per cent in the Palestinian territories and 14 per cent in Israel. Thus, women (as mothers, daughters or sisters) in Palestinian society are the core of the Palestinian family. They are the clearing house for economic and social ties inside the fragmented transnational Palestinian family. However, this positive image of the status of women, one that confirms the Islamic and Arabic value placed on *silate al arham* (maintaining the ties with the relatives) and *a'rd* (honour), should not blind us to the effect of a patriarchal society in which men are still favoured in education and receive the most significant gifts from their family. The gender-constructed reality of ties is very important for return migration; it concerns a refugee population in which women are the most vulnerable due to early marriage, as well as a high proportion of widowed, divorced, and single middle aged and elderly women.[16] This might indicate a *propensity for more families who have ties to Palestine/Israel through maternal relatives to return than those who have ties through paternal relatives.*

The survey also reveals that men have very few contacts with their step-families and families-in-law. The same observation pertains to contact by phone: in the Palestinian territories men make more phone calls to their sisters than to their brothers. The increased number of ties that surveyed women had to their relatives can be explained by their greater emotional attachment to the family.

Thus, the decision to return will be shaped by the kind of relatives with whom the refugees have ties. Proximity of age plays a major role in so-

---

[16] Giacaman/Johnson, see note 6, 9; see also R. Isotalo, *Gendering the Palestinian Return Migration: Migrants from the Gulf and Marriage as a Transnational Practice*, paper presented at the Third Mediterranean Social and Political Research Meeting, Florence, 20-24 March 2002.

cial connectivity, but less so in terms of economic ties. This is partly because the generational gap between children and their parents and elderly siblings has widened rapidly, especially in people with transnational experience. This was obvious from Shaml's survey: some young people who had grown up in the United States expressed a cultural conflict with their relatives who did not have the same transnational experience.

The geographical location of the interviewees is also very relevant. In the Gaza Strip, 43 per cent do not visit (or receive visits) with their close relatives outside the Strip. This percentage increases for those living in camps, as their relatives are more likely to be refugees who live outside Palestine. In Israel, 82 per cent of interviewees from big cities like Haifa have lost direct contact with close relatives. Visits decrease as people age. Whereas the economic situation seems irrelevant to the frequency of visits, better-educated people seem to visit their close relatives more often. It seems then that education increases the possibility of travel to meet with transnational relatives.

The use of telephones does not seem to compensate clearly for the absence of physical meetings; there are very few phone calls between people who do not exchange visits. Generally speaking, most speak on the phone about once every two months. Those who have property in Palestine tend to meet more often. It seems that the presence of property encourages them to maintain contact with their families.

The border is a major cause of the lack of physical contact; approximately 56 per cent of the people who cannot visit Palestine/Israel have lost contact with the first cycle of relatives. The geographical location of relatives also impacts on the meetings: Palestinian refugees in Jordan and Egypt are more likely than those who live in the Gulf States to maintain contact, but even they meet only about once every two years. Further, it is practically impossible to meet relatives in Lebanon and Iraq. Palestinians living in Europe and the United States, however, are able to meet with their Palestinian relatives in Palestine/Israel more easily than those living in Arab countries, due to the fact that travel between Arab countries and Palestine/Israel is difficult, even impossible in some cases.

In addition, the second *Intifada* has sharply affected the ability of Palestinians living in the Palestinian territories to maintain physical contact with one another let alone with those living abroad. The situation is especially acute in Gaza, which Israel has sealed off since the beginning of the *Intifada*. Majdi Malki has poignantly argued that Israeli closures and invasions often increase the importance of geographical and local solidarity, as family ties become less important when such a harsh situation affects all members of nuclear and extended families.[17] According to Lisa Taraki, it is in this context that we also witness the emergence of a new middle class, which rejects lower class refugees and camp-dwellers. Thus, fragmentation and segmentation of Palestinian society has a negative impact on establishing and maintaining ties throughout the Palestinian territories.

Telephone Contact: most calls are to sons and daughters dwelling abroad, and occur about once every two months or more. Phone calls to relatives abroad vary according to the location: they are very important in Bethlehem, Walaja (a suburb of Jerusalem), Ramallah, and refugee camps and less so in Nablus and the Gaza Strip. Calls from Israel abroad are very rare, except for Um al Fahm where they seem to be an act of solidarity with relatives in the West Bank and Jordan. In the Palestinian territories, men and women maintain phone contact with relatives abroad at the same rate, but in Israel, women use the phone less frequently. Overall, those who are less educated tend to use the phone less often. Conversations by phone with close relatives living abroad are more important with Europe and the United States than with the Gulf, Egypt, and Jordan. This can be explained by the cost of the call; it is cheaper to call from the United States or Europe. Communication with Lebanon is very rare, as it is impossible to phone from Lebanon (and from Syria) to Israel/Palestine. One female interviewee declared that she used to give money to cover the equivalent of twelve phone cards a year to her sick and poor uncle living in Jordan so that he could call the family in Palestine.

E-mail communication among immediate family members in Palestine/Israel is infrequent; only one third of close relatives are connected by e-mail with those who live in the Palestinian territories, and are mostly those under 40 years old. In Palestine, women use e-mail less often than men; whereas, in Israel it is the reverse. Several modes of communication, such as Internet chatting, Short Messenger Service (SMS), and sending pictures through the Internet are used to connect people across geographical borders.

Marriage Patterns: Endogamous marriage, i.e. marriage within the same lineage, sect, community, group, village, or neighbourhood, is an important indicator of connectedness. Marriage between first cousins and blood-related kin is the most common form of endogamy in the Arab

---

17 M. Malki, 2003.

world.[18] Many studies show the persistence of a high rate of endogamy in the Palestinian family. The Fafo study[19] states that "[t]he family, and in particular the parents, play an important role in the process of finding an appropriate marriage partner in Palestinian society." Fafo researchers found that only 36.6 per cent of women born between 1940 and 1949 and 43 per cent of women born between 1960 and 1969 married outside of the family or the *hamula*. Marriages are often arranged, as is the case in most of the Arab world.[20]

The Shaml survey and Riina Isotalo's work[21] also show that endogamous practices exist even at the transnational level (i.e. between family members in different countries), but much less so than when other relatives live in the same country. This allows many unexpected groups to join the family. The small number of transnational endogamous marriages can be explained by its high cost; in contrast, local endogamous marriages are economical since dowries are smaller.[22] However, in some cases, transitional endogamous marriages are encouraged to sidestep bureaucratic and mobility problems as we will see in the Barta'a case.

Economic Assistance: Social capital refers to the capacity of the individual to command scarce resources through adhesion to networks and broader social structures. These resources include economic favours, such as the reduction of price, credit without interest, and information on business conditions. These resources in themselves are not a social capital, but the concept does refer to the ability of individual to mobilise it in case of need. People, especially migrants, do not only need jobs; they also need companionship, emotional support, help with everyday problems, care when ill, and other forms of social support.

---

18 L. Holy, *Kinship, honour and solidarity: cousin marriage in the Middle East*, 1989.

19 J. Pedersen et al. (eds), *Growing Fast. The Palestinian Population in the West Bank and Gaza Strip*, 2001, 83-84.

20 M. Heibergand/G. Ovensen, *Palestinian Society in Gaza, West Bank and Arab Jerusalem: A survey of Living Conditions*, FAFO-report 151, 1993. The mother plays a more informal role in this process, while the father is the one who makes the final decision.

21 R. Isotalo, "Yesterday's Outsiders, Today's Returnees – Transnational Processes and Cultural Encounters in the West Bank", in: A. Linjakumpu/K. Virtanen (eds), *Under the Olive Tree. Reconsidering Mediterranean Politics and Culture*, 1997.

22 L.B. Jacobsen/M. Deeb, "Social Network", in: Ugland, see note 7.

In terms of help between relatives, this study distinguishes between two forms of aid: non-mutual and reciprocal. According to exchange theory, the network is much stronger when help is non-mutual. It is argued that networks characterised by non-mutual help are more connected and stable because "in the hiatus between giving and the reciprocation of an item, obligation, trust and cooperation are created and extended among exchangers."[23]

Solidarity between Palestinians in the territories and abroad is important. A third received financial and non-financial help from abroad that began before the start of the current *Intifada*; such assistance is therefore not related to the increased economic hardship experienced during the *Intifada*.[24] This help is mainly among parents, children, and siblings. It includes small gifts and the occasional major gift, such as the cost of education or health treatment. While payment for health treatment is extended to all relatives, payment for education is usually extended only to male members. Religious holidays, such as the *Eid* and Christmas, are also occasions when gifts are given. This result is confirmed also by the Birzeit University Survey: there is a regular financial link with 15 per cent of migrants, defined as giving or receiving money every three months or less, with 8 per cent of emigrants sending money to their families in Palestine, 6 per cent of families in Palestine sending money to their relatives abroad, and 1 per cent both sending and receiving money depending on the situation. Villagers score highest in terms of receiving money from relatives abroad (20 per cent), probably related to the higher proportion of relatives in Western countries.[25]

Face-to-face contact is very important for economic transactions and especially for receiving and giving help. A Fafo study[26] shows that a family living in the Palestinian territories typically relies on members abroad, but that the lack of physical communication hinders transactions. The Shaml study found that half of the transfers do not go

---

[23] E. Uehara, "Dual Exchange Theory, Social Networks, and Informal Social Support.", *American Journal of Sociology* 96 (1990), 521 et seq., 524, quoted in Jacobsen/Deeb, ibid., 223.

[24] 82 per cent of those surveyed said they received the same as before the *Intifada*.

[25] Giacaman/Johnson, see note 6, 36-38.

[26] P. Sletten/J. Pederson, *Coping with Conflict. Palestinian communities Two Years into the Intifada*, 2003, 47.

through banks but are transmitted during familial visits. The study also found that money is brought as presents.

It is interesting, however, to note that around half the assistance now is transferred through banks, a radical change from the 1970s and 1980s when most financial help was transferred in person.

Few Palestinians in Israel receive help from their relatives abroad, which is probably due to their relatively good economic situation and to the weakness of transnational social ties.

Concerning reciprocal help though, the survey found very few cases on the transnational level. Help not only enters the Palestinian territories, but is also sent from the territories to close relatives living abroad (a third of the interviewees). However, this is not necessarily reciprocal or economically based assistance, as in the case of parents who give financial help to their daughters living abroad.

While solidarity is important, at least between the Palestinian territories and abroad, economic ties based on partnership are very problematic in the current situation (economic partnerships with the diaspora seem to be a hazardous enterprise). However, there is some financial help for small entrepreneurs who are setting up their business.

It seems that help in Palestine/Israel has an altruistic motivation, i.e. transferring resources for general moral imperatives or solidarity with in-group needs and goals.[27]

This will have an important impact on facilitating the establishment of eventual returnees back home, especially in the initial period.

In short, the outcome of our Shaml survey shows *less social connectedness and solidarity exists than expected in Palestine/Israel and especially in Israel. This will make the use of kinship ties to assist return less important than generally assumed for a nation whose source of cohesion is its ongoing plight.* Thus, the negative impact of borders and the implications of Israeli practices on Palestinians' local and international ties are far reaching.

Fractured Nuclear Family

Recent field research presents a profile of fractured networks inside the nuclear family in the Palestinian territories, but not in Israel.[28] Mothers

---

[27] A. Portes, *Latin journey: Cuban and Mexican immigrants in the U.S.*, 1985.

and children may reside in one country, husbands and fathers may live and work in another, and grandparents and more distant relatives may live elsewhere. The fractured family experience indicates that *return will not necessarily involve the entire family initially.*

This pattern also exists among other diaspora groups. Awhio Ong[29] found that cultural norms dictate the formation of trans-local business networks in the case of Chinese living abroad: males possessed mobility while women and children remain the disciplinable subjects of familial regimes. Here, it is the men who tend to decide whether to relocate to Palestine/Israel or whether to choose other options for the family. In particular, the person who has found suitable employment typically brings the family to join him/her and makes the decisions concerning the family's mobility; though international migration statistics show that the percentage of females who are international migrants is increasing; currently, 47.5 per cent of international migrants are female. The decision to migrate is also based on the availability of affordable educational opportunities for children. In the Palestinian case it was evident from an electronic discussion on PALESTA (Network of Palestinian Scientists and Technologists Abroad, an independent Internet-based network seeking to connect Palestinian professionals in the diaspora with Palestinian Territories) that many discussions revolve around the existing education structure and the language of instruction for children.

2. Mode of Entrepreneurship Favourable to Return

If some returnees will consume from the resources of the place to which they return, then others will bring capital and expertise sufficient to generate improvements to the economy. Some studies have demonstrated that the capital influx and investment that accompany the return of professionals generates investment. This type of investment is significantly different from the classical model of remittances studied in the

---

[28] S. Hanafi, *Hona wa honaq: nahwa tahlil lil 'alaqa bin al-shatat al-falastini wa al markaz (Here and There: Towards an Analysis of the Relationship between the Palestinian Diaspora and the Center)*, 2001, in Arabic; Isotalo, see note 16; B'tselem/Ha'Moked, *Families Torn Apart: Separation of Palestinian Families in the Occupied Territories*, 1999.

[29] A. Ong, *Flexible Citizenship. The Cultural Logic of Transnationality*, 1999, 20.

Arab world,[30] which were dominated by limited economic benefits and negative effects of migration, weak investment of remittances in productive activities, and inflation provoked by the transfer of currency.[31]

Contrary to studies that view returnees as a future burden[32] and that examine the absorptive capacity of Palestinian refugees from a narrow and short-term economic perspective, other studies illustrate a great potential benefit, considering the new dynamics and positive externalities that might be established by the absorption of refugees.[33] The Oslo transition period generated a high rate of growth in the Palestinian territories. Gross domestic product and gross national product before the *Intifada* were higher than in neighbouring countries, with the exception of Israel. If this level is regained, then the Palestinian territories might well attract refugees from Jordan and Egypt, especially if family members contribute initially. Some Palestinians might also move from the Gaza Strip to the West Bank, where income is higher. This also applies to Israel, where future government policy will determine whether Palestinian workers, engineers, and information technology professionals can reside there.

The decision to move people or capital is subject to a complex set of factors, especially in the era of globalisation. Thus, one should reject a

30 S. Hanafi, "Penser le rapport diaspora, centre. La contribution de la diaspora palestinienne à l'économie des Territoires", in : H. Hassan-Yari (ed.), *Le processus de paix au Moyen-Orient*, 2000.

31 I. Saad Al Din/A. Fadil, *Intiqal al 'amalah al 'arabiyya: (The Movement of Arab Labor)*, 1983; N. Fergany, *Sa'yan wara' al rizq. Dirasa maydaniyya 'an hijret al masriyyin ll'amal fi al aqtar al arabiyya (Striving for Subsistance)*, 1988. In 1978, a sample survey conducted by Khader and Badran in Jordan found that about half of the remittances from Jordanian workers in Kuwait were channelled towards investment purposes, including 20.5 per cent to education alone, B. Khader/A. Badran, *The Economic Development of Jordan*, 1987, 41, cited in J. Husseini, *Current socioeconomic status of the West Bank camp refugees*, paper presented to the Shaml Workshop "Palestinian Return Migration: Socio-economic and Cultural Approaches", Ramallah, 2-4 March 2000.

32 See for example the European Union report, commissioned in 1999, T. Charalambos/A. Huliaras, *Prospects for Absorption of Returning Refugees in the West Bank and the Gaza Strip*, unpublished report, Institute of International Economic Relations, December 1999.

33 N. Van Hear, *Reintegration of the Palestinian Returnees*, 1996.

straightforward relationship between transnationalism and global capitalism, a position advocated by Basch et al.[34]

What I will show here is that the potential return of the refugees (especially the entrepreneurs and professionals) is structurally constrained; at least more so than a model of pure economic choice geared to optimal benefit would indicate. The recycling of de-territorialised Palestinian capital reveals fault lines in the international global market; and unlike some like to believe, it does not show the beneficial workings of globalisation. For instance, the geographical de-localisation of Palestinian economic transactions can best be understood to mean that it is possible to improve the fragile legal status of the refugees, regardless of their wealth. Thus, most of their investments reflect more of an economy of survival than the exercise of real political and economic power in the economy of globalisation and the world system.

As Grillo, Riccio, and Salih argue, "[e]conomic dislocation in both developing and industrialised nations has increased migration, but made it difficult for migrants to construct secure cultural, social and economic bases within their new settings."[35] Thus, transnationalism, whether in reaction to global capitalism or in preceding its triumph, as in the case of the Senegalese communities in Italy, does not exhibit a straightforward relation to global capital.[36] The experience of Palestinians recruited through the UNDP's TOKTEN programme[37] indicates that many people came to Palestine due to their precarious situation in their host country. Accordingly, any return must be expressed by a model in which a constrained people seek to improve their flexibility, rather than

---

34 L. Basch/N. Glick Schiller/C. Szanton Blanc, *Nations Unbound: Transnational Projects, Postcolonial Predicaments, and Deterritorialized Nation-States*, 1994, 22; see the critique by R. Grillo/B. Riccio/R. Salih, "Introduction", in: R. Grillo/B. Riccio/R. Salih (eds), *Here or There? Contrasting Experiences of Transnationalism: Morrocans and Senegalese in Italy*, 2000, 19.

35 Grillo/Riccio/Salih, *idem.*

36 *Idem.*

37 Transfer of Knowledge Through Expatriate Nationals (TOKTEN) is an interesting mechanism for tapping into national expatriate human resources and mobilising them to undertake short-term consultancy work in their countries of origin. The UNDP, which founded it, demonstrated that specialists (who had migrated to other countries and achieved professional success abroad) were enthusiastic about providing short-term technical assistance to their country of origin.

point to a straightforward choice between the country of residence and the country of origin.

There are two interconnected considerations that must be taken into account at this juncture. First, the nature of the investment and the motivations for it are driven by non-economic factors more than by economic ones in the region; and, second, the familial mode of entrepreneurship predominates in the Palestinian territories and Israel. From this perspective, therefore, one can clearly see that the Palestinian economy in Palestine/Israel will be strongly affected by certain forms of refugee repatriation.

a. Diaspora Investment

During the Oslo transitional period, local and international economic links were re-established after a long period of conflict and separation. Already partially tied to their native community, the Palestinian diaspora contributed to the reshaping and the emergence of new transnational economic networks. The proportion of investments by the Palestinian diaspora in the Palestinian territories to the volume of the Palestinian capital abroad was modest,[38] although it was vital for the Palestinian economy. As an indicator, according to Palestinian economist

---

[38] For example, my findings in the United Arab Emirates are significant in this respect. Few Palestinian businesspeople have any strong conviction that they should leave the Emirates and return to Palestine, even though the partial right of return (family reunification) now exists, albeit to a limited extent. They decided instead to express their feelings of nationalism by contributing to the construction of the Palestinian entity. However, such investment, made in a delicate economic and political situation, indicates that the rationale is not just economic: It concerns prestige and the acquisition of position. 34 economic projects have started since Oslo. From the 75 members of the sample selected for the survey, more than a third invested in territories. This number is considerable, taking into consideration the attitude of the Palestinians in relation to Palestinian-Americans. It seems, in any case, that there is a correlation between proximity and investment. The type of investment is also related to the origin of the people in question. Those of 1948 territories origin (eight in the sample) were stakeholders in many holding companies, such as PADICO and International Salaam Company, since they did not have physical access to the territories. Palestinians of West Bank and Gaza origins behave differently. They associate a relative or a friend in their projects in locus after paying a visit to these territories. Table 3 shows the chosen sectors. For further analysis see S. Hanafi, *Business Directory of Palestinian in the Diaspora*, 1998; and *idem*, 2001b.

Fadl Naqib[39], from 1993 to 1999 average annual investment growth was 12.3 per cent.

To give an idea of the size of the diaspora's contributions during times (i.e. before the *Intifada*), one need only consider that contributions in terms of investment and philanthropic activities were valued at US$ 408.006 million in 1996 (of which 74 per cent was investment) and US$ 410.211 million in 1997 (of which 76 per cent was investment).[40] This was a significant resource for Palestinian society and its economy. Indeed, diaspora provided 74 per cent of total international assistance (US$ 549.414 million) in 1996 and 95 per cent in 1997 (US$ 432.259 million).[41] However, their contributions remained insufficient for a young entity ravaged by 30 years of de-development;[42] and arguably such contributions were well below what Palestinian businesspeople could contribute. In fact, these investments did not necessarily come from wealthy people, but often came from the middle classes, especially in the Gulf, because of the familial nature of entrepreneurship in the Palestinian territories.

---

39 F. Naqib, *Absorption of the Palestinian Refugee: Economic aspect*, unpublished paper, 2003, 45.

40 S. Hanafi, "Contribution de la diaspora palestinienne à l'économie des Territoires investissement et philanthropie", *Maghreb-Machrek* 161 (November 1998), Paris, Documentation française. The Palestinian economy and economic development are now so uneven that generalisations based on central data are extremely hazardous. To trace investments from the host countries into the homeland, 600 interviews with Palestinian businesspeople (mainly from Jordan, the United Arab Emirates, Egypt, Syria, Israel, Lebanon, Saudi Arabia, the United States, Canada, Chile, the United Kingdom, and Australia) were conducted during 1995-1997.

41 MOPIC (Ministry of Planning and International Cooperation), Aid Coordination Department, *MOPIC's 1997 Fourth Quaterly Monitoring Report of Donor Assistance*, 1998, <http//www.pna.net>; see table 2.

42 S. Roy, *The Gaza Strip: The Political Economy of Development*, 1995.

Table 1: Financial Contribution of the Palestinian Diaspora (US$ million)[43]

Total Contribution	1996	1997
Total Investment	303.8	311.1
Philanthropic and Familial Aid	104.206	99.111
Total Contribution of the Diaspora	408.006	410.211
Donors' Foreign Aid	549.414	432.259

The impact of these contributions by diaspora can be measured on both a quantitative and qualitative basis. For example, a holding company permits strategic and long-term investment, as well as the creation of substantial projects that are beyond the capacity of one entrepreneur. This would be a new model introduced into a country dominated by family-based, small or medium enterprises. Infusing vitality into the Palestinian economy at its initial stages of development is essential to any future prospect of stability and sustainable development. Such an approach would not only relieve the economic, social, and political tensions that are now a fact of daily life, but would also initiate a process of capital accumulation into a low-resource based economy with high levels of imports.

The leader of such companies is PADICO, which was founded by 140 prominent diasporic Palestinian businessmen with working capital of US$ 500 million. One of its objectives is to help channel new capital, either directly or through affiliated or subsidiary companies,[44] towards projects that can create jobs while providing competitive, financial returns to investors; in short, it tries to attract and use investment to help rebuild the economic infrastructure in the territories.

A collective mobilisation of resources has also taken place alongside efforts such as PADICO. To that end, a number of stockholding companies have been founded; chief among them is the Arab Palestinian Investment Company (APIC), whose activities include the joint efforts of Palestinian businesspeople in Israel and the territories. The Arab Pales-

---

[43] Diverse sources. See Hanafi, see note 40.

[44] PADICO has bridged the gap between local and diaspora Palestinians by establishing subsidiaries in which home investors can participate even with small amounts.

tinian Financial Foundation (Beit Al-Mal Al-Arabi Al-Falestini), the Palestine Bank for Investment and the Arab Islamic Bank are but a few other examples. The impact of such societies, however, has been limited when compared to PADICO.

However, this new pattern of big companies is not necessarily the best model for progress. Within developed countries it is clear that some challengers to corporate hegemony have appeared. Small businesses, in decline, and universally stereotyped as dependent, backward and low-skilled until the 1970s, have begun to increase in number again. Some have been highly successful and innovative self-starters, developing the latest technology and design for the newest markets. Silicon Valley and Third Italy (famous emerging information technology areas in USA) have become models to imitate, as they denote mutually supportive communities. Few, however, have thought of these small firms as actual or potential actors on a global stage or as nascent rivals to the international operations of the multinationals.[45]

Yet, the involvement of diaspora in the territories has its limits. This is partly because of the nature of their niches, which are mainly trade and construction. These niches do not constitute value-added benefits to local expertise. This has encouraged diaspora to separate know-how and capital. Those with capital have teamed up with those who have expertise externally, in order to start businesses in the territories or in Israel. The creation of holding companies has resolved such structural problems. In the Oslo period, many Palestinian citizens of Israel who lacked the access and relationships to invest in the territories invested through such companies.

As for motivation, Palestinian diaspora investors have said that they do not expect to achieve any quick profits. According to those sampled, some also felt that almost any other region in the Middle East would be a wiser location for investment, particularly in the industrial sector. Most decisions in favour of investment in Palestine were made for social rather than strictly economic reasons. Such economic behaviour, however, cannot be explained by simply portraying diaspora as "patriotic." For the Palestinian investor is neither purely a *homo economicus* nor a *homo patrioticus.*

---

[45] C. Lever-Tracy/D. Ip/T. Noel, *The Chinese Diaspora and Mainland China. An Emerging Economic Synergy*, 1996.

b. Transnational Familial Entrepreneurship

Transnational familial entrepreneurship does not imply a fixed behaviour or a kind of economic mentality, as it is a dynamic concept. This mode of entrepreneurship represents how capital, know-how and the sustainability for business are required.[46] Such entrepreneurship concerns not only businesspeople, but also entrepreneurs in general, including the self-employed and the employer.[47] According to this definition, Palestinian diaspora (whether refugees or not) are quite entrepreneurial, where 20 per cent of the labour force is self-employed or an employer.[48] According to the PCBS, this percentage is more like 15 per cent in the Palestinian territories.[49]

Various fieldworks conducted previously by myself and by Shaml, identify two different types of Palestinian entrepreneurship: individualist and communitarian, both of which operate on a transnational level. Businesspeople diversify their business in different fields and across geographical areas, using mainly capital transfers rather than physical re-location.

This diversification thus does not stem from business attitudes toward new markets or new methods of production designed to benefit from the economic environment in the host countries; rather this diversification seeks out economic activity in new geographical areas and new sectors in order to ensure the security of capital in case one sector within a country encounter difficulties. Such insecurity is typical of a diasporic and refugee population best characterised by permanent liminality, a psychology of transition and impermanence.

---

[46] More precisely we can define entrepreneurship as "an attempt at new business or new venture creation, such as self-employment, a new business organisation, or the expansion of an existing business, by an individual, a group of individuals, or an established business" (P.D. Reynolds/M. Hay/S.M. Camp, *Global Entrepreneurship Monitor, 1999 Executive Report*, 1999, 23).

[47] ILO, *Resolution concerning the Measurement of Underemployment and inadequate employment situations*, The Sixteenth International Conference on Labor Statistics, Geneva, 1998.

[48] Khawaja/Tiltnes, see note 7, 99. Here we use the ILO classification and the definition of the entrepreneur (ILO, *idem*).

[49] H. Al-Rimmawi/H. Bukhari, *Population Characteristics of the PopulationRefugee Camps, Ramallah: PCBS and Dissemination and Analysis of Census Findings*, 2002, 54, in Arabic.

The nature of this sectoral diversification and investment strategy by Palestinian entrepreneurs does not depend solely on a rational economic model or a complex set of calculations of different factors related to the size of markets, labour costs, technological performance, and the presence of infrastructures that facilitate investment. Palestinian economic diversification is dependent on the vagaries of social and political criteria such as the impact of the Oslo peace process, the juridical status of the investor in the host and investment countries, mobility, and access, in addition to the difficulties associated with obtaining visas. As a result of such factors in the Gulf States, for example, Palestinians were unable to convert and recycle the capital they acquired during the golden age in the Gulf when they migrated to North America after the Gulf crisis in 1990-1991.

If the peace process explains the Gulf capital flow toward Palestine and Jordan, then the movement towards Canada and the United States demonstrates the inability of the Middle East to absorb investment; it likewise underscores the difficulty in keeping pace with the process of economic globalisation. Since the 1980s, inter-Arab migratory trade and investment has shrunk substantially when compared to general economic activity. Most economic activity and patterns of capital ownership have unfortunately been confined within Arab states. The trend prevails, despite some signs of change since 1994.

Kinship networks between diaspora and the resultant gravitational centre have assumed critical importance, although the trend is not necessarily self-evident. In the Gulf countries, political instability and limited investment opportunities have only increased the value of economic kinship networks, while in other countries diaspora individualist entrepreneurship has assumed a greater role.[50] While Palestinian ethnic and kinship networks are not *per se* necessary for the success of investment and recycling of capital in recipient countries, the situation in the territories leans toward the entrepreneur-family, rather than entrepreneur-individual relationships. Many interviewees indicated the importance of role models (i.e. other successful entrepreneurs) in their social networks. Many family stories show that people who engaged in micro- or macro-enterprise creation have close relatives who operate businesses. The experience of many Palestinian families depicts a typical transnational entrepreneur. Difficulties caused by being diaspora means that transnational strategies are a way of ensuring economic continuity in spite of diverse crises.

---

50 Hanafi, see note 30.

Transnational networks are not the expression of global capital, but rather constitute strategies for survival. In many transnational experiences around the world, such as the Chinese in the United States,[51] the quest for the accumulation of capital and for social prestige in the global arena emphasises the need for practices favouring flexibility, and mobility, in addition to a general repositioning in relation to markets, governments, and cultural regimes. In the Palestinian case, the acquisition of capital reflects a struggle for economic survival. For example, a New York businessman might well make a million dollar transaction with relative ease, thanks to the time-space compression enabled by new information technologies;[52] whereas a Palestinian transnational refugee in many countries in the Middle East will likely need to spend days to make a much more modest transfer, rendering his/her transaction cost much higher. In contrast to many euphoric transnational studies, our fieldwork highlights the importance of class and even cultural stratification, as they are often linked to global systems of production.

Shaml's socio-anthropological survey in 2003 focused on forty entrepreneurs, mostly in Ramallah. The results illustrate the economic importance of Palestinian refugees: half of the entrepreneurs are refugees, although few live in camps. The Oslo process seems to have generated around 40 per cent of the entrepreneurial activities. The capital mobilised mostly came either from inheritances or was family assistance. Very few cases indicate the use of bank credit, due mainly to the conservative policies of banks in the territories; but also because using the familial partnership privileges a mode of trust that reduces the cost of economic transactions. The familial partnerships before Oslo tended to involve the families living in the territories more than those of the diaspora (the transnational family). The peace process created connections between the West Bank and Gaza and encouraged many partnerships, and the locations of these partnerships went beyond the territories: a quarter of the entrepreneurs interviewed had investments abroad. The Shaml survey also shows that the social familial ties entrepreneurs maintain are more important than other socioeconomic stratagems. Telephone and travel encourage such connections. However, ties with distant relatives (aunts, uncles, and their offspring) are weak. Some entrepreneurs use their relatives abroad to facilitate export and import, especially if those relatives live in Jordan. This is important, as the ma-

---

51 Ong, see note 29, 6.

52 D. Harvey, *The Condition of Postmodernity*, 1990.

jor constraint to developing businesses in Palestine is the Israeli occupation, travel restrictions, and travel route closures.

The mobilisation of the family to support a business does not mean that this fits a model of "ethnic" business that some tend to describe in a euphoric manner. Many entrepreneurs are reluctant to employ people from their village of origin. They are afraid that their enterprise will become a welfare project, with relatives expecting handouts without having to work.[53] The situation in the Palestinian territories could even be more complex than in Indonesia (where Geertz conducted his study); since despite it likely being bad business to employ relatives, the pressures here to do what is socially appropriate is arguably much higher.[54]

Meanwhile, economic ties between Palestinians in Israel and those abroad with the Palestinian territories are unlikely to flourish if the situation remains as it is. As for investment within Israel, the absence of an independent Arab economy will discourage many Palestinians, as they are not willing to help the Israeli economy. For Palestinians it seems that the only legitimate economic ties are those with members of the family. As for outward trade from Israel to the Palestinian territories or to the Arab world, many Palestinian entrepreneurs complain about the risk of investing as holders of Israeli nationality, which they feel makes them vulnerable. One should not forget that the territorial restrictions Israel enforces against the Palestinians of the territories also encompasses Palestinians from Israel who cannot travel to Palestinian cities and to the Gaza Strip. As a result, many economic ties have been severed, as the testimony of many interviewees in Beer Sheva and Nazareth bore out.

Comparing the potential Palestinian case with other return experiences is crucial. Many studies, like those of Nicholas Van Hear,[55] provided very instructive conclusions drawn from case studies about return migration that depict it as a generator of employment that also encourages an economy to flourish. Van Hear studied four return experiences. The first examined the expulsion of 50,000 Asians from Uganda in 1972 and

---

53 C. Geertz, *Peddlers and Princes*, 1993.

54 Many entrepreneurs indicate difficulties in dealing with employees and complain about the absence of a work ethic. This can be explained by the weak institutionalisation of regulations concerning work as well as weakness in the workers union and the fragmentation of other unions like the Engineers Union, in which each branch functions as an independent entity.

55 N. Van Hear, 1997.

their subsequent, albeit limited, return (some 7,000) two decades later, an important factor in the recovery of the Ugandan economy. The second case dealt with the forced exodus of 300,000 ethnic Turks from Bulgaria back to Turkey in mid-1989. In this case, external assistance aided integration greatly. The third case concerned the exodus of 350,000 of Palestinians from Kuwait and other Gulf States, most of whom went to Jordan. The mass migration from Kuwait and the Gulf represented a 10 per cent growth in Jordan's population, increasing it to approximately 3.8 million. While the immediate consequences of the mass arrival were negative and disruptive, some long term benefits with great potential for the national economy became apparent within the first two years. Two factors played a major role in the positive economic impact: First, the majority of returnees were well-educated and skilled professionals who immediately entered the labour market; secondly, the migration was accompanied by a large influx of capital.[56] The economic behaviour of the returnees and the manner of their social integration could tell us much about what to expect in the territories. In all these three cases, external assistance was a positive factor in integration. In comparison, the expulsion of 800,000 Yemenis from the Gulf States, with no external assistance in the late 1990s, showed a negative impact on the society of origin.

One can also draw lessons from the Israeli experience. Israel had a high rate of investment during its peak period of migration. Between 1950 and 1955, the investment rate was an impressive 13 per cent, and during the waves of Soviet Jewish migration between 1988 and 1992 the rate reached 13.6 per cent.[57]

3. Migration Culture

According to human capital theory, migration occurs if the discounted expected returns in a potential destination country minus the migration costs are larger than the discounted expected returns in the current country of residence. However, this theory has been challenged by analyses that focus on the importance of migrant networks that make the decision to migrate. Moreover, the consequences of the migration, and the sending and receiving societies go beyond simple socioeco-

---

[56] Estimated at some US$ 1.5 billion (Central Bank of Jordan, 1992).

[57] Naqib, see note 39, 45.

nomic impact. Migration increases the tendency toward the individualisation of society and the number of female-led households.

Shaml's socio-anthropological survey covered both lifetime migration and circular/temporary migration both within Palestine/Israel and internationally. For the last type, a complete migration history of adults, aged 15 and over, was collected. The migration history data includes the timing of each move, places of origin and destination.

Generally, we can talk about a migration culture among Palestinians in certain areas. All the villages to the east of Ramallah (Deir Dibwan, Mazraa Sharquiyya, Tormos Aiyya, etc.) have a great number of migrants in the United States, while the western villages tend to send their male members to Israel as labourers. This is mainly due to the culture of migration: the social networks between the villagers and their relatives in the USA were very useful in facilitating and encouraging migration. The consequences of this migration in the socioeconomic and cultural features of these sets of villages are enormous, as migrants aid the rest of family who stay in the village.

Not surprisingly, Palestinians in the territories were much more mobile than Palestinians inside Israel, but less mobile than refugees outside. This indicates that many migration movements were caused by political disturbances and border restrictions. Some 60 per cent of respondents had moved at least once, with three moves being the average, and where the Gulf countries were the favourite destination abroad. For Palestinians in the territories the most important reasons to move are work, education, marriage, and improved housing, especially for refugees who wish to leave the camps and move to the cities. For Palestinians in Israel, marriage is an important reason, followed by work and then education. In more than 90 per cent of the cases, women follow men in marriage-related moves. The same pattern is detected in family reunifications; 77 per cent of the cases in the territories involve women following their male relatives.

The highest incidents of mobility are within the Palestinian territories with 57 per cent of total moves; while the favourite destinations abroad are the Gulf countries with 10 per cent of the total moves (inside and abroad).

Although the Oslo peace process decreased the tendency to move (only 18 per cent of the moves reported were during the period of 1993-2003), the process also created opportunities for people to move inside the Palestinian territories. In fact, 94 per cent of the moves during this period involved people moving inside the territories, particularly on the part of the most educated people.

The importance of migration with family support has been similarly confirmed by other various surveys. In the Birzeit University Survey, of the 2,254 households surveyed, 2,774 migrants were recorded (1.2 migrants per household) with direct relation to the head of the household. Of the total emigrants, 55 per cent were male and 45 per cent female. The majority of migrants were listed as siblings of the household head (76 per cent) followed by children (20 per cent) and other categories (4 per cent). More males from the central region (Jerusalem, Ramallah and Bethlehem) suffer enforced migration as a result of expulsion and Gazans generally migrate in search of study opportunities. The migratory destinations vary: more camp-dwellers move to Jordan, more villagers move to the United States and Canada, and the more educated people go to the Gulf States. Mobility is noticed also in Jordan: according to the Fafo survey in 1996,[58] half the adults had moved at least once, although not necessarily outside Jordan.[59]

This tendency to migrate seems to have increased during the second *Intifada*, with some leaving the territories because of the insecurity and its attendant economic situation. Some 100,000 Palestinians are thought to have left the West Bank for Jordan and the West since late 2000,[60] marking a significant increase in migration rates.[61] Compare the annual migration rates that prevailed under the Israeli occupation from 1967 to 1993 (0.5-2 per cent, or some 5,000-15,000 from the West Bank and 3,000-7,000 from the Gaza Strip).[62] It is very hard to find current statistics on migration, as it is a silent migration with people ashamed to

58 The Fafo Survey concerns migration history data, and covers the entire life-span of a representative sample of this population.

59 Khawaja/Tiltnes, see note 7, 28-29.

60 Sletten/Pederson, see note 26, 31.

61 Many indications show Palestinian outward bound migration during the *Intifada*. The prestigious and expensive Al Mustakbal primary and secondary school in Ramallah, whose class rosters are a who's who of the Palestinian elite, lost more than one-third of its students as their families moved abroad. Moreover, according to information received from the anthropologist Riina Isotalo based on her fieldwork, a number of Palestinian-Chilean nationals from Bethlehem, Beit Jala and Beit Sahour left the territories during the new *Intifada* (personal communication with her).

62 ICBS, *Statistical Abstract of Israel*. Jerusalem: Central Bureau of Statistics, 1993, 760.

leave during the national struggle. People who leave are likely to be from the well-educated middle class and not from the working class. Some of those who leave suffer from the protracted, low-intensity conflict and have left because of proximate cause rather than the conflict itself. What all this illustrates is the eventual ease with which Palestinian refugees in the future may either emigrate abroad or return home.

One can conclude, therefore, that two main categories of people are likely to migrate to Palestine/Israel. First, there are those without kinship ties. Their "home"-coming is subject to (1) the political push factor from the host country; (2) their legal status in the host country; (3) sociological and economic push factors from the host country; and (4) sociological and economic pull factors from Palestine/Israel. The second category comprises people who have access to social capital through kinship ties in these areas, who are influenced by the same push and pull factors, but who can also use their social capital to encourage and facilitate their return.

Social capital, however, will also motivate Palestinian refugees' propensity to move to Palestine/Israel. Taking into consideration the fact that many Palestinians from both categories also have connections with Canada and the United States,[63] the possibility of migrating there is significant. Canada or the United States (and Europe and Australia) will be favoured both for kinship reasons and for educational systems. Around a third of those interviewed in the Gulf in 1990-1995 went to Canada and the United States to benefit from the educational systems there.

4. Positive Experience of Returnees

Some lessons can be learned from the experience of "returnees" to the Palestinian territories during the Oslo period. This return took the form of a collective influx during two distinct periods, as opposed to an organised or planned individual return. The first, forced movement was provoked by the outbreak of the Gulf War and entailed the emigration of some 350,000 Palestinians from Kuwait and other Gulf countries.[64] However, only 37,000 of those who had preserved their rights as per-

---

[63] According to different Fafo surveys. See note 7.

[64] S. Hanafi, *Entre deux mondes. Les hommes d'affaires palestiniens de la diaspora et la construction de l'entité palestinienne*, 1997; ESCWA, *Return Migration. Profiles, Impact and Absorption*, 1993.

manent residents in the West Bank and Gaza returned to these territories.[65] The second period followed the launch of the peace process and involved a return migration from Arab countries, Egypt, and Jordan, as well as Tunisia. Palestinians with a precarious legal status or those who benefited from a quota agreed upon between Israel and the Palestinian National Authority (PNA) comprised the majority in this latter period.[66] Cases of individual return from various countries were also observed.[67] These migrants, belonging to different socio-professional categories, were often qualified university graduates possessing technical skills acquired in the host countries.[68]

Although there are no reliable estimates of the number of returnees residing in the Palestinian territories, there are some indicators. According to the 1997 census by the Palestinian Central Bureau of Statistics (PCBS), the total number of returnees was 267,355, constituting 10.5 per cent of the total population.[69] Interviews with representatives of the

---

65 Isotalo, see note 16.

66 Those who returned with the PLO were mostly PLO members and their families. They returned in the beginning of 1994 to be involved in building the institutions of the PNA. By now there are tens of thousands of people on the state payroll (if one includes the security services). They are among the higher rank of the PNA administration. R. Heacock, "Al-mahalliune wal 'aidune: Locals and Returnees in the Palestinian National Authority (PNA): A Historical Perspective", <http://www. birzeit.edu/academics/research/locals>, 2001, described their weight as following: "In the ministries, the directors general are 460 in number according to the archivist of the presidential office, in fact, more like 1000. Up to 65 percent are returnees, depending on sources. The same goes for the perhaps 2000 directors in the ministries. They dominate the executive branch. On the other hand, the inside heavily dominates the PLC, Palestinian Legislative Council or parliament elected in 1996. Although the numbers vary depending on the number of years of exile which define a person as a returnee rather than a local, there are by all counts well over fifty locals in the 88-member body. But its head, speaker Ahmad Qrei', a returnee who was elected to the PLC from Jerusalem, in turn heavily dominates that body."

67 Some were admitted in accordance with family reunification or temporary visitor visas. The latter have remained despite their irregular status *vis-à-vis* Israeli regulations.

68 E. Zureik, "The Trek Back Home: Palestinians Returning Home and their Problem of Adaptation", in: A. Hovdenak et al. (eds), *Constructing Order: Palestinian Adaptation to Refugee Life*, 1997.

69 M. Malki/Y. Shalabi, *Internal Migration and Palestinian Returnees in West Bank and Gaza Strip*, 2000.

PLO's Department of Refugee Affairs indicate that at least 200,000 of those may have returned during the Oslo process. According to surveys by Shaml and the Birzeit University Households,[70] returnees are more highly educated than non-returnees.[71] They also have more members in civil service employment and less in the private sector. Indeed, the government, UNRWA, and/or NGOs employ 57 per cent of returnees.

Any discourse concerning Palestinian return to the West Bank and Gaza Strip incorporates its share of paradox. "Returning" Palestinians who hail from areas that became Israel in 1948 have not realised a return to their native villages or cities; in their cases, "return" signifies a new migration. Furthermore, the "return movement" remains ephemeral as Israel still controls immigration to the territories and rarely grants residency to returnees: returnees, who generally possess a foreign passport, are considered tourists and are given three-month visas or often only one month visas when travelling across land borders. Even when they work in Palestinian areas, they can rarely acquire a work permit or residency; and they must repeatedly exit and re-enter the country before the expiration of their visa in order to obtain a new one. Those who overstay their visa risk being permanently barred entry into Israel, and, consequently, the territories.

These above distinctions are important because they will have an impact on the character of any eventual Palestinian state. As Roger Heacock has noted, if the return is to a "remembered" land (the West Bank and Gaza Strip) and not to the historical one (pre-1948 Palestine), then it is not a returnee state, but a settler state. The case of Bosnia-Herzegovina demonstrates that a state based on a merely liveable experience (and this at the expense of history) is not necessarily a successful one; in contrast, Israel, with its half-century of existence based on a discontinuous

---

70 Giacaman/Johnson, see note 6.

71 Generally, refugees in the Palestinian territories have higher levels of education than non-refugees. Fewer refugees are illiterate or with elementary skills (23 per cent) compared to non-refugees (25 per cent) and have more secondary education (17 per cent) compared to non-refugees (15 per cent) and more post-secondary education (11 per cent) compared to non-refugees (8 per cent). This confirms the importance of UNRWA support for refugees; education and perhaps the refugee population's ambition to seek educational capital where other forms of capital do not exist. (Ibid., 12).

memory and reconstructed history, has undoubtedly been a successful case of settler state-building.[72]

The return to the Palestinian territories pre-dates the Oslo process, and, if anything, was sparked by the Iraq-Kuwait War. However, three quarters of those who responded to the Shaml survey indicated a post Oslo return. Half of those interviewed returned with the PNA while 13 per cent were beneficiaries of the family reunification policy. What is important here is that around a quarter of the returnees lack proper papers as they came as visitors and Israel has not permitted the renewal of stays in the Palestinian territories since the beginning of the *Intifada*. Return seems to have taken place in consultation with their families (81 per cent); in only 10 per cent of the cases did the family oppose a return, mainly because of spousal commitments abroad. In one case, the family accepted the decision of the father, but the women imposed the condition that they do not take Palestinian IDs and keep their status as foreigners. It also appears that the opposition to return migration was not generally from spouses, but mainly from the older children, who did not want to return.

According to the Shaml survey, returnees' situation improved after their return, although the nature of their jobs changed. While half previously worked as employees, 80 per cent did so upon their return. Three quarters declared themselves satisfied with their work and only one quarter said their economic situation had worsened. These percentages should be read in the context of the general instability as a result of the *Intifada*. Only a third received help from family members when they moved, largely because the majority were not originally from the West Bank or the Gaza Strip; therefore, they did not have family members there or a family who financially was able to help them.

Overall, three quarters declared that they were satisfied with their return, despite the difficulties. Older people were more satisfied than young people. The latter complained particularly about the level of health services, housing, and the quality of education.[73] Two-thirds still rent their apartments ten years after arrival.

---

72 R. Heacock, "Returnee State", in: T. Hentsch et al. (eds), *The Becoming of Returnee States: Palestine, Armenia, Bosnia*, 1999, 57.

73 65 per cent of the returnees interviewed spoke of encountering difficulties, mainly social ones, during their initial time. Around 41 per cent said health services in the Palestinian Territories were poor and only 22 per cent said they were good. Many returnees complained about Palestinian universities as too

Most importantly, even though two-thirds had expectations about the "homeland" (*al-watan*), which were different from what they encountered, this did not hinder 95 per cent of them to advise others to come to the territories. Homeland becomes not just a "natural" place of return or a symbol of the *Intifada* and political alienation, but a real place, where there are job opportunities and scientific and technological development. One female returnee called it the "country of interest and of love ... the last refuge for people after the tiring exile in countries that did not respect refugee rights." Many came to the homeland even if they were originally from Historical Palestine. "It is not the homeland I had dreamed of and not my people to whom I thought I belonged," said one frustrated man, who returned on the PLO list after 1993.

Even if returnees are satisfied, the return experience was and will be problematic. Many have said that the local population did not welcome them or seemed not to want their return, especially on the West Bank. They saw the economic advantage of returning, but viewed it as difficult to adapt socially to Palestinian society. An employee with the PNA administration stated, "We are different in culture and mode of thinking." Nonetheless, most respondents, especially in Gaza, viewed the return phenomenon as providing important advantages, including an increase in the number of educated people and intellectuals, the presence of multiple cultures in Palestine, and a revival of Islamic values. It is curious that in an overcrowded Gaza, return migration was seen as a way to increase the Palestinian population in the territories, an argument not made by Western Bankers and peace brokers.

III. Conclusion

During the last 100 years it seems there has been a major shift in what kinship implies. Kinship relations used to include a strong tribal structure whereby two putative allegiances, such as the Qaysi and the Yamani before the 1950s, would form important social allegiances and networks.[74] In the 1960s, 1970s and 1980s the extended family became the most important network. But since the beginning of 1990s, the ma-

---

commercial but more than the half expressed satisfaction with their children's schools.

74 S. Tamari, "Palestinian Society", in: P. Matar (ed.), *Palestinian Encyclopaedia*, 2000, 370.

jor social network has been reduced to the level of the nuclear family. The historian Nazmi Jo'bi argues that the nature of the habitat and internal and outside migration has affected ties among cousins. He remembered that in the 1980s he used to visit his cousins during the *Eid*, but does so much less now. His father's house could host 40 people; his own is far too small for that.[75]

The most striking finding of the current research is that social ties between the Palestinians of Palestine/Israel and their relatives abroad after this protracted period of conflict is shaped more by rupture than continuity. The duration of the exodus, now more than 55 years, and the impact of the borders have hampered ties between relatives. Arabs used to say *al bo'd Jafa* (distance ends the relationship). Reality is not far removed from this. The Israeli system of bio-politics, with its methods of surveillance and control, has created a huge distance between the two sides; while the number of ties is less, their depth is still very important. Some transnational families have resisted the borders and the length of separation while others have been tremendously affected. The result is that the mode of entrepreneurship in Palestine, and to a lesser extent in Israel, was kept familial. For this reason, the remaining transnational social ties were used to mobilise capital, know-how and information to help families in the Palestinian territories. One can reasonably suspect, therefore, that return shall remain transnational, i.e. refugees shall keep their ties to both their place of return and their previous host country.

Generally speaking, there is a huge difference between Palestinians in the territories and those in Israel, as pertaining to the impact of the many factors that shape the eventual movement of Palestinian refugees. The Palestinian transnational kinship ties, for instance, in the territories are more important than those in Israel.

Power Structure: the Encounter between Palestinians from Different Sides of the Green Line

Palestinian sociologist Aziz Haidar observed that after the 1967 War encounters between Palestinian refugees living in the newly occupied West Bank and Gaza Strip and their relatives within the 1948 borders were problematic. After many years of separation, people quickly real-

---

75 Interview with Nazmi Jo'bi, Jerusalem, November 2003.

ised the differences.[76] Occupation, surveillance, and control had created a new Palestinian world inside Israel. In addition to the impact of the political system, a social class issue had arisen. The Palestinians inside Israel had become much wealthier than their relatives who were living as refugees in the West Bank and Gaza Strip. Haidar notes that the visits stopped quickly. One interviewee who lives in Haifa explained that he became too upset when he accompanied people to their former homes in Wadi Salib and other parts of Haifa, and that he had to stop doing this.

There are many explanations for this rupture between the two sides of the Green Line. The Palestinians of Israel channelled the power from the hegemonic Israeli society, absorbed it and then exercised it against the Palestinians living under occupation in WBGS. Moreover, the differences in their socioeconomic situation created a feeling of superiority. The sociologist Nabil Saleh argues that the Palestinians of Israel did not worry about what the occupation meant for the WBGS. He remembered from his childhood how the Palestinians of Israel would say "when the West Bank was *opened*" and not "*occupied.*"

On their first trip to East Jerusalem, Palestinians of Israel took pictures with Israeli soldiers in their uniforms and their guns.[77] The historian Adel Manaa considered the case of 350 Palestinian families from the north of Israel who moved to East Jerusalem to be closer to the Palestinian universities; there was a lot of subtlety as to the desire of these people to be close to the Palestinians under occupation. This desire did not prevent a number of complications arising. Some of them felt the double marginality: the marginality of a minority in a racist Israeli society and marginality with the Palestinian Jerusalemites who did not wish to integrate them.

One can argue that these prejudices among different groups are no different when a Palestinian Bedouin of Beer Sheva goes to live in Jaffa or Nazareth. In a highly segmented and tribal Palestinian society, prejudices among different groups are only aggravated by border separation and not created by it. Nor must one underestimate how much the current Israeli politics of space also hinders connections between Palestinians inside the West Bank and Gaza Strip. The result in the long term is very significant in creating borders in the minds of people. A border does not necessarily change a national identity, but it does change the

---

76 Personal communication with the author.

77 Interview with Nabil Saleh, Haifa, November 2003.

everyday practices of people, including their willingness to move to their places of origin. Similarly the current fragmentation of the Palestinian population, mainly through the exercise of Israeli bio-politics, creates local identities in the population. This will not necessarily cancel the national identity, but it will interact with it, sometimes harmoniously and sometimes in conflict.

Consider the story of Barta'a, a village that straddles the border between Israel and the West Bank. In 1949, Israel[78] divided Barta'a into two sections separated by an armistice line. Although Barta'a has a tribal structure composed mainly of one family (the Kabha family), its family ties were torn apart. From 1949 to 1967, meetings between people were rare, with both Israel and Jordan hindering people from interacting.[79] Villagers would hold funerals and weddings close to the border to allow the other side to participate (the same thing applies to ties between Palestinian Rafah and Egyptian Rafah, even if the separation date there was only 1983). In 1967, the village was informally reunited when Israel occupied the West Bank; although, initially warm meetings quickly faded as cultural, economic, and political differences between the divided families became apparent. The ties were now structured by "power relations and disputes"[80] and those divides have continued until today. While West Bank Barta'a was a bastion of the two *Intifadas*, 57 per cent of the population of the Israeli half in 1995 voted for a Zionist party (Labor Party) in the eleventh Knesset elections, which was vastly different from the general trend in other Palestinian localities in Israel.[81] This vote should not be overanalysed in terms of group identity. In the ninth Knesset elections, 44 per cent of Barta'ans voted for the Arab Front, and the rest of the vote was for Labor because the party had chosen a candidate from Barta'a for the Hestadrut General Secretary election.[82]

---

[78] After the Rhodes Agreement with Jordan in 1949, Jordan handed many villages in the triangle area, including half of the village of Barta'a over to Israel.

[79] Z.M.D. Kabha, *Barta'a. The Divided Heart*, 2003, 69.

[80] M. Totary, *The Political Attitude in a Divided Village. The Case of Western Barta'a/Eastern Barta'a*, 1999, 13.

[81] This contrasted with Arab voting in general: 51 per cent of Palestinians of Israel supported Arab parties who obtained only 17 per cent of the vote in Barta'a (ibid., 18).

[82] *Idem.*

Due to the separation between the two sides of Barta'a, there have been very few inter marriages between the two sides. Barta'a, with (in 2002) 7,356 inhabitants (4,174 and 3,182 in east and west respectively), can count only 12 marriages between the sides in the years 1967 and 1968. That number has since increased to 30 marriages after restrictions on the entry of Palestinian workers were imposed during the first *Intifada* encouraged. In other words, endogamous marriages were motivated by an interest to obtain Israeli Ids and access to Israel proper. Currently, the Barta'ans are alienated by the construction of the separation wall that will once again isolate the two sides of the village from each other.

West Barta'ans do not want their village to fall under PNA control. There is a very complex relationship between the two sides. During the Oslo process, the main topic of discussion in Barta'a's coffeshops was the future of the village. The Palestinian side wants to unify Barta'a within a Palestinian state, something the other side refuses categorically. And although they assist their West Bank relatives when the Israeli army demolishes homes, this solidarity resembles Palestinian American support for the Palestine cause or American Jewish financial support for Israel, support that is offered without wanting to be identified. The border and the power relationship have created a new identity for the inhabitants of Western Barta'a. They will be happy to reunite their village, but only without the undermining of their privileges.

Palestinian refugees in WBGS, as well as the diaspora, have a much stronger feeling of *nostalgia for the land* of Palestine than for the people of Palestine. For example, refugees insist on talking about property, land, and the Mediterranean Sea, in addition to the Al Aqsa mosque, Khader tomb, Deir Bor'om Church ... and when confronted with questions about with whom and how they would live, they become evasive. Any reflection on the return of refugees should be a reflection on the society of return and not only the land of return. The Palestinian refugees should not create a myth of a *land without a people for refugees without land* that is nothing more than a parody of the Zionist myth.

The Spatial Outcome of the 1948 War and Prospects for Return

Arnon Golan

I. Introduction

Variations of the spatial outcome of fought wars in the 20th century in different areas of the world were the result of different political, socio-economic, cultural, and geographical realities. In most cases, however, the established settlement picture of war-stricken areas changes at a speed impossible in peacetime. Modern war affects human settlements and environment, urban and rural, in large areas both close to and far away from the front. The devastating power of modern weaponry, the demands of the war economy, the need to provide shelter for refugees, the maintenance of a large military organisation, as well as other wartime realities, cause an immense shift in human spatial systems that occurs in a relatively short period of time. Postwar spatial formations and landscapes in various areas around the world are the result of formidable wartime transformation, although the short-lived traumatic character of war and the long-term dynamics of postwar development veil war's impact on the transformation of pre-war human landscapes.[1]

The Arab-Israeli conflict is no exception in the context of wartime spatial transformation. But, its ongoing nature has kept the 1948 wartime trauma alive; it was never marginalised by the involved societies, and its outcome was not obscured by postwar spatial dynamics. The vast transformation of landscapes included in the territory of Israel, and the myth

---

[1] P.F. Lewis, "Axioms for Reading the Landscape", in: D.W. Meining (ed.), *The Interpretation of Ordinary Landscapes*, 1979, 23; J.W. Konvitz, *The Urban Millennium*, 1985, 167-187; G.J. Ashworth, *War and the City*, 1991, 83-111, 137-145; S. Kostof, *The City Assembled*, 1992, 254-266.

of Palestinian return, namely the expectation of the restoration of pre-1948 spatial realities, still coexist and clash five and a half decades following the end of the 1948 War.

II. The 1948 War: Fundamental Facts and Spatial Imagination

The establishment of the State of Israel in the course of the 1948 War induced the drastic spatial transformation of the human geography of British Mandatory Palestine. The victorious Jewish/Israeli forces took over extensive Palestinian Arab areas, including about 400 villages, the Arab neighbourhoods of five mixed-populated cities and towns, and six Arab towns. Most former Arab villages were eventually demolished and their lands redistributed among pre-1948 and newly established Jewish settlements.[2] Former Arab urban areas, whose physical structure remained almost intact, were repopulated by Jews and incorporated into the emerging Israeli urban system.[3]

Following the signing in the spring and summer of 1949 of the armistice agreements with its Arab neighbours, the newly established State of Israel included about 76 per cent of the territory of British Mandatory Palestine. The remaining area was either annexed by Jordan (the West Bank) or came under Egyptian military rule (the Gaza Strip). The vast majority of the Arab Palestinian population that had lived in the territory now included within the borders of Israel, became refugees. Most of these 700,000 uprooted Palestinians found refuge either in the West Bank (about 38 per cent), becoming Jordanian citizens, or in the Egyptian-controlled Gaza Strip (about 26 per cent). Others were scattered among neighbouring Arab countries: Lebanon (14 per cent), Syria (10 per cent), and Jordan (10 per cent), while smaller numbers of Palestinian Arabs found refuge in Egypt and Iraq. Many among the refugees

---

[2] For different accounts of the number of former Arab villages, see W. Khalidi (ed.), *All That Remains*, 1992, xvii-xx; for different views of the reasons for the demolition of villages see G. Falah, "The 1948 Israeli-Palestinian War and Its Aftermath: The Transformation and De-signification of Palestine's Cultural Landscape", *Annals of the Association of American Geographers* 86 (1996), 256 et seq.; A. Golan, "The Transformation of the Abandoned Arab Rural Areas", *Israel Studies* 2 (1997), 94 et seq.

[3] A. Golan, *War and Spatial Transformation: The Case of the Former Arab Area in Israel, 1948-1950*, 2001, in Hebrew.

were housed in refugee camps within and without the boundaries of British Mandatory Palestine.[4]

During and following the 1948 War, and until the end of 1951, Israel absorbed about 700,000 Jewish immigrants, including Holocaust survivors and others from Europe and a large number of refugees from Arab and Muslim countries. Post-1948 Jewish immigrants were initially settled in former Arab urban areas, as were Jewish refugees of the 1948 War. Later, during the 1950s and 1960s, immigrants and others were housed in public housing estates, many of which were built on former Arab-owned lands. Most former Arab villages were razed to make room for the establishment of about 400 new Jewish collective and co-operative villages, many of which were populated by immigrants. Most of their agricultural land was redistributed among pre-1948 and new Jewish villages, while the remainder was allocated either for forestry or for the development of new Jewish urban areas.[5]

The vast majority of the Palestinian Arab refugees were not given permanent housing solutions. Many continued to live in destitute refugee camps, hoping to return to the homes they were forced to leave during the 1948 War. The return became a fundamental factor in the reconstitution of the Palestinian national identity in exile.[6] The persistence of the Arab-Israeli conflict on the one hand, and the formation of a new spatial reality in Israel on the other, as well as the integration of Palestinians in their places of refuge, gave the return an illusive character. It was the 1993 peace process that renewed Palestinians' hopes of return, as part of a future peace agreement.[7]

The prospects of a reconstitution of the map of pre-1948 Arab Palestine, which had become somewhat imaginary following the war, seemed

---

4 M. Gilbert, *The Arab-Israeli Conflict: Its History in Maps*, 1984, 4th ed., 47.

5 T. Goren, *From Dependence to Integration*, 1996, in Hebrew; Golan, see note 3; *idem*, see note 2; Khalidi, see note 2.

6 D.E. Arzt, *Refugees into Citizens: Palestinians and the End of the Arab-Israeli Conflict*, 1997, ch. 2; D. Rubinstein, *The Fig Tree Embrace*, 1990, 9-54, in Hebrew; M. Hassassian, "The Evolution of the Palestinian Refugee Problem", *Palestine-Israel Journal* 2 (1995), 29 et seq., 30-31.

7 Hassassian, ibid., 33-34; E. Zureik, "Palestinian Refugees and the Right of Return", *Palestine-Israel Journal* 2 (1995), 35 et seq.; A. Shiblak, "A Time of Hardship and Agony: Palestinian Refugees in Libya", *Palestine-Israel Journal* 2 (1995), 41 et seq.; R. Khalidi, "The Palestinian Refugee Problem: A Possible Solution", *Palestine-Israel Journal* 2 (1995), 72 et seq.

more realistic to the Palestinian side. Many among them consider it an essential part of the solution to the conflict as the restoration of just national rights.[8] Yet the possibility of such a process might seem a complex question, in respect of the spatial consequences of the 1948 War and the subsequent rapid development of the State of Israel. The effect of total or even the partial return of Palestinian refugees would not be the restoration of the past, but the formation of a new spatial reality. It might crucially impinge on Israel's political, cultural, economic, and social geography, resulting in the exacerbation rather than the settlement of the Israeli-Arab conflict.

The first aim of this paper is to present the Jewish repopulation process of former Arab rural and urban areas of Palestine, and its spatial consequences, during and following the 1948 War. The fundamentals of Israel's present spatial patterns are in many respects the outcome of the drastic wartime process, although the direct consequences of the 1948 War are hardly present in its contemporary landscape, in which former Arab areas are present mainly as relics. Some of them, especially those remaining as ruins, contrast and contest the modern Jewish-Zionist features of the landscape. Others have been integrated into the Israeli landscape, signifying a romanticist trend in the Israeli society that praises the aesthetic qualities of the pre-Zionist landscape, ironically considering it as (re)presenting "original" landscapes of Biblical periods. The second and consequent aim is to display Israel's present spatial reality as an apparent indication of the impracticality of mass repatriation of Arab Palestinians, and of the need for alternative solutions to the Palestinian refugee problem, rather than return.

The paper concentrates on the formation of Israel's post-1948 spatial reality, especially the "Israelisation" of pre-1948 Palestinian Arab areas and its effect on the feasibility of the return of former Arab residents or their descendants. It does not seek to present alternative solutions, which may include the resettlement of Palestinians in host Arab countries and in the territory of a future Palestinian state. The formulation of a sustainable spatial solution for the Palestinians needs further research.

---

[8] M. Benvenisti, *Sacred Landscape: the Buried History of the Holy Land since 1948*, 200 and 322-323.

III. The 1948 War: Depopulation and Repopulation

1. Depopulation: the Historiographic Debate

The academic discourse on the depopulation of Arab Palestinians is dominated by a heated debate between Israeli and Palestinian historical narratives of the 1948 War. This ongoing debate has an important impact on both Palestinians and Israelis regarding the relevance of the question of return.

The fundamental, not to say official, Israeli version places responsibility for the war with untrustworthy and incompetent Palestinian and other Arab leaders who refused to accept the 1947 UN partition resolution. The events and outcomes of the war initiated by them caused many Palestinians to flee. Moreover, many fled at the behest of these leaders, who promised a swift victory by the Arab regular armies over the Zionists and an immediate return.[9]

This narrative was utterly rejected by Palestinians and their supporters within and outside the Arab world. Palestinians blamed the Jewish-Zionist/Israeli leadership for a well-orchestrated deportation venture carried out according to a pre-war transfer plan that was brutally and efficiently implemented during the 1948 War by Jewish/Israeli military forces.[10]

Following the opening to the public in Israel and in Great Britain of archival materials relating to different aspects of the 1948 War, Israeli, Palestinian, and other scholars have been able to reconsider both the Israeli and the Palestinian Arab narratives.

Most notable in this context was the trail-blazing work of Benny Morris that concentrated on the role of the Jewish Zionist/Israeli leadership and armed forces in the creation of the Palestinian refugee problem. Many Israelis, including those who doubt most or some of his conclusions cannot deny that Morris has successfully contested the old Israeli narrative. Still, Morris found no evidence for a pre-war Zionist transfer plan and the subsequent systematic deportation of Palestinians by Jewish military forces, and he does not support the Palestinian narrative.

---

9 Y. Cohen, *The Arabs Hold the Key: How to Solve the Refugee Problem*, 1962, in Hebrew.

10 W. Khalidi, "Plan Dalet: Master Plan for the Conquest of Palestine", *Journal of Palestine Studies* 18 (1988), 3 et seq.

His book illustrates a complex set of causes for the uprooting of Palestinian Arabs, asserting that neither side is completely to blame.[11]

The publication of Morris' book initiated a bitter debate among Israeli academics and the wider public, which was not limited to the origins of the Palestinian refugee problem. History and contemporary reality intermingled as the debate spread to other episodes in the history of Zionism and the State of Israel, and to questioning the moral aspect of Zionism as a whole.[12]

New research trends affected the Palestinian narrative as well, but in a totally different way. The exposure of documents in Israeli archives revealing cases of deportation and massacre of Arabs that took place during the 1948 War, oral testimonies by villagers and townsfolk regarding such cases, as well as the growing debate among so-called old and new Israeli historians over the events of that war in particular and the general debate among various academics regarding Zionism's moral justification as a whole, seemed to support the Palestinian narrative. It strengthened Palestinians' sense of being victims, asserting that their misfortune was the outcome of an initial plan for deportation and a well-orchestrated set of massacres intended to terrorise Palestinian rural and urban populations.[13]

The Palestinians' myth of martyrdom resulted in turning the right of return into a fundamental of Palestinian nationalism. The 1948 events are known as *Al-Nakba*, the catastrophe. That is, the Palestinian Arabs were a passive group who suffered terrible injustice. Justice would be restored once Israel took full responsibility for the deportation of the Palestinians, recognised their right to return, and allowed the refugees and their descendants actually to go back to their places of origin.[14]

---

[11] B. Morris, *The Birth of the Palestinian Refugee Problem, 1947-1949*, 1987; see also D. Gutwein, "Left and Right Post-Zionism and the Privatization of Israeli Collective Memory", in: A. Shapira/D.J. Penslar (eds), *Israeli Historical Revisionism From Left to Right*, 2003, 9 et seq., 14-20.

[12] On different ramifications of the debate see articles published in Shapira/Penslar, ibid.

[13] As depicted in Falah, see note 2.

[14] E. Webman, "Al-Nakba – a Founding Myth in the Palestinian National Identity", in: T. Yegns (ed.), *From Intifada to War*, 2003, 107 et seq., in Hebrew; S. Abu Sitta, *The Unfolding of the Holocaust*, 2001, <http://www.palestineremembered.com/Acre/Right-Of-Return/Story433.html>.

The similarity to the Jewish Holocaust is no coincidence.[15] The Palestinian view elaborates on modern Jewish history to demand a full restoration of the rights of the victims (i.e., return), who like the Jews during World War II, took no part in the conflagration, but sustained the lion's share of suffering. Therefore their rights should be restored, regardless of the political solution of the Arab-Israeli conflict.

2. Wartime Depopulation and Repopulation of Rural Areas

The spatial outcome of the 1948 War is far less contested. Although there is a debate concerning the exact number of refugees and of abandoned Arab villages, the almost total eradication of the landscape of former Arab areas included within the boundaries of the State of Israel is indisputable. Almost all Arab villages abandoned during the 1948 War were demolished: during the war, in the months following it, and the last as late as the mid-1960s. Only few and sparse remains of some villages are still evident, mainly in remote areas of the Israeli periphery.[16]

The rationale for the eradication of Arab rural landscapes in Israel lay on three levels: the political-strategic, the socioeconomic, and the cultural-symbolic.

On the political-strategic level, some villages were partly or wholly demolished during the fighting. These were located at strategic sites, near main roads and junctions, and were demolished to prevent Arab forces from using them as logistic bases and for attacking Jewish villages, towns and transportation. This took place according to Plan D (Dalet) of the Hagana general staff of 10 March 1948 initiated to block the anticipated invasion by Arab regular armies following the termination of the British Mandate on 15 May 1948.[17] Plan D is considered by some scholars as the pre-emptive plan for the deportation of Palestinian Arabs;[18] nevertheless, demolition and deportation were not considered a

---

15 This is explicitly put forward by Abu Sitta, ibid., in the heading of his paper "The Unfolding of the Holocaust".

16 Morris, see note 11, 155-169; Golan, see note 3, 243-254; A. Shai, "The Fate of Abandoned Arab Villages in Israel on the Eve of the Six-Day War and its Immediate Aftermath", *Cathedra* 105 (2002), 151 et seq., in Hebrew.

17 For a detailed account of wartime demolition of villages: Morris, *idem*.

18 Explicitly by Khalidi, see note 10.

default, as the number of villages destined for demolition according to the plan was small.[19]

It was the demand presented to Israel by the UN Palestine Conciliation Committee (UNPCC), in the spring of 1949, following the termination of fighting, to allow the return of refugees that encouraged the Israeli government to decide on the systematic demolition of tens of abandoned Arab villages. Most of these were located in the strategic areas of the southern coastal plain and the Jerusalem corridor. While wartime demolition originated in strategic and tactical needs, postwar demolition was aimed to support a policy of preventing the possibility of the return of original residents to these areas.[20]

On the socioeconomic level, Jewish authorities preferred not to resettle sites of abandoned Arab villages, as the traditional clustered pattern of Arab villages did not comply with modernist meticulously planned patterns of the collective (*kibbutz*) and cooperative (*moshav*). Therefore, many abandoned Arab villages were demolished to clear the area for cultivation or building a new site for a Jewish village. Some villages were pillaged by Jewish looters, who dismantled whole houses, including bricks, rafters, roof tiles, doors, faucets, etc., for building or repairing their own houses, mainly in poor Jewish neighbourhoods of urban concentrations. In several cases debris from demolished villages was used for paving new roads. In other cases abandoned villages were left alone to deteriorate, due to the negligence of maintaining houses and infrastructure.[21]

On the cultural-symbolic level, in the eyes of the Zionist leadership and rural settlers, the Arab village stood for the underdevelopment and poor condition of the old Jewish homeland, neglected and impoverished by its "unworthy" Arab population. The *kibbutz* and *moshav* depicted the diametrical opposite, symbolising the merits of the modernist Jewish-Zionist (re)settlement venture and the return of the worthy to their homeland. Not only were the built-up structures demolished. Arable land of former Arab villages was redistributed among Jewish cultivators. This resulted in the removal of stone and cactus fences typical to the rural Arab landscape. They too depicted the "improper" situation and underdevelopment of the Promised Land, in contrast to the Jewish

---

[19] The original full Hebrew version of the plan is found at the Hagana Archives in Tel Aviv, file 73/94.

[20] Golan, see note 2, 102-103.

[21] Ibid., 103-104.

collective and cooperative ownership of land, as well as intensive cultivation methods that formed a modern landscape of rural areas, depicting the merits of Zionism.[22]

Rural Arab populations, as well as their traditional landscapes, remained in three different areas of Israel. The largest concentration of Arab villages was that of central Galilee. Next were the Arab villages of Wadi Ara and the eastern Sharon plain, the area known as the "Little Triangle." Jordan ceded this area according to the April 1949 armistice agreement, while Israel agreed to refrain from the expulsion of its Arab population. The third was the nomad and semi-nomad Bedouin population of the Negev desert, concentrated in the northern and northeastern part of this area.[23]

3. Wartime Depopulation and Repopulation of Urban Areas

Former Arab urban and urbanised areas were treated in a totally different way. The need to settle tens of thousands of Jewish immigrants arriving during the emergency of the 1948 War and thousands of Jewish war refugees, mostly from front-line neighbourhoods of Tel Aviv, Haifa, and Jerusalem, resulted in the preservation of most built-up structures and urban infrastructure systems.

In the case of the Tel Aviv-Jaffa metropolitan area, the villages of Jammasin, Sheikh Muwannis and Salama, located northeast and east of Tel Aviv, were the first to be abandoned by Arabs and used between February and May 1948 for housing Jewish war refugees. Later, between December 1948 and February 1949, all three were formally annexed to the municipal area of the Jewish metropolis. During the autumn of that year and until the summer of 1949 thousands of new immigrants were housed in former Arab neighbourhoods of Jaffa, which was formally incorporated into Tel Aviv in April 1950. Between October 1948 and June 1949 Jewish new immigrants also resettled the towns of Lydda and Ramla and villages such as Yazur, Yhudia, and Beit Dajan. The two towns, and the three villages that underwent a process of rapid urbanisation, became part of the rapidly developing Tel Aviv metropolitan

---

22 *Idem.*

23 On Arabs in Israel since 1948 see U. Benziman/A. Mansour, *Subtenants*, 1992, in Hebrew; I. Lustick, *Arabs in a Jewish State: Israel's Control of a National Minority*, 1980.

area. The remaining Arab population of this area was concentrated in the Ajami neighbourhood south of the old city of Jaffa, and in segregated sectors of Lydda and Ramle.[24]

Most former Arab neighbourhoods of Haifa were also initially populated by Jewish war refugees and later by a large number of new immigrants. Jewish immigrants were also housed, from the summer of 1948, in adjacent villages such as Ballad al-Sheikh and at-Tira, which became small immigrant towns, and in the town of Acre. All formed part of the developing metropolitan area of Israel's main port city. The remaining Arabs were concentrated in the Wadi Nisnas neighbourhood of Haifa and in the old quarter of Acre.[25]

Former Arab neighbourhoods of western Jerusalem: Qatamon, Talbiya, Deir Abu-Tor, Musrara, the German Colony, and Baqa'a, were all populated first by Jewish war refugees, and from September 1948 also by new immigrants. With the widening in the mid-1950s of the area of Israel's capital city westward, former Arab villages of Ein Karem, Maliha, Deir Yasin and Lifta, all of which had already been resettled from late 1948 or early 1949 by Jewish immigrants, were incorporated into the city limits. The remaining Arab population of Jerusalem included the residents of the northern part of the village of Beit Safafa, which was transferred to Israeli hands following the signing of the armistice agreement with Jordan in April 1949, and later annexed to the municipal area of Israel's capital city.[26]

Peripheral former mixed and Arab towns also experienced the process of wartime spatial transformation. Among the first were Tiberias and Safed, the repopulation of whose former Arab neighbourhoods began with the housing of Jewish war refugees, followed by new immigrants arriving in growing numbers since the summer of 1948. The resettlement by Jewish immigrants of peripheral former Arab towns, Beisan, Al-Majdal, and Beersheba, took place in the spring and summer of 1949. The remaining members of the Arab community of Al-Majdal were deported to the Egyptian-controlled Gaza Strip during the second half of 1950. Some peripheral large former Arab villages were also left intact, becoming Israeli towns. These were the northern village of

---

24 Golan, see note 3, chs. 2, 3; *idem*, "Lydda and Ramle: from Palestinian-Arab to Israeli Towns, 1948-67", *Middle Eastern Studies* 39 (2003), 121 et seq.

25 Goren, see note 5, 154-157; Golan, see note 3, 177-183.

26 Golan, ibid., ch. 1; Y. Ben Arieh/A. Vager, "The Development of Western Jerusalem between 1948 and 1967", *Idan* 18 (1994), 91 et seq., in Hebrew.

Khalisa whose built-up structures housed the first Jewish immigrants that settled in what later became Qiryat Shemona, and the southern villages of Yibna and Aqir, resettled by Jewish immigrants and renamed Yavne and Qiryat Eqron.[27]

Nazareth and Shefar'am remained the only Arab towns included within the boundaries of the State of Israel that preserved their original character. Except for these urban areas, Arab neighbourhoods that remained were in large and small Israeli urban centres, and the old quarters of Haifa and Tiberias which were demolished almost completely by local Jewish authorities in 1948 and 1949. Jews resettled almost all former Arab urban areas located within Israel's territory.

IV. Demolition, Development and Preservation: Former Arab Areas Between 1950 and Recent Years

Since the end of the emergency of the 1948 War, de-Arabisation and Israelisation of former Arab areas took place in three forms: demolition, redevelopment, and preservation. In rural areas demolition was dominant while in urban areas all three modes of operation were used.

1. Demolition

As mentioned above, Jewish populations housed in former Arab urban neighbourhoods included mainly impoverished new immigrants and war refugees. Following the war, the strongest among the residents were inclined to move to more attractive dwellings. Their places were taken mainly by other newly arrived impoverished immigrants. Consequently, during the 1950s many former Arab urban areas, including former middle and upper class neighbourhoods deteriorated into slums. The poor socioeconomic situation of the residents resulted in the deterioration of built-up structures and of urban infrastructure systems due to poor maintenance. Obsolete neighbourhoods, mainly the *nuclei* of former Arab towns whose poor physical condition was apparent before

27 Golan, ibid., ch. 3.

the war, mostly deteriorated and some of their houses collapsed, causing casualties among the recently housed Jewish population.[28]

Jewish municipalities of former mixed cities and towns, as well as new municipalities established in former Arab towns, sought the demolition of deteriorating urban sectors for the purpose of slum clearance and urban redevelopment. In the 1950s the Israeli government was reluctant to support such initiatives due to the shortage in housing. Most urban areas demolished in this decade were delapidated urban areas such as the old city of Lydda. Many houses, either obsolete or damaged during the war in Jaffa, Yahud, Ramla and Safed, were also demolished.[29]

The turning point in government policy was the outbreak of the 1959 Wadi Salib riots. Wadi Salib was a former Arab neighbourhood of Haifa, inhabited by indigent Jewish immigrants. The poor socioeconomic and physical conditions prevailing in the neighbourhood, whose population included a majority of immigrants from Morocco, stimulated the formation of a local leadership whose protest took the form of violent demonstrations censuring the discrimination against the residents by the Israeli authorities. Riots spread to other urban concentrations of new immigrants, revealing the plight of many among this population, for the most part Jews of Middle Eastern and North African origin, to Israeli public opinion. A discussion of the riots and their effect on Israeli society is beyond the scope of this paper. Suffice it to say that the disturbances motivated the government to initiate a slum clearance and rehabilitation policy.[30]

Among the slums destined for demolition were three of Tel Aviv's slum areas: Manshiya, a former Arab neighbourhood of Jaffa, Givat Amal, pre-1948 Jammasin, and Kfar Shalem, pre-1948 Salama. Eviction met the resistance of many of the slum dwellers, who demanded larger compensation than that offered by the authorities, and the pace of demolition was rather slow. The demolition of Manshiya was completed only in the mid-1970s, and that of the two other areas is still in progress. Hundreds of former Arab structures located in other main cities and peripheral towns, as well as many obsolete structures of pre-

---

[28] Y. Almogi, *A Plan for Evacuation and Reconstruction of Slum Areas*, 1963, in Hebrew.

[29] Golan, see note 3, ch. 3; *idem*, see note 24.

[30] On the Wadi Salib riots see H. Dahan-Kalev, *Self-Organizing Systems: Wadi Salib and "The Black Panthers" – Implications for Israeli Society*, 1991, in Hebrew.

1948 Jewish slums, have been demolished since the early 1960s to afford further urban redevelopment projects. As a result, the number of former Arab built-up structures has been greatly reduced, and the impact of former Arab urban areas on the Israeli urban landscape is diminishing.[31]

2. Development

The former Arab built-up area did not supply all housing needs for immigrants to Israel in the early 1950s, whose number more than doubled the newly formed state's Jewish population. Many among them, numbering about 250,000 in 1952, were housed in immigrant transit camps known as *ma'abarot* (plural of *ma'abara*). Arabs formerly owned most land allocated by the Israeli authorities to the transit camps. In many cases these were agricultural lands located on the margins of large and small urban concentrations, pre-1948 Jewish, former Arab, or new towns.

The large-scale construction of public housing estates for new immigrants began in 1953. It took place in Tel Aviv and Haifa and their metropolitan areas, as well as in Jerusalem and in various peripheral towns. Housing estates were constructed also for various pre-1948 Jewish urban populations. The government also sold land to private contractors who built for the middle and upper class population. Most of these lands were formerly owned and cultivated by Arabs. The landscape of these areas was urbanised, as houses, roads, commercial centres and industrial zones replaced cultivated fields and olive and orange groves.

The rapid growth of the Jewish urban population and the rise in living standards enhanced further urban development. The transformation of rural into urban landscapes in both central and peripheral areas has been accelerating since the late 1960s. A large portion of the land allocated for further urban development was owned by Arabs before 1948 or confiscated from Arab cultivators during the 1950s and 1960s.

---

[31] A. Golan, "Redistribution and Resistance: Urban Conflicts During and Following the 1948 War", *Modern Jewish Studies* 1 (2002), 117 et seq.; *idem*, "The Politics of Urban Demolition and Human Landscape Transformation", *War in History* 9 (2002), 431 et seq.; *idem*, "From Abandoned Village to Urban Neighborhood, Kafr Salama 1948-1950", *Merhavim* 4 (1991), 71 et seq., in Hebrew.

Moreover, former Arab land allocated to Jewish rural settlements has also been redistributed for urban development.[32]

3. Preservation

In general, the Zionist Jewish-Israeli establishment and elite regarded the Arab landscapes of Palestine/Israel as obsolete and representing the underdevelopment and degeneration of the Jewish ancient homeland. Yet, a romantic view of Arab landscapes also persisted among some Zionists, especially those of the cultural elite, who regarded them as the depiction of Biblical landscapes.[33]

Those who adhered to the romantic view initiated the preservation of what they considered picturesque Arab landscapes such as that of Jaffa's old quarter. There were also some modernist-nationalist-functionalists who appreciated the qualities of several former middle-class Arab urban neighbourhoods planned and built in a hybrid (modernist and traditional) architectural style and modern construction methods. The quality of planning and construction of houses in neighbourhoods such as Qatamon and Talbiya in Jerusalem excelled those in most Jewish modern neighbourhoods.[34]

Both romantics and modernists sought to preserve former Arab neighbourhoods by permanently settling them. Artists settled the Arab quarter of Safed and in the old quarter of Jaffa, recognising the value of their pre-modern qualities. Resettlement saved both areas from demolition, different from the cases of the old quarters of Haifa, Tiberias and Lydda. Senior Israeli government officials, university professors, and other members of the elite settled in Talbiya and redeemed this neighbourhood from deteriorating into a lower middle class or poor urban area inhabited by war refugees and immigrants. From the 1960s until recently, other former Arab neighbourhoods of Jerusalem such as Qatamon, Deir Abu-Tor, the German Colony, and Baqa'a, underwent a process of gentrification, becoming middle and upper middle class ar-

---

32 For a detailed overview of the recent debate regarding land use in Israel see the different articles published in *Karka* 52 (2001), in Hebrew.

33 For the cultural elite's view see G. Ofrat, *On the Ground: Early Eretz-Israeli Art*, 1993, 483-500, in Hebrew.

34 D. Kroyanker, *Jerusalem – Conflicts Over the City's Physical and Visual Form*, 1988, 315-317.

eas. Gentrification of former Arab neighbourhoods originally settled by war refugees and immigrants was somewhat unique to Jerusalem, while in most other cities and towns they are still among the poorer urban areas or have already been demolished.[35]

Well-preserved former Arab neighbourhoods were integrated into the Jewish Israeli urban fabric. The old quarter of Jaffa and the area preserved as the artists' quarter in Safed serve as major tourist attractions. They contrast and contest modernist urban values and landscapes developed by the Zionist movement and the State of Israel, but on the cultural inner-Jewish level, not on the national level, as they are not identified with their Arab former residents. Although given Hebrew names, former Arab neighbourhoods of Jerusalem are familiar to most Jewish residents of the city by their original names,[36] but are not identified with their original residents. For the recent Jewish population, names such as Talbiya and Qatamon depict high economic and social status and upper middle-class living standards, rather than their Arab past.

V. Concluding Remarks

The 1948 War and Israel's dynamic development in over five decades of independence resulted in an almost total spatial transformation and an extensive change of the landscape of former Arab rural and urban areas. Hundreds of new modern planned Jewish villages replaced traditional rural Arab villages. Most former Arab urban areas were incorporated into the rapidly developing Israeli urban system. The growth of Israel's Jewish urban population brought about the reallocation of former Arab agricultural land for the development of housing estates and new neighbourhoods. Redevelopment of run-down urban areas, including former Arab neighbourhoods, resulted in their demolition and replacement by modern built-up structures. Modernisation and rise in living standards also resulted in the rapid development, not to say westernisation, of urban and rural sectors inhabited by Israel's Arab minority.

---

35 A. Gonen, *Between City and Suburb*, 1995, 95-97.

36 Officially these neighbourhoods were given Hebrew names, which hardly anyone uses, not even scholars in their books, as related in Kroyanker, see note 34, 315-317.

Returning refugees would find it a challenge, in most cases, to locate their old home or its original site. They would also realise that the landscapes they knew and remember, and which probably form a set of spatial images bequeathed to their descendants, have long disappeared or have been utterly transformed. The return to original homes and tracts of land, which have by now disappeared, been transformed, or occupied by other residents, might prove illusory. The mass implementation of the right of return demands the allocation of land for alternative housing and developing means of living. This might be illusory, too.

Allocation of space to a mass of repatriated refugees would hamper the daily practices of the Israeli population, Jewish and Arab, and its capability to use the space for the fulfilment of different economic, social, and cultural needs such as travelling to work places and schools, socialising with family and friends, and recreation and leisure. Moreover, Israel's relatively small territory and high population density[37] produce many conflicts over land uses for housing, industry, commerce, public amenities, leisure and recreation. These arise between national and local government, and between government and interest groups.[38] The adding of a new and large interest group such as returning Palestinian Arabs would produce a new set of conflicts over land use, accelerated by ethnic and cultural differences, economic inferiority, long-lasting animosity, and hostile political views regarding the fundamental existence of a Jewish state.

Nevertheless, it is not the practical implementation of a mass return but the concept of return that causes apprehension among the Jewish majority in Israel. The Palestinian imaginary map conceals a future threat, whose realisation may be attempted, resulting in the eradication of the Jewish map. It is rather similar to the threat that the imaginary Jewish Biblical map holds for the Palestinians living in the West Bank and the Gaza Strip. No wonder that the attempt at the latter's implementation, namely the settlement project, raises overwhelming Palestinian resistance and imperils any chance of reconciliation. Palestinians should accept that the spatial reality formed during the 1948 War and consecutive years of Israeli independence is irreversible, and that the mass return of refugees and their descendants is impossible. Israelis should see that a stable and lasting peace will not be achieved without relinquishing the Biblical map and acknowledging the need for a Palestinian independent

[37] Central Bureau of Statistics, Statistical Abstract of Israel 2002, No. 53, <http://www.cbs.gov.il/shnatonenew.htm>, Table 2.4.

[38] Different articles published in *Karka* 52, see note 32.

state, in which at least some Palestinian refugees will be settled. The abandoning by both sides of illusive maps can help bring about the realisation of what still seems an elusive peace.

Zionist Massacres: the Creation of the Palestinian Refugee Problem in the 1948 War

Dr. Saleh Abdel Jawad[*]

> "Palestine is the cruellest, most difficult cause to uphold, not because it is unjust, but because it is just and yet dangerous to speak about ... honestly and concretely."
> Edward Said[1]

> "Things will come out in the end. The question is how to live with this."
> Aryeh Yitzachi[2]

I. Introduction

The Arab-Israeli War began on Monday, 5 June 1967. By the next morning a long column of men, women, and children coming from nowhere began to crowd the streets of my home town, el-Bireh, heading

---

[*] I want to thank the following institutions and individuals for supporting this work in a variety of ways: the Program for Scholars At Risk and the Department of History, Harvard University, especially Jacqueline Bhaba and Professor John Womack, Professor Joel Perlmann, Levy Institute Research Professor at Bard College; Professors Joseph Massad of Columbia University, Professor Suad Joseph of the University of California at Davis, Rosemary Sayigh, Linda Butler of the *Journal of Palestine Studies*, and Professor Eve Spangler of the Boston College Department of Sociology for invaluable editorial suggestions and insightful ideas.

[1] Quoted in B. Harlow, "Remember the Solidarity Here and Everywhere", *Middle East Report* 229 (2002), 4 et seq.

[2] G. Ehrlich, "Not only in Deir Yassin", *Ha'ir*, 6 May 1992, 22.

toward Amman. Some were in their cars, but most were on foot. My father, who was the Mayor of el-Bireh at that time, tried to stop the fleeing refugees with the help of local scouts. He noticed that the bulk of the mass was composed of people who had fled their homes in 1948 fearing war atrocities, and were now refugees for the second time. I was struck by the agony in their voices and the grief on their faces. I also observed their extreme fear of the Israelis whose only appearance in the town had been for a short strafing "visit" by three Israeli airplanes, which killed five people. My interest in the Palestinian refugee tragedy during the 1948 War dates from this moment when I, as a boy of 15, began to wonder about the nature of an enemy who could strike such terror into the hearts of the adults I knew.

Since then, I have dedicated my work to "the study of the inhuman use of power ... determined to uncover the essence of the system that produced it."[3] Today, I argue the following: The number of documented massacres[4] perpetrated by Zionists and Israeli forces against the Palestinians during the 1948 War is much larger and more important than previously thought. Furthermore, the false perception of the size and the significance of the massacres is not only by the general public, but even historians, including Palestinian historians.[5] The size and significance of these incidents transcend the scope previously given to it by historians. For the time period between the beginning of the war, December 1947, and January 1949 at the end of the war, I documented *nearly 70 massacres.*

This relatively large number is a conservative count for many reasons. First, it does not cover the entire period of the war.[6] Second, there are locations for which I have no data at all, like the Bedouin settlements in

---

3 S. Power, "The Lesson of Hannah Arendt", *New York Review of Books* 51 (2004), 34 et seq., uses this language to describe the work of Hannah Arendt and it perfectly describes why I greatly admire her intellectual work.

4 I will offer a definition of a massacre below.

5 This contradicts both the old Israeli historiography that recognises only Deir Yassin, as well as the work of Benny Morris who continues to insist that "atrocities were limited in size, scope and time" (B. Morris, *The Birth of the Palestinian Refugee Problem Revisited*, 2004, 2nd ed., 482).

6 The war itself began in December 1947 and ended in 1949 with the signing of multiple armistice agreements. The expulsion of the Palestinians from their land, however, continued for many years after the war. For example, the population of the city of Majdal was expelled in 1950; the Bedouin tribes' expulsion continued up to 1953.

the Negev. Third, there are other areas for which I have little information. This especially holds true for the villages in Southern Palestine where, I suspect, war crimes were particularly intense because the area was, as is the Gaza strip today, less frequented by press and international observers in comparison to other parts of Palestine. People were also less educated in this area and had little access to world media.[7] Fourth, I have not listed the hundreds of war crimes involving only one or two fatalities. Fifth, there are archives that I have not yet been able to visit, archives that have not yet yielded all their information (for example "sensitive" documents in the UN and Israeli archives),[8] and Arab archives that have not been made accessible as of yet. Sixth, Arab societies often failed to collect or, when collected, failed to protect documents that would attest to massacres even after all the eyewitnesses had died. Seventh, some massacres are still under investigation, and they, too, are omitted from my list. Eighth, for purposes of this paper, I have also eliminated most terror attacks which, while part of the 1948 dirty war, were not often aimed at populations that had already surrendered, as one of the conditions of my definition of a massacre.

My work is intended to make the following contributions in regards to the events I cover: to offer a definition of the term "massacre;" to uncover some new incidents; to demonstrate the power of grafting oral testimonies with documentary sources; to offer a preliminary typology of massacres; and eventually, for future work, to provide the first systematic and integrated census of massacres in a field where information has previously been fragmented, scattered, and faceless. The latter can be at times a strategy of "containment" by which massacres may be simultaneously admitted and minimised. When the pattern of massacres is considered in its entirety, I argue that it is enough to demonstrate a

---

[7] For the harsher behaviour against people in Gaza, G. Levy, "The IDF's Shooting Range", *Ha'aretz*, 15 February 2004, <www.haaretz.com/hasen/spages/394153.html>, and, in general, Amira Haas' reports from the Gaza strip in *Ha'aretz*.

[8] The United Nations archives in New York, which I visited in March 2004, contain rich documentation about the war. However, the UN archives continue to classify certain documents even 55 years after the events that they describe. The question is: who is protected by this discretion? M. Palumbo, "What Happened to Palestine? The Revisionists Revisited", *The Link* 23 (1990), argues that the UN limits access to documents that might damage its own reputation – but the implication of this standard for particular research questions is unclear. Similarly, Israeli archives are open but continue to censor many of the documents which relate to atrocities and war crimes in 1948.

centralised Zionist/Israeli policy of ethnic cleansing, even without "smoking gun" documents attesting to such a centralised policy.[9]

I arrived at these conclusions gradually, over a long period of study. A retrospective view may be the most suitable for explaining my methodology and course of work. The starting point of my study was in mid 1993, when I was appointed Director of the Birzeit University Research Center,[10] and was charged to pursue the programme of publishing monographs on the destroyed Palestinian villages. This work was begun by my colleagues.[11] I introduced a new approach to the work. I fo-

[9] The existence of central plan or intent of ethnic cleansing is, of course, a matter of intense controversy, with the Israelis arguing, despite their recognition of archival censorship, that no documentary evidence of such a plan has ever been produced. However in personal correspondence to the author, Harvard historian John Womack writes: "reading of the missing 'black box' or 'smoking gun,' I thought of Hitler's missing orders for extermination of European Jewry, the lack of which has not yet stopped historians from arguing that the orders we know he did give certainly warrant the argument that he intended to wipe out Jews and others in the way of German rule westward and German demographic expansion eastward – and that his intention in these orders was perfectly clear to his subordinates all the way down to the lowliest German policeman assigned to military duty. Likewise, I think of the current uproar over torture in U.S. prison camps. We (historians) have a pitifully narrow and childish idea of how 'statesmen' proceed, as if we did not want to know. Not even General Pinochet said, 'Kill him', or 'kill them.' The real political order to kill is always a euphemism. Only in stories and plays do we have to say it, as children say it in their play." The self-same logic – that mass killings can be organised without centralised written orders – applies to other instances of mass killing in the Russian gulag, the Chinese "Great Leap Forward," the killing fields of Cambodia, the Bosnian and Rwandan genocides.

[10] The Birzeit Research Center, especially at that time, struggled to do its work with an extremely modest budget (apart from salaries) of approximately US$ 15,000-US$ 20,000 per year.

[11] The idea of a "memorial" monograph series about the destroyed Palestinian villages was proposed in 1979 by Dr. Kamal Abdel Fattah and Dr. Sharif Kanaana. In 1983 the idea materialised, beginning with Dr. Abdel Fattah's publication of the first map of the Palestinian destroyed villages. And in 1985 the Birzeit University Research Center began to publish its monograph series under the supervision of Dr. Kanaana. Dr. Kanaana, an anthropologist himself, took an anthropological approach – recording how respondents perceived events and basing his work totally on oral testimonies. Research continued in this way until the closing of Birzeit University on 9 January 1988 by a military order which struck all Palestinian universities for years. Work on the series resumed only in mid 1993.

cused on the 1948 exodus using a historical rather than an anthropological approach to ensure that we had not only people's impression of events, but also independent corroboration of facts. This involved cross-checking the information we gathered, adding a significant number of new interviews, and matching eyewitness accounts with written sources, especially Israeli archival material and secondary sources. The average monograph thus increased from approximately 60 pages to 250 pages in length.

At the outset of the project, we at Birzeit University Research Center focused on ten villages, mainly from the central area of Palestine. The refugees came to the West Bank from the following villages: Qaqun, Abu Shusha, Zir'ein, Teiret Haifa, Qissaria, Sheikh Muwanass, Beit Jibrin, Al-Dawayimah, Beit Nabala, and Zarnuqa. These villages were chosen for the research mainly because of the availability of their refugees in the West Bank camps.[12]

When we, at Birzeit Research Center, began, we already knew that there had been a massacre in Al-Dawayima. But, to my total astonishment, we soon discovered that three more villages – Abu Shusha, Teiret Haifa and Zarnuqa – had also suffered massacres, which were then unknown to scholars. My second discovery was that three villages – Qissaria, Sheikh Muwanass, and Zarnuqa – had always had good relations with their Jewish neighbours.[13] This find ran counter to the myth of eternal enmity between Palestinians and Israelis which many people of

12 The Palestinian exodus had a geographic pattern. Due to the fear and panic, people from the north of Palestine went to Syria and Lebanon. People from the south went to Gaza, and those from the central area, especially the plains near the Judean hills, came to the West Bank. Zarnuqa is a special case because only a small part of its refugees came to the West Bank.

13 The history of friendship between Arab villagers and Jewish settlers remains a matter of controversy to this day. For example, in November 1995 I gave a lecture in Birzeit University, at the First International Conference on Palestinian Studies. The paper was entitled "Non-Aggression and Good Neighbor Oral Agreements between Palestinian Villages and Jewish Settlements during the 1948 War." In it, I focused on the case of five villages – Sheik Muwanas, Deir Yassin, Qireh, Abu Zureiq, and Caesaria. These villagers had complex relations with neighbouring Jewish settlements, based on mutual interests. In the last case the villagers worked as faithful guards on Jewish farms for decades. Despite all this, they were expelled. In three of these five villages, villagers were not only expelled but also massacred. Nevertheless, this paper was criticised by the Arab audience, especially those who came from the villages I mentioned, because they were afraid of being painted as collaborators.

both groups believe. Nevertheless, despite such favourable relations, one of the villages, namely Zarnuqa, was massacred and all three were completely depopulated. A few years later, we learned from Israeli sources that a massacre was also committed in Qissaria.

This led me to believe that if I had found five massacres in ten randomly chosen villages, then the massacre in Deir Yassin could not be as exceptional as it was commonly claimed to be.[14] Rather, it was the rule. This was the first stage of my understanding of the massacres, which I reflected upon in two papers.[15] When I reached this phase of my research I also arrived at two conclusions: first, there had been numerously more massacres than was generally acknowledged; and second, Jewish settlers expelled and massacred Palestinians irrespective of the Palestinians' stance toward their Jewish neighbours. These conclusions led me to a further, more general observation, one which is that the pattern of massacres suggested a central Zionist policy of ethnic cleansing.

At this stage of my research I also became committed to the use of eyewitness testimonies, used in conjunction with documentary sources, to tell the story of the Palestinian expulsion. The village of Abu Shusha (massacre, 14 May 1948) provided a good case study in the development of a substantive argument and methodology. The villagers of Abu Shusha, even after Deir Yassin and despite their isolation, chose to stay and fight for their land and homes. Interviewed refugees from Abu Shusha recounted to us the complex story of the expulsion in their vil-

---

[14] For various reasons it was impossible for mainstream Zionist leaders to deny the Deir Yassin massacre. Instead, they represented it as an exception and as an atrocity perpetrated by "dissidents." Despite the partial involvement of the Haganah in the massacre, the Jewish Agency responded to news of Deir Yassin as follows: "The Jewish Agency received now more details about the occupation of Deir Yassin by groups of dissidents. It expresses shock and disgust at this barbaric action. This operation substantially contradicts the spirit of the Yishuv ... [and] the regulations of the Geneva Convention which was accepted by the Agency without reservation" (in the translated version of Y. Slotsky, "Sefer Toldot Ha Haganah" [The History of Haganah], 3 *From Struggle to War, Part II*, 1972, 1548, Hebrew version, translated into Arabic by A. Kalifah as *The Palestine War 1947-1948: An Official Israeli Account*, 1986, 1441-1442). The IPS introduced two systems of numbering: one which reflects the translated Arabic version (hereafter: AV), the second which reflects the original Hebrew work (hereafter: HV).

[15] S.A. Jawad, *Deir Yassin: Exception or Rule*, paper given at a meeting commemorating the anniversary of Deir Yassin in April 1996 in el-Bireh's Town Hall, and *idem*, see note 13.

lage, which went on over a period of a week beginning with an occupation. We were given 64 names of murdered individuals, a list from which all except two were killed on the day of Abu Shusha's occupation. We painstakingly reconstructed the massacre, name by name. We noted the victim's ages, family background, and plotted where they had been killed. We interviewed respondents first at their homes and then, under oath, at Birzeit University. In general, the information provided by multiple respondents proved to be highly consistent and accurate. Despite the consitency and accuracy of the gathered information, the final Birzeit Research Center monograph on Abu Shusha contained a conservative estimate of casualties, mentioning only 50 of the 64 names we had on file. We omitted murders for which we had no corroborating details and individuals for whom names could not be ascertained. For example, we did not use a name when there was a chance that the same person was referred to under multiple names such as their own, as someone's parent, and as a clan member. My own names illustrate this point in more detail. I can be referred to as Saleh Abdel Jawad, Abu Maher (Maher's father), or even Saleh Hamayel under the Israeli system of requiring clan names. The work on Abu Shusha is typical in the labourious attention to detail required to reconstruct a massacre. We sent the final monograph on Abu Shusha to some Israeli scholars of the 1948 War, who never acknowledged it until they "found" Israeli archival material confirming our work.[16]

The two most important lessons I learned from my work on Abu Shusha and the other villages I studied soon thereafter, continued to hold true. First, eyewitness oral testimonies, when subjected to rigorous scholarly cross-examination, continued to provide accurate, valid, and reliable information.[17] Such testimonies proved their utility when they

---

[16] For a description and for sources about Abu Shusha, see Census of Massacres, 14 May 1948, below. Unfortunately, the entire Birzeit series on the destroyed villages is available only in Arabic (except the work on Abu Shusha, which has a long English abstract) and this, among other factors, has limited its impact.

[17] For a discussion of the credibility of Palestinian oral testimonies see "Le Témoignage des Palestiniennes Entre l'Historiographie Israélienne et l'Historiographie Arabe: Le Cas de 1948", in: C. Coquio (ed.), *l'Histoire trouée, négation et témoignages. Travaux du Colloque à la Sorbonne, Septembre 2002*, 2004, 627-640. For a more detailed and complete discussion, see S.A. Jawad, "The Arab and Palestinian Narratives of the 1948 War", in: R. Rotberg (ed.), *The Intertwined Narratives of Israel-Palestine: History's Double Helix*, forthcoming, 93-142.

were often confirmed years later by Israeli archival sources upon accessibility to archives. Omar Bartov, a well-known specialist on the subject of war crimes, confirms the importance of eyewitness accounts. He argues that eyewitness testimony has become inherent in and indispensable to the historical study of war crimes.[18] His argument has been supported more recently by the actions of the U.S. State Department, namely by the department's reliance on oral testimonies to assess the genocide in Sudan.[19] And, second, when we systematically asked the survivors of the 1948 War about the violence they had witnessed, we discovered that many of them had experienced events that could properly be defined as massacres.

Inspired by the results of our early work, in 1995 I suggested a project, entitled "A Race Against Time," which consisted of interviewing as many survivors of the 1948 War as possible. Unfortunately, the Birzeit University, its Research Center, and other Palestinian institutions could not offer material support. Therefore, over a five year period, I conducted 300 interviews with the help of my students.

These interviews gradually confirmed the existence of more massacres and shed new light on the many forms of massacres in Palestine. Some, like simple firing squads, conformed to popular images and were well known. Others, like the aerial bombardment of fleeing civilians, remain untold or incompletely understood to this day.[20]

In the second stage of my research, the emerging information convinced me that there was a central guiding brain, which unified all the individ-

---

[18] O. Bartov, "Recherches Historiques sur l 'Holocaust et Etudes Comparatives", in: C. Coquio (ed.), *Parler des camps, penser les genocides*, 1999, 116-121.

[19] See M. Lacey, "U.S. Report on Violence in Sudan Finds a Pattern of Atrocities", *New York Times*, 25 August 2004. The State Department's finding of a pattern of atrocities was based exclusively on 257 eyewitness accounts.

[20] Based on the interviews I conducted with survivors, I estimate that aerial bombardment was one of the deadliest forms of killing since July 1948, especially in southern Palestine and the central Galilee in the north. While my interviews cover only a very limited number of villages from these areas, the testimonies are all in agreement about the high casualty rates produced by aerial bombardment. My respondents' observations are consistent with data reported by Benny Morris on the bombing of Tarshiha in Morris, see note 5, 479. Morris' account, based on Israeli army records, acknowledges a higher level of devastation than is found in Nafez Nazzal's coverage of the same events based on eyewitness testimonies in N. Nazzal, *The Palestinian Exodus from Galilee*, 1978, 97 et seq.

ual massacres into a coherent policy of ethnic cleansing. Our interviews revealed in a highly visible way that the massacres were disciplined and the chain of command was clear. The killings were also carried out more to create an environment of terror and result in the flight of the population, than to maximise the number of casualties.

Due to this aim, the massacres were often conducted in a manner, which appeared to go beyond the immediate objective of taking a particular village. Villages were encircled, bombarded, and residents were sent through openings in the line of attack toward Arab areas. The choice of a certain village was also not at random. Often, there was a clear relationship between the timing of a brutal massacre in an outlying village and the assault on a major nearby town or city. For example, the massacre in Nasir al-Dien was just a few days before the Tiberias was besieged.[21] Also, the multiple massacres in Ein Zaytoun were used to "soften up" Safad directly before the final assault on the city.[22]

The brutality in Deir Yassin must be understood within the struggle for Jerusalem. Huge massacres, like the one in the village of Al-Dawayima where between 100 and 200 people were killed and raped with exceptional brutality, were part of Ben-Gurion's strategy to control the whole Hebron area.[23] The intensity of massacres in Central Galilee on 29 and 30 October in the year 1948, during Operation Hiram, was a clear solution to Ben-Gurion's worries a month earlier concerning a pocket of civilian population in this area. This population was problematic for Ben-Gurion because it attracted forcibly removed refugees who were attempting to return to Lebanon.[24]

Ben Gurion's repeated telegraphs and instructions to IDF commanders 24 hours before the occupation of Nazareth, requiring extreme restraint (even to the point of shooting looting soldiers) reveals the level of vio-

---

21 B. Morris, *1948 and After, Israel and the Palestinians*, 1990, 177-178, also cites Nahmani's dismayed reaction.

22 For a more detailed discussion of Ein Zaytoun, see the section of the massacre of prisoners in the typology of massacres, below. The use of the assault on Ein Zaytoun to soften up Safad see M. Kelman, in: IDF Archives, file no. 1226/922/75, 121/4.

23 D. Ben-Gurion, *Yumann Hamilhamah, 1947-1949 (Diaries of War, 1947-1949)*, 1984, G. Rivlin/E. Orren (eds), Samir Jabbour (trans.), 1993, see especially footnotes for 27 October 1948, 597 in the Arabic version (hereafter: AV) and on 779 in the Hebrew version (hereafter: HV).

24 Ibid., Entries for 13 September 1948, 521, and for 26 September 1948, 556 (AV), 683 and 721 (HV).

lence which was accepted as normal in the Israeli army when it was unconcerned with Western, Christian opinion, and the degree of control central command could exercise over it when it chose.[25] I believe that the Israeli army was unconcerned with Western and Christian opinion. Furthermore, the central command picked and chose the degree of control it exercised over the army depending on the situation.

I also discovered that the geographic distribution of the massacres indicated centralised planning that orchestrated massacres across the length and breadth of Palestine. I expressed this new knowledge in a series of lectures beginning in late 1997. I, then, argued that for the first time my data permitted me to describe Israeli leaders of 1948 as war criminals and to call for an International Tribunal to assess their crimes.[26] The German newspaper *Die Frankfurter Allgemeine Zeitung* published the most complete version of this research in early 2001.[27] The article drew an angry response from Benny Morris almost a year later.[28] Although Morris did not agree with the article, he understood that Palestinian researchers were, in their own way, finally using empirical research to document what happened in 1948 and were not limiting themselves to the Zionists analysis expressed in documentary sources. Also, although he ferociously denied a master plan of ethnic cleansing in 2001, he now admits that the events during 1948 constitute a "justifiable" ethnic cleansing.[29]

A number of different elements have advanced my research this past year.[30] These elements have also allowed me to have a more complete

---

25 Ibid., Entries for 15 July 1948, 454 (AV), 591 (HV). Ben-Gurion also urged extreme restraint in the occupation of Jerusalem, for similar reasons.

26 Lecture, in Baladna Center, el-Bireh/Ramallah, 30 October 1997.

27 S.A. Jawad, "Ein Fall von 'ethnischer Säuberung': Warum haben die Palästinenser 1948 ihre Heimstätten verlassen", *Die Frankfurter Allgemeine Zeitung*, 9 January 2001, 14 et seq.

28 B. Morris, "Vertreibung, Flucht und Schutzbedürfnis. Wie 1948 das Problem der palästinensischen Flüchtlinge entstand", *Die Frankfurter Allgemeine Zeitung*, 29 December 2001, 8.

29 B. Morris, "The Survival of the Fittest", *Ha'aretz* interview by A. Shavit, 9 January 2004, <http://people.na.infn.it/~clarizia/palestina/giusti/Morris_intervista_9-1-04.pdf>.

30 Essential to my work in the past year has been access to the transcripts of the bulk of the interviews completed by 2002, the vast secondary sources of western libraries and a glimpse at the materials in the UN archives, and the peace to reflect and write without tanks in the streets.

picture of the subject. I presently view the subject to have three main features:

Massacres should be viewed as a common phenomenon in nearly every Palestinian village and Bedouin settlement from which people involuntarily fled. Jaffa and Haifa, the major cities and centre of Palestinian intellectual and cultural life, and Lod, were the sites of the most destructive forms of ethnic cleansing. Documents and responses converge to show that in "... each village occupied by the Israeli army we could smell the stench of a massacre."[31]

Villages were subjected not only to massacres. To understand the exodus, it is necessary to consider, not just a refugee's last day in a village, but also the long cumulative process of harassment and terror. In many villages, civilians suffered repeated attacks before the final assault and occupation. In such attacks, people were killed, and houses as well as livestock were destroyed. Subsequently, aerial and artillery bombardments were carried out. The residents were also attacked with psychological warfare and propaganda. Under occupation, they suffered indiscriminate massacres and survivors were forbidden to bury the dead. Furthermore, in villages, towns, and cities, looting was systematic. Any attempt by residents to claim property was punished by death. Some villages were mined and dead bodies were booby-trapped, as in the case of Beit Jibrin and al-Dawayima.

While young people fled, the elderly stayed behind in the villages for several reasons. They were unable to walk, had been abandoned, or wanted to live their last days in the place of their birth. In many villages the elderly were executed and in some cases they starved to death. Furthermore, some of their bodies did not receive proper burials. In some cases they were eaten by wild animals and in others they were trucked to Arab borders and abandoned.

Villagers often witnessed first-hand the destruction of the houses, in which they had lived all their lives. People were also killed in limited numbers, while fleeing and if they were able to escape they hid in nearby caves or orchards. They always tried to return to harvest a crop, retrieve food, or to rescue an old family member. In many cases, such attempts resulted in deaths by mines and ambushes. Refugees were un-

---

[31] Here we are using a quote from Aryeh Yitzachi, a historical researcher whose job enabled him to see all censored materials in the IDF archives where he worked, in Ehrlich, see note 2, 22.

safe even in tents located in not-yet occupied villages, which were also subject to further bombings.

I can imagine the whole of Palestine, the villages and towns many of which I know personally, subject to an infernal machine of massacre, terror, looting, humiliation, and death marches. I can see the towns filled with people who became homeless and penniless in a matter of a single day. This result was not brought about by simply military means, but was also carried out systematically: Villagers experienced subversion, sabotage, rumour mongering, and propaganda designed to create panic. There was also the meticulous planning of the expulsions, reflected in Ben-Gurion's diaries, which was accompanied by an equally meticulously planned cover-up. The cover-up consisted of deliberate fabrication of myths by a Foreign Ministry, which was finely attuned to world opinion and wholly dedicated to the displacement of Palestinians. Finally, the Palestinians were – just as the machine wanted them to be – dust trampled under the heel of the powerful.

Within this larger framework, I view massacres as a tool, probably the primary tool, of a total war through which Zionists and later Israelis sought to expel the Arabs from their lands by means of ethnic cleansing.[32] Such action was designed to produce an exclusively Jewish state in the place of the Arab-dominated, multi-ethnic society which once flourished there. I argue, that the Palestinians in 1948, inundated by massacres, were left, as Elias Sanbar said, with only two choices: flee or die.[33]

This story is told unapologetically from facts, which include the voices of the Palestinian exiles. Israeli expulsions, viewed from the Palestinian side, are recalled in stories like the one below of Haj As'ad Hassouneh, a survivor of the death march that followed the expulsion of Palestinians from Lod, in July 1948. In my interview with him, Hassouneh recalled:

---

32 Elsewhere, I have written about the historiography of this period and the use of different terms by Palestinians and Israelis at different points in time to describe the events of 1948. In brief, Palestinians refer to these events as genocide, expulsion, and catastrophe, while Israelis refer to 'Transfer,' abandonment, and flight. Among Israelis, Ilan Pappe is the first to use the term ethnic cleansing. For further details on this point see Jawad, see note 17. See also S. Slyomovics, "The Rape of Qula, a Destroyed Palestinian Village", in: L. Abu-Lughod/A. Sa'di (eds), *The Claims of Memory: Palestine 1948*, forthcoming.

33 E. Sanbar, *Palestine 1948, l'expulsion*, 1984.

The Jews came and they called among the people: "You must go." "Where shall we go?" "Go to Barfilia." At first they let people walk on the asphalt road that led east, but later they corralled people forcing them off the paved roads and onto, stony, hard to walk in areas. The taking of cars was prohibited. The riding of an animal or cart was permitted, although not a single step could be taken westwards. In other words, the spot you were standing on determined what if any family or possession you could get; any to the west of you could not be retrieved. You had to immediately begin walking and it had to be to the east. The people began to depart – among them the sick, paraplegic, handicapped, children, pregnant women who may have given birth at any time, and even those who were heavy and old. They all had to begin walking. Most people of Lod were peasants and did not have money. Very few of them were traders or shopkeepers. It was very rare that one of them owned ten pounds. Many were in debt and it was the beginning of summer. No one had collected the produce off of their land or sold it. The Jews were taking the jewelry and any money from the women. Only a few women could escape their searches and seizures.

I heard a story, although I did not see it with my own eyes, of an area where people left a water generator, which provided water for the town. It was a western generator. The Jews let the water flow out onto the road, producing mud on which people began to slip. The people were fatigued even before they began their journey or could attempt to reach any destination. No one knew where Barfilia was located or its distance from Jordan. Perhaps one or two individuals had heard of it. The people walked and among them some carried a daughter, a son, or some food. Some did not know what to carry. After a little while, they reached the stones and rock. Those who were riding animals let them go and the animals fled back to Lod, because the farm animals always know their way back home. The people were also fasting due to Ramadan because they were people of serious belief. There was no water. People began to die of thirst. Some women died and their babies nursed from their dead bodies. Many of the elderly died on the way. The distance to Barfilia can be travelled in four hours, but it took the people three days. They were very thirsty and many died of thirst. Many buried their dead in the leaves of the corn.[34]

---

[34] The interviewee, from a well-known Lod family, became a trader in el-Bireh and, from 1992 until his death, he served as the head of the Chamber of

In the context of a conference designed to address the contemporary problems of Palestinian refugees, one may ask whether it is necessary or even useful to recall such painful material. Certainly Israeli politicians, who are on other occasion dedicated to remembrance, often argue that when it comes to the Palestinian refugees, it is better to say that "we may never agree on the past, but we can agree on the future"[35] or, more ominously, "what's done is done."[36] Thucydides, the famous Greek historian, goes even further in advocating a purely pragmatic stance, quoting the Athenian representatives to Melos as saying: "[W]e will not make a long and unconvincing speech, full of fine phrases, to prove that our victory ... justifies our empire ... Let ... us say what we really think and reach a practical agreement. *You know and we know, as practical men, that the question of justice arises only between parties equal in strength, [for] the strong do what they can and the weak submit.*"[37]

The cynical tone of Thucydides' Athenians can be used to suggest why the history of the Palestinian refugee problem continues to be important, even in the face of the immense practical and political difficulties facing the refugees today. Indeed, the problem may be important due to those very difficulties. Without an accounting for where the problem began, there can be neither an assessment of responsibility with its associated obligation to bear the burden of creating a solution, nor a realistic evaluation of the intentions of the parties involved in crafting a settlement.

Moreover, it is unlikely that a just and lasting solution to the refugee problem can be achieved amidst ongoing lies and evasion. The psychiatrist Robert Jay Lifton, regarding the American conduct in Vietnam, argues that bearing witness even to the worst moments in history is essential to healing and integrity at the personal level.[38] I argue that in the

---

Commerce in Ramallah and el-Bireh. Interview in his house in el-Bireh, November 1996.

[35] For a critique of this point (paraphrasing Yossi Beilin) see M. Bishara, "The Geneva Accord: A Critical Assessment", *Daily Star*, 1 December 2003, <http://www.shaml.org/ground/geneva/marwan%20bishara.htm>.

[36] Author interview with E. Sanbar, Paris, 5 January 1995. Sanbar used in French "partir ou mourir."

[37] Thucydides, *The History of the Peloponnesian War*, 1960, 267. Author's emphasis.

[38] R.J. Lifton, "Looking into the Abyss: Bearing Witness to My Lai and Vietnam", in: D.L. Anderson (ed.), *Facing My Lai, Moving Beyond the Massacre*, 1998, 19-26.

context of the Palestinian refugee problem, using history as a starting point is also essential to integrity and healing at the societal level.[39] Current psychological thought concerning trauma and recovery supports my view. Judith Lewis Herman[40] shares with us that recovery from trauma of any sort, personal or political, is a three step process. First, the victim must find a place of safety. Second, the victim must narrate the trauma until it becomes a contained and coherent story, rather than a set of fragmented and overwhelmingly intense vignettes. Third, the victim must be able to integrate the coherent narrative into an ongoing life, which includes, but is not limited to, the trauma. For Palestinians in refugee camps even the first condition of recovery has not been met, which makes the construction of a coherent narrative for Palestinian historians a work in progress.

II. Defining a Massacre

To understand the Palestinian refugee problem, it is necessary to have a clear definition of what constitutes a massacre. This concept is central to my work. Dictionary definitions which emphasise the simple fact of brutal killing are not very helpful and nor is the huge literature on the Arab-Israeli conflict. It does not even provide an attempted definition. The absence of such a definition poses problems for researchers, which are intensified when ideological and political motives intrude. A definition that can be used consistently and rigorously in research is needed. It is also necessary that this definition allow for the differentiation between massacres and more general violence from both sides in a war.

On the Israeli side, political and ideological reasons dictate the lack of a definition of the term "massacre." The old Israeli historians never use the word, except in the case of Deir Yassin. Revisionist historians use it rarely and they are inconsistent in their application of the term. For ex-

---

39 Edward Said expresses a similar point of view when he says: "For the Palestinians, a vast collective feeling of injustice continues to hang over our lives with undiminished weight. If there has been … one particular delinquency committed by the present Palestinian leaders for me, it is their supernally gifted power of forgetting … [O]ne of them … reported blithely, 'We are prepared to forget history.' That is a sentiment I can neither share nor, I hasten to add, easily forgive" (E. Said, "Introduction: The Right to Return at Last", in: N. Aruri (ed.), *Palestinian Refugees: The Right of Return*, 2001, 1).

40 J.L. Herman, *Trauma and Recovery*, 1992.

ample, they will call the same incident a "massacre" on one occasion and an "operation" or a "battle" on another. Israeli historians also contradict each other. Uri Milstein, a right wing revisionist, does not consider the massacre in Deir Yassin, committed by a right wing militia, to be a massacre.[41] However Benny Morris disagrees with Milstein.[42] Amidst the controversy, it is easy to lose sight of the fact that the absence of a definition is almost certainly intentional. Any clear and appropriate definition of the concept would oblige Israeli historians to admit more massacres than they are prepared to acknowledge.

Palestinians, too, struggle with the term, but for very different reasons. The lack of definition at the popular level may result from the commonness of massacres, making them hard to distinguish from regular life. For example, I noticed that some older Palestinians consider the killings committed in their villages, especially when only men of fighting age were targeted, as an inescapable fate and a widespread consequence. In many cases, villagers describe the attack on Deir Yassin as a massacre, but do not use the same term when describing similar events in their own villages or neighbouring towns. The massacre in Deir Yassin became the national symbol of massacres because of the media and because it was the only case in which the rape of women was publicly acknowledged.

On an intellectual level, I note that there is no systematic, coherent, and complete Palestinian narrative of the 1948 War. Perhaps for this reason, creating a clear and consistent definition of massacres has also been deferred. Furthermore, I am unable to find an explanation for why scholars like Aref al-Aref and Nafez Nazzal, neither define nor use the term in most of the cases in which it can properly be applied.[43] Their work documents multiple instances of massacres without raising the question of a definition for the term "massacre." It also should be noted, that in much of Palestinian discourse the term "massacre" means something

---

[41] U. Milstein, *The War of Independence Vol. IV: Out of Crisis Came Decision*, 1991, 255- 276.

[42] Morris, see note 21, 36.

[43] A. al-Aref, *Nakbat Filastin wa al-Firdaws Mafqud (Palestinian Nakba and the Lost Paradise)*, 1956-1958. Originally published in Lebanon. Page citations in this article are taken from a pirated copy (Dar al-Huda publishers, in Kofr Qar', Israel, n.d.) in the author's possession. Aref's work represents the first Palestinian attempt to create a complete account of the war. He relates many atrocities, but rarely uses the term 'massacre.' Nor does Nazzal, see note 20, in his recounting of the exodus.

more general – it is a shorthand way of invoking a more complex series of events called the *Nakba* (the Catastrophe), which is the Arab term for describing what happened to Palestinians in 1948.

One additional problem the researcher faces is the determination of the extent to which the definition of a massacre depends upon the number of people killed. During the 1948 War, killings varied from 1,000 casualties, for example in the many phases of the Lod massacre (our estimation),[44] to one person. While I have decided to omit the killing of one or two individuals from what constitutes a massacres, I agree with Catherine Coquio, a professor at the University of Paris-IV and the president of the Association Internationale de Recherche sur les Crime contre l'Humanite et Les Genocides, who argues that the number of victims is less important than the intentions of the killers and their patterns of activities. She emphasises that the importance of the number of fatalities rests in the imagination of victims and observers. For example, although the "Boston Massacre" involved only approximately ten fatalities, it is central to the American narrative of The War of Independence.[45] In the case of Palestine, it is important to note that most people lived in small villages and that the killing of five or ten people was significant to those who remained in the village after the conquest. The loss of some individuals of a village was especially difficult because such it occurred after the residents already bared the terror of bombardment, crop destruction, psychological warfare.

I settled on the following definition of a massacre. *It is the killing of unarmed civilians or combatants who have surrendered and who have come under the authority of the conquering force, by an armed military or para-military force. Massacres also involve the use of lethal force in a variety of forms (terror attacks, aerial bombardment, "reprisals" etc.) against civilians, unrelated to military necessity, but nevertheless occurring in the context of a total war and with the aim of producing ethnic cleansing.* The definition of "massacre" requires three key elements to be present: (1) the perpetrators are state agents or quasi-state agents; (2) the victims are individuals who, according to the international rules of war, are not to be killed even if hostilities exist; and (3) the killings are

---

[44] For the source of the casualty estimate in Lod, see the discussion of Lod below.

[45] For an early eyewitness account of the 'Horrid Massacre in Boston,' which lists five dead, two mortally wounded, and four more seriously wounded, see N. Harris et al. (eds), *The History of The United States, volume I: 1600-1876, Sources Readings*, 1969, 168-169.

not the result of any military necessity or threat posed by the victims, but, instead, are part of another greater strategy.[46] In offering this definition I ignore the inclusion of not only the numbers of victims and the technology used for killing, but also specifics such as population density and the topography of Palestine. The more general definition organises my data and lends itself to historical and comparative work.

III. Ideological Context

In order to understand massacre as one of the main tools of the ethnic cleansing in the *Nakba*, we must comprehend the ideological context that allowed the architects of such a policy to proceed. The history of Zionism has been aptly described by both Palestinian and Israeli scholars[47] and it is beyond the scope of this article to recapitulate. For the purpose of understanding the massacres, however, it is essential to note that the Zionist political leaders who designed and led the project to create a Jewish state operated from the outset on the premise that this state would be exclusively Jewish.[48] Long before the 1948 War, Zionist logic had committed the Jewish settlers to expel Palestinians, by force if necessary. The commitment to an exclusionary Jewish state derived from a variety of sources. The historic Jewish experience of exclusion

---

[46] R. Gellately/B. Kiernan, "The Study of Mass Murder and Genocide", in: R. Gellately/B. Kiernan (eds), *The Spectre of Genocide: Mass Murder in Historical Perspective*, 2003, 9-11, summarise the theoretical frameworks used for describing genocide. They identify the "intentionalist" approach that focuses on the plans of the leaders of genocidal armies or nations and the "interactive" approach which places more emphasis on the understandings of field commanders in producing genocidal outcomes. These two interpretive traditions have in common the presumption that genocide, mass murders and massacres are committed by state actors.

[47] For a Palestinian interpretation, see N. Masalha, *Expulsion of the Palestinians: The Concept of Transfer in Zionist Political Thought 1882-1948*, 1992, Arabic version hereafter AV, English version hereafter EV. For an Israeli interpretation, see A. Shapira, *Land and Power, The Zionist Resort to Force, 1881-1948*, 1992.

[48] French historian Henri Laurens describes this premise in these words: "Pro-Palestinian historians projected the expulsion of the Palestinians in 1948 as the achievement of a long envisioned project. In some manner, the expulsion of the Palestinians is part of the genetic code of Zionism." Notes given to author from a lecture given at the French Cultural Center, Jerusalem, 1998.

and persecution; the prevailing ideology of nationalism in 19th century Europe that emphasised religious, cultural and ethnic homogeneity; the practical need to integrate secular Western and religious Eastern European Jews; and even a socialist aversion to creating an immigrant elite which could oppress an indigenous working class – all contributed to the aspiration to build an exclusively Jewish state. Accordingly, Zionism shared an important premise with other forms of nationalism that were its contemporaries.

Zionism also shared some features of the European ideology of colonialism. In general, colonial powers moving into an area used three arguments to justify their actions: that the land they were appropriating was empty; that therefore it rightly belonged to those who "discovered" it; and that the colonial power thereby acquired the right, indeed the obligation, to "civilise" the natives who were conquered. It is safe to say that powers intent on colonial projects were content to ignore the contradiction between the statements that a land was empty and that there was a responsibility to "civilise" its natives.[49]

Zionism shared the belief in the existence of "empty land" with the ideology of colonialism. Accordingly, Zionist leaders quickly adopted Lord Shaftesbury's famous slogan: "a land without people for a people without land"[50] despite the fact that internal documents, especially a speech entitled "The Hidden Question,"[51] illustrate that they were troubled by the presence of the Palestinians. As other colonialists had done on other lands, Israelis were intent to declare Palestine an empty land, which could be used to receive the scattered Jewish people.[52]

---

[49] A way of reconciling this contradiction was to argue that the land, while not physically empty, was empty of civilisational achievements. Zionists used this variant of the 'empty land' argument as well. M. Rodinson, "Israel: Fait Colonial", *Les Temps Moderns* 253 (1967), 51 et seq., emphasises this second sense of 'emptiness.'

[50] For a history of the term, see A.M. Garfinkle, "On the Origin, Meaning, Use and Abuse of a Phrase", *Middle Eastern Studies* 27 (1991), 539 et seq., <http://members.dca. net/sotireew/garfinkle.html>.

[51] Shapira, see note 47, 45.

[52] The insistence on the 'emptiness' of Palestine is not limited to 19th century Zionists. For example, in his book (B. Netanyahu, *A Place Under The Sun*, 1993, 40) Benjamin Netanyahu adopts the image of physical emptiness. He quotes Arthur Stanley, the British "map expert" who wrote in 1881 "In Judea it is hardly an exaggeration to say that for miles and miles there was not appearance of life." But, in a contradictory testimony conveniently ignored by

Although Zionists voluntarily argued that Palestine was empty before their arrival, the second and third premises of traditional European colonialism – the right to conquer previously undiscovered places and to convert the natives – was not on the agenda of the Zionist project. For clear reasons, the Holy Land of biblical narrative hardly needed to be "discovered" in the late 19th or early 20th century. Furthermore, Zionists were not interested in converting the Muslims.

In the absence of these two legitimations, the Zionist movement, which claims to be secular, found it necessary to embrace the idea of "the promised land" of Old Testament prophecy, to justify the confiscation of land and the expulsion of the Palestinians. For example, the speeches and letters of Chaim Weizmann, the secular Zionist leader, are filled with references to the biblical origins of the Jewish claim to Palestine, which he often mixes liberally with more pragmatic and nationalistic claims.

By the use of this premise, embraced in 1937, Zionists alleged that the Palestinians were usurpers in the Promised Land, and therefore their expulsion and death was justified. The Jewish-American writer Dan Kurzman, in his book *Genesis 1948: The First Arab-Israeli War*, describes the view of one of the Deir Yassin's killers:

> "The Sternists followed the instructions of the Bible more rigidly than others. They honored the passage (Exodus 22:2): 'If a thief be found ... and be smitten that he die, there shall be no blood shed for him.' This meant, of course, that killing a thief was not really murder. And were not the enemies of Zionism thieves, who wanted to steal from the Jews what God had granted them? He didn't hate the Arabs as he did the British, who had no business at all in Palestine. But they were nevertheless 'thieves.'"[53]

It should also be noted, however, that Zionism has a long and complex history. Its followers have always had a more conciliatory impulse toward the Palestinians. For example, there were humanist intellectuals like Ahad Ha'am (Arthur Ginsberg), who, since the end of the 19th century, criticised the *Yishuv's* (the prestate Jewish society in Palestine) treatment of Palestinians. Professor Yehuda Magness, the head of He-

---

Netanyahu, Zionist preacher Israel Zangwill talked about a dense Palestinian population. I. Zangwill, *Speeches, Articles and Letters*, 1937, 210, complains that "Palestine is already twice as thickly populated as the United States ... and not 25 per cent of them [are] Jews."

[53] D. Kurzman, *Genesis 1948: The First Arab-Israeli War*, 1992, 43.

brew University when it was created in 1925 and during the Mandate period, favoured a bi-national state that had room for the Palestinians, as did Martin Buber, the famous writer and philosopher. The Palestinian Communist Party, composed of Arab and Jewish members, also favoured a bi-national state. Furthermore, "there was also a strand of Yishuv culture that tended to rebel against European Jewish 'sickness' by claiming to return to a Semitic, Arab-like culture."[54] Unfortunately, these humanist voices remained a minority and did not shape the ultimate Zionist policy.

But, perhaps because the humanist voice was always a part of Zionism, religious justifications for expelling the Palestinians were not entirely persuasive of their own accord. Therefore, along with religious arguments, Zionist leaders chose to dehumanise Palestinians and to emphasise the cultural differences between Jews and Arabs – all in the service of legitimating a plan of expulsion.

Dehumanisation of the Palestinians began early and continued unabated into the period of my study. For example, Abraham Yair, known by the nickname "Stern" who was the leader of the terrorist Jewish group Lehi, described the Arabs as "beasts of the desert not a true people."[55] In another article he states that "[t]he Arabs are not a nation but a mole that grew in the wilderness of the eternal desert. They are nothing but murderers."[56] With the passing of time, Palestinians were compared to many of the harmful animals in Noah's ark: scorpions, snakes, cockroaches, moles, etc. This type of name calling and the beliefs they reveal permit us to understand why individuals of the IZL or Lehi group disguised themselves as Arabs, walked into popular markets, and detonated bombs among family groups of shoppers.

The dehumanisation is not limited to an earlier period. The 1966 Nobel Laureate for literature, Shmail Agnoon, writes in his novel *Before Yesterday* (written in 1945) that the Arabs are people "without dignity, accepting humiliation, exploiting the settlers, cause of the destruction of the land, annoying, filthy, cheating the Jews, hating civilization, resembling dogs."[57]

---

[54] Private communication from Professor Joel Perlmann of Bard College to the author.

[55] A. Perlmutter, *The Life and Times of Menachem Begin*, 1987, 212.

[56] Masalha, see note 47, 30 (EV).

[57] Quoted in A. Shalhat, *An Introduction to the Study of the Arab Personality in Zionist Literature, el-Karmel, Vol. 7*, 1983, 379.

Along with the dehumanisation of Palestinians, cultural differences were also emphasised. This took two forms. First, the unity of a diverse Jewish population was greatly exaggerated, which ignored the 2000 year diaspora in which Jews lived in a variety of countries, spoke many different languages, and evolved along entirely different paths. In fact, it was only according to 19th century Zionism that Jews were considered a single people. Second, the differences between Jews and their Arab neighbours were greatly exaggerated, especially by ignoring the historical experiences of Arabic-speaking Jews.[58]

The enforcement of cultural distance between the two communities was not only at the level of rhetoric. Separation was enforced in every institution, including the entire Jewish education system under the British Mandate. In 1937, it was noted with dismay in the Peel Commission Report's (generally pro-Zionist document) chapter on education, that Jewish education was dedicated to "glorifying the homeland as a work accomplished only by Jews ..." It further stated that "the idea of sharing their lives with Arabs is never present in any shape or form. To grow up to be citizens, companions, and friends of Arabs in a shared Palestinian state – this is something that does not exist [in the Jewish curriculum]. The Jewish education system does not try to create any understanding between the two peoples."[59]

Cultural distance, dehumanisation, and emphasis on the alleged cruelty of the enemy were used not only to create an iron wall of separation between Jews and Arabs, but also to facilitate the expulsion of the Palestinians. Such techniques are used intensively in the training of special killing units within all modern armies and are major elements in the psychological conditioning of men. When successfully implemented, the techniques produce reactions such as this one from the poet, Abba Kovner, an anti-Nazi partisan and left-labour activist, who wrote about military operations for his Brigade's Combat Page:

> "Suddenly, the ground was soft [under the wheels of the jeeps of 'Samson's Foxes,' Giv'ati's command unit] – bodies! Tens of bodies under their wheels. The driver was put off, human beings under his

---

[58] For example, M. Rodinson, "Israel and the Arabs", in: G.V. Smith (ed.), *Zionism, the Dream and the Reality*, 1974, 259 et seq., notes that Yemeni Jews, who spoke a form of Hebrew closest to Arabic were shamed and "reprogrammed" into speaking a form of Hebrew closer to that spoken by European immigrants with no knowledge of Arabic.

[59] Royal Committee for Palestine 1937, #5479 Full Report, Official Arabic version, White Paper, 1937, S. 440. Author's translation.

> wheels! [But] wait a minute. He remembered [Kibbutz] Negba [and] Beit Daras [in both Arab troops killed Jews] – and he ran them over! Do not be deterred sons: murderous dogs – their punishment is blood! And the more you run over bloody dogs, the more you will love the beautiful, the good and *liberty*."[60]

Under different circumstances, reactions such as those expressed by Kovner might well have supported genocide. But, after World War II, the world had become more informed, aware, and sensitive to large scale atrocities. Changes in international media coverage also promoted such awareness. The evolution of the human rights principles absolutely precluded genocide in the period immediately following the Holocaust. Also, Palestinians were part of a greater Arab world, which would not allow their extermination. For these and other reasons extermination became an unacceptable way of ridding the land of its original inhabitants. Therefore, Zionist leaders were forced to develop new methods.

The new method made systematic use of violence and killing, without taking the "classic" form of genocide. Massacres and terror became a well planned and carefully orchestrated practice that produced a cloud of terror. Terror spread all over Palestine, even though the body count of the massacres was kept within acceptable limits to the international community. The new method succeeded in creating ethnic cleansing similar to that previously produced, except that it was created through the use of genocide. At the same time, ironically, Zionist propaganda succeeded, for a variety of reasons, to present Israeli behaviour as an act of self-defence.

The way in which terror was used during the 1948 War could not have occurred without the belief that the Arabs had no right to live in Palestine, and that they were subhuman or at least immeasurably different from the Jewish settlers. These ideas nourished the Zionist killing machine. Once the use of violence appeared to be successful, the Zionists were trapped in an indefinite addiction, because state-sponsored terror became their main instrument in achieving power and hegemony.

---

[60] Morris, see note 5, 437. Morris, who added the reference to Arab troops killing Jews, did not mention that Beit Daras was a Palestinian village which was attacked four times and the Jews who were killed there were military aggressors.

IV. Typology of Massacres

Israeli massacres were carried out before, during, and immediately after the occupation of a village or a city. In some cases massacres also occurred in waves for longer periods of time. For example, when the initial pressure was not enough to uproot the population, such waves were utilised. Massacres also took a variety of forms and varied in intensity depending on the phases of the war. For example, during the period of British Mandate rule (and especially when British troops were present in the immediate area), the Haganah was generally more restrained in attacking civilian targets than it was after their departure. Variations in the intensity of killing also were shaped by presence or absence of public scrutiny – hence massacres tended to be more severe in the northern and southern sections as in comparison to the central section of Palestine near Jerusalem, which is the centre for international media and organisations such as the Red Cross. This explains the violent, but at the same time hypocritical denunciation of the massacre in Deir Yassin by the Jewish Agency.

Taken as a whole, massacres were a pervasive reality for Palestinians in 1947 and 1948. In the following text, I describe the seven principal forms of massacres and illustrate their occurrence. I then proceed to use this typology to analyse a still-evolving census of 68 massacres recorded in a variety of official, popular, and scholarly sources. I also include another seven terror attacks, not numbered in the census, which are important for their role in precipitating the war.

One view of massacres presents an analysis of the degree to which a killing is selective or indiscriminate. Selective massacres target limited numbers of people or specific populations such as combatants, while indiscriminate killings are directed at anyone in the line of fire – the elderly, women and children are not spared. Indiscriminate killings can involve widespread executions or more specific sub-types such as reprisals against whole villages, terror attacks using explosives, aerial bombardments of refugees and forced expulsion that lead to mass fatalities. Regardless of the type of killing, all have the characteristic of putting everyone in harm's way. "Apparently, various officers who took part … understood that the expulsion order they received permitted them to do these deeds [massacres] in order to encourage the population to take to the roads. The fact is that no one was punished for these acts of murder."[61]

1. Type I: Selective Killing

After the occupation of a village, the invading forces selected a few individuals, mostly men described by Israeli documents as being "of the age of fighting" (from 15 to 55 years old). They were lined up against a wall and shot. In most cases, the executions were carried out in front of villagers to create the desired psychological impact. These executions, designed to create a local exodus, were a message aimed to be more convincing than any words: "Leave this place and never return." In reaction to such massacres, Israeli "new" historian Benny Morris has said: "[T]here was an unusually high concentration of executions of people against a wall or next to a well in an orderly fashion. That can't be chance. It's a pattern."[62]

An example of a selective killing occurred in the village of Majd al-Krum. The village arranged an official surrender on the morning of 30 October 1948, after the Arab Liberation Army (ALA) had withdrawn the night before. A few militants from the village, who were also directly involved, left. Some went to the caves near the village. The Israelis gathered arms in two successive rounds. On 5 November, one week after the surrender, an officer and two soldiers appeared with the *Mukhtar* at the square near the village's spring. They demanded the surrender of all rifles within the next half an hour. The *Mukhtar* argued that even if some villagers still possessed arms, the allowed time for their surrender was too short. The soldiers then selected five men from the village, lined them up in front of a wall, and shot them before the eyes of hundreds of male villagers who subsequently panicked. In the ensuing search of the houses four more people were killed – two men from Sha'b who came into the village apparently unaware of the happening there. They were bayoneted repeatedly and left for half an hour in an injured condition, before soldiers shot them. One woman was killed while she watched the soldiers and another was murdered because she was thought to have fled from an attempted rape. The UN observers who appeared on the scene were at first obstructed by IDF,

---

61 Morris, see note 29.

62 *Idem.*

but they later succeeded in their attempt to exhume bodies and to document photographically their findings. Unfortunately the IDF later stopped the UN observers and confiscated the films. The selective killing was contributed to the flight of some of the villagers. Later, V. Rabinowitch, a Haifa area intelligence officer (who used the Arab name Khawaja Ghazal in his undercover work) ordered the expulsion of hundreds of villagers in direction of the West Bank, which was far from the nearest Arab lines in Lebanon.[63]

2. Type II: Prisoner Massacres

All massacres of prisoners are in some sense selective, insofar as they target particular populations, either captured combatants or men of fighting age. Nevertheless, it is worth distinguishing them from the selective killings mentioned above, which all have an eerie similarity to one another.

There were, in fact, three different types of massacres directed at prisoners. The first occurs after the occupation of a locale. Those who defended the area, are rounded up after they surrender, tied up, and shot.

The second kind of massacre involves the killing of prisoners – usually young men – who were not even combatants; in some cases, those killed were from villages that offered no resistance to Israeli forces.

The third type of massacre is carried out behind the walls of a detention centre. After a speedy interrogation, sometimes using torture, a military court gives the orders for execution. These prisoners were considered by the military court as people who committed murders against Jews. In one case, summary executions were performed on the field of battle.

An example of the first kind of massacre against prisoners, who had already surrendered and were disarmed, occurred in the village of Abbas-

---

[63] Al-Aref, see note 43, Vol. 6, 125, was the first to mention this massacre. He is followed by Nazzal, see note 20, 92; and M. Palumbo, *The Palestinian Catastrophe, The 1948 Expulsion of a People from their Homeland*, 1987, 171-172, who provides the comprehensive version, quoting UNA13/3.3.1, box 11, Atrocities September-November. The most detailed account is provided by A. Mana', *The Memories and Historiography of the Events of the Nakba : The Example of Madj al-Krum, al-Dhakira w-al-Ta'rikh li Ahdath al-Nakba, Majd al-Krum Mathalan*, forthcoming. Compare Mana's treatment to Morris. Mana used eyewitness accounts and interviews with Palestinians and Israelis, as well as documentary sources, and offered to show them to Morris, who declined.

siyeh, near Lod, on 10 July 1948.[64] Retreating Palestinian combatants from the village were encircled in an open plain and were in clear view of Israeli troop carriers who ordered them to surrender. After 32 Palestinians threw down their arms and raised their hands in the air they were searched, handcuffed, and blindfolded by Israeli soldiers. They were then taken to a vacant house in the neighbouring Arab village whose inhabitants had already fled. After a few hours, the area was bombarded by the Iraqi artillery. The Israelis shot all prisoners just before they withdrew from the village. Two of the prisoners lived in spite of their wounds. The first one is Abdel Rahman Darweish and the second is Abdel Rahemm Mustafa Hamoude Kanash. The first victim was able to reach the Arab lines, but the second man was never seen again and is presumed to have bled to death. Darweish, who knew that the prisoners had been shot, could not bring himself to tell the other villagers of men's fates, and thus the villagers of Abbassiyeh, who became refugees, continued to hope for many years that their lost sons were alive. Only after the war of 1967 was the complete story revealed.[65]

An example of the second type of prisoner massacre occurred in Ein Zaytoun on 2 May 1948. On 1 May 1948 the Israeli forces began to prepare their occupation of Safad.[66] As part of these preparations, the village of Ein-Zaytoun was attacked by the third Palmach battalion. After an attack at dawn with mortar, heavy machine guns, and grenades, the Palestinian men in the village immediately withdrew. A few days prior to the attack, the residents of the village had agreed that, when resistance was no longer possible the armed defenders and other men would leave the village and allow only women, children, teenagers, and the elderly to remain. The Israelis killed one man as they entered the village. Then, as they had previously done on such an occasion, they demanded that the population of the village gather in the central square.

---

64 Author interview with Mahmoud Mohammad Ghabish, el-Bireh, 29 October 1997. In addition to the interview above, see also al-Aref, see note 43, Vol. 3, 582. Al-Aref says 32 prisoners were missing. H. Hamoudeh, Al-'Abbasiyeh 1921-1948: The Struggle of a Palestinian Village, Abbasiyeh Villagers Association, n.d., 47-50, in Arabic, supplies the names of 25 men killed. Hamoudeh is also the source of the names of the two survivors.

65 *Idem*; and author interview with Anis Abu Hakmeh, Ramallah, 1997.

66 For the battle of Safad, see M. Abbasi, "The Battle for Safad in the War of 1948: A Revised Study", *International Journal of Middle East Studies* 36 (2004), 21 et seq.

37 males were selected, mostly teenagers.[67] They were handcuffed and subsequently executed outside the village. The Israelis then shot over the heads of the crowd causing them to flee. Next, the Israeli forces began to demolish the houses of the village, wiping the village off the face of the earth. The demolition was done rapidly and in full view and hearing distance of the town of Safad. Safad's residents were able to observe what took place from the hills of the town. The goal of the Haganah was to demoralise them and make the attack on Safad easier for the Israelis.[68]

The citizens of Ein Zaytoun did not know the fate of the 37 prisoners from their village. Some believed that the prisoners had been killed although there were rumours and whispers that some had survived. The survival of the prisoners remained a part of the hopes of their families for many years.[69]

In 1985, thanks to the memoir of an Israeli soldier in the battalion that carried out the attack, we learned that the 37 young men from Ein Zaytoun were combined with other prisoners together numbering 70,[70] all

---

67 Nazzal, see note 20, 34-37, was the first to report the massacre.

68 Moshe Kelman, the military leader of this massacre was quite candid in his reports. He wrote "Safad was the [Arab] nerve-center ... in the Galilee region, and to some extent it was a symbol for all the Arabs in the country. It was clear that once we succeeded in conquering Safad, it would undermine the whole basis for the secure existence of Arab settlement in Galilee, and the control over the entire eastern part of that region would come into our hands very easily" (M. Kelman, Hagana Archives, file no. 65/13, 22). Kelman wanted to use the effect of the conquest of Ein Zeitun and decided, as he says, "To blow up the village buildings [of Birya and Ein Zeitun] one by one during daylight hours so that the Arab residents of Safad who were on the opposite ridge could see what was in store for them" (Kelman, see note 22). Kelman is quoted in Abbasi, see note 66, 34.

69 Palumbo, see note 63, 111-112, and Nazzal, see note 20, 34-37.

70 This information comes from N. Ben-Yehuda, *Passed the Ropes*, 1985, 243-248, in Hebrew, quoted in Morris, see note 5, 289, note 427, who describes removing the handcuffs from executed prisoners. Two other massacres account for the difference in numbers between the 37 young men from Ein Zaytoun and the total of 70 prisoners killed there. In 1992, Ehrlich, see note 2, quoted Milstein, who interviewed soldiers who were at Ein Zaytoun. They told him that there were two more massacres. Milstein has testimony from Aaron Yoily who said that three people from Safad came to Ein Zaytoun, demanded 23 Arab prisoners, claiming they were murderers. The men from Safad took the prisoners watches and pocketed them and then marched them behind the hill and

of whom were executed while handcuffed on 3 or 4 May in the valley between Ein Zaytoun and Safad. The executions were carried out according to the orders of Moshe Kilman, the head of the Palmach battalion.

In her memoir, Nitivah Ben-Yehuda devoted several pages to the massacre.[71] She described the events, which preceded and followed the execution of the prisoners. According to her testimony, some officers from the battalion refused to participate in this execution. Kilman then selected two soldiers, who claimed to have personal grievances against the Arabs, to carry out the executions. When the news reached the Israelis that the Red Cross was about to visit the area, Kilman requested that Ben-Yehuda untie the hands of the murdered men so that the Red Cross would not learn that a cold-blooded massacre had taken place. Today we also know from Israeli sources that Moshe Kilman, who ordered the massacre near Ein Zaytoun, was additionally responsible for two other massacres in Lod.[72]

The third type of massacre is the execution of prisoners – with or without a summary court martial. In some of these killings, the Israelis alleged acts of war and atrocities against Jewish civilians (e.g. the refinery case or the ambush of busses on the roads), thus creating legal cover for their executions.

These types of war crimes are quasi-secret. In general, there is far too little written about the Israeli prison camps and detention centres of 1948. The International Red Cross (IRC), which was later given access to the prison camps, has no record of the summary executions of prisoners. Apparently, some of the detention centres remained secret, and were thus unknown to the IRC. The testimony of Jum'a Ahmad Ghanam, a young village combatant from Tieret Haifa, gives us a hint of what was going on in these detention camps.

---

killed them. Another soldier, Yitzah Golan talked about 30 other prisoners who were taken for questioning at Kanaan by the Shai (Haganah) Intelligence Service who killed them after interrogating them because they "were attempting to flee."

71 Ben-Yehuda, quoted in Morris, *idem.*

72 Different Israeli sources, including Moshe Kilman's letters, confirm his role in killing of dozens of Palestinians, some even say as many as 250, in the Dahmash mosque in Lod. Ehrlich, see note 2, documents Kilman's role in ordering the execution of those who buried the dead from the Dahmash mosque.

> In Tabariya they interrogated me. They asked for the prisoners to come one at a time in the court. They take them to the room off the courtyard and there are officers there, sitting at a table and, with them, guards – of course. And they question us. We who are in the room, we hear the sound of shots. In the beginning, we did not know what these shots were. Did they make us hear, to frighten us, or so that we confess to what we were accused of? But then we knew that they were executed, because they never came back. And I was the only one who returned. Those who saw me in the room thought that there was a miracle. And the story of my continuing to live will be written. I stood before the judge and he asked me, yelling, if I were guilty or not. I told him "God knows, my lord, all is written in front of you from the questioning." The judge looked at the papers in front of him and said "Are you the son of Ahmad Ghannam?" so I responded "yes." I thought in the beginning that he wanted to belittle me, because I knew that my name was before him. But then he said "Do you remember when you fell in the well when you were small?" I said "Which well?" He said "the well of the railroad station. Do you not know me? I am Khawaja (Mister) Berman." It turned out that he was an employee of the railroad. So the worker of the railroad is now a Judge passing judgment on me. When I was small I went with my father to his work on the railroad. At night came a wagon, emptying water. The water was dirty. Another wagon came and I ran to my father. And at night the well was not visible. I did not see it, and a second later, I was at the bottom. When I began to scream, the workers ran to me and one of them was him. The Jew who told me "I knew you when you were small" was one of those who saved me. So Khawaja Berman told them in the court that I am too young to kill. He talked with those around him and told me that the courts passed judgment on me as innocent. "Go back to your place and if you see your father give him my regards."[73]

Many executions of prisoners did not even have a summary "court martial." Youssef Sayigh, now a retired professor from the American University of Beirut, was arrested in Jerusalem in mid May 1948. After his arrest, he was transferred with 23 other prisoners to Ijlail Detention Centre, in a Palestinian village, which was by then depopulated. He became the representative of the 5,000 Arab prisoners held at Ijlail. In his testimony he gave an account of the killing of selected prisoners. Pris-

---

[73] Author interview, Askar Refugee camp near Nablus, 1995.

oners were killed based on the allegation that they were attempting to escape. In particular, he recounted the example of a Palestinian prisoner, who felt that he was targeted and tried desperately not to go outside the camp to work (prisoners were made to work, sometimes even in military efforts). The day the prisoner did not return, Sayigh insisted on seeing an IRC representative. He finally succeeded, but only after he exhumed the body. The autopsy indicated that the bullet, which killed the young man entered from the chest, thus falsifying the allegation of flight.[74]

3. Type III: Indiscriminate Killing

Indiscriminate killing as a type of massacre has two distinguishing features. First, no distinction is made between men and women, or between adults, children and the elderly. Second, the objective is the extermination of either a large number of people or a high percentage of the people remaining in an area. Such killings – involving many people killed, women raped, as well as pregnant women and children being among the murdered – typically created a climate of terror and fear beyond the borders of the village where the crime occurred. The impact created a regional exodus.[75]

The number of fatalities is not always the defining feature that distinguishes selective killings from indiscriminate killings. Given differences in the size of villages and cities, some indiscriminate killings in tiny villages may produce fewer casualties than selective killings in large cities. Thus, for example, the killing of all ten elderly men and women remain-

---

[74] Testimony of Youssef Sayigh, representative of the Arab POW in Ijlaiel Detention Center, in: W.R. Khalidi, *Ramlehh Tataklam. Ramlehh Talks*, 1991. Dr. Sayigh later became a renowned world economist.

[75] A student interview with Amneh Mohammad Tomlieh (known as Umm Jihad) from 'Inaba, near Ramleh, conducted in the Am'ari refugee camp, 14 November 1999, shows one way the regional effect was created – by refugees from one massacre carrying their tales to surrounding villages. "They just hit us with a few shells from the Gezer settlement. The people heard and ran. They had taken Abu Shusha before us and the women and girls of Abu Shusha, when they arrived, they were crying how they saw, this one her brother, this one her father – they saw them killed." Stories like that told by Amneh Mohammad Tomlieh repeated themselves in many villages around Abu Shusha, and led to widespread demoralisation and flight after the first shells fell.

ing in a village would be an indiscriminate killing, but the execution of 20 men of fighting age in a large captive population would be a selective killing. The distinguishing feature is the inclusion of women, children and the elderly as victims and the intent to kill all or at least most of the people in a particular location.

An example of such an indiscriminate killing occurred in the village of Al-Dawayima (Hebron area) on 29 October 1948. Al-Dawayima was famous all over southern Palestine. Its Friday *souk* was one of the important regional markets. It was also known as a base for the Darawiesh (Suffis), who maintained their own mosque (Zawya). At noon on Friday, during the Friday prayer, the village was occupied by the mechanised Battalion No. 89 of the eighth brigade of the IDF. This was the best armed unit of the Israeli Army. It is known among Israeli New Historians that the battalion's leaders were eager to accomplish a Palestinian transfer by force, even without the nicety of psychological warfare. Leaders, like the battalion chief and his deputy, had a long history, going as far back as 1938, of inflicting death and destruction on Arab neighbourhoods.[76] The invaders occupied the village almost without resistance.

The massacre at Al-Dawayima was carried out in several stages. Initially, soldiers marched into the small mosque of the village. Many villagers were in the mosque at the time for two reasons. First, the army arrived during the Friday prayer. Secondly, many people, especially the elderly, took refuge in the mosque due to their awareness of army's presence. The following is an excerpt from the published testimony of Khalil Muhammad Mahmoud Salime Hudeib. From his home, which adjoined the Mosque, he recounted the troop-carriers approaching:

> The soldiers were laughing and joking loudly as they marched in. The Sheikhs and Daraweish began to plead with the soldiers for mercy. One of the soldiers said "Arabs you have to die so that you go to God." I heard the shooting and simultaneously the calling of "There is but One God" by the Sheikhs, giving their religious witness as they died. The voice of the Mosque's Imam, Sheikh Muhammad Mutlak Al-Ghawanme, calling with pain "God" and then I heard a shot and the voice was extinguished. And I heard one of the Daraweish saying "Oh God, Oh great one" and a soldier shouted

76 Palumbo, see note 63, xii.

> "die because you are great." After that a frightening silence engulfed the Mosque.[77]

Khallil's parents did not dare to open the door of the house to examine the mosque till much later in the day, when darkness began to fall after 5:30 pm. In the mosque, they found Daraweish and all the old men who had been there to pray, dead.

The second stage of the massacre occurred in the streets and in some of the village houses, where killing was indiscriminate. It is almost certain that four girls were raped and killed. Three such atrocities are mentioned in the eyewitness account below.

The third stage of the massacre took place in front of a large cave in the village, named Tor Il-Zagha. Several families of village had sought refuge at this site. One of the Israeli units discovered the cave, apparently after one or two of the youths, who were fleeing the village, fired upon the unit. The soldiers first dragged out those who had taken refuge in the cave, which were mostly women and children, and then they indiscriminately shot all the escapees. Entire families were executed. Two injured persons escaped this particular incident and bore witness to what had taken place.[78] They recalled:

> "We began to hear the sound of shooting approaching the cave. Everybody flattened themselves against the walls and floor of the cave, and they thought that their hour had come. A terrible silence reigned. Each woman began to hug their children to their breasts, kissing them with deep compassion, but without crying. Fear dried their tears. When the soldiers came to the entrance, one of them shouted, ordering people to come out. At this moment, children burst out crying. They grabbed their mothers' *jalabiyyas*. There is nothing warmer than a mother in the moment of death. One of the men took his white headdress in his hands and the people in the cave came out, one after the other, men, women, and children in a nightmare scene. Their eyes, now, were full of tears, not knowing if they will die. Two men fled. The soldiers turned shot at them, but they

---

[77] There are three main sources for the Al-Dawayima massacre. M.A.S. Hudeib, *Al-Dawayimah Village*, 1985; A. 'Atharbeh, *Al-Dawayimah*, Birzeit Research Center, The Palestinian Destroyed Villages, 21 April 1997, 215-216; "Olive Season Massacres: This is How They killed The People in al-Dawayima Mosque During the Friday Prayer", *Sawtt al-Haq wa-al-Huriya*, 21 October 1994, 9.

[78] 'Atharbeh, ibid., 212-216.

escaped. Then the soldiers led us to the nearby well and we were asked to stand in two lines, one of men and one for women and children. One soldier came from the troop carrier with a long weapon, but he was wearing shorts ... Everybody was standing absolutely motionless. I was on the far side. I was very young and I was saying to myself silently 'Hey, Khalil Allah [Abraham of God] hey, Khalil Allah' but I didn't say it out loud. I had my baby boy in my arms. This man, he went up to a woman, Fatmeh el-Maqdisyeh who was an old woman with children. They approached her and they took the three girls, Mariam, and the daughter of Moustafa al-Haj and another girl from the village of al-Qubaybah [a nearby village], – they took the three girls to the troop-carrier. The daughter of Ibrahim Joudeh was carrying her brother in her arms. They took him and threw him to the people standing around. And the woman said 'Hey, Khawajah, my daughter – where are you going to go with her?' She just said that and one bullet hit her heart. We heard their voices. She said 'Ah' and she fell to the ground as if she were kneeling for prayer. In her arms were her grandson (the son of Mariam Moustafa) and granddaughter. And then they got an order from the man in the tank and began to shoot first the men's line. Oh my god! Bang, bang, bang. It was like seeing a flock of pigeons being shot by hunters. The boy was in my arms and all I kept saying was 'Oh, Khalil Allah.' And they continued to shoot. I fell to the ground, not even daring to look around. Only hearing the shooting. Then they left. My husband Salim said 'I'm thirsty.' From where should I bring him water? I took the shoes from his feet and I covered him with my shawl. He was only a small distance from me. And there was a man with a little girl. She remained between his knees, her head turned toward the ground ... with her father's leg over her. The girl was unconscious. I came and pushed his leg aside. The girl was not breathing."[79]

4. Type IV: "Reprisal" Raids

"Reprisal" raids were carried out in villages, which had not yet been occupied. Therefore, almost all such attacks occurred at the beginning of the war, before the departure of the British armed forces from Palestine in May 1948. The pretext used for these raids, was that it was in reac-

[79] Ibid., 212-213.

tion to a particular incident, in which there was a Jewish victim. It was also allegedly done to punish a community for behaviour, such as attacking Jewish vehicles on the roads. "Reprisals" cannot just be understood in such limited contexts, but instead they should be understood as part of a more general plan of expulsion. They were indiscriminate for two reasons. First, both women and children were included among the victims. Secondly, the targets of reprisal raids were rarely the people who might actually have acted against the Jews. The people chosen by the Israelis as targets were so chosen because they were easy to reach.

This type of raid was usually accomplished during the night when people were asleep. These types of attacks were also executed by military units, which were well trained in night warfare behind enemy lines.

"Reprisal" raids were utilised by the Haganah. It was trained for this type of attack by a British officer, Ord Wingate, who was an expert in counter-revolutionary warfare.[80] During the 1936-1939 Arab Revolt, the Haganah's "reprisal" raids were directed as much as possible at militant targets. Unfortunately, by 1947 the policy of "*hafflaga*" (restraint, or proportionate response) was eroding, in favour of killing indiscriminately when the opportunity arose.[81] After the Arab Revolt, Palestinian relations with Jewish settlers returned to a more peaceful pattern. The Haganah policy of reprisals, used in 1947, was meant to return the level of tension between the native Arab and Jewish settler communities back to the levels during the Arab Revolt. It succeeded in doing so. One British Mandate officer described reprisals as follows: "Haganah men used to sneak into the village and put explosive charges around the stone houses while people slept. They threw petrol on the wooden

---

[80] The Israeli military academy is named in his honour. C. Burgess, "Ord Wingate; Rebellious Misfit", *Quarterly Journal of Military History* (1999), 68 et seq., recounts that Wingate was extremely pious, [in today's terms, a fundamentalist Protestant], obsessed by the idea of revenge. Wingate's fanaticism about the Old Testament led him to support the Zionists against the Arabs.

[81] For example, in one of these reprisal attacks, on 15 July 1947, 11 Palestinians, all innocent civilians, were killed, including seven from a single (Abu Laban) family. See Masalha, see note 47, 143-144 (AV). Another attack, in Feja, in May 1947 was characterised by U. Milstein (with A. Amit), *The Rabin File, An Unauthorized Expose*, 1999, 45, in these words: "Allon's contention that the Arab dead [in Feja] were later identified as gang members, can be treated as the propaganda it was."

frames of windows and doors, and then opened fire, and dynamited and burned the sleeping people to death."[82]

Reprisal raids also continued after the 1948 War. During the fifties the newly established Battalion 101, under the leadership of Ariel Sharon, continued to attack unarmed Palestinians in the same manner. It also committed well-known massacres, such as those in Qibya and Nahaleen.[83] The events at Qibya and Nahaleen provoked international condemnation of Israel's actions and thus Israel dissolved Battalion 101.

An example of a reprisal raid occurred in Khassas on 18 December 1947.[84] During the night, a force from Palmach penetrated the village after a settlement police car was attacked, which killed one man. There was, however, no connection between the residents of the village and the car attack. Furthermore, Haganah intelligence knew that the attackers had come from the Lebanese village of Kofr Kalla when the attack occurred. According to British sources, during the raid on Khassas, led personally by Moshe Dayan, the villagers did not fire a single shot. The next morning, the police found ten Arab dead under two demolished houses. Among the dead was a mother who had five children. Moshe Dayan claimed that the raid was justified. He stated "that it led to desirable results."[85] Ben-Gurion commented on the Khassas operation in his *Diaries* on 1 January 1948. He stated:

> The question is not if there is a necessity to retaliate ... We need strong and harsh retaliation ... When the family is known, we must be merciless in hitting them; including women and children, or our

---

[82] From the Arabic translation of Major R.D. Wilson, *Cordon and Search*, 1952, quoted in I. Abu-Loghod (ed.), *The Transformation of Palestine*, 1972, 201 (AV).

[83] In Qibya, in the West Bank, during one night of May 1953, 63 civilians, most of them women and children, died when their houses were dynamited by Israelis. They had no connection to the violent event in which three Israelis died. At Nahaleen a similar operation took place.

[84] This is a well-known massacre, cited in most writing about the war, including Milstein, see note 41, 113, who acknowledges eight fatalities; Morris, see note 21, 169, acknowledges ten fatalities; in B. Morris, *The Birth of the Palestinian Refugee Problem*, 1987, 33, Morris cites "about a dozen" fatalities; *Palestine* (newspaper), 20 December 1948, 1.

[85] Quoted in Ben-Gurion, see note 23, 99 (AV), 97 (HV). Author's translation.

> retaliation will not be efficient. No need to differentiate ... between the guilty and the innocent.[86]

Major General Bennike, Chief of Staff of the Truce Supervision Organization in Palestine, described years later the result of such a "necessary" retaliation in the Qibya. He recalled: "Bullet-riddled bodies near the doorways and multiple bullet holes on the doors of the demolished houses indicated that the inhabitants had been forced to remain inside until their homes were blown up over them."[87] Yosef Nahmani, the Head of Jewish National Fund in the north, was a rare Zionist who not only understood, but also deplored the new function of reprisals in the service of expulsions. Regarding the massacre in Khassas, he commented:

> "This matter causes horror and nausea. Such acts ... will only increase the number of those who hate us. How were the children to blame? If [we] want to punish, the guilty must be punished ... Such acts persuade the Arabs that we hate them ... [and] help the extremists among them to throw the whole country into a bloody maelstrom ... The situation in Galilee had been tense, but this was not expressed in attacks on the Jews, and Khassas will be the cause of untimely eruptions."[88]

5. Type V: Terror Operations

Explosives are the main instrument utilised in terror operations. Bombs were placed in urban areas, public buildings, and transport services. Small undercover groups committed such action. The people of such groups familiarised themselves with target locations prior to their attack. They were also fluent in Arabic and knew how to disguise themselves, either in Arab dress or as British soldiers.[89] They penetrated

---

[86] *Idem.*

[87] Report by the Chief of Staff of the United Nations Truce Supervision Organization in Palestine, Major General Vagn Bennike (of Denmark) to the UN Security Council, in particular to the incident at Qibya on 14-15 October, p.5.

[88] Yosef Nahmani quoted in Morris, see note 21, 169-170.

[89] These elite units, formed by the Palmach in 1942, were known in Hebrew as "mustarivim" meaning "like Arab." Slotsky, see note 14, 160-161 (AV), 1316 (HV).

Arab civilian areas typically in stolen British or Arab cars. Before the withdrawal of British forces, such terror attacks were carried out dominantly by wearing disguise. The Haganah typically executed such operations. The Irgun and the Lehi group introduced this type of action to Palestine in 1938. The Haganah learned from their example. Terror attacks were largely used against the British in the forties and on a large scale during the first six months of the 1948 War. In the period leading up to the 1948 War, terror attacks aimed at Palestinians were used as instruments of provocation. They also created fear and panic, which met another desired goal of the Israelis.

On 11 and 12 December 1947, the village of Tieret Haifa suffered a terror attack. In the following excerpt, Umm Riyad recalled the operation.[90]

> We were sitting one day ... after the afternoon *muezzin* call to prayer when someone knocked on the door. Three young men in tattered clothes looking like beggars told us that they were hungry and wanted to eat. My father told me "Get up girl and get them food." I was small. I brought them food and placed it in front of them. They started eating and carefully examining the house and exclaiming "What a house! Is this an important centre?" Our house was at the outskirts to the north of the village. When they finished my mother said to my father "I am afraid of these men, they are not beggars." He responded "You are the only one to be afraid; all the cannons of Europe cannot enter El-Tieret." She said to him "But I am afraid." We forgot the event but a few nights later we found our home besieged. Our house was big, two stories high. We lived on top and below were the sheep and between us and my uncle's home there was a wall. My brother opened the door and ran to my uncle's home. But he was not able to reach them. He went to hide in the *taboun* (bread oven) which was beside the wall at the back of the house. They broke down the door. I and my sister and mother and my uncle's daughter-in-law who came from Haifa saw them enter the room and place a crate [of explosives]. So we fled, some of us to the veranda and some downstairs. There was an explosion and stones flew even as far as the fields. When the bomb exploded I was outside the house. The house fell on those who were in it and

---

[90] Oral testimony from Umm Riyad, Far'a refugee camp, 1995, 192-193; A.R. al-Mudor, *Tieret Haifa*, Berzeit Research Center, Palestinian Destroyed Villages, series #19, 1995.

> burned. My uncle's home did not fall. My mother died and my sister and my brother died.

I have omitted most terror attacks from the census below, even those for which I have sufficient documentation. Many of these attacks do not fit the purposes of the census, because they were normally used before a village was conquered and therefore could be considered as a technique of war – albeit dirty war. My census is largely limited to massacres that occurred after a village was conquered, even if the subjugation was temporarily. Massacres which occur after conquest make clear the killers aim to carry out ethnic cleansing.

6. Type VI: Aerial Bombardement of Civilians

The Israelis had almost no air force in the beginning of the war. Until April 1948, there were only a few air attacks reported. That unfortunately changed during the first truce (June/July 1948) when the IDF was able to acquire fighter planes and bombers (including B-17s) on the European and American black markets. Aerial and land bombardment created great loss of civilian life and widespread demoralisation due to its indiscriminate character and because Palestinians, who had never experienced aerial bombardment before, had no defences against it. Air raids brought the "industrialisation of massacres"[91] (mass killings on a wide and speedy basis and from a distance) to the Middle East. Such raids killed many in the Gaza strip and in the villages like Tarshiha, Safsaf, Suhmata, Faluja, Isdood, Juret Askalan, Ijzem, Ein Ghazal, Ittiere, Beit Daras, Beit Jibrine, Lubia, Qaqoun, and dozens of others.

An example of the use of aerial bombardment, entirely without military justification and as a tool of expulsion, is the attack on the town of Beisan in May 1948. In a testimony of Musa Goldenberg, regional director of the Jewish National Fund in the District, he recalled:

> "One fine day, the instruction came from the [Haganah] headquarters, to evacuate immediately the town ... of its Arab residents, as a

[91] V. Nacquet, "Instruments Industriels de la Mort en Serie", in: G. Wacjman (ed.), *L'Objet du Siecle*, 1998, 37; O. Bartov et al. (eds), *Crimes of War, Guilt and Denial in the Twenthieth Century*, 2002, 4, says "Guernica's bombardment in 1937 and the bombardment of Barcelona in 1938 pushed the League of Nations on September 30, 1938 to adopt a resolution condemning indiscriminate bombing."

> defence centre for the whole region was to be organized there. I knew that the grounds given for the evacuation were not logical, [Beisan had surrendered and there was an official written agreement between its leaders and Haganah commanders] but I could not appeal and did not even have the opportunity to think about the matter. The battles still continued, and an order is an order. I travelled to Beisan because I had to explain to the inhabitants – 7,000 in number – the importance of this arrangement, and I thought that I could sweeten the bitter medicine with a few concessions and promises that would make it easier for them to carry out the order. The day came and it was announced in the streets that every resident could choose whether to travel to Nazareth in a bus provided by the government or to emigrate to Transjordan, and our army would ensure their safety up to the Shaikh Hussein Bridge. In any case, the town must be evacuated by the next evening. There was a great deal of fear in the town, and fierce criticism could already be heard of the Jewish state which needlessly oppressed its inhabitants. I tried to explain that this was only a temporary order, and that things would quickly be sorted out, but no one would listen to me. In order to enforce the evacuation order, a Piper aeroplane appeared and dropped two bombs in the courtyards where there were concentrations of people, causing deaths and injuries. After this, soldiers went through the town in a sort of demonstration of strength and hastened the departure of the inhabitants."[92]

Golenberg does not mention what is perhaps the most chilling detail in the Beisan massacre, which is that Arab inspectors were required to wear yellow armbands and to tag empty shops with yellow tags after the Jewish occupation. The labelling facilitated the acquisition of Arab property by the Jews.[93]

The massacre at Beisan is the only incident of aerial bombardment included in the census of massacres because it occurred long after the city and its Arab population came under Israeli authority. Although I find aerial bombardment to be one of the deadliest forms of assault, I have omitted all other incidents of this type, as in the villages and towns mentioned above. The reason I have not included such attacks in my census is because, while oral testimonies give a sense of what happened, individual respondents are rarely able to see the "big picture" in such

---

[92] M. Goldenberg quoted in W. Lehn (in association with U. Davis), *The Jewish National Fund*, 1988, 245-246.

[93] Morris, see note 5, 228.

incidents. Therefore respondents do not provide comprehensive accounts of events, including reliable estimates of fatalities.

7. Type VII: Deaths Resulting from Expulsions and the Execution of Old People

The Israelis used a variety of methods to accelerate the flow of refugees and to empty the Palestinian land of its population. The expulsions went far beyond a mere transfer of populations and were often fatal for the people who were subjected to the forced relocations. For instance, my interviews contained stories of Palestinian women who were so terrified, that they grabbed pillows, but left their children in the midst of forced evacuations. This happened in a number of villages and towns. Issbir Munier, for example, recalled how he found the bodies of two small children less than two years old in their cradles in a condition of decomposition after their family had been forced to flee el-Lod.[94] Terrified and unable to think clearly, fathers and mothers forgot or were forced under fire to leave some of their children to save their other children. Sometimes parents were able to return to seek their children, but if this was not possible their children died or were lost.

Some deportees drowned when overcrowded ships sank in the Jaffa port. Others were killed in the Natir neighbourhood of Jaffa, by Israeli snipers, as they attempted to flee. Still others, among them 20 young

---

94 Student interview with Issbir Munier, 1999. There are many patterns surrounding the abandonment of children or the elderly. In some cases, parents were killed and no one knew that babies had been left behind. In some cases bombardment caused panic fleeing. Sa'id Rashid Bakir from Abbasiyeh left his village on 4 May 1948 and took refuge in Beit Nabala until mid July, when this village also fell. He says: "The planes came [to Beit Nabala] and bombarded the people. Some fled and left their parents. Some fled and left their children. I saw old people abandoned by the trunks of the trees. Young kids, some women were not able to carry them. They put them near the road, and they left" (student interview of Bakir, Jalazon Refugee Camp, 3 October 1999). We also have Nimr Sirhan from Sindiyani telling the story of Mahmoud al-Sheikh whose wife could not carry all of their children to safety. She took two children in her arms and another on her back. Her young son remained behind until the next day when his grandmother was able to fetch him (student interview with Sirhan, in his home in Nabi Saleh, 15 December 2000).

men from the town of Sha'ab in Galilee, died trapped in the mud that obstructed their retreat.[95]

Perhaps the best known example of the murderous effects of expulsions is the case of Lod, the site of one of the worst war crimes of the 1948 War. The town was bombarded by mortar and airplanes. The occupation was brutal. Many civilians who fled in panic were shot in the streets. Israeli reports confirm the oral testimonies, which stated that hundreds of bodies "littered" the roads.[96] One woman thought that people were asleep in the street because she could not believe that she had walked past so many dead bodies.

After the capitulation of the city, three Jordanian troop carriers entered the city for a very short time. They gave the wrong impression that Jordanian forces had returned. Some of the Palestinian militia, who were still armed, opened fire on Israeli forces thinking that the Jordanians had recaptured the city. Israeli reprisals were immediate and disproportionate. The number of persons killed included some 175-250 persons who were machine-gunned down in the Dahmash Mosque, which was the second most important mosque of the city. Only one injured man survived to tell the story. Israeli sources later acknowledged the high number of casualties in the mosque, but claimed that their action was justified because it was in reaction to the bombardment of combatants. Later, many of the Palestinians who were ordered to dig the graves and bury the dead were subsequently gunned down. The aim of this section is not to discuss in detail the massacres in Lod, but instead to discuss the exodus and how the exodus turned into a death march for the citizens of Lod. The following testimony comes from two men I interviewed: Haj As'ad Hassoune (quoted in the introduction, above) and Father Odeh Al-Rantisi, who later became the Vice Mayor of the town of Ramallah.

Father Odeh Al-Rantisi recalled:

> That morning the Jews knocked on the doors of the houses, one by one, and my mother went to the door. I was standing behind her. There were three soldiers with blond hair and blue eyes and their facial type appeared European and they spoke English fluently. My

---

[95] Elias Khoure, communication to the author, Berne, Switzerland, August 1997.

[96] Morris, see note 5, 434, writes: "Hundreds of unburied corpses littering [Lod's] streets and houses and the road between Lod and Ramleh during 12-15 July."

mother used to know English and German and so she understood them when they demanded that we leave all the doors open and depart. During the six month general strike of 1936 the British asked the people of the town to leave their houses and leave the doors open and we returned at the end of the day. We thought that things would be similar. We decided to go to the church of Mar Giryes (Saint George) in Lod to take refuge there until the end of the search. And then we thought we would go back home. However, this time things were different. The Jews prevented us from returning and forced us to join a flood of people towards the eastern exit. We walked with the people until the end of the town and there the Jews prevented us from walking on the automobile road and directed us to the mountains. We had nothing with us, because we believed that we could return. But it was an exodus without a return. People heard what had happened in the Mosque and thus people thought that the Jews would kill them in the mountains and thus the morale of the people was awful. We walked in the mountains until we reached a large vegetable farm. In front of the farm was a big gate, which had a cement pediment, and on this there sat three Israeli soldiers. They began to shoot over our heads. And this increased the fear in the hearts of people. When we turned to the gate there were hundreds there, wanting to enter. I was holding my grandfather's hand who was holding in his pocket a box of sugar. In his other hand he had some milk, because my cousin, who was only two years old, had typhoid and I remember it as a sight which is impossible to forget. There was, in front of us, a woman holding her small baby and a cart with large wheels pulled by a horse. From the greatness of crowding and anxiety and fear, the child fell from his mother's arms to the ground and the wheel went over his neck. It was the first of this type of scene which passed before my eyes. When we entered this gate, we saw Jewish soldiers spreading sheets on the ground and each who passed there had to place whatever they had that was valuable on the ground or be killed. I remember that there was a man whom I knew from the Hanhan family from Lod who had just been married barely six weeks and there was with him a basket which contained money. When they asked him to place the basket on the sheets he refused – so they shot him dead before my eyes. Others were killed in front of me too, but I remember this person well because I used to know him. We continued walking after this and we had no food or drink. In the farm the people had taken to walking quickly to pick fruits and eat them raw. We filled what we could with water, and rejoined the march. In the evening, we reached the district Jimzo and there, in the mountains, we gathered wood and lit a fire so we could warm ourselves. And a bit later we heard airplanes approaching us and the people yelled "Put out the fires." Whoever had a bit of water used it to throw on the fire but then we had not a drop of water left to drink. In the morning we woke to the sound of shooting in our direction. There came a group of armed Jews, approaching on horseback and firing in our direction. The people scattered and fled in all directions and, in this way, families were divided. And because we were on the mountain, we began to run to the valley. Suddenly I looked around me and found myself alone. I could not find my father and brothers or relatives. Each person had run in a different direction. I took to asking people if they saw my relatives, but none had. All of them were suffering from the same problem and all were searching for their family. Suddenly a bullet scraped me and ended up in a donkey standing behind me and killed him. So I ran away as fast as I could. I continued to walk and to inquire and, to my great luck, I found my uncle and his family. My oldest sister was with them. I asked about my mother and father and brothers. They indicated that they had not seen them, but that they would probably follow us and catch up with us in time. I stayed with them and we walked all day until we went a long distance. Nightfall came and we found a place among the rocks to lie down and protect ourselves from the cold. I could not accept the idea that our parents would catch up with us and thus I left my uncle's family and I marched the other way in the dark. From a distance I heard my father's voice and it was a deeply affecting moment when I actually met up with them and I took them to where my uncle and his family were, and there we spent the night. We continued walking on the third day and the things I saw that third day had a big effect on my life. Hundreds lost their lives due to fatigue and thirst. It was very hot during the day and there was no water. I remember that when we reached an abandoned house, they tied a rope around my cousin's child and sent him down into the water. They were so thirsty that they started to suck the water from his clothes … The road to Ramallah had become an open cemetery.[97]

---

[97] Compare the testimony of Rantisi, above, with Benny Morris' bloodless summary: "The atrocities were limited in size, scope and time. And, as immediately after Hiram, movement by inhabitants between villages was curtailed, news of massacres probably moved slowly. Moreover, atrocities did not occur in many, perhaps most, of the villages captured. In most, the primary causes of flight were those that had precipitated previous waves: Fear of being caught up

Forced expulsions were directed at entire populations and therefore they are a sub-type of indiscriminate killing. It should be noted though, that forced expulsions disproportionately harmed the old and the weak in at least two ways. First, it was difficult for the elderly to keep up with the pace of forced marches and second some elderly were blind or so old they could not walk at all. Therefore, many could not leave by themselves and their children were unable to aid them in doing so. Others were afraid of dying in a strange place and thus refused to leave the villages of their birth. They thought that they would only need to stay alone in the village for a few days, until those who had left would return.

The Israelis encountered remaining elderly in most of the villages they occupied. There was no well-defined policy for how to handle such a group. The Israelis killed them and burned their bodies in most cases. Sometimes the Israelis left half-charred remains of those they killed.

Many eyewitnesses recounted that they found the half-burned bodies of five old women and two old men in Qula. Qula was the site where the Jordanian army counter-attacked a few days after the fall of the village in mid July 1948. The soldiers used kerosene from a neighbourhood shop to set the bodies on fire, but the flames did not completely consume the corpses.[98] Those who returned to Saris (occupied on 15 April 1948) only a few hours after the fall of the village, discovered the remains of four old women. The women had been lined up against a wall and each had been shot in the forehead.[99] Similar executions of the elderly occurred in many villages, such as Abbasiyeh, Daniyal, el-Burj, Barfilia, Bier Ima'ein, 'Ajur.

The elderly were not always killed. One eyewitness from Isdood stated that an old, blind woman was spared. Siryeh, the mother of Suleiman al-Ashkor, was also found alive by returnees who came back to harvest their wheat. They had left food for her and so did some of the Israelis who had occupied the village. Nevertheless, she died. No one is certain

---

and hurt in battle, fear of the conquerors and of revenge for past misdeeds or affiliations, a general fear of the future and of life under Jewish rule, and confusion and shock" (Morris, see note 5, 482).

[98] Author interview with Samara Rantisi, el-Bireh, 7 January 2000; student interview with Hassan Abu Ghanim, Birzeit, 20 December 2000; student interview with Mohmmad Mahmoud Ibrahim, el-Bireh, 2 January 2001; student interview with Tawfiq Hussein Saleh, Birzeit, 2000.

[99] Student interview with Hadj Mahmoud Jaber Mahmoud Abu Khairy, Beit Hanina, November 2000.

how she passed away. One returnee recalled that dogs ripped pieces of flesh from her body. He said "Dogs who were left in the village were hungry too."[100] In 'Inaba, an old injured woman was even taken to the hospital by the soldiers who found her.[101] She was treated there and then subsequently sent to Lod. In the village of Ez Zib, which is in the north, old people were also spared.[102]

Although I believe that the killing of the elderly should also, perhaps, be considered a distinctive form of massacre, I do not include such incidents in my census. I have omitted the cases because either only one or two old people were killed, or because the documentary evidence is too contradictory. I have deferred the question of whether the killing of the elderly is a distinctive type of massacre to my forthcoming work.

V. Census of Massacres

It is important to note, again, that the list of the total number of massacres is a conservative estimate as explained in the first section of this article. Furthermore, one should be aware that terror attacks were eliminated from the census, except for seven incidents, which occurred between 11 and 13 December 1947. These events are the first seven items on the list. The attacks have been described by the British High Commissioner Sir Alan Cunningham as "an offence to civilisation." They also played a crucial role, as I have argued elsewhere,[103] in triggering the war. Nevertheless, I only consider the events in Khassas (18 December 1947) and onward massacres. Additionally, a terror attack on the Haifa Oil Refinery was included in the census to put the two massacres, which occurred in Balad al-Sheikh and Hawassa al-Fuqa, into context.

The full analysis and evaluation of the listed massacres is not included in this article. Such work is still in progress. The purpose of this article is to create the empirical basis for analysis.

11 December 1947: Balad al-Sheik (Haifa area)

---

[100] Student and author interview with Mohmmad Batrawi of Isdood, Ramallah, 7 May 2000.

[101] Student interview with Abed Wahdan Abu Khalid, Jalazoon Refugee Camp, 9 December 2000.

[102] See Nazzal, see note 20, 74, for Kuweikat whose elderly people were expelled to the Druse village of Abu Sinan, and 56, for Ez Zib.

[103] Jawad, see note 17.

11-12 December 1947: Tieret Haifa (Haifa area) and Ramlehh

12 December 1948: Nabi Yosha' (Galilee panhandle)

13 December 1947: 'Abassiya (Jaffa area), Damascus Gate, Jerusalem and Jaffa near Cinema al-Hamra, King George Street

18 December 1947: Khassas (Galilee panhandle)

19 December 1947: Qazazeh (south of Ramlehh)

30 December 1947: Haifa Oil Refinery

31 December 1947: Balad al-Sheikh (Haifa area), Hawassa al-Fuqa (Haifa area), and Mansurat al-Kheit (also known as Mansurat al-Hula – Upper Galilee)

Early February 1948: Caesaria (Haifa area)

14 -15 February 1948: Sa'sa (Safad area, on the Lebanese border)

12 March 1948: Husseiniya (Tiberias area)

17 March 1948: Huseiniya (Tiberias area).

April 1948: (11). Al-Manshiya (Tiberias area)

9 April 1948:

(12). Deir Yassin (Jerusalem suburbs): Indiscriminate mass killings and killings of prisoners take place. 100 villagers are killed. Some are killed during battle and others are killed subsequently. Women are raped and killed. Survivors are paraded through Jerusalem's Jewish neighbourhood and subsequently men are machine-gunned down in a quarry near Deir Yassin.[104]

12 April 1948:

(13). Nasir al-Deen and Sheikh Qadumi hill (Tiberias area): Indiscriminate killings occur. The two locations are attacked by Haganah's Golani Brigade to aid the demoralisation of the besieged city of Tiberias. 12-20 civilians are massacred by machine guns and homes in Nasir al-Deen

---

[104] This massacre is universally recognised. However, most sources (e.g the Red Cross) estimated the fatalities at 254. Palestinian sources (al-Aref and my oral histories) put the number at 100. The best study available is W. Khalidi, *Deir Yassin*, 1998, in Arabic. Khalidi drew extensively on the work of S. Kanaana/N. Zitawi, *Deir Yassin*, Birzeit Research Center, Palestinian Destroyed Villages, series #4, 1987. See also Milstein, see note 41.

and Sheikh Qadumi are blown up. The majority of the dead are women and children.[105]

(14). Abu Zureiq (Haifa area): Selective killing occurs. Abu Zureq is considered friendly to Jewish settlers at the time of the massacre. The village is mortared, but no retaliation ensues. The Haganah kill at least ten men fleeing the village.[106]

16-17 April 1948:

(15). Sariss (Jerusalem corridor): Indiscriminate killings occur. The Haganah attacks the village at dawn. At that time, at least four elderly women remain in the village as other villagers flee in panic. Later in the same day, returnees discover the corpses of four women. The bodies are all in one spot and each is shot in the forehead.[107]

19-20 April 1948:

(16). Beit Surik and Bidu (two neighbouring villages in Jerusalem area): Palmach troops, commanded from Jerusalem by Yitzak Rabin, occupy the two villages without confronting resistance. Sappers blow up occupied Arab houses. According to *Ha'aretz*, "the houses collapsed on dozens of Arabs," who are falsely presumed to be fighters (author's comment: according to Arab oral sources).[108]

---

[105] Al-Aref, see note 43, Vol. 1, 205; Ehrlich, see note 2; Morris, see note 21, 177, quoting Yossef Nahmani, gives the highest number of casualties (20) for Nasir al-Deen alone.

[106] Morris, see note 5, 242-243, quotes a letter from Eliezer Bauer, Mapam member to Mapam leaders, attributing the killing in Abu Zureq to Jewish settlers from nearby settlements. Bauer writes: "When the village was conquered, the villagers tried to escape ... Forces from the nearby settlements sortied out and outflanked them ... [of those who] surrendered or were captured unarmed, most were killed [i.e. murdered]. And these were not gang members as was later written in [the Mapam daily] ... but defenceless, beaten peasants ... Also in the village, when adult males were discovered hiding hours after the end of the battle – they were killed." For good relations between Abu Zureq and surrounding Jewish settlements, see M. Benvenisti, *Sacred Landscape, the Buried History of the Holy Land since 1948*, 2000, 74-77.

[107] Student interview with Hadj Mahmoud Jaber Mahmoud Abu Khairy, Beit Hanina, November 2000.

[108] Milstein, see note 41, 211; Ben-Gurion, see note 23, entry for 21 April 1948, 273 (AV), 361 (HV), "Beit Surik was occupied and destroyed. Nothing remained except the Mosque. The same is in Bidu." Oral testimonies indicate that those killed were civilians, student interview with Hassan Dawud al-

21-22 April 1948:

(17). Haifa: Mass indiscriminate killings occur. After the fall of Haifa, the Haganah continued to bombard civilian gatherings, especially near the port. They create panic and cause looting. Prisoners of war are executed. The number of casualties is unknown.[109]

27 April 1948:

(18). Haifa: Extra-judicial executions occur. Seven of the oil refinery workers, who are suspected of having been present at the 30 December 1947 killings (see above), are executed by the Haganah.[110]

28 April 1948:

(19). Jaffa, Manshieh neighbourhood: Indiscriminate killings occur. Following heavy bombardment and a fierce battle, which lasts several days, IZL forces from Tel Aviv occupy al-Manshieh. They systematically massacre both combatants and remaining civilians. Casualties are estimated to be around 50.[111]

29 April 1948:

Khatib, head of the village local council, 11 November 2000. However, our interviews failed to give an estimate of the number of fatalities.

[109] This is a well-known massacre, al-Aref, see note 43, Vol. 1, 222, is the earliest source, but for more complete information, see especially Palumbo, see note 63, 62-81; W. Khalidi, *Fifty Years After the Partition Plan, 1947-1997*, 1998, 29-134; Masalha, see note 47, 173-176 (AV); E. Childers, "The Other Exodus", *The Spectator* (a London weekly), 12 May 1961; Morris, *Birth*, 76-77, especially the "22 Battalian (Carmeli Brigade) orders to its troops ... 'to kill every ... Arab encountered' and to set alight with fire bombs 'all objectives that can be set alight';" for the killing of Arab prisoners, Ben-Gurion relates a case in which a guard ordered prisoners not to speak and when they spoke anyway, he shot them, see note 23, 284 (AV), 378 (HV). B. Farah, *Min al-'uthmaneya ila adawlat al-'ibrya* (From Ottomanism to the Hebrew State), 1985, 197, documents details of individual Jews expelling individual Palestinians and taking their houses.

[110] Masalha, see note 47, 176 (AV), quoting British document: "Section 257 and 317F.S, Weekly Report No. 3", for the week ending 28 April in PRO, WO 275-79, 3.

[111] Al-Aref, see note 43, Vol. 1, 258-260. Dr. Hassan Hathut, an Egyptian doctor, collected eyewitness accounts from Egyptian fighters in Jaffa, in H. Hathut, *Diaries of an Egyptian Doctor, Palestine the First Disaster of 1948*, 1988, 32; student eyewitness interview with Abed Aziz Abu Raya, village of Silwad, 1979.

(20). Jerusalem, Qatamoun neighbourhood: Indiscriminate killings occur. After the fall of this western neighbourhood in Jerusalem, the Haganah forces kill an unknown number of people.[112]

(21). Ein Zaytoun (Safad area): Multiple prisoner massacres occur.[113]

4 May 1948:

(22). Kofr Ana (Lod area): Indiscriminate killings occur. The village is demoralised and occupied after a period of resistance. Ten civilians are killed on the day of the occupation. Those murdered are either elderly people, who remained in the village, or men, who attempted to flee.[114]

(23). As Samakiyya ('Arab al-Samakiyya near Tiberias): Indiscriminate killings occur. The Haganah fires on fleeing civilians and kill at least three individuals from Tabigha, who had taken refuge in As Samakiyya. Among the dead are Ahmad Muhammed, Ahmad Abu-Fadil, Hamdih Khadrah, and the sister of Ahmad Yousef Ali.[115]

9 May 1948:

(24). Qanir (Haifa area): Indiscriminate killings occur. The village is attacked for the first time on 2 March, according to Masalha. Most of the houses in the village are destroyed. On 9 May, according to Haganah reports, Alexandroni troops raid the village and kill at least four Arabs. They blow up the remaining 55 houses.[116]

Mid May 1948:

(25). Beisan (Jordan Valley): Aerial bombardment occurs.[117]

---

[112] Palumbo, see note 63, 100, cites the report of the Red Cross doctor who, despite obstruction from the Haganah, followed the smell of rotting flesh to a cave where he found "A group of bodies piled in a heap, including soldiers, women and even a mule." Six men who tried to help the doctor were overcome by the stench and were unable to go on.

[113] See section of massacres of prisoners, above.

[114] Student eyewitness interview with testimony of Ahmad Abdullah Abu Sheikh, Ramallah, 5 April 1995.

[115] Nazzal, dissertation, Vol. II, 260-264, interviews with Ahmad Yousef Ali and Ahmad Shahadi Muhammed.

[116] For details about 2 March, see Masalha, see note 47, 155 (AV), quoting British documents; for the events of 9 May, see Morris, see note 5, 244; according to Morris' map legend, xviii, Qanir fell on 25 April 1948. We can assume that the events of 25 April constituted a second attack on Qanir and the raid of 9 May a third attack, probably aimed at those who returned.

[117] For details, see comments under aerial bombardment, above.

12 May 1948:

(26). Um Chouf (Haifa area): Massacre of prisoners after extra-judicial "court martial" occurs. "An IZL officer at Umm al Shauf later recalled searching a column of refugees and finding a pistol and rifle. The troops detained seven young adult males and sent the rest of the column on its way. The troops demanded to know who the weapons belonged to. When the detainees refused to own up, the IZL men threatened them with death. When no one owned up, the IZL officer held 'a field court martial that sentenced the seven to death.' The seven were executed."[118]

(27). Khubbeiza (Haifa area). Arab sources refer to a massacre. Israeli sources make no mention of a massacre, but acknowledge that Khubbeiza was one of four villages attacked by the IZL. In the same operation which attacked Khubbeiza, Sabbarin, Umm Shouf and Bureika massacres did occur in two of these four.[119]

12-14 May 1948:

(28). Sabbarin: Indiscriminate killings occur. A section of the IZL attack four villages (see Khubbeiza above). Civilians who flee are massacred after a short battle. About 20 people die. Over 100 people remain. All or a part of the elderly, women and children are forced into a house, which is blown up by troops.[120]

13 May 1948:

(29). Burayr (Gaza): Indiscriminate killings occur. The Haganah occupies the school, where most of the Palestinian combatants from the village and other volunteers from the Gaza area barricade themselves. All the people inside the school (mainly combatants) are killed. Then civil-

---

[118] Morris, see note 5, 244.

[119] S.H. Abu Sitta, *The Palestinian Holocaust (Al Nakba) 1948, The Register of Depopulated Localities in Palestine, Preliminary draft*, 1997, 10, is the Arab source. Morris, see note 5, map, identifies 12-14 May as date of IZL occupation. On 243-244, Morris reports: "IZL forces ... on 12 May attacked and cleared the last Arab villages in the Hills of Menashe ... The dissidents attacked Sabbarin, al Sindiyana, Bureika, Khubbeiza and Umm al Shauf." The Haganah often tried to distance itself from IZL and Lehi by describing them as "dissidents," though the British High Commissioner for Palestine, Sir Alan Cunningham, discounts this claim.

[120] Two eyewitness accounts offer different details, but confirm the massacre. Muhammad Adel Qadir al-Azziz Nazzal, student interview, Qabattia, 23 October 1999, provided an eyewitness report of the blowing up of houses. Ra'ouf al-Hadj Yehya, interview, 2001, provides details of approximately 20 people killed while fleeing.

ians, including women, children and the elderly, are systematically massacred in the surrounding houses. 20 combatants and 50 civilians are killed. Among the massacred, four are women, five are children and eight are over 60. Only a ten-year-old boy from the group of injured survives. Morris mentions the rape and murder of a teenage girl.[121]

(30). Sumsum: Indiscriminate killings occur. Sumsum is a village with a reputation for being a home for collaborators. Oral testimonies provide information about the imprisonment and torture of some people, during the war, by Egyptian forces for treason. Regardless of the residents' connection to the Israelis, they are expelled more than once from the village. They rely on their past connections, though, to return to their fields and village. The Negev Brigade is ordered to expel the remaining and returning villagers and to burn the fields and granaries. It kills five to 20 people (according to Haganah documents quoted in Morris), blows up granaries, and destroys a well. Morris uses the terms "resistance" and "skirmishes" to describe the behaviour of the Sumsum residents. The resistance was only a refusal to obey the expulsion orders and not the use of an armed force by the villagers.[122]

(31). Jaffa: Indiscriminate killings and forced expulsions occurred. A siege and bombardment lasted months. The city falls. It is the theatre of extensive looting by Jewish civilians and militias. The combination of massive bombardment, looting, and summary executions lead to panic. Many drown in their attempt to board overcrowded boats in the harbour. Oral histories paint an apocalyptic vision of summary executions in the cemetery and on the beach. Mainly poor foreign workers (Egyptians and Syrians from Huran), who are suspected of being resisters, are the targets of such executions. Prisoners are killed on the spot. There

---

[121] The most important and detailed source for this massacre is M.H.A. Hussein, *Burayr Village*, 1999, 142-147, which includes the names of all the villagers who were killed. The author is the son of the *Mukhtar* of Burayr and also the headmaster of the village school. Morris, see note 5, 258, implies the massacre when he says: "The 9th Battalion troops killed a large number of villagers, apparently executing dozens of army-age males."

[122] Oral testimonies delivered to us by Rashad Madani from Gaza who conducted oral history interviews with refugees in the south of Palestine for Birzeit Research Center and Amneh al-Najar, student interviewer from Beit Affa, el-Amari Refugee Camp, 1999; and Morris, see note 5, 258.

are also reports of the execution of surrendered. In some cases, civilians, who refused to surrender their belongings or houses, are also shot.[123]

14 May 1948:

(32). Bassa (Acre area, Western Galilee): Indiscriminate killings occur. The Haganah rounds up fleeing civilians in the Greek Orthodox Church and kills at least five people inside the church. A larger group, which includes the young Salim Darweish and his sister Elaine, is taken outside the church and those present are killed. At least 14 are killed. Three men, who attempt to return to the village later, are also killed.[124]

(33). Ghabisiyya (Acrea area): Indiscriminate killings occur. The village "maintain[s] close ties with their Jewish neighbors and ha[s] even signed an agreement to provide information to them, in return for which the Jewish forces undert[ake] not to enter the village or harm its residents. In spite of the agreement, the village [is] occupied; eleven of its inhabitants [are] killed."[125]

(34). Abu Shusha (Ramlehh area): Selective killings and forced expulsions occur. The Haganah bombard the village and seven men are killed. Men are shot, bayoneted, and axed after the fall of the town. Women and children who take refuge in a cave are discovered three days later. Some of the women are injured by mines planted by the Haganah and at least one woman is raped. 50 people were killed, including ten from the neighbouring village of Sidon, who had taken refuge in Abu Shusha. Women and the elderly are forced to abandon the village.[126]

---

[123] Al-Aref, see note 43, Vol. 1, 250-268, estimates that 700 people were killed in the battle of Jaffa and 7,000 injured. Student eyewitness interview with Abed Aziz Abu Raya, village of Silwad, 1979; student eyewitness interview with Tamam Ahkal Shammoutt, 2001; other oral testimonies from people who still live in Jaffa and who wish to remain anonymous were given to the author. Palumbo, see note 63, 87-94, summarises the fall of Jaffa. See also W. Khalidi, *Khamsun 'aman' ala harb 1948, ula al-hurub al-sihyuniyya al-'arabiyya [Fifty years since the 1948 War, the First of the Arab-Zionist wars]*, 1998, 134-138; for the looting in Jaffa, see an Israeli account by D. Kimchee, in: W. Khalidi (ed.), *From Haven to Conquest*, 1992.

[124] Information communicated to the author by Elham Bayour, 1997, and Yousef Haddad, 1999 in California. Both are intellectuals from Bassa who did important work on village history. See also Nazzal, dissertation, Vol. II, 386; Benvenisti, see note 106, 140.

[125] Benvenisti, *idem*.

[126] N.Yakub/F. Shalabi, *Abu Shusha*, Birzeit Research Center, Palestinian Destroyed Villages, series #18, 1995. This monograph dedicated one whole

(35). Kofr Saba (Qalqilya area): Indiscriminate killings occur. According to eyewitnesses, 11-20 people are killed after the occupation of the village by the Haganah. After the capitulation of the village, a young man, who tries to help his elderly father leave the village, is shot.[127]

16–18 May 1948:

(36) Acre: Indiscriminate killings occur. After the fall of Haifa, Acre is inundated by tens of thousands of refugees from Haifa and the neighbouring villages. A large number of refugees are from Balad al-Sheikh and Hawassa Fuqa. Atrocities are committed in Acre during the time it is conquered,[128] but they are on a smaller scale than in Lod, Haifa and Jaffa.[129]

20 May 1948:

(37). Kabri (Acre area, Western Galilee): Selective killings occur. Haganah forces occupy the village under Moshe Carmeli's orders (dated 19 May) "to attack with the aim of conquest, the killing of adult males, destruction and torching." Seven young men are murdered the following day by two Israeli soldiers; Yehuda Rashef and his brother. In the presence of their commander, Dov Shetch, the soldiers order the seven men to fill up some ditches. The men are then lined up and shot dead. The story of one of these men is told in the testimony of his widow, Aminah Mohammad Musa. She recounts that they, along with others, had already fled the village. They were stopped by Jewish troops on the Kabri-Tarshiha road. She was then robbed of her gold jewellery by a soldier, who told her he would give them to his *habibti* (his girlfriend). Subsequently, an armoured car picked them up and brought them the long way back to Kabri. There her husband was questioned. He denied

---

chapter to the massacre. Later the author published more advanced accounts of the massacre in a number of newspaper articles – for copies, contact the author.

[127] Five oral testimonies from the village, author and student interviews; S. Kanaana/B. al-Ka'bi, *Kofr Saba*, Birzeit Research Center, Palestinian Destroyed Villages, series #11, 1991, 59.

[128] Al-Aref, see note 43, Vol. 2, 416 dates the fall of Acre as 16 May; Slotsky, see note 14, 480 (AV), 1585 (HV), dates it on 17 May and Morris, see note 5, 231 on 18 May.

[129] Al-Aref, see note 43, Vol. 2, 424, talks about the death of 91 persons including fighters and many civilians. In one case, seven people he names, mainly old, were machine-gunned when they went out to welcome the Haganah troops who were disguised as Arabs. Morris, see note 5, 231, talks about the rape and the murder of a girl and her father. Saleh Idriss Titi, communication to the author, confirms atrocities, saying that most of those killed were refugees.

that he was from the village, but an Arab collaborator identified him as a Kabri villager and that sealed his doom. Musa then tells of finding her husband's body: "He was shot in the back of the head. I pulled him into the shade and went to bring 'Umm Hussain to help me bury him. We carried him on a piece of wood to the cemetery and buried him sideways in his mother's grave ... Until today I worry and pray that I buried him the right way, in the proper position [i.e. facing Mecca]." Musa also reports an Israeli soldier showing her a picture of someone named Faris, telling her, "Tell him, we will occupy Palestine and we will follow him into Lebanon." In another incident, the Israeli commander and other officers shot a youth fleeing the village with an 18 year old girl whose fate is unknown.[130]

21 May 1948:

(38). Beit Darass (Gaza): Forced expulsions and indiscriminate killings occurred. Israelis open fire on women and children being evacuated from the village.[131]

23 May 1948:

(39). Tantoura (Haifa area): Selective killings occurred. Despite its complete isolation, the village resists many attempts at conquer. In the last battle, which ends with its occupation, the IDF execute the men they capture. Casualties, including those killed in battle and those massacred, are estimated to be between 52 and 85. Later, individual executions are committed against Tantoura prisoners in detention centres as well.[132]

---

[130] Nazzal, see note 20, 62-63, documents the first and most important killing along with the names of the victims. Morris, see note 5, 253, documents the kill orders. Ehrlich, see note 2, confirmed the massacre and provided the names of soldiers and their commander and details about the second incident.

[131] Al-Aref, see note 43, Vol. 3, 536, talks about 33 casualties and also documents one rape. He also talks about an earlier attack in which 80 persons from the village were killed in battles. Amneh Najar (oral testimony, previously cited, see note 122) provides the name of the rape victim. Morris, see note 5, 256, mentions 100 people killed and wounded from the earlier attacks.

[132] The massacre was first mentioned in 1951 by M.N. al-Khatib, *From the Events of the Disaster or the Palestinian Disaster*, 1951, 204-205, who presented a complete eyewitness account from a survivor, Marwan 'Iqab al-Yahya. Al-Aref, see note 43,Vol. 6, 124, talks about 85 people killed in the village, but, as was his habit, does not use the term massacre; in the early 1990s an Arab newspaper in Israel, *Kull al-Arab*, published two testimonies about the massacre. In 1998, an Israeli leftist, Teddy Katz, submitted a soon-to-be controversial MA Thesis, "The Exodus of the Arabs from the Villages at the Foot of the Southern

(40). Zarnuqa (Ramlehh area): Indiscriminate killings occur. Zarnuqa is known for its friendly relations with neighbouring Israeli settlements at the time. Workers from Zarnuqa continue to work in Jewish citrus groves throughout the war. Nevertheless, multiple small massacres occur before and during its occupation. Six Egyptian citrus workers and residents of the village, who worked in Jewish-owned groves, are shot in front of villagers who had worked in the same grove earlier February. Only one individual survives. During the village's occupation, troops kill an old man, his wife, and grandson, inside a residence. In another incident, a family of three is killed in a Muslim sanctuary. Men who flee are killed. Many villagers are killed in air attacks on refugee gatherings in Jorat Askalan and Isdood, which is in the Gaza strip.[133]

25 May 1948:

(41). Kaufakha (Negev): Indiscriminate killings occur. Many civilians are killed for non-military reasons.[134]

11 June 1948:

(42). Jules (Gaza): Indiscriminate killings occur. The village of Jules is attacked by Israelis directly after the beginning of the first truce on 11 June. Women and children are slaughtered, as well as houses set on fire.[135]

Carmel in 1948", to Haifa University. For two opposed views of Katz's work, see I. Pappe, "The Tantura Case in Israel: The Katz Research and Trial", *Journal of Palestine Studies* 30 (2001), 19 et seq.; and Morris, see note 5, 299-301, note 671.

133 Oral testimonies taken by Rashad al Madani, for Birzeit Research Center document the killing of the Egyptian workers and the killing in the Muslim sanctuary; Benvenisti, see note 106, 137, describes what happened during the expulsion as "serious atrocities;" Morris, *Birth*, 127, documents the killing in the home.

134 S. Kanaana/R. al-Madani, *Kaufakha*, Birzeit Research Center, Palestinian Destroyed Villages, series #8, 1990, 43. Morris, see note 5, does not acknowledge fatalities – however, his map, xx, confirms a military assault on the settlement whose villagers "had earlier repeatedly asked to surrender, accept Jewish rule and be allowed to stay, to no avail" (ibid., 258).

135 In the Jamal Husseini report, dated 13 July 1948, entitled "Memorandum to the Secretary General of the United Nations on the Violation of the Truce by the Jews." Morris, see note 5, 260, quoting a Gi'vati report talks about forces deployed in the area for "cleansing that was carried out to completion." Morris says that on the eve of the first truce there were orders "to create facts of political importance" and to "clean" all the Arab villages that were occupied by the

29 June 1948:

(43). Qalqilya: Selective killings occur. Israelis execute four men in front of villagers and a Jordanian Army unit, which does not respond.[136]

9 July 1948:

(44). Beit 'Affa (near Majdal): Selective killings occur. After the village is occupied, dozens of men are handcuffed, blindfolded, and held face down on the ground. When an Egyptian unit counter-attacks, the Israelis machine-gun dozens of blindfolded men down.

10 July 1948:

(45). 'Abbasiyeh (Lod area): Massacre of prisoners occurs.[137]

10 July 1948:

(46). Tall as Safi (Hebron area): Indiscriminate killings occur. According to Israeli testimony, Battalion 51 of the Givati Brigade (IDF) finds ten Palestinian peasants, including a very old man, and "liquidate[s] [them] in cold blood."[138]

11-13 July 1948:

(47). Lod: Indiscriminate killings occur in multiple forms.[139]

12 July 1948:

(48). Daniyal (Ramlehh area): Indiscriminate killings occur. IDF shelling induces most villagers to flee. All who remain are killed. Two Egyptian stable hands and three old women are instantly killed. Troops find one elderly man hiding with his wife in a cave. The couple is shot. The man is killed, but his wife is only injured. She receives medical treatment from the Israelis. Another three old women remain in the village for a relatively long time, but are also subsequently killed.[140]

Egyptian forces. Here the reference was particulary to the villages of Jules and Yasur, which were to be occupied several hours before the start of the truce so that, according to Morris the Egyptians would have no time before the truce took effect to recapture them.

[136] Al-Aref, see note 43, Vol. 4, 903.

[137] See discussion in section on massacres of prisoners, above.

[138] Menachem Attar (soldier)'s letter to editor, 2 May 1972, *Yedi'ot Ahronot*, quoted in Ehrlich, see note 2, 25.

[139] See details in section on forced expulsions, above.

[140] Student interview with oral testimony of Amneh Ahmad Khalil Danyali, Bireh, 1999; student interview with Abdel Jabir Bajiss (Abu 'Izat), Rafat, near

(49). Qula (Ramlehh area): Indiscriminate killings occur. The IDF occupy the village. Seven people, who are too old to flee (five women and two men), are killed and their bodies are burned. Two of the female victims are refugees from Abbasiyeh and Kofr Ana. The Jordanian Army counter-attacks and defeats the IDF. The Jordanian soldiers and the villagers find semi-charred corpses in the village.[141]

16 July-3 August 1948:

(50). Illut (Nazareth area): A series of massacres occur.

16 July: Selective killings occur. After the fall of Nazareth, the surrounding Arab villages are demoralised. The Golani Brigade occupies the village and selects 20 young men to be executed in front of the villagers. Villagers are ordered to leave without burying the dead or taking their clothes.[142]

21 July: Selective killings occur. Some villagers returned to 'Illut after their expulsion. The IDF rounds up the remaining/returning civilian population and separates the men from the women. The women are stripped of their jewellery. One man is run over and killed by an IDF vehicle. 24 men are fired upon by a machine-gun. 22 of 24 die. The two survivors are Hadr Ali Abou Ras and Mustaffa Mamour.[143]

Early August: Selective killings occur. The IDF arrests 20 men who are taken to a nearby settlement. After a few days, 17 men are released and the remaining three are killed. Awad Ali Abou Ras, Salim Mohammed Abou Ras, and Ali Odeh Aboud are the three killed men.[144]

Ramallah, 20 October 1999; student interview with Ahmad Rashid, Qalandia Refugee Camp, 10 November 1999.

[141] Author interview with oral testimony of Samara Rantisi, el-Bireh, 2001; student interview with Hassan Abu Ghanim, Birzeit, 20 December 2000; student interview with Mohmmad Mahmoud Ibrahim, el-Bireh, 2 January 2001; student interview with Tawfiq Hussein Saleh, Birzeit, 2000. See also Slyomovics, see note 32.

[142] Originally reported in al-Aref, see note 43, Vol. 3, 631, and later confirmed with some difference in numbers and details by oral testimonies published in *al-Itihad* (Haifa newspaper), 6 January 1998, 11; and, finally mentioned by Morris, see note 5, 422-423.

[143] Oral testimonies in *al-Itihad, idem*; Morris, *Birth*, 2nd ed., 422-423, using Golani documents, acknowledges the killing of ten inhabitants "while trying to escape."

[144] *Al-Itihad, idem*. In all, the sources agree that there were three atrocities committed in 'Illut within three weeks and that they involved an initial expul-

17 July 1948:

(51). Tieret (Haifa area): Indiscriminate killings occur. Tieret Haifa is a village which plays an important role in the 1948 War and resists its occupation many times. Most of the fighters succeed in leaving the village before the village falls. After the village is conquered by the IDF, the remaining men of fighting age are taken to detention camps. 28 elderly and paralysed men and women remain. They are supposed to be taken by a bus to Arab areas for evacuated people, but instead they are burned to death in a field using dry plants and kerosene. The Arab League brings charges concerning this massacre before the UN and the massacre is vigorously denied by the Israelis. The Israelis claim that the "story may have originated in the burning of 25-30 bodies 'in an advanced state of decomposition' found near 'Ein Ghazal. For lack of timber ... the bodies were only partially consumed." The IDF responds to the charges in the UN by challenging all the names on the list. Morris paraphrases the IDF denial in his work, which deals with this case, and writes in a referencing footnote: "an enigmatic, partly censored document that indicates that something amiss had indeed occurred." Morris never questions this partially censored army document, which refers to an ongoing IDF "trial" concerning the killing of "the 28" Palestinians.[145]

Early August 1948:

(52). Umm al Zinat (Haifa area): Selective killings occur. The village does not take an active part in the war. Ben-Gurion notes in his Diaries on 25 April 1948 the following: "Umm al Zinat asked to surrender its weapons and asked for a Jewish garrison in the village."[146] According to Safa Mohammad Ali Sheikh Yusef,[147] a few villagers, including Safa, remain in the village after its occupation. Most of them, mainly women and children, live in one house with the *Mukhtar* of the village, who

---

sion and then continued raids against returnees. The sources differ on the number of fatalities, dates, and details. Morris, see note 5, 422, argues that "The available documentation does not paint a clear picture of what exactly happened."

[145] The Palestinian account of the massacre can be found in al-Mudor, see note 90, especially 28-30. Efrat ben Ze-ev, author interview, Hebrew University, 1996, translated and gave me copies of some of the correspondence between the IDF and the UN. For Morris, see note 5, 440 and 458, note 167.

[146] Ben-Gurion, see note 23, 278 (AV), 369 (HV).

[147] Student interview, Jalazoun Refugee Camp/Ramallah, 22 December 2000.

apparently hopes that Israelis would let them stay. Later, (unknown date) the Israelis kill four people to force a final expulsion. Two of the four are killed on the street, one of whom is the richest man in the village, Sheikh Abdel Ghani. The third victim is killed outside of the house, which contains his family, by the Haganah with a rifle for local defence. The fourth young man, Safa's cousin, is slaughtered in a house two days after the expulsion. The oral testimony does not provide an exact date. Morris recognises the killing of at least two men who remained in the village in early August.[148]

21 October 1948:

(53). Bier Sab' (Negev area): Indiscriminate killings and prisoner massacres occur. Two massacres are committed during the occupation of the city. In one massacre, 19 civilians are killed. In the second at least 20 Egyptian soldiers are killed after they surrender.[149]

29 October 1948:

(54). Al-Dawayima (Hebron area).[150] See above.

(55). Jish (Acre area): Indiscriminate killings and killings of prisoners occur. Sources emphasise different details, but agree that civilians and fighters who had surrendered are rounded up and killed. Those killed include four Maronite Christians, a woman and her baby, ten Morrocan prisoners, and surrendered soldiers. There are at least 100 fatalities (author's estimate). Of particular interest are the traces of the murder of prisoners. "It is worth noting that the initial IDF intelligence report after the capture of Safsaf and Jish sp[eaks] of the capture of '150-200 prisoners'."[151] The next report[152], written a day later states: "The num-

---

148 Morris, see note 5, 244.

149 For the massacre against the civilians see al-Aref, see note 43, Vol. 3, 736, who talks about a massacre and names some of the victims, but to reconstruct a more complete picture, see Vol. 6, 29-30, 36-37, 39, 43, 51, 62-63, 72, 92, 94; for the massacre of the Egyptian soldiers see Ehrlich, see note 2, 25, citing Abraham Adan who was an IDF officer and eyewitness.

150 Details in text, see section on indiscriminate killings, above.

151 G. Gil'ad, "Hiram" Report Activites 'B' 290800-292000', undated, IDFA 7249/49/170.

152 G. Gil'ad, "Hiram" Report Activites 'C' – 292000-300800', undated, IDFA 7249/49/170.

ber of prisoners given in report Activities 'B' is based on a mistake. [Only] a small number of prisoners is in our hands."[153]

(56). Safsaf (Safad area): Indiscriminate killings occur. The assault on Safsaf begins with heavy aerial and artillery bombardment in which many civilians are killed, including refugees from other villages.[154] After the occupation, there is a massacre (according to Israeli and Palestinian sources) of approximately 70 villagers. Those killed are mainly assembled men, who are executed by shooting, bayoneting and drowning. Another 30-40 men are reported missing by the *Mukhtar* of the village. Israeli documents[155] acknowledge four rapes, including one of a 14 year old girl, although the complaint of the *Mukhtar* suggests widespread rape. He writes: "All this is nothing compared to the savage acts committed against the women and young girls, violating their virginity."[156]

30 October 1948:

(57). 'Eilabun (Acre area): Selective killings occur. The IDF enters the village. A soldier kills one worker with his pistol. Two other people are injured. Then the army chooses 20 men from among the villagers, who are taking refuge in a church. Four to six of these men are later used as human shields against mines outside the village. A heap of 14-16 bodies, all gunned down in a church, might indicate a massacre; the remaining

---

[153] Morris, see note 5, 501, note 120, on the massacre of prisoners; S. Kanaana/M. Eshtieh, *Kofr Bir'am*, Birzeit Research Center, Palestinian Destroyed Villages, series #13, 1991, 28; Palumbo, see note 63, 171, documents the killing of individuals who asked for receipts for their property from looting Israeli soldiers; Morris, *Birth*, 230; *idem*, see note 5, 474.

[154] Nazzal, see note 20, 43.

[155] In Morris, *Birth*, 230.

[156] Al-Aref, see note 43, Vol. 6, 125, was the first scholar to report the massacre. Later, Nazzal, see note 20, 93-95, provided a more accurate and detailed report compared to al-Aref. "About 70 of our men were blindfolded and shot to death, one after the other, in front of us. The soldiers took their bodies and threw them on the cement covering the village's spring and dumped sand on them." The testimony by Mouhamed Karim, *Mukhtar* of Safsaf in UN documents, # S-0636-003-002, "Subject files – UN Military Observer Records 9/8/48 – 23/03/4" reported by Major Loheac and Captain Ballanie on 13 December 1948, describes all the killings and rape. The first Israeli document to acknowledge the massacre is Israel Galili, a Mapam party leader and Israeli cabinet minister, quoted in Morris, *Birth*, 230, who reports: "52 men tied with a rope, and dropped into a well and shot. Ten were killed. Women pleaded for mercy. [There were] three cases of rape ... A girl aged 14 was raped. Another four were killed."

men are executed in groups of two to three, apparently to simulate battle casualties for the benefit of UN observers who were in the area. The population is expelled. The massacre is memorialised in a popular song by famous Egyptian singer Abdel Halim Hafez.[157]

(58). Bi'neh and Deir al-Asad (Acre area): Selective killings occur. The IDF occupies both villages without encountering resistance and asks villagers to assemble in a meadow between the two villages. Two young men are chosen at random from each village, presumably to bring water for the villagers, but instead, they were executed in an olive grove. The villagers, who are forced to leave, see the bodies of the men as they walk past them. UN observers describe the killings as "wanton slaying without provocation."[158]

(59). Hula (Lebanon): Mass indiscriminate killings occur. The Karmeli Brigade occupies the village without meeting any resistance. Commander Shimuel Lahiss forces all the men from the age of 15 to 70 into a house which he then blows up. 89 men are killed. Lahiss "justifies" these killings by claiming that it is revenge for Palestinian acts. He is put on trial, but is pardoned by the president before he can serve his

---

157 All sources confirm the massacres, but differ on whether the executions were performed in front of the assembled villagers. Sources also differ on what triggered this massacre. Morris claims an element of reprisal, but this is denied by Srour. The best primary source is E.S. Srour, *Eilaboun: History and Memory*, 1997, using the diaries of Fr. Marcos, the village priest who was an eyewitness and who interceded with the IDF. The UN documents (UNA (old numbers) 13/3.3.1, box 11, Atrocities September–November) are cited in Palumbo, see note 63, ch. 10, note 225. For the IDF denial to UN officers of this now well-known massacre, see Morris, note 5, 499, note 109, quoting IDFA 1261/49/4; additional eyewitness sources include an interview with Butrus Shukri Mata (Abu Hana), *Sunara* (newspaper), supplement, 31 October 1997, 6, who was wounded during the massacre and helped to bury the dead; and E. Srouji, "The Fall of a Galilean Village during the 1948 Palestine War: An Eyewitness Account", *Journal of Palestine Studies* 33 (2004), 74 et seq., who explains the attempt to deceive UN observers. *Al-Ayyam*, in an article, 15 May 2000, reports on a monument in 'Eilaboun to 28 villagers killed during the war.

158 The massacre was first disclosed by Nazzal, see note 20, 89, who talked about two men being executed. However, in an interview with the author, in Irvine, California, 6 June 1999, Saleh Edriss Titti, an eyewitness originally from Bi'neh, named four victims: from Bin'eh: Hana Elias Farhud and Ali Mohamad 'Abed and from Deir al-Asad: Ahmad 'Abdallah 'Issa Assadi and Subhi Mahmoud Thabah. Morris, see note 5, 477, also gives four as the number killed. Palumbo, see note 63, 168, cites the UN reaction: UNA13/3.3.1, box 11, Atrocities September-November.

time. He is later promoted to the position of Director General of the Jewish Agency.[159]

(60). Sa'sa (Safad Area, on the Lebanese border): Indiscriminate killings occur. Many villagers, including cripples, are massacred after the surrender of the village. This is the second massacre in the village (the first is reported above, 14-15 February).[160]

(61). Saliha (Safad area, Lebanese border): Indiscriminate killings occur. 60-94 people are killed after being forced into a house which is blown up.[161]

(62). Kofr Annan (Acre area): Selective and indiscriminate killings occur. Al-Aref states, "40 people were lost." He sometimes uses this phrase to describe a massacre. Morris acknowledges that villagers "left by expulsion." An account sent to the UN, probably by the *Mukhtar* of "Kafar Hanay," (which is Kofr Annan, see discussion in note 163) relays that seven young men whose full names are listed in the document, are executed and then burned in front of other villagers. Soldiers then take another 88 young men to an unknown destination. The sound of

---

[159] Al-Aref, see note 43, Vol. 6, 125, documents 89 killed, but without any other details. Ehrlich, see note 2, mentions "all men from 15 to 70." UN Document S-0636-0002-003 Subject Files – Senior UN Military Observers Records 28 July 1948 – 30 November 1948 Field Observer's Group: Beirut, "19 Septembre, 1948 No. 17/F: Reference votre lettre du 15 septembre 1948" reads: "The Jews of the Al Manara post have the habit, since August, to come and steal the grapes from the vineyards which belong to the villagers of Hula. Slowly, slowly they got bolder and they wanted to prevent the villagers from leaving their village to come the vineyards, which are in Lebanese territory. Deciding to defend their property, the villagers surprised the Jews in their vineyards in the Lebanese territory and they killed two on 2 September (Daily report of 4 September, 1948)."

[160] Details from Israel Galili who reports: At Sa'sa there were cases of "mass murder [though] a thousand lifted white flags [and] a sacrifice was offered [to welcome] the army. The whole village was expelled." Morris, *Birth,* 230 (and 354, note 37; Ben-Gurion, see note 23, 844 et seq., entry for 25 November 1948; Weitz, Diary, III, 357, entry for 25 November, 1948). For details on the killing of cripples, see report by Emmanuel Yalan (Vilensky) cited in Morris, *Birth,* 501, note 122.

[161] Al-Aref was the first to report the massacre in Saliha, see note 43, Vol. 6, 125, with 45 casualties. In UN document # S-0636-003-002, the *Mukhtar* also reports 60 deaths by firing squad "Subject files – UN Military Observer Records 9/8/48 – 23/03/49 reported by Major Loheac and Captain Ballanie on 13 December, 1948"; Morris, see note 5, 481 and note 118.

machine-guns is heard from a nearby field soon after their departure. The soldiers then assemble all the remaining women, children, and elderly. After beating the villagers, the soldiers expel them, and destroy the village. Israeli officers tell the people to "'go to Lebanon because we don't have to feed you here[!]'. They opened fire and another child and one woman was killed."[162]

31 October 1948:

(63). Nahaf (Acre area): Selective killings occur. When the army enters the village, some of the men flee to surrounding areas. Soldiers kill a few men in the streets and round others up. Most villagers flee except a few old men and women. The dead include Sgt. Saleh Moustafa 'Abas, a refugee from Damoun, and Qasim Ahmad 'Ayasheh, a widower, who is killed while escorting his blind mother and young son. Fatmeh Othman Hassan 'Abas finds the mother weeping and the son wailing "Father, wake up, please, I'm hungry."

We have the names of two more victims and two more possible victims. The total number killed is four to six, but others might also have been killed.

The old women, who remained in the village, furnish a moving description of how they were unable to bury the dead. Eventually they use ropes and a donkey to drag the corpses into a cave and barricaded the entrance.

I found a letter of complaint of "a villager from Nahaf" to the UN, which claimed that 50 to 100 civilians were killed. I think this letter is false. Other reliable sources denied all knowledge of the killings.[163]

Late October 1948:

(64). Arab al Jubarat (Hebron area): Selective and indiscriminate killings occur. Nine people are executed, including one individual who is "murdered with pleasure in front of his wife." The exact date of this massacre is unknown. One survivor recounts, that after he fled to Hebron, the

---

[162] Al-Aref, *idem*; Morris, see note 5, xvii, map notes. The village account in UN document, # S-0636-003-002, "Subject files – UN Military Observer Records 9/8/48 – 23/03/49" refers to Kafar Hanay, probably Kofr Annan. Kafar is definitely Kofr, and the French observer might well have transcribed the 'ein sound as an "h."

[163] Author interview with Saleh Idriss Titi, quoting his aunt Fatmeh Othman Hassan 'Abas, Irvine, California, 6 June 1999. For Said Mouhamed's letter to the UN Observers, see UN documents, # S-0636-003-002, "Subject files – UN Military Observer Records 9/8/48 – 23/03/49".

refugees in Al-Dawayima heard about the massacre. Based on this account, the event likely occurred in late October or early November.[164]

2 November 1948:

(65). Khirbet Wa'ra as Sauda (Acre area, inhabited by *Bedouins of Arab al-Mawasi*): Massacre of prisoners occurs. After the occupation, the destruction of the village, and the expulsion of the villagers, "19 adult males [are] arrested and taken to Israeli army HQ in Maghar. There the prisoners [are] sorted out and 14 [are] determined to have taken part in enemy activity against our army, they [are] taken away and liquidated."[165]

5 November 1948:

(66). Majd al-Kurum.[166]

15 September 1948:

(67). Sha'b: Forced Expulsion/Death march in the mud occurs. The village resists Israeli occupation and is admired by a UN observer due to this feat. According to Nazzal, it is occupied on 21 July. There is an expulsion, but a woman, Rim Muhammad al-Haj As'ad, insists on returning to the village to get food for her children. They are hiding in the nearby orchards. Her insistence inspires the villagers to launch a counter-attack and to reoccupy their village during August and September. Unfortunately, Sha'b is re-taken by the Israelis as part of Operation Hiram on 29 October. Another round of expulsion follows in the following days, weeks, and months. The Israelis hold the village and repel all those who try to return. In one case, 20 people (mainly young men), are expelled toward the village of Zububa (near Jenin). They subsequently die by getting stuck in mud. They cannot disentangle themselves.[167]

---

[164] Oral testimony of Abu Ishaq al Daqs, 85 years old when interviewed by Kadija Abu 'Arqoub for *Wattani* (newspaper), No. 25.

[165] Morris, see note 5, 481, quoting army report.

[166] See discussion of selective killing, above.

[167] For the story of Sha'b's resistance see Nazzal, see note 20, 87. This is confirmed by UN document # S-0636-0002-003 "Subject Files – Senior UN Military Observers Records", 28 July, 1948 – 30 November, 1948 Field Observers' Group Beirut 21st September 1948 No. 21/F Reference votre lettre du 15.9.48 paragraphe 2. Incidents de Sha'b (173-255). Details of the deaths of the young men in the mud from Elias Khoure in personal communication to author. Nazzal, see note 20, 90, tells a story which implicitly confirms Elias Khoure's account.

Early November 1948:
(68). Farradiya (Safad area).

VI. Conclusion

The massacres and atrocities reflect the intensity of the war in this conservatively compiled census of 68 massacres. Such events display the international, regional and local balance of power. Furthermore, they illustrate the resolve of the Israeli leaders, to construct an expansionist and exclusionary Jewish state, through the use of force. The massacres also shaped the winning of the war, as well as the losing of the peace. The refugee problem is a direct result of the massacre strategy.

Although the final count of massacres is surrounded by controversy, there is little doubt that it continues to grow. The main intellectual arguments have moved away from the question of sheer quantity and instead choose to explore the question of how best to understand the pattern of massacres in its totality.

Israeli researchers are divided into three groups. The old school and its contemporary adherents continue to deny the reality of massacres. This group uses the tired and discredited arguments of old Israeli mythology. This group is mentioned, but will not be discussed in this article. The second group consists of a small number of Israeli scholars who are actually willing to confront the implications of the massacres. Unfortunately, the members of this group are too few, they do not consistently exploit all the potential sources of useful data, and they are marginalised in Israeli society. The third and most influential group is made up of Israeli apologists who accept massacres as fact, but tend to minimise their significance. For example, Benny Morris' important work in the Israeli archives confirms many massacres, yet he continues to resist the term and its implications. Unfortunately he also considers ethnic cleansing justified and calls implicitly for its completion. Also, a closer look at his work shows that, for the most part, the massacres, which he confirms in his research, have already been shown to exist by Palestinian and foreign scholarship. Works in foreign archives have also stated their existence.[168]

---

[168] For example, the massacres at Lod, Haifa, Kabri, Khassas, Safsaf, Jish, 'Eilaboun, Dawayima and Majd al-Krum had already been shown to exist in the work of Palestinian and foreign scholars such as Aref al-Aref, Walid Khalidi,

Five years ago, I came to believe that the main task of Arab historiography is to confront the apologist narrative. This view was contrary to my earlier perspective. Today, apologists use four main strategies (separately and in combination) to respond to the massacres. These strategies are used as an attempt to exempt the Israelis from having to address the injustices done to Palestinians. Some apologists argue that the Palestinians refused to uphold the UN Partition Plan and in turn initiated the war. Furthermore, according to this argument, since Palestinians are the source of the start of the war, they are responsible for all the ills, including the massacres, which are a consequence of it. Crudely put, this can be called the *"they brought it on themselves"* argument.[169] Other apologists try to explain and tacitly justify each massacre as a reprisal for some Palestinian wrong doing. For example, Morris describes the events at 'Eilaboun and Wara al Sauda as responses to the decapitation of two Israeli soldiers. Additionally, he considers that the massacre in Madj al Krum was a consequence of villagers' lying and not surrendering all their arms, and Jish and Safsaf because they offered military resistance. Crudely put, this is the *"they deserved it"* justification. A third allegation is that Palestinians are killers as well. Israel suffered 6,000 casualties during the war, which is 1 per cent of their total population. Crudely put, this is the *"well, they did it too"* argument.[170] Finally, some apologists fall back on the argument that Jews, in the wake of the Holocaust, are entitled to use all possible means to defend their interests. This position is almost always coupled with the assertion that compared to the Holocaust, the expulsion of Palestinians is a small and insignificant matter. This is the "*necessity*" or the "*so what?*" argument.[171]

Nafez Nazzal, the authors of the Birzeit Research Center Destroyed Villages series, and Michael Palumbo.

[169] This is a very common discourse, exemplified by the comment of Yigal Allon who, in denying Yitzah Rabin's narrative about the expulsions of Arabs from Lod, ends his denial with the assertion that "If a war had not been imposed on us, all this suffering could have been avoided" (quoted in D.K. Shipler, *Arab and Jew: Wounded Spirits in a Promised Land*, 1986, 35).

[170] This, too, is a common position, threaded through the most recent discourse of Benny Morris in *Ha'aretz.*

[171] See Z. Sternhell who says "The founding fathers and those who immediately followed them knew that if the Jews wanted to inherit the land, they would have to take it by force. Until the War of Independence they had no other choice" (Z. Sternhell, "The logic of body counts", *Ha'aretz*, 2 April 2004).

While I do not seek to address the polemics surrounding the discussion of the 1948 War, I recently published a study in which I contest the idea that Palestinians initiated the war.[172] Furthermore, even if Palestinians had started the war, such an act would hardly justify the war crimes against surrendered civilians. I would like to underscore this idea further by pointing out that most Israeli massacres occurred when the Arab forces no longer represented any threat. The application of the Israeli myth of a "fight for survival" is also not fitting in such cases. It is ludicrous to argue, that the most powerful, well-equipped, and disciplined Middle Eastern fighting force was driven beyond its limits of endurance, by the Palestinian peasants' desire to hold on to their villages and orchards. Can one compare the possible guilt of poor Palestinian peasants to the guilt of the Nazis?

The third, *"well they did it too,"* argument has some basis in fact. Palestinians committed atrocities as well. They looted whenever it was possible. They also mutilated Jewish combatants, but typically the killings by Palestinians were very different from Israeli massacres, for a number of reasons. The killings were not part of an aggressive annexation or expulsion strategy; they were not perpetrated by organised military forces, but were spontaneous mob actions; and, finally, in comparison to the number of Israeli massacres, they were rare events. While these explanations do not justify the killings perpetrated by Palestinians, they challenge the attempt to put Israeli and Palestinian killing on an equal footing. This issue continues to be relevant today. Take the matter of suicide bombings, which I have publicly and vigorously condemned. To suggest that the actions of a minority within a stateless population living under military occupation can be judged on the same grounds as the implementation of a declared policy of oppression by the highly militarised armed forces of the occupying state is to approach the realm of the absurd. Moreover, unlike the suicide bombings of the second *Intifada*, the Israeli massacres in 1948 were not born of despair, exile, and dispossession, but instead were instruments of nation building. Some of the massacres were carried out by people who, according to today's standards, may be described as right wing zealots. However, other massacres were carried out by those, who on some issues may be identified as liberals.

I began this article with the question of why the Palestinians fled from their villages in 1948. My research has focused for many years on the role of massacres in the Palestinian exodus. I have addressed the occur-

---

[172] Jawad, see note 17.

rence of the massacres and documented their frequency, type and, briefly, their human impact. In the assessment of the human impact, it is important to note, that massacres and expulsions cast a long shadow. For every village, where a massacre occurred, refugees spread the story of their villages in more distant lands. There were also many villagers killed on the road to exile and in the places where they sought refuge. Therefore nearly every Palestinian family, even those living abroad, felt the impact of Israel's total war against the Palestinians.

I strongly argue that the massacres, along with the other techniques used to acquire Palestinian land, were so consistent, comprehensive, and effective that the existence of a central guiding intelligence can be inferred. Perhaps most chilling is that the leaders of the massacres, such as Dayan, Kilman, Shaham, Lahis, and Sharon, not only went unpunished, but were promoted to the highest positions in Israeli public life.

I find the lack of a "smoking gun," which documents a policy of ethnic cleansing, irrelevant for the purposes of my research. By any reasonable standard of intellectual inference, moral reckoning, and international law, the array of facts allows us to assign responsibility for massacres to the Israeli state. The guilt of the Israeli state is apparent, even without documented proof of their plans to produce such a series of events.

I do not seek to enter a debate concerning Israeli intentions, but instead I aim to demonstrate empirically the pervasiveness of the massacres. I argue that massacres were the principal instrument of ethnic cleansing, which, in turn, was part of a total war against the Palestinians. Ethnic cleansing continues to this day, by other means. My objective in this chapter is to illustrate the importance of the massacres of 1948 in producing the refugee problem, which we continue to face today. I seek to achieve this aim through typology and a (still evolving) systematic census of massacres.

Political Aspects

Palestinian Perceptions of the Israeli Position on the Refugee Issue

Elia Zureik

I. Introduction

While the Israeli-Palestinian debate surrounding the refugee issue has undergone discernable changes since the early 1990s, certain important elements have remained constant throughout. Hebrew literature from 1991 to 1995 on the subject of Palestinian refugees offers a meagre 15 references in the public domain, and these include newspaper articles and opinion pieces. Repeating the exercise for the period 1995 to 1999 reveals 275 such references, which includes academic and popular writings – a clear rise in interest in the subject. And if one were to update this figure, in order to cover the last four years, Israeli interest would be reflected in even higher numbers.[1]

Today, hardly a week goes by without comment, as Israeli public figures, political pundits, and others all tend to chime in on the subject of Palestinian refugees. But are there any significant qualitative changes in the Israeli position in the midst of what appears to be a quantitative leap in writings on the subject? The official position has arguably remained in fossilised form since 1948, although as of late one detects minor admissions surrounding Israel's role in creating the refugee problem.

Hence, this paper examines whether Israeli discourse on the refugee issue is still dominated by power and demographic considerations, given that these two venues are unlikely to resolve the conflict. Reconciliation that is based on admission of the injustice suffered by Palestinian refugees is a viable alternative for dealing with this intractable conflict. The

---

[1] E. Zureik (ed.), *Palestinian Refugees: An Annotated Bibliography Based on Arabic, English, French and Hebrew Sources*, 2000.

point here is that given the lack of honesty in its own internal discourse, gradually, Israel is inching towards a unitary, bi-national state.

II. Israeli Consensus on the Refugee Issue

There is unanimous agreement among Israeli writers belonging to the right and left of the ideological spectrum that no Palestinian refugees should be allowed to return to their homes in what is now Israel under the auspices of United Nations General Assembly Resolution 194. In May 2003, and in conjunction with its highly qualified endorsement of the Road Map that was accompanied by no less than 14 main reservations about the plan, the Israeli government unanimously passed a resolution that affirmed that the 1948 refugees would not be allowed to return to their homes.

Why is this? The answer is both ideological and pragmatic. On the pragmatic level, the claim is made that there is simply no room to accommodate returning refugees. The country is crowded as it is, the argument goes, and refugee property has already been expropriated for use by incoming Jewish immigrants. On the ideological front, which is more central to the Israeli argument, the inflow of Palestinian refugees to Israel would change the Jewish character of the state, and would defeat the whole idea of establishing a *Jewish* homeland. Within this ideological construct there are certain nuances. Those on the left and those who are members of the peace movement would be willing, for symbolic purposes, to admit a limited number of refugees under a family reunification scheme. Although this number would reach the tens of thousands, it is still nowhere near the estimated number of more than four million Palestinian refugees who are registered with United Nations Relief and Works Agency (UNRWA). Belatedly, a minority within this camp has acknowledged the need for the Israeli government to accept some responsibility for the expulsion of the refugees in 1948, and the subsequent prevention of their return.

III. The Palestinian Position

On the Palestinian side, the crux of the issue rests not with pragmatic or ideological considerations as such, but with issues of justice. In the words of Israeli academic Ilan Pappe, "a fair peace in the eyes of the

Palestinians can only be based on healing of past wounds and far more important [insuring] the security against future desolation."[2] For Palestinians, this position is compelling in its simplicity: "why is it," they ask, "that people who were expelled and/or left their homeland because of war and fear should not be allowed to return?" After all, this is a basic natural law principle and a human rights issue.

Within this justice-cum-rights-based approach, which most Israeli human rights advocates reject,[3] Palestinians have been willing to entertain several modalities of the right of return. To begin with, and in line with abundant historical data, Israel should accept its role in creating the problem and preventing the refugees from returning to their homes. Second, that the implementation of the right of return need not be to the same places from where the refugees came, but alternate places could be suggested within Israel itself. Third, why assume that all the refugees would want to go back? An improvement in the status of Palestinian refugees in their places of dispersal (in terms of citizenship rights, living conditions, etc.) would go far in opening up new vistas for them in terms of where they want to reside. Why should Palestinian refugees not behave like any other refugees after 50 years of displacement? Fourth, those who can be accommodated and absorbed need not all return at the same time. Rather, their return could be prioritised and staggered over a period of time (depending on need, age, resources, absorptive capacity, etc.) to cause minimum disruption in conditions on the ground.

IV. Demography and Refugees

At the heart of the Israeli position regarding the return of Palestinian refugees is the issue of demography. No wonder then that Israeli demographers, policy makers, and researchers in various think tanks and academia have been busy pontificating on the subject, as, for example, in the recent research efforts of the Hertzliya Interdisciplinary Centre.[4]

---

2 I. Pappe, *The Post-Territorial Dimensions of a Future Homeland in Israel and Palestine*, 2002.

3 As it was announced for instance by R. Gavison at the Heidelberg conference on refugees in July 2003.

4 See E. Zureik, "Demography and Transfer: Israel's Road to Nowhere", *Third World Quarterly* 24 (2003), 619 et seq.

The salient aspects of the demography debate compelled me to compare population balance under various scenarios that are based on constant fertility and infant mortality rates. These are summarised in the table below. If, as supposed in Scenario 2 (Israel's preferred scenario), one million Jews were to immigrate to Israel during the period 2003-2012, and no Arabs are allowed to return, the two populations will balance out in 2090. If one million Jews and a quarter-million Arabs were to enter Israel between 2003 and 2012, parity will be attained in 2078. If, on the other hand, one million Jews and half a million Arabs enter, parity will be achieved in 2075, so on and so forth.

Let us now compare Scenario 2, as preferred by Israel, to Scenarios 3 and 4, which are plausible from the Palestinian vantage point. If Israel persists in advocating no return of the refugees, it would have delayed population parity either by 12 years (from 2078 to 2090) or 15 years (from 2075 to 2090), depending on the number of Palestinians who are allowed to return. I ask: "is it worth embarking on the second 100-year war between Arabs and Jews in order to postpone the inevitable by 12 or 15 years?"

Equally important, and assuming that no refugees are allowed to return, in the short term (extending over the next ten to 15 years), the Arab component of the population in Israel, even though it will continue to be a minority (around 23 per cent[5]) will exceed the magical number of 20 per cent. Yet, if Israel continues to hold on to the West Bank and Gaza, Arab-Jewish population parity West of the Jordan River will be attained within a decade, as Lebanese demographer Yousef Courbage shows in his thorough demographic analysis.[6] All this justifies reopening a serious debate over the perennial question: "Should Israel remain the state of the Jewish people, or should it become the state of its citizens?" Indeed, the logical outcome of such a development is a unitary, bi-national state in which both Jews and Arabs will exercise their political and national rights.

5 See *Statistical Abstract of Israel 2002*, No. 53, Table 2.27, 2 et seq.

6 See Y. Courbage, "Reshuffling the Population Deck of Cards in the Middle East: The Demographic Future for Israel/Palestine", *Majallat al-Dirasat al-Filastiniyah* 38 (1999), 56 et seq., in Arabic.

Population Parity between Arabs and Jews in Israel*
(1998-2098)**

Scenario	Entry into Israel		Parity Interval	Mid-Point Parity
	Arabs	Jews	(in years)	(year)
1	0	0	2078-2083	(2080)
2	0	1 million	2088-2093	(2090)
3	250,000	1 million	2078-2083	(2080)
4	500,000	1 million	2073-2078	(2075)
5	750,000	1 million	2063-2068	(2065)
6	1 million	1 million	2058-2063	(2060)
7	1.5 million	1 million	2048-2053	(2050)
8	2 million	1 million	2038-2043	(2040)

* The population projections are based on 1998 Israeli census figures of 4.74 million Jews, and 1.00 million Arabs, and the following rates:

Total fertility rate for Jews: 2.6

Total fertility rate for Arabs: 4.5

Infant mortality rate for Jews: 5.2 per thousand

Infant mortality rate for Arabs: 9.3 per thousand

** Entry of newcomers is prorated for the period 2003-2012

Of course, Israeli researchers (a sample of whom would include demographers Arnon Sofer of Haifa University, Sergio de Ila Pergola of the Hebrew University, and policy analyst Itzhak Ravid of the Hertzliya Centre) have highlighted what they call the demographic threat, or what Ehud Barak called at Camp David the "existential threat" and its consequences. Palestinians, who are well aware of Israeli thinking on the subject, extrapolate several ominous conclusions from the demography argument.[7]

---

[7] See for example, I. Ravid, *The Demographic Environment of Israel*, paper presented in April 2001 at a conference organised by The Institute of Policy and Strategy, the Interdisciplinary Centre, Herzliya, Israel. Herzliya Conference, The Balance of National Strength and Security, Policy Directions, April 2001,

In order for Israel to perpetually maintain overwhelming numerical majority, it is necessary for it to contain the growth and even deplete the Arab component of pre-1967 Israel. Four factors could come into play here. First, under the guise of resolving the refugee issue and implementing the right of return, Israel could offer to "exchange territory" with the new Palestinian entity. For example, Um El-Fahm, with its densely Arab population, would be turned over to the new Palestinian entity, in addition to parting with an empty tract of land in the Negev in which Palestinian refugees would exercise their "right of return" in an area that would become part of the new Palestinian entity. Some Labour politicians floated this position, but it may not be to current Prime Minister Ariel Sharon's liking as he could end up one day having Arab neighbours across the fence in the Negev! Furthermore, Um El-Fahm residents would also reject such a swap, as indicated by public opinion polls.

Second, Sharon is on record as supporting the proposal of denying citizenship rights to Arab offspring born in Israel if one of the parents originates from the territories. In spite of various protests from Israeli civil rights advocates and Palestinians themselves, the Interior Ministry responsible for managing population registration continues to strip identity cards from spouses originating from the territories. Third, if it is the case that 300,000 immigrants from the former Soviet Union who came to Israel in the 1990s are in fact not Jewish, as claimed by the Israeli Census Bureau, one can see a move in Israel to construct a new definition of Jewishness. This definition may not be to the liking of the Orthodox elements of the Israeli body politic, but it would enlarge the size of the Jewish majority by incorporating these non-Jews in the head count of the Jewish population. In conjunction with this, discussions are already underway to make the process of conversion to Judaism easier to accomplish by removing it from the jurisdiction of Orthodox rabbinical authorities. Finally, there are those, in Sharon's current and former government, who publicly call for transferring a portion of the Palestinian population from its homeland, a proposal that is not far-fetched if one follows the Israeli public debate on the subject, and bearing in mind that such a proposal has not been publicly condemned by Sharon.

Herzliya, Institute of Policy and Strategy, Lauder School of Government, Diplomacy and Strategy, The Interdisciplinary Centre; and L. Galili, "A Jewish Demographic State", *Ha'aretz*, 28 June 2002.

V. Israeli Response

While I could imagine what the Israeli response would be to such demographic scenarios, a confirmation of my hunches came when attending a recent conference on Palestinian refugees that was held by the International Development Research Centre (IDRC) in June 2003 in Ottawa. In reflecting the liberal position in Israel, Yair Hirschfeld, a major player in facilitating secret negotiations of the Oslo Agreements, was quick to provide an answer to the following question, "What will happen to the concept of a Jewish state in the event of Arab-Jewish population parity within Israel?" His reply was unequivocal: should the Palestinian population become a majority within four to five generations, even without any refugees returning to their homes within Israel, Israel will continue to be a *Jewish* state. Thus, the concept of majority rule was thrown out the window.

The rationale for this was that Israel must remain a haven from anti-Semitic flare-ups. When, in a further discussion, I raised the issue with a colleague of Hirschfeld's, Gidi Grinstein of the Economic Cooperation Foundation in Tel-Aviv, the latter provided the following answer to my prodding. I asked: "Under such a demographic eventuality of population parity, will Israel unload areas with heavy Arab population concentration on the new Palestinian entity, as part of thinning out the Arab population in Israel?" "Why not?" was his answer. "There is nothing sacred about borders," he added. Of course, as I said earlier, nowhere are the opinions of Israel's Arab population meant to be taken into account in carrying out such a scheme. Grinstein, a typically self-assured liberal Israeli, went further and advocated replacing the PLO as an interlocutor if it did not abide by the rules of the Israeli game. This sounded to me like a revival of the discredited "village league" concept of more than two decades ago – the brainchild of orientalist Menachem Milson. Indeed, it is astonishing to encounter such viewpoints given the Israeli feeling of righteousness buttressed by the arrogance of power.

VI. The Will to Power

It is clear from the Palestinian perspective that the Israeli position is wedded to a Nietzschean notion of the "will to power."[8] There is no

8 F. Nietzsche, *The Will to Power*, edited by W. Kaufman, 1968.

room here for practising what Jürgen Habermas appropriately called communicative action based on undistorted forms of communication that are devoid of asymmetrical power relations.[9] Discussion of Palestinian refugees is now situated within an ideological straightjacket in which "red lines" are drawn by Israel, and of which Israel constantly reminds its Palestinian interlocutors of. The purpose here is to bracket out any discussion of the right of return. One may surmise that this may work for the short run, but that it shall eventually collapse under the weight of its own naked power.

Hence, allow me to suggest a way around the "will to power" approach. For it is high time that both Israelis and Palestinians embark on establishing what Ian Lustick called "shared truth." Unlike other writers, Lustick does not spend any time discussing the legal nuances of the right of return. Instead, he focuses on formulating Israel's moral responsibility towards Palestinian refugees in a way that would satisfy notions of justice – without Israel assuming the sole culpability for what happened in 1948. By drawing upon the arrangement worked out between Israel and Germany, which secured for Israel reparations for the Holocaust without requiring from post-war Germany a public admission of full moral responsibility for what the Nazi regime did, Lustick has argued that the Palestinians and Israel should be able to agree upon a formula which would enable them to reach an agreement, even though they lack a shared "truth" of what happened in 1948. Drawing upon the press reports of the final agreement reached by the Israelis and Palestinians at Taba, Lustick sees reason to be hopeful that it is possible to close the gap between the two sides.[10]

VII. Truth and Conciliation Commission

We need to go beyond the legalese surrounding United Nations General Assembly Resolution 194, a discourse that is usually burdened with hair splitting exercises of whether the right of return is supported by public international law and whether such law is binding or not. For every Ruth Lapidoth, Eyal Benvenisti, Ruth Gavison, and many others

---

9 J. Habermas, *The Theory of Communicative Action*, Vol. I, translated by T. McCarthy, 1984.

10 I. Lustick, *Negotiating Truth: The Holocaust, Lehavdel, and al-Nakba*, available at <http://www.arts.mcgill.ca/MEPP/PrrN/papers/lustick.html>.

on the Israeli side (see in this book the contribution of Yaffa Zilbershats) who see no basis in international law for the right of return, there is a Thomas Mallison, John Quigley, Susan Akram, or other young Palestinian legal scholars to argue the contrary (see for instance the contribution of Gail Boling in this book). But above all, and transcending any legalese, there are the refugees themselves in their millions whose voices are drowned in the mumbo jumbo rhetoric of denial of rights. A Truth and Reconciliation Commission should be established at the citizen level, which will not be run by formal political actors on either side. Modelled after the South African experience, but structurally different from it, the idea here is to let Israelis and Palestinians narrate their stories. Yes, let us hear not the grand narratives of political leaders, but the petite narratives of the people most directly affected by what happened in 1948 and after. I am not offering this as a new, patented idea. Ilan Pappe referred to a similar version in the paper cited above. He referred to Howard Zehr's book *Changing Lenses* (1976) to argue for a non-retributive, restorative form of justice through truth commissions. The idea is not to mete out punishment, but to guarantee that future relationships between the two communities are built not on punishment but on reconciliation. But the victimiser must face its victims. It is a process that is not intended to whitewash what Danny Rabinowitz called Israel's "original sin" in an op-ed piece he wrote for *Ha'aretz* in 2000.[11] It should be stated that the moral constitution of the problem does not by any means negate material forms of compensation and restitution for the refugees.

Let these encounters be open to the refugees themselves. In order to give credibility to such an organisation, experienced actors who have the moral clout and are interested in narrowing the gap between the two narratives should chair it. Such a Commission, anchored in civil society, if it were to hold meetings in Israel, Palestine and beyond, will go a long way towards circumventing the ineffectual so-called second- and third-track conflict resolution encounters which have typified the conflict-resolution approach so far – so much so that a whole industry of refugee scholarship and workshop meetings have been created.

Unlike the South African experiment, such a Truth and Reconciliation Commission should precede any formal agreement on the refugee issue – if such a formal agreement does materialise. Indeed, it can be argued that the Commission will facilitate much needed political work by

---

[11] See D. Rabinowitz, "Recognizing the Original Sin", *Ha'aretz*, 17 October 2000.

highlighting the issue and creating mutual empathy between the two sides. It will definitely contribute to the emergence of shared truth, something that is essential for any durable agreement. With a Truth and Reconciliation Commission in place, the Israeli monolithic stand on Palestinian refugees may begin to show internal variations: difference will replace sameness.

Transitional Justice and the Right of Return of the Palestinian Refugees

Yoav Peled & Nadim N. Rouhana***

All the efforts undertaken so far to establish peace between Israel and the Palestinians have failed to seriously address the right of return of the Palestinian refugees. This failure stems from a conviction that the question of historical justice in general has to be avoided. Since justice is a subjective construct, it has been argued that allowing it to become a subject of negotiation only perpetuates the conflict. However, the experience of these peace efforts has shown that without solving the problem of the Palestinian refugees an agreement cannot be reached; and the problem cannot possibly be solved without addressing the key Palestinian demand on this issue – the right of return. For both sides, the right of return, more than any other issue, touches on the essence of their respective histories. The national narrative of each side thus centres on its version of the 1948 Arab-Israeli war, in the course of which the Palestinian refugee problem was created. And each side maintains the fundamental belief that its future national existence hinges on whether, and how, the issue of the right of return is resolved.

For the Palestinians, the right of return is an inalienable right that defines their national identity and their struggle for liberation. For Israeli Jews, the right of return signifies an existential threat to the Jewish character of their society, if not to its very existence. It is not surprising, therefore, that within each of the two societies a national consensus has been built around this issue and that the position of each society seems

---

* Department of Political Science, Tel Aviv University.

** Department of Sociology and Anthropology, Tel Aviv University.

The authors gratefully acknowledge a research and writing grant they received from the MacArthur Foundation for the purpose of this study.

to stand in complete opposition to that of the other. However, we argue that a morally and politically sound basis could and should be established for a middle ground between these two positions and that such a basis can be provided for by the notion of "transitional justice." Transitional justice stresses two major steps as necessary for reconciliation between parties involved in an historic conflict: recognition and restitution. Recognition entails revealing the historical truth about the injustices committed, according their victims dignity, and granting respect to them as rights-bearing human beings. Restitution is meant to alleviate some of the material deprivation suffered by the victims and is also a form of recognition. Reconciliation is achieved when both sides recognise each other as historical, fallible human beings and agree to establish relations of mutual respect between them.

In the Israeli-Palestinian case, recognition by Israel of the right of return entails an assumption of responsibility for the uprooting of the majority of Palestinian society in 1948. This would satisfy a demand that has become a fundamental element in Palestinian national identity. Recognition would then enable the two parties to enter negotiations over restitution, including the implementation of the right of return. In these negotiations, as many Palestinian political leaders have indicated, the concerns of Israeli Jews for security and for their own national identity would be taken into account. Only if the fundamental concern of the two parties, i.e., the right of return, is addressed as herein described can the road towards reconciliation between Israeli Jews and Palestinians be opened.

I. Introduction

By most accounts, the refugees' right to return to the part of Mandatory Palestine[1] which now constitutes the State of Israel, has been the most obstinate stumbling block preventing the resolution of the conflict between Israel and the Palestinians. Because the right of return, more than any other issue, touches, for each, on the essence of its respective history since the conflict began, and on its prospects for the future, the national narrative of each side is centred on its own version of how things turned out in the 1948 Arab-Israeli war. Both sides believe that

[1] The territory currently encompassed by Israel, the West Bank, and the Gaza Strip.

their national identities and future national existence hinge on how the issue of the right of return is resolved.

The 1993 Oslo Accords designated the question of the Palestinian refugees a "final status" issue, meaning that it was one of the issues that Israel and the Palestinians would have to resolve for a permanent peace to be established. This issue was central to the failure of the Camp David summit in the summer of 2000. It figured even more prominently in the talks held in Taba, Egypt, in early 2001, where some progress on this issue was reportedly achieved.[2] The progress achieved at Taba was supposedly reflected in the Geneva Accord, a mock peace agreement authored by a number of liberal Israeli politicians and unofficial representatives of the Palestinian National Authority in December 2003.[3] The Accord, however, failed to address the issue of the right of return in a straightforward manner and has been soundly criticised accordingly.[4]

The failure of these peace efforts to seriously address the issue of the right of return is a reflection of the fact that the broader question of historical justice in general has been avoided in the various attempts to solve the Israeli-Palestinian conflict. A key argument in support of this avoidance has been that justice is a subjective construct and allowing it to become a subject of negotiation would only perpetuate the conflict. As articulated by the Israeli scholar of international relations, Yaakov Bar-Siman-Tov,

> Since fairness and justice are not self-defining and objective terms, it may be difficult for the parties to agree what is fair and just. The assessments of what is fair and just are often biased by self-interest. The resulting conflict in perceptions of what constitutes fair and just

---

[2] See N. Ju'beh, "The Palestinian Refugee Problem and Final Status Negotiations: A Review of Positions", *Palestine-Israel Journal* 9 (2002), 5; A. Eldar, *The Refugee Problem at Taba, Palestine Israel Journal* 9 (2002), 12; Y. Beilin, *A Guide for a Wounded Dove*, 2001 (Hebrew); O. Shinar, *Making Silent Voices Heard: Non-Official Truth and Reconciliation Commissions in the Israeli – Palestinian Conflict*, 2001, New York University, unpublished manuscript, on file with the authors.

[3] The Accord itself can be found at <http://www.heskem.org.il>. References in the present paper are to the hard-copy Hebrew edition: The Geneva Initiative: A Model for an Israeli-Palestinian Permanent Agreement (Nov. 2003), available at <http:// www.heskem.org.il>.

[4] See, e.g., M. Levine, "The Trouble With Geneva", *Tikkun*, 25 October 2003, available at <http://www.tikkun.org/index.cfm/action/current/article/195.html>.

> agreement may create barriers to peace implementation and relations.[5]

However, the negotiating framework established in Oslo in 1993, that studiously avoided considerations of justice, has brought the parties to an historic dead-end, resulting in unprecedented dynamics of violence that have posed existential threats to both parties.

II. Transitional Justice

Our argument in this paper is that considerations of historical justice are essential for achieving reconciliation in the Israeli-Palestinian (like any other) conflict and that a morally and politically sound basis could and should be established for a workable solution to the question of the right of return. We believe this could be achieved on the basis of a conception of justice that is not merely *corrective* or *compensatory*, but rather *transformative*. This conception, usually referred to as "transitional justice," does not seek to achieve a balance between violated rights and compensatory measures. It aims, rather, to establish the principles that should govern the transition from a morally deficient ("barbaric") society or situation to a morally superior ("minimally decent") one.[6] A successful transition is what endows the measures necessary for its achievement with moral value. In other words, in transitional justice, the practical outcome that is being sought should itself be the basis in which the moral arguments are grounded.

While transitional justice necessarily addresses past injustices, it is future-oriented rather than past or present-oriented in terms of where its moral emphasis lies. It seeks to "affirm and restore the dignity of those whose human rights have been violated; hold perpetrators accountable, emphasizing the harm they have done to individual human beings; [and] *create* social conditions in which human rights will be respected."[7]

---

[5] Y. Bar-Siman-Tov, *Dialectics Between Stable Peace and Reconciliation*, 2001, paper presented at the Leonard Davis Institute, Hebrew University, 8 February 2001, on file with the authors.

[6] See R. Bhargava, "Restoring Decency to Barbaric Societies", in: I. Rotberg/D. Thompson (eds), *Truth v. Justice: The Morality of Truth and Reconciliation Commissions*, 2000, 45 seq.

[7] E. Kiss, "Moral Ambition Within and Beyond Political Constraints", in: Rotberg/Thompson, see note 6, 68, emphasis added.

Here, therefore, the "practical" is not a limiting condition of the "moral," but rather its foundation.

While the principles of transitional justice seek to transcend mere power relations, in order to achieve its ultimate goal – establishing the conditions for greater respect of human rights – transitional justice must take the power balance between the parties into account. Its virtue, therefore, lies not in its being absolute, but rather in its being *attainable*. It is for this reason that transitional justice privileges reconciliation over retribution – which would satisfy solely the victims of past injustices – and forgetfulness – which would benefit only their perpetrators. Still, transitional justice must walk a thin and very treacherous line between ignoring the existing power relations and subjecting justice to them.

1. Recognition

To achieve reconciliation, transitional justice relies on what may be termed its two other R's: recognition and restitution. Recognition of the narrative told by the victims of injustice is a necessary precondition for reconciliation. This narrative forms an essential component of the victims' identity and is usually denied and de-legitimated by their victimisers.[8] In many cases, recognition of that narrative, that is, of the injustice that was committed, and validation of their experiences, memories, and identity are the primary objective sought by victims of historic injustice.

> When political victims suffer violence, they are not merely harmed physically ... The act of violence transmits an unambiguous, unequivocal message, that their views on the common good – on matters of public significance – do not count, that their side of the argument has no worth and will not be heard, that they will not be recognized as participants in any debate, and, finally, that to negoti-

---

[8] For the place of the *Nakba* (the Palestinian catastrophe of 1948) in Palestinian identity, see, among many other sources, R. Khalidi, "Observations on the Right of Return", *Journal of Palestine Studies* 21 (1992), 29; A. Sa'di, "Catastrophe, Memory and Identity: Al-Nakbah as a Component of Palestinian Identity", *Israel Studies* 7 (2002), 175; D. Rabinowitz, *Morality, Identity, Demography, Return: Thoughts on the Future of Palestinian Refugees*, 2003, paper presented at The Hagop Kevorkian Center for Near Eastern Studies, New York University, on file with the authors.

ate, or even reach a compromise with them, is worthless. In effect, it signals their disappearance from the public domain.[9]

It is this situation that is most often in need of rectification.

Recognising the victims of historic injustice requires, first and foremost, that the historical truth about the injustice that was committed against them be revealed.[10] However, if the victims' truth entails the complete denial of the perpetrators', then, unless the power relations between the two sides have been reversed, the perpetrators, who are still the more powerful party, will refuse to accept the victims' truth. Therefore, the primary function of truth and reconciliation commissions has been to enable the victims, as well as the perpetrators, to air their historical narratives.

The work of truth and reconciliation commissions is designed to acknowledge the distinctive identity of the victims, to strive to repair the damage done to them through violence, stigmatisation, and disrespect, and to include their histories in the collective memory of the relevant political community.[11] Revealing the truth about past injustices can be very traumatic, of course, to both victims and perpetrators, as well as to their descendants and sympathisers. This trauma has been exemplified in the acrimony generated by the "historians' debate" about the 1948 Arab-Israeli war and, most recently, by the controversy surrounding the claim that a massacre was perpetrated by Israeli forces in the Palestinian coastal village of Tantura. What the appearance of the "new history" in Israel also points to, however, is the greater readiness of new generations, farther removed from the original injustice, to face the historical truth.[12]

---

[9] Bhargava, see note 6, 47.

[10] See N. Rouhana, "Identity and Power in the Reconciliation of National Conflict", in: A.H. Eagly et al. (eds), *The Social Psychology of Group Identity and Social Conflict: Theory, Application, and Practice*, 2004.

[11] See Kiss, see note 7, 73.

[12] See T. Katz, *The Exodus of Arabs from Villages at the Foot of Southern Mount Carmel in 1948*, 1998, unpublished Master's thesis, University of Haifa, in Hebrew, on file with authors. In his thesis, Katz argued, mainly on the basis of oral history, that the Jewish forces committed a massacre in the process of occupying the Palestinian village of Tantura. The public and academic outrage that this thesis stirred continues until today. The author was taken to court by veterans of the brigade that had occupied the village, and Haifa University established a special committee to investigate the thesis and eventually disqualified it. See also J. Brunner, "Pride and Memory", *History & Memory* 9 (1997),

2. Restitution

One way of according recognition to victims of historic injustice, as well as compensating them for their real material losses, is through restitution. The question of restitution raises the issue of responsibility: Who is the agent responsible for the injustice? Can the present generation, or immigrants who arrived after the injustice had been committed, be held accountable for the actions of their predecessors? Is the political community the responsible agent, regardless of its changing human composition? Similarly, how far can the right to receive restitution be transmitted across generations? Does that right inhere in individual members of the victimised community or in the community as a whole? Are the rights of the victims ever superseded and under what conditions? Different schools of thought in moral philosophy and political theory give different answers to these questions.[13]

A major issue to be considered in discussing restitution is not only the form it should take – restoration of citizenship status and expropriated property, repatriation, monetary compensation, etc. – but also its magnitude. The passage of time makes the monetary evaluation of the damage done to the victims of injustice extremely difficult, but not impossible. However, the factors that should be included in this evaluation are in contention among scholars, as are the principles that should govern their determination. Should restitution aim to restore a hypothetical *status quo ante*? Should it aim to compensate the victims or their descendants for all they could have achieved had the original injustice not been committed? For all that the perpetrators gained from their injustice? Is it even possible to calculate those things? Or should restitution

---

256; J. Brunner, "Contentious Origins: A Psychoanalytic Comment on the Public Debate over Israel's Creation", in: J. Bunzl/B. Beit-Hallahmi (eds), *Psychoanalysis, Identity, and Ideology: Critical Essays on the Israel/Palestine Case*, 2002, 107; I. Pappe, "The Tantura Case in Israel: The Katz Research and Trial", *Journal of Palestine Studies* 30 (2001), 19; S. Esmeir, "1948: Law, History, Memory", *Social Text* 21 (2003), 25; J. Isacoff, "Writing the Arab-Israeli Conflict: Historical Bias and the Use of History in Political Science", *Perspectives on Politics* 3 (2005), 71.

[13] See, e.g., J. Waldron, "Superseding Historic Injustice", *Ethics* 103 (1992), 4; W.J. Booth, "Communities of Memory: On Identity, Memory, and Debt", *American Political Science Review* 93 (1999), 249; S. Dodds, "Justice and Indigenous Land Rights", *Inquiry* 41 (1998), 187.

serve as merely the material signifier of recognition and involve only symbolic compensation?[14]

3. Reconciliation

If recognition means acknowledging the identity of the victims as rights-bearing human beings, reconciliation entails recognition *by* the victims of the humanness of their oppressors, rather than attributing to them absolute evil. The historicity of the injustice committed should be taken into consideration, without being turned into a justification for the injustice. In other words, as much as reconciliation demands remembering, it also demands letting go of the psychologically comforting tendency of the victims to picture themselves as "the 'good people': the ones who, from now on, will have the absolute right to command because they were absolutely right in the way they suffered."[15] Going through a psychological transformation of this kind is no less traumatic for the victims than revealing the historical truth is for the perpetrators, and victims tend to show a great deal of resistance to this demand.

III. Transitional Justice and the Right of Return

Transitional justice has usually been applied to transitions *within* particular societies, rather than to inter-societal relations. It could be argued, therefore, that transitional justice is not applicable to the case of the Israeli-Palestinian conflict, which is a conflict between two distinct societies. We, however, believe that the principles of transitional justice can provide useful guidelines for analysing the Israeli-Palestinian con-

---

14 See Waldron, *idem*; E. Barkan, *The Guilt of Nations: Restitution and Negotiating Historical Injustices*, 2000; T. Cowen, "Discounting and Restitution", *Philosophy & Public Affairs* 26 (1997), 168; A. Kubursi, "Valuing Palestinian Losses in Today's Dollars", in: Naseer Aruri (ed.), *Palestinian Refugees, The Right of Return*, 2001, 217; R. Klinov, "Reparations and Rehabilitation of the Palestinian Refugees: Analyzing the Costs of Implementing a Form of Return", *Palestine-Israel Journal* 9 (2002), 102.

15 B. Van Roemund, "Rubbing Off and Rubbing On: The Grammar of Reconciliation", in: E. Christodouldis/S. Veitch (eds), *Lethe's Law: Justice, Law and Ethics in Reconciliation*, 2001, 183, 186.

flict in general and the issue of the right of return in particular. The Israeli-Palestinian conflict has features of both an intra-societal and inter-societal dispute, and its very nature in this respect has been a subject of controversy and has changed over the years.

Since the Zionist movement claimed Palestine as the homeland of the Jewish people, that land came to be the site of conflict between the Palestinians and the Zionists. Thus, at the core of the Israeli-Palestinian conflict, at its current stage, is a disputed but shared territory – that of Mandatory Palestine – with which the history and identity of both sides are inextricably intertwined. This despite the fact that on each side there are people who do not currently reside in that territory, have never resided in it in the past, and may never reside there in the future. The obvious asymmetry, that members of one national group – the Palestinian refugees – are prohibited from returning to that land, because their right of return is not recognised, while members of the other group, the Jewish people, are welcomed under a Law of Return,[16] is the outcome of power relations: the defeat of the Palestinian national movement in 1948. Due to the Arab defeat in the subsequent Arab-Israeli war of 1967, the disputed territory in its entirety is currently under the control of one side, which has established an internationally recognised state on part of it, while the other side has failed to achieve this goal. The question of what kind of state the Palestinians seek to establish and may eventually succeed in establishing – a separate state in the occupied territories or one bi-national or non-national state in all of Mandatory Palestine – is still unresolved. Its resolution would determine, retroactively as it were, whether the conflict is (was) an intra-societal or inter-societal one.

More concretely, the issue of the right of return bears not only on the relations between Israel and the Palestinians outside the borders of Israel's formal sovereignty. It bears also, at least in part, on Jewish-Palestinian relations within the sovereign State of Israel. Israel's Palestinian *citizens* are implicated in the issue of the right of return in several ways:

1. As members of the Palestinian nation whose society was decimated in 1948, resulting in a very large portion of its members becoming refugees;

---

[16] The Israeli Law of Return, 1950, 4 L.S.I. 114 (1949-1950), confers on every Jew, with some minor exceptions, the right to immigrate to Israel and become an Israeli citizen upon arrival.

2. as citizens of a state that encourages the immigration of Jews, but blocks almost completely the immigration of Palestinians (since 2003, even of those married to Israeli citizens), among other reasons, for fear of recognising the right of return "through the back door"; and

3. because at least 15 per cent of Israel's Palestinian citizens, or about 150,000 people, are "internal refugees" (known officially as "present absentees"), displaced from their original places of residence since 1948 and not allowed to return to those places, mostly for fear, again, of implicitly recognising the Palestinian right of return.[17]

This complicates even further the question of whether the conflict is an intra-societal or inter-societal one, adding credence to our determination that the principles espoused by the conception of transitional justice are relevant to its resolution.

For Palestinians, the outcome of the 1948 War was a national disaster, referred to as the *Nakba* in Palestinian historiography. It brought about the dismantling of Palestinian society, the loss of their homeland, and the dispersion of most Palestinians from the part of their homeland that became Israel to neighbouring countries as refugees. For them, the *Nakba* was an historic injustice inflicted on them by the Zionist project; an injustice that, in their view, can be rectified only through recognition of the refugees' right of return.[18] If the *Nakba* was indeed an historic injustice, which we take as our starting point,[19] then it is hard to see how

---

[17] The best known of these cases is that of the Christian communities of Ikrith and Bereim, a case that has been in adjudication in the Israeli courts for the past 50 years. On 26 June 2003, Israel's Supreme Court rejected yet another appeal by the former residents of Ikrith to be allowed to return to their village, on the grounds that such a return could enhance the Palestinians' claim to a general right of return (A. Barkat/Y. Ettinger, "High Court of Justice Denies the Appeal of the Displaced of Ikrith to Order that They Be Allowed to Return to Their Village", *Ha'aretz*, 27 June 2003, A1, in Hebrew; see also M. Benvenisti, "Bagatz and the Fear of Return", *Ha'aretz*, 3 July 2003, B1, in Hebrew). For a general discussion of the "present absentees," see H. Cohen, *The Present Absentees: The Palestinian Refugees in Israel Since 1948*, 2000, in Hebrew.

[18] Khalidi, see note 8, 31 et seq.

[19] We take this as our starting point, rather than arguing why the expulsions of 1947-1948 were, indeed, an injustice. The burden of argument that expulsion of the Palestinians from their homeland and preventing them from return are just should be on those who maintain this view. The view that their expulsion is unjust is shared by all Palestinians and is, therefore, the view that needs to be addressed if reconciliation is to be achieved.

the right to return to ones homeland can be denied to Palestinian refugees. However, some might argue that in the half-century that has passed since the original injustice was committed, the right of the refugees to return has been superseded.

Jeremy Waldron has most eloquently articulated the argument that historic injustice may be superseded with time.[20] Waldron's argument is sophisticated and multi-layered, but the crux of it is the contention that an act that may have constituted an injustice at a certain point in time might not constitute an injustice at a later point, due to changed circumstances. When that happens, the right of the victims of the original act to restitution has been superseded.

If one were to apply Waldron's argument to our particular case, one would have to argue along the following lines: the expulsion of about 750,000 Palestinians from Israel and the expropriation of their land in 1947-1948 by 600,000 Jews, who then comprised one-third of the population of Palestine, was, indeed, unjust. However, in the intervening years, millions of additional Jews arrived in the country, both because their national identity is intimately connected with it and because they had nowhere else to go. Today, Jews, broadly defined, outnumber Palestinians at a ratio of about 3:2 within the area of Mandatory Palestine, so their control of about 75 per cent of the territory is not as blatantly unjust as it was in 1948. Moreover, Jewish settlement has resulted in economic development that would have been unimaginable without it, so that property values have soared and even small amounts of property can now guarantee their holders a decent standard of living. If only the Palestinians had agreed to accept the Jews and live in peace with them since the beginning of Zionist settlement in 1882, all of Mandatory Palestine, whether divided politically into two states or not, could have been a peaceful and prosperous land.

This argument, we believe, would be difficult even for Waldron to accept. For even if by some theory of justice it could be convincingly argued that the Palestinians now have a moral duty to share their land with Jews or even that they had that duty in 1947 (because Jews were persecuted and had nowhere else to go), this would in no way diminish the injustice committed by the forceful expulsion of the Palestinians from their homes and homeland, the destruction of their society, and the disruption of so many individual and family lives. Moreover, many of the refugees of 1948, and their descendants, still live in refugee camps

---

20 Waldron, see note 13.

in miserable conditions (for example, in Lebanon) and have not been able to reconstruct their lives. Thus, the injustice committed against them is still ongoing, and the question of supersession has not become relevant. Even according to Waldron, his supersession thesis "applies only if an honest attempt is being made to arrange things justly for the future. If no such attempt is being made, there is nothing to overwhelm or supersede the enterprise of reparation."[21]

Yet, a morally valid argument can be derived from the changed circumstances, to wit: with the passage of time Jews living in Israel have acquired the right not to be displaced and the right to maintain an Israeli Jewish national community in Palestine. For these Jews, the prospect of a massive Palestinian return and the demographic transformation it would entail raise a profound and acute fear that has to be addressed, namely: that their lives, as individuals and as a national community, will be irrevocably and dramatically disrupted.[22] Therefore, just like the Palestinians, they maintain the fundamental belief that their future national existence hinges on whether, and how, the issue of the right of return is resolved.

Taking these realities into account, the principles of transitional justice would suggest, we argue, the separation of the *right of return*, which is non-negotiable for the Palestinians, from the means and ways of *realisation* of that right in practice, which could be negotiated between the two sides. The only *right of return* that can be meaningfully recognised by Israel is the right of the refugees to return to the State of Israel within the borders of its formal sovereignty, whatever these borders may be following a future Israeli-Palestinian peace agreement. Since recognition of a right necessarily creates an obligation and since there is no moral value in creating an obligation for somebody else, Israel cannot meaningfully recognise the right of the refugees to return to a third country, not even to the future state of Palestine. In this respect, the Geneva Accord, which gives the Palestinian refugees the *right* to return only to territories that will be under the sovereignty of the future Palestinian state and denies them the *right* to return to their original places of residence in Israel, fails to meet the moral challenge that, in our view, must be met for reconciliation between the two peoples.[23]

---

21 Ibid., 27.

22 Rabinowitz, see note 8.

23 Geneva Initiative, see note 4, 33, Article 7 para. 4 (d)(iii); see also *idem*, 8, Article 5; cf. Levine, see note 4.

By the same token, if Israel were to recognise the *right* of return, this would satisfy an essential demand of the Palestinians and would enable them to recognise Israelis' acquired right to continue their national existence in their part of the disputed territory. This would mean that the actual means of realisation of the right of return could be negotiated in a way that would take the concerns and interests of Israeli Jews into account. This much has been made clear already by many Palestinians, including people in positions of authority, from Yasser Arafat on down.[24] So far, however, neither present nor former Israeli officials, not even those actively engaged in seeking an understanding with the Palestinians, have agreed to recognise the Palestinian right of return. They have maintained, erroneously we believe, that the Palestinian demand for recognition of the refugees' right of return signifies, in and of itself, a denial of the right for a national Jewish existence or the right of the State of Israel to exist.

Recognition by Israel of the *right* of return would meet many of the goals stipulated by transitional justice as necessary for achieving reconciliation:[25]

1. *Truth*. The Palestinian narrative of 1948 will become legitimate in Israel, leading to recognition of the *Nakba* and of the Palestinians' identity as its victims. This is a necessary first step towards the construction of a joint historical narrative, an important goal of transitional justice. Preparatory work could begin even before Israel recognises the right of return, by non-official or semi-official truth and reconciliation commissions that would clarify and acknowledge the historical truth. The biggest task of these truth commissions would be to document the specific histories of the refugees, in order to establish a pattern, which will expose the "hidden history" of the region. As Hanan Ashrawi has stated, "[A]llowing the truth to come out will go a long way to starting a process of reconciliation."[26]

2. *Recognition* of the moral worth of the Palestinians as human beings that has been denied since 1948. (This denial of their moral worth has been more pronounced in the case of non-Israeli citizen Palestinians under Israel's military rule and of the refugees in some of the Arab

---

24 Khalidi, see note 8; Y. Arafat, "The Palestinian Vision of Peace", *New York Times*, 3 February 2002, A15; Eldar, see note 2, 17 et seq.

25 See D.A. Crocker, "Transitional Justice and International Civil Society: Toward a Normative Framework", *Constellations* 5 (1998), 492.

26 Shinar, see note 2, 52 et seq.

countries than for those who are citizens of Israel.) Recognising their historical narrative will go a long way towards affirming their humanity and moral worth.

3. *Responsibility,* both collective and individual, of Israel and of Israelis for the *Nakba* in general and for individual atrocities (e.g., Tantura) will be established. Israel might well maintain that the Palestinians, as well as the Arab states, shared in the responsibility, etc.[27] Given the passage of time though, recognition of responsibility is not likely to lead to demands for the prosecution of individual perpetrators of crimes (on either side).

4. *Public Discussion.* This has been stifled in Israel due to the fear of recognising the right of return. That fear will, obviously, be removed once the right of return is recognised, and this will open up the possibility of airing the history of the 1948 War, including the opening up of still-classified material in various official Israeli archives.[28]

Of course, recognition of the right of return will not be sufficient in itself to achieve reconciliation, but it will meet many of the preconditions for it. Reconciliation could be achieved only after some measures of restitution are affected as well. Of these, compensations and reparations could begin to be assessed (although recognition of the right of return is not necessary for that), while the most difficult aspect of restitution, return of refugees, begins to be negotiated.

IV. Conclusion

Most people who are interested in achieving reconciliation between Israelis (or actually Israeli Jews) and Palestinians recognise that the Gordian knot tying the Palestinians' demand for recognition of the refugees' right of return to the Jews' absolute determination to maintain a substantial Jewish majority in Israel must be severed. Most liberal Israeli politicians and scholars, as well as some Palestinians, such as those involved with the Geneva Accord, believe the knot can be cut by distinguishing between a collective right of "return" and self-determina-

---

[27] See Z. Sternhel, "Settler Post Zionism", *Ha'aretz*, 20 June 2003, B1, in Hebrew.

[28] See B. Morris, "Revisiting the Palestinian Exodus of 1948", in: E.L. Rogan/A. Shlaim (eds), *The War for Palestine: Rewriting the History of 1948*, 2001, 37, 49 et seq.

tion in a future Palestinian state and an individual right of return that could be redeemed (without being openly recognised, according to most versions) through monetary compensation. Others have suggested that the right of return itself should be curtailed in various ways or that a distinction should be made between Israeli *citizenship*, including social benefits, which would be granted to Palestinian refugees who would opt for it, and *residence* in Israel, which would be denied to most of them.[29]

It is significant, we believe, that none of the authors making these suggestions have been able to provide a morally persuasive argument for dividing the right of return in any particular way (e.g., between generations of refugees, between the residents of different host countries, between those whose former places of residence are still vacant as compared to those which are not, by socio-economic status, etc.). In our view, the right of return is indivisible (as is clearly evident in the way Israel conceptualised and implemented its own Law of Return), and, therefore, the only way to cut the Gordian knot that is both morally sound and politically practicable would be to conceptually separate the *right of return* from the negotiations over the *means of actual return* of refugees.

In the spirit of transitional justice, recognition by Israel of the right of the 1948 Palestinian refugees to return to their previous places of residence within the State of Israel would be a formidable step towards achieving reconciliation between Israelis and Palestinians. The moral significance of this act would be lost, however, if its meaning were circumvented by designating the future Palestinian state as the target area of the "return" or by trying to balance off the rights of the Palestinian refugees against the rights of the Jews who left the Arab countries in the wake of the 1948 War and subsequent Arab-Israeli wars. Still, as is the case with all individual and collective rights, the right of return will have to be balanced against other relevant rights that must also be recognised.

Regardless of the original justice or injustice of Zionism, present-day Israelis have acquired the right not to be displaced from their homes inside Israel's pre-1967 borders. (In this sense there is a great deal of difference between Jewish residents of pre-1967 Israel and of the territories occupied in that year. The latter have been settled in territories that are under belligerent occupation, in clear contravention of international

---

29 Rabinowitz, see note 8.

law.) Liberal political theory also recognises Israeli Jews' right of national self-determination, especially if the solution to the Israeli-Palestinian conflict is envisioned as a two-state solution. (The moral force of Israeli Jews' claim of the right to national self-determination will be greatly weakened, however, if the national minority rights of Israel's own Palestinian citizens are not recognised. Thus the two sets of rights – Israeli Jews' right to self-determination and the Palestinian citizens' national minority rights – will have to be negotiated in the context of a two-state solution, to the extent that such a solution is still possible.) In addition, the social, economic, and environmental rights of Israelis and of the refugees themselves must be recognised.

One area where the relations between the right of return and its implementation are unproblematic is that of the internal Palestinian refugees within Israel. The internal refugees' return to their original places of residence (or to locations nearby if the original places are inhabited by others), accompanied by an adequate compensation programme, would not enhance the Palestinian demographic presence that Israel considers to be a threat and could be effected immediately and unilaterally by Israel. This very act would signal recognition of the injustices committed by Israel since 1948 and at least some assumption of responsibility for these injustices. The Israeli Supreme Court's recent decision alluded to above[30] is clearly a significant step in the wrong direction.

Another possible, and partial, way for the conflicting rights/aspirations/fears of Jews and Palestinians to be reconciled could be negotiation over the abolition/modification of the Israeli Law of Return, in conjunction with the negotiation over the implementation of the refugees' right of return. Despite the different moral foundations of these "returns," the Law of Return could be used by Israel in negotiating the practical implementation of the Palestinians' right of return.[31] As it is, from a Zionist point of view, the Law of Return is already defeating its own declared purpose in that the majority of immigrants entering Israel under its provisions right now are religiously non-Jewish.[32] Thus, it should not be too difficult for Israel to agree to abolish that law and replace it with an equitable civil immigration law. In return, Israel can ask Palestinians for concessions on the number of Palestinian returnees.

---

30 See note 17.

31 Eldar, see note 2, 18 et seq.

32 See I. Lustick, "Israel as a Non-Arab State: The Political Implications of Mass Immigration of Non-Jews", *Middle East Journal* 53 (1999), 417.

Palestinians might be able to make such concessions on practical grounds: data based on survey research conducted by Palestinians show that the number of refugees who would actually want to implement a right of return if recognised is not as high as was originally expected. Thus, it should be possible for Palestinians to make "practical" concessions on the number of returnees, given the actual number of refugees who will opt to return.

Finally, since the question of how many refugees would be allowed to return is paramount in most Israelis' minds, we would like to point out that if and when Israel gives up its occupation of East Jerusalem, the number of Palestinians within the State of Israel will decline by 250,000 to 300,000 people. This amount of Palestinians leaving Israel and joining a Palestinian state is significant in Israel's "demographic balance," given that the number of Palestinian refugees who are likely to be interested in returning to Israel is not particularly great.[33] We point this out not in order to legitimise Israel's "demographic fear," which we consider to have racist overtones, but as a way of showing that the conceptual decoupling of the recognition of the right of return – a *sine qua non* for reconciliation – from the negotiation in good faith over the means of its implementation hides a potential yet unexplored for resolving the conflict. Furthermore, our suggestion is based on sound moral foundations derived from the approach of transitional justice.

If the implications of Israel's recognition of the Palestinian right of return could be shown to have no negative effect on the question of the continued Israeli-Jewish national existence, while the benefits of recognising that right, in terms of enhancing the prospects for reconciliation, could be immense, some of the fears blocking Israelis' ability to even consider this issue might be alleviated. To the extent that this would facilitate reconciliation between Israelis and Palestinians, a political outcome of great moral value would be achieved.

---

[33] K. Shikaki, "The Right to Choose", *Al-Ahram*, 28 August 2003, op. ed.; K. Shikaki, "The Right of Return", *Wall Street Journal* 30 July 2003.

Palestinian Return: Reflections on Unifying Discourses, Dispersing Practices and Residual Narratives

*Riina Isotalo**

I. Introduction

This article is a short excursion into the relationship between return as a cultural notion and part of Palestinians' normative repertoire[1] and those meanings this notion is invested with, in Palestinian return migrants' lives. I will try to show that different manifestations of "right of return" connote phenomena which refer to different levels or domains of Palestinian communities' and individuals' social realities. One of these domains is formed by the notions people hold and communicate to one another, and the other by the actions they actually perform. The first two parts of this paper focus on how return discourse is invested with

---

* Institute of Development Studies, University of Helsinki. The first draft of this article was written in the framework of "The Impact of Social Capital on the Eventual Repatriation Process of Refugees: Study of Economic and Social Transnational Kinship Networks in Palestine/Israel" research project, the Palestinian Refugee and Diaspora Centre, Shaml and IDRC. The author would like to thank Dr. Sari Hanafi as well as Rula el-Rifai and Dr. Pamela Scholey. A revised version of the text was published in R. Isotalo, *Many Routes to Palestine. The Palestinian Return, Forged Transnationalism and Gender*, 2005.

1 This concept has been discussed mainly in legal pluralism writings of legal science, anthropology of law and sociology of law. In those contexts, the concepts "normative repertoires" and "normative pluralism" refer to norms that govern society parallel to and sometimes in competition with "law" as issued by the state and enforced in the courts. See for example B. Dupret/M. Berger/L. al-Zwaini (eds), *Legal Pluralism in the Arab World*, 1999.

different meanings of return by different groups of Palestinians at a transnational level and how this relates to Palestinians' identity politics. I will look at this process against the background of first, politicisation of culture, and second, right-of-return discourses in the light of the so called "Nusseibeh controversy." The third part of the paper discusses the notion of return in the lives of some people who have returned to live in Palestine. In short, this part is a discussion about the relationship between those meanings that "return" has been invested with in the hegemonic discourse, and the return move in four women's lives. I will see if in my example people invoke those meanings that have been invested in return in the unifying return discourse in connection to actions that they have actually performed, and if not, why, and what kind of meanings are invoked when they talk about their returning to Palestine. I will argue that in this context not only different notions of return meet, but also different gendered subjectivities.

New speech genres are claimed to have emerged from new and fundamental disruption of social structure and social experience.[2] My understanding of the phenomenon of particular speech genres in the context of the relationship between the notion of the "right of return" and the Palestinian return migration refers to discursive forms where either some message is being conveyed to the "outer world," or to the internal others within Palestinian communities. In the Palestinian context, the major fundamental disruption of social structure and social experience has undoubtedly been *Nakba*, "the catastrophe." This means that the foundation of Israel, which was followed by the mass expulsion of 700,000-900,000 Palestinians,[3] has shaped the Palestinian social reality and culture so profoundly that expulsion and conflict have become a part of the symbolic and cultural capital. Hence it has become a cultural notion where all Palestinians regardless of whether they live in exile, refugee camps, today's PNA-areas or in Israel, can relate to in different ways.[4] In other words, cultural processes common to Palestinians since

---

2 W. Hanks, "Discourse Genres in a Theory of Practice", *American Ethnologist* 14 (1987), 668 et seq.

3 In 1949, the United Nations Conciliation Commission estimated the number of Palestinian refugees at 726,000, whereas in 1950, the newly-established United Nations Relief and Works Agency put the number at 957,000.

4 Following Holy and Stuchlik, by "cultural notion" I mean a notion that is part of the actors' discourse and not of the researcher's analytical discourse. It is a notion of which the actors are aware, which they are usually able to formulate

1948 have *Nakba* as one of their points of reference. Thereby "the catastrophe" can be seen as a time-out in the Palestinian history that created a discursive space for new speech genres to emerge, most notably to the discourses on expulsion and consequently, return.

The Palestinian return refers to the coming back of those Palestinians who were directly or indirectly forced to leave the country against their will as a result of the war that followed the founding of the Israeli State in 1948, and further, the Israeli occupation of the West Bank and Gaza Strip as a result of the war in 1967. In international law, political negotiations and public parlance, "return" and "right of return," are part of "the Palestinian refugee issue" or "the Palestinian refugee problem." Thus the return is perceived to concern first and foremost the Palestinian refugees, even though its actual connotations are far more numerous. The Palestinian refugee issue has remained unresolved for more than 50 years, and its longevity makes the plight of approximately 4 million UNRWA[5]-registered refugees one of the largest unresolved mass displacement problems in the world. In the meantime, a process that can be characterised as return migration – and in some cases repatriation under conflict – has brought approximately 250,000[6] Palestinians to the West Bank and Gaza Strip. The number of returnees has been difficult to estimate accurately, due to the political tension implicit in the concept "returnee," the relative lack of statistics until recently, the partial illegality of the move from the Israeli perspective, and the transnational back-and-forth lifestyle of some return migrants.[7]

---

verbally and which they are able to communicate to one another. L. Holy/M. Stuchlik, *Actions, norms and representations - Foundations of anthropological inquiry*, 1983; L. Holy, *Kinship, honour, and solidarity: cousin marriage in the Middle East*, 1989, 14.

5 United Nations Relief and Works Agency for Palestine Refugees in the Near East.

6 Drawing on the census material collected during 1995, the Palestinian Central Bureau of Statistics provided similar numbers to the author in March 1999, that were published in M. Malki/Y. Shalabi, *Internal Migration and Palestinian Returnees*, 2000.

7 For example A. Nour, *Coming Home: A Survey of the Socio-Economic Conditions of the West Bank and Gaza Returnees Following the 1991 Gulf War*, 1993 ; A. Hovdenak, "On the Gulf Road: Palestinian Adaptations to Labour Migration", and E. Zureik "The Trek Back Home: Palestinians Returning Home and Their Problem of Adaptations", in: A. Hovdenak/J. Pedersen/ D.Tuastad/E.Zureik (eds), *Constructing Order: Palestinian Adaptations to Refugee Life*, FAFO Report 236, 1997; R. Isotalo, "Yesterday's Outsiders, To-

II. Return and Culturalism

Ever since the 1948 War, "return" has remained a powerful symbol that at the same time draws all Palestinians together as well as divides them: as a unifying national signifier it has been chosen in Palestinian discourses to represent a variety of aims and activities. Let me mention a few: a PLO newspaper, refugees' right to return to their pre-1948 home-areas, Palestinian football team in Kuwait and a *debka*-band in Peru have all been named *Awda*, "return." Ala Hamarneh even calls "the culture of return" those conscious efforts of the diaspora Palestinian – mainly refugee – organisations and groups to keep the issue of the right of return on the political agenda by cultural means. These cultural means include projects of collecting oral histories of 1948-refugees and their descendants, documentary films, autobiographies and novels, and an effort to reconstruct a pre-1948 Palestinian village for an exhibition "as it was."[8] This "culture of return" seems to suggest, when culture is understood as contested meaning-making,[9] a comprehensive ideological and political effort around which key-concepts such as "identity," "memory," "exile" and "homeland" are consciously and explicitly brought together. Hence, it appears to me as an objectification of culture[10] in a manner rather similar to the politicised folklore movement in

---

day's Returnees – Transnational Processes and Cultural Encounters in the West Bank", in: A. Linjakumpu/ K.Virtanen (eds), *Under The Olive Tree. Reconsidering Mediterranean Politics and Culture*, 1997; R. Isotalo, *Gendering the Palestinian Return Migration: Migrants from the Gulf and Marriage as a Transnational Practice*, paper presented at the Third Mediterranean Social and Political Research Meeting, Florence, 20-24 March 2002; S. Hanafi, *Flexible Transnational Survival Practices of Palestinian Transmigrants/Returnees, and Inflexible State Policies: Crafting the Palestinian Extra-territorialized Nation-State*, paper presented at the Third Mediterranean Social and Political Research Meeting, Florence, 20-24 March 2002.

8 A. Hamarneh, *The Culture of Return of the Palestinian Refugees: Identity, Memory, Exile, and Homeland*, paper presented at an International Conference on Israel and the Palestinian Refugees, Max Planck Institute for Comparative Public Law and International Law, Heidelberg, 11-13 July 2003.

9 S. Wright, "The Politicisation of Culture", *Anthropology Today* 14 (1998), 7 et seq.

10 For an overview of a conceptual discussion, see for example P. Werbner/T. Modood (eds), *Debating cultural hybridity: multi-cultural identities and the politics of anti-rasicm*, 1997; see also S. Wright, see note 9; and R. Handler, *Nationalism and the Politics of Culture in Quebec*, 1988.

the West Bank where folklore collection, writings, and different forms of its presentation in festivals and exhibitions gained nationalistic significance from the late 19th century until the Oslo Accords.[11] Ted Swedenburg calls these efforts "projects to rescue the past."[12] In the footsteps of European ethnology and folklore, as it developed in the 19th century, the latter Palestinian scientific discipline of folklore and folklore enthusiasm alike acted almost in unison toward the construction of a national past.[13] For example, an effort to reconstruct a pre-1948 Palestinian village appears to reflect a vision where the past lifestyle of the Palestinian peasant is seen as encapsulating shared values worthy of preservation, and it provides a picture of traditional life "as it was" prior to the disaster of 1948.[14]

In her study on Palestinian refugees in Lebanon before the Israeli invasion in 1982, Julie Peteet maintains that Palestinians were vitally aware of the implications of presenting their culture to outsiders. According to her, Palestinian refugees' readiness to present their culture and the calculations that accompanied it were a means of reclaiming the past and asserting control over their own future.[15] In the case of the folklore movement inside historical Palestine, perhaps "salvage folklore" in its aim to "pickle heritage"[16] was a means to legitimise presence as well. Since the mid 1990s, a coherent folklore movement as such no longer exists in the West Bank and Gaza. At the end of the 1990s, different folklore festivals and other folkloristic events still flourished during the summer months. But instead of reflecting a unifying national goal, folkloristic events rather articulated organisers' views on societal matters and competed with each other in entertaining a paying audience.[17] Therefore the focus of politicised culture in its different forms seems to have shifted around "the refugee issue," whereas folklore as such con-

---

11 R. Isotalo, *Different Meanings of Palestinian Nationalism: The Politicisation of Culture*, 1999.

12 T. Swedenburg, *Memories of Revolt. The 1936-1939 Rebellion and the Palestinian National Past*, 1995, 95.

13 Isotalo, see note 11; Swedenburg, *idem.*

14 Swedenburg, ibid., 22.

15 J. Peteet, "Authenticity and Gender: The Presentation of Culture", in: J. Tucker (ed.), *Arab Women: Old Boundaries, New Frontiers*, 1993, 49 et seq.

16 "Pickled heritage" is a pithy expression used by Salim Tamari for the above described phenomenon.

17 Isotalo, see note 11.

tinues to preserve a kind of "rootedness" and even nationalistic feelings in the diaspora. Palestinian exiles and migrants often arrange their hometown associations' activities around folkloristic events.

The politicisation of culture as described by Hamarneh and Peteet can be seen as part of a culturalist movement at the transnational level. Arjun Appadurai's notion of culturalism refers primarily to "identity politics,"[18] and seems suitable to characterise the Palestinian "culture of return" as well. According to Appadurai, culturalism is conscious mobilisation of cultural differences in the service of broader national or transnational politics. It is frequently associated with extraterritorial histories and memories, sometimes with refugee status and exile, and almost always with struggles for stronger recognition from existing nation-states or from various transnational bodies. Culturalist movements are self-conscious about identity, culture, and heritage, all of which tend to be part of the deliberate vocabulary of culturalist movements as they struggle with states and other culturalist focuses.[19]

III. Unifying Discourse, Contested Meanings

The concept, the thought of return is thus common to all Palestinians, but at the same time it divides people into several categories, positions, and statuses in their relation to it. These categories, positions, and statuses partially overlap with the divisions of Palestinians' dispersal to different geographical locations and sovereignty zones.[20] Since 1948 it is self-evident that not all Palestinians are in the same position in relation to return. They have totally different possibilities or willingness to the actual return move, a fact that obviously influences their constructions

---

[18] A. Appadurai, *Modernity at Large. Cultural Dimensions of Globalization*, 1996.

[19] Ibid., 15.

[20] By "different sovereignty zones" I am referring to the fact that in the West Bank, Gaza and those neighbouring Arab countries where there are Palestinian refugee camps, the administration, services provided, etc., of the camps has been handed over to an international organisation, namely UNRWA. The camp inhabitants cannot participate in municipality-level policy-making of the surrounding towns and cities. Further, the areas that are today governed by the Palestinian Authority form contested sovereignty zones of different degrees in regard to their legal status, in a world that remains organised as nation-states with recognised borders.

of identity and nation, as well as their views on the future. In regard to the relationship between the discourse and practice of return, this is a point where many misunderstandings and confrontations occur. A number of discussions not only ignore the bifurcation between symbolic and practical dimensions of return but hesitate to make the separation for reasons this paper in part aims to discuss.

That "return" is a cultural notion for Palestinians, suggests that it can be discussed as a part of a normative repertoire common to all Palestinians, which is not to say that all Palestinians would share a similar understanding of the concept's meaning. The development of different notions of return has been perpetuated parallel to a complementary if contradictory process, namely, that of the fragmentation of Palestinian identity. Locality-tied specificity as a feature of Palestinian identity that can also be seen as a kind of fragmentation has not occurred as a direct consequence of Palestinians' dispersal. One may rather see it as a continuum of the tradition of localism/territoriality (common habitat and belonging in *hamula,* lineage, and clan-system based patron-client relationships that are at times called "traditional loyalties") and urban/rural division as part of the Palestinian society's traditionally rather hierarchical social structure. Glen Bowman's remarks on Palestinians' identity may help us to estimate whether the recent Palestinian debates – or controversies – concerning the right of return are about a real shift in the right-of-return discourse or rather about (movements of) including or excluding elements inside a discursive formation without fundamentally changing or challenging it.

Using different diaspora sites and subject positions as a starting point, Bowman argues that the imaginings of Palestine by Palestinians located within the various sites of the diaspora differ substantially and may lead Palestinians from one domain to see those from another as foreigners or even as enemies.[21] The "nation" in the discourse of an established national entity is an imprecise and nebulous concept which is, precisely because of that imprecision, open to appropriation of all its readers. Thus, the concept of "nation" retains its grip on the imagination of its population by remaining unfixed, because, in this way, a wide range of persons and collectivities (such as the different communities of the Palestinian diaspora) can identify as constituent parts of it without having

---

[21] G. Bowman, "A country of words, conceiving the Palestinian nation from the position of exile", in: E. Laclau (ed.), *The Making of Political Identities*, 1994, 138 et seq., drawn from electronic form at <http://www.kent.ac.uk/anthropology/department/staff/bowman/laclau.html<, 1 et seq., 1-4.

their readings and their allegiances to it challenged or denied by particular and exclusionary definitions.[22] However, this "unfixity" can only be maintained, asserts Bowman, as long as the persistence of the nation is taken for granted. As soon as the nation is discursively posited as endangered, battle lines are drawn and processes of selective exclusion/inclusion are set in motion. When a nation is lost or unrealised, just as when it is perceived as threatened, the issue of what impedes its realisation becomes salient. Persons who perceive themselves as nationals without a nation, like those who feel their national identity is endangered, will interpret all manifestations of antagonism affecting their "subsidiary" identities as symptomatic of the denial to them of their nation. The "problem" in the Palestinian case, according to Bowman's analysis, is that their identity as Palestinians is built on these denials. In Bowman's words, "in the absence of any generalising positivity defining the Palestinians as a whole, the experience of antagonism itself comes to provide the determinative marker of identity."[23] Notwithstanding my belief in the contextuality and fluidity of identities, I would like to apply Bowman's notion by suggesting that part of Palestinians' identity as Palestinians appears to be built on *particular* denials and antagonisms that each group or community experiences by virtue of being Palestinian. Can we assume that there may be a lack of mutual understanding, or even knowledge, between different groups about each others' particular antagonisms? What does this have to do with discourses on return?

Since the 1948 dispersal, there have been few "time-outs" in the Palestinian history which would have carved space for new speech genres to emerge, for example those of the 1967 War, the first *Intifada*, the Oslo process, and as it seems now, the second *Intifada*. Admittedly, new speech genres on return have emerged where the return has been invested with new and competing symbolic and political meanings; but they have mainly appeared in particular contexts, such as in camp communities in Lebanon, and have often been inter-generational in nature. In these discourses where return has been treated, for example, the political choices of the older generation have been called into question and indirectly criticised.[24] Also, it is noteworthy that the 1948-generation's personal narratives of *Nakba* and return seem to be very

---

22 Ibid., 5.

23 Ibid., 6.

24 D. Tuastad, *Aere eller ikke vaere. Slektskap og politisk orientering I en palestinsk landsby i Israel*, 1993, 77.

locality-, class-, and event-specific. People who now inhabit the place where the narrator returns to, whether Palestinians or Israelis, are seldom present in these narratives.[25]

Hence it seems that the only discourse that would have seemed to be broad and imprecise enough to be open to all its readers regardless of geographical location, status in relation to return or the consequent particular group antagonisms, has been that of the right of return. The corpus of "authoritative texts" of the unifying right-of-return discourse consists basically of the UN resolutions and international law (and in some cases interlocutors' religious interpretations). Public parlance and political parlance have, however, until very recently, made no distinction between the symbolic, legal, and practical aspects of the (right of) return.

The discursive field of return thus allows a number of different interpretations. Suffice it to say that, while the symbolic and practical dimensions of return are obviously intertwined, the reasons for being explicitly conscious of them at the level of analysis and policy-making alike, are many. For example, as mentioned earlier, many discourses on return refer as their resource texts to the several UN resolutions or international political agreements or even religious sources. These as such legitimate resource texts either tend to have an administrative top-down perspective[26] or, alternatively, point to a particular moral framework. All of them can be regarded as situated corpuses of knowledge[27] that concern the refugees and the return from a particular vantage point, and thereby each of them invests their notion of return with different meanings. The particular notion of "return" that each "authoritative text" contains has stipulations as to how people, whom the return concerns – and that means almost all Palestinians – make symbolic use of "return" in order to achieve practical goals. Controversies occur when interlocutors from different diaspora sites, from the international community or

---

[25] See for example S. Tamari, *Bourgeois Nostalgia and the Abandoned City*, 2003, and the numerous autobiographies, novels, short stories and poetry of Palestinian writers.

[26] See for example L. Malkki's critical analyses of expert knowledge and other discourses that "mute," depoliticise and dehistoricise refugees who become the mere objects of help and knowledge. L. Malkki, "Speechless emissaries: refugees, humanitarianism, and dehistoricization", in: K. Fog Olwig/K. Hastrup (eds), *Siting Culture. The Shifting Anthropological Object*, 1997.

[27] D. Haraway, "Situated knowledges: The science question in feminism and the privilege of partial perspective", *Feminist Studies* 14 (1989), 575 et seq.

even the official representatives of the parties in conflict, use specific "authoritative texts" as bases for general claims that concern "return" in its entirety; notwithstanding that they would perhaps mean or prioritise the specific dimension of return. The resource texts are separate discursive formations but the unifying right-of-return discourse incorporates them all: it often looks like the interlocutors who use them in the above described manner would end up strengthening their particular positions instead of carving space for dialogue. As an example, the efforts to solve a political conflict over the return of the refugees with the help of argumentation that is solely based on international law have been unsuccessful. This characteristic of communication concerns mainly the discourses on refugees, but also those on migrants, whether forced migrants, voluntary migrants or something in-between, and has spill-overs and stipulations to many other areas of Palestinians' lives. Putting it provocatively, perhaps this intentional and unintentional delay to deconstructing return is part of the policy of return hierarchy[28] by all stakeholders, including refugees who are not a homogenous group.

In the framework of political factuality, a discourse formation that touches upon return, namely "pragmatism," or, as its advocates call it, "realism," appeared in the late 1980s and 1990s.[29] "Pragmatism" discourse did not openly challenge the rights-based discourse, but rather became part of it, under the umbrella of nationalism, since its interlocutors or proponents never deconstructed the return at a discursive level. In other words, "pragmatic" and "realist" politicians preferred to refer to the return as "the refugee issue" that must yet be resolved in the future. It appears that there remained a balance of fear between the so-called *realpolitik* and the right of return in the ways "the refugee issue" was talked about. That may have been possible because *realpolitik* was in fact from the very beginning being formed under the imprecision of the right-of-return discourse, which was profoundly silent as to the exclusive nature of any nation-state project. Precisely because of this imprecision, right-of-return discourse was still broad enough to embrace

---

28 R. Isotalo, *Some Theoretical and Methodological Issues within the Field of Palestinian Return Migration*, paper presented at Brainstorming Workshop on Palestinian Return Migration: Socio-economic and Cultural Approaches, Ramallah, 13-14 June 2001.

29 That reflected, for example, the 1988 PLO decision to accept a two-state solution to the conflict over Palestine; the mutual recognition of the PLO and Israel and the so called "Oslo Accords," Israel-PLO Declaration of Principles on Interim Self-Government Arrangements, 13 September 1993, in its entirety.

all its readers – that is, Palestinians beyond the demarcation lines of their particular antagonisms.

"Nusseibeh controversy": the right of return vs. refugee's choice?

Return continues to be a paradox: it is a force of dispersion and cohesion alike. It was not until late 2001 that a new speech genre emerged on return and caused what some may think of as disproportionate controversy, in other words, the battle lines were drawn. The initiative came from Sari Nusseibeh, a long-time professor of the al-Quds University in East Jerusalem and a well-known Palestinian intellectual, who had recently been posted as the Palestinian Authority's diplomatic representative in Jerusalem. He declared in several interviews and articles in the Israeli media (and later, in Palestinian media) that the Palestinians cannot demand the return of refugees to areas inside today's State of Israel. According to him, in a two-state solution there should be one state for the Israelis and one state for the Palestinians; not one state for the Israelis and two states for the Palestinians. Nusseibeh also mentioned that Israel should recognise its responsibility for the refugees' plight and thus, according to his own interpretation, his proposal did not mean giving up the *right* of return. This assurance did not satisfy Nusseibeh's Palestinian critics to whom it looked like giving up the right of return was exactly what he was doing. A lively debate followed by mainly Palestinian but also Israeli commentators, but in relation to the right-of-return discourses the *intra-Palestinian discussion* is of more relevance.[30]

One may ask what caused this controversy, since there is actually nothing new at the factual level inside the so-called "Nusseibeh declarations" and the debate that followed. Or, to put it another way, why could the persistence of the nation no longer be taken for granted? Why did some interlocutors feel that now that the processes of exclusion/inclusion are underway, it is time to draw the battle lines? The battle lines were indeed drawn, since war rhetoric was part of the debate from the very outset: while declaring himself and those who were like-minded as "level-headed," "sane" and "rational"[31] Nusseibeh thereby

---

[30] For a comprehensive overview in English of the so-called Sari Nusseibeh controversy, see <http://www.shaml.org/ground/Nusseibeh>.

[31] See for example S. Nusseibeh, "What Next", *Ha'aretz English Edition*, 24 September 2001.

appeared to define significant numbers of interlocutors – alas, those who disagreed with him – as "hotheads," "insane" and "irrational." "Quick and decisive" (to quote Salman Abu-Sitta)[32] responses from different sites of the Palestinian diaspora as well as the West Bank and Gaza followed. Nusseibeh's position was perceived as a threat to a number of things: identity, history, moral and legal rights, and national consensus or unity. This underlines that Palestinians argue many aspects of their reality in relation to return. It is noteworthy also that referring to history and identity is characteristic for culturalist movements where cultural and symbolic means are often used in the absence of other powerful political tools.[33] Other political tools besides cultural and symbolic ones were also used. For example, al-Awda network, which is an advocate of the refugees' right to return to their pre-1948 homes, demanded in a petition addressed to PA chairman Yasser Arafat the dismissal of Nusseibeh from his post. Arafat deposed Nusseibeh in late 2002. Prior to that, Nusseibeh had gradually reformulated the emphasis of his views so that he increasingly addressed the Palestinians to waive their right of return to Israel as part of a so-called "Nusseibeh-Ayalon Plan" that he formulated together with former head of the Israeli Shin Bet security service Ami Ayalon. In so doing he did not pay much attention to his former demand of Israel's acknowledgment of refugees' plight – i.e. symbolic recognition of their right of return. Exchange of opinions continued to polarise to the point of declaring: "These are our enemies!", as did some activists in an international al-Awda convention,[34] addressing most members of the PA and the Palestinian *intelligentsia* and *academia* alike.

More petitions and open letters were exchanged, and the message can be generally summarised as: "This is no time to break the national consen-

---

[32] Salman Abu-Sitta is a Palestinian scholar who has published several studies of what he calls "the sacred, legal, and possible" return of all Palestinian refugees to their pre-1948 homes in today's State of Israel. See, for example, S.H. Abu-Sitta, *The End of the Palestinian-Israeli Conflict. From Refugees to Citizens at Home*, 2001. He is also one of the main interlocutors of the recent diasporic intra-Palestinian debates regarding the right of return and its implementation scenarios. "Quick and decisive response" is his expression for the negative response that he thought Nusseibeh's proposals would receive among the refugees from 1948-areas.

[33] "Cultural means" in regard to the Palestinian folklore movement and nationalism are discussed in Isotalo, see note 11.

[34] International Convention on al-Awda, organised by the al-Awda Coalition, 20-22 June 2003, Canada.

sus and besides, who are you to speak since you are an outsider anyway." This figurative sentence sums up many comments' argumentation and illustrates a paradox that in my mind is characteristic to this debate and the conditions that are peculiar to Palestinian societal discussion in a crisis-ridden and beleaguered atmosphere. On the one hand there is a strong need to show national unity and cohesion, because the lesson learnt the hard way from the past has been that "the enemy" will exploit the slightest hint of society's seam lines. Precautions against disrupting the "national unity" and "national consensus," which have been numerous in the debate, can be interpreted in this light. On the other hand, many comments in the debate have reflected on positions such as: who is speaking on whose behalf and in what official position, which reminds of our earlier discussion about particular antagonisms as internal demarcation lines of the Palestinian society.

To cite Bowman: "When a nation is unrealised, as when it is perceived as threatened, the issue of what impedes its realisation becomes salient."[35] What became salient in this debate was the refugees' right to return, which was formulated as "refugee's choice" by Nusseibeh and his proponents or "giving up the right of return" by his opponents. So is the right of return to pre-1948 areas the issue that impedes the realisation of the Palestinian nation in a state framework or what is at stake in this debate? Let us try to unfold the issue by looking at it from the perspective of the broad and unifying right-of-return discourse. As an official PA-appointed diplomatic representative in Jerusalem, Nusseibeh differentiated between moral, legal, political, practical and symbolical aspects of return – i.e. there was a significant effort to deconstruct the return *within* the discourse of right of return. To sum up Nusseibeh's argumentation very roughly: He was basically saying that admittedly Israel does have a *moral* obligation; *legally* we can interpret the right of return to Israel. *Politically*, however, it is not feasible to push this right, so we should *practically* interpret the *legal* right of return as being to a Palestinian State, and *symbolically* it is to live under Palestinian rule. To deconstruct something is to make it visible and as Foucault has shown us in many of his works, the project of "making visible" is integrally linked to operations of power and practices of subjection. This deconstruction of return made visible an interpretation of its elements that could no longer fit inside the unifying discourse: the right-of-return discourse allowed the elements of "pragmatism" to be brought into it, but only as far as they surrounded the discursive silence about the pro-

---

35 Bowman, see note 21, 5.

cesses of exclusion/inclusion. Although Nusseibeh tried to embrace the pragmatism discourse that is aligned with the right-of-return discourse, he broke the discursive silence about the processes of exclusion/inclusion.

Without going into nuances of exclusion (like those that would separate families), one categorical exclusion/inclusion issue that became visible in Nusseibeh's deconstruction of return was a deconstruction of "refugees" as a group by privileging the rights of the 1967 refugees (the displaced) at the expense of the 1948 refugees. Once these processes were brought to light in the terms of the right-of-return discourse, as they were in Nusseibeh's argumentation, they could no longer be inclusive in the same discourse. Instead, they started forming another discursive formation in the guise of "refugee's choice." Despite the fact that these two discursive formations (right of return and refugee's choice) contain opposite arguments, they are not counter discourses because both are based on the rights-premises. Looking at these discursive formations, it remains outside the scope of this article to analyse their political factuality and details. In light of the debate that has continued since the "Nusseibeh controversy,"[36] a discourse on return that so far appears hegemonic is rights-based: it contains the refugees' right of return to their former homes as a positive legal right *or* a moral right to be acknowledged. Given that, a *unifying* right-of-return discourse that was open to all Palestinians no longer exists.

The refugee's choice discourse does not challenge the rights-premises, given the attention it has paid to the separation between a quest for the Israeli acknowledgement of its responsibility on the one hand, and the refugee's choice to exercise a return (as defined in the discourse; to the Palestinian State but not to Israel) or accept another solution, on the other. Hence the "right" is connected to a symbolic Israeli apology and de-coupled from the "return" understood as the repatriation of refugees to their original homes. Thus the discourse refers to a notion of return that is stripped of many of its dimensions – alas, the contents of "the

---

[36] For example, the so-called Nusseibeh-Ayalon plan and "People's campaign;" discussion that preceded and followed publishing the results of the Palestinian Centre for Policy and Survey Research conducted poll, 2003, where 4,500 refugee families were asked to express their support or opposition to different alternatives for their permanent place of residence as designed in the so-called Taba-based solution; and, discussion around the Yasser Aboud Rabbo and Yossi Beilin initiated "Geneva Accords" peace proposal can all be seen as bench-marks of the ongoing discussion.

choice." The dimensions that are connected to *Nakba*: war, history and a locality-specific identity now become parts of the notion of "right," not the notion of "return." The "right" becomes symbolic while the "return" becomes a practice.

In line with the Palestinian mainstream nationalism, even "refugee's choice" discourse aims to be unifying. It promotes a notion of identity that is based on the nation-state: it is the future Palestinian State that is home to all Palestinians, not one's original village or town. Opponents to the "refugee's choice" discourse insist on a different notion of return, but the opponents cannot be seen as a homogenous group. As mentioned earlier, the project of "making visible" is integrally linked to operations of power and processes of subjection. Explaining well why the battle lines were drawn in the first place, at least two important questions are at stake in the ongoing process. First, what is the notion of return that remains or becomes hegemonic; and second, who is to decide which notion remains part of the drawing the lines of the nation? Some well-placed diaspora activists insist on a notion of return that is linked with their history and identity, despite the fact that personally, repatriation would be of secondary interest to them. Refugees, to whom also the practical dimension is of acute interest, are no less concerned about the questions of identity and history. Active constructions of national identity and history are part of maintaining the "imagined community," as the nation has been called.[37] Refugees' and diaspora Palestinians' reading of the nation becomes seriously threatened when their origin and, consequently, their identity as Palestinians based on antagonism is cut off from the hegemonic discourse of the nation.

IV. Return in Normative Repertoires

Let me now go back to my earlier notion about return as a part of Palestinians' normative repertoire.[38] In the following pages, I discuss how

---

[37] B. Anderson, *Imagined Communities. Reflections on the Origin and Spread of Nationalism*, 1983.

[38] "Normative repertoire" is a cluster of formal resources around legitimising principle. It is possible to call upon a multitude of justifying principles and use them according to the needs of the situation or contexts of interaction. The normative repertoire's particularity is that its principal aim is to account for the discursive forms used in the construction of the action claiming to be founded on a norm and expressed in a norm. The repertoire is determined not so much

return as a part of the normative repertoire boils down to today's return migrants' lives. I will connect some features of particular individuals' return to the questions of recent Palestinian research regarding refugees' eventual repatriation process in the light of contemporary return migration. More particularly, my discussion reflects recent research scenarios regarding the probability of family or individual return and the role of kinship and other networks in the eventual return. I will also try, to some extent, to bring into our discussion what kind of "choice" may be meant by a refugee's or a migrant's choice. While doing that, I will also consider the gender-specificity of these issues. Drawing on an ethnographic example, I have chosen as my point of reference a few excerpts from four women's lives.

Positioning residual voices

"Amal" returned to Palestine in 1997. In many ways, particularly in the light of what can be called hegemonic discourses on return, it is doubtful whether she really "returned" at all. However, according to her own perception, she did return. She is middle-aged, academically educated, a refugee born in one of the camps in Lebanon, and her family originates from Jaffa. We became acquainted in Ramallah where she had resided since her return. The fact of settling in Ramallah, in itself, questions the nature of her return if we look at it in the light of the hegemonic right-of-return discourses: Instead of Jaffa, she was only able to return to the West Bank, whereas her parents of the 1948-generation and her siblings with their families remain in one of Lebanon's refugee camps. Amal is divorced and she returned alone. Her young unmarried adult daughter chose to stay in the United States where Amal and her husband had migrated about 20 years ago. In the context of today's limited return migration, it is not uncommon that return actually separates families.

Amal's return was facilitated by two things: her American citizenship and her profession. The latter made it possible to move initially to the

by the circumstances but by the argumentative tactics chosen by its user. The number of repertoires any individual can use will be influenced by the individual's own choices and the constraints of the social environment. See B. Dupret, "Legal Pluralism, Normative Pluralism and the Arab World", in: Dupret/Berger/al-Zwaini, see note 1.

West Bank through the TOKTEN-programme.[39] The facilitators of Amal's return were not, however, the same as her motives to return. After the TOKTEN-assignment was over she found a well-paid job, but this did not fulfil the expectations that she had associated with return. These expectations were not of an economic nature, but she had hoped to influence positively the development of her professional field while at the same time making a "contribution to the homeland." However, she never found her "professional community" in Palestine, and claimed that her office in the West Bank was filled with nepotism and, consequently, mediocrity. Amal had channelled many of her expectations regarding return into her work, through which she had hoped to contribute to the homeland and to become part of the (professional) community. Thus, one might ask whether her sharp criticism also articulated a more general sort of disillusionment, resorting to professional issues as a vehicle through which most freely to express the gap between her dreams and the reality of the homecoming.

Amal had already resided some years in Palestine when the second *Intifada* began. Conditions of the uprising did not shock her in the beginning, since she was accustomed to the hardships of war from her years in Lebanon. However, the Israeli invasion of Ramallah in the spring 2002 caused her to bitterly regret that she had just moved to a new apartment in the vicinity of the *muqata* headquarter "because it had a lovely view" – indeed she had a room with a view onto an Israeli war helicopter constantly hanging three metres outside her bedroom window. During the weeks of the siege, women who lived in the small apartment building occasionally met in the staircase. Amal knew that I was writing my PhD research on the Palestinian return and that I was interested in how, and indeed if, gender organises the return move. She therefore later recounted to me in detail one discussion she had with her neighbours, thereby advising me to be mindful about drawing too hasty conclusions from how the return is spoken of in public, mostly by men, who set the tone for national discourses for Palestinians on a transnational level.

This is mainly the contents of what she memorised. Once four neighbours of them started to chat about how awful the circumstances

---

[39] TOKTEN (Transfer of Knowledge Through Expatriate Nationals) is a programme implemented by UNDP (United Nations Development Programme) to utilise the expertise of expatriate nationals through providing short-term technical assistance to their country of origin. For Palestinian TOKTEN in electronic form, see http://www.tokten.org/palestinian.html.

had turned in comparison to how they were only some years earlier. One topic led to another, namely, what had brought them – newcomers all – to the West Bank. One of the ladies told of her husband being a pilot who used to work in the Gulf. When the Gulf crisis unfolded he lost his steady job and did not manage to replace it. When a new airport was opened in Gaza, he considered himself quite fortunate to find employment there. According to his wife, his salary in Palestine was not as good as it had been in the Gulf prior to the crisis, but at least he would not be made to leave the country once he reached the retirement age. Gaza airport was destroyed by the Israeli army in early 2001, but in the mid 1990s moving to Palestine had improved this family's standard of living and brought them some stability. The second neighbour explained that she did not actually have a choice since her husband was employed by the Palestinian Authority; they had returned as part of the PLO-quota. She went on to explain that they had previously lived in South Yemen where, in her view, the atmosphere had deteriorated after the unification of the South and North in 1990. She had liked Yemen very much but she now preferred that her daughters go to school in Ramallah. The third woman had moved to Ramallah from Jordan. Living in Amman had not been bad, but her husband's dental practice had been quite successful in Ramallah before the *Intifada*. Now that business was going slowly.

In all three neighbours' narratives about coming to Palestine, circumstances in Palestine were considered in comparison with the conditions in the former host countries. Return to Palestine was not seen as an isolated event taking place in a vacuum, but in retrospect, was viewed through a lens of continuum and comparison. Conditions in Palestine were not evaluated *per se*; in other words, return was not considered an end in itself but was evaluated against the background of the respective former host country as an alternative.

"Pay attention," Amal told me before she continued her story, "Not once did they [the neighbours] mention nation or patriotism or even Israel." By this she meant that despite the crisis-ridden atmosphere where patriotic feelings in general were running high (the presidential headquarter was being destroyed by the Israeli army just a few hundred metres away), none of Amal's three neighbours mentioned anything connected with patriotism, nationalism, or right of return in the context of their repatriation. All of them referred to return in terms of material costs and losses for themselves, *through* their families. Return was described in relation to their husbands' jobs and children's education. Migrant's or refugee's "choice" was mentioned once by a woman who had explained that in practice she had no choice but to return to Palestine. It is interesting to note that this woman belonged to the so-called PLO-returnees, who are usually perceived as a privileged category by the surrounding society. Nevertheless, in describing her return as the absence of real choice, she couched her narrative *in the idiom of the family* instead of that of nationalism, despite the fact that the family was part of the "homecoming of the revolution," as the return of the PLO-members was often called in the 1990s.

Then it was Amal's turn to tell what had brought her to Palestine. She told her neighbours how as a refugee she had felt that it was an important part of her identity to come and live in Palestine, at least for a while, and that is why she had quit her work in the United States, thinking that her professional skills would benefit the Palestinian society. According to Amal, the three other women stared at her in disbelief. Then, in order to verify that they had understood correctly, they asked if she had actually quit a perfectly good job in the US to come to Palestine. Amal confirmed that this was indeed the case. Several detailed questions followed. The fact that Amal's unmarried daughter had remained in the US raised such astonishment that Amal, who already suffered tremendously for being unable to be in regular contact with her concerned daughter during the siege, interpreted the astonishment as indirect criticism of her mothering. To summarise the neighbours' reactions: Amal's decision to come alone, for ideological and professional reasons that were personal rather than collective, was strongly called into question by her three neighbours.

In this staircase discussion, none of Amal's neighbours spoke of their return as deriving from the public normative repertoire where Palestinian nationalism plays a role and can thus be used in public to justify and explain different actions. Amal's return story as recounted to her neighbours, however, was very similar to some accounts that I have heard from return migrant men (refugees and non-refugees alike) at the beginning of a discussion or an interview. Independent of the content of the life history and narrative contents that follows later, quite a few narratives have begun with a statement that links the return to "the cause" such as: "I came to help my people." "I wanted to contribute to the country." "It was always my dream to return to the homeland." But in this particular context, Amal's explanations, which would have perhaps sounded perfectly "acceptable" or "natural" if uttered by a migrant man, particularly to a foreigner or a stranger, were rejected by her neighbours. Women regarded Amal's motives as a justificatory norm. When it became apparent that the circumstances in the US were not what motivated Amal to leave, since they were "better" than in Palestine, the women were left with their original question: "Why did you return?"

Where can we situate Amal's neighbours' voices in the field of return? Should they be seen as representing some kind of counter discourse? After all, not only did they make no reference whatsoever to Palestinian nationalism, identity, or "homeland", but they questioned the one person's narrative who was actually applying these concepts. In my view they should not be seen as representing a counter discourse to the hegemonic discourses on return. Neither should their gender specificity be interpreted in a manner that would contribute to conventional generalisations that tend to see female narratives as "gender specific," while those uttered mainly in public by men are considered to speak for the whole group or "society."[40] Rather, we should look at how gender relates to (and is constructed in) the practices and discourses on return.

What do these women's "arrival stories" tell us about how gender features in the practices of return? In Amal's neighbours' "arrival stories," gender related to the return migration (especially from the Arab world but also in general) in a way that confirms a trend that is typical not only for the Palestinian return migration, but for Middle Eastern family migration in general: namely that normally the woman follows the man. The latter is, or is considered to be, the main or sole breadwinner of the household.[41]

Further, I suggest that gender in the practices of return relates to the questions of agency and subject-formation. Following Saba Mahmood,

---

40 Accordingly, surveys that measure, for example, Palestinian refugees' housing needs, willingness to move, etc., often present gender-diversification of answers as "women's special needs" in the results of those studies where women have been addressed.

41 See, for instance, Hovdenak, see note 7; Palestinian Central Bureau of Statistics (PCBS), *Women and Men in Palestine: Trends and Statistics*, 1998; Isotalo, "Yesterday's Outsiders, Today's Returnees – Transnational Processes and Cultural Encounters in the West Bank", see note 7; *idem*, *Gendering the Palestinian Return Migration: Migrants from the Gulf and Marriage as a Transnational Practice*, see note 7; and S. Hanafi, *The Impact of Social Capital on the Eventual Repatriation Process of Refugees: Study of Economic and Social Transnational Kinship Networks in Palestine/Israel*, 2003.

"agency" is here understood as the capacity of action that, historically, specific circumstances (of subordination) enable and create.[42]

Sari Hanafi asserts in a recent survey-based analysis that "males tend to decide on the relocation of their families" and that in 81 per cent of the responses "the return seems according to declaration of the respondents to be done with the consultation with their family."[43] In the Middle East, family is usually a major concern for both spouses; family, not the individual, is seen as the basic unit of the society.[44] Without simplifying the complex process of social change and modernisation as it is understood locally in urban Middle Eastern societies, one may nevertheless generalise that a familial ideology based on gender complementarity prevails in the Middle East. The idea of gender complementarity does not imply a hierarchy between the sexes. Rather, this enduring familial ideology motivates everyone's duties and obligations from a perspective that places the individual at the service of a functioning family. However, the duties and obligations that women and men are expected to perform are different, and this ideology also results in women and minors in the family putting aside their needs and wishes on behalf of the "common good."[45] This matter is of relevance when issues of repatriation and return migration are examined. The above citations from a recent survey should not be interpreted to mean that women have no say in the decision-making regarding return, or that their views would not count but be merely "consulted" in the familial decision-making. How-

---

[42] S. Mahmood, "Feminist Theory, Embodiment, and the Docile Agent: Some Reflections on the Egyptian Islamic Revival", *Cultural Anthropology* 6 (2001), 202 et seq., 203.

[43] Hanafi, see note 41, 13, 16.

[44] See for example S. Altorki, "The Concept and Practice of Citizenship in Saudi Arabia", in: S. Joseph (ed.), *Gender and Citizenship in the Middle East*, 2000; A. Amawi, "Gender and Citizenship in Jordan", in: *idem*; S. Joseph, "Women and Politics in the Middle East", in: S. Joseph/S. Slyomovics (eds), *Women and Power in the Middle East*, 2001.

[45] For instance, S. Joseph, "Theories and Dynamics of Gender, Self, and Identity in Arab Families", in: S. Joseph (ed.), *Intimate Selving in Arab Families. Gender, Self, and Identity*, 1999; *idem*, "Searching for Baba", in: *idem*; *idem*, "Connectivity, Love and Power in Reproduction of Power in Lebanon", in: *idem*; R. Giacaman/I. Jad/P. Johnson, "For the Common Good? Gender and Social Citizenship in Palestine", in: Joseph/Slyomovics, see note 44. Many chapters in M. Heiberg/G. Ovansen, *Palestinian Society in Gaza, West Bank and Arab Jerusalem: A Survey of Living Conditions*, 1993, illustrate how this familial ideology is reflected in different areas of Palestinians' lives.

ever, the questionnaire or survey-based studies where women have been addressed – such as the Fafo surveys (for example, 1993, 1997) – or the above-cited Shaml survey (2003), have been mainly conducted at a household-level. Given that the respondent has often been "the head of the household" and that the household approach places the emphasis on a conjugal unit, women's attitudes or opinions as individuals (or as part of a larger kin network that includes their natal homes), for example towards repatriation and integration, remain almost unexamined.[46] In my example of Amal and her neighbours, where the women spoke privately among themselves, the latter linked their return to their husbands' income and children's schooling. Husbands' income earnings and families' legal statuses in their former countries of residence were shaped by political developments. Amal's three neighbours' framing of return articulated both structure and agency in the context of a culturally specific welfare contract. Familial ideology and lifestyle set frames for culturally constructed familial welfare contracts.[47] *The Impact of Social Capital on the Eventual Repatriation Process of Refugees* also confirms that economic investments and support inside the family remain gender-structured and based on an idea about complementarity of gender roles. The "big gift" is gendered, i.e. the major investment in offspring's education goes to boys and, later on, brothers are expected to support their sisters in the form of gifts in money or goods.[48] Thus the assumption of the families continues to be that of a man as the provider. What questionnaire-based research may perhaps not show, due to its methodological premises, is what is going to happen with this trend in the future and what are the younger generation's gendered individual readings of this collective ideology. This gains importance particularly

---

[46] In the conclusions of his research, Palestinian sociologist Najeh Jarrar mentions that his study deals almost exclusively with male leaders and residents of refugee camps. He adds that he feels strongly that research should be conducted on women's role in decision-making regarding integration and repatriation. N. Jarrar, *Palestinian Refugee Camps in the West Bank. Attitudes Towards Repatriation and Integration*, 2003; see also J. Rogge, "Repatriation of Refugees. A Not So Simple 'Optimum' Solution", in: T. Allen/H. Morsink (eds), When Refugees Go Home. African Experiences, 1994.

[47] See U. Vuorela's key-note lecture "Global Families" given at the "Family Relations and Intimacy in the Globalising World" Conference, held in Kylmäpihlaja, Finland, 4-6 September 2003. As a concept, welfare contract reflects on Carol Pateman's critique toward social contract.

[48] Hanafi, see note 41.

in cases where the return separates the family according to the lines of generations as it did in Amal's case.

What do these women's talks about their return tell us about how gender enters into the discourses on return? A number of studies have characterised Palestinian nationalist discourses as male. Women have characteristically been defined not as agents or national subjects but in terms of their relation to men as their mothers, wives, sisters and daughters in these discourses.[49] Most public discourses on return are no exception.[50] This often includes even academic and policy-oriented writing, despite the urge for "gender mainstreaming" in post-conflict reconstruction and political transitions, in the sense that they accept the received wisdom of such basic elements of culture as family and gender roles almost as "immovable." That does not mean of course that women would not be co-producers of these patriarchal discourses.[51] I would thereby suggest that Amal's "arrival story" was questioned by her neighbours owing to her being a woman, while drawing in the context of her actual return move on a public discourse that connotes identity politics at a transnational level. We can see in the ways in which women couch their actual return moves in different idioms – a meeting point of different feminine subjectivities, and, gendered agency in its relation to return and a familial ideology peculiar to Palestine and in the Middle East more generally. Also the interplay of individual and collective in

---

[49] For discussions on gender in Palestinian national and nationalistic discourses, see for instance S. Haj, "Palestinian Women and Patriarchal Relationships", *SIGNS: Journal of Women in Culture and Society* 17 (1992), 761 et seq.; Peteet, see note 15; J. Massad, "Conceiving the Masculine: Gender and Palestinian Nationalism", *Middle East Journal* 49 (1995), 483 et seq.; T. Mayer, "Heightened Palestinian Nationalism. Military Occupation, Repression, Difference and Gender", in: J. Tucker (ed.), *Arab Women. Old Boundaries, New Frontiers*, 1993; R. Giacaman/I. Jad/P. Johnson, "Transit Citizens. Gender and Citizenship under the Palestinian Authority", in: Joseph, see note 44.

[50] "The old man glanced back at his village and went on the road to exile ... The boy survived al *Nakba* and became *fedayi* ... The child grew up in a refugee camp, ignited the *intifada* and prepares to return home, armed with his grandfather's memory, his father's sacrifice and his own relentless determination to return. To all three generations, this Book of Return is dedicated." Abu-Sitta, see note 32, 1.

[51] Katila and Meriläinen, reflect on women's roles as co-producers of patriarchal structures and discourses in: S. Katila/S. Meriläinen, "A Serious Researcher or Just Another Nice Girl?, Doing Gender in a Male-Dominated Scientific Community", *Gender, Work and Organization* 6 (1999), 163 et seq.

this encounter deserves close attention. Amal was under the impression that her neighbours indirectly criticised her for not being a good mother, in a situation where Amal linked her return to the nation, instead of family, discursively and quite concretely by leaving her daughter behind. For Amal's neighbours, return in its relation to themselves and to the collective boiled down not to the relationship between themselves and the homeland or nation, but themselves and their family members. The resonance over different meanings of return between these female returnees centered on their relation to the familial ideology and its hierarchical order, with return in the given moment and in the limits of their individual agency. The order of things was different for these women, but the place of return within this order in regard to different domains of reality can shift in different stages of a person's life span. Also a returnee's former host society where she or he may have lived surrounded by people committed to a welfare contract of another kind, and where her or his legal status in the society has been safer than generally for the Palestinians in the Arab world, may influence how discursive notions of return relate one's feelings of belonging in the discursive nation on the one hand, and actions on the other hand. Divorced and with an adult child, when Amal returned she was the head of her own household, and her "arrival story" related to the approaches of male returnees to Palestine, those associated with: identity, homeland, and contribution to the society and nation through work. Apart from culturally specific welfare contract and Amal's economically independent status, let us also remember that her refugee status was central to her identity.

Drawing on my ethnographic material from the West Bank, I would argue that gender is an important organiser of the Palestinian return migration. However, this does not justify a claim that women and men would somehow form separate entities in relation to discourses and practices on return. The contemporary return migration is in part "repatriation under conflict,"[52] where return takes place despite the fact that the conflict that originally caused the dispersal remains unresolved. As such, repatriation under conflict is not uncommon. However, the Palestinian case of repatriation under conflict does not concern the major bulk of the population that was dispersed: the refugees. Given that fact, the unifying discourses on return, as discussed earlier, point to the

52 See K.B. Wilson/J. Nunes, "Repatriation to Mozambique. Refugee initiative & agency planning in Milange District 1988-1991", in: T. Allen/H. Morsink (eds), *When Refugees Go Home. African Experiences*, 1995, 172 et seq.

return of the refugees. Thus, it would be unwise to draw straightforward or unambiguous parallels between any discourses on and practices of return, keeping in mind that discourses construct social reality rather than reflect it. Neither is the public/private dichotomy very helpful in analysing the relationship between discourses and practices of return and the place of gender in them, if it is understood as the sociological categorisation of society into separate fields of public and private.[53] Even cases where people's ways to talk about the return appear at first sight to divide along the lines of public/private dichotomy deserve closer analyses. Nevertheless, the dialectical relationship between the discourses and practices of return is informative of much stratification in the Palestinian society.

The ways in which today's return migrants speak about the return are situational and contextual but not random. In the example of Amal and her neighbours, two notions of return met – but it remains to be seen if the meeting will produce new meanings. Amal was drawing from a pool of meanings that is familiar from the discourses on right of return: identity, homeland. Her neighbours, for their part, spoke of their return in a matter-of-fact manner that is similar to women who returned from Kuwait to live in their Palestinian home villages after the unfolding of the Gulf crisis, most of whom connected their mobility to the decisions of their husbands. Also in their narratives, in moving back to the West Bank the women did not have many personal choices.[54] Instead of identity and homeland, the meanings of return that the three of Amal's female neighbours invoked in the discussion were linked to their relations with family members and different aspects of their families' well-being. It would, however, be an analytical shortcoming to reduce the meaning of return in their lives to its practical aspects. To the contrary; given that there is no single and unambiguous meaning of return and that normative notions constitutive in discourse are not always activated, we might focus on potential and actual returnees not only as parts of nationalistic projects or subjects for expert concern but as active social agents in the fields of their lives, whereas complexity of return challenges people's

---

[53] In terms of state intervention at the transnational level, the Palestinian return migrants' family relations are influenced and regulated by nation-state policies and legislation like any aspect of the "public sphere." Isotalo, see note 7. For recent critiques of the public/private dichotomy's applicability in the Middle East, see, for example, Joseph/Slyomovics, see note 44.

[54] See Isotalo, *Gendering the Palestinian Return Migration: Migrants from the Gulf and Marriage as a Transnational Practice*, see note 7.

agency and shapes not only identity but also their life-strategies. Given that agency in the context of prevailing familial ideology remains gendered, identity and life-strategies in relation to return are divided not by the meanings of return only, but distinctions such as social history and class. The fact that returnees, in talks of their move, invoke family, emotional as well as material well-being and security, as shaped and constructed in a mutually constitutive relationship between external circumstances and investments in relationships inside family, is not in contradiction with meanings of return related to identity, homeland and nationalistic project. Indeed, people draw upon discursively constructed norms in the context of their return move, but as my example illustrated, the norms that are motivating (rather than justifying) the return move can point to other aspects of their reality than those cognitive structures that all Palestinians embrace regarding the catastrophe, expulsion, and consequent discourses on return.

Amal found it surprising that her neighbours never mentioned anything connected to nationalism or conflict in their "arrival stories." This, however, is understandable in the circumstances of repatriation under conflict: conflict is a taken-for-granted part of the return and its absence from the narratives reflects other issues rather than lack of consciousness regarding national issues. The continuance of occupation and conflict at some level is not a taken-for-granted part of the return for the refugees, whose return supposedly is pending the conflict's solution. For Amal's neighbours, return did not appear to be an end in itself. For Amal, a refugee whose family was first dispersed by migration and then further by return, it was. During our acquaintance she never compared the conditions in Palestine with those in the US or in Lebanon. Instead, she sometimes discussed her present circumstances in relation to the return itself – her expectations and experiences of it. The neighbours' surprised and critical attitude towards the way Amal phrased her return and her answer to their question "why did you return?" not being satisfactory to them, point to many directions, as we have already seen. We can only wonder how much their attitude was influenced by the then current intense conflict situation. Accordingly, Amal's return – despite the fact that she was relatively free from material "push-factors" in the US – may have appeared as an enigma. Moreover, in a family-oriented society where family is considered to "cushion" the external hardships and provide the person with social, material and emotional support, it may have looked in her neighbours' eyes that Amal had paid a very high price for her return. Finally, they reflect the sensitive relation between the discourses and practices of return as it boils down to return migrants' lives. It seems likely to me that Amal and her neighbours were conscious of the normative repertoire where Palestinian nationalism – and consequently return – remain a part. However, they contextualised the situation differently, and return played a different part in their lives. Amal's three neighbours appeared to assume that they were having a conversation among people who basically share the same antagonisms and, consequently, identity, and basically the same meaning of the notion of return. Amal's response seemed to surprise and make them even uncomfortable. Amal had responded by using an identity-based return discourse, where Palestine is not just a place but the homeland, with its consequent claims, rights, and duties. The three other neighbours, again, had spoken of the return in terms of how it benefited their families' well-being and security.

In relation to hegemonic discourses on return, Amal's neighbours' voices could be seen as residual narratives. They could be interpreted from the point of view what Ted Swedenburg calls potentially oppositional memories and practices in his analyses of the relations between the popular memories and national past of the 1936-1939 rebellion.[55] Swedenburg's analysis links Gramsci's notion of "common sense"[56] with "commonsense memory." Unlike the accounts under discussion here, dissidence to official views was, in Swedenburg's material, usually couched in the idiom of nationalism, the accepted framework within which to conduct political discussion. Even in this case, however, the four women's discussion that at first maybe not appears as political regardless of its politically charged topic, return, reflects the feminist theory claim about personal being political. Oppositional memory takes two basic forms. The first involves interviewees' use of nationalist categories to make negative judgements about the elite. The second form concerns those remembered popular practices that official historical discourse neither criticises nor celebrates but simply ignores. Swedenburg notes how authoritative historical accounts have relegated a whole range of peasant activities during the revolt to the margins because they were regarded as "prepolitical" and insignificant.[57] This could be applied to the relationship between return migration and the issue of refu-

---

55 Swedenburg, see note 12, 110 et seq., 138.

56 As ambiguous, contradictory, multiform and strangely composite, "common sense" is characterised by distinctive local and regional differences. See A. Gramsci, *Selections from the Prison Notebooks*, 1971, 324, 423.

57 Swedenburg, see note 12, 110.

gees return. "Official discourses" have hardly touched upon the silent migration that has so far taken place before the resolving of the refugees issue. Williams' concept of residual narratives[58] characterises the second type's oppositional memories that tackle practices which official discourses have ignored. Because they stand "outside" or "adjacent" to national histories, they are often recounted unselfconsciously. All four neighbours' narratives can be seen as residual narratives in at least two senses. First, in practice, all four of them tackled return migration. Three of them stood outside the official discourses by not deriving from nationalism-based normative repertoires that refer to the return of the refugees; and all four women's experiences fall outside the scope of hegemonic discourses because return migration *per se* is still largely ignored by those discourses. Second, being "outside" or "adjacent" reflects the place of women's narratives in relation to Palestinian national histories and narratives more generally. In national discourses women remain defined in relation to men, and consequently their experiences, attitudes and opinions still remain mainly absent from the official discourses on return and largely unexamined in studies concerning return. Swedenburg argues that since residual narratives have remained relatively unaltered by dominant discourses, they represent potential rather than overt counter-discourses to the official nationalist views.[59]

V. Conclusions

The discursive field of return is an area where different aims linked to return meet in a process where they construct distinctions and alignments to each other. What I still consider as the hegemonic discourse of the return is constitutive in the refugees' right for return and, accordingly, Palestinians' general awareness of the absence of refugees' access to Palestine and camps' existence as tokens of Palestinianness and communities under threat. Consequently, in the framework of today's limited return migration, it is generally not normatively acceptable to present one's actual return as economically beneficial. Looking at the debate among the Palestinians at a transnational level, where competing notions of return meet, it is worth pointing out the existence of residual

---

58 R. Williams, *Marxism and Literature*, 1977, 122 et seq.; cf. Swedenburg, ibid., 111.

59 *Idem.*

narratives and the gender-specificity of received knowledge. In this context the grey area between "the right" and "the return" remains filled with almost hidden voices that link the return with its practicalities – its costs and losses. These voices often belong to the return migrants (for example, to women who privately discuss their return in the idiom of the family). Increasingly, these voices can also be those of some refugee women and men, according to studies where the refugees' opinions have been questioned with the help of scenarios in which the practical alternatives have been dissociated from the major issues of rights, history, and, identity. These potentially oppositional discourses are sensitive and easily suppressed, and that is why they are often not uttered in public.

While norms can be understood as "background or backcloth of understanding,"[60] behind this sensitivity is a backcloth of non-returnees' (local residents) and refugees' (in diaspora and Palestine alike) critical comments regarding the Oslo Accords and the PLO-returnees – namely, that "they signed the papers only that they themselves could return."[61] This criticism is in line with the formerly unifying right-of-return discourse in the sense that it sees the return in itself as beneficial and rewarding. Interestingly, it also precedes the recent debates caused by the attempts to deconstruct "return" in political declarations and research because it reveals a painful connection between the contemporary return migration and the exclusiveness of the nation-state project. In the latter sense this criticism can be seen as a form of potentially oppositional discourse that links "common sense memory" with nationalism, given that the criticism over some elements of national elite is couched in nationalism. There may, however, be important regional differences between the West Bank and Gaza and rural/urban divisions that my discussion in the scope of this article may have passed unnoticed. At the heart of this criticism are the PLO-returnees, but it also touches upon other groups whose return migration was even indirectly made possible by the "peace process." It directly points to the privileged returnees who are seen as corrupted by other members of society. At the normative level, even other return migrants are aware of this criticism. Even those return migrants whose lives are marked by economic insecurity, total ambivalence, ephemerality and forged transnationalism, were nevertheless somehow able to return – unlike the big

---

60 Dupret, see note 38, 4.

61 Particularly during the first half of the year 2000, I often heard similar versions of this comment in the West Bank.

bulk of the refugees. Hence, the relationship between the hegemonic discourse on return and the return migration remains sensitive, and the return migrants are careful to draw from what they perceive as the commonly acceptable normative repertoire when they discuss their return. Otherwise it could appear as if their return would take place at the expense of those who cannot return, one more reminder of the hierarchy of the return[62] and the exclusive nature of any nation-state project.

62 Isotalo, see note 28.

International Law and Precedent

International Law and the Palestinian Right of Return to the State of Israel

*Yaffa Zilbershats**

I. Introduction

Palestinians argue that according to international law, they have a legal right to return to the State of Israel. They refer to the UN General Assembly Resolution 194 (III) of 11 December 1948 to explain what this right entails. Article 11 states the following:

> "... the refugees wishing to return to their homes and live at peace with their neighbours should be permitted to do so at the earliest practical date, and that compensation should be paid for the property of those choosing not to return and for loss of or damage to property which, under principles of international law or in equity, should be made good by the governments or authorities responsible."[1]

A careful reading of this article illustrates that the right of return can be fulfilled in two major ways:

(1). an economic route – which includes restitution of property and/or payment of compensation; and

---

* Dean of the Faculty of Law and Associate Professor of Law, Bar-Ilan University. I would like to thank Prof. Shlomo Avineri for his helpful comments and Prof. Yedidia Z. Stern, Dr. Gidon Sapir and Dr. Shachar Lifshitz for reading the article and supporting my arguments. Thanks to Nimra Goren, Rahel Rimon and Ruth Ben-Zvi for all their assistance. I would likewise wish to express my gratitude, for the referencing of historical sources, to Dr. Shelly Fried, who unfortunately passed away before the finalisation of this publication.

1 A/RES/194 (III) of 11 December 1948.

(2). repatriation – which entails entry into the State of Israel for the purpose of settling there and becoming a citizen of the state.

A refugee may pursue the economic and repatriation routes concurrently. He or she may choose to enter the state, may become a citizen, and could thus recover his/her property and/or compensation for damage to his property. The refugee may also choose to only partially fulfil a right of return. He or she may repatriate to the state without seeking restitution and/or compensation. Alternatively, the refugee may seek restitution and/or compensation without actually settling in the State of Israel and becoming a citizen.

This paper is concerned solely with the repatriation aspect of the right of return. We argue that according to international law, Palestinians have no legal right to repatriate to the State of Israel.

There are two main sources of international law norms: treaty and custom.[2] While it is quite simple to trace treaties, define their scope, and decide who is bound by their norms, it is more difficult to make such determinations when dealing with customary norms of international law. The assertion that a certain norm is binding because of its customary character, places the burden of proof on the proponent of that assertion. The proponent must successfully show that over a considerable period of time, states have followed a general practice, which has conformed to a norm which then takes on the binding aspect of a law.[3] Failure to prove this will prevent the norm from being regarded as binding according to customary international law. A state which from the outset persistently objects to the practice of states and makes it clear that the norm is not binding upon it, will not be bound by that customary norm.[4]

---

[2] Article 38 para. 1 of the Statute of the International Court of Justice, <http://www.icj-cij.org/icjwww/ibasicdocuments/ibasictext/ibasicstatute.htm>. See also Restatement of the Law (Third) The Foreign Relations of the U.S. 1986, Vol. I , § 102, 24 et seq.

[3] According to Article 38 para. 1 (b) of the Statute of the International Court of Justice, ibid., custom is defined as "evidence of a general practice accepted as law." See also Restatement, ibid., comments (b) and (c), 25, and reporters' note 2, 26.

[4] See M.N. Shaw, *International Law*, 1997, 4th ed., 89 et seq.; I. Brownlie, *Principles of Public International Law*, 1990, 4th ed., 10; M. Akehurst, *Akehurst's Modern Introduction to International Law*, 1997, 7th ed., 47 et seq.; R. Jennings/A. Watts (eds), *Oppenheim's International Law*, 1992, 9th ed., 29.

According to the current development of international law, the decisions of the International Court of Justice, like the decisions of other international law tribunals, are not by themselves binding sources of legal norms. The resolutions of international organisations and scholarly works are also non-binding. These sources are merely subsidiary means of determining the rules of law.[5] Additionally, UN Resolutions are also not binding rules of international law. They are considered to be recommendations only.[6] Thus, in recent years, there has been a tendency to assert that a massive *opinio juris* concerning a norm, stated repeatedly in a series of treaties or in a series of UN Resolutions, establishes a customary norm.[7] This assertion will only be made if the various treaties or UN Resolutions set out precisely the same norm. Therefore, customary norm cannot emerge, unless the repetition of a norm is identical.[8] Regardless of this requirement being met and consequently a customary norm being formed, a state which persistently objects to the norm cannot be bound by it.

In the discussion of the Palestinian right to repatriate to the State of Israel, the following sources should be referenced:

(1). UN Resolutions (both of the General Assembly and of the Security Council), which deal with the issue of the Palestinians;

(2). Sources of general international law, which deal with:

a) Human rights law

b) Citizenship and nationality law

c) Refugee law

---

[5] See Article 38 para. 1 of the Statute of the International Court of Justice, see note 2, and Restatement, see note 2, comment (g) and reporters' note 3, 26 et seq.

[6] See Akehurst, see note 4, 378; Shaw, see note 4, 89 et seq.; Brownlie, see note 4, 14, 699.

[7] See Jennings/Watts, see note 4, 48 et seq.; Akehurst, ibid., 40; Shaw, ibid., 75 et seq., 90 et seq.; Restatement, see note 2, comment (i), 26, and reporters' notes 5, 7. In the Nicaragua case, ICJ Reports 1986, 14 et seq. (99-100, para. 188), the court noted that: "… *opinio juris* may, though with all caution, be deduced from, *inter alia*, the attitude of the Parties and the attitude of States towards certain General Assembly Resolutions, and particularly Resolution 2625(xxv) entitled 'Declaration on Principles of International Law Concerning Friendly Relations and Co-operation among States in Accordance with the Charter of the UN.'"

[8] Akehurst, ibid.,41-42; the Nicaragua case, ibid., p. 98, para. 186.

d) Humanitarian law

We will reference the above sources in this article and show that none of them establishes a binding legal right of the Palestinians to repatriate to Israel. Furthermore, the State of Israel is under no legal obligation to enable the repatriation of Palestinians to its territory.

II. UN Resolutions with Special Reference to the Palestinian Issue

General Assembly Resolution 194 (III) of 11 December 1948 was the first resolution to address the Palestinian right of return.

It should be noted again that according to international law, a UN Resolution is merely a recommendation and not a binding legal norm.[9] Furthermore, neither the Israelis nor the Palestinians agreed to abide by Resolution 194 (III). Additionally, neither group considered the adherence to the resolution's recommendations obligatory.[10]

Consequently, today, it is bizarre to call the resolution a binding legal obligation.[11]

---

[9] See note 6.

[10] See K.R. Radley, "The Palestinians Refugees, The Right to Return in International Law", *AJIL* 72 (1978), 586 et seq., 599 et seq.; R. Lapidoth, "Israel and the Palestinians: Some Legal Issues", *Die Friedens-Warte, Journal of International Peace and Organization* 76 (2001), 211 et seq., 235; M. Klein, "Between Right and Realization: The PLO Dialectics of the 'Right to Return'", *Journal of Refugee Studies* 11 (1998), 1 et seq.; D.E. Arzt/K. Zughaib, "Return to the Negotiated Land: The Likelihood and Legality of Population Transfer Between Israel and a Future Palestinian State", *Journal of International Law and Politics* 24 (1992), 1399 et seq., 1437; J. Singer, "No Palestinian 'Return' to Israel", *Human Rights Brief* 8 (2001), 5 et seq. See also the UN Study, "The Right of Return of the Palestinian People", 1 November 1978, ch. V, ST/SG/SER.F/2. There is a Palestinian allegation that Aba Eban, Permanent Representative of Israel to the UN made a statement in the UN where he agreed to Resolution 194 (III). This is inaccurate, see the statement he made on the issue of the refugees on 4 May 1949, in Y. Rosenthal (ed.), *Documents on the Foreign Policy of Israel*, Vol. 4, 1986, 15 et seq.

[11] The Palestinians only began to move towards the acceptance of the UN resolutions during the mid-1980s (in 1985, in an agreement between the PLO and Jordan it was agreed to solve the refugee problem in accordance with the UN resolutions). See Klein, ibid., 4 et seq.; and Arzt/Zughaib, ibid., 1433 et seq.

Moreover, the content of the resolution is not clear and the scope of the alleged obligations it imposes are widely debatable. The resolution states that refugees wishing to return to their homes "should be permitted" to do so.[12] This language is ambigious. The resolution does not state that the refugees have a legal right to return, but only that they should be permitted to do so; apparently with the State of Israel's authorisation.[13]

The resolution includes a condition, that only those refugees, who wish to live in peace with their neighbours, should be permitted to return to Israel. The Palestinians negated the legitimacy of Resolution 194 (III), for decades, because of this added condition. They alleged that the condition indirectly forced them to recognise the existence of the State of Israel, by compelling them to live at peace with the Israelis.[14] Israel, on the other hand, understood this condition as relieving it of an obligation to repatriate Palestinians refugees. Israelis believed that as long as a general peace had not been reached with all the Arabs in the area and the Palestinians' return could jeopardise Israel's security, the allowance of repratriation was not obligatory.[15] The resolution also provides explicitly that the return of the Palestinians should only take place at the "earliest practicable date," which strengthens the above interpretation. Israel insisted that as long as no general peace had been attained with the Arab world, it could not be claimed that such a practical date had arrived.[16] The Palestinians interpreted the words "earliest practicable

---

12 Resolution 194 (III) spoke of "refugees" and not only "Arab refugees," whereas the text of the Report of the UN Mediator Count Bernadotte of 18 September 1948, referred only to "Arab refugees." See E. Benvenisti, *The Right to Return in International Law: An Israeli Perspective*, 2003, 2, note 4, <http://www.tau.ac.il/law/ members/benvenisti/work.html>.

13 Count Bernadotte spoke of "right." See Benvenisti, *idem.*

14 See Radley, see note 10, 600.

15 This statement was made by Prime Minister David Ben Gurion at the meeting of the United Nations Conciliation Commission for Palestine on 7 April 1949. See Y. Freundlich (ed.), *Documents on the Foreign Policy of Israel, Vol. 2*, 1984, 561; and see also Radley, ibid., 610; Y. Tadmor, "The Palestinians Refugees of 1948: The Right to Compensation and Return", *Temp. Int'l & Comp. L. J.* 8 (1994), 403 et seq., 424, notes 203, 204; UN Study, see note 10, ch. V, note 2 and ch. VI, note 6.

16 See Tadmor, ibid., 424; UN Study, ibid., ch. V, text accompanying note 4.

date" to impose an immediate duty upon Israel to allow repatriation of Palestinians.[17]

Resolution 194 (III) does not alone obligate Israel to any specified action, since it is only a recommendation. The language of the resolution is also unclear and debatable. Furthermore, the two parties (the Israelis and the Palestinians) did not accept the resolution when it was adopted by the UN General Assembly.

An additional argument for a Palestinian legal right to return states, that although Resolution 194 (III) is by itself not legally binding, the norms of customary international law, which it expresses, are legally binding.[18] Such an assertion will be disproven later in this paper. We argue that in 1948, when Resolution 194 (III) was adopted, there were no customary international law rules imposing an obligation upon states to allow the repatriation of refugees. In fact, the practice of states at that time supports the opposite contention: that transfer of populations from one state to another was permissible and that there was no obligation upon states to let refugees return to their states of origin.[19]

A careful reading of Resolution 194 (III) reveals that it only bases the requirement of compensation payment, instead of or in addition to, restitution, on the principles of international law and equity. The resolution does not also state that the return of Palestinians is based on principles of international law and equity. Therefore, one cannot argue, that regarding repatriation, Resolution 194 (III) embodies existing customary international law.

Resolutions adopted subsequently to Resolution 194 (III) were not identical to Resolution 194 (III). Already in 1950, General Assembly Resolution 393 (V) offered an additional possible solution. It stated that "... without prejudice to the provisions of paragraph 11 of General Assembly Resolution 194 III of 11 December 1948, the reintegration of the refugees into the economic life of the Near East, either by repatriation or resettlement, is essential..."[20] According to the General Assembly, the refugee problem could be resolved either by repatriation or resettlement. This idea was repeated by the General Assembly in fu-

---

[17] See G.J. Boling, *The 1948 Palestinian Refugees and the Individual Right to Return, An International Law Analysis*, 2001, 13, note 36.

[18] See Boling, ibid., 10 et seq.; J. Quigley, "Displaced Palestinians and a Right to Return", *Harv. Int'l L.J.* 39 (1998), 171 et seq., 211 et seq.

[19] *Infra*, text accompanying notes 34-35.

[20] A/RES/393 (V) of 2 December 1950, emphasis added.

ture resolutions.[21] Nevertheless, these resolutions also referred to Resolution 194 (III), and therefore they were persistently resisted by Israel.[22] Therefore, again, the existence of a customary norm imposing an obligation upon Israel to repatriate Palestinians cannot be inferred.

The Six Day War of 1967 encouraged additional voices in the General Assembly to address the Palestinian issue,[23] as did, even more forcefully, the Yom Kippur War of 1973.[24] The General Assembly stated the right of the Palestinian people (abandoning its former more specific reference to the Palestinian-Arab refugees) to self-determination, national independence, and sovereignty. It also reaffirmed the inalienable right of the Palestinians to return to the homes and property from which they had been displaced and uprooted.[25] Bearing in mind that actual restitution of property might be impossible because of third-party rights, repatriation was not necessarily linked to the restitution aspect. The repatriation contemplated meant entry to any part of former Mandatory Palestine. Once a Palestinian State was established in the West Bank and Gaza, which were in the past part of Mandatory Palestine, it could allow all Palestinians wishing to return to the area to repatriate to it based on their right of return.

Interestingly, the approach adopted by the Security Council is quite different from that of the General Assembly. The first resolution, No. 233 of 6 June 1967, implores the facilitation of "the return of those inhabitants who have fled the area since the outbreak of hostilities."[26] The language of the resolution is soft – "facilitate return" – and there is only reference made to refugees from the West Bank and Gaza Strip, who fled the area due to the 1967 War. The resolution does not refer to the refugees who fled in 1948.

The subsequent resolution is the Security Council Resolution 242 of 22 November 1967.[27] This resolution was adopted again after the 1973 War

---

[21] A/RES/513 (VI) of 26 January 1952, 6 GAOR, Suppl. (No. 20) 12, UN doc. A/2119(1951), *id.*

[22] See Klein, see note 10, 2.

[23] A/RES/2535 (XXIV) A-C of 10 December 1969; A/RES/2672 (XXV) of 8 December 1970; A/RES/2792 (XXVI) A-E of 6 December 1971; A/RES/2963 (XXVII) A-F of 13 December 1972.

[24] A/RES/3089 (XXVIII) A-E of 7 December 1973.

[25] A/RES/3236 (XXIX) of 22 November 1974.

[26] S/RES/233 (1967) of 6 June 1967.

[27] S/RES/242 (1967) of 22 November 1967.

in the Security Council Resolution 338 of 22 October 1973.[28] These resolutions call for the withdrawal of Israeli armed forces from territories occupied in the recent conflict, for the termination of all claims or states of belligerency, and for the respect of the sovereignty of every state in the area (including Israel). The resolution also mentions the "achiev[ement] [of] a just settlement to the refugee problem." This resolution refers to the refugees in general, not only Arab refugees, and the term "just settlement" does not impose any duty to reach a solution based on Resolution 194 (III) of the General Assembly.

Regardless, as previously mentioned, UN Resolutions are merely recommendations and are not considered compulsory legal norms. The issue of the Palestinian refugees was raised in the Peace Treaties Israel signed with Egypt, Jordan and the Palestinians. As opposed to UN Resolutions, these are binding legal sources. All these treaties contain an agreement concerning the right of Palestinian refugees, who had fled the West Bank and Gaza Strip, to return to those areas.[29] These agreements do not provide any of the refugees, who fled in 1967 or 1948, with a right to return to the State of Israel.[30] In 1993, in Oslo, the Palestine Liberation Organization (hereinafter: PLO) acting as the representative of the Palestinian people, agreed in the Israeli-Palestinian Mutual Recognition Agreement to provide several commitments to Israel. These commitments included the PLO's acceptance of UN Security Council Resolutions 242 and 338, and the PLO undertaking to annul the provisions in the Palestinian Covenant, as well as other similar provisions, which called for Israel's destruction.[31]

UN Security Council Resolutions 242 and 338, which the PLO accepted, are the only UN Resolutions referred to in the Oslo Agreements. As such, these Resolutions, and not General Assembly Resolution 194 (III), are the only agreed arrangements to be applicable within the framework of the Israeli-Palestinian permanent status negotiations.

---

[28] S/RES/338 (1973) of 22 October 1973.

[29] See Arts A3, A4 of the Peace Treaty between Israel and Egypt, 1978, UNTS Vol. 1138 Nos 39-45; Article 8 of the Peace Treaty between Israel and Jordan, 1995, *ILM* 34 (1995), 43-66; Declaration of Principles on Interim Self-Government Arrangement between Israel and the Palestinians, 1993, *ILM* 32 (1993), 1525-1544.

[30] See Lapidoth, see note 10, 238; Singer, see note 10, 2.

[31] See Preamble and Article XXX para. 9 of the Israel-Palestine Interim Agreement on the West Bank and the Gaza Strip, 28 September 1995, <http://www.israel. org/mfa/go.asp?MFAH00qa0>.

As mentioned above, UN Security Council Resolution 242 affirms the necessity of achieving a just settlement of the refugee problem, but it does not mention the right of return or any other arrangement as a mandatory solution to the refugee problem.

III. General International Law Norms and the Alleged Palestinian Right to Repatriate to the State of Israel

1. Introductory Comment

Palestinians base their demand to repatriate to the State of Israel on various sources of human rights law. Each of these sources will be elaborated in this section and the reasons why they cannot serve as a legal basis for the Palestinian demand to repatriate to the State of Israel will be explained.

Prior to a detailed analysis of the relevant laws, one should note that the Palestinian refugee problem began in 1948, after the British left and this occurred only three years after the end of World War II and the establishment of the United Nations Organization in 1945. Until 1945, international law did not concern itself too much with the issue of human rights. International law, at that time, was primarily a law that regulated the relations between states and it did not confer rights directly upon individuals, who could claim that such rights were not respected by states. The UN Charter provided for the international protection of human rights in broad and general terms.[32] It was only in 1948 that the General Assembly Universal Declaration of Human Rights established the framework of this protection and provided it with meaning.[33] Consequently, it is apparent that all the human rights, which the Palestinians refer to as international legal sources in support of the right to repatriate to the State of Israel, were not customary international law rights in 1948. The refugee laws that they point to, were developed after World War II.[34] Issues of nationality and citizenship have not been regulated

---

[32] Arts 1 para. 3, 55, 56 of the UN Charter, 1945, <http://www.un.org/about un/charter/index.html>.

[33] Universal Declaration of Human Rights, 1948, A/RES/217 of 10 December 1948.

[34] Convention Relating to the Status of Refugees, 1951, UNTS Vol. 189 No. 137. The UN High Commissioner for Refugees draws his power from the Stat-

by agreed international law norms to this day.[35] Even if such norms had been developed within the second half of the 20th century, it is not clear whether they could have conferred rights upon Palestinians because the alleged damage occurred before these rights existed.

Notwithstanding reservations, the following section will examine the various international law sources upon which the Palestinians base their right to return to the State of Israel. The section will also prove that irrespective of the fact that human rights norms cannot apply to the Palestinian refugee problem since they did not exist when the problem was created, these sources do not provide the Palestinians with such a right.

2. Human Rights Law and the Right of Return

The 1948 Universal Declaration of Human Rights, like other universal and regional human rights conventions concluded by states, provides for the right of return. The scope of the right is debatable in regard to the identity of the holder of the right. While the Universal Declaration and the African Charter provide a right of "return,"[36] all the other instruments mention the right to "enter" the state.[37] While the term "return" only refers to persons who have already been in the state and seek to come back to it, the term "enter" is broader. The latter term confers a right also upon persons who have never been present in the state to now enter its borders for the first time.[38]

---

ute of the General Assembly Resolution 428 (V) of 14 December 1950, <http://www.unhcr.ch/cgi-bin/texis/vtx/home?page=search>.

35 *Infra*, text accompanying notes 56-64.

36 Article 13 para. 2 of The Universal Declaration of Human Rights, see note 33, and Article 12 para. 2 of The African Charter on Human and Peoples' Rights, 1981, O.A.U. Doc. CAB/LEG/67/3 Rev. 5, reprinted in: I. Brownlie, *Basic Documents on Human Rights*, 1992, 3rd ed., 556.

37 Article 12 para. 4 of The International Covenant on Civil and Political Rights, 1966, UNTS Vol. 999 No. 171; Article 3 para. 2 of the Fourth Protocol of the European Convention of Human Rights, 1950, reprinted in: Brownlie, ibid., 347; Article 22 para. 5 of The American Convention on Human Rights, 1969, reprinted in: Brownlie, ibid., 504.

38 See H. Hannum, *The Right to Leave and to Return in International Law and Practice*, 1987, 56.

Another aspect of the dilemma concerning the identity of the persons upon whom the right of return is conferred, relates to the term "his own country."

While the European and American Conventions state that no one shall be deprived of the right to enter the state of which he is a national,[39] the Universal Declaration, like the International Covenant on Civil and Political Rights, mentions the right of a person to enter "his own country."

Scholars have discussed extensively the proper way to interpret the term "his own country." While Jose Ingles and Paul Sieghart[40] insist that the right to enter the state is assigned solely to citizens of that state, Manfred Nowak argues that this term should be interpreted more broadly. The broader interpretation includes permanent residents and others who might not even be permanent residents but who subjectively feel attached to the state and argue that a state is their home.[41] Hurst Hannum believes that the term "his own country" should be interpreted more broadly than the term "the state of which he is a national," but it should not include persons who subjectively see themselves as belonging to the state:

> "The only additional category besides citizenship or nationality to which reference is made in the *travaux* is that of permanent residence. The interpretation advanced by Jagerskiold that Article 12 includes nationals, citizens and permanent residents – thus seems to be the most consistent with the ordinary meaning of the words in the text and with at least portions of the *travaux préparatoires*...
>
> The expansive definition proposed ... finds no support in the *travaux préparatoires* and, if accepted, would be of such wide scope that it would imply a right to 'return' or 'enter' to any number of persons who seek to return 'home'."[42]

---

[39] Article 22 para. 5 of The American Convention of Human Rights, see note 37, provides: "No one can be expelled from the territory of the state of which he is a national or be deprived of the right to enter it."

[40] J. Ingles, Special Rapporteur: Study of Discrimination in Respect to the Right of Everyone to Leave Any Country, Including His Own and to Return to His Country, UN Sales No. 64 XIV 2, UN Doc. E/CN/4 Sub.2/220/Rev.I (1963); P. Sieghart, *The Lawful Rights of Mankind*, 1985, 115.

[41] M. Nowak, *CCPR Commentary - U.N. Covenant on Civil and Political Right*, 1993, 219 et seq.

[42] Hannum, see note 38, 59.

The Human Rights Committee is a body of experts whose task is to supervise the implementation of the Covenant on Civil and Political Rights. It has stated that the right to enter according to the Covenant is attributed to any person who has an effective link to the state. Such a link entails a person living in a particular state, working there and having his family, friends, and other social, as well as, public interests in that state.[43]

The argument, which claims that there exist genuine links between the Palestinian population and the State of Israel, would only be valid, if the Palestinian problem had occurred recently. Today, such an argument, which refers to the links between Palestinian refugees and the State of Israel, is quite artificial. There is no doubt that Palestinians have much stronger effective links to the states, in which they have resided for decades.[44]

Earlier, many scholars commonly believed that the right of return applied to individuals who wished to return, but it did not apply to the mass relocation of populations.[45] This view seems to have changed in recent years and the right of return provided by international human rights law is now also applicable to cases in which a large population wishes to return to the state it has left.[46] Nevertheless, only the citizens, permanent residents and others who can prove genuine links to the

---

[43] UN Doc. CCPR/C/21/Rev.1/Add 9, 2 November 1999, 5 et seq.

In the Nottebohm case (Liechtenstein, Guatemala)(second phase), ICJ Reports 1955, 4 et seq. (23), the court defined nationality as "a legal bond having as its basis a social fact of attachment, a genuine connection of existence, interests and sentiments, together with the existence of reciprocal rights and duties ... [It is the] juridical expression of the fact that the individual upon whom it is conferred is more closely connected with the population of the conferring State than with any other State."

[44] See K. Lawand, "The Right to Return of Palestinians in International Law", *International Journal of Refugee Law* 8 (1996), 532 et seq., 556.

[45] See Lapidoth, see note 10, 235; Benvenisti, see note 12, 5; Lawand, ibid., 542 and notes 43-45; Quigley, see note 18, 211 et seq., notes 232-229; S. Jagerskiold, "The Freedom of Movement", in: L. Henkin (ed.), *The International Bill of Rights,* 1981, 166, 180.

[46] See Lawand, ibid., 543, notes 47-49. Lawand notes that even though the right of return is an individual right, at the end it may be a massive return of many individuals. Therefore there is no reason why not to apply it in the case of a large-scale return. See also Quigley, ibid., 213 et seq., 233 et seq.

state possess the right to return in such larger groups. As mentioned earlier, the right of return does not exist for groups of Palestinians.

One might argue for an exception to the above statement, which is regarding family reunions. If Palestinian refugees are married to Israeli citizens, they possess a right to be united with their spouses and small children.[47] Whether such right to family unification creates necessarily a right of entry of the refugee to the state of his spouse is not clear under international law norms.

The right of return is not an absolute right. It can be both derogated and limited. According to Article 4 of the Covenant on Civil and Political Rights, a state can derogate from considering most of the rights valid, including the right to enter the state, in time of emergency. Emergency has to be officially proclaimed.[48] Such derogation must not exceed the extent, which the exigencies of the situation require.

Israel still does not live at peace with her neighbours. It is under an officially proclaimed state of emergency.[49] As long as this situation exists, human rights law does not impose upon Israel any obligation to enable the return of people who might threaten its security.

Article 12 para. 4 of the Covenant on Civil and Political Rights provides that "[n]o one shall arbitrarily be deprived of the right to enter his own country." Prevention of entry is not considered arbitrary when it is imposed upon a person as a punishment for a crime by a court of law as an alternative to the punishment of arrest.[50] The common view is that any other restriction on the right of entry is arbitrary and represents a violation of that right.[51] One may consider such a narrow interpretation

---

47 Article 16 para. 3 of the Universal Declaration on Human Rights, see note 33; Article 10 para. 1 of the International Covenant of Economic, Social and Cultural Rights, 1966, UNTS Vol. 993 No. 3; Article I 16 of the European Social Charter, 1961, ETS No. 035, §I, Art.16; Arts 18 para. 1, 27 para. 1 of the African Charter on Human and People's Rights, see note 36.

48 International Covenant of Civil and Political Rights, see note 37.

49 The Declaration on Emergency State of 15 May 1948 went on until 1997. Beginning with 1997, according to Article 49 of the Basic Law: the Government, 1992, S.H. 1396, 214, and the Basic Law that substituted it (Article 38 of the Basic Law: The Government, 2001, S.H. 1780, 158), a state of emergency should be declared every year – and so it is practically done.

50 See Nowak, see note 41, 219; Y. Zilbershats, *The Human Right to Citizenship*, 2002, 48.

51 See Zilbershats, *idem*; Lawand, see note 44, 547 et seq. It should be noted that "arbitrary" in Article 12 para. 4 of the Covenant of Civil and Political

of the limitation of the right of return as proper, as long as the right is not applied to masses of people. But once the scope of the right is enlarged and it is applied to masses of refugees and displaced persons, one may rethink what the proper limitations of that right should be. A return to the State of Israel of all, or most people who consider themselves Palestinian refugees, may hamper the right of the Israeli people to self-determination. This is a right that the Israelis possess like any other people of a nation and which is declared in Article 1 of the Covenant on Civil and Political Rights. Therefore, the restriction of the rights of the Palestinian refugees to return to the State of Israel may not be arbitrary.

3. The Right of Return and the Laws of Citizenship

Palestinians, who resided in British Palestine before 1948, were Palestine citizens, like any other Jewish or Arab resident.[52] Consequently, Palestinian refugees argue that they must be granted Israeli citizenship. They claim that their right to Israeli citizenship is supported by the norms of international law, which deal with the issue of citizenship.[53] Israeli citizenship naturally allows its holders to legally enter Israel.[54]

Palestinian refugees feel that Israel denied them Israeli citizenship to prevent their possible repatriation. Furthermore, they claim that this deprivation was arbitrary and therefore a violation of their right to return, though this claim is untrue.[55] Israel did not revoke the Palestinian refugees' Palestine citizenship. This citizenship simply expired once the British terminated their Mandate over Palestine on 15 May 1948. The

---

Rights is considered a narrower limitation than the limitation on the right to leave any country and the right to liberty of movement within a state, that is provided in Article 12 para. 3 of this covenant.

[52] A. Zimmermann, "The Nationality of the Inhabitants of the Palestinian Autonomous Territories", in: M. Tabory/A. Shapira (eds), *New Political Entities in Public and Private International Law: with special reference to the Palestinian entity*, 1999, 231, 233 et seq., 234, note 16; Quigley, see note 18, 208 et seq.

[53] See Quigley, ibid., 210. Zimmermann, *idem*, analyses the Palestinian citizenship but does not necessarily come to the same conclusion as Quigley does. See Boling, see note 17, 21.

[54] See Boling, ibid., 24, notes 75-79.

[55] Ibid., 24 et seq., notes 80-81; Lawand, see note 44, 555.

relevant issue is whether, according to international law, Israel has an obligation to grant citizenship to the Palestinians who fled its territory.

The right to citizenship (or the right to nationality)[56] is an ambigious and under-developed right in international law. In Article 15 of the Universal Declaration of Human Rights the right is stated in a very general manner: "everyone has a right to a nationality ..." Scholars commonly view the right, conferred by Article 15 of the Universal Declaration, as weakly drafted. They also believe that Article 15 fails to impose a clear duty upon states to ensure that every person in every state shall possess a nationality.[57]

It should be noted, that neither the European Convention on Human Rights of 1950,[58] nor the 1966 International Covenant on Civil and Political Rights[59] impose upon states any obligation to grant nationality. Furthermore, the Convention on the Status of Refugees (1951)[60] and the Convention Relating to the Status of Stateless Persons (1954)[61] also do not impose any such duty upon states. The International Convention on the Elimination of All Forms of Racial Discrimination (1966) merely sets out state parties' broad undertaking to prohibit and eliminate all forms of racial discrimination. Most notably, the document addresses the enjoyment of rights, including the right to nationality.[62] The general, soft language of this recommendation is similar to that of the European Convention on Nationality (1997).[63] No general international law con-

---

[56] These two terms are considered to have the same meaning and may be used interchangeably. See Zilbershats, see note 50, 4 et seq.

[57] H.F. Van Pamhys, *The Role of Nationality in International Law*, 1959, 222; P. Weis, *Nationality and Statelessness in International Law*, 1979, 198-199; J.M.M. Chan, "The Right to a Nationality as a Human Right", *HRLJ* 12 (1991), 1 et seq.

[58] ETS No. 105.

[59] See note 37.

[60] See note 34.

[61] UNTS Vol. 360 No. 117.

[62] UNTS Vol. 660 No. 195.

[63] ETS No. 166. Article 5 para. 1 of the convention provides: "The rules of a State Party on Nationality shall not contain distinctions or include any practice which amount to discrimination on the grounds of sex, religion, race, colour or national or ethnic origin."

vention imposes a duty upon states to grant citizenship in any particular manner.[64]

International law has additional conventions, which deal specifically with issues of citizenship and nationality.[65] These conventions also do not confer a general obligation upon states to grant citizenship. They only impose a duty on states to confer citizenship upon stateless persons, basing citizenship on the place of birth of the stateless person and making it conditional upon his reaching a certain age and residing in his state of birth.[66] In some circumstances citizenship of stateless persons is dependent upon the status of their parents.[67]

Most general international law instruments do not impose an obligation upon states to grant citizenship and treaties, which deal specifically with issues of citizenship, have not emerged with any broad or clear rules. This is true because state leaders still tend to believe, that it is their sovereign prerogative to decide who may aquire their states' citizenship. International human rights law has not yet restricted a state's sovereignty, by imposing upon it a duty to grant citizenship.

This is the legal context today and therefore this was, of course, the legal context in 1948. No state, including the State of Israel, was under any international law obligation to grant citizenship to any person.

---

[64] There is one exception: Article 20 para. 2 of The American Convention on Human Rights, see note 37, which provides that "Every person has the right to the nationality of the state in whose territory he was born if he does not have the right to any other nationality."

[65] Convention on Certain Questions Relating to the Conflict of Nationality Laws, 1930, L.N.Doc.C.24M.13 1931 V; Convention on Nationality of Married Women, 1957, UNTS Vol. 309 No. 65; Convention on the Reduction of Statelessness, 1961, UNTS Vol. 989 No. 175; Article 3 of Declaration of the Rights of the Child, 1959, A/RES/1386 (XIV) of 20 November 1959; Article II of the International Convention on the Suppression and Punishment of the Crime of Apartheid, 1973, UNTS Vol. 1015 No. 243; Article 9 of the Convention on the Elimination of All Forms of Discrimination Against Women, 1979, UNTS Vol. 1249 No. 13; Arts 7, 8 of the Convention on the Rights of the Child, 1989, UNTS Vol. 1577 No. 3.

[66] Harvard Draft Convention on Nationality, 1929, *AJIL* 23 (Special Suppl. 1929), 11; Convention on the Reduction of Statelessness, 1961, ibid.

[67] Convention on Certain Questions Relating to the Conflict of Nationality Laws, see note 65.

Article 10 of the Convention on the Reduction of Statelessness (1961)[68] and the later European Convention on Nationality (1997), both deal with the question of citizenship and succession of states. Although these conventions came into effect long after 1948, they provide relevant ideas. The European Convention on Nationality (1997)[69] adopts the approach of the 1961 Convention. It conveys that in cases of state succession, state parties to the Convention shall endeavour to regulate matters relating to nationality, by agreement among themselves and where applicable, in their relations with other states. In the event that no agreement is reached, states shall endeavour to avoid statelessness. Each state shall take into consideration the genuine and effective link of a person with the state. They shall also consider the person's habitual residence at the time of state succession, his will and his territorial origin.[70]

In cases of succession of states, these conventions call for a regime to be flexible in dealing with issues of citizenship. They recommend that states reach a voluntary agreement. When an agreement cannot be reached, a wide margin of discretion is left to states to resolve problems of statelessness. Issues which deal with the past, such as place of birth and place of residence at the time of state succession, should be balanced against issues relating to the present link of the person to the state.

The issue of the succession of states in general, and in relation to matters of citizenship in particular, became a prominent issue in the last decade of the 20th century. Following the dissolution of the Soviet Union and the formation of new states within its territory, the matter caught the interest of many people. This historical event influenced the International Law Commission's adoption of the Draft Articles on Nationality of Natural Persons in Relation to the Succession of States.[71] The Draft was adopted by a General Assembly Resolution,[72] but has still not become a binding international law agreement. The Draft does not codify any customary international law rule on the matter because, as shown in this article, international law has not yet developed to the

---

68 See note 65.

69 See note 63.

70 Arts 18, 19 of the European Convention on Nationality, ibid.

71 Report of the International Law Commission, 1999, ch. IV, <http://www.un.org/law/ilc/reports/1999english/chp.4.htm>.

72 A/RES/55/153 of 12 December 2000.

stage where it encompasses any agreed customary norms on the obligation of states to grant citizenship in general, and in relation to the succession of states, in particular.

The last paragraph of the Preamble of the Draft states that the General Assembly is: "Convinced of the need for the codification and progressive development of the rules of international law concerning nationality in relation to the succession of states ..." This proves that the International Law Commission was aware that its task was not limited to codify customary existing norms. It knew that it also had a duty to establish new norms, which were not yet adhered to by the international community. An examination of Article 14 para. 2 of the Draft, which provides for the return of people who were forced to leave their habitual residence because of events connected with succession of states,[73] and Article 5 of the Draft, which provides for the acquisition of the nationality of the successor state by people having their habitual residence in the territory affected by the succession,[74] shows that the Draft's rules differ from the rules of the European Convention on Nationality and the Convention on the Reduction of Statelessness. Accordingly, the provisions of the Draft cannot be binding rules of customary international law.

4. The Right of Return in Refugee Law

After World War II, international law developed treaties, which dealt with the rights of refugees and stateless persons. The major instrument handling these issues was the Convention Relating to the Status of Refugees (1951).[75] The main defence afforded to refugees was the right of *non-refoulement*. According to this right, "[n]o Contracting State shall expel or return (refouler) a refugee in any manner whatsoever to the frontiers of territory where his life or freedom would be threat-

---

[73] Article 14 para. 2 provides: "A state concerns shall take all necessary measures to allow persons concerns who, because of the events connected with the succession of states, were forced to leave their habitual residence on its territory to return thereto."

[74] Article 5 provides: "Subject to the provisions of the present draft articles, persons concerned having their habitual residence in the territory affected by the succession of states are perused to acquire the nationality of the successor state on the date of such succession."

[75] See note 34.

ened..."[76] The state of refuge is permitted to send the refugee to a third state that is willing to grant admittance and provide refuge, but only if the latter state is also committed to the obligation of *non-refoulement*.[77]

The 1951 Refugee Convention does not require that refugees be granted permanent asylum in the sense of permanent admission to the state of refuge. The Convention also does not explicitly impose upon the states of origin the obligation to repatriate nationals who have found refuge in other states.

Article 1 (c)(5) of the Convention may be read as indirectly imposing an obligation upon refugees to return to their state of origin, when the reasons for their right to asylum cease to exist. This article reads: "This Convention shall cease to apply to any person falling under the terms of Section A if: he can no longer, because the circumstances in connection with which he has been recognised as a refugee have ceased to exist, continue to refuse to avail himself of the protection of the country of his nationality."[78]

Nevertheless, the message of Article 1(c)(5) was not visible in states' practices. For decades after World War II, states of refuge refrained from returning refugees to their state of origin. Instead, despite the absence of a legal obligation to do so, they granted refugees permission to stay within their borders permanently and gave them the opportunity to become citizens of the state.[79] The Refugee Convention was neither interpreted to include a right of return nor was it implemented with this concept in mind. Consequently, it is not surprising that the 1967 Protocol to the Refugee Convention, also failed to mention the right of return or the concept of repatriation.[80]

---

[76] Article 33 of the Refugee Convention, ibid.

[77] Arts 32 and 33 of the Refugee Convention, ibid.

[78] Ibid.

[79] E. Rosand, "The Right to Return Under International Law Following Mass Dislocation: The Bosnia Precedent", *Mich. J. Int'l L.* 19 (1998), 1091 et seq., 1116 et seq.; J. Hathaway, "The Meaning of Repatriation", *International Journal of Refugee Law* 9 (1997), 551 et seq., 551 et seq.; S. Takahashi, "UNHCR Handbook on Voluntary Repatriation, The Emphasis of Return over Protection", *International Journal of Refugee Law* 9 (1997), 593 et seq., 597 et seq.

[80] Protocol Relating to the Status of Refugees, 1967, <http://www.unhchr.ch/html/menu3/b/o_p_ref.htm>.

Another major instrument, which addresses refugee problems, is the Statute of the High Commissioner for Refugees. This statute was adopted by the General Assembly in December 1950 and establishes the office of the High Commissioner for Refugees.[81] Article 1 of the statute defines the aims of the Office of the High Commissioner: to "... facilitate the voluntary repatriation of refugees or their assimilation within new national communities." The statute actually offers three alternative ways of solving the problem of refugees: voluntary repatriation, absorption and resettlement.[82] Also, the statute conveys that there is no duty imposed upon states to confine themselves strictly to the solution of voluntary repatriation. Over the years, the High Commissioner for Refugees has tried to apply the solution of repatriation as widely as possible and has considered it to be the preferred course of action. Nevertheless, since repatriation is not a legal right held by refugees, it could not be imposed by the Commissioner upon the refugees' states of origin without the latter's consent. Consequently, the Commissioner encouraged repatriation agreements to be signed between himself, the states of refuge, and the states of origin.[83]

---

[81] See note 34.

[82] James Hathaway comments that there should be a mandatory duty upon refugees to repatriate to their state of origin. He advocates a clear rule stating that asylum be temporary and that refugees be required to return to their state of origin because in the last decade of the 20th century, states ceased to consider refugees as immigrants or, more accurately, were reluctant to allow refugees asylum for fear that they would stay permanently in the state. No right of return practice exists, and therefore no rules about how to implement the right exist either. There are no answers to basic questions regarding the right, such as when is the proper time to return, what safeguards must exist, who will supervise the implementation of those safeguards, what happens if the refugee refuses to return etc. See Hathaway, see note 79, 554 et seq. See also Takahashi, see note 79, 601 et seq.; S. Bagshaw, "Benchmarks or Deutschmarks? Determining the Criteria for the Repatriation of Refugees to Bosnia and Herzegovina", *International Journal of Refugee Law* 9 (1997), 566 et seq., 573 et seq., 591.

[83] M. Zieck, "UNHCR 'Special Agreement'", in: I. Klabbers/R. Lefebre (eds), *Essays on the Law of Treaties – a Collection of Essays in Honour of Bert Vierdag*, 1998, 171, 182 et seq.; see also Arzt/Zughaib, see note 10, 1450.

5. Return According to Humanitarian Law and International Criminal Law

Humanitarian law deals with the protection of combatants' and civilians' rights during wartime and sometimes even in the aftermath of war.

International humanitarian law developed extensively after World War II in two ways:

(1). It augmented the protection of combatants and civilians in the Four Geneva Conventions of 1949, as well as in the two 1977 Additional Protocols to the Conventions.

(2). It imposed individual responsibility upon persons who committed grave breaches of the Geneva Conventions, crimes against peace, war crimes and crimes against humanity, and in turn established international criminal law.

Repatriation of post-war refugees is not explicitly stated in humanitarian law. It cannot be inferred from Article 46 of the Hague Regulations, which states that "[f]amily honour and rights must be respected,"[84] or from Article 26 of the Fourth Geneva Convention, which states that "[e]ach Party to the conflict shall facilitate inquiries made by members of families dispersed owing to the war, with the object of renewing contact with one another and meeting, if possible."[85] These articles make family reunion after the war a humanitarian goal, but they do not clarify how this reunion should occur. Regardless, they do not impose a duty upon the state of origin to allow repatriation.

Humanitarian law mentions two specific categories of persons upon whom it confers the right to repatriate: prisoners of war[86] and internees[87]. However, no general rule of repatriation, which considers all refugees, can be inferred.

Article 6 para. 4 of the Fourth Geneva Convention states that "protected persons whose release, repatriation, or re-establishment may take place after such dates [the dates that the Convention ceases to be ap-

---

[84] Regulations Concerning the Laws and Customs of War on Land, The Hague, 18 October 1907, USTS 539, *AJIL* 2 (1908), Supp. 90.

[85] Convention (IV) Relative to the Protection of Civilian Persons in Time of War, 12 August 1949, UNTS Vol. 75 No. 287.

[86] Article 20 of Hague Regulations, see note 84; Article 118 of Geneva Convention (IV), ibid.

[87] Article 134 of IV Geneva Convention (IV), ibid.

plied] shall meanwhile continue to benefit by the present Convention ..." Article 158 para. 3 of the same Convention provides that a state cannot denounce the Convention until operations connected with the release, repatriation and re-establishment of the persons protected by the Convention have been carried out. The existence of a general right of refugees to repatriate cannot be inferred from these two articles of the Convention. In contrast, it can be established that upon the explicit provision of Conventions for repatriation, as in the case of prisoners of war and internees, a state cannot denounce the Convention or stop applying it, until such persons repatriate.

The Hague Regulations and the Fourth Geneva Convention, which deal with occupied territories, are irrelevant to the case of the Palestinian refugees who fled in 1948. The refugees left the State of Israel, which was not an occupied territory at the time. Therefore, neither Article 43 of the Hague Regulations, which deals with an occupying powers' limits of power in an occupied territory, nor Article 49 of the Geneva Convention, which forbids deportations from an occupied territory, should be applied when dealing with refugees who left the State of Israel in 1948.[88] There exist explicit agreements, which allow refugees who left the West-Bank and Gaza Strip after the war of 1967, to return to those areas. Nevertheless, these refugees cannot return to the State of Israel.[89]

Deportations and forced expulsions are forbidden according to international criminal law even if the territory expelled from is not occupied territory. This principle is enshrined in the Charter of London of 1945 establishing the International Military Tribunal at Nuremberg,[90] Article

---

88 See Radley, see note 10, 597 et seq.

89 See Peace Treaty between Israel and Egypt, see note 29; Peace Treaty between Israel and Jordan, ibid.; Declaration of Principles on Interim Self-Government Arrangement between Israel and the Palestinians, ibid. See also J.R. Weiner, "The Palestinian Refugees 'Right to Enter' and the Peace Process", *Boston College International and Comparative Law Review* 20 (1997), 1 et seq., 3 et seq.; G. Halley, "Issues Confronting the Return of Palestinian Arab Refugees after the 1993 Declaration of Principles on Interim Self-Government Arrangements", *Geo. Immigration Law Journal* 8 (1994), 149 et seq., 152 et seq.

90 Article 6 (c) of The Charter of the International Military Tribunal (IMT) in Agreement for the Prosecution and Punishment of the Major War Criminals of the European Axis (London Agreement), 8 August 1945, UNTS Vol. 82 No. 280.

147 of the Fourth Geneva Convention of 1949,[91] the Statute of the International Tribunal for the Former Yugoslavia (1993),[92] the Statute of the International Tribunal for Rwanda (1994),[93] and the Rome Statue of the International Criminal Court (1998).[94]

These prohibitions against deportations cannot be applied as legal sources imposing a duty upon Israel to repatriate Palestinian refugees to her territory. The historical facts regarding the creation of the Palestinian refugee problem in 1948 are controversial. Israel insists that it did not expel the Arabs from its territory and instead claims that they chose to flee; either because they were persuaded to do so by neighbouring Arab states or because they feared the independent State of Israel. They joined the Arab elite that had already fled Israel at the end of 1947, after General Assembly Resolution 181 created the partition of the British Mandate Palestine into Jewish and Arab states. Contrary to what Israel claims, the Arabs insist that they were forcibly expelled from areas controlled by Israel.[95]

It is important to note that the Arab population's flight from Israel occurred concurrent to the emigration of Jews from neighbouring Arab states. The Jews were either expelled or left because fear motivated them to do so. Many Jews found refuge in Israel and received citizenship there.[96] Therefore, the actual result of the political changes in the Middle East and the war in 1948 was a transfer of populations. Following the establishment of the State of Israel, Jews went to Israel from

---

91 See note 84.

92 Article 2 of the Statute of the International Tribunal for the Prosecution of Persons Responsible for Serious Violations of the International Humanitarian Law Committed in the Territory of Former Yugoslavia since 1991, S/RES/827 (1993) of 25 May 1993.

93 Article 3 of Statute of the International Tribunal for the Prosecution of Persons Responsible for Genocide and Other Serious Violations of the International Humanitarian Law Committed in the Territory of Rwanda and Rwandan Citizens Responsible for Genocide and Other Such Violations Committed in the Territory of Neighbouring States between 1 Jan. 1994 and 31 Dec. 1994, S/RES/955 (1994) of 8 November 1994.

94 Article 7 of Rome Statute of the International Criminal Court, 17 July 1998, UN Doc. A/CONF.183/9, *ILM* 37 (1998), 999.

95 See Radley, see note 10, 589 et seq.; Lawand, see note 44, 536 et seq.; L. Takkenberg, *The Status of Refugees in International Law*, 1998, 334; Weiner, see note 89, 15 et seq.; Arzt/Zughaib, see note 10, 1421 et seq.

96 *Encyclopaedia Judaica, Vol.* 2, 1971, 335-336.

Arab states and the Arabs who lived in British Palestine left for Arab states.

It should be stressed that, in that period, the transfer of populations in consequence of political changes was not considered to be wrong according to international law. For example, the agreement adopted by Greece and Turkey in their 1923 peace treaty resulted in an exchange of populations. This exchange occurred after a long war between the two states, which ended in the defeat of Greece. Two million Greeks, who held Turkish citizenship, were obligated to leave for Greece and half a million Turks were required to move to Turkey.[97] Another example, which illustrates how states solve the problem of post-war ethnic tensions by the transfer of populations is the Potsdam Declaration made by the Allied powers in 1945. It transferred millions of Germans, who lived in Eastern Europe, Austria, Poland, Czechoslovakia and Hungary to Germany.[98]

Another transfer of population occurred in 1947. British India was divided into two states (India and Pakistan) when the British left the region. The division was in order to separate the Hindus (India) from the Moslems (Pakistan). This split resulted in a massive transfer of populations. Today, such a practice would be regarded as ethnic cleansing and would be absolutely prohibited. At the time however, it was a welcomed idea.[99]

Although the 1948 Arab refugees' narrative is one of forcible expulsion from their homes, in reality their group underwent a population transfer. Arabs insist that forcible expulsion was forbidden in 1948 and that it was already considered a crime against humanity.[100] Therefore, they

---

97 Convention Concerning the Exchange of Populations, 30 July 1923, Greece-Turkey, LNTS Vol. 28 No. 11, reprinted in 2 *The Treaties of Peace, 1919-1923*, 1924, 653. See Benvenisti, see note 12, 7; and E. Benvenisti/E. Zamir, "Private Claims to property Rights in the Future Israeli-Palestinian Settlement", *AJIL* 89 (1995), 295 et seq., 321 et seq.; and Rosand, see note 79, 1115 et seq.

98 The Berlin (Potsdam) Conference Protocol, 1 August 1945, section XII, reprinted in: C.I. Bevans, *Treaties and Other International Agreements of the United States of America 1776-1949, Vol. 3*, 1969, 1207, <http://www.yale.edu/lawweb/avalon/decade/decade17.htm>; see Benvenisti, ibid., 7 et seq.; and Benvenisti/Zamir, ibid., 322; and A. De Zayas, *Nemesis at Potsdam,* 1990, chs. 1, 5-6.

99 See Benvenisti, ibid., 8; Benvenisti/Zamir, ibid., 323.

100 This is based on the principles of the IMT, see note 90.

claim that Israel is under an absolute obligation to allow repatriation of Palestinian refugees.

This allegation is not supported by international law. Although international law prohibits forced expulsion, the remedies it provides against such expulsions do not include an explicit or implicit duty upon a state to repatriate expellees. A state, which forcibly expels people from its territory, bears state responsibility for its actions and the perpetrators of the expulsion bear individual responsibility.[101] Nevertheless, there are no provisions in international law, which require a state to offer repatriation as a remedy for a wrongful act of expulsion.

State practice proves this assertion. Examples, which support the assertion, are remedies accorded to refugees after World War II. The perpetrators of crimes in World War II, including the crime of forced deportation and expulsion, were prosecuted in both domestic and international tribunals. In many cases such individuals were convicted and punished. Germany had to eventually pay compensation to the victims, but it was not obligated to repatriate refugees to its territory. This duty was also not imposed later on any Eastern European states. Jews sued to be compensated for their lost property in Eastern Europe, but they did not seek repatriation to the states from which they had been expelled. Had they wanted to return, there was no legal rule imposing upon the various States they fled from the duty to open their borders for them.

Professor Eyal Benvenisti[102] points out two more recent attempts to solve the refugee problem in a recent article. The approaches are different from those in the previous examples. The two attempts to reach a solution regard events in Bosnia and Herzegovina and in Cyprus.

The Dayton Peace Agreement of 1995, which ended the conflict in Bosnia and Herzegovina, explicitly states (in its Annex VII) the right of refugees and displaced persons to return to their homes.[103] Annex 7, Article I states that "[a]ll refugees and displaced persons have the right freely to return to their homes of origin ... The parties shall ensure that

---

[101] Here lies the idea of individual responsibility, additional to state responsibility. This means that the performers will stand trial. The basis for this principle lies in the IMT, Article 6, ibid.

[102] See note 12.

[103] General Framework Agreement for Peace in Bosnia and Herzegovina, 14 December 1995, UN Doc/1995/999, Ch. 1, Article I para. 1 of Annex 7, <http://www.ohr.int/docu/d951208a.htm>.

refugees and displaced persons are permitted to return in safety, without risk of harassment, intimidation, persecution or discrimination, particularly on account of their ethnic origin, religious belief or political opinion."[104]

The Dayton Peace Agreement represents the current trend of the international community to call for repatriation when people leave their homes as a result of wars in which ethnic cleansing takes place.[105]

However, there is a big difference between stating that repatriation must occur and making the process a reality. Many refugees and displaced persons, who have international legitimacy to return, do not wish to do so. It is also possible that they cannot fulfil the right because of domestic legal constraints, because they still fear human rights violations, or because they would not be able to earn a living in the areas which they fled.[106]

The statement recently published by the United Nations High Commissioner for Refugees reveals that the obstacles to the fulfilment of the

---

[104] Ibid.

[105] J. Quigley, "Repairing the Consequences of Ethnic Cleansing", *Pepperdine Law Review* 22 (2001), 33 et seq., 33 et seq.; Rosand, see note 79, 1098, 1131 et seq. For the call for return see for example Security Council Resolution 1034 (1995) which states in Article 18: "Also urges all the parties to the conflict in the territory of former Yugoslavia to fully cooperate with these efforts with the view to create conditions, conductive to the repatriation and return of refugees and displaced persons in safety and dignity." Security Council Resolution 1491 (2003), dealing with the former Yugoslavia, emphasises in the preamble that "... a comprehensive and coordinated return of refugees and displaced persons throughout the region continues to be crucial to lasting peace." Security Council Resolution 1239 (1999) dealing with refugees from Kosovo, reaffirms in Article 4 "the right of all refugees and displaced persons to return to their homes in safety and in dignity." In connection with the Republic of Tajikistan too, the Security Council in Resolution 999 (1995), Article 14, "[w]elcomes the obligation assumed by the Government of the Republic of Tajikistan to assist the return and reintegration of refugees as well as the obligations by the parties to cooperate in ensuring the voluntary return, in dignity and safety, of all refugees and displaced persons to their homes." A similar attitude may be found in recent decisions of the Security Council regarding Georgia. See Resolution 1462 (2003), S/RES/1462 (2003) of 30 January 2003, Article 14, and Resolution 1494 (2003), S/RES/1494 (2003) of 30 July 2003, Arts 9, 10, 14, 15, 17.

[106] Rosand, see note 79, 1101 et seq., 1111; M. Cox, "The Right to Return Home: International Intervention and Ethnic Cleansing in Bosnia and Herzegovina", *ICLQ* 47 (1998), 599 et seq.; Bagshaw, see note 82, 573 et seq.

right of return still exist and that many refugees have not yet repatriated.[107]

In the aftermath of the events in Cyprus, the approach to reach a solution was different than in the case of Bosnia and Herzegovina. As a consequence of the conflict in Cyprus between the Greek-Cypriots and the Turkish-Cypriots, which began in 1963, Turkey invaded the northern part of Cyprus in 1974. Greek Cypriots who lived in the northern part of the island left their homes and moved to the south. Their homes were taken over by Turkish-Cypriots, who moved northwards from the south.

On 1 April 2003, Kofi Annan, the Secretary-General of the UN, issued a report on his mission to Cyprus.[108] In the report Annan distinguished the Cyprus case from that of Bosnia and Herzegovina and explained why repatriation and restitution did not seem suitable for Cyprus:

"In making any suggestions, I took into account these developments and the positions adapted recently by the UN and the international community in the former Yugoslavia, but also the fact that events in Cyprus happened 30 to 40 years ago and that the displaced people ... have had to rebuild their lives and their economies during this time."[109]

In accordance with this rationale, Kofi Annan suggested the establishment of a property board that would give priority to claims made by current occupiers, who had themselves been displaced and now wished to exchange property titles. The reinstatement of property was allowed only to a limited extent, namely, 20 per cent of the residences and land in any village or town and no more than a total of 10 per cent reinstatement of the residences and land in either constituent state. Annan concluded with the remark that "the territorial adjustment described below strides a fair balance between competing legitimate interests and individual human rights and respects the principle of bi-zonality and international law."[110]

The Cyprus case proves that according to international law there is no rule which imposes a duty to solve the problems of refugees and dis-

---

[107] UNHCR General Report 2002 on the Federal Republic of Yugoslavia including Kosovo, on Croatia and on Bosnia and Herzegovina, <http://www.unhcr.ch/cgi-bin/texis/vtx/home>.

[108] Report of the Secretary-General on his mission of good offices in Cyprus, 1 April 2003, S/2003/398, <http://www.un.org/Docs/sc/sgrep03.html>.

[109] Ibid., 24.

[110] *Idem.*

placed persons by returning them to their original homes. If such a compulsory rule had existed, Kofi Annan would not have been able to offer such a proposal. In cases where ethnic conflict has caused the movement of populations, and no agreement has been possible for decades, it is unrealistic to demand restoration of the past. The situation is different if an agreement is reached immediately after hostilities end. In such cases, like in the case of Bosnia and Herzegovina, the past is recent and it is logical at least to try to ensure that each person returns to his home and property, although such attempts have been shown to be impracticable in far too many cases.

Kofi Annan also mentioned in his report the recognition of bi-zonality as a basis for avoiding the return of people to earlier homes. Bi-zonality can be a solution in the Israeli-Palestinian conflict, once a Palestinian State is established and the Palestinians exercise their right of return to the Palestinian State.

IV. Conclusion

Return, in the context of repatriation, is not a legal right according to the present development of international law. It is not enshrined in general human rights law, the law of nationality, the law of refugees or humanitarian law. Accordingly, Palestinians cannot speak of a "right" to return based on international law.

Palestinians can neither base a right to repatriate on international law documents which deal specifically with the Palestinian problem. These documents are General Assembly or Security Council Resolutions which are not binding legal sources, but merely offer recommendations. The content of the resolutions is controversial and they offer alternative solutions to repatriation, such as resettlement and a "just solution."

Any negotiations between Israel and the Palestinians should take into consideration that repatriation of Palestinians to the State of Israel is not imposed upon Israel by international law.

The Question of "Timing" in Evaluating Israel's Duty Under International Law to Repatriate the 1948 Palestinian Refugees

*Gail J. Boling**

I. Introduction

In July 2003, I participated in the Max Planck Institute's International Conference on Israel and the Palestinian Refugees in Heidelberg, Germany. For that symposium, I submitted a 50-page monograph that I had written previously, titled *The 1948 Palestinian Refugees and the Individual Right of Return: An International Law Analysis.*[1] That paper is rather detailed, with full legal citations, and there is no need (or space) to repeat the same arguments here. However, the basic thesis argued in the monograph is that the 1948 Palestinian refugees have a legal *right* – based upon customary international law as existing in 1948 and as strengthened through the progressive development of international law since then – to return to their homes of origin in what is now the State of Israel. If my assertion is correct, then the existence of such a

---

* Gail J. Boling is a U.S.-licensed attorney and legal researcher working in the West Bank, including in association with Birzeit University's Institute of Law and the Palestine Yearbook of International Law, as Assistant Editor. J.D., Ohio State University College of Law; B.A., University of Chicago; member of the Illinois Bar.

1 The monograph was published by BADIL Resource Centre for Palestinian Residency and Refugee Rights, in Bethlehem. It is available on the BADIL web site at: <http://www.badil.org/Publications/Legal_Papers/RoR48.pdf>. The monograph has been translated into Arabic. Shorter versions of the monograph have also been published by BADIL as "briefs" in English, Arabic and Hebrew.

right would necessarily imply the existence of a corresponding legal *duty* on the part of Israel to readmit the 1948 refugees, as a matter of international law (as distinguished from power politics, or *realpolitik*).[2]

At the symposium in Heidelberg, I was pleased to receive extensive comments[3] on my monograph. I would like to take this opportunity to reply to one of the most recurring challenges to my argument raised at the symposium – the issue of "timing" in evaluating the existence *vel non* of what I assert is the duty owed by Israel to repatriate the 1948 Palestinian refugees.

The objection essentially runs as follows: what Israel (and its pre-state paramilitary predecessor organisations, both regular and irregular) did in 1948 in stampeding Palestinians from their residences in systematic military campaigns that succeeded in driving over 700,000 Palestinians outside what eventually became the 1949 armistice lines (i.e., the current *de facto* borders for Israel), and then subsequently refusing to allow those Palestinians to return to their homes (refusing to readmit them), *was permissible behaviour for states back in 1948.* (Actually these events spanned 1947 to 1949, but we will use 1948 for shorthand.) This argument assumes that refusing to repatriate civilian refugees was not expressly prohibited by positive international law *binding upon Israel in 1948*, whether customary or treaty-based. Therefore, it is asserted, Israel was permitted, as a matter of law, to refuse to readmit the refugees (questions of morality aside, and some supporters of the Israeli position will concede that the 55-year-long forced exile of the 1948 Palestinian refugees is unfortunate from a humanitarian point of view, at least for the refugees).

It is interesting to note that the question of "timing" is very much embedded in this argument, even if it is not explicitly spelled out. Observe the consequences of this argument once again: it is asserted that as a matter of law, Israel *in 1948* was not under any legal duty to admit the

---

[2] Note that my argument is strictly confined to the legal realm – as an analysis of whether the right exists or not – and does not venture off onto the path of policy recommendations concerning the best possible methods of implementing (or denying) such a right, if it does exist.

[3] The most sustained commentary came in the form of a paper submitted by Prof. Yaffa Zilbershats, who is Associate Professor and Vice Dean of the Faculty of Law at Bar-Ilan University. Prof. Zilbershats' paper, which reads very much like a point-to-point rebuttal of my original monograph, will form a part of this collection of papers from the symposium. For that reason, it can be useful to read the two papers together.

refugees and therefore Israel – it is assumed – has not come under any legal duty to readmit since then *because the actions occurred in 1948* and, accordingly, *no subsequent developments in international law could impose upon Israel (or strengthen) a duty to readmit.* In other words, the legality of Israel's actions should be judged only in light of the state of the law that existed in 1948, and the matter remains frozen in time legally since then. Subsequent developments in international law are irrelevant and cannot impose any duty upon Israel *vis-à-vis* the 1948 refugees.

It is the purpose of the present paper to examine the above assumption in light of two relevant doctrines of international law related to the issue of "timing." The first – which is a choice of law rule – is known as the "intertemporal doctrine." The second – which relates to characterisation of the time period (duration) of the breach of an international obligation – is known as the "continuing violations doctrine."

After reviewing the development of these two legal doctrines, this paper will conclude by suggesting the implications of applying them to the case of Israel, in section IV, below.

II. The Intertemporal Doctrine

1. The Two Prongs of the Huber Formula

Time is linear, and is always moving forward. Actions occur at various points in time creating facts. Facts can be mapped along a timeline. Law can also be mapped along a timeline, since law is constantly evolving and changing over time. What is the relationship between facts and law as mapped against time?

Actions occur, creating facts that can comprise a breach of an international obligation. Later, such a breach can become the subject of a dispute based on international law. If there has been a change in the relevant rules of substantive international law during the time period from when the breach arose to when the dispute is presented for judgment, the question will arise of which law to apply: the "old law" (law in effect when the breach arose) or the "new law" (law in effect when the dispute is presented)? This is a "choice of law" question. International law has developed a mechanism for dealing with this question, known as the "intertemporal doctrine."

For purposes of this discussion, I would like to suggest that two parallel bars on a horizontal timeline be used to illustrate the concept that substantive rules of law evolve over time, while at the same time – as an independent process – state actions also occur over time, giving rise to facts that can comprise breaches of obligations of international law. (While these processes occur independently, the process of deciding whether a breach has occurred involves considering them together. In order to determine which state actions comprise a *breach* of obligations, it is necessary to refer to the relevant rules of international law in effect. This is a very important point for purposes of our discussion.) Such a graphic would look like the following:

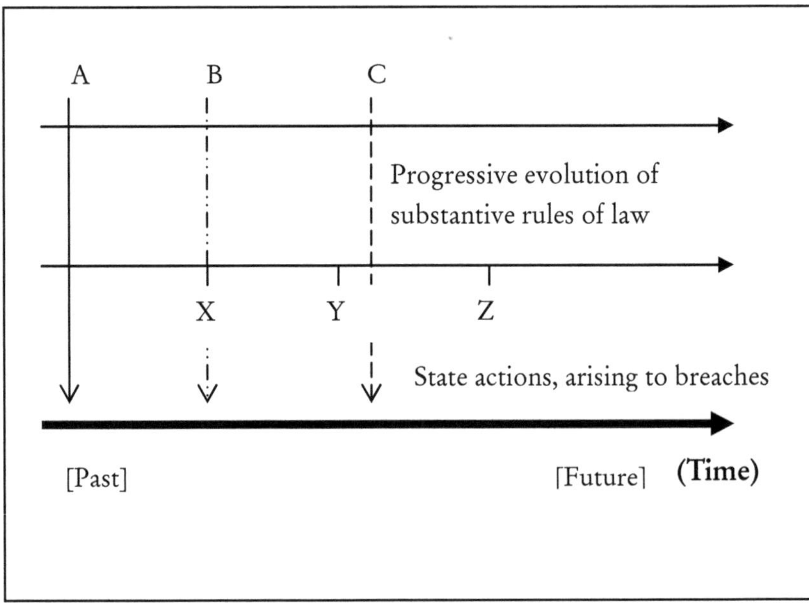

The intertemporal doctrine was articulated by the Swiss jurist Max Huber, who was the selected arbitrator acting for the Permanent Court of Arbitration in the Island of Palmas dispute between the United States and the Netherlands, decided in 1928. Huber was faced in that case with a situation in which sovereignty over the Island of Palmas (also known as Miangas), situated roughly halfway between the islands of Mindanao in the Philippines and Nanusa in the Netherlands Indies, was disputed. The U.S. claimed title, based on acquisition from Spain in a treaty of cession, and Spain had originally claimed title based on "discovery" in the 16th century. In the meantime, while the U.S. had not exhibited any actual display of sovereignty there, the Netherlands established a claim to the island and did display an exercise of sovereignty. Thus in the arbitration, the Netherlands claimed it had acquired title based on its more recent actual display of sovereignty (which, in the 20th century, when the dispute was presented for decision, was a more modern rule of law than the discovery rule). The question before Huber was which of the two rules of law to apply to determine sovereignty as between these two claimants. Ultimately, Huber decided that the U.S. had not maintained its right over the island in a sufficiently obvious way. Thus he held that that sovereignty had passed to the Netherlands. In other words, Huber chose to apply the more recent rule of law to decide the case. His finely nuanced reasoning for doing so continues to set the standard for deciding intertemporal questions to this day.

Huber formulated his famous doctrine in two parts, or prongs. The first prong of the doctrine states: "a juridical fact must be appreciated in the light of the law contemporary with it, and not of the law in force at the time when a dispute in regard to it arises or falls to be settled."[4] This first prong establishes that facts must be judged in light of the law then in effect when the breach occurred. This could be referred to as the "freeze frame" prong because it isolates a particular moment in time (which I will refer to as the "critical date")[5] as the date to be used to identify the relevant legal principles then in effect. Those are the principles to be used to analyse the case. The rule of Huber's first prong freezes the dynamic, evolutionary and streaming development of law (constantly rolling throughout time, like a movie projector) and allows

---

[4] Island of Palmas Case (Netherlands, United States), Reports of International Arbitral Awards 2, 831 et seq. (845), award of 4 April 1928.

[5] There are various uses of the phrase "critical date." I am using it with reference to the process of determining when a breach arose. It can also be used with reference to the process of determining what the cut-off date for jurisdiction is under a jurisdictional limitations clause *ratione temporis* (which is actually the more common usage of the phrase). Because I am focusing on the choice of law function of the intertemporal doctrine, I would like to follow T.O. Elias in using the term "critical date" to refer to the point in time at which the state actions comprising the breach of an international obligation occurred, because that time period will determine which substantive rules of law to select. See T.O. Elias, "The Doctrine of Intertemporal Law", *American Journal of International Law* 74 (1980), 285 et seq., 292.

the decision-maker to select a discrete moment in time from which to identify the relevant legal principles (the freeze frame, in this analogy).

The purpose of this rule is to promote "stability."[6] It is evident that the rule is based upon straightforward logic. Time is linear and always moves forward. Decision-makers, when presented with cases, cannot apply the law of the future, which is unknowable to them since it has not yet occurred. That being so, it is only possible to select from the law of the present or the law of the past. For cases that are based on recent facts, it is not only fair but more appropriate to use the law of the present to decide the case. The current law is the most capable of being known by the parties and usually will contain the most evolved expression of social policies. Thus the *law of the present* is the preferred, and therefore the default, choice of law. The only time when it would be appropriate to use the law of the past is when the facts giving rise to the breach occurred sufficiently long ago that the law has *changed* during the period of time between when the facts originally occurred and when the case is presented for decision. In such cases, procedural fairness requires that the parties' actions should be judged by what they then viewed the law to be when they acted (the future development of the law being unknowable to them then, although it is clearly revealed to us in hindsight). Hence, in such cases, the *law of the then-present* (i.e., the law of that particular point in time in the past when the facts occurred giving rise to the breach) must be used as the default reference point by which to analyse the case.

This seems to be a rather straightforward matter of logic and fairness, and frequently the analysis stops there. It is rather common to see reference to the intertemporal doctrine as if it contained *only* to Huber's first prong, and nothing more. However, matters are – not surprisingly – rather more complex. Huber elaborated upon his doctrine by formulating a second prong, which, commentators, have noted, could have the potential to "wipe out" the effects of the first prong. Huber formulated the second prong of his doctrine as follows:

> "As regards the question which of different legal systems prevailing at successive periods is to be applied in a particular case (the so-called intertemporal law), a distinction must be made between the *creation* of rights and the *existence* of rights. The same principle which subjects the act creative of a right to the law in force at the

---

6 See R. Jennings, *The Acquisition of Territory in International Law*, 1963, 30.

> time the right arises, demands that the *existence* of the right, in other words *its continued manifestation, shall follow the conditions required by the evolution of law.*"[7]

It thus transpires that Huber's doctrine is really a two-step analysis. The first step analyses the *creation* of a right (the "freeze frame" prong). The second step analyses the *maintenance* of the right (which I will refer to as the "responsibility" prong).

The responsibility prong appears predicated upon appreciation of the basic reality underpinning the entire international legal system which holds that states have rights, but that those rights also impose corresponding duties upon states. A state may not assert a right without acting in accordance with the corresponding duty. To assert the right without acting in accordance with the corresponding duty (even if the requirements for fulfilling this duty might change over time, with the progressive evolution of law) would be to violate the social contract between states that comprises the very fabric of the system of international law.

The responsibility prong, therefore, does look at the actions of a state in maintaining a right *over a period of time*, i.e., up to the point in time when a dispute is submitted for decision. To do so, the responsibility prong requires that the evolutionary development of the law during that passage of time – the intertemporal law – be taken into account.

Is Huber's second prong unfair? Does it hold states to an unreasonable standard by requiring them to comply with future-developed standards of law, about which they could have no knowledge whatsoever at the time they performed (or initiated) their actions? Some prominent critics of Huber's formulation have objected to the second prong on the basis that "states that had acquired territories might find later on, according to the second element [of Huber's doctrine], that they could subsequently lose the territory by operation of a new rule of international law."[8]

---

7 Island of Palmas Case, see note 4, 845. Emphasis added.

8 Elias, see note 5, 286 (citing P. Jessup and W.J.B. Versfelt, who published a 1928 article and a 1933 book, respectively, on the Island of Palmas arbitration decision and both expressed this fear); Jennings, see note 6, 30:

"If indeed the second branch of the rule of intertemporal law is allowed to mean more than this, the result is not only that title ceases to have significance, it also means that the first part of the rule is itself virtually cancelled of its effect. It means that title has so to speak to be earned again at every moment of time.

In contrast, however, T. O. Elias, who was the Vice-President of the International Court of Justice (ICJ), has written an eloquent endorsement of Huber's formulation of the intertemporal doctrine, in both its parts.[9] Elias argues forcefully that the doctrine represents a finely nuanced balancing of interests:

> "The intertemporal law seems to have been designed to govern a situation in which the necessary stability in relations between states is to be preserved, *while at the same time the necessity for evolution in these relations and in the law regulating them is recognized.* There is no real antithesis between the first and second element in Max Huber's formulation of the rule in the Island of Palmas case, and the more we have regard to this consideration, especially in the light of disputes that have arisen since that case, the better we can appreciate the *delicate balance* aimed at in the formulation of the doctrine as now generally accepted."[10]

Elias sustains this thesis through a rigorous and detailed examination of relevant case-law interpreting the intertemporal doctrine – whether explicitly or implicitly – ranging from jurisprudence of the International Court of Justice,[11] arbitral awards, and three prominent domestic jurisdiction cases (U.K. and Germany). Elias concludes that Huber's formulation is not only valid but is required by logic. He reads the ICJ interpretation of the doctrine as upholding both parts of the Huber formulation, i.e.,

> "the principle that the creation of a right must be appreciated in the light of the law contemporaneous with the acts creative of the right

---

Under these conditions no title would be secure and the supposed aim of the law – stability – would be utterly defeated."

9 Elias, see note 5.

10 Ibid., 305. Emphasis added.

11 See, e.g., The Minquiers and Ecrehos Case (France, United Kingdom), ICJ Reports 1953, 47 et seq. (where the ICJ followed the rule of Huber's second prong in deciding that maintenance of territorial title, as distinct from its abstract acquisition, must be in conformity with the relevant rules of law as they evolve over time and not merely with the law contemporaneous with the acquisition of title); Aegean Sea Continental Shelf Case (Greece, Turkey), ICJ Reports 1978, 1 et seq. (where the ICJ interpreted specific terms in Greece's jurisdictional reservation to the 1928 General Act for the Pacific Settlement of International Disputes in light of their "evolving" meaning over time, since they were generic terms, rather than viewing their meaning as frozen in content as of the filing of the reservation in 1931).

> *and* that the *continued validity of that right at any future date must depend on the state and requirements of international law at that particular moment.*"[12]

Another judge of the ICJ, Rosalyn Higgins, has also written about the intertemporal doctrine.[13] She demonstrates that in cases involving human rights obligations, in particular, courts have been very supportive of the approach that permits consideration of standards of law contemporaneous to when the dispute is submitted, if there is a dispute between "old law" and "new law." She cites case-law from the ICJ[14] and the European Court of Human Rights in support of this approach.

Referring specifically to Huber's second prong, Higgins states:

> "Some have interpreted [Huber's] second limb as providing that a right, even if lawfully obtained by reference to the law of the era, will be lost if a later rule of international law evolves by reference to which the basis of the 'right' would no longer be lawful ... Our understanding [of the second prong] should flow from the realisation that it was a *dictum* offered in the context of establishing and maintaining territorial title. The second element may then be seen as providing that *the creation of an initial right does not of itself suffice to maintain it up to the moment of the claim. Perpetuation of that right ... (as required by later law), is necessary.*"[15]

It may well be that Huber's second prong is actually an intuitive attempt to fold into the intertemporal doctrine a logical corollary of a related doctrine of international law, namely the "continuing violation"

---

12 Elias, see note 5, 307. Emphasis added.

13 R. Higgins, "Time and the Law: International Perspectives on an Old Problem", *ICLQ* 46 (1997), 501 et seq.

14 See, e.g., South West Africa cases, ICJ Reports 1966, 294 et seq. (where Judge Tanaka rejected the suggestion that the mandate should be interpreted only by the law of 1920, and that contemporary law did not apply, stating "In the present case, the protection of the acquired rights of the Respondent is not the issue, but its obligations, because the main purposes of the mandate system are ethical and humanitarian. The Respondent has no right to behave in an inhuman way today as well as during these 40 years."); Legal Consequences for States of the Continued Presence of South Africa in Namibia, ICJ Reports 1971, 31 et seq. (where the ICJ took the position that the League of Nations Covenant Article 22 guarantees that the mandate was a "sacred trust for civilization" should be assumed to be understood by the parties as having an evolving, rather than static, content); Aegean Sea Continental Shelf Case, see note 11.

15 Higgins, see note 13, 516. Emphasis added.

doctrine. As is discussed in the following section, the continuing violation doctrine – which is usually formulated in terms of analysing "breaches" of the law, rather than analysing states' claims to "rights" – expressly allows the intertemporal law to be taken into account for the entire intertemporal period, i.e., from the beginning of the breach of the international obligation until the time the dispute is presented for judgment. Huber's second prong, by contrast, is phrased in the language of states' "rights," and thus addresses the situation of "rights maintenance" *over a period of time*. However, as we have already discussed, since every right imposes a corresponding duty upon states, whenever a "right" is asserted but such right is not maintained in accordance with its corresponding duty, then necessarily the state that is asserting the right is in fact doing so wrongfully, which means it is actually committing a violation. In such cases, the wrongful assertion of a right over a period of time is actually a "continuing violation," since it is done without any legal basis. Therefore, invocation of Huber's second prong (allowing the intertemporal law, including the law of the present, to be taken into consideration) would be entirely correct, as well as consistent with the rule as formulated in the "continuing violations" doctrine.

Thus, Huber's formula might make more sense and arouse less objection if the first prong is viewed as reserved for cases where the violation was "instantaneous" and occurred sufficiently long ago in the past that the rules of law have changed since then. In contrast, the second prong could be viewed as reserved for cases where either the right asserted or the breach alleged is a *continuing* one, i.e., continuing up until the moment it is presented for judgment. For cases involving such "continuing" situations, in which the breach (or the wrongful assertion of a right) is still ongoing at the moment of judgment, the dispute is necessarily very much a "current" one to which the application of the "law of the present" (which is the preferred default rule, anyway) would be entirely appropriate. Thus, the intertemporal law (including the law of the present) should logically be considered in deciding such cases.

The dangers inherent in rejecting this approach can be demonstrated by turning this argument around. To require the decision-maker to ignore the intertemporal law would be effectively to freeze time – and to freeze with it the evolving status of the law – thus handing state violators the perfect excuse to prolong their violations. They would argue that the current standards of law do not apply to their conduct, since it began "long ago when this conduct was permitted." As a policy matter, there would be little incentive for states to act to bring their behaviour into conformity with modern standards if they could argue that the intertemporal doctrine forbids the decision-maker from referring to modern law because the second prong of Huber's formulation is dispensable and endangers "stability."[16]

2. Non-Retroactivity in International Law

The non-retroactive application of law is, then, considered a foundational principle of procedural fairness in international law, as it is in domestic law.[17] The "intertemporal doctrine" thus incorporates the non-retroactivity guarantee, in Huber's first prong. Indeed the non-retroactivity principle is cited as a central organising principle in the International Law Commission's Draft Articles on Responsibility of States for Internationally Wrongful Acts, and Huber's first prong is cited as the source for the rule.[18]

---

[16] State stability, if maintained at the expense of individual rights, seems inherently unjustifiable and artificial from a policy perspective. It also seems inherently unstable, if not in and of itself actually destabilising, as a practical matter.

[17] The basic principle of non-retroactivity in law is expressed by the maxim *nullum crimen sine lege praevia* (a party cannot be held liable for an act that was not prohibited at the time of commission).

[18] Draft Articles on Responsibility of States for Internationally Wrongful Acts, in Report of the International Law Commission on the Work of Its Fifty-third Session, GAOR 56th Sess., Suppl. No. 10, at 43, UN Doc. A/56/10 (2001), available at <http://www.un.org/law/ilc>, hereinafter "ILC Draft Articles on Responsibility" (this document also contains the official ILC commentary on the draft articles). The ILC's commentary to Article 13, para. 1 reads as follows:

"Article 13 states the basic principle that, for responsibility to exist, the breach must occur at a time when [the] State is bound by the obligation. This is but the application in the field of state responsibility of the general principle of intertemporal law, as stated by Judge Huber in another context in the Island of Palmas case:

'A juridical fact must be appreciated in the light of the law contemporary with it, and not of the law in force at the time when a dispute in regard to it arises or falls to be settled.'

Article 13 provides an important guarantee for States in terms of claims of responsibility. Its formulation ('does not constitute ... unless ...') is in keeping with the idea of a guarantee against the retrospective application of international law in matters of State responsibility." Citations omitted.

And yet, as will be discussed further in the following section, the non-retroactivity principle logically cannot apply in the context of continuing violations. As I have already suggested, Huber's first prong seems more applicable to cases of the "instantaneous" violations. In contrast, Huber's second prong may best be viewed as applying to special cases where the dispute concerns the *continuing* breach of an obligation or the ongoing wrongful assertion of a right, whereby the state actor itself has "kept the issue alive" by breaching the obligation or asserting the right wrongfully on a continuing, ongoing basis. In such cases, there can be no argument against applying the intertemporal law, including the law of the present, to decide the case because the state actor brought the applicability of the later-in-time law upon itself. The state actor could have avoided application of the later law by suspending the breach or ceasing the wrongful assertion of a right earlier in time, thereby cutting off the application of the "then-future law" to its actions. However, by keeping the issue alive, the state actor has left itself open to application of the law of the present. Thus, there is *no retrospective* application of the law in *continuing* cases because the actions giving rise to the breach or the wrongful assertion of a right are still *ongoing*. Thus, the non-retroactivity principle is not violated by Huber's second prong. This principle is made clear by the widespread acceptance of the "continuing violation doctrine" in international law.

III. The "Continuing Violation" Doctrine

As we have just seen, the intertemporal rule is a choice of law rule that seeks to isolate the relevant principles of law that a decision-maker should apply. It does not deal with the related, but separate, question of determining factually when the breach of an international obligation has occurred or its duration, i.e., whether it is continuing in nature. There are separate rules that deal with the equally important issue of the characterisation of the actions (facts) that give rise to the breach of an international obligation – e.g., as "instantaneous" or as "continuing" in time – and the consequences that flow from that characterisation.

The "continuing violations" doctrine is well-established in international law, including case-law of the International Court of Justice, the European Court of Human Rights, the UN Committee on Human Rights (charged with monitoring the International Covenant on Civil and Political Rights) and the Inter-American Court of Human Rights. It has been incorporated into the 1969 Vienna Convention on the Law of

Treaties, as well as the International Law Commission's Draft Articles on Responsibility of States for Internationally Wrongful Acts, adopted by the ILC in November 2001 and endorsed by the UN General Assembly. It can also be found in major systems of domestic law (e.g., the U.S.,[19] France and Belgium, to name just a few).

The "continuing situation" doctrine, of which the continuing violation doctrine is a logical corollary, is expressly incorporated into the Vienna Convention on the Law of Treaties in Article 28, titled "Non-Retroactivity of Treaties":

> "Unless a different intention appears from the treaty or is otherwise established, its provisions do not bind a party in relation to any act or fact which took place or *any situation which ceased to exist* before the date of the entry into force of the treaty with respect to that party."[20]

What this rule means in practical terms is that if a "situation" does *not* cease to exist before the coming into effect of a new treaty, then the situation – because it is a *continuing* one – will be covered by the terms of the new treaty. This is logical, since any new treaty is intended to cover acts which occur subsequent to the date of execution, which would logically include continuing situations (whether they constitute *breaches* of international obligations, and hence continuing "*violations*," or whether they constitute action in conformity with interna-

---

[19] In U.S. law, the "continuing violations" doctrine is most commonly invoked in the context of employment discrimination and sexual harassment lawsuits, where the plaintiff will often need to demonstrate a "pattern" of prohibited acts in order to make out a complaint. As long as one of the complained of acts falls within the statute of limitations period, the complaint will be considered filed timely. Each of the United States Circuit Courts of Appeal have recognised the validity of the continuing violation doctrine in the context of sexual harassment cases. See, e.g., *Sabree*, 921 F.2d at 400; *Quinn*, 159 F.3d at 165; *West v. Philadelphia Electric Co.*, 45 F.3d 744, 754 (3d Cir. 1995); *Tinsely v. First Union Nat. Bank*, 155 F.3d 435, 442-443 (4th Cir. 1998); *Huckabay*, 142 F.3d at 238-239; *Jackson v. Quanex Corp.*, 191 F.3d 647, 667-668 (6th Cir. 1999); *Filipovic v. K&R Exp. Systems, Inc.*, 176 F.3d 390, 395-396 (7th Cir. 1999); *Jenson v. Eveleth Taconite Co.*, 130 F.3d 1287, 1303 (8th Cir. 1997); *Fielder v. UAL Corp.*, 281 F.3d 973, 983 (9th Cir. 2000); *Bullington v. United Air Lines, Inc.*, 186 F.3d 1301, 1310-1311 (10th Cir. 1999); *Calloway v. Partners Nat. Health Plans*, 986 F.2d 446, 448 (11th Cir. 1993); *Palmer v. Kelly*, 17 F.3d 1490, 1496 (D.C. Cir. 1994).

[20] Vienna Convention on the Law of Treaties, opened for signature 23 May 1969, Art. 28, UNTS Vol. 1155 No. 331. Emphasis added.

tional obligations, and hence a continuing situation that does not constitute a continuing violation).

The Vienna Convention includes another indirect provision for the "continuing situation" doctrine in para. 2 (b) of Article 71, which is titled "Consequences of the Invalidity of a Treaty Which Conflicts with a Peremptory Norm of General International Law":

> "71(2): In the case of a treaty which becomes void and terminates under article 64, the termination of the treaty:
>
> ...
>
> (b) does not affect any *right*, *obligation* or *legal situation* of the parties *created through the execution of the treaty prior to its termination*; provided that those rights, obligations or situations may thereafter be maintained *only to the extent that their maintenance is not itself in conflict with the new peremptory norm* of general international law."[21]

This article of the Vienna Convention on the Law of Treaties can be thought of as a "knock-out" article, whereby those parts of a treaty that conflict with a peremptory norm are invalidated ("knocked out"), whereas in contrast those rights, obligations or legal *situations* that were created by the parties under the terms of the treaty and that do not conflict with the peremptory norm *will continue to exist,* even though the treaty itself has been invalidated as a legal matter. Thus, those continuing situations created under the subsequently invalidated treaty that are nevertheless in conformity with the peremptory norm that invalidated it will continue to have legal effect, since they were not the cause of the treaty's invalidation. This constitutes further recognition of the "continuing situation" doctrine whereby continuing situations are recognised to survive the change of legal rules surrounding them.

The law of state responsibility – which has benefited greatly from the International Law Commission's completion in November 2001 of its Draft Articles on Responsibility of States for Internationally Wrongful Acts – makes a clear distinction between "instantaneous" violations and "continuing" violations.

Article 14 para. 1 of the Draft Articles on Responsibility defines "instantaneous" acts: "The breach of an international obligation by an act of a State not having a continuing character occurs at the moment when

---

[21] Ibid., Art. 71 para. 2 (b). Emphasis added.

the act is performed, even if its effects continue."[22] Thus, an important distinction is made, in this definition, between the "act," which is instantaneous in character, and its "effects," which may be prolonged or continuing in nature.

In contrast, a "continuing" violation is defined in Article 14 para. 2: "The breach of an international obligation by an act of a State having a continuous character extends over the entire period during which the act continues and remains not in conformity with the international obligation."[23] The definitive difference between the instantaneous violation and the continuing violation is that for the latter, the *act* itself causing the breach "continues" in time and "*remains* not in conformity with the international obligation" relevant to it.[24]

As a practical matter, it can often be difficult to distinguish between an instantaneous act whose *effects* continue over time as opposed to a continuing violation where the *breach itself* continues over time. Courts have also struggled with this distinction, sometimes coming up with seemingly inconsistent results. A useful rule of thumb suggested by one commentator is to look at the conduct and to ask whether "cessation" of the action, which is one of the remedies provided for in Article 30 of the Draft Articles on Responsibility, would provide relief to the injured party.[25] Another typical identifier of a continuing violation is whether the state action "affects the legal status of a person during a certain period in time."[26] If so, it will normally be regarded by courts as a continuing violation.

The case-law under the European Convention on Human Rights has developed particularly clearly on this point. The European Commission

---

22 ILC Draft Articles on Responsibility, see note 18, Article 14 para. 1.

23 Ibid., Article 14 para. 2.

24 The ILC defines a second type of continuing violation in Article 14 para. 3 as the failure of a state "to prevent a given event." Such a breach lasts for as long as the prohibited event occurs in violation of the obligation. See ibid., Article 14 para. 3. Emphasis added.

25 J. Pauwelyn, "The Concept of a 'Continuing Violation' of an International Obligation: Selected Problems", *BYIL* 66 (1995), 415 et seq., 448, (an *a contrario* interpretation of this rule (that cessation can only be ordered if the violation still continues) offers a useful criterion to determine whether a continuing violation exists at all. Indeed the remedy of cessation is only of any use if the violation is a continuing one.")

26 Ibid., 421.

of Human Rights (the "Commission"), which, until it was phased out in 1999, received initial applications under the Convention and was generally responsible for making findings of fact, would generally examine the question from the perspective of the aggrieved individual plaintiff:

> "From the outset, one of the decisive elements in the Commission's decision on whether a continuing situation exists has been whether the position in which the victim is placed represents a continuing situation in violation of the Convention or, on the contrary, a violation of its rights and freedoms which clearly dates from the past (i.e., an instantaneous fact). In other words, the Commission focuses on the *effects* on the *victim* of the act (*in casu* the individual), taking into account all relevant circumstances of the case, rather than on the objective qualification of the *act* as such or the subjective intentions of its *author* (*in casu* the State). In this sense all the rights and freedoms protected by the Convention can be the object of a continuing violation."[27]

This was the approach adopted in the De Becker case,[28] the first "continuing situation" case decided by the organs of the European Convention on Human Rights. There the applicant argued that a prior conviction under Belgian law barred him from certain rights for life, including practising his profession as a journalist. The Commission found that the applicant "finds himself to be in a continuing situation in respect of which he claims to be the victim of a violation of Article 10."[29] Thus the Belgian *legislation*, by changing the applicant's *status* over an *ongoing period of time* and in a manner alleged to be in violation of an international obligation, had created a continuing situation which the Commission found it had jurisdiction to consider.

In addition, there is a third type of violation listed in the ILC's Draft Articles on Responsibility, namely the "composite act," which is a special kind of continuing violation. The "composite act" is defined in Article 15 as follows:

> "1. The breach of an international obligation by a State through a series of actions or omissions defined in aggregate as wrongful, occurs

---

[27] *Idem*. Emphasis in original.

[28] *De Becker v. Belgium*, *Yearbook of the European Convention on Human Rights* 2 (1958-1959), 214 et seq.

[29] Ibid., 231.

> when the action or omission occurs which, taken with the other actions or omissions, is sufficient to constitute the wrongful act.
>
> 2. In such a case, the breach extends over the entire time period starting with the first of the actions or omissions of the series and lasts for as long as these actions or omissions are repeated and remain not in conformity with the international obligation."[30]

The ILC's commentary to Article 15 explains that "composite acts" are meant to cover breaches of obligations concerning "some aggregate of conduct and not individual acts as such."[31] Thus their focus is on "a series of acts or omissions defined in the aggregate as wrongful."[32] The commentary lists the following as examples of obligations covered by the category of composite acts: "genocide, apartheid or crimes against humanity, systematic acts of racial discrimination, systematic acts of discrimination prohibited by a trade agreement, etc."[33] Thus, in the words of the ILC, "[s]ome of the most serious wrongful acts in international law are defined in terms of their composite character. The importance of these obligations in international law justifies special treatment in article 15."[34]

Regarding the intertemporal doctrine, it is interesting to note that the ILC's Draft Articles on Responsibility phrase the doctrine in a straightforward and generic way that applies to all three categories of violations identified above, i.e., the instantaneous, continuing and composite violations (as a special subset of continuing violations). The intertemporal doctrine is set forth in Article 13: "An act of a State does not constitute a breach of an international obligation unless the State is bound by the obligation in question *at the time the act occurs.*"[35] This formulation is a great simplification from earlier versions of the rule, i.e., the former Article 18 in previous drafts of the ILC articles on state responsibility, which had provoked much commentary and critique. Apparently the main reason that the rule could be simplified so dramatically was the distinction that the ILC eventually drew between what it termed "primary" rules of law (meaning rules of substantive law) and "secondary" rules of law (meaning essentially procedural or interpretive rules). After

---

[30] ILC Draft Articles on Responsibility, see note 18, Article 15.

[31] Ibid., commentary to Article 15 para. 2.

[32] *Idem.*

[33] *Idem.*

[34] *Idem.*

[35] Ibid., Article 13. Emphasis added.

struggling for 40 years to include (and harmonise) both sets of rules in the Draft Articles on Responsibility, the ILC eventually abandoned that approach and settled for including only "secondary" rules in the draft articles. This jettisoning of the primary substantive rules is credited for enabling the ILC to complete its work on this topic in November 2001.

As we have already seen, for instantaneous violations, the obligation must be in force at the time the act occurs. The timing of the act, then, is the "critical date" for selecting the applicable law by which to judge whether a breach has occurred or not.[36]

As for continuing violations, the operative time period during which a "continuing violation" is said to exist is that period of time during which the action of the state coincides in time with the existence in international law of a legal obligation binding upon the state actor. Referring back to the graphic at the beginning of this article, there are two parallel lines moving forward in time, one representing the progressive development of international law and one representing the actions of the state. The actions of state may take place either before, during or after the coming into existence of a binding norm of international law. Therefore, for a *breach* of an obligation to exist, the *action* must *coincide* in time with the existence of an applicable *norm*. If that breach (i.e., the coinciding of state action with the existence of an applicable obliga-

---

[36] Unfortunately, there is something a bit circular in this logic, and it may simply be unavoidable. Since the intertemporal doctrine is a choice of law rule, in all likelihood the outcome of the entire case will turn upon the choice of substantive law selected, so everything hangs upon this selection. However, observe the process by which the "critical date" is selected by which to identify the appropriate law. First, the "act of state" is isolated, in order to identify the "critical date," i.e., time period from which to select the relevant principles of applicable law. Once the applicable law has been identified, it is used to analyse whether an obligation bound the state and if so, whether the state breached it. In making this analysis, the substantive law itself is used to identify the relevant facts to be used in characterising the conduct of the state actor. This characterisation in turn may well extend to the issue of the characterisation of the facts of the initial "act" itself, including its initiation, duration and completion. However, this rather circular logical process simply points to the difficulty of characterising facts in any case. This is a reality with which legal decision-makers have to deal routinely. In the case of the intertemporal doctrine, then, Elias is correct in pointing out that "the doctrine of intertemporal law may be regarded as a substantive rule of law in one sense, and as a rule of interpretation in another sense." See Elias, see note 5, 285.

tory norm) is a continuing act extending over time, then a continuing violation exists.

There are a variety of issues associated with continuing violations, most of which relate – not surprisingly – to matters of timing, namely determining starting points and ending points (if any) for continuing violations. The questions are particularly interesting in cases of only partial overlap between the period of time of the state action and the period of time that the obligation is in force.[37]

For purposes of this discussion, it is only necessary to illustrate four basic theoretical patterns encountered by courts when dealing with continuing violations:

1. *Complete coverage of action by obligation*: cases where the state's action is completely covered in time by the existence of an obligation, and hence the entire action is considered a continuing breach;

2. *Partial coverage of action by obligation*: cases where the obligation arose after the action began but both the action and the obligation are continuing at the time that the dispute is presented for settlement; and

3. *Cessation of State Action (Former Continuing Violation Ceases)*: cases where the state action (and hence the breach) ceased (although the obligation continued to exist) before the dispute was presented for settlement (in which case the court would probably be asked to consider the sufficiency of reparations made, if any).

4. *Cessation of Obligatory Norm (Former Continuing Violation Ceases)*: cases where the obligatory norm (and hence the breach) ceased (although the state action continued) before the dispute was presented for settlement.[38]

---

[37] There are also interesting timing questions concerning the relationship between continuing violations and jurisdictional limitations clauses *ratione temporis*, as well as the appropriate way to calculate damages incurred by a continuing violation (and in particular where the court only has jurisdiction over part of the time period during which the violation occurred). Elaboration upon these topics is beyond the scope of this article.

[38] In these cases, liability accrues for the period during which the prohibited state action coincided with the international obligation. Since the breach has ceased before the dispute is brought for settlement, the aggrieved party must strive to file in a timely manner to avoid a bar by laches or unreasonable delay. There are two commonly discussed international cases that fit this category. The first is the Rainbow Warrior case (arbitral award of 30 April 1990), where France was held to be in continuing violation of its obligations to New Zealand, but only for a specific time period in the past, for refusing to return two of its

As already noted we are leaving aside the related issue of whether a court has jurisdiction over the entire continuing violation or only part of it, which is beyond the scope of this paper.

Following the form of the graphic presented at the beginning of the discussion, these four basic scenarios could be illustrated in the following manner.

First Scenario: Complete Coverage of Action by Obligation:

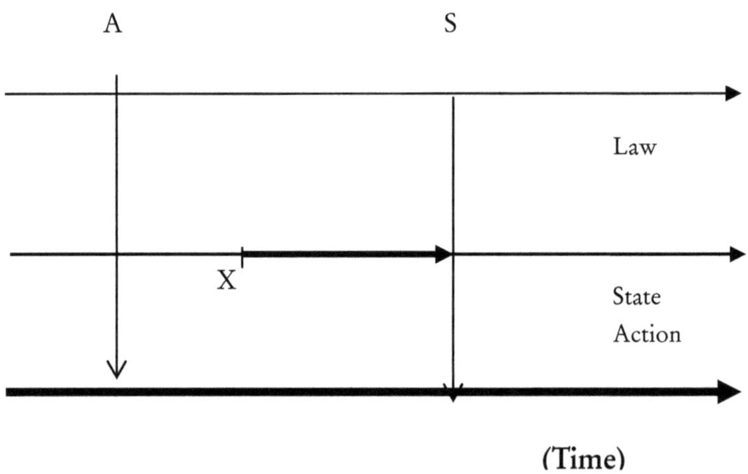

A = establishment of binding international obligation upon state.
X = state action begins after obligation comes into force and continues to presentation of dispute for settlement (S).

agents responsible for the sinking of the Rainbow Warrior to the Island of Hao. The second case is the ICJ decision in Certain Phosphate Lands in Nauru, where the ICJ ruled admissible a decades-old claim based on Australia's joint administration of the trust territory of Nauru (1947-1968), even though the Trusteeship Agreement upon which the claim was based had terminated in 1968 when Nauru achieved independence. See Rainbow Warrior (New Zealand, France), *Reports of International Arbitral Awards* 20 (1990), 217 et seq.; Certain Phosphate Lands in Nauru (Nauru, Australia), Preliminary Objections, ICJ Reports 1992, 240 et seq.

Second Scenario: Partial Coverage of Action by Obligation:

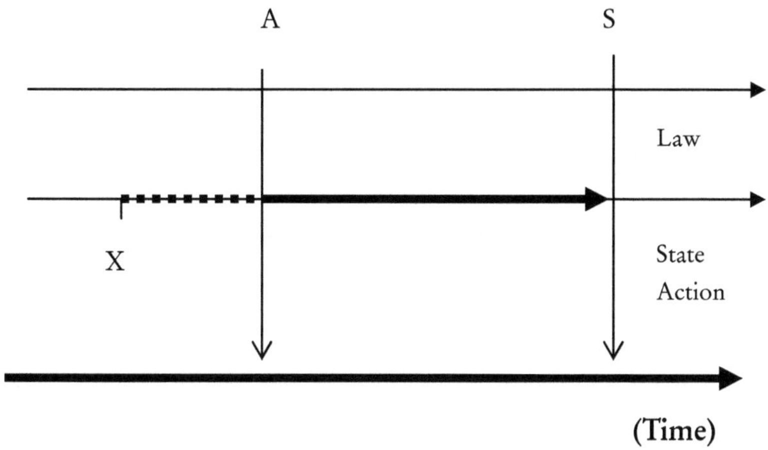

A = establishment of binding international obligation upon state.
X = state action begins before obligation comes into force and continues to presentation of dispute for settlement (S).

Third Scenario: Cessation of State Action (Former Continuing Violation Ceases):

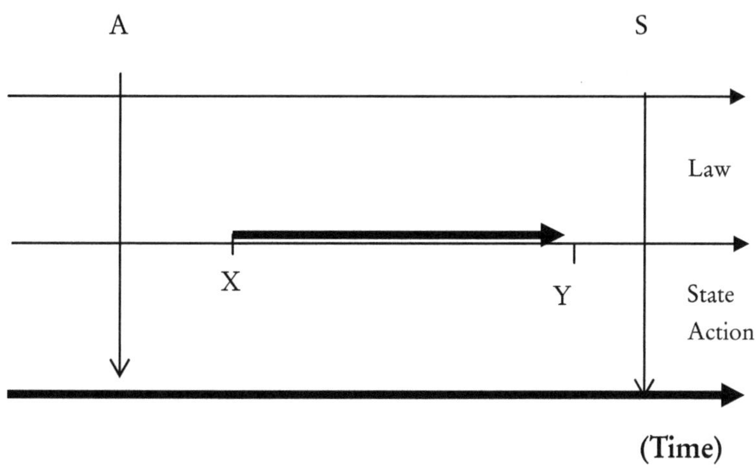

A = establishment of binding international obligation upon state.
X = state action begins after obligation comes into force and ceases (Y) before presentation of dispute for settlement (S).

Fourth Scenario: Cessation of Obligatory Norm (Former Continuing Violation Ceases):

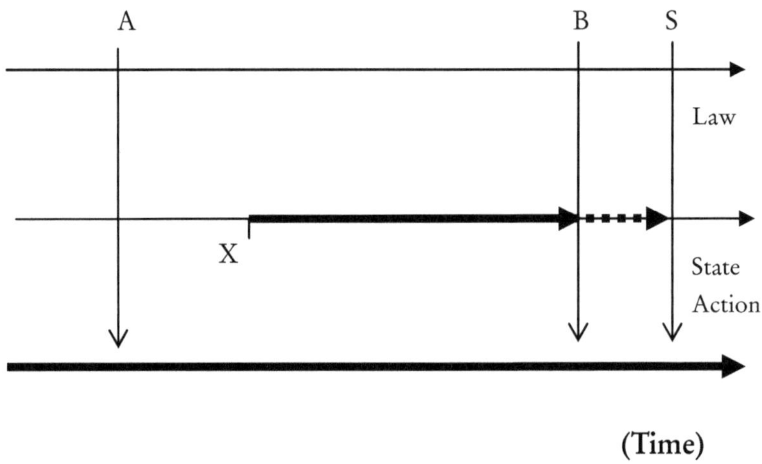

A = establishment of binding international obligation upon state.
B = international obligation ceases to exist.
X = state action begins after obligation comes into force and continues beyond cessation of international obligation (B), continuing until presentation of dispute for settlement (S).

Following is one of the better summaries of the abstract principles demonstrated by means of the above three graphics:

> "[R]egarding *continuing acts* ... [t]here is a breach of obligation if, and in respect of the period during which, a State's conduct contradicts an obligation binding upon it. The 'moment of breach' thus occurs alternatively either with the commencement of the conduct or with the entry into force of the obligation whichever comes later. The 'time of commission,' on the other hand, extends from this initial moment to a later stage when either the conduct ceased or the obligation expired whichever comes earlier ...
>
> If the law undergoes a change while a *composite act* is being performed ..., the consequences are not so obvious. Composite acts, such as a systematic violation of human rights, normally occur as soon as a common intention or a common effect emerges from a series of separate actions or omissions. This is the 'moment of breach.' The 'time of commission,' on the other hand, normally extends from

> the first to the last instance of such a practice. Where the law changes during this practice *it is clear that only the portion of practice contemporaneous with the obligation represents the wrongful act.*"[39]

Another commentator reiterates the common principles underlying these various patterns:

> "[D]ifficulties of application arise if the continuing conduct coincides only partly with the period during which the obligation is in force for the state concerned. In this event, there will be a breach only in so far as, and only for the period during which, the continuance of the act of the State and the existence of the obligation incumbent on it are simultaneous ... This will be the case even if the continuing situation started before the obligation entered into force or continued after the obligation ceased to exist. *Whether or not the newly imposed obligation is more stringent for the respondent State involved is irrelevant.*"[40]

For composite acts, the principles are, not surprisingly, similar, although there is one important difference:

> "In other international obligations a certain degree of repetition or a so-called practice is required before it can be breached. In these cases ... only those individual cases or acts which occurred *after* the obligation came into force can be taken into account to determine whether the obligation in question has at all been breached, i.e., whether, for example, a 'discriminatory practice' or 'consistent violation' has been established. *Indeed, once it has been determined that the 'composite act' breaches the obligation, the breach will necessarily operate retroactively and start from the date of the first act of the series of acts taken into account ...*"[41]

A detailed analysis of the special rules governing composite acts is beyond the scope of this paper. For our purposes, it is enough to note that the general principle applicable to all continuing violations applies to composite acts well, namely that where an obligatory norm arises after the start of continuing state conduct, that portion of the state conduct

---

[39] K. Wolfram, "The Time Factor in the Law of State Responsibility", in: M. Spinedi/B. Simma (eds), *United Nations Codification of State Responsibility*, 1987, 107 et seq. Citations omitted, emphasis added.

[40] Pauwelyn, see note 25, 443. Citations omitted.

[41] Ibid., 446 et seq. Citations omitted, emphasis added.

that coincides in time with the existence of the norm will be considered a continuing violation.

Let us now examine some representative cases and authoritative analysis from the first two categories represented in the preceding set of four graphics. Since proponents of the Israeli position are more concerned with arguing that the events of 1948 did not constitute a breach *at that time*, we would do well to focus our attention on case-law and analysis that addresses the question of when breaches arise. Thus, we will be focusing our attention on the left-hand side of the time spectrum (the beginning of the breach).

1. First Scenario: Complete Coverage of Action by Obligation

Examples from the ICJ include the case concerning U.S. Diplomatic and Consular Staff in Teheran,[42] where the detention of American diplomatic and consular staff was found to be a continuing violation. Similarly, in the case concerning Military and Paramilitary Activities in and against Nicaragua,[43] U.S. actions towards Nicaragua were held to constitute a continuing breach of obligations.

The Inter-American Court of Human Rights has also advanced the continuing violations doctrine. In the Blake case,[44] an American journalist, Ned Blake, and his companion disappeared in Guatemala in March 1985. Guatemala filed a declaration accepting the Court's jurisdiction some two years later in March 1987 for "cases" taking place after the date of the filing of the declaration. The Court held that because the government of Guatemala had concealed information and evidence of the deaths from the families and had later tried to dispose of the remains, the disappeared status of the victims continued beyond the filing of Guatemala's declaration. Thus the Court had jurisdiction to hear the case. The Court cited its own jurisprudence on continuing violations, the Inter-American Convention on the Forced Disappearance of Persons, and Article 17 para. 1 of the United Nations Declaration on the

---

[42] U.S. Diplomatic and Consular Staff in Teheran, ICJ Reports 1980, 3 et seq.

[43] Military and Paramilitary Activities in and against Nicaragua, ICJ Reports 1986, 14 et seq.

[44] Blake Case, Preliminary Objections, Inter-American Court of Human Rights, Judgment of 2 July 1996, Ser. C, No. 27.

Protection of All Persons from Enforced Disappearance, in addition to Guatemala's own penal code, as authority for the applicability of the continuing violations doctrine in the case of disappearances.

A recent and quite high profile case under the European Convention on Human Rights is the case of *Loizidou v. Turkey*.[45] The case involved land in northern Cyprus owned by a Greek Cypriot who, since Turkey's occupation of northern Cyprus in 1974, had been prevented from accessing or enjoying it. Turkey asserted that the land had been lawfully expropriated from the applicant by virtue of Article 159[46] of the Constitution promulgated in 1985 by the "Turkish Republic of Northern Cyprus," an entity not recognised as a state except by Turkey. On 22 January 1990, Turkey had accepted the Court's jurisdiction with respect to facts occurring subsequent to the date of deposit of its declaration of acceptance. Turkey therefore argued that the operative facts had occurred prior to its acceptance of the Court's jurisdiction and, consequently, that the Court did not have jurisdiction over the case.

The Court had joined the preliminary objection *ratione temporis* to the merits phase and thus decided on the continuing violation question in its judgment on the merits. The Court specifically "recall[ed] that it has endorsed the notion of a continuing violation of the Convention and its effects as to temporal limitations of the competence of Convention organs,"[47] citing several recent cases.[48] The Court then noted the issue in the instant case: "the present case concerns alleged violations of a continuing nature *if* the applicant, for purposes of Article 1 of Protocol No.

---

45 *Loizidou v. Turkey*, Merits, RJD 1996-VI, 2216.

46 Article 159 para. 1 (b) reads:

"All immovable properties, buildings and installations which were found abandoned on 12 February 1975 when the Turkish Federated State of Cyprus was proclaimed or which were considered by law as abandoned or ownerless after the above-mentioned date, or which should have been in the possession or control of the public even though their ownership had not yet been determined ... and ... situated within the boundaries of the TRNC on 15 November 1983, shall be the property of the TRNC notwithstanding the fact that they are not so registered in the books of the Land Registry Office; and the Land Registry Office shall be amended accordingly."

As cited in decision of *Loizidou v. Turkey*, see note 45, para. 18.

47 Ibid., para. 41.

48 The Court cited *Papamichalopoulos and Others v. Greece*, judgment of 24 June 1993, Series A no. 260-B, 20 et seq., 46; *Agrotexim and Others v. Greece*, judgment of 24 October 1995, Series A no. 330, 22, 58.

1 and Article 8 of the Convention, can still be regarded – as remains to be examined by the Court – as the legal owner of the land."[49] The Court then proceeded to examine the question of ownership of the land and found that the asserted expropriation of land by the TRNC could have no legal validity under international law: "[a]ccordingly, the applicant cannot be deemed to have lost title to her property as a result of Article 159 of the 1985 Constitution of the 'TRNC.'"[50] The Court then concluded: "It follows that the applicant, for the purposes of Article 1 of Protocol No. 1 and Article 8 of the Convention, must still be regarded to be the legal owner of the land. The objection *ratione temporis* therefore fails."[51] Hence, the Court held that the actions of the TRNC and of Turkish troops that prevented the applicant from accessing her property had continued after Turkey's acceptance of the Court's jurisdiction and – since these actions violated Article 1 of Protocol 1 – constituted a continuing violation, thus sustaining the jurisdiction of the Court.[52]

Thus the Loizidou case, in sustaining jurisdiction on the basis of a continuing violation which at the time of judgment was 22 years old, constitutes a landmark reaffirmation by the European Court of Human Rights of the importance and power of the continuing violations doc-

---

49 *Loizidou v. Turkey*, see note 45, para. 41. Emphasis added.

50 Ibid., para. 46.

51 Ibid., para. 47.

52 The voting on the decision rejecting Turkey's preliminary objection *ratione temporis* was eleven to six. Judge Bernhardt filed a dissenting opinion on this decision, in which he was joined by Judge Rocha and with whom Judges Jambrek, Pettiti, Baka and Gölcüklü in substance agreed. Judge Bernhardt agreed that the legality of the asserted expropriation by the TRNC was doubtful. However, he did not feel that this was sufficient to decide the matter. He viewed the operative fact to be the closure of the border between northern and southern Cyprus in 1974, which was, in his view, an "instantaneous" act not giving rise to a "continuing violation." He stated that he was "unable to base a judgment of the European Court of Human Rights exclusively on the assumption that the Turkish presence is illegal and that Turkey is therefore responsible for more or less everything that happens in northern Cyprus." Nevertheless, the majority opinion cited and relied upon extensive authority from the UN Security Council and various other international organisations that had expressly declared that the invasion of northern Cyprus was illegal and should not be recognised. See ibid., dissenting opinion of Judge Bernhardt.

trine in making the "law of the present" applicable to decades-long continuing breaches of international law by state actors.[53]

2. Second Scenario: Partial Coverage of Action by Obligation

The ILC commentary on Article 15 ("composite acts") gives a very fine example of how to deal with conduct that at its beginning was not prohibited by a legal norm but which during the course of the conduct became prohibited and hence constitutes a continuing breach from that point in time forward:

> "The word 'remain' in paragraph 2 is inserted to deal with the intertemporal principle set out in article 13. In accordance with that principle, the State must be bound by the international obligation for the period during which the series of acts making up the breach is committed. In cases where the relevant obligation did *not* exist at the beginning of the course of conduct but came into being thereafter, *the 'first' of the actions or omissions of the series for the purposes of State responsibility will be the first occurring after the obligations came into existence*. This need not prevent a court taking into account earlier actions or omissions for other purposes (e.g. in order to establish a factual basis for the later breaches or to provide evidence of intent)."[54]

An example of a continuing violation only partially covered in time by the applicability of an obligatory norm comes from the UN Human Rights Committee (HRC), responsible for monitoring states' compliance with the International Covenant on Civil and Political Rights (ICCPR). This is the case of *Lovelace v. Canada*.[55] The ICCPR entered

---

[53] In a subsequent 1998 ruling, the European Court of Human Rights ordered Turkey to pay compensation and to restore possession ("peaceful enjoyment," as guaranteed by Protocol I of the European Convention) of her property to the applicant, Titina Loizidou. Turkey has subsequently paid US$ 1.4 million in compensation to Loizidou, but only after the Council of Europe threatened sanctions. Turkey has been allowed to delay restoration of Loizidou's "peaceful enjoyment" of her property until 2005. See M. Jansen, "An Invaluable Precedent", *The Jordan Times*, 11 December 2003.

[54] ILC Draft Articles on Responsibility, see note 18, commentary on article 15, para. 11. Emphasis added.

[55] *Lovelace v. Canada*, *Human Rights Law Journal* 2 (1981), 158 (decision of 29 December 1977).

into force with respect to Canada on 19 August 1976. The HRC found that it could not adjudicate on actions prior to that date but stated that "the situation may be different if the alleged violations, although relating to events occurring before 19 August 1976, *continue, or have effects which themselves constitute violations, after that date.*"[56] The HRC thus found that it had jurisdiction to pass upon the applicant's legal status as from 19 August 1976 onward (which, as the date when the obligation entered into force for Canada, was the date when Canada's action gave rise to a breach). It further found that Canada, by denying applicant Lovelace legal status as an Indian, had violated ICCPR Article 27 (right of a member of a minority to enjoy own culture, religion and language).

This was also the approach adopted in the De Becker case, the first "continuing situation" case decided under the European Convention on Human Rights, which concerned the continuing change in status of the applicant resulting from his conviction in 1946 under the Belgian penal code. The Convention entered into effect with respect to Belgium on 14 June 1955. The Commission concluded that:

> "the applicant cannot legally claim, for the period in question [the period prior to 14 June 1955] to have been the victim of a violation of the rights guaranteed by the Convention, even if the state of affairs complained of is of a permanent nature ... [However,] the application, in so far as it concerns this continuing situation extending after 14 June 1955 is not inadmissible *ratione temporis.*"[57]

This approach has been consistently followed in a solid line of cases.[58] The Commission, not surprisingly, has also followed this approach for acceptances of jurisdiction by declaration under Article 25. Thus in *Roy and Alice Fletcher v. United Kingdom*,[59] the Commission considered the complaint admissible for the time period the alleged violation continued *after* the date of acceptance of jurisdiction, but deemed inadmissible the portion of the claim for the time period *prior* to that date.

---

56 Ibid., 166. Emphasis added.

57 *De Becker v. Belgium*, see note 28, 234.

58 See, e.g., *X and Y v. Switzerland*, decision of 8 October 1976, Decisions and Reports 6, 107; *X v. Switzerland*, decision of 12 July 1976, Decisions and Reports 6, 124; *X v. Belgium*, decision of 3 December 1979, Decisions and Reports 18, 250.

59 *Roy & Alice Fletcher v. United Kingdom*, Decision of the Commission, *Collection of Decisions* 25 (1968), 76.

In conclusion, it may be worthwhile to reflect upon a useful summary of this matter:

> "[T]he establishment of a continuing violation, in cases where a jurisdictional limitation clause *ratione temporis* can be invoked, is of major importance. If the applicant can prove a continuing violation which existed *subsequent* to the [jurisdictional] critical date, the international tribunal will confirm its jurisdiction even though the violation dates back or started *before* that critical date. If, on the contrary, the tribunal decides in these circumstances that a claim only concerns an instantaneous act, even one with lasting effects, the claim will necessarily be defeated *ratione temporis*."[60]

Thus once again, the power of the continuing violations doctrine to make the "law of the present" applicable to ongoing, continuing violations that started in the past – even if the entire course of state conduct does not comprise a breach, due to the later coming into effect of the obligatory norm of law – demonstrates the importance of this doctrine in giving courts jurisdiction to adjudicate disputes concerning longstanding violations committed by state actors.

IV. Applicability to the Case of Israel's Duty to Readmit the 1948 Refugees

It is now clear how much is at stake in the characterisation of a state action as a "continuing violation" as opposed to an "instantaneous act." In cases where a significant amount of time (e.g., in the case of Israel, 55 years, from 1948 to 2003) has lapsed between the initial commission of the breach of an international obligation and the bringing of a dispute for settlement, the chances are greater that there will have been a change in the relevant rules of law during the intervening period. Furthermore, the "new law" will generally tend to be more favourable to individual aggrieved parties than the "old law," since the general trend in the evolution of international law since the beginning of the "human rights revolution" in 1945 (which began with the Nuremberg prosecutions, the founding of the United Nations, and the promulgation of the UN Charter) has been to widen the range of protections afforded to individuals and to limit the range of actions permitted by states (which have come under corresponding duties to respect the rights of individuals).

---

60 Pauwelyn, see note 25, 440. Emphasis in original.

In addition, important norms relating to sovereignty rights – such as the all-important right of self-determination – achieved a clear position in positive international law through the human rights revolution.

As mentioned at the outset, I argued in my monograph (see text at notes 1 and 2, above) that the 1948 Palestinian refugees had a right under customary international law in 1948 to return to their homes of origin inside what eventually became the State of Israel. That being so, then Israel had a corresponding duty to readmit them. I argued that the right/duty polarity is grounded in four separate bodies of international law: the law of nationality as affected by state succession; humanitarian law; human rights law; and refugee/displaced persons law.

To give just one example of the customary law basis of the duty to readmit, this one taken from international humanitarian law, let us examine the prohibition against forcible expulsion, which has its basis in Article 46 para. 1 of the Hague Regulations.[61] Pierre Mounier, an assistant prosecutor for the Allies in the criminal prosecution of the Nazi leaders in the IMT at Nuremberg, stated in his opening arguments on 20 November 1945 that "deportation" violated Article 46 of the Hague Regulations, as well as customary international law in general.[62] For that reason, the Charter of the International Military Tribunal[63] (the IMT Charter) included "deportation" in the definition of both "war crimes" (in Article 6 (b) of the IMT Charter) and "crimes against humanity" (in

---

61 Hague Convention (IV) Respecting the Laws and Customs of War on Land, and Annex: Regulations Respecting the Laws and Customs of War on Land, UST.S 539, 1 Bevans 631, signed at The Hague, 18 October 1907, entry into force 26 January 1910. Article 46 para. 1 reads:

"Family honour and rights, the lives of persons, and private property, as well as religious convictions and practice, must be respected."

62 See 2 Trial Of The Major War Criminals Before The International Military Tribunal, Nuremberg, 1945-1946, 49 (42 vols. 1947-1949) (statement of Pierre Mounier, assistant prosecutor for the French Republic, in opening remarks on 20 November 1945: "These deportations were contrary to the international conventions, in particular to Article 46 of the Hague Regulations, 1907, the laws and customs of war, the general principles of criminal law as derived from the criminal laws of all civilized nations, the internal penal laws of the countries in which such crimes were committed, and to Article 6 (b) of the Charter [of the International Military Tribunal at Nuremberg]").

63 See Charter of the International Military Tribunal, Annexed to the London Agreement for the Prosecution and Punishment of the Major War Criminals of the European Axis, 1945, reproduced in D. Schindler/J. Toman (eds), *The Laws of Armed Conflict*, 1988, 3rd ed., 911.

Article 6 (c) of the IMT Charter). *Barring the return of forcibly expelled persons (i.e., refusal to readmit) was similarly condemned as illegal.*[64] Consequently, the Hague Regulations were definitively interpreted by the prosecutors of the IMT to include a right of return under customary humanitarian law and *refusal to readmit constituted a breach of that right/duty.*

Since the 1945 London Charter of the IMT explicitly criminalised deportation, which the prosecutors read to include the obviously related action of refusing to readmit, there is no way that these actions could have been considered "legal" in 1948. This argument seems rather conclusive.

Furthermore, the Fourth Geneva (Civilians) Convention of 1949 expressly categorised "deportation" and the broader category of "transfer" in Article 147 as "grave breaches" (also known as "war crimes") giving rise to universal jurisdiction to prosecute on the part of the High Contracting Parties to these conventions. Hence, the criminal illegality of Israel's actions in 1948 was further clarified and amplified, in a rather rapid and widespread fashion, given the large number of states that have ratified the 1949 Geneva Conventions (including Israel).

Assuming that Israel did have a duty of readmission, then Israel has been in violation of that duty ever since 1948, by continuing to deny reentry to the refugees. Furthermore, this violation is a continuing violation. Israel has enacted legislation – specifically its Nationality Law of 1952[65] – that purported to denationalise the Palestinian refugees, based on the fact of their displacement, and thereby alter their national *status* specifically in order to deny them the ability to return to their homes of origin. Maintenance of this discriminatory law and the concomitant governmental policy of refusing to readmit the refugees since 1948 therefore constitutes a continuing violation of Israel's duty to readmit, as grounded in the four above-mentioned bodies of international law.

So what is the value of Huber's second prong and the continuing violations doctrine in this analysis? The issue relates to the standard of proof

---

[64] See 3 Trial of the Major War Criminals Before the International Military Tribunal, Nuremberg, 1945-1946, 596 (42 vols. 1947-1949) (Captain S. Harris, assistant prosecutor for the United States, introduced evidence on 14 December 1945 on the illegality of preventing the return of forcibly expelled persons: "The first expulsion action was carried out in Alsace in the period from July to December 1940; in the course of it, 105,000 persons were either expelled or prevented from returning"). Emphasis added.

[65] Nationality Law, 5712/1952, *Official Gazette* 93 (1952), 22.

that the plaintiff needs to make out in arguing that a legal duty existed and was violated by the state actor in 1948.

Putting it simply, if Israel's actions in 1948 violated at least one viable, existing customary norm of international law in 1948, that is sufficient basis to start the clock running on a continuing violation. The violation of one valid existing norm will serve to *ground* the claim of illegality. However, since the violation is a continuing and ongoing one, as newly emerging norms crystallise and as treaty obligations are undertaken by the state concerned, such "subsequent" norms and treaty obligations will serve to *buttress* and strengthen the claim of illegality over time. (One clear example of this from treaty law is Israel's undertaking of clear obligations to repatriate under Article 12 para. 4 of the International Covenant on Civil and Political Rights.) Thus, Huber's second prong and the continuing violations doctrine demonstrate rather strikingly that the passage of time – rather than "eroding" or "diluting" a violation and the concomitant obligation to remedy, as many people tend to assume – actually has quite the opposite effect. *Passage of time reinforces the duty to provide a remedy, since the law has gained greater strength and clarity over time.* This is the importance of the two doctrines in the case of Israel's duty to readmit the 1948 Palestinian refugees.

As I demonstrated in my monograph, the right of return has only gained strength in the intervening passage of time since the initial period of forcible displacement in 1947-1949 up through the present. The strong articulation of the right of return in modern law and state practice (see monograph) is a clear indication of the continued existence of the right of return in modern international law. The striking similarity in the formulation of the principles of return/restitution/compensation which figure in United Nations General Assembly Resolution 194, for the Palestinian refugees, and the famous Annex 7 of the Dayton Accords, concerning the rights of the refugees and internally displaced persons in the Bosnian context, indicates that the rights of the Palestinian refugees were established, well-recognised by states and binding in 1948. They have become only more so with the intervening passage of time.

Therefore the fact that Israel's violation is a continuing violation, unresolved up to this day, serves to expose Israel to the entire range of binding norms of international law which have existed from 1947 up through the present time. *Israel cannot escape responsibility by delaying its compliance with international law.* Such delay only serves to increase Israel's liability for reparations owed under the law of state responsibility for the immense scope and duration of time over which the continuing violation has been, and continues to be, committed.

This conclusion is consistent with the commonly held understandings of both the intertemporal doctrine (namely Huber's second prong) and the continuing violations doctrine. It is to be hoped that this matter might be submitted to an impartial international tribunal so that the applicable rules of international law may be used to hold Israel to account both to cease its continuing violation and to provide the full range of remedies to the victims for which it is liable under the law of state responsibility for internationally wrongful acts.

Philosophical Perspective

The Palestinian Right of Return and the Justice of Zionism

*Chaim Gans**

Abstract

Supporters of a Palestinian right of return assume that Israeli Jews bear responsibility for both the past and present suffering of the Palestinian refugees. Accordingly, the Palestinian claim for return is a demand to realise this responsibility (*inter alia*) by way of the return of the refugees to their places of origin or to uninhabited regions in the Land of Israel/Palestine. The purpose of this article is to examine the responsibility of the Israeli Jews for the Palestinian suffering and whether this responsibility ought to be realised by way of return of the refugees in light of the question of the justice of Zionism. Part I of the article presents various approaches rejecting or affirming Zionism. The subsequent parts investigate the implications of the disparities between these approaches rejecting/affirming Zionism and Zionism's actual history as it unfolded in terms of Jewish responsibility for the Palestinian plight and the question of Palestinian return. I argue that some of the approaches to Zionism are irrelevant to the dispute over the Palestinian right of return as it is understood within the framework of Israeli internal discourse and the Israeli-Palestinian dialogue. However, my main point is that those approaches rejecting/affirming Zionism that are relevant, though they may vary in their implications for the scope of Jewish responsibility for Palestinian suffering, nevertheless lead to very similar conclusions with respect to discharging that responsibility by way of Palestinian repatriation.

---

* I am grateful to Eyal Benvenisti, David Enoch and Andrei Marmor for their many important comments on an earlier draft of this article.

I. Introduction

Supporters of a Palestinian right of return assume that Israeli Jews bear responsibility for both the past and present suffering of the Palestinians. Accordingly the Palestinian claim for return is a demand to realise this responsibility (*inter alia*) by way of the return of the Palestinian refugees to their places of origin or to uninhabited regions in the Land of Israel/Palestine.[1] There are several dimensions to this claim and to its underlying presupposition concerning the responsibility of Israeli Jews for the plight of the Palestinian diaspora. One such dimension pertains to the types of damage for which responsibility should be borne (property damage, loss of residence, pain and suffering, loss of livelihood, and so on). Another dimension pertains to the scope of the people to whom responsibility is owed: only and strictly those exiles who were forcibly expelled by the Jews? all exiles, including those who fled out of fear? or an intermediate category of displaced persons? A third dimension of the Palestinian demand concerns the group of exiles towards whom responsibility will be realised by allowing their return either to their places of origin or to uninhabited areas in the Land of Israel/Palestine and to the possible future political-cultural character of these areas. For example, should all Palestinian refugees be allowed to return to their places of origin or just some of them? And if this right to return is to be restricted to only some refugees, then how will they be defined? Furthermore, should the remainder then be permitted to return to uninhabited areas in the Land of Israel/Palestine currently controlled by

---

[1] In this article, the term "the Land of Israel" (which is the English translation of the Hebrew *Eretz Yisrael*) designates both the territory lying west of the Jordan River up to the Mediterranean Sea (which today encompasses the territories of the State of Israel and the Palestinian Authority) and the territory east of the Jordan River (which is part of Jordan today and in the British Mandate period was Transjordan). In the Jewish faith, the Land of Israel is the territory that was promised to Abraham, the forefather of the Jews. "Western Land of Israel" refers to that part of the Land of Israel that lies west of the Jordan River and which is also known as "Palestine." The Palestinian demand for the return refers to return within the territory of Israel's recognised borders, that is, the state's borders from the end of the 1948 Israeli War of Independence until the outbreak of the Six-Day War in June 1967. The Palestinian refugees originate from these territories. Any official Jewish willingness today to the return of Palestinian refugees relates not to a return to these territories but, rather, to territories in Western Land of Israel/Palestine that were conquered by Israel during the Six-Day War, some of which were transferred to the Palestinian Authority under the Oslo Agreements.

the primarily Jewish state but that eventually will constitute part of a primarily Palestinian state? And there are further possibilities: return to uninhabited regions of a bi-national state or return to uninhabited areas in a state that is culturally neutral.

The most ambitious interpretation of the right of return and of the assumption of Jewish responsibility for the Palestinian refugee situation is that Jews in Israel are responsible for *all of the past and present suffering of all members of the Palestinian diaspora resulting from* Zionism and the establishment of the State of Israel. Under this interpretation, responsibility for the Palestinian plight can only be properly discharged (in addition, *inter alia*, to providing monetary compensation for the suffering in all its forms) by way of allowing the return of all members of the Palestinian diaspora to their places of origin in a state that is entirely Palestinian and expelling all the Jews living in those places, or at least those who live there as a consequence of Zionism. The antithesis to this interpretation of Jewish responsibility for Palestinian suffering is the absolute denial of any such responsibility and the total rejection of any Palestinian right of return, of any scope – and perhaps even beyond this: the exacerbation of the problem by transferring those Palestinians still resident in the Land of Israel, at least the western part. These are the two polar positions of the spectrum, between which numerous intermediate possibilities fall. The central intermediate position supports the return of all or part of the Palestinian diaspora to Israel within its pre-1967 borders. Under this position, Israel is meant to continue its role as the manifestation of the Jewish right to self-determination. The Israeli consensus rejects this position, but at least refers to it and regards it as worthy of response in its internal discourse and in its dialogue with Palestinians. The focus of this paper is on the right of return as conceived under this intermediate approach.

The array of considerations for assessing the scope of Jewish responsibility for the Palestinian diaspora and whether that responsibility should be realised in some form of Palestinian return is complex. It comprises individualist and collectivist moral considerations, historical and a-historical considerations, and retrospective and prospective moral considerations. I focus primarily, though not exclusively, on the individualist and collectivist moral considerations deriving from historical and present justice concerns. These considerations cannot be properly identified without addressing the different approaches affirming and rejecting Zionism and their respective justifications and underlying assumptions. In Part II below, I present some of these approaches for and against Zionism, and in the subsequent parts, I investigate the implications of the disparities between the different approaches and Zionism's actual history as it unfolded in terms of Jewish responsibility for the Palestinian plight and the question of Palestinian return. I argue that some of the approaches denying or affirming Zionism are irrelevant to the dispute over the Palestinian right of return as it is understood within the framework of Israeli internal discourse and the Israeli-Palestinian dialogue. Both these discourses presuppose that the dispute revolves around the question of the existence of a Palestinian right of return to Israel as a state that realises the Jewish right to national self-determination. I argue that although the approaches affirming or rejecting Zionism that are relevant to this specific point of dispute may vary in their implications for the scope of Jewish responsibility for *Palestinian suffering*, they nevertheless lead to very similar conclusions regarding discharging that responsibility by way of *Palestinian repatriation*.

II. Different Forms of Zionism and Different Approaches Rejecting It

In the framework of the present discussion, Zionism is understood as a cultural-nationalist ideology. This type of ideology is not necessarily devoid of political aspirations,[2] but its focus is on the interest of members of particular national cultures in adhering to their cultures, sustaining them through the generations, and securing political support to do this. Nationalism of this type first originated in Central and Eastern Europe and should be distinguished from what historians and sociologists refer to as "civic nationalism," which I prefer to call "statist nationalism."[3] The latter originated in Britain and France and is concerned not so much with people's interest in adhering to their cultures as with the interest that states have in ensuring the cultural homogeneity of their populations.[4] Zionism is a cultural nationalist movement of Jews, but not the only such movement. The *Bund*, too, was a cultural nationalist ideology that focused on enabling the Jews to adhere to and sustain their culture. However, in contrast to Zionism, it did not aspire to realise these goals in the Land of Israel. This latter aspiration – to establish

---

2 See C. Gans, *The Limits of Nationalism*, 2003, ch. 1.

3 *Idem.*

4 *Idem.*

Jewish self-determination specifically in the Land of Israel – can be regarded as a constitutive component of Zionism.[5]

One possible basis for rejecting Zionism is the rejection in principle of cultural nationalism. This rejection could originate from political ideologies such as socialism, cosmopolitan liberalism, or neutralist liberalism. Neutralist liberalism does not necessarily dispute cultural nationalism's claim that people have an interest in adhering to and sustaining their cultures, but it does contest the notion that the State should actively promote such an interest.[6] The other two political ideologies noted – socialism and cosmopolitan liberalism – reject the thesis that there is any such real interest.[7] Another possible basis for rejecting Zionism, rather than deriving from the rejection in principle of cultural nationalism, can be the denial of the right of any national group to protect its culture within the boundaries of a territory already inhabited by another group or groups (even if the former has a preceding historical link to that territory).[8]

Zionism can be affirmed on the basis of a principle according to which the aspiration of the Jews for self-determination in the Land of Israel should be realised in a non-territorial form or, alternatively, in a territorial form. Each of these two possible forms has a number of variations. The non-territorial form of Zionism can be understood as prescribing the establishment of either a spiritual centre or a bi-national state in Palestine/the Land of Israel, where Jewish and Arab populations would be intermixed. The territorial approach can be conceived of as advocating the creation of a bi-national state that will designate separate territories for each group. Alternatively, it could be interpreted as supporting the establishment of a Jewish state in part of the Land of Israel/Palestine with a Jewish hegemony, populated primarily – but not exclusively – by Jews, or even a Jewish state in the entire territory of Palestine with a Jewish hegemony. Yet a third version of the territorial approach would call for the establishment of a Jewish state in part of the Land of Israel

---

[5] This is so despite the Uganda Plan, which proposed Uganda as the Jewish national homeland, and, *inter alia*, also because of its total rejection.

[6] See, e.g. B. Barry, *Culture and Equality: An Egalitarian Critique of Multiculturalism*, 2001.

[7] Regarding the socialist rejection, see Nimni's discussion relating to Marx and Engels in E. Nimni, *Marxism and Nationalism*, 1991, especially chs. 1, 3; for the cosmopolitan liberal's rejection, see J. Waldron, "Minority Cultures and the Cosmopolitan Alternative", *U.Mich.J.L. Reform* 25 (1991-1992), 751 et seq.

[8] This matter is discussed in Gans, see note 2, ch. 4.

exclusively for (all) Jews. Almost all of these approaches, both those advocating Zionism and those rejecting it, had their supporters at various stages of Zionism's history. The dominant form of Zionism, however, the approach that occupied and continues to occupy central stage in the history of the Zionist movement, is the aspiration to establish a Jewish state in part of the Land of Israel, with a Jewish hegemony, that is (or strives to be) a homeland for all Jews.

III. The Right of Return and the Anti-Nationalist Rejection of Zionism

Those who reject Zionism on the basis of an outright rejection of cultural nationalism (which I will hereafter refer to as "nationalism") will hold Israeli Jews responsible for all the suffering that was and still is the lot of the entire Palestinian diaspora. They can do this because even the most minimalist form of Zionism supports the establishment of a binational state in Palestine, an aspiration rejected by anti-nationalists as not legitimate. Accordingly, the argument goes, Zionism is responsible for the creation of the Palestinian diaspora in its entirety and not merely for the exile and hardships suffered by Palestinians forcibly expelled during the 1948 Israeli War of Independence. Consequently, at least from the perspective of retrospective considerations, the entire Palestinian diaspora is entitled to return.

However, those who reject Zionism for anti-nationalist reasons cannot support the removal of all Jews from the Land of Israel. The anti-nationalist stance is grounded in arguments drawn from socialist or liberal political moralities. Proponents of these moralities are necessarily humanists. As such, they will not advocate the banishment from Palestine of all Jews living in Israel today as a result of Zionism, for this would entail the immoral expulsion of people born and/or raised in Israel since the advent of the refugee problem. Since their lives are deeply rooted in Israel, on the one hand, and since they bear no personal responsibility for the emergence of the Palestinian diaspora, on the other, a strong individualistic argument can be made against their displacement and removal from their homes. Because these points, grounded in contemporary realities, act as a bar to any demand by opponents of nationalism to remove all Jews from Israel, they also preclude the return of *all* members of the Palestinian diaspora to their places of origin. The most that anti-nationalists can demand is the return of some of the Palestinian refugees to their places of origin and the return of others to unpopulated areas of Palestine/the Land of Israel.

It should be recalled, however, that an anti-Zionist stance deriving from the rejection of nationalism grounded in socialism, cosmopolitan liberalism, or neutralist liberalism must, for consistency, reject also the establishment of a state that would realise the Palestinian right to self-determination in Palestine. It can only support the establishment of a culturally neutral state in Palestine where Jews and Arabs coexist. Yet I am sceptical as to the defensibility of the various theses upon which this rejection of nationalism rests. I doubt whether the cosmopolitan ideal is universally suited to all human beings.[9] I am also sceptical as to the feasibility of an ideal of a culturally neutral state in which there is no clear preference of one or a very limited number of national cultures over other cultures to which citizens of the state belong.

In the context of the debate between neutralist liberals and nationalist liberals on this matter, it has often been observed that states cannot be neutral *vis-à-vis* culture in the same way as they conceivably can be with regard to religion. The reason for this is that there is no way to avoid giving preference to, for example, one or several of the state's dominant languages over languages that are the first language of many citizens. Such a preference, which results from practical necessity, engenders a partiality that may be prejudicial to the interests of individuals belonging to cultural minorities who wish to adhere to their cultures and live within the framework of those cultures.

It can certainly be argued in the Marxist vein that these interests are based on false consciousness and that people should be re-educated so that they no longer identify with these interests. Since this is not the appropriate forum for addressing this claim, I will note only that insofar as the Jewish-Palestinian struggle is concerned, the belief of both sides in the importance of their interests in their respective cultures is so entrenched that any attempt to reshape their consciousnesses in the foreseeable future would be doomed to fail. Since there is an urgent need to resolve the Palestinian refugee problem in the foreseeable future, understandings of the right of return based on a rejection of Zionism that derives from the outright rejection of cultural nationalism must be set aside for the time being.

---

[9] These questions are discussed in W. Kymlicka, *Multicultural Citizenship: A Liberal Theory of Minority Rights*, 1995; Gans, see note 2, 160-165.

Furthermore, as stated above, both the Israeli internal discourse regarding the Palestinian right of return and the discourse between Israeli Jews and those Palestinians willing to discuss the issue presuppose the return of members of the Palestinian diaspora to the borders of a state that is the framework for Jewish national self-determination – namely, to Israel. Denial of the feasibility of such a state is incompatible with the presuppositions of these two discourses. Hence, even if it were tenable to reject Zionism on the basis of anti-nationalism, such a stance would, in practice, be irrelevant to the present Israeli-Palestinian dialogue.

IV. The Right of Return and Rejecting the Realisation of Jewish Nationalism in Palestine

Zionism can be rejected not only on an anti-nationalist basis; it can also be rejected by nationalists who object to the realisation of Jewish self-determination specifically in Palestine/the Land of Israel.[10] Such an objection could be grounded in the denial of any historical connection between the Jewish People and the Land of Israel. Alternatively, an actual historical connection can be admitted, but the normative significance of that connection could either be completely denied or deemed insufficient to justify the politically-motivated return of the Jewish People to a particular territory that, up until their return, had been populated by individuals constituting a cultural group entirely distinct from the Jews.[11] If, indeed, the Jews have a right to national self-determination,

[10] The former approach will find no distinction between Zionism and any other colonialist movement. The latter will concede the possibility of a distinction, but of no normative significance for the justification of Zionism. The truth is that the question of whether or not Zionism is a colonialist movement is irrelevant to its *post-facto* justification, since even the colonialist nations were never seriously requested to leave the locations in which they had settled (e.g. the European nations that had settlers in New Zealand, the United States, Australia, etc.). In other words, it can be argued that just as the historical connection did not justify the Jews' return, its absence does not justify their removal. Accordingly, it is of no consequence, whether or not Zionism is identified as a form of colonialism.

[11] They can in fact reject Zionism and Jewish cultural nationalism through yet a third avenue: that of Palestinian chauvinism, according to which only Palestinian nationalism is of intrinsic value and any other cultural nationalism is a sham. I do not discuss this possibility since it is clearly incoherent (in that it as-

proponents of this position would argue, they should have realised it in the territories in which they were residing at the relevant time. Since members of another, non-Jewish culture already inhabited the territory comprising the Land of Israel, Jewish migration to that land for the purpose of establishing a Jewish entity there was inappropriate insofar as it entailed the usurpation of land from its inhabitants. The principled position that this approach presupposes is that the right to territorial self-determination belongs only to groups that already constitute a majority in a given territory; it is not the right to create such a majority in a territory already settled by other nations.[12]

Which particular version of the Palestinian right-of-return supporters of this position will adopt depends on whether they are liberal nationalists or nationalists to the right of liberalism. The former do not assume normative priority of the national "collective" over its individual members, nor do they assume normative priority of one national group over other such groups. On the contrary, their understanding of the relationship between national groups and their members rests on individualistic assumptions, while their understanding of the relationship among different national groups rests on egalitarian assumptions. Non-liberal nationalists do the opposite: they assume normative priority of national groups over their individual members and normative priority of their own national group over other groups.[13] However, there are both liberal nationalists and more right-leaning nationalists who reject Zionism because they deny either the very fact of the historical connection between the Jews and the Land of Israel or the normative significance of that link. Such critics will attribute responsibility to Zionism for the Palestinian diaspora in its entirety and for all the various types of suffering borne by its members. Yet they may differ significantly on the matter of Palestinian return.

---

cribes value to one group and denies it to another, despite admitting the relevant similarities between the groups), as well as patently racist (in that it characterises one group as inferior to another).

[12] For a detailed discussion of this issue, see Gans, see note 2, chs. 4, 5.

[13] Regarding philosophical characterisations of nationalism that is right of liberalism, see I. Berlin, "Nationalism: Past Neglect and Present Power", in: I. Berlin, *Against the Current: Essays in the History of Ideas*, H. Hardy (ed.), 1980, 333-355; Barry, see note 6. For characterisations of historians, see P. Alter, *Nationalism*, 1994, 2nd ed., ch. 2. Philosophers refer to these forms of nationalism as romantic; historians often call them integral.

Non-liberal nationalists who reject Zionism based on their rejection of any factual or normatively significant link between the Jews and the Land of Israel might subscribe to the first version of the right of return, i.e., the return of the entire Palestinian diaspora and the expulsion of the Jews. They will derive this position from their presumption of the normative priority of the national group over its individual members. Under this presumption, they will find it irrelevant that the lives of Jewish individuals are currently rooted in Palestine and that those individuals are not responsible for the fact that their lives are now rooted there. Since their moral ontology is comprised primarily of collectives and not individuals, they will ascribe responsibility to the Jewish collective inhabiting Palestine, regardless of the innocence of the majority of the individuals comprising that collective. The Jewish collective is certainly responsible for the fact that its existence is rooted there, as well as for the fact that this existence began "in sin" as it were. Under this approach, therefore, it is legitimate to expel the members of such a collective. Thus a rejection of Zionism that stems from a right-wing rejection of the legitimacy of realising Jewish self-determination in Palestine inevitably produces the most extreme version of the Palestinian right of return: the return of the entire Palestinian diaspora and the removal of all Jews from the territory of Palestine if their presence is the result of Zionism.[14]

Liberal nationalists who reject the realisation of Jewish self-determination in Palestine cannot adopt this extreme interpretation of the Palestinian right of return. As liberals, they base their nationalism on individualistic interests, and they therefore would be compelled to attribute significant weight to the interests of the Jewish individuals currently living in Palestine/the Land of Israel to continue living there and not to be uprooted even if their presence in Israel is the result of Zionism. These individual interests must merit protection at least with respect to those individuals who are not responsible for the fact that they were born and raised in Israel. Since the interests in question are significant, the liberal nationalist has no choice but to support the right of these individuals to remain in Israel, or at least to concede that there is no justi-

[14] I must stress that this could be their position, but it is not necessarily their position, the reason being that even if they ascribe ultimate value to collectives, they can simultaneously ascribe similar value to individuals. Conceivably, they could ascribe a degree of importance to individuals that would lead them, in this case, not to favour the interests of the Palestinian collective and its component individuals to inhabit Palestine on their own over the interests of individual Jews to continue living there.

fication for expelling them. In addition, acknowledgement in this way of the right of numerous individual Jews currently residing in Israel to continue to do so will also lead to recognition of the right of those same individuals to self-determination in areas in which they constitute the majority. In other words, the liberal nationalist rejects the all-embracing claim regarding the Jewish People's right to establish their self-determination in the Land of Israel at the time of the inception of the Zionist movement. Yet at the same time he or she must acknowledge the moral right to national self-determination of Jews born in Israel and/or those who immigrated there as infants and who, therefore, bear no personal responsibility for their lives' being rooted there. In other words, while liberal nationalism allows its proponents to reject Zionism, it nonetheless requires their *post-facto* assent to Zionism's normative consequences – consequences that are consistent at least with the most rudimentary, modest form of Zionism. By rejecting this rudimentary form and denying the historical justification for its adoption by the mainstream Zionist movement, liberal nationalists can hold the Jews accountable for all the Palestinian refugees' trials and tribulations. They do recognise that Zionism has had certain consequences which, *post-facto*, provide a normative basis for Jewish self-determination in the Land of Israel. Yet they must not translate the responsibility ascribed to the Jews for all the Palestinian exiles and for all their suffering into a correlative right of return for all members of the diaspora to their places of origin.[15]

Liberal nationalists certainly would not resort to individualistic arguments in order to justify the return of Palestinian refugees to areas currently inhabited by Jewish individuals, since the latter are not individually responsible for the expulsion of the Palestinians or for the fact that

---

[15] Obviously, liberal nationalists could acknowledge that their liberal stances could be exploited and manipulated by, for example, nationalist movements such as Zionism that create on-the-ground facts with normative significance, facts that liberals will have to recognise. If these liberals are consequentialists, they can, in principle, recognise the legitimacy of supposedly non-liberal steps that might, in the long run, maximise the realisation of liberalism. Problems of this kind cast a shadow also on such legal institutions as statutes of limitations. Yet I believe that ultimately these institutions are justified and more plausible from a liberal standpoint. For a convincing argument, see J. Waldron, "Settlement, Return, and the Supersession Thesis", *Theoretical Inquiries* 5 (2004), LXXX.

their lives are rooted in these places.[16] However, with respect to uninhabited areas, individualist considerations could, in the eyes of the liberal, justify allowing the return of the Palestinian refugees to the places from which they were uprooted, regardless of whether they were expelled or left voluntarily. Later in this article, I deal with the question of whether this argument is decisive with respect to this kind of Palestinian return. As argued above, no member of the Palestinian dispersion, whether he/she was exiled or left willingly, is entitled to return to his or her former home if inhabited by Jews who are not responsible for the fact that they currently reside there. The question is, are such refugees entitled to return to presently uninhabited areas in the Jewish state from which they were not uprooted in the past? There seem to be no individualistic considerations that work in favour of this particular way of realising Jewish responsibility for the refugee problem. The determination of the appropriate way of realising responsibility for the Palestinians' exile and suffering is contingent on what form is deemed appropriate for realising the right to self-determination of both nations that today, as a point of fact, reside in the Land of Israel/Palestine.

---

[16] A distinction must be made between a person's lack of responsibility for the fact that his life is conducted in a particular place and his lack of responsibility for the expulsion of the previous residents from the same place. The former entails the latter, but not *vice versa*. No responsibility for living in a particular place does not imply no responsibility for the expulsion of previous residents. Hence, Jews born on Palestinian property or brought there as infants are not responsible for the fact that their lives are rooted in those places and, thus, are not personally responsible for the Palestinian exile. Jewish adults who were opposed to the Palestinian expulsion, or who were even opposed to the actual realisation of Zionism, are not personally responsible for the Palestinian diaspora. If, as adults, however, they purchased property that was once Palestinian, they are most certainly responsible for the fact that their lives are rooted there. The situation becomes more complex when we consider that many Jewish individuals who are not responsible for the fact that part of their lives are rooted in formerly Palestinian property, since they have been there since infancy, do bear responsibility for other parts of their lives being rooted in such property since this has occurred in adulthood, when they chose to conduct certain aspects of their lives in these places. For example, at the age of three, I was brought to the lands of Sumeil (where a part of North Tel Aviv is located). But it was only in my adulthood that I began spending time in Sheikh Monis (where Tel Aviv University is located). The only way of overcoming this problem is *via* the claim of necessity. Many adults conduct parts of their lives on formerly Palestinian property, to which they arrived as adults, since the requirements of conducting a normal life, including following a career and earning a livelihood, leave them no other option.

Those favouring a single bi-national political framework for this self-determination in the territory between the Jordan River and the Mediterranean Sea ("Western Land of Israel"), without any territorial distinction between the two nations, would certainly argue that all Palestinian exiles should be permitted to return to the areas currently within the boundaries of the State of Israel, just as they are entitled to live in areas of Palestine outside those borders, since all of Western Land of Israel constitutes the Palestinians' historical homeland.

However, if, for reasons stemming from the desirable interpretation of the right to self-determination in general or from its desirable realisation in the context of the Israeli-Palestinian dispute, liberal nationalists were to contend that Jewish self-determination and Palestinian self-determination should be realised today in mutually distinct territorial frameworks (either in two separate states or in one state with a territorial division between the two cultures, as in Belgium and Switzerland), then under such an arrangement, the place of Palestinian return would be contingent, first and foremost, on how Palestine/Western Land of Israel is divided between the two nations. This question is a thorny one, for Zionism's "birth in sin" casts a shadow not only on its demographic consequences but also on its territorial consequences. From this perspective, Israel's 1948 borders (in force from the establishment of the state until 4 June 1967, the beginning of the Arab-Israeli Six-Day War) would have no legitimacy. The same would be true of the borders set out in the 1947 UN Partition Plan or the borders running along the demographic lines set by the Jewish settlements in the Occupied Territories (Judea and Samaria and the Gaza Strip) since the 1967 War. At this stage of the discussion, I will not examine the relevant criteria for determining the appropriate borders under the territorial-separation solution to the Jewish-Palestinian dispute. Suffice it to say that if territorial separation is the appropriate resolution, then there would be obvious advantages to a solution whereby Jewish responsibility for the Palestinian refugees is fully realised through compensation for their suffering and through their repatriation exclusively within Palestinian territories, at least with regard to those unable to return to their places of origin because they are currently occupied by other individuals. Palestinians' residence in areas designated as Palestinian territories would be considered residence in their homeland at least to the same extent as their residence in territories designated for Jewish self-determination.[17]

---

[17] It is important to remember that whether or not Jews' residing in one or another part of the Land of Israel can be considered residence in their homeland

However, since Palestinian culture would be more fully expressed in exclusively Palestinian territories and since the Palestinian right to self-determination would be realised primarily there, collectivist considerations would favour Palestinian return specifically to those territories. These considerations would be decisive, in light of the individualistic considerations against allowing exiles to return to areas now inhabited by Jews who are not responsible for the fact that their lives are rooted there. Admittedly, it could be argued that Palestinian refugees whose places of origin are currently occupied by Jews could conceivably prefer living in geographic proximity to their former homes, even if located in the territory of Jewish self-determination, to living in a territorial entity controlled by Palestinians where they would enjoy national self-determination. However, I am sceptical as to how compelling such a preference could be. For, ultimately, most of the places in close physical proximity to the refugees' original homes have changed beyond recognition in terms of physical appearance and character. Accordingly, even if a certain weight is ascribed to proximity to places of origin, it certainly cannot be of a decisive nature.

The position of liberal nationalists who reject Zionism but accept its *post-facto* consequences can be summed up as follows: They call for Israeli recognition of the Jews' collective responsibility for the emergence of the Palestinian diaspora in its entirety, not just for those expelled, and for all the Palestinians' subsequent suffering. They point to significant individualistic grounds for recognising a *prima facie* right of return for Palestinians, which would mandate that all Palestinian exiles be

---

depends on whether one attributes normative significance to the historical connection between the Jews and the Land of Israel. If one denies such normative significance, then it is clear that the borders of the Jewish state cannot diverge from the areas in which Jews actually reside. The reason is that if the historical connection is not a consideration, then the justification for a Jew living in the Land of Israel is identical to the justification for a settler of European origin living in New Zealand. Colonialists should not be expelled from the places where their lives are now rooted. Their right to receive territories that they do not actually occupy is subject to considerations of distributive justice, which take natural reproduction into account. However, if one attributes normative significance to the historical connection between the Jews and the Land of Israel, then vacant areas in that Land can be included in the framework of the Jewish state. Furthermore their claim to these territories will not be based exclusively on considerations of distributive justice between them and the Palestinians that rest on natural reproduction alone, but also upon the exigencies created by the return of members of the Jewish diaspora to the Jewish state.

given the right to return to their places of origin on the *proviso* that Jewish individuals do not reside there (or that those who do are personally responsible for the expulsion of Palestinians). Those liberal nationalists who view a bi-national state in all of Western Land of Israel as the appropriate solution to the dispute will demand Palestinian return to any uninhabited place, regardless of whether it falls within the current borders of Israel or not. However, if they deem territorial separation the appropriate solution, their demand will be restricted to a right of return to those areas that are designated to be part of the Palestinian territory.

The question to be asked, then, is whether the Jewish People's historical connection to the Land of Israel is of sufficient normative significance to justify their return to that territory for the purpose of realising their self-determination. This is a watershed question, separating those who reject Zionism without an accompanying outright rejection of nationalism from those who support Zionism. Those who deny any normative significance to the Jewish people's connection to the Land of Israel or claim that it is insufficient to justify the return of the Jews to territory already inhabited by another nation will reject Zionism. I have just discussed the conclusions such nationalists should arrive at with regard to the Palestinian right of return. However, those who take the position that the Jews' historical connection to the Land of Israel can provide a sufficient ground for their return to that territory, despite its being inhabited by Arabs, would subscribe to one or another form of Zionism. I mentioned two such streams at the beginning of the article, and I will now proceed to discuss their implications for the Palestinian right of return.

V. A Non-Territorial Version of Zionism and the Palestinian Right of Return

According to the first and very modest version of Zionism mentioned above – the version subscribed to by *Ahad Ha'am* and later by the *Brit Shalom* movement – Jews should have been allowed to realise national self-determination in the territory comprising the Land of Israel, but not within the framework of a Jewish nation-state and probably not even within an independent territorial framework. On the one hand, this version of Zionism is based upon the recognition of the normative significance of the historical connection between the Jews and the Land of Israel and perhaps also upon the understanding that national self-determination is viable only within an historical homeland. On the other hand, it recognises that the territory comprising the Land of Israel is simultaneously the Palestinian homeland, and accordingly, Palestinians have the same entitlement as Jews *vis-à-vis* that territory – namely, to realise their right to national self-determination there. At the inception of the Zionist movement, the Palestinians were dispersed throughout the entire territory. However, their degree of concentration at the time did not preclude the parallel settlement of a large Jewish population, large enough to warrant the realisation of sub-statist and non-territorial Jewish national self-determination. Therefore, in accordance with this version of Zionism at that point in time, the Jews were entitled to aspire to this kind of self-determination in Palestine/the Land of Israel. They were not, however, justified in aspiring to statist self-determination or sub-statist territorial self-determination, because, given the existing demographic circumstances of the Land, this would have meant imposing Jewish government on the entire Arab population, or at least a large proportion of it, thereby turning the latter into foreigners within their own homeland. The Palestinians, for their part, also would have to content themselves with sub-statist and non-territorial national self-determination. All this pertains to the principle that Zionism *should* have been adopted and that, *had* it been adopted, the Arabs would have had to come to terms with it.[18] History, as we know, took a different path.

[18] It should be stressed that this claim does not imply that the right of the Jews to return to the Land of Israel is justified by considerations of corrective justice, i.e., that the persecution of Jews primarily in Europe justifies the compensation of the Jewish People by allowing them to establish their self-determination in the Land of Israel. Many hold this view, but its foundations are rather shaky given that the Arabs were not a party to the persecution of the Jews, so there is no reason why they should have to pay the price. The claim is an a-historical distributive justice claim based on the general principle that every nation is entitled to self-determination in its historical homeland, even if this means that the other nations in that homeland must content themselves with less than statehood (see Gans, see note 2, ch. 4). It should also be stressed that this principle need not be interpreted as asserting a right to nation-statehood. It can also be interpreted as referring to a right to sub-statist self-determination (see the Australian and Canadian decisions regarding indigenous peoples' right to self-determination: *Mabo v. Queensland* (No. 2) (1992) 175 CLR1; *Delgamuukw v. British Columbia* (1997) 153 DLR (4th) 193 (SCC)). This principle can be further qualified: Nations that were uprooted from their homeland and persecuted are entitled to return to their places of origin even if not entirely vacant. In the Jewish-Palestinian case, this would mean that the Palestinians are

On the one hand, mainstream Zionism aspired to establish a Jewish nation-state in the Land of Israel and was not content with sub-statist and non-territorial self-determination. On the other hand, the Arabs gave the impression that they were opposed not only to the establishment of an independent Jewish state, but also to any other form of Jewish national self-determination in the Land of Israel, even sub-statist and non-territorial. If, indeed, these are the facts, then to the extent that the Palestinian exile was voluntary, the Jews and Arabs share equal responsibility for the emergence of the Palestinian diaspora and its accompanying suffering. The Jews bear sole responsibility only towards those Palestinians who were forcibly expelled.[19] This, then, concludes the issue of the allocation of responsibility.

---

paying the primary price of this principle of distributive justice and that they are doing so not as a result of their own culpability but due to simple bad luck (their homeland is also the homeland of others). This fact lays the basis for international responsibility to solve the Palestinian refugee problem, with particular responsibility borne by the European nations who persecuted the Jews, which led to the applicability of the a-historical distributive justice principle in this context.

[19] Obviously, this description is a simplistic one. Ultimately, we can assume that amongst both the Jews and Arabs different stances were adopted by different sectors regarding the opinions and actions of the other side and that these actions and reactions had a dynamic reciprocal effect. Accordingly, the opinions of the different groups and the groupings themselves are perpetually in a state of flux. In order to provide comprehensive answers to questions concerning the responsibility of one party for the reactions of the other, one must provide answers to factual historical questions relating to states of affairs in infinite points in time and to complex theoretical questions relating to the justness of the responses of one side to the other. This should be done in light of the weight of the different opinions of the different sectors of both sides regarding the actions of the other. Obviously, I am unable to deal here with either these factual historical questions or the theoretical moral ones.

Applying the distinction between those who were forcibly expelled and those who voluntarily left is also problematic. The term "forcibly" also includes explicit threats to use force and implicit threats, for example, those that are the product of rumours regarding threats of force and a general atmosphere of a threat to use force. One must assume that the overwhelming majority of the Palestinian exiles would be able to claim that they left due to direct or indirect threats of force. This notwithstanding, I assume that there may have been those who left not as a result of a direct or indirect threat to their physical existence, but because they did not want to live in Jewish surroundings or in a region in which Jews and Arabs were at war.

The way in which this responsibility should be realised rests primarily on which framework is the most appropriate today for both nations currently living in Palestine/Israel to realise their self-determination. The options will resemble those proposed by liberal nationalists who reject Zionism by virtue of their rejection of the Jews' historical connection to the Land of Israel, options that have already been addressed. The relevant approaches to this matter are those proposed by liberal nationalists and not those proposed by right-wing nationalists, since the latter would presumably not endorse the moderate version of Zionism. It is reasonable to assume that Jewish non-liberal nationalists (i.e., nationalists to the right of liberalism) would support more extreme versions of Zionism, whereas their Palestinian counterparts would reject Zionism outright. Liberal nationalists who support the moderate version of Zionism might, under current conditions, support a bi-national state without territorial distinctions, as a possible but not necessary implication of their accepting this version of Zionism. Such liberal nationalists could also accept territorial separation between the two nations (whether within the framework of one state or two) as a solution necessitated by the history of the dispute and its demographic and territorial realities. Liberal nationalists holding this latter position would reject the right of Palestinian exiles to return to their places of origin if populated, but would find powerful grounds for favouring the right of all Palestinian exiles, whether they left voluntarily or were forcibly expelled, to return to their places of origin if unpopulated. This position with regard to those who were expelled follows from the exclusive Jewish responsibility for these exiles. With regard to the return of those who left voluntarily, the argument will be that since Israeli Jews collectively bear partial responsibility for these exiles and since most are unable to return to their places of origin because they are now populated by others, there are compelling grounds for allowing the return of those whose places of origin are vacant. All of this, however, depends on whether it makes any sense at all to speak of "vacant" places, an issue addressed in Part VI.

In the framework of a bi-national solution in which the Palestinian and Jewish populations would not be distinguished from each other territorially, all Palestinian exiles would, of course, be permitted to return to unpopulated areas of Palestine/Western Land of Israel. In the framework of a bi-national solution with territorial separation or, alternatively, a two-state solution, return would be allowed only to territories designated as Palestinian. I will leave open the question of which territories are Palestinian and which Jewish for the time being, reserving this discussion for Part VII.

To sum up, the position of those liberal nationalists who endorse the moderate version of Zionism on the Palestinian return will be similar to that of liberals who reject Zionism on the basis of a denial of the historical connection between the Jews and the Land of Israel. Under the latter position, the Israeli Jews are responsible for *all of the suffering* of *all members* of the Palestinian diaspora. Under the moderate version of Zionism, the Jews and Arabs share *equal* responsibility for all of the suffering caused to those Palestinians who were not expelled, whereas the Jews are *exclusively* responsible only towards those who were forcibly expelled. With respect to the question of how the responsibility for the Palestinians' loss of residence and property should be discharged – compensation or return – the answers are identical to those arrived at in the previous part. There are strong individualistic grounds for recognising the right of all members of the Palestinian diaspora, not only of those forcibly expelled, to return to their places of origin if the lives of other individuals have not taken root there. Those Palestinian exiles who cannot meet this condition should be entitled to return to unpopulated areas, either in a mixed bi-national state – if that is deemed the appropriate solution to the dispute, – or to unpopulated areas in territories designated for the Palestinian People, if territorial separation is deemed the appropriate solution.

VI. A Territorial Version of Zionism and the Palestinian Right of Return

According to a more ambitious version of Zionism, Jews at the end of the 19th century had not only a right to sub-statist, non-territorial self-determination in the Land of Israel, but also the right to realise their self-determination within a distinct territorial framework. The historically dominant stream in Zionism sought to realise that right within the framework of an independent state. The legitimacy of this stream of Zionism from the perspective of liberal nationalism depends primarily on the answers to two types of questions. First, there are factual questions concerning the concentrations of Arab populations at the end of the 19th century in Palestine/the Land of Israel, their numbers, and the patterns of their geographical dispersion. Second are questions of principle and empiric assessment regarding the scope of territory and size of population necessary to constitute a viable political entity. If the size and dispersion of the Arab population in Palestine at the time could have enabled the establishment of two viable, separate territorial entities, one primarily Arab and the other primarily Jewish, then liberal nationalists could even have supported the more ambitious version of Zionism. If, however, the establishment of two such entities in Palestine was not possible at the time, then the Jewish attempt to do so would, by definition, have been an attempt to subjugate at least some of the Arab population to Jewish rule, making them foreigners in their own land. Liberals could not condone such an attempt.

As mentioned above, apart from the factual questions pertaining to the size and dispersion of the Arab population in Palestine at the end of the 19th century, the justification of this version of Zionism is dependent also on the demographic and territorial criteria for constituting a viable political entity. This dependence makes any attempt to decisively determine whether or not this version of Zionism is justified a hornets' nest.[20] I will avoid making such an attempt, but for argument's sake, I will assume the legitimacy and justifiability of this version of Zionism. This version has two implications for the resolution of the Palestinian refugee problem that distinguish it from the previous versions.

First, under this version, while Israeli Jews may bear exclusive responsibility for the suffering of those Palestinians who were forcibly expelled, the primary responsibility for all "self-exiled" Palestinians lies with the Palestinians themselves. Responsibility cannot be equally divided between the sides as it is under the more moderate versions of Zionism, because the actual historical realisation of Zionism does not deviate much from Zionism, as it should have been in principle realised under the territorial version. For if we assume, in accordance with mainstream territorial Zionism, that the Jewish People were justified in their (subsequently successful) aspiration for self-determination in a territorial manner in a part of the Land of Israel, then the Palestinian

---

[20] Assessments on this matter are dependent on innumerable variables, such as the economic industriousness of the group wishing to form a state, how pampered its members are and their willingness to suffer, and the technological means available in the particular period. All of these are factored in with, amongst other variables, the topography of the region, the character of the populations in territories neighbouring on the territory where the new group seeks to form its state and the relations with them, the international connections of the particular group and those of their neighbours, and the intensity of the international community's commitment to morality and international law.

opposition to that aspiration was unjustified. Consequently, Palestinians who departed in fear of the war they forced upon the Jews in order to prevent them from realising that right bear responsibility for their fleeing, along with the Arab states that encouraged them to do so. Israel cannot be held responsible for these actions or their consequences. It should be noted that the ramification of this approach is that Israel is not required to compensate all of the Palestinian exiles for their suffering.[21] Accordingly, Israel would be responsible for compensating only those who were forcibly expelled.[22] However, the denial of Israel's responsibility for the departure of all of the Palestinian exiles, if this version of Zionism is justified, does not entail that the exiles, whether they were expelled or left voluntarily, are not entitled to compensation or to the right to return to their former property. Ultimately, even if they left of their own volition, they are entitled to change their minds, in which case a very strong argument could be made for allowing them to return to their former homes if unpopulated. For on the individual level, the issue concerns property rights and residence rights, where the act of vacating the concrete objects of those rights is not tantamount to a waiver of the rights themselves (at least if the right-holders have continued to demand restitution, as have the Palestinians). And if the original concrete objects of these rights cannot be restored, the right-holders are entitled to alternative compensation in the form of compensation.

A second difference in the implications of the ambitious version of Zionism and the moderate non-territorial version *vis-à-vis* the Palestinian right of return is that the former provides a clear method for instituting the respective rights of the Jews and Arabs to self-determination in Palestine/the Land of Israel. Under the latter version of Zionism, Zionism should realise its aspiration to self-determination within the framework of a bi-national state without any territorial distinctions. The exigencies of the history and geo-demographic conditions that were created in the area, however, entail a need to re-examine the question of how this

---

21 However, if we assume that certain exiles immediately regretted their departure and requested to return but Israel rejected these requests, then Israel is not only responsible for their loss of property, but also for all damage they suffered, from the moment they were refused return. Israel could raise a counter-argument that, in the absence of a resolution to the dispute, considerations of security and public order precluded granting permission for their return. This argument might be of real substance, though it is not obviously so. It represents yet another complication in the tangled way towards a moral solution to the problem of the Palestinian diaspora.

22 See note 19, para. 2.

form of Jewish self-determination should be realised today. Under the territorial version of Zionism, there is no need to re-examine the question of realising the right to Jewish self-determination, for if the geo-demographic conditions in Palestine at the end of the 19th century justified the Zionist aspiration for territorial self-determination, then it is certainly justified in the geo-demographic conditions that obtain at the beginning of the 21st century. What may, in fact, require re-examination is the matter of the just division of the territory of Western Land of Israel between the Jews and the Palestinians. This question remains an open one, as it did in the context of the moderate, non-territorial version of Zionism and in the context of the rejection of Zionism based on the denial of the normative sufficiency of the Jewish historical connection to the Land of Israel to justify the return of the Jews. Consequently, the question of which vacant areas of Western Land of Israel should be designated for the return of Palestinian exiles who cannot, on an individual basis, return to their places of origin also remains open.

At the outset, I noted additional forms of Zionism. They revolve around the establishment of a Jewish state in all of the Land of Israel or in parts thereof designated exclusively for Jews. These forms of Zionism do not merit discussion, not only because they cannot be justified under a humanistic interpretation of nationalism, but also because their presuppositions are diametrically opposed to those of any possible Israeli-Palestinian dialogue on the subject of return. Such a dialogue would concern the return of members of the Palestinian diaspora, which emerged as a result of the creation of the State of Israel, to the territory occupied by a state that would continue to manifest the Jewish People's right to self-determination. The ideal of a state only for Jews necessarily entails the outright rejection of any possibility of Palestinian return. This conception of Zionism is the mirror image of those approaches that reject it (and the right to self-determination in the Land of Israel of those Jews living there as a result of Zionism) for reasons stemming from non-humanist forms of Palestinian nationalism. As mentioned above, these forms of nationalism demand the return of all members of the Palestinian diaspora to their places of origin, in conjunction with the removal from the Land of Israel of all those Jews whose lives are rooted there as a consequence of Zionism, even if they bear no personal responsibility for the injustices suffered by the Palestinians. It should be recalled that the rejection of Zionism on the basis of the outright rejection of cultural nationalism, while justifiable on humanistic grounds, cannot serve as the starting point for any dialogue on the Palestinian right of return. In rejecting the very possibility of political support for national cultures, this approach also excludes any possibility of a state serving as the framework for Jewish self-determination. Palestinian return is, of course, possible under this approach, but it could definitely not be to territories located in a state that realises the Jewish right to self-determination. As noted, the Palestinian return discourse presupposes the possibility of return to a state that realises that right.

Most of the approaches from the gallery of versions accepting and rejecting Zionism (whose implications *vis-à-vis* Jewish responsibility and the right of return are discussed above) were rejected as undesirable for normative reasons, and the approach just discussed was discarded for pragmatic reasons. Thus, three approaches remain that warrant serious consideration: (1) the liberal nationalist rejection of Zionism based upon the denial of the normative significance of the Jews' historical connection to the Land of Israel; (2) the moderate version of liberal Zionism, which supports Jewish non-territorial self-determination in the Land of Israel; and (3) the ambitious version of liberal Zionism, which advocates territorial self-determination for Jews in parts of Western Land of Israel.

Each of these three positions has distinct implications for the question of the scope of Jewish responsibility for the Palestinian plight, both in terms of the categories of suffering and the categories of Palestinian exiles towards whom responsibility is borne. However, all three approaches have almost identical implications *vis-à-vis* a Palestinian right of return. With respect to the scope of suffering for which Jews are responsible, those rejecting Zionism will assert Jewish responsibility for all of the suffering endured by all Palestinian exiles. Supporters of Zionism in its moderate form will ascribe special responsibility to the Jews for all the suffering of those Palestinians who were forcibly expelled and joint responsibility with the Palestinians and perhaps other entities for all of the suffering of all other Palestinian exiles. Proponents of the territorial version of Zionism will assign special responsibility to the Jews for the suffering of all those forcibly expelled, but will exempt them from any responsibility towards other exiles (except with regard to the suffering entailed by the continued separation from their property and places of origin). All these positions acknowledge weighty grounds for recognising a Palestinian right of return on an individual basis for all Palestinian exiles to their places of origin in Jewish territories if uninhabited. If territorial separation (in the framework of either one state or two) is the preferred arrangement for establishing Jewish and Palestinian national self-determination, then on collectivist grounds, none of these approaches will recognise a Palestinian right of return to unpopulated Jewish territories if they are not the site of the places of origin of those seeking to return.

As noted, under the ambitious version of Zionism, the appropriate arrangement for setting up Jewish and Palestinian self-determination today is the same as was the case at the inception of Zionism: territorial separation. It seems that today this option should also be accepted by those who claim that Zionism should have been rejected from the outset, since they deny any normative significance to the Jews' connection to the Land of Israel, as well as by those who maintain that, from the start, only the moderate version of Zionism should have been accepted, with its aspiration only for non-territorial Jewish self-determination. The reasons that both groups should now embrace territorial separation do not rest, of course, on the view that national self-determination must necessarily and always take a territorial form, but rather on the fact that the constraints of the particular history of the Jewish-Palestinian dispute over the last 120 years make this solution the most likely to succeed. This claim is not only a moral claim; it is factual prediction. Since we can presume that very few will dispute this claim, I will adopt it as it is.

Thus, all three approaches to Zionism warranting consideration in the context of the debate over a Palestinian right of return have identical implications for this right. First, they all acknowledge powerful reasons for supporting the return of exiles to their places of origin if unpopulated, reasons that stem from people's right to their property and to residence in their places of origin. Second, they support the return of all other exiles (i.e., those whose places of origin are not vacant) to unpopulated areas of Palestine/Western Land of Israel designated to be Palestinian territory. However, this stance leaves open two significant points of contention regarding the right of return. The first pertains to the vagueness of the term "unpopulated" (or "vacant") areas and the conclusiveness of the reasons for supporting the return of Palestinian exiles to unpopulated places of origin. The second point pertains to the appropriate territorial division of Western Land of Israel.

VII. Return to Unpopulated Places of Origin

Consider the case of a house that serves as a restaurant or the warehouse of an Israeli institution in an area that has completely transformed in character since the original owners left the house and went into exile: Should this be considered a "vacant" place? Is the answer to this contingent on the use made of the place by the institution and on the possible existence of alternative sites for such use? Can a village that was destroyed and a forest planted on its land, and its agricultural lands once tilled by the exiled villagers and now providing the livelihood of others, be considered vacant? And what about a village that was not destroyed, but since its original inhabitants either fled or were driven away, its agricultural lands now provide a livelihood for others? These are places that are not privately owned or possessed by Jewish Israeli individuals in the sense that the majority of their lives are conducted there. Rather, they are places that were previously owned or possessed by Palestinian individuals or entities that are now state-owned by the State of Israel. The State nationalised them and either directly changed their character or indirectly did so by giving them to private or public Israeli entities that changed their character – places which are now used by Israelis with varying degrees of intensity. Can these places be regarded as vacant? Is it even at all possible to speak of unoccupied places in Israel after the Israelis have changed, to varying extents, the character of almost all of the physical sites left by Palestinian exiles more than 50 years ago and are making some use of the majority of them?

It could be claimed that since there are no clear answers to these questions, in those situations in which they arise, the general logic underlying the eventual settlement of the Israeli-Palestinian dispute should be followed to solve the problems. If the arrangement chosen is one of territorial separation, then the members of the Palestinian diaspora ought to relinquish their right to return to territories designated for Jewish self-determination, even if those territories include Palestinian places of origin that are vacant in some sense. However, this claim can only be consistently made if, under the territorial separation arrangement, no Palestinians are to be left in the areas designated for Jewish self-determination. It cannot be consistently made by those who maintain that all or at least some of the Palestinians who have been Israeli citizens since the establishment of the State of Israel ("Israeli Arabs") should be allowed to continue to reside in these areas (a position for which I will later make my case), since, under their view, Jewish-designated areas would, in any event, not be populated exclusively by Jews. The moral vagueness of the term "vacant areas" cannot provide the ground for the absolute and overall exclusion of any Palestinian return. But it can provide a reason for the parties to reach a compromise solution with regard to return to these areas so as to avoid becoming entangled in disputes over moral issues lacking clear solutions. Such a compromise would entail recognition of the right of return for a non-negligible number of people, but not the mass return of Palestinian exiles to areas within the borders of the Jewish entity.

Yet another argument can be put forth in support of this type of limited Palestinian return, which derives from Israel's duty to acknowledge its responsibility for at least part of the wrongs suffered by the Palestinians in the wake of its establishment. This responsibility arises not only under the position rejecting Zionism that stems from a rejection of the normative significance of the Jews' historical connection to the Land of Israel or under the moderate non-territorial form of Zionism. It arises also under the ambitious version of Zionism, according to which, at the end of the 19th century, Jews were entitled to territorial self-determination in Western Land of Israel. Such responsibility certainly follows from the first two positions (i.e., the rejection of Zionism based on a denial of the Jewish connection to Palestine and the affirmation of the non-territorial form of Zionism), since the actual realisation of Zionism deviated from its acceptable parameters under these positions: Zionism attempted and succeeded in forming a Jewish state in the Land of Israel. However, for a number of reasons, Israel also bears this responsibility under the ambitious version of Zionism. One reason stems from the fact that believing in the justness of this version of Zionism cannot be free of all doubt. As I argued above, its justifiability is contingent not only on factual matters such as the size and dispersion of the Arab population in the Land of Israel at the end of the 19th century, but also on the answers to questions such as the minimum demographic and territorial conditions for establishing a viable state. In many cases, the question of whether these conditions obtain is hard to answer. Since the aspiration to establish a Jewish state in Palestine at the end of the 19th century is one such case, the justness of this aspiration must also be subject to doubt. Even if this doubt does not lead to an abandonment of this version of Zionism, it does require a consideration of the price paid by the Palestinians for the realisation of this version of Zionism and the acknowledgement of a certain degree of responsibility for it, a responsibility that must be discharged in some substantial form.

The second reason why, under the ambitious version of Zionism, Israel should acknowledge its responsibility for wrongs suffered by the Palestinians stems from the nature of the conceivable justifications of this version. Such justifications could certainly not be based exclusively on corrective justice considerations relating to the persecution of the Jews throughout history. Many have already observed that if the establishment of the Jewish state was based upon the persecution of Jews, then there was no justification for the Palestinians to pay the price, since they played no part in this persecution. As I hinted at above, the justification for establishing a Jewish state in the Land of Israel is based on distributive justice considerations regarding the division of territory among nations for the purpose of realising their rights to self-determination. It derives from the principle that every nation is entitled to a piece of territory in its historical homeland where it can exercise its right to self-determination.[23] Some might argue that this principle is only valid in cases in which the territory designated for the exercise of the right to self-determination is actually settled by members of the nation wishing to exercise that right.[24] Those who reject Zionism based on the claim that the Jews' historical link to the Land of Israel is not sufficient to justify their return to that territory would surely adopt this position. Moreover, even those who accept Zionism based on this link must concede that its realisation inflicted a huge sacrifice on the part of the Palestinians, the dominant nation in the Land of Israel at the end of the 19th century: they were forced to give up lands they naturally regarded as their own. The sheer magnitude of their sacrifice may provide the basis for appreciating their opposition to Zionism, even if this opposition was not justified. The magnitude of their sacrifice should be the basis for the requirement to take actual measures to appease them, for example, by returning some of the exiles to their original locations.

The third and the most important argument for holding Israel at least partially responsible for the suffering of the Palestinians even if the ambitious version of Zionism is justified pertains to the fact that Zionism in practice was more ambitious than was justified even under this ambitious version. In other words, even if at the end of the 19th century there was *ex ante* justification for the Jewish People to strive for territorial self-determination in the Land of Israel, there was certainly no justification for striving to do so within the borders created following the 1948 Israeli War of Independence. Even if the War was forced upon the Jewish state and was therefore a just one, there was no justification for expelling Palestinians, or for seizing the property and places left by those who fled the War.[25]

---

23 See Gans, see note 2, ch. 4.

24 *Idem.*

25 See A. Marmor, "Entitlement to Land and the Right of Return: An Embarrassing Challenge for Liberal Zionism", in: L.H. Meyer (ed.), *Justice in Time: Responding to Historical Injustice*, 2004.

Conceivably, even if some of these actions are excusable due to the particular circumstances of the Jewish People in 1948 and the fears that arose out of such circumstances (the justified fears of the Jews in the wake of World War II and in the face of the refusal of the Arab states to accept the establishment of a Jewish state under the UN Resolution of 29 November 1947), this does not mean they are justified, wholly or in part. Therefore, there is good reason to hold Israel at least partially responsible for the Palestinian suffering even if we regard the ambitious version of Zionism as just and the Arab opposition to its realisation as unjust.

VIII. Return to Israeli Territory and Territory that Will Cease to Be Israeli

The discussion thus far has shown that all three of the approaches to Zionism warranting consideration within the framework of the right-of-return discourse support the return of Palestinian exiles to their places of origin within the territory of the Jewish state only if those places are vacant. However, the discussion has yet to clarify whether the justifiable borders of the Jewish state are the pre-1967 borders or whether they should be an expanded or narrower form of those borders. The reason for this lack of clarity is that if, under the three relevant approaches to Zionism, Zionism as it has actually unfolded is responsible for its demographic consequences, then there is no reason not to hold it similarly responsible for its territorial consequences.

Andrei Marmor illustrates this point in the following manner: If I purchase a piece of land and others trespass on it, conceivably I am entitled to take violent measures to remove them. However, their act of trespass does not entitle me, the landowner, to seize additional territory. If this claim is correct, then the claim that Palestinian refugees who cannot be repatriated to their places of origin should not be repatriated to vacant areas in the Jewish state does not entail the conclusion that they should not be allowed to return to vacant areas that are *currently* within the borders of the State of Israel. Conceivably, they should be allowed to return to the latter vacant areas, and at the same time, these areas should be transferred to a Palestinian state.

But is this, in fact, an appropriate solution? An overwhelming majority of the Israeli left rejects such a solution, for they reject any form of Palestinian return to territory within the borders of the Jewish state set following the 1948 Israeli War of Independence – borders sacred to them. On the one hand, they oppose withdrawal from these borders to the narrower borders of the Partition Plan under the UN Resolution of 29 November 1947, regarding the establishment of a Jewish state in the Land of Israel. On the other hand, they oppose expanding these borders to include Jewish settlements resulting from Israeli settlement activities in the territories conquered in the 1967 War. In their view, the Palestinian refugee problem must be resolved within the framework of a Palestinian state to be established in those parts of Western Land of Israel falling outside of Israel's pre-1967 borders.

The central reason for this position regarding the territorial division of Western Land of Israel is the international recognition of Israel's pre-1967 borders and the prospects such a division holds for reaching a peaceful arrangement between a Jewish state and a Palestinian state. Borders wider than the pre-1967 borders will not enjoy these two advantages. First, such expanded borders have never been accorded international recognition, and under current conditions there is no chance of this ever occurring. Second, such borders preclude any possibility of an agreement between the Jews and Palestinians that will provide the Palestinians with a minimal measure of self-respect *vis-à-vis* what they have endured due to the dispute with the Jews thus far, as well as with regard to the possibility of their independent and respectable existence in the future. It could of course be argued that while these are valid reasons for preferring the pre-1967 borders to expanded borders, they do not provide the basis for preferring the pre-1967 borders to narrower borders. Obviously, narrower borders would similarly accommodate the possibility of peace between the Jews and Palestinians – it would almost certainly enhance its prospects (the well-known aphorism "Give them a finger, they'll take a hand" notwithstanding), and there is no reason to assume that such borders would not enjoy international recognition.

But this argument overlooks the reason why the international recognition of the pre-1967 borders makes them the appropriate line along which Western Land of Israel should be divided between the Jews and Arabs. It is not that these borders are inherently just, but, rather, that there is no clear answer (from an infinite number of possible reasonable answers) to the question of the just territorial division of Western Land of Israel between the Arabs and Jews, specifically, and of territories between national groups, in general. In drawing the territorial boundaries of national entities for the purpose of self-determination, complex moral considerations of distributive justice must be weighed, relating to the size of the national groups, the nature of their cultures, and the collective and individual needs of their members. These factors must be evaluated relative to other national groups in the world – and their comparative needs – and in consideration of the limitations of global territorial resources. Clearly, widespread agreement on comprehensive and perfect moral solutions to these questions (even if, in principle, such solutions exist) is well nigh impossible due to the limitations of human intelligence and nature. This is certainly the case regarding the Jewish-Palestinian dispute. When determining the appropriate size of the Palestinian state relative to the size of the Jewish state, the only things that should not be in dispute are a *prima facie* presumption against mass transfers of populations, an unequivocal presumption against forming suburb-size states, and a *prima facie* presumption in favour of the territorial continuity of states. However, even these undisputed points are formulated in language that can open them up to debate. For example, what constitutes "mass" population transfer? What conditions overcome any one of the *prima facie* presumptions?

Other considerations to be weighed in deciding upon the territorial division between national groups are even more controversial. For example, should the territorial borders of the Jewish state be based solely on the size of the current Jewish population in Israel or should the fact that Israel perceives itself as the home for all Jews be taken into consideration and the borders set in anticipation of their possible absorption? Should the territorial borders of the Palestinian state be set in light of the possibility of all members of the Palestinian dispersion settling there? Should consideration be given to the significant political and cultural support that would be given to such a state by its neighbours, whose cultures are very similar to the Palestinian culture? How much unpopulated space is necessary to accommodate the recreational needs of each of the states' populations?

Even if there are clear and precise answers to these questions, there is still dispute among the members of each party to the Jewish-Palestinian conflict, as well as between the two parties themselves, as to how to arrive at these answers. In cases where there are moral ambiguities and disagreements of the sort discussed here, the parties bear a moral obligation to reach a compromise. Israel's pre-1967 borders provide a firm foundation for such a compromise by virtue of the international community's recognition of their legitimacy. Any attempt to reach a compromise based on other borders, whether narrower or wider, will open up disputes with no ready resolutions for which consensus can easily be secured. Moreover, since both sides bear a grave moral duty to prevent the further perpetuation of the violence, any attempt to formulate a compromise based on anything but the pre-1967 borders must be rejected, as it will only lead to a stalemate between the two sides and further violence.

In other words, the pre-1967 borders are the best territorial line along which to separate the Palestinians and Jews, not because they are inherently more just than any other option in the infinite range of reasonable possibilities for just borders, but because it is difficult to point to any relevant reason for preferring any one of these solutions over the rest; the advantage of the pre-1967 borders lies in the international recognition they already enjoy.[26] The fact that international recognition for any other borders will be secured *after* a territorial agreement has been reached between the parties regarding those borders cannot assist the parties in setting the borders *before* this recognition. The existing international recognition of the pre-1967 borders provides moral grounds to favour these borders not only because it is *international* recognition but also, and perhaps primarily, because it is an *already existing* recognition. It can constitute a conventional anchor for the resolution of a moral dispute whose solution is an urgent moral imperative, with only a slim chance of finding any solution other than territorial separation along these borders given the limitations of human intelligence and nature.[27]

---

[26] It is important to remind supporters of this position (the Israeli left) that this international recognition is accompanied by two additional positions taken by the international community: Israel's duty to absorb at least a certain number of Palestinian refugees (UN General Assembly Resolution 194 (III)) and the refusal to recognise Jerusalem as the capital of Israel. Reliance on the international recognition of the pre-1967 borders as the grounds for adopting them entails taking into consideration the other two stances, which also touch on the very heart of the Israeli-Arab dispute. These international decisions are inextricably interwoven and constitute parts of a whole; rejecting one of them means rejecting them all and reopening the points of dispute.

[27] Moral problems for which there are several possible solutions, none of which is considered better than the other, and whose resolution is morally urgent can be regarded as similar to convention problems. Ordinary convention problems are those in which the parties have an interest in cooperating with each other. There are a number of ways of cooperating, but none is necessarily superior to the other from the perspectives of the parties; indeed, often the differences among the alternative means of cooperation are relatively insignificant). The problem, therefore, is which mode of cooperation to choose. In our context, the problems are not of a kind that the parties are *necessarily* interested in solving, but *should be* interested in solving them for moral reasons. The problem is that there are an infinite number of reasonable moral solutions to

The upshot of these last comments is that the preclusion of return for the Palestinian refugees to areas in the Jewish state means no return to areas within Israel's pre-1967 borders. The general conclusion of my discussion on Palestinian return is that the stance rejecting Zionism based on the rejection of any normative significance to the link between the Jews and the Land of Israel (the non-territorial version of Zionism) and the more ambitious (territorial) version of Zionism can all justify, on individualistic grounds, the return of Palestinians to their places of origin within the pre-1967 borders, provided these places are vacant. They also can justify a collectivist Palestinian demand for the return of at least some of its members, based on the Jewish state's obligation to realise its responsibility for at least some of the suffering caused to the Palestinian People with the establishment of Israel. Since the issue of what constitutes a "vacant" area in the context of the right of return is open to significant interpretative debate and since the question of how many Palestinian returnees will suffice to constitute a manifestation of Israel's responsibility has no precise moral solution, here, too, the parties bear a moral obligation to reach a compromise. This compromise must be guided, on the one hand, by the general logic of the chosen solution to the dispute and, on the other hand, by all the details of its implementation. The fact that the solution is a territorial division of Western Land of Israel between Jews and Arabs is good reason for not allowing the mass return of Palestinian refugees. The fact that an important detail of this territorial division is that the size of the territory to be allocated to the Jews is much larger than the territory to be allocated to the Palestinians serves as good reason for allowing the return of a non-

---

the matter of the territorial division between the Jews and Arabs in Western Land of Israel. There is a moral obligation to choose one of them, for otherwise the violence will continue. Which should be chosen? International recognition of a particular territorial division can determine the choice. Obviously, there can be other ways of reaching the decision. However, even within the scope of reasonable territorial divisions, the possibilities are endless, and the parties could spend the rest of their days trying to decide only on the preliminary questions of which of these possibilities will go into the hat from which the final solution is to be drawn. For example, let us assume that the parameters of a reasonable solution extend between one of the partition plans from the 1930s and the borders that current Israeli Prime Minister Ariel Sharon intends to propose within the framework of the "Roadmap" process initiated by President Bush. Even within those parameters, there is an infinite number of variations, because one can forever add or remove different variations from the stockpile that differ only fractionally from any option for borders.

negligible number of Palestinian exiles.[28] Within certain parameters of reasonableness, neither morality nor justice provides any guidance as to what constitutes a "mass" return and what constitutes a "negligible" return. However, this does not strip the principle I have formulated of all content. Vagueness is characteristic of many concepts of natural languages, not only moral concepts. Just as the assertion "He is tall" is not devoid of content, nor is the statement "The Palestinian return should be neither *en masse* nor negligible" devoid of content.

IX. Andrei Marmor's Position on the Right of Return

In his article *Entitlement to Land and the Right of Return: An Embarrassing Challenge for Liberal Zionism*,[29] Andrei Marmor argues for a more generous right of return than the one I argue for. But as I will immediately show, his arguments, if carried through, imply a right of return even more generous than he himself actually supports. Marmor advocates the return of members of the Palestinian diaspora who were exiled as a result of ethnic purges and who have remained refugees, regardless of whether or not their places of origin are currently vacant. The frequent challenge to this claim, voiced also by Liberal Zionists, is that such a return would endanger the Jewish character of the state. Marmor's response is that if ethnic cleansing can be a legitimate means of securing the cultural character of a state, then why not ensure this character by placing restrictions on the political and civil rights of minorities (or even the majority)? The Zionist "Left," Marmor implies, does not have too many options: it must either abandon its opposition to the Palestinian right of return or else it must admit that it is not truly liberal. Furthermore, in Marmor's view, Israel's borders prior to 4 June 1967, are morally no more defensible than the (expanded) borders that include post-1967 settlements in the Occupied Territories. In both cases, the borders were the result of a war; and war, however justified, is not a legitimate means of acquiring territory. Although not explicit, Marmor's position is that not only must Israel permit the return of Palestinians to unpopulated locations inside its borders, but the Israeli

---

[28] Conceivably, such a return will have to be postponed by a decade from the day that the peace treaty comes into force and will have to be contingent upon compliance with the other parts of the agreement for the duration of that decade in order to assuage Israeli security concerns.

[29] Marmor, see note 25.

borders themselves should be far narrower than the pre-1967 borders. Thus, the Palestinians should be permitted to return to at least some of the unpopulated parts of Israel inside its pre-1967 borders, and their return to those parts should be accompanied by Palestinian statehood being bestowed upon those places.

The arguments presented earlier in the article indicate that these conclusions are invalid. I will first address Marmor's claim supporting the right of return for those members of the Palestinian diaspora whose exile is the product of ethnic purges. At the basis of this claim is the argument that just as Liberals cannot consent to limiting freedom of speech and suffrage rights in order to preserve Israel's Jewish character, they cannot agree to the continued perpetuation of a situation that is the result of ethnic purges toward the same purpose. There are numerous possible responses to Marmor on this count. For example, we can point to the fact that the ethnic cleansing of the Palestinians from certain territories in Palestine was not a planned future policy but, rather, was an exceptional, one-time occurrence over 50 years ago. Thus, preventing the perpetuation of its tragic consequences does not necessitate the repatriation of all its victims. On the other hand, imposing limitations on the political rights of Israeli Arabs in order to preserve the Jewish character of the state constitutes a permanent arrangement that impacts on the future, the consequences cannot be mitigated by anything less than its total abandonment.

Furthermore, compensation for the suffering that was and still is the product of the 1948 ethnic cleansing of the Palestinians may indeed be imperative, but the choice of the means of righting this wrong must reflect other components of the moral situation. For example, the Jews in Israel harbour well-founded security concerns regarding the presence of a large population that bears resentment against the very establishment of the state, born of bloodshed and injustices suffered; and quite naturally, such seething hostility is not likely to be placated by any Israeli actions intended to atone for those wrongs. We can also point to the fact that not all ethnic purges are the same. The Serbs' ethnic purge of the Moslems in Bosnia in the beginning of the 1990s did not resemble the ethnic purge of the Sudeten Germans by the Czechs in the aftermath of World War II, for example. Although not justifying it, the circumstances of the 1948 ethnic purge of the Palestinians by the Jews may be excused, provided the Jews acknowledge the wrongs committed and compensate by means other than actual return.

However, my arguments in the preceding parts of this paper offer a far more fundamental response to Marmor. For, in essence, his claim has force only because he plays on the vagueness of the term "preserving the Jewish character of the state" and on the moral dangers inherent to the use of this term because of this ambiguity. In the context of the problem of Palestinian return, the "character of the state" argument can be given an entirely clear and lucid interpretation; in fact, the argument's objective can be reached in complete disregard of the argument itself. Following the lines of my previous arguments, the return of refugees is warranted only when their original locations are vacant, since, on the one hand, there are individualistic reasons to support return to their former homes and, on the other hand, there are no individualistic reasons that preclude this (i.e., no innocent individuals live – and are rooted – on that property). In all other instances, however, the wrongs must be redressed by settling refugees not in their original locations, but in other areas in Western Land of Israel. If the Palestinian-Jewish dispute is to be resolved by establishing separate territorial units of self-determination for the two nations, the internal logic of this solution supports the conclusion that where individualistic reasons preclude the return of Palestinian refugees to their original homes, they ought to be resettled in territories designated to be Palestinian. In other words, if Zionism is justified or, alternatively, the realisation of its aspirations retroactively morally justified in light of current conditions, and if there is a similar nationalist justification for the establishment of a Palestinian state, it is not clear why Marmor supports allowing refugees unable to return to their original locations to return to vacant areas in Israel and not to vacant Palestinian areas. For in any event, whether these refugees return to areas in the Jewish state or the Palestinian state, they will be returning to parts of their historical homeland and nearby their original locations. Thus, it is difficult to understand why they should return specifically to areas inside the Jewish state. This objection to the return of Palestinian refugees to vacant areas in the Jewish state does refer at all to the "Jewish character of the state" argument. Alternatively, it could be understood as giving the argument very clear meaning in the context of the right of return, thereby avoiding the moral pitfalls of its vagueness.

The second implicit aspect to Marmor's argument is that the pre-1967 borders are no more morally justifiable than borders that include settlements created after 1967, since both are the product of wars, which, even if they were just, cannot justify territorial acquisition. Consequently, the argument goes, the return of Palestinian refugees to at least part of the unpopulated areas in Israel must be accompanied by the transfer of these areas to a future Palestinian state. This claim is problematic because it takes for granted that the borders of the 1947 Partition Plan are *the* morally justified borders of the Jewish state.

The Partition Plan can be regarded as having established morally legitimate borders for the Jewish state for two alternative reasons. One reason is that it constitutes an international solution to a problem lacking any clear moral solution, and given its potential to prevent the continuation of violence, there is a moral obligation to adopt this solution. Alternatively, the Plan can be regarded as having enunciated the morally appropriate solution given the relevant parameters at the time: it divided the areas with a Jewish majority on the one side and those with an Arab majority on the other. However, neither of these justifications has force with regard to the period leading up to the Six-Day War in June 1967 or to the period immediately thereafter. Whereas in 1947 the Partition Plan offered a desirable solution because it was then a reasonable solution and an international solution to a problem with no one right solution, this was not the case in 1967 in terms of international recognition. In 1967, Israel, as a state perceiving itself as Jewish, enjoys international recognition within the borders of 4 June 1967, which replaced the international recognition of the Partition Plan provided in 1947. If the Plan had offered an appropriate solution for the territorial division of Western Land of Israel because of the moral justification of its content – namely, the existence of a Jewish majority in the area designated for Jews and the existence of an Arab majority in the areas designated for Arabs – then the demographic reality in Palestine/the Land of Israel in 1967 mandated a different territorial division. Of course, such a division would not necessarily have had to follow the lines of the pre-1967 borders; narrower borders might conceivably have been appropriate. But either way, it would not have been along the Partition Plan lines of 1947. And in 2004, wider borders than the pre-1967 ones might be required. Indeed, the situation is such that there is no clear moral criterion for determining whether, in 2004, the borders should be narrower or wider than the pre-1967 borders, for there is international consensus only with regard to the pre-1967 borders. Given this background, it makes a lot of sense to claim that the latter should be the recognised borders.

Not only does Marmor ignore and belittle these considerations, he also claims that borders stretching beyond the pre-1967 ones seem more legitimate than those exceeding the territorial lines of the Partition Plan, since the former would be drawn in accordance with settlements on lands not attained by way of ethnic cleansing, whereas the latter were based on borders that were largely the consequence of ethnic cleansing.

He argues that therefore any moral divergence between the borders that were set after 1947 and those that were set after 1967 tilts in favour of the latter. The only reasons for compromising on the post-1967 borders are pragmatic and prospective, not principled. Despite his admission in one place that these reasons also have a moral tinge to them, in deriving their impetus from the moral imperative to resolve conflicts in general, Marmor underplays the significance of this moral duty by generally describing the considerations it reflects as of a pragmatic nature.

This presentation of matters must be rejected. Admittedly, seizing lands by way of ethnic cleansing is perhaps graver than attaining land in a manner that does not involve this crime. Yet there are strong reasons for maintaining that the ethnic cleansing of 1948 was less morally reprehensible than the ongoing settlement activity following the 1967 Six-Day War. First, the ethnic cleansing of 1948, even if intended by part or all of the Jewish political leadership in the Land of Israel, is attributable to the Jews' post-World War II fears and the understandable urgency with which they sought a state that would provide them with protection, a state whose establishment the Arabs rejected. Though this claim is, to a certain extent, part of the Zionist narrative, it is not necessarily a fabrication. In contrast, the settlements following the 1967 War were on behalf of, or at least under the aegis of, an existing state; they were established for the purpose of territorial expansion under circumstances that provided no basis for the fears that may have been justified in 1948.

Second, and more importantly, the post-1967 settlements were intended to plant almost insurmountable obstacles on the way to peace and the resolution of a violent conflict. The moral duty not to obstruct any possibility for terminating the conflict is, in my view, no less principled than the duty not to thwart the Partition Plan of 1947. Taking cold and calculated measures to prevent any possibility of complying with that moral duty, as in the manner and circumstances of the settlements, will prepare the ground for future ethnic cleansings, which will be unpardonable in the circumstances.

To sum up, Marmor accuses those who identify themselves as "Liberal Zionists" of two inconsistencies. The first relates to their use of the "Jewish character of the state" argument in order to justify their objection to the return of the Palestinians to places that are not their original locations. Marmor maintains that this objection is inconsistent with the Liberal Zionists' opposition to imposing restrictions on the political rights of Israeli Arabs. Second, he takes issue with their objection to borders that exceed the pre-1967 borders. This objection, he argues, is inconsistent with their opposition to returning to the 1947 borders. The above discussion has shown that these charges are unfounded. Indeed, inconsistency in fact seems to be the hallmark of those supporting positions such as that of Marmor. For if they oppose any kind of nationalism, whether by dint of their being socialists or neutralist liberals, then they cannot speak of the materialisation of Palestinian return within the framework of the State of Israel as a state perceived of as realising the Jewish right to self-determination. They can speak only of a culturally neutral state in Western Land of Israel, the return to which should not be limited to those members of the Palestinian diaspora that were the victims of ethnic cleansing, but, rather, should extend to all members of the Palestinian diaspora. This argument, however, is incommensurate with Marmor's presuppositions, for he seems to regard the right-of-return discourse as revolving around the question of the appropriateness of Palestinian return to a state that realises the Jewish right to self-determination. The question of whether this possibility merits support will similarly compel the supporters of a position such as Marmor's to address the dispute between liberal nationalists and neutralist liberals and not take for granted that liberalism can be neutralist with respect to national cultures. The question of whether liberalism is compatible with some sort of nationalism will compel them to attribute greater significance to the distinction between Liberal Zionists and Romantic Zionists (those to the right of liberal nationalism), a distinction Marmor ignores (for he refers to Zionism as though it were wholly romantic). Furthermore, Marmor is mistaken in directing his accusations at the so-called "Liberal Zionist" consensus; in 2003, humanistic nationalists, even if they are not Zionists, can also be partners in the consensus regarding the pre-1967 borders and the opposition to Palestinian return. For within the geo-demographic reality that Zionism created in Western Land of Israel, even non-Zionist nationalists can argue that this territory should accommodate both Jewish self-determination and Arab self-determination. Furthermore, they also can support territorial separation between the two entities of self-determination, either because they believe that self-determination ought, in principle, to be territorial or else because they believe that, in the particular context and history of the Jewish-Palestinian dispute, territorial self-determination for the respective parties is the best solution.

My position regarding the right of return, therefore, lies somewhere between that of Marmor and that which he ascribes to the Liberal Zionist consensus. It will be recalled that I support a restricted right of return for Palestinians as an expression of the collective Jewish responsibility for the Palestinian refugees' plight and based on the individual rights of some of the members of the Palestinian diaspora to return to their original locations if vacant. My position diverges from the Liberal Zionist consensus not because I maintain that the latter position reflects inconsistent moral stances, but, rather, because I believe that it does not take into account some important considerations.

Historical Injustice and the Right of Return

Lukas H. Meyer[*]

I. Introduction

Do present-day Palestinians living in refugee camps[1] have a right of return to their homes and to have their property recovered namely in virtue of the history of having been forcefully and deliberately expelled from their homeland? This essay presents two comments on doubts one might have with respect to the validity of the Palestinian claims to reparation. These doubts reflect the two sets of questions that have defined, at least in part, the philosophical subject of *Historical Injustice*: First, addressed shall be the questions arising from the non-identity problem as introduced by Derek Parfit in his work *Reasons and Persons*,[2] and, second, the questions arising from Jeremy Waldron's supersession thesis as presented in his article "Superseding Historic Injustice."[3] My com-

* I would like to thank Ruth Gavison and other participants of the conference and, especially, Chaim Gans and Alon Harel for their helpful criticisms and comments. Comments and criticisms are most welcome; please send them to lukas.meyer@philo.unibe.ch

1 I follow Andrei Marmor in assuming that the needs of these refugees are particularly urgent and compelling and in stressing that the argument is not restricted to the refugees in the camps. See A. Marmor, "Entitlement to Land and the Right of Return: An Embarrassing Challenge for Liberal Zionism", in: L.H. Meyer (ed.), *Justice in Time. Responding to Historical Injustice*, 2004, 319 et seq., 325, note 13, and see note 28, below.

2 D. Parfit, *Reasons and Persons*, 1984, part iv.

3 J. Waldron, "Superseding Historic Injustice", *Ethics* 103 (1992), 4 et seq. (an earlier version of this paper was published as "Historic Injustice: Its Remembrance and Supersession", in: G. Oddie/R.W. Perrett (eds), *Justice, Ethics and New Zealand Society*, 1992); and most recently J. Waldron, "Redressing

ments are meant to show that the non-identity problem is of little practical significance for assessing the validity of the right of return of the Palestinian refugees, where the same holds true for the supersession thesis.

II. The Irrelevance of the Non-Identity Problem

The non-identity problem gives rise to the following general question: how can individuals today have a just claim to compensation owing to what was done to others in the past when the claimants would not exist today had the latter not suffered these harms?[4] For example, do African-Americans, whose ancestors were subjected to the terrible injustices of being kidnapped in Africa and subsequently enslaved, have a just claim to compensation?[5] Let us set aside a host of specifically legal questions concerning, for example, the laws of limitation and liability.

Historic Injustice", in: Meyer, see note 1. Waldron's "Superseding Historic Injustice" is likely the most often discussed and cited paper in the debate about the moral validity of claims to reparation owing to historical injustices. David Lyons holds a similar view on historical entitlements. See D. Lyons, "The New Indian Claims and Original Rights to Land", *Social Theory and Practice* 4 (1977), 249 et seq., republished in: J. Paul (ed.), *Reading Nozick: Essays on Anarchy, State and Utopia*, 1982.

4 See C. Morris, "Existential Limits to the Rectification of Past Wrongs", *American Philosophical Quarterly* 21 (1984), 175 et seq.; R. Kumar/D. Silver, "The Legacy of Injustice: Wronging the Future, Responsibility for the Past", in: Meyer, see note 1, 145 et seq., 148 et seq.

5 For the claims of descendants of slaves in the USA see, e.g., H.A. Bedau, "Compensatory Justice and the Black Manifesto", *The Monist* 56 (1972), 20 et seq.; B.R. Boxill, *Blacks and Social Justice*, revised edition, 1992; R.L. Brooks (ed.), *When Sorry Isn't Enough. The Controversy over Apologies and Reparations for Human Injustice*, 1999, parts 6 and 7; W. Soyinka, *The Burden of Memory, the Muse of Forgiveness*, 1999, 44 et seq.; R. Fullinwider, "The Case for Reparations", *Report from the Institute for Philosophy and Public Policy* 20 (2000), <http://www.puaf.umd.edu/IPPP/reports/vol20sum00/case.html> (25 August 2005); D. Lyons "Unfinished Business: Racial Junctures in US History and Their Legacy", in: Meyer, see note 1.

To illustrate the point here one need only consider the case of Robert, a modern day descendant of slaves.[6]

People can make claims to compensation for harms they have suffered. As a descendant of slaves, has Robert been harmed owing to the injustices suffered by his ancestors? First, consider briefly the most common interpretation of harm,[7] which requires that the existence of the harmed person or people *qua* individuals be independent of the harming act or policy. This interpretation of harm can be expressed in the following formula:

(1). Subjunctive-historical: An action (or inaction)[8] at time t_1 harms someone only if the agent causes (allows) this person to be worse off at some later time t_2 than the person would have been at t_2 had the agent not interacted with (or acted with respect to) this person at all.[9]

---

[6] See J.S. Fishkin, "Justice between Generations: Compensation, Identity, and Group Membership", in: J.W. Graham (ed.), *Compensatory Justice*, 1991, 85 et seq., 91 et seq.

[7] For a discussion of different notions of harm in the intergenerational context see Parfit, see note 2, 487 et seq.; J.S. Fishkin, "The Limits of Intergenerational Justice", in: P. Laslett/J.S. Fishkin (eds), *Justice Between Age Groups and Generations*, 1992, 62 et seq., 63 et seq.; S. Shiffrin, "Wrongful Life, Procreative Responsibility, and the Significance of Harm", *Legal Theory* 5 (1999), 117 et seq.

[8] For a defence of the view that certain types of inactions, namely omissions, can be harmful see, e.g., J. Feinberg, *The Moral Limits of the Criminal Law. Vol. 1. Harm to Others*, 1984, ch. 4.

[9] "Acted with respect to this person" is meant to include the act that is the cause of this person's existence. It is difficult to interpret such acts as interactions. We prefer "had we not interacted with (or acted with respect to) this person at all" to David Gauthier's "in our absence" (D. Gauthier, *Morals by Agreement*, 1986, 203 et seq.). Both formulations are problematic and it is beyond the scope of this entry to discuss their respective problems at length. Gauthier himself points out that his formulation runs into difficulty in dealing with situations in which a person has assumed a certain social role, e.g., the role of a life-guard that is, in part, defined by positive duties *vis-à-vis* others. If a person assumes such a role her "absence" in a situation where she is duty-bound to intervene can render the situation of others worse (ibid., 205). For the purpose of the formulation we prefer it seems plausible to suggest that assuming such a role does constitute an "interaction" of the then duty-bound person with those to whom she is bound where fulfilling the duties of her role is concerned.

Under this interpretation of harm, a person can be understood to be fully compensated for an act or policy (or event)[10] when he/she is as well off as he/she would be if the act had not been carried out. Under this interpretation of harm, Robert cannot be said to have been harmed by the kidnapping and enslavement of his ancestors, for had his ancestors not been kidnapped and enslaved, he would most likely not exist. His existence is the product of a certain genealogical chain not being broken. Hence, the initial kidnapping in Africa, the transporting to America, and the enslavement of his ancestors are (very likely) necessary conditions for Robert's having come into existence at all. Indeed, he would not have been better off had his ancestors not been badly wronged. Thus, we cannot rely upon this interpretation of harm and its accompanying interpretation of compensation to ground the claim that Robert has been harmed and should be compensated. The required state of affairs implies the non-existence of the person claiming compensation.

To this claim we can respond in a number of ways.[11] The response I find most plausible is to allow for an identity-independent notion of harm in addition to the common identity-dependent notion of harm.[12] Such an identity-independent notion of harm can be expressed in the following formula:

---

[10] People can be harmed by events, say, by a natural catastrophe. The following reasoning applies when such an event occurs before the person who makes the claim to being compensated owing to the event comes into existence.

[11] Currently living African-Americans might well have just claims to compensation based on the subjunctive-historical reading of harm because of harm done to them or to their more recent ancestors. See my discussion of the claims of the Palestinian refugees, below, and Lyons' analysis of continuing discrimination against African-Americans, see note 5.

[12] See L.H. Meyer, "Past and Future: The Case for an Identity-Independent Notion of Harm", in: L.H. Meyer/S.L. Paulson/T.W. Pogge (eds), *Rights, Culture, and the Law. Themes from the Legal and Political Philosophy of Joseph Raz*, 2003. A different type of response relies on a non-consequentialist interpretation of the relation of wronging a person and harming a person. If we can wrong a person without harming the person, a person can have a claim to rectification without having incurred any harm. A claim to rectification for past wrongs may not give rise to the non-identity problem – as R. Kumar argues in "Who Can Be Wronged?", *Philosophy and Public Affairs* 31 (2003), 99 et seq. For a different interpretation of the ethical significance of past wrongs see L.H. Meyer, "Obligations Persistantes et Réparation Symbolique", *Revue Philosophique de Louvain* 101 (2003), 105 et seq.

(2). Subjunctive-threshold:[13] An action (or inaction) at time t_1 harms someone only if the agent thereby causes (allows) this person's life to fall below some specified threshold.

Under this interpretation of harm, a person can be considered to be fully compensated for an act or policy (or event) if she or he does not fall below the specified standard at a particular time. Robert can be understood as having incurred harm because his ancestors were kidnapped and enslaved. Whether Robert has been harmed due to the way his ancestors were treated depends upon whether the way they were treated has led to Robert's falling below the specified standard of well being. However, whether or not this is the case will turn on his current state of well being. Employing this interpretation of harm and its accompanying interpretation of compensation requires a forward-looking assessment of what others ought to do today in terms of providing measures of compensation.[14]

When we analyse historical claims on the basis of such a subjunctive-threshold interpretation of harm, the normative relevance of past wrongs will depend upon their causal relevance for the well-being of currently living (and future people). Fulfilling our duties toward both

---

[13] For the wording of these notions of harm see T.W. Pogge, "'Assisting' the Global Poor", in: D.K. Chatterjee (ed.), *The Ethics of Assistance: Morality and the Distant Needy*, 2003.

[14] The relevance and importance of the forward-looking assessment of the normative significance of past wrongs has been stressed by, e.g., Lyons, see note 3; Waldron, "Superseding Historic Injustice", see note 3; B.A. Ackerman, *The Future of Liberal Revolution*, 1992, 72 et seq.; *idem*, "Temporal Horizons of Justice", *Journal of Philosophy* 94 (1997), 299 et seq. For a theory of justice that grounds our obligations in backward-looking reasoning see R. Nozick, *Anarchy, State, and Utopia*, 1974, 152 et seq. The theory relies upon counterfactual reasoning. For critiques of this theory, see Lyons, *idem*; G. Sher, "Ancient Wrongs and Modern Rights", *Philosophy and Public Affairs* 10 (1981), 3 et seq.; Waldron, *idem*. For epistemic reasons only, Nozick proposes Rawls's difference principle – a forward-looking principle, specifying what the future should be like – as a "rough rule of thumb for rectifying" historical injustice (*Anarchy, State, and Utopia*, 231). This idea does not address the problem of the inapplicability of a non-comparative notion of harm as discussed in the text. For alternative *impersonal* interpretations of how the past matters normatively, see P. Vallentyne, "Teleology, Consequentialism, and the Past", *Journal of Value Inquiry* 22 (1988), 89 et seq.; T.E. Hill, "The Message of Affirmative Action", *Social Philosophy & Policy* 8 (1990/1991), 108 et seq.; F. Feldman, *Utilitarianism, Hedonism, and Desert*, 1997, chs. 1, 4.

the latter might well require compensation for the consequences of the fact that their predecessors were badly wronged. However, the fact that their predecessors were wronged does not, in itself, give rise to justified claims to compensation for their descendants today.

The compensation claims of the Palestinian refugees are relevantly different, however. The non-identity problem is of little practical significance for assessing the validity of the right of return of the Palestinian refugees – and for two reasons. First, the non-identity problem does not arise with respect to surviving victims of wrongs. Among those present-day Palestinians living in refugee camps are a good number of those individuals who were forcefully and deliberately expelled from their lands by the Israeli fighting forces. The harm done to them can be understood in accordance with the common understanding of harm: the Israeli policy caused these people to be worse off than they would have been in the absence of that policy. These individuals would be fully compensated for the harm done to them were it the case that, as a result of measures of compensation undertaken, they were as well off as they would have been had the policy not been carried out.

Second, for the descendants of those who were expelled from their homeland it might well be true that they would not exist had their parents and (great-)grandparents not been expelled. However, the descendants can be said to be victims of the additional wrong that their parents did not receive compensation for the wrongs inflicted upon them. The individual descendants can be said to have been harmed from conception or birth because of the lack of sufficient compensation to their parents. Again, the harm done to them can be understood in accordance with the common understanding of harm: having refrained from providing sufficient measures of compensation to the first generation of Palestinian refugees, those entities who are under obligation to provide such measures of compensation harmed the descendants of the first generation of Palestinian refugees by causing those descendants to be worse off than they would have been had the relevant entities fulfilled their obligations. And, again, the second generation of Palestinian refugees would be fully compensated for the harm done to them if, as a result of measures of compensation undertaken, they are as well off as they would have been had the first generation of Palestinian refugees received the compensation they were entitled to. And this line of argument can be similarly extended for the third and fourth generations of Palestinian refugees.

Thus understood, the later generations' claims to compensation do not have to contend with the non-identity problem.[15] However, the legitimacy of people's claims can depend upon their actions (and inactions) and the impact these have on their well being. For these actions can be attributed normatively to people only insofar as they decide to act (not act) and take responsibility therefore. The strength of later generations' claims to compensation – derived from the failure to provide a sufficient measure of compensation to the first generation that suffered the initial harm – is thus likely to wane over time. The more the descendants' well-being can be attributed to actions or inactions for which they themselves or members of the intermediate generations are responsible, the less the hypothetical state of affairs that would obtain had the direct victims received adequate compensation[16] is relevant for the determination of the claims of the indirect victims.[17] This insight is, however, of little practical significance in assessing the strength of the claims of the descendants of the Palestinians who were expelled from their homeland. Most of them are the children or grandchildren of the direct victims. The harm done to their ancestors is not ancient. Thus, here the descendants' claim to compensation – based on the harm inflicted on them due to the failure to provide adequate compensation so far for the initial harm – is strong.

III. The Irrelevance of the Supersession Thesis

Let us now turn to the second source of doubts about the validity of historical claims to reparations. Injustices committed against people in the past may not give rise to claims to reparations today if such claims can be understood to presuppose an indefensible interpretation of property entitlements. David Lyons and Jeremy Waldron argue that the view that once we acquire entitlements they continue until we transfer or relinquish them is indefensible since there are reasons of principle[18]

---

[15] See G. Sher, *Transgenerational Compensation*, paper presented at the conference "Historical Justice", Potsdam, Germany, 19-20 July 2000.

[16] Assuming we could know what that state of affairs would be.

[17] See, e.g., Sher, see note 14.

[18] Here we are not concerned with pragmatic reasons for, e.g., statutes of limitations and the doctrine of adverse possession. Marmor, see note 1, 319 et seq., 325.

for holding that entitlements and rights are sensitive to the passage of time and changes of circumstances. According to Waldron, entitlement to land is based upon the idea that such entitlement can be an integral part of people's life plans and projects as individuals and as members of groups. Entitlements to land can be important for people being able to autonomously realise particular goods of their way of life.[19] When circumstances change, the entitlement might no longer be important in that sense or may decrease in normative significance. For example, the entitlement of original owners might weaken over time if they are separated from the land. Having been separated from the land, entitlement to the land might no longer be important for those original owners in autonomously realising their way of life. Thus, generally speaking, entitlements are sensitive to background circumstances and they are vulnerable to prescription. As Waldron argues, property entitlement is a set of claim rights, liberty rights and powers that are "circumstantially sensitive."[20]

Further, if legitimate entitlement is sensitive to changes in background changes, it is possible that the ongoing effect of an illegitimate acquisition and, more generally, of unjust violations of rights of others can become legitimate when circumstances change. This is Waldron's principal argument for the thesis that historical injustices may be superseded.[21]

---

19 See, e.g., L.H. Meyer, "Transnational Autonomy: Responding to Historical Injustice in the Case of the Saami and Roma Peoples", *International Journal on Minority and Group Rights* 8 (2001), 263 et seq., sections 10 (discussing the normative significance of sub-sovereign transnational control over their homeland for the political and cultural autonomy of the Saami people) and 11 (discussing the non-territorial claims of the Roma people to securing the status of a minority in the countries in which they reside and to recognition as a transnational minority for protecting a group identity that transcends national borders).

20 Or as David Lyons, see note 3, 370, puts it: "property rights themselves, and not just their exercise or contents, are relative to circumstances."

21 See Waldron, "Superseding Historic Injustice", see note 3, 24; and *idem*, "Redressing Historic Injustice", see note 3, section 7. The supersession thesis concerns the ongoing effect of past injustices only. Claiming that injustices are superseded implies neither that the past unjust violations of rights were not unjust nor that they should no longer be considered unjust. Even if certain injustices are superseded, we may well stand under obligations to publicly acknowledge the wrongs committed and to provide, say, measures of symbolic reparation toward the victims. See Meyer, "Obligations Persistantes et Réparation Symbolique", see note 12.

He gives an example in which the violation by one group of the legitimate rights of another group to a given waterhole is superseded by ecological catastrophe such that the interlopers acquire a right to share what they had wrongly begun to use. In these circumstances, "they are entitled to share that water hole. Their use of [the waterhole] no longer counts as an injustice; it is now in fact part of what justice now requires. The initial injustice by [the first group] against [the second] has been superseded by circumstances."[22] Hence, justice may require that original owners of land share their land with others, and they may be required to share even with those who unjustly appropriated the land. However, even if supersession of injustice is possible, the claim that it has occurred in any given situation "depends on which circumstances are taken to be morally significant and how as a matter of fact circumstances have changed."[23] The argument for the possibility of supersession rests on a hypothetical case of ecological disaster such that the need of others to use of the resource is both extreme and brought about by circumstances beyond their control.

If we assume that the Palestinians were unjustly expelled from their lands by the Israeli fighting forces and that the appropriation of these lands was unjust, it seems implausible that these historical injustices are superseded today so that their ongoing effect – namely, Israeli exclusive sovereign control of the land – is to be considered legitimate.[24] Israel cannot plausibly claim either to have an extreme need to exercise exclusive sovereign control over the land or that such a need has been brought about by circumstances beyond their control.[25] Further, and according to Waldron's account of property rights, supersession of the historic injustices will turn on whether for the Palestinian refugees loss

---

[22] Waldron, "Redressing Historic Injustice", see note 3, section 7.

[23] *Idem.*

[24] I do not mean to imply that Jeremy Waldron or David Lyons hold that these more recent injustices are superseded. Both claim that some colonial injustices committed two hundred years ago can plausibly be said to be superseded given dramatic changes that have taken place. But see Paul Patton's critique of the claim colonial injustices in Australia and New Zealand are superseded. P. Patton, "Colonization and Historical Injustice – The Australian Experience", in: Meyer, see note 1, 167 et seq..

[25] See Chaim Gans' subtly nuanced analysis of the just claims to self-determination of both the Jewish and the Palestinian peoples. C. Gans, "The Palestinian Right of Return and the Justice of Zionism", in this volume; *idem, The Limits of Nationalism*, 2003, ch. 4.

of their homeland and the lost property is of significance for their sense of who they are and who they want to be. In actuality, the loss is highly important to them, namely, to their individual and collective identities. We can explain this in terms of the importance of a shared communal life that allows the members of an ongoing cultural and ethnic group to autonomously participate in the realisation of the particular goods of their way of life.[26] For a people to realise this value, they typically need a meaningful degree of autonomous control over land, and for the Palestinians, there is no available substitute for their homeland. This is not an atypical situation either.[27] Further, and as Andrei Marmor has stressed, in the case of the Palestinian refugees, the claim to a right of return is particularly pressing owing to the miserable conditions under which they live in the refugee camps, with, as Andrei Marmor puts it, "very limited opportunities to escape such a predicament."[28] In the case of the Palestinian refugees it seems clear that their yearning for their lost homes "is not just a sentimental matter,"[29] but something which is closely related to the person's individual or communal sense of identity.

This is not to deny the Jewish right to self-determination.[30] Also, changes of circumstances do matter: a number of considerations can be distinguished that are relevant for specifying the contents of the Palestinian right of return and to how that right ought to be exercised.[31] These considerations reflect, first, how best to serve the interests under-

---

[26] Marmor, see note 1, 328.

[27] See, e.g., S. Wiessner, "Rights and Status of Indigenous Peoples: A Global Comparative and International Legal Analysis", *Harvard Human Rights Journal* 12 (1999), 57 et seq.; B. Kingsbury, "Indigenous Peoples in International Law: a Constructivist Approach to the Asian Controversy", *American Journal of International Law* 92 (1998), 414 et seq.; Meyer, see note 19.

[28] Marmor, see note 1, 328.

[29] *Idem.*

[30] See note 25.

[31] Ibid., section 3.3; A. Føllesdal, "The Special Claims of Indigenous Minorities to Corrective Justice", in: Meyer, see note 1, section 4; H. Hannum, *Autonomy, Sovereignty, and Self-Determination. The Accommodation of Conflicting Rights*, 1990. See especially A. Harel, "Whose Home Is It? Reflections on the Palestinians' Interests in Return", *Theoretical Inquiries in Law* 5 (2004), 333 et seq. (Harel argues that the Palestinians' interests correctly understood do not support their right of return, while I would argue that they ought to exercise their right of return in a way that reflects, *inter alia*, (some of) the considerations as most helpfully discussed by Harel).

lying the Palestinians' right of return; second, how to respect and to accommodate the legitimate interests and rights of others who might be affected by recognition of that right; and, third, pragmatic or strategic concerns of how best to serve the goal of establishing a legitimate and stable political order in the region. This essay does not even attempt to inquire into these normatively and empirically difficult questions. Such an inquiry might lead us to the conclusion that (many of) the Palestinians should not return to their homeland, that, instead, Israel ought to provide measures of material and symbolic compensation and that (many of) the Palestinians should accept, say, control over the West Bank as a sufficient territorial base for realising the particular goods of their way of life. However, such a conclusion could not rest on the mistaken premise that the Palestinian right of return has been superseded. Rather, such a conclusion would reflect an assessment of how (the) Palestinians ought to exercise their right of return and – or alternatively – it would reflect the view that (the) Palestinians have good or even compelling reasons to waive their right of return as a measure of political strategy.

IV. Concluding Remarks

The argument presented in this essay has been theoretical and mainly negative: the two main sources of doubt about the validity of claims for reparation owing to past injustices do not undermine the validity of the right of return of the Palestinian refugees. Neither the questions arising from the non-identity problem nor those arising from the supersession thesis significantly undermine the Palestinian refugees' claims to reparations and their right of return. First, the common understanding of harm and its accompanying notion of reparation and compensation are applicable to those Palestinians who were forcefully and deliberately expelled from their homeland as well as to their descendants with respect to the harm done to them owing to the lack of effective measures of reparations for the initial harm. Second, even if we allow for the conceptual possibility of historic supersession of injustices, it seems highly unlikely that the Palestinians' right of return has been superseded. Morally speaking, there does not seem to be a compelling case for considering the ongoing effect of the expulsion of the Palestinians from their homeland as just given current circumstances. However, this essay has not addressed the question of how the Palestinians ought to exercise their right of return or whether they (or many of them) might have good or compelling reasons to refrain from realising their right of return. Responding to this question would require consideration not only how best to serve the interests underlying the Palestinians' right of return, but also how to respect and to accommodate the legitimate interests and rights of others, including the Jewish right to self-determination. Last but not least, we would need to pragmatically assess how best to serve the goal of establishing a legitimate and stable political order in the region.

Economic Aspects

Palestinian Refugee Property Claims: Compensation and Restitution

Salim Tamari

I. Introduction

Assessment of refugee property losses should be tackled in the wider context of addressing refugee grievances, which include residency options, rehabilitation, restitution and repatriation. In this chapter I will isolate the issues of property compensation and restitution for analytic purposes and with the assumption that this approach will be part of the larger body of refugee claims. My working assumption is that it is essential to distinguish between the constellation of issues related to refugee rehabilitation, residency and compensation for states undertaking refugee absorption on the one hand (including Israel and the future Palestinian State), and issues of property compensation/restitution on the other. This approach is obviously problematic since Israel and some European countries have proposed that a package be comprehensive and that an international fund deal with refugee claims for material compensation. In addition, Israel proposed in the first and second Refugee Working Group (RWG) plenary meetings in the context of multilateral negotiations that refugee property claims be dealt with in relation to an exchange with Jewish refugee property claims in the Arab countries, notably Iraq and Egypt.[1] This position was flatly rejected by the Palestinian side, which adopted the position that these claims should be dealt with on a bilateral basis with the respective Arab states concerned.

---

1 See S. Tamari, *Palestinian Refugee Negotiations: From Madrid to Oslo II*, 1996, 43.

Similarly, the proposal for creating an international fund for compensation – while suitable for certain aspects of refugee rehabilitation, including support for states undergoing revalidation – has been deemed unacceptable for several reasons:

(1). It takes the issue of refugee property out of the domain of Israel's legal accountability and transfers it into the realm of international voluntary donations.

(2). It absolves the State of Israel from accountability for property that it has appropriated for Jewish immigrants with the resultant ethnic displacement. That rewards this displacement.

(3). It establishes a false parallel between the rights of Palestinian refugees and those of Jewish immigrants. To the extent that Arab Jews were expelled from their countries of origin, those claims of lost property should be dealt with bilaterally between the respective Arab states and these Jewish emigrants, including those who did not go to Israel but rather sought refuge in other European countries and the United States.

II. Scope of the Problem

Palestinian refugee property includes the bulk of private and public real estate, buildings, communal/public property, and *waqf* property acquired by Israel in two broad areas:

(1). Land within the territory designated for the Jewish State in the 1947 Partition Plan.

(2). Areas added to the State of Israel by military conquest and consolidated by the armistice agreement of 1949.

Land acquired in the 1967 War, which may be consolidated by any future accord to be signed by Israel and the Palestine Liberation Organization (PLO) is not within the scope of this chapter. A distinction should be made between claims of compensation/restitution for public/state property within the boundaries of the Jewish State according to the Partition Plan and those areas that were annexed in 1949 to the expanded Jewish State. For example, railway lines, public buildings and forest land in the Jaffa area, which was designated as part of the Arab state, would be subject to compensation claims, whereas the same categories of properties in Haifa would not. Compensation/restitution claims for refugee property would apply to those who were either displaced during and after the war of 1948 or in its immediate aftermath and found themselves outside the boundaries of the state and those Palestinian refugees who became citizens of the state but whose land was taken over by the state involuntarily.

Until recently most studies of refugee compensation claims have focused on the issue of valorisation of lost property. One of the first to address this issue seriously was Sami Hadawi in his *Palestinian Rights and Losses*.[2] The assessment was based on his work with the United Nations Conciliation Commission for Palestine (UNCCP) and contained a critique of the UN's categories, which were based essentially on tax declarations. By Hadawi's estimates those properties amounted to US$ 11.5 billion in 1990 prices.[3] Since then, Atef Qubursi and Yusif Sayigh attempted separately to update and refine these assessments. Among the international assessors, Frank Lewis came up with supplementary assessment for agricultural lands, which amounted to US$ 2.3-2.8 billion in 1993 prices.[4] Nevertheless, global figures for property losses, as we shall see, must be subjected to assumptions that are rarely clarified in these estimates. For example do they include *waqf* properties? Do they include public and communal properties in the area designated as the land of the Jewish State in the Partition Plan? If not, would they include such properties in the areas that were *de facto* annexed to the State of Israel by virtue of the armistice of 1949? These and many other questions should be clarified before we begin the attempt to assess the value of lost Arab property in Palestine.

The procedure for filing compensation claims will also have to take into account several factors that are related to the elapse of time, as well as bureaucratic steps, which are bound to result in inequities:

First, poorer refugees are less equipped than better off claimants with documentation and authentication for their property. Landless refugees and former sharecroppers (about 20-25 per cent of all rural refugees) do not have any land claims but do have claims of material grievances – now recognised by a number of important precedents. Since a compensatory fund is likely to be based on an Israeli or international fund with finite resources, refugees with more substantial land claims are more likely to benefit from such a fund than those with little or no such

2 S. Hadawi, *Palestinian Rights and Losses*, 1985.

3 See R. Klinov, *Reparations and Rehabilitation of Palestinian Refugees*, paper presented at the Max Planck Institute's conference on Palestinian Refugees, Heidelberg, 11 July 2003.

4 See the contribution of R. Klinov in this book, 340-341.

claims. In other words, richer claimants who are already living comfortably will get the lion's share of this compensation, rather than poorer refugees who suffered more in the war itself and subsequently in the refugee camps.

Second, unlike the situation in Germany after World War II or the former Yugoslavia in the 1990s, where refugee claims were supported by a coalition of international forces favourable to their predicament, no similar compulsion impels the State of Israel today to deliver on any obligations it will incur towards the Palestinians either during the negotiating process itself or in the implementation of an agreement. Indeed the current Israeli position under the Sharon government is that Palestinian refugee property has already been "exchanged" for the losses of Jewish emigrants from Arab countries (sometimes Iran is added for good measure) after the war of 1948.

Third, bureaucratic setup for most procedures of compensation means that the state and agencies representing the refugees (including the battery of international lawyers acting on their behalf) will siphon off the bulk of those benefits owed to their clients/subjects.

The gradual opening of important data archives that delineate the nature of property and land claims as well as the social composition and distribution of Palestinian refugee population has made the issue of documenting refugee claims much more feasible than at any previous time. We can say without exaggeration that these data bases – and the UNRWA and UNCCP files in particular – contain the most extensive and reasonably reliable information about the social attributes as well as socioeconomic and property claims of the Palestinian refugees, more reliable than similar data on any other refugee population in modern history.

III. Problems Inherent in the Documentation of Property Claims

But these databases are not without problems, including the problem of missing components, lack of longitudinal depth, and lack of proper access. Most importantly, for the purpose of this analysis, they tend to reinforce an element of unjust distribution of claims for historical losses. I will discuss this component of bias for each database separately.

1. Bias in the UNRWA Archives

Archives of the United Nations Relief Works Agency for Palestine Refugees in the Near East (UNRWA) contain demographic data, prepared for the purpose of the administration of welfare among refugee population, for close to 3.8 million individual refugees in five refugee areas: Palestine (West Bank and Gaza), Jordan, Syria, and Lebanon. Most of this data has been available in a computerised data system known as the Unified Registration System (URS) since 1979 and is updated by field offices on a daily basis. A more extensive data source is contained in a sub-system of the URS covering elaborate attributes of the most destitute of the refugee population households (about 15 per cent of the total households in the URS) originally known as the "special hardship cases."

A separate, but non-computerised, source of data is the family files. These are currently (2003) prepared for digitisation and hence searchability. They contain data on the original process of registration of refugee families, reasons for flight from Palestine in 1948 – as reported in 1950 by the head of household – and changes that affected the family fortunes in the process of relocation to the host countries. They also contain a key section, but not properly or systematically entered, on losses incurred by the refugee family as a result of the war of 1948 and documentation of these losses, again not systematically provided.

Together these databases provide an extensive profile of the demographic profile of refugee families, their composition, their educational achievement, their health conditions and their habitat and location. The amount of data is relatively accurate (compared to census data gathered by the state) and very detailed.

What are the main pitfalls in the UNRWA data basis?

(1). It is basically a record of poor refugees. The professional strata, the middle classes, and a substantial section of skilled workers are absent as are the bulk of the landed elements, namely the people with the most substantial compensation claims.

(2). It does not cover refugees who settled outside the "confrontation states" – Syria, Lebanon, Jordan, and the Palestinian territories. That is, refugees in Egypt, the Gulf States, North Africa, and abroad do not appear in the record; nor do "internal refugees" from Israel.

(3). It has no historical depth. That is, UNRWA data is not longitudinal. Computerised data is continuously being replenished with updating and deletion and expunging of earlier information. People who die, who move outside the system, whose records are few years old, etc. are removed from the record. This may be essential for the purposes of administering welfare dispensation, but it is a disaster for proper examination of social change, mobility, and the evolution of the refugee problem.

(4). An important component of this data, the family files, is not computerised, and therefore is not searchable. This includes data about original claims and conditions of flight. Recent commitments (in the summer of 2003) by certain European states, most notably Denmark, to extend the computerisation of the UNRWA archives will improve this situation considerably.

(5). Self-reporting of property losses does not lend itself to authentication and therefore to the external legitimising of these claims. By contrast, social conditions and claims for current material assistance are rigorously investigated since they fall under the mandate of UNRWA as a service provider for the health, educational, and welfare needs of refugees.

2. Bias in the UNCCP Records

The UNCCP databases in New York are currently digitised and contain the most elaborate record of Palestinian refugee property and land losses in the war of 1948, systematically gathered by an expert land team in the period of 1951-1961. The records are for individual (personal) title deeds and for communal and religious endowments. They are tabulated by title deed owner, size of land, and locational coordinates. They contain map linkages for easy determination of location.

One of the most important features of the UNCCP land records is that exact replicas of the database are owned by the five regional Arab states (as well as Palestine) in addition to Israel. Thus, claims based on this source are verifiable and subject to immediate authentication. Its verifiability is further buttressed by the fact that the land records are all derived from regional land registry offices (the *Tapu*), currently located in Israeli territories.

But the UNCCP database has a number of pitfalls in terms of its applicability to material claims by refugees.[5] First, it does not cover the conditions of hundreds of thousands of refugees who were either landless or sharecroppers with long-term cropping contracts with landlords. It also does not cover the claims of former peasants who lost their property because it was not properly registered in the *Tapu*.

Second, it is a record frozen in one moment of history. It does not reflect changes in the status of properties, real estate, and land plots since 1948. These changes include confiscation, leases, resale by the State of Israel and by some former owners, and changes in the physical status of the property, such as changes in agricultural land into urban property and the abolishing of *waqf* land and its transformation into state, communal, or private property.

Third, large areas of refugee property do not appear in the UNCCP records. Those include a substantial area of southern Palestine (the Negev area), which was deemed communal property as a result of common law practices by Bedouin tribes. Significant sections of urban real estate (e.g. Jaffa) are also missing for obscure administrative reasons. Areas not surveyed and settled into the land registry by 1947 are included, but proper coordinates for their location make those sections of the UNCCP in need for modification. This is true of areas in West Jerusalem, which have been digitised most recently by the mapping section in Orient House.

Fourth, a technical problem with the UNCCP record is the lack of bilingual entries. Since Arabic names are transliterated this may produce problems of recognition.

3. Integrating the Demographic and Property Databases

At the risk of oversimplification we can say that while the URS (UNRWA) constitutes a demographic record of poor refugees in the countries of the Arab East, the UNCCP records provide a basis for claims by the propertied classes. There is obviously a substantial degree of overlap in the two social categories, but this overlap is deceptive. UNRWA records, intended primarily as a frame for the provision of welfare

[5] For a discussion of these flaws see E. Zureik/S. Tamari (eds), *Reinterpreting the Historical Record: The Uses of Palestinian Refugee Archives for Social Science and Policy Research*, 2000.

services for camp and non-camp needy refugees need substantial modification before they can become a suitable frame for compensatory claims. In contrast, the UNCCP was established for exactly this purpose. Having said that, there is a lot to be gained from the creation of a single digitised database from the two sources of refugee archives; such an integration would help in rectifying the absence of a "poor refugee" component in the UNCCP archives and would supplement the UNRWA-URS with a property record that has so far been poorly documented in the family files. It will also help buttress the UNRWA records with an important element of replicability and verifiability – a condition that has been perceived as lacking (at least by the Israelis and Americans) in UNRWA files.

One assisting factor is that both the URS and the UNCCP records have individual coding features that can act as the linkages between the two data sets. In order to integrate the two archives, certain measures have to be taken:

(1). A political decision on the part of the PLO that an integrated data set should be created as a basis for refugee compensation claims.

(2). A joint committee made up of UNRWA and UNCCP technical staff to work out conceptual and technical modalities for the integrated framework.

(3). The protocols for codes of identification of individual and collective (family, communal) refugee units must be approved by the Arab host countries and Israel, since those parties' cooperation will be needed to facilitate this technical process.

IV. The Issue of Equity in Refugee Property Claims

The Palestinians have hesitated in developing a strategy for compensation/restitution since that might lead to questions about the resilience of the leadership in defending refugee political rights. Israel has used this absence as an instrument in claiming that the Palestinians have been using the refugee issues as a means of potential demographic destabilisation of the Jewish State. Some Palestinians (e.g. Rashid Khalidi) have put forth the position that Israeli acceptance of moral culpability for the dispossession of the refugee will be the basis of a historical settlement of this issue,[6] – but most Palestinian negotiators on refugees have taken the position that a combination of options must obtain (restitution, repatriation, naturalisation, and compensation) so that closure for the refugees can be achieved. In all of these cases the refugees themselves should be an essential party to the determination of their future based on concrete choices.

Similarly, Michael Fishbach suggests that Palestinian property claims should be considered within the context of Jewish global claims for property lost in Arab states in the 1950s. The rationale for this position lies in the assumption that the Israeli Palestinian refugee settlement will be part of a wider process of negotiating the Arab-Israeli conflict. But if this is the case then it makes equal sense to bring the issue of German-Israeli reparations into this global picture: first, because these reparations can set important precedents for the ways and means of implementing refugee compensation, and second, because Palestinian refugees were themselves the indirect victims of the German displacement of Jews.

1. Separating Refugee Repatriation from Refugee Compensation

I argue that it is essential *to distinguish and separate* the issue of resolving the future repatriation of refugees from the question of the disposition of their property. Considerations dealing with the question of residency emanating from repatriation (return, naturalisation, and settlement) are likely to affect some refugees, while issues of compensation will affect all refugees. In the former case, the modalities of the practical implementation of the right of return were discussed at Taba in December 2000: return to Palestine, to Israel, to territories ceded the future Palestinian State, naturalisation and resettlement. The issue of material compensation on the other hand, needs to be addressed in terms of documentation of property claims and compensating losses in life-chances, e.g. employment, normality, physical and psychological suffering.

One significant feature of the compensatory paradigm, if taken on the basis of documented losses of property, is that it tends to replicate a highly skewed social structure. A claims strategy in which refugees will

---

6 R. Khalidi, "Toward a Solution", in: Center for Policy Analysis on Palestine (ed.), *Palestinian Refugees: Their Problem and Future*, 1994, 24 et seq.

simply reiterate their demands for compensation on the basis of material property losses is highly favourable to the owners of large estates and their descendents and very unfavourable to those who were either landless or had small properties, the latter constituting the vast majority of refugees. Furthermore, if we assume that the collective fund for restitution will be limited and considerably smaller than the actual value of dispossessed land and real estate, this inequity will be further accentuated.

2. The Issue of Demographic Attrition

Two essential historical factors contribute to the process of inequity in compensation claims:

(1). Refugees with smaller property (e.g., those households that individually used to possess less than 50 dunums) will have property claims that are extremely fragmented and parcellised by demographic attrition, four generations later. One can visualise interfamilial squabbles over such rights, whose return will be further reduced by the passage of time and the intervention of a battery of lawyers who will get the lion's share of such indemnities.

(2). Establishing material claims for landless refugees and those with small amounts of property will be much more difficult to ascertain and authenticate than for those with substantial property. The rich have always been better in preserving their records than the poor in the condition of war. Moreover, the UNCCP records – the most systematic in archiving these records – have nothing to say about landless refugees and those sharecroppers whose land was unjustly appropriated by big landlords.

V. A Strategic Approach Toward Material Compensation

Israeli acknowledgement of its role in the historical dispossession of Palestinian refugees in the war of 1948 should not be seen as act of contrition in lieu of concrete settlement, but as the first step in a process of negotiations over material settlement that will bring closure to the issue of the refugees. So far, with precious few exceptions (e.g. Shlomo Ben Ami in the Ottawa multilateral meeting in 1991 and Yossi Beilin's proposal for a joint narrative in Taba 2001) Israeli official pronouncements have been that Israel and its armed forces are not culpable for the displacement of the refugees in the 1948 War and that the appropriation of Palestinian absentee property is held in lieu of the "exchanged" Jewish property confiscated in Iraq, Egypt, Tunis, Lebanon, and so on.

I propose here a three-pronged approach to material compensation, which will follow a process of acknowledgment of historical injustice. The essential feature of this process is that it will give the refugees concrete options to choose from, including repatriation in Palestine, repatriation to areas of Israel that will be annexed to Palestine (on a swap basis), repatriation to Israel, naturalisation in the host countries, and third state migration. The compensation/restitution modalities apply independently to all of these options.

(1). During the first stage, the PLO and Israel, in coordination with the Arab host governments, will agree on the procedures necessary to authenticate the documents needed to approve property claims. It is necessary at this stage to separate the procedures of repatriation/resettlement from those pertaining to material compensation. It is not the objective of this paper to address the question of repatriation/naturalisation, which has been dealt with at length elsewhere.

(2). Collective *versus* Individual Claims: It is essential that Palestinian refugees are able to have two venues for claims of material compensation. A collective claim will go for the state (e.g., state to state), earmarked for the rehabilitation of repatriated refugees and the building of a national infrastructure (housing, roads, and economic and social base) for the absorption of refugees. Individual claims, on the other hand, will be cleared through an autonomous organisation (possibly UNRWA), which will assess, authenticate, and process individual claims for property losses. Refugees who are residents of countries outside the regional host countries will be able to file claims worldwide.

(3). Restitution: This is an essential component of a just solution to the refugee problem. One major argument used against restitution of property is that such an act would dispossess current (i.e. Israeli) occupants. But precedents in other areas, including Germany and Bosnia, indicate that a model of restitution would enable the owners to repossess their former properties while allowing for long-term leases for the current occupiers.

Precedents need to be examined in order to see which recent historical examples are appropriate. One of the most relevant cases in this regard is the Dayton Peace Agreement concerning the repatriation of refugees from Bosnia Herzegovina (1995), which involved millions of Bosnian,

Serb, and Croat refugees. Although the schemes for repatriation and compensation were only partly successful, the Dayton Agreement contained the three elements of success necessary for the Palestinian-Israeli case: international intervention by the European Union and the United States, border delineation, and a mechanism for repatriation of refugees and restitution/compensation for their lost properties, supervised by the UN High Commissioner for Refugees (UNHCR) and the UN International Task Force. One can benefit from both the benefits and mistakes made by this agreement. In Mick Dumper's study in this volume, he noted:

> "As a result [of the agreement] by 2000 only 10 per cent of the Serbs from Croatia, 5 per cent of Muslims and Croats from Western Bosnia and Herzegovina and only 1 per cent of those expelled by Serbs from eastern Bosnia and Herzegovina (Republica Srpska) returned to their homes."[7]

This case is particularly relevant to the Palestinian case because it involved the issues of borders, displacement, and restitution in a new state that ceased to be the national state of the original refugees. Most other international cases involving repatriation (e.g. Guatemala, Afghanistan and Somalia) involve refugees' repatriation to the country that still represents them or third party relocation.

(4). Cutting Point in Property Claims: In this case it will enhance refugee claims to propose a strategy (successfully adapted in Yugoslavia, among other recent cases) in which landless refugees and those with minimal property claims (say owners of areas below 40 dunums in rural areas and single properties in urban areas) group their claims into a single package-deal in which they will receive a standard package of monetary compensation (or a number of standard packages) per family. Although on the surface, this proposal may not meet the standards of justice, its consequences meet conditions of fairness. For once claimants will shorten prolonged waiting periods for the bureaucratic procedures of authentication of claims, which could take years and quite likely decades, judging from precedents. They will also ensure that the bulk of this compensation goes directly to the claimants and not to attorneys and bureaucrats representing them.

---

[7] M. Dumper, *Comparative Perspectives on Repatriation and Resettlement of Palestinian Refugees: The cases of Guatemala, Bosnia and Afghanistan*, unpublished paper, 2004.

But there is a more important reason for adopting this procedure already referred to above. Namely, the cumulative increase in the size of the households of those claimants, four generations after the event, will most likely ensure internal family disputes over individual rights that can be spared through the suggested procedure. It is quite likely that this procedure will allow a substantial proportion of Palestinian refugee property claimants (perhaps as much as 80 per cent of the total refugees) to expedite their claims within months of the implementation of an accord on such claims, leaving room for effective concentration of legal and administrative resources for the remaining 20 per cent.

Why is it possible to achieve an equitable resolution for refugee claims despite inequitable power relations between the protagonists? Now we come to the thorniest of the questions of equity raised above: why would the State of Israel feel compelled to respond to these issues of justice and equity raised above? So far it has had three standard answers:

(a). That Israel is not accountable for the fate of refugees during the war.

(b). That Palestinian property confiscated from exiled refugees has been "exchanged" by the sequestered property of Jewish emigrants from Arab countries.

(c). That the status of refugees is a humanitarian issue of global concern, largely the product of Arab countries themselves intent on perpetuating the conditions of misery for their own political objectives, and in this context Israel will contribute, voluntarily, to solving this situation through an international fund of compensation.

The first of these answers has already been superseded by the intellectual work of the "new" Israeli historians, whose contribution has already become acceptable to important sections of the Israeli establishment such as Shlomo Gazit, Beilin, Shlomo Ben Ami and indeed to public opinion worldwide. It is ironic that the same claims, when made by the victims themselves for decades were seen as propaganda. It took the work of few courageous Israeli scholars, especially renegade historian Benny Morris, to make this point acceptable.

The second response, concerning the exchange of property, has acquired recent weight since it has been officially adopted by both the Netanyahu and Sharon governments. Nevertheless, it has been sufficiently challenged during the multilateral peace negotiations to warrant its shelving. The main argument here is that Palestinian restitution claims cannot be reduced to the status of "generic Arab claims" and pertain to Israeli actions during the war and its aftermath and that Jewish property claims belong to the arena of bilateral negotiations between Israel (or individual Jewish emigrants and refugees) and the concerned Arab states.

My main contention is that, despite the lack of equity in power relations, Israel will most likely respond to claims of accountability with regard to refugee property for two important reasons:

First, Israel wants to achieve closure on the question of refugees more than any other issue. This is partly due to the need to bring about an "end of claims, end of conflict" resolution in negotiations, which was at the heart of the collapse of the Camp David/Taba negotiations in 2000 and which is impossible without addressing refugee property claims. It is also to forestall individual refugee claims for property rights by making a collective deal on this issue with the PLO/PNA acting on behalf of the global refugee population.

Second, Israel seeks the ultimate legitimacy and its acceptance as a state within the Arab world. It is impossible to do this without resolving the refugee claims, especially as far as Jordan, Syria, and Lebanon are concerned.

Israel will most likely resist any deal that will involve the repatriation of refugees inside Israeli territory and will insist that refugees be either repatriated to the future Palestinian State or naturalised in the host country. Even if a symbolic deal is struck over repatriation of refugees to Israel, the Israelis will try to undermine it in the process of implementation.

But even here there is room for flexibility. If the process of naturalisation of refugees in the Arab states is to succeed, Israel must be party to this absorption. Having said this, it will make more practical sense for the Palestinians to insist that refugee repatriation in the context of implementing General Assembly Resolution 194 (III) be accomplished primarily in territories in Israel to be annexed/swapped to the Palestinian State.

Reparations and Rehabilitation of Palestinian Refugees

*Ruth Klinov**

I. Introduction

The payment of financial reparations to Palestinian refugees[1] has been widely recognised as an essential component of any resolution of the Israeli-Palestinian conflict. The purpose of this memorandum is to suggest a framework of analysis for a proposed package of such reparations.

No paper on these issues can be free of basic political, controversial assumptions, and this paper is no exception, so it is best at the very outset to articulate that, in this paper, the basic assumption is that returning titles of ownership to refugees as a major form of reparations is both politically and practically impossible. (The practical difficulties will be dis-

---

* Work on this memorandum was financed by the Institute for Social and Economic Studies in the Middle East, at the Kennedy School, Harvard University, in the framework of its Refugee Project. The first draft was written in 1999. The present memorandum incorporates many of the comments made by Tayseer Abdel Jaber, Shmuel Amir, Isaac Diwan, Ephraim Kleiman, and Elias Tuma. I thank each of them. Revising the data set out in the 1999 paper, I modified the section on investment. For lack of updated data, economic figures date from 1995, and in order to adjust them to some future year, use was made of the annual growth rate of the refugee population (circa 3 per cent).

[1] The paper does not address the issue of reparations to Jewish refugees from Arab countries. Such claims may affect the net amount available for Arab refugees, i.e. their budget constraints, but once this is dispensed, its uses and distribution can be discussed independently of the amount given to Jewish refugees. Since the paper considers scenarios with *different* budget constraints, we ignore the Jewish aspect.

cussed later). This leaves financial compensation as the main form of reparation.

In addition, the solution of the refugee problem is viewed as a primarily political, rather than purely humanitarian effort, where the political realities lead to the following assumptions: first, that even after a peace settlement the majority of refugees will not immigrate to Israel; secondly, that their rehabilitation will occur in either their present host countries, or in Palestine; thirdly, that resettlement in other countries – whether in America, Europe or the rest of the Middle East – cannot form a major part of reparations package. By the same token, most Israeli settlements in the West Bank and Gaza will be dismantled. Lastly, this paper assumes that no external limitations, by Israelis or others will be put on the number of returnees to Palestine.

There are three central economic issues regarding reparations: the overall sum to be allocated; the types of expenditures to be financed (private consumption, public consumption, investment); and distributive issues – by location, by level of income, by region, and between the public and private sectors. There is a sequence to these issues. Arguably the first is the most important. As Benvenisti and Zamir[2] demonstrate, in most international claim settlements the preferred mode is to determine the lump sum due to the claiming government, and leave its allocation to the respective government's discretion. In the Palestinian case a discussion of allocation seems to be in order, for at least two reasons. First, because it is not clear which government should be compensated: Some of the refugees are expected to move to Palestine, but others may prefer to stay at their present location, or move to other countries. Assuming that such a decision is voluntary and that mobility may extend over several years, the right to compensation must be vested, at least partly, in the refugees themselves.[3] The second reason for discussing allocation is to glean past experience of other countries and, regardless of which body administers the money, to draw lessons about the efficiency of various modes of allocation. We shall discuss allocation between uses for the same reasons.

---

[2] E. Benvenisti/E. Zamir, "Private Claims to Property Rights in the Future Israeli-Palestinian Settlement", *AJIL* 89 (1995), p. 295 et seq.

[3] The official PLO economic development programme for Palestine (1993) assumed the return of only 500,000 refugees from the 1967 War until year 2000, leaving the issue of the number of returnees of 1948 – and some of those of 1967 – moot.

Accordingly the paper has two parts: Part II discusses various approaches for determining the overall sum of reparations, and provides orders of magnitude implied by each approach; part III addresses the allocation of funds between uses and between recipients.

A comment on this paper's title: the terms "reparations" and "rehabilitation" imply two different rationales of the resources given to refugees: the first implies compensation for past damages, while the second implies a contribution to the solution of current problems. As will be seen, the two will be compared, but to avoid monotony both terms, as well as "compensation," will be used interchangeably. Last, the paper uses the term Palestine to denote the West Bank and the Gaza Strip.

II. The Range of Overall Reparations

There are several ways to approach the estimation of the overall sum required. They are not alternative, but rather complementary, and the final sum should reflect a synthesis of all these approaches.

Availability of international funds: For a long time this was considered to be the central limiting factor. It is still necessary to get a realistic idea about the amount available from the international community, and how flexible it is. Who are the potential donors? What determines the size of their donations? Can in-kind donations (e.g. readiness to absorb immigrants, giving refugees residing in camps a title of ownership on their house) be part of the overall sum?

Refugee needs: Another approach is to sum up the "demand" for reparations by starting from a micro base and asking: who is a refugee, what are the needs of the various refugee communities, and how much will it cost to fill these needs. A reasonable criterion for the extent of needs is the amount of resources necessary to bring refugees up to the prevailing norms of the population of their country of residence. On the whole, and except for Lebanon, refugees are not very different from non-refugees, in their employment rate and in educational and health standards.[4] Their obvious specific needs are for housing for camp-dwellers and for replacement of UNRWA expenditures on health, education, training and welfare for camp and non-camp-dwellers alike. As to em-

[4] R. Klinov, *Reparations and Rehabilitation of Palestinian Refugees*, draft report prepared for the Harvard Institute for Social and Economic Policy in the Middle East, 1999.

ployment requirements: not only are there only minor differences between refugees and non-refugees in their labour force characteristics, but it is very difficult to imagine refugee-specific job-creation activities. Only in Lebanon does a degree of labour market segregation exist, but even there any settlement is likely to include desegregating measures. Therefore, employment requirements should be determined on the basis of forecasted population growth in each country, regardless of refugee status, and the role of reparations to refugees should be considered within the general development targets of the various countries. This is discussed in section 3 below. The needs approach is thus confined to specific refugee needs for housing and social services.

Development requirements: Investment in refugee housing and employment constitutes a part of the overall investment in each country. Rather than consider it separately, this approach asks: What is the feasible overall domestic investment in each country in housing and in non-housing? How much of this can be financed through reparations and how much is expected from other sources – domestic savings, foreign aid other than reparations, foreign loans, and foreign investment.

On the allocation side: how much of the total should be allocated to housing, and how much to other forms of physical capital? Should a part of reparations be used for current consumption, and if so, what part? This approach emphasises the importance of reparations for creating employment and housing in the general framework of the country's economic development. It also has to confront the general tendency characterising the Middle East (including Israel) of over-investing in housing relative to infrastructure and productive capital. In sum, this approach involves an integrative view of the various sources and uses of the economy.

In this context, several additional aspects have to be considered: (1) the spread of investment over time from a technical viewpoint (the marginal cost of investment in each year rises with its overall annual amount; hence an optimal investment policy may require a spread of investment activities over a longer period); (2) the channelling of reparations toward investment requires good savings channels; (3) the experience of successful international transfers of resources, and particularly the Marshall Plan, prove that the effect on growth and employment depends not so much on the overall sum transferred as on the institutional structure of such transfers, and the accompanying conditions imposed on spending there from.

Compensation for property loss and issues of equity: An alternative, and the prevalent approach in the existing literature on reparations, is to take past losses as a departure point for determining the overall sum of reparations. This is the most common but also the most controversial approach. It requires heroic assumptions about the items to be included, the revaluation of the price of capital abandoned 50 years ago, and the discount rate to be used over these 50 years.

Set out below are very rough estimates of the sums involved in each of these approaches. As will be explained, some of the estimates are outdated.

1. Availability of international funds

I first began studying the issue in 1997. The estimates at the time were extremely low – between US$ one and two billion. Since then, and particularly at the Camp David talks in 2000, President Clinton mentioned US$ 10-20 billion as possible amounts.

The most thorough recent paper on the issue is by Rex Brynen[5] of McGill University, Montreal. Three potential groups of donors are identified: Israel, whether in the form of the restitution of refugee properties, cash payments, or capital resources in the West Bank and Gaza; contributions from Arab donors; and contributions from international donors. It is argued that, on the one hand, the ability and willingness of Arab and international donors to finance a compensation scheme has often been overestimated. On the other hand, the restitution of titles to former refugee property, however morally appealing, is politically and practically unfeasible. As a result Brynen concludes that the major portion of any compensation scheme will necessarily take the form of financial and capital resources contributed by Israel.

Brynen quotes several overall sums: The Harvard-based Joint Working Group on Israeli-Palestinian Relations, in a paper written by Joseph Alpher and Khalil Shikaki, suggested that individual compensation to Palestinians, largely financed by Israel, might total US$ 15-20 billion. Rashid Khalidi suggests that reparations might total some US $40 billion (based on *per capita* payments of around US$ 20,000), or several times this amount, based on the current value of both material and non-material losses. Shlomo Gazit has suggested that Israel might assume a

---

5 R. Brynen, *Financing Palestinian Refugee Compensation*, workshop paper; workshop title: Compensation as a Part of a Comprehensive Solution to the Palestinian Refugee Problem, 2003.

substantial portion of a refugee compensation scheme totalling US$ seven to ten billion.

Brynen examines various levels of Israeli compensation commitments relative to the size (1999) of the Israeli population, economy, and government expenditure, on the assumption that these amounts are raised over ten years. A total of US$ ten billion represents, relative to GNP, about the same level of generosity evident in the current Saudi and Kuwaiti foreign aid programmes, and only slightly more than Denmark's ratio of ODA/GNP, and might also be considered economically feasible. On the other hand, a total ten-year contribution of US$ 25 billion is equivalent to more than one quarter of the entire Israeli defence budget, and can only be considered the extreme upper boundary of what is economically possible.

2. A need-based approach: housing and social services

This approach requires a definition of the universe of beneficiaries. Between the non-controversial group of camp-dwellers and that of self-proclaimed refugees there are numerous possible definitions. Here we adopt the official UNRWA data on camp and non-camp-dwellers.

UNRWA's[6] definition, prevailing to date, was formulated in 1953/1954. "A person whose normal residence was Palestine for a minimum of two years preceding the conflict in 1948, and who, as a result of this conflict, lost both his home and his means of livelihood and took refuge in one of the countries where UNRWA provides relief." Refugees within this definition and direct descendants of such refugees are eligible for Agency assistance if they are registered with UNRWA, living in an area of UNRWA operations, and in need.[7]

---

6 UNRWA Annual Report 1953/1954, GAOR 9th Sess., Suppl. No. 17 (A/2717).

7 Originally the definition was broader: "A needy person who lost his home and livelihood as a result of the Palestinian conflict," see Progress Report of the UN Acting Mediator on Palestine, GAOR 3rd Sess., Suppl. No. 11A, 1948, p. 5.

a. Housing

At this stage we engage in an extremely crude exercise. Before presenting the estimates it is important to emphasise the distinction between the cost of land and that of other inputs into construction and infrastructure. Land *per se* is a fixed production factor, its price is totally demand-determined. While it constitutes a very large component of the price of a house to the buyer, it constitutes a real cost to the economy as a whole, insofar as its transfer requires giving up alternative production (e.g. when land is urbanised and involves loss of agricultural production). Otherwise it is an internal transfer between the buyer and seller, cancelling out for the economy as a whole. A real cost to the economy occurs where the use of land requires additional resources, not available at present, or when these resources have to be pulled out from other lines of production, decreasing them elsewhere in the economy. The real cost of residential construction to the economy is thus composed of inputs other than land. These are labour, machines, roads, sewage systems, construction materials, etc., all of which require additional labour, capital and materials. Reparations can finance these additional costs by providing the means to buy machinery and materials. But if given for buying land, they will simply inflate the money supply, and eventually will either be used for imports in other sectors or left as surpluses in the balance of payments. The following estimates of the housing cost thus exclude land prices.

Let us assume that improvement in housing, including the necessary infrastructure, but excluding land price, requires US$ 20,000-30,000 per household. The estimated price of a low-middle-class apartment in Amman in January 1997 was (according to estimates of local real-estate dealers) 25,000-30,000 Jordanian Dinars (US$ 40,000), and outside Amman 80 per cent of that amount. This includes land price. Our assumption of a US$ 20,000-30,000 cost per apartment minus the price of land is thus reasonable. A typical apartment is 125 square metres, is connected to all utilities, and accommodates six persons.

What is the overall sum of investment required for rehabilitating camps? UNRWA's estimates of the refugee population in and out of camps for June 2002 are summarised in Table 1. The total number of refugees is 3.973 million, and that of camp-dwellers is 1.263 million. UNRWA itself warns that "the number of registered refugees present in the Agency's area of operations is almost certainly less than the population recorded," and both numbers were strongly challenged by other researchers.[8] Here we take them at their face value.

Based on an average family size of 7.5,[9] the order of magnitude of the total sum needed for housing rehabilitation of camp-dwellers alone is US$ five billion.

b. Housing in Jordan: a comment

According to Table 1, refugee requirements of apartments in Jordan amount to US$ 1.2 billion. An alternative is to base the estimates on the recent Jordanian Employment and Housing Survey of 1996. According to this survey 7.65 per cent of the population of Jordan, Jordanian and non-Jordanian alike, including camp-dwellers, live in over-crowded conditions of four or more persons per room. In Amman itself, where nearly 60 per cent of all refugees live, the proportion of the population living in a density of over four persons per room is 7.1 per cent.[10] Though some in the high-density group are in all likelihood non-refugees, camp-dwellers form a large part of this population, and improving their housing conditions is a golden opportunity to solve the housing needs of the poorest of the Jordanian and Palestinian population alike.

7.5 per cent of the 4.6 million Jordanian persons (including Jordanians and Palestinians) amount to 350,000 persons. Assuming a household size of seven persons, the number of apartments needed (including camp-dwellers and others) is 50,000, costing US$ 1-1.5 billion.

---

[8] M. Efrat, *The Palestine Refugees: The Dynamics of Economic Integration in their* Host Countries, 1993; D. Peretz, *Israel and Palestine Arabs*, 1958; R. Weller/W. Serow, "Indirect Estimates of the Birth and Death Rates and Age Composition of Palestinian Refugees", Population Bulletin of ECWA No. 29 (1986), 8; J.L. Abu Lughood, *Demographic Characteristics of the Palestinian Population: Relevance for Planning Palestine Open University*, Annex 1 of Palestine Open University Feasibility Study, Part II, UNESCO, Paris, 30 June 1980.

[9] M. Heiberg/G. Ovensen, *Palestinian Society – a Survey of Living conditions*, FAFO Report 151, 1993, 364.

[10] Further unpublished material from the survey shows that non-camp refugees and Jordanians have an almost identical room-density distribution, while camp-dwellers have a much higher proportion of persons living at a density of over two persons per room.

Recently Dr. Abdel Jaber and I made some progress regarding suggestions towards rehabilitation of camps in Jordan, and I believe some of our conclusions could apply to Palestine as well. The basic idea is that, in addition to the compensation money, some of the resources required for housing projects can be mustered from the local private sector. Giving titles to apartments to their present residents can cover a part of camp rehabilitation expenditures. In the case of camps located in desirable areas, selling construction permits in the free market could cover the cost of building new apartments plus their infrastructure. This may save reparation resources for productive investment.

In conclusion it is necessary to reiterate, that the cost of housing considered here is real investment alone, excluding land prices. The redistribution of ownership need not necessarily be connected to external resources for compensating refugees.

c. *UNRWA assistance*

The most important services are health care, education, vocational training, social welfare assistance, and food rations. Nowadays most UNRWA sources are used for education and health services. Refugees who reside in camps serviced by UNRWA are entitled to receive all services. Other UNRWA-registered refugees may receive some or all services depending on need, as determined by family size, income, and similar qualifications.

Table 1: Housing Needs of Camp-Dwellers, June 2002.[11]

	Refugees ('000)	Camp-dwellers ('000)	Housing needs of camp-dwellers (US$ '000)[12]	Percent of refugees not in camps
Jordan	1,680	293	1,172	83
West Bank	626	168	672	73

[11] Source for refugees and camp-dwellers is the Report of the Commissioner-General of the UNRWA for Palestine Refugees in the Near East, GAOR 57th Sess., Suppl. No. 13 (A/57/13), 2002; the authors of the table warn that the number of refugees is almost certainly lower than recorded.

[12] The calculation is based on a 7.5 average household size, and a price per unit of US$ 30,000, excluding residential infrastructure and land prices.

	Refu-gees ('000)	Camp-dwellers ('000)	Housing needs of camp-dwellers (US$ '000)	Percent of refugees not in camps
Gaza	879	468	1,872	46
Lebanon	387	217	868	44
Syrian Arab Republic	401	116	464	71
Total	3,973	1,262	5,048	63.4

UNRWA's total regular budget for 2002 was US$ 331 million, and actual expenditures in 2001 were US$ 278 million.

The real cost to the economy of transferring UNRWA's functions to the host governments involves an equalisation of the quality of public education and health services between UNRWA and the host governments. In Jordan, for example, educational services for refugees are below the standards provided by the government to the resident population, while health services for refugees are above them. The net effect of equalisation of service standards is not known at this stage.

Table 2: UNRWA's Actual Expenditures in 2001 and Budget for 2002 – Regular Budget (in US$ Millions)[13]

	Actual 2001	Budget 2002
Education	164.4	172.3
Health	50.6	58.9
Relief and Social services	29.1	33.6
Other	33.8	65.9
Total	277.9	330.7

The transfer of UNRWA functions to governments should, *pari passu*, include the cost of relocation of workers, many of whom are teachers,

13 UNRWA, see note 11.

social workers and medical personnel, presently employed by UNRWA. Phasing them out could take several years. Assuming a five-year period of adjustment, plus set-up costs of services for migrants to Palestine, an order of magnitude would be US$ 1.5 billion.

3. Development requirements approach

The need to treat the employment of refugees as a separate topic arises only if their labour market status is unique. This happens if it is segregated from that of the population at large, if they are denied access to a certain range of jobs, if they suffer from an especially high level of unemployment, or if their education or typical occupations are different from those of the indigenous population. Otherwise the creation of jobs for refugees is inseparable from the creation of jobs in general. The starting point here is that labour markets of refugees and non-refugees are, except for Lebanon, integrated. Facts supporting this claim are summarised elsewhere.[14] In particular, unemployment among refugees is not significantly higher than that of non-refugees. Hence there is no way of defining refugees' employment needs apart from the general population.

Reparations can therefore be viewed as a unique opportunity to combine personal compensation with a *quantum* leap in the economic progress of the region. To this end it is vital that personal compensation be channelled into investment and, as much as possible, to non-housing investment, raising the *per-capita* income of the population as a whole. To the extent that refugees (including those already living in Palestine) choose to stay at their present locations, the framework of analysis is the economic development of the present host country, rather than specific refugees' needs.

a. The maximum feasible investment approach

This section suggests a crude way of estimating overall "needs" for gross domestic investment, to be financed by reparations.[15] To this end

---

14 Klinov, see note 4, appendix 1.

15 Real gross domestic investment is defined as the additions, during a given year, to a country's capital stock, namely additions to its stock of machinery, buildings (residential and other), infrastructure, and inventories. These are rele-

we suggest the concept of maximal annual investment. The basic assumption behind it is that, beyond a certain point, shortages of managerial power, labour, capital and materials raise the marginal cost of investment and make it overly expensive. Thus, beyond a certain limit, further demand for investment will result mainly in price rises and not in real additions to capital. Too rapid an increase in the demand for investment can therefore cause inflation or channel the money into a rise in real estate prices or into a massive import of durable consumer goods, with little left for investment. We ask what levels of investment are consistent with economic stability. This approach does not put an upper ceiling on the overall present value of capital accumulation, but does suggest a ceiling on the maximum annual rates of investment. In what follows we treat the horizon for settling reparations as a ten-year time period.

The ceiling on annual investment is not an absolute concept: the production of some investment goods is more easily expanded than that of other types. Yet international experience indicates that, in the long-term, e.g. as a ten-year annual average, countries do not exceed a certain average annual increase in their overall investment activity. The average annual growth rate of real gross domestic investment for middle-income countries in East Asia and the Pacific, which is the fastest growing region in the world, were 9.7 for the period 1970-1980, and 10.1 for 1980-1991. For Japan it was 2.5 in the first and 6.0 in the second decade. The average for OECD high-income countries was 1.9 and 4.0 respectively. Israel's annual rate of increase in gross domestic investment in periods of rapid population increase was 3.1 per cent for 1950-1955; and an unprecedented 13.6 per cent for the period of mass immigration from the former Soviet Union, 1988-1992, followed by negative investment growth in subsequent years. The average for 1980-1991 was 3.6 per cent.[16] For our calculations we assumed, alternatively, a 5 and a 10 per cent annual growth rate in the level of real domestic investment, and the first stage is to forecast investment in each year over 1995-2005, given these ceilings.

The estimate is outdated, for lack of up-to-date national accounting data for Palestine. However, even if they were available, they might not be useful for the purpose of this exercise: Recent years were very bad

---

vant to a country's productive capacity. The definition excludes all forms of financial investment.

16 World Bank, World Development Report 1993, 252 et seq.; Israel, Central Bureau of Statistics: Statistical Abstract of Israel 1994, Tables 2.1, 6.5.

for the Palestinian economy, and investment levels during those years may be under the longer-term investment potential.

The calculation, shown in Table 3, was done for Jordan and Palestine separately, and assumes zero migration. The next section will discuss the modifications required under the assumption of migration between the countries. The first stage is, as mentioned, the forecast of gross domestic investment levels, assuming alternative annual growth rates of investment of 5 and 10 per cent. The next stage is to deduct from these figures the 1995 level of investment, and then calculate the present value of additional investment (over the base period) in 1995 US$. It is assumed that the 1995 level of investment can be financed in the future as it was financed in the base period, and that reparations are needed only if the level of annual investment is to increase. Hence, ignoring the possibility that other sources of investment financing will increase as well, investment needs over the period 1995-2005 are equal to the discounted (at 5 per cent) present value of additional investments over this period.[17]

[17] Let I_0 = initial level of domestic investment (in dollars) in 1995; g = annual growth rate of I, and r = the discount rate. The present value (PV) of additions to the 1995 level of investment over ten years is: $PV = I_0\, \Sigma\{(1+g/1+r^t - (1/1+r)^t\}$. We assume that r=5%.

The value of the expression $\Sigma(1+g/1+r)^t$ depends on the value of g. For g = 5% this expression is equal to 10. For g = 10% this is equal to 13.02993.

The value of the expression $\Sigma\ 1/(1+r)t$ is 7.72173.

The final values of PV are I_0 times 2.27827 for g = 5%, and I_0 times 5.3082 for g = 10%.

Table 3: Forecasted Present Value at 5 Per Cent Discount Rate of Additions to Investment Between 1995-2005, at 1995 Prices, in Millions of US$.

Palestine and Jordan.[18]

	5 per cent annual growth rate of total investment	10 per cent annual growth rate of total investment	Level of gross domestic investment, 1995
Jordan – total	3,395	7,909	2,210
Jordan – residential	2,264	5,273	1,474
Jordan – non-residential	1,131	2,636	736
West Bank and Gaza – total	1,443	3,364	1,244
West Bank and Gaza – residential	1,035	2,414	865
West Bank and Gaza – non- residential	408	950	379
Total residential	3,299	8,137	2,339
Total non-residential	1,539	3,586	1,115
Total residential and non-residential	4,838	11,273	3,454

As shown in Table 3, the present value of investment funding, both residential and non-residential, assuming a 10 per cent annual growth,

18 Palestinian Central Bureau of Statistics, National Accounts 1995-1996, Preliminary Estimates, March 1998, Code no. 261 Table 1-4-1, 70; Jordan, Central Bank of Jordan Annual report 1998, Table 2.

reaches about US$ 11 billion, or about 1.1 billion a year. This corresponds to Brynen's minimal estimate. Given that unemployment is currently high, it is possible to use an additional part of reparations to increase both investment and consumption, and activate the existing underutilised capital and labour. Brynen's suggestion of a range between US$ 10-20 billion is thus consistent with our estimates.

An important issue is the housing/non housing trade-off. As can be seen from Table 3, a disproportionate per cent of total investment goes to residential building. High priority for construction may be supported by a number of considerations: supply of housing to immigrants is necessary, and expansion of housing for camp-dwellers is also an acute need. In addition, residential construction can supply employment without delay, has low capital-labour intensity, and does not require much foreign exchange. However, from a long-term viewpoint, production-oriented physical and human capital investments are more important: although housing projects do create a demand for workers in the short-term, it tapers off, while other types of investment provide a long-term basis for employment and growth, and, subsequently, housing as well. In addition, housing is not tradable on the international market, and long-term development requires a strengthening of the tradable sector. This requires a much more developed financial market than the existing one.

b. The regional context

The estimates in Table 3 ignore additional costs of two types: the investment involved in relocating immigrants from Jordan to Palestine, and the reparations to Lebanese and Syrian refugees. Since the approach in this section is macroeconomic, it ignores Syria and Lebanon, because of the negligible size of the refugee community as a source of investment funds. In the next section, however, where the approach is that of compensation for losses, the refugee communities in these countries should be included.

The cost of immigration from Jordan is another matter. There is much controversy as to the expected size of this immigration. Borjas and Rodrik[19] suggest that the expected flow is between 250,000 and 750,000,

---

[19] G. Borjas/D. Rodrik, *The Harvard Project on Palestinian Refugees*, summary report draft, Institute of Social and Economic Policy in the Middle East, Harvard University, 1997.

with a likely number of 500,000, spread over several years. This amounts to less than three years of Palestinian natural increase, and should thus not cause major economic dislocations.

Additional investment due to immigration consists of housing and of productive capital. Housing needs may be financed by reparations received by the immigrants, who also add to the total labour supply available for construction. By the same token, their emigration will reduce the housing needs in Jordan.

Employment-creating investment *cannot* be discussed by multiplying alternatively estimated numbers of immigrants, by some key capital/labour ratio. The World Bank has estimated the investment in productive (i.e. non-housing) capital needed to create a job in the Occupied Territories at US$ 33,000. Under the assumption of 500,000 immigrants and without regard to the fact that a capital surplus may be created in Jordan, this will require an amount of US$ 16,500 billion in non-residential investment alone. This is far beyond the investment capacity of Palestine, and is, moreover, a waste of resources. A joint labour market with Jordan will require far less investment, and will create fewer imbalances by migration.

The question must be analysed in a regional context, for additional reasons. First, any immigration to Palestine also affects the labour markets of the present host countries, and they might require resources to make the adjustment. Furthermore, differences in capital/labour ratios in the region will themselves affect the propensity to migrate. Last, Jordan, where the majority of potential immigrants to Palestine live, is within commuting distance from Palestine, and absorption resources may be utilised far more efficiently if labour mobility between the two countries is allowed.

In Jordan, refugees constitute a third of the population, and, on the other hand, comprise 65 per cent of all refugees living outside Palestine.[20] A separation of the Palestinian and Jordanian labour markets will create a shortage of capital and a surplus of labour in Palestine, and the reverse in Jordan. In particular, separate labour markets will create a difficulty for the private sector in Jordan. Palestinians tend to work in

[20] This and the following sections are based on T. Abdel-Jaber/R. Klinov, *The Impact of the Return of Refugees to Palestine, on the Jordanian Economy*, draft paper prepared for the Institute of Social and Economic Policy in the Middle East, Harvard University, 1997.

this sector more than do Jordanians. Their emigration will therefore affect it disproportionately.

Another imbalance that characterised the pre-*Intifada* period can be seen in relative wages. Before the closures, many Palestinians worked in Israel. Wage differentials by occupation and education were smaller in Palestine than in Jordan: work in Israel has raised the wages of less skilled labour, while the small size of the civilian public sector and lack of work opportunities in Israel have reduced the wages of professionals. If the Jordanian and Palestinian labour markets are separate, unskilled workers will be over-represented among immigrants. Therefore, immigrants to Palestine should be allowed to continue working in Jordan, while Jordanians may be incorporated into the Palestinian and Israeli labour markets.

Indeed, there are indications that refugees prefer very close relations between the two countries. A poll survey, carried out by the Institute of Strategic Studies at the University of Jordan in the camps, shows that the overwhelming majority of camp-dwellers favours close relations between Jordan and Palestine with free movement. A related question is the degree of labour mobility from Palestine and Jordan to Israel. The cost of absorbing immigrants to Palestine will be lower if they have employment opportunities in the Israeli market. In short, given investment in transportation and communication facilities between the two countries, and given labour and capital mobility, the additional cost of absorption should be small.

4. Compensation for property loss[21]

The issue of reparations has had a long history. As early as 1949 UN General Assembly Resolution 194 (III) called for two types of reparations to refugees: one for "choosing not to return to their homes in Israel;" the second "for loss of damage to property which under the principles of international law or equity should be made good by the governments or authorities responsible."

In 1950 the UN General Assembly passed Resolution 394 (V) calling upon the Conciliation Commission for Palestine (CCP) to set up a refugee office to "make such arrangements as it may consider necessary

[21] This part draws heavily, and some times quotes *verbatim*, Peretz, see note 8.

for the assessment and payment of compensation." A committee of experts, attached to the refugee office, came up with an estimate of the overall value of abandoned property by first calculating the worth of the total property of the Arab community in Palestine as of 29 November 1947, and then taking three quarters of it as an approximation to refugee-owned property. The total value of property abandoned within the 1949 armistice frontiers, estimated to be 120 million pound sterling at 1947 prices, is equivalent to approximately 1.85 billion 1990 US$.[22] The value of land was estimated by crop productivity in rural areas and by rent in urban areas, as of 29 November 1947. Movables were estimated as a proportion of land and real estate, based on a formula developed for the Greek-Turkish settlement. CCP has not been officially dissolved, but ceased operations in 1957. It has accomplished two things: (1) it established a global estimate of the value of Arab abandoned property; (2) it identified individual refugee property that was abandoned in Israel that was worth a large amount.

Arab economists challenged this estimate, arguing that it omitted a number of critical items such as human sufferings and loss of human capital and of public property. An evaluation of Arab property in Israel was made by Yusif A. Sayegh and later by Hadawi.[23] Hadawi's estimate for abandoned property, exclusive of human capital, was 743 million pounds for 1948 (6.2 times the UN estimates); but, after adding human capital losses, the total rose to 1.182 billion pounds – nearly ten times the UN estimate.

Recently Frank Lewis[24] has offered a new estimate of the loss of agricultural property, based on the value of the agricultural output produced on that property, and making a series of assumptions on the contribution of land to the value of production, and on the discount rate to be used in capitalising the flow of the land's marginal product to its present value.

He is apparently unaware that the UN committee used a similar method.[25] It is therefore instructive to see that the results are of the

---

[22] Peretz, see note 8, 88.

[23] Y.A. Sayegh, *The Israeli Economy*, 1966; S. Hadawi, *Palestinian Rights and Losses in 1948*, 1988.

[24] F.D. Lewis, "Agricultural property and the 1948 Palestinian refugees: Assessing the loss", *Explorations in Economic History* 33 (1996), 169 et seq.

[25] The summary of the Committee's work is derived from Peretz, see note 8, 88, but no direct source is given by the author.

same order of magnitude, though Lewis's are somewhat higher. Lewis estimates the lost value as of 1948 of the agricultural property (land and capital) at US$2.3-2.8 billion in 1993 dollars (the difference between the two figures is arrived at by using 8 and 10 per cent discount rates alternatively).

The wide range of estimates highlights the difficulty of using this criterion. The first and most important issue is: what counterfactual should be used? In particular, what would the productivity of capital have been under different political scenarios? Suppose it were possible to calculate the value of property as it was in 1948. In particular, land prices would have grown because of population increase, beyond their 1948 value, but probably less than their present actual value.

In a series of articles and in his recent book, Kurbursi[26] calculates the overall sum due to Palestinian refugees as a compensation for their losses in 1948. There emerges a huge range of estimates, depending crucially on the items to be included, and on the counterfactual taken. There are three headings: material wealth, human capital, and psychological suffering.

The material loss, adjusted for inflation alone, is estimated at US$ 6.4 billion at 2000 prices, but assuming a 4 per cent annual real increase, the sum reaches US$ 102 billion. Similarly, human capital losses adjusted for inflation alone are estimated at US$ 13.2 billion, but assuming a 4 per cent increase, we reach US$ 173 billion. Adding psychological suffering to the 4 per cent annual growth assumption leads to the final estimate of US$ 327 billion.

Another calculation, mentioned by Kurbursi and cited in many other articles assuming the equity approach, takes as a criterion the compensation given by Germany to the Jewish victims of the holocaust.

There are so many ways to calculate such a sum, that in all probability there is no single "correct" estimate, and the final sum decided upon will be determined by a compromise between the different criteria. It is, however, necessary to point out that equity considerations cannot be dissociated from the economic realities presented previously, namely the ability of donors to pay on the one hand, and the ability of the economies involved to absorb the compensation in a stable, growth-oriented way. Kurbursi's final estimate is at least ten times bigger than that implied by any of the criteria discussed above.

---

[26] A. Kurbursi, *Palestinian Losses in 1948: Calculating Refugee Compensation*, 2001.

In summary, it seems to the author that the most reasonable approach to the overall sum is the maximum feasible investment – US$ 11 billion – plus the replacement of UNRWA services which amounts to US$ 1.5 billion. The overall sum is thus in the range of US$ 15 billion, which is also feasible from the donors' viewpoint.

III. Principles for the Distribution of Reparations

This section addresses three questions: (1) who should be in charge of distribution? (2) should reparations be given to households or to governments? and (3) should the use of reparations be at the discretion of the recipient, or should it be limited?

1. Who should be in charge?[27]

In most international compensation schemes, the right to monetary compensation was recognised. However, except for German compensation to Nazi victims, compensation of private persons was relegated to their respective governments. Negotiations resulted in the transfer of lump sums to governments, who took charge of their distribution. In a book reviewing 168 settlements of international claims, Lawlike and Weston[28] conclude that in the last 40 years this arrangement became the paramount vehicle for settling international claims. For the claimant state they result in prompt payment, less costly procedures for distributing the funds, and control over these procedures. For the paying state there is a final sum and a final release of obligations, since individual claims are then processed at the national level.

It seems to the author that this is also the proper form in which to proceed in the Palestinian case, except that instead of a state, a central authority of refugees, elected by the latter, or established in cooperation with them by the UN, should be in charge. In addition to the abovementioned reasons, it will also save endless debates between the Palestinians, UNRWA and Israel on the proper definition of a refugee, and hence on eligibility. Such debates will take place when overall sums are

---

27 The discussion draws liberally on Benvenisti/Zamir, see note 2.

28 R.B. Lawlike/H. Weston, *International Claims: Their Settlement by Lump Sum Agreements*, 1975.

discussed, but once decided upon, eligibility rules will be determined by the refugees themselves, or by an international body, *via* the authority. It will also be in charge of allocation rules.

However, even if it is decided to follow this pattern, it may be appropriate to discuss the underlying economic considerations determining the private-public distribution, and the allocation into final uses, simply to learn from past experience in similar cases.

2. Allocation between private and public compensation

a. Reasons for preponderance of private compensation

There are two main reasons: The first is that governments are suitable to carry out only a limited range of investment projects – mostly in housing and infrastructure. If they administer the funds, investment will be biased towards these projects. Obviously infrastructures such as water, roads and communication systems are necessary. But even here two arguments in support of private reparations could be made: first, there are other sources of public funding; secondly, in due time, if a well organised stock-exchange is set up, it could induce individuals to save in government bonds, which can be used to invest in infrastructures.

The second argument in favour of private compensation is that psychologically the public will feel at least partly compensated only if there is a direct benefit at the individual level.

b. Arguments for allocating some of the reparations for public expenditures

1). The rehabilitation of refugees requires public investment in residential infrastructure and in providing services, which are currently administered by UNRWA.

2). The Palestinian government may not have other sources to finance public investment, at least until a viable capital market and a tax system are established.

3. Free or limited use of compensation to households?

The main argument in favour of limiting the uses of compensation money is that it leads to a higher savings rate than free-use compensation would, and therefore guarantees a larger investment rate. In countries lacking a fully developed capital market, such savings may enhance development. The main argument against such monitoring is that, by the very existence of limitations, it will detract from the welfare provided to households through reparations.

Here is an example of the way in which limited-use funds may operate: One possibility is that special agencies are established in each country-region to administer saving funds, opening personal accounts, and setting the specific rules for releasing money to households. These funds will, in turn, buy financial assets in the stock exchange, including foreign financial assets.[29] Individuals will be allowed to withdraw funds only for specific purposes: investing in housing, in a business, acquiring higher or vocational education, and pensions. Each region would put ceilings on the various uses according to local conditions: e.g. in Gaza the ceiling for withdrawal for housing may be higher than in Jordan.

4. Instead of conclusions, some lessons from the Israeli experience

In numerous private discussions of the suitable design of reparations to Arab refugees, three Israeli episodes are mentioned as a possible guideline: the absorption of mass immigration in the fifties; German compensation (to individuals) and reparations (to the Israeli government); and the absorption of recent Jewish immigration from the USSR. Based on these it is possible to address several relevant issues.

a. Should the German-Israeli model of reparations to the government be followed?

It is necessary to distinguish between reparations paid to the Israeli government, and compensation, which was paid out to individuals regardless of their location.

---

[29] There may be a time lag between the receipt of reparations and the expansion of domestic investment. Foreign investment may bridge over this gap.

The total amount of reparations to the government of Israel was US$ 820 million (about US$ 3.5 billion at 2000 prices), paid over a period of 12 years, mostly in the form of German investment goods. The time span was necessary in order to stay within the limits of the Israeli economy's capacity of annual investment, and I believe that this should be a major consideration in the Arab case as well. Moreover, as in the German case, it is important to adhere to an arrangement whereby reparations are used for investment, not consumption. On the other hand, the form of reparations – they were in kind rather than in money – may be outdated. It was characteristic of the basically protectionist economies of both Germany and Israel at the time, but in today's freer-trade world, reparations may better be given in money, not in machines.

b. Should the German-Jewish model of private compensation be followed?

I hesitate to discuss this analogy. Though none of us has a yardstick by which to compare human sufferings, I do maintain that the horrors of the holocaust are unique. Yet if one limits the discussion to narrow technical aspects, it is possible to learn some lessons.

In the German-Jewish case, the amount of compensation was computed, for each claimant, on the basis of a list of personal suffering of losses *other than the loss of property*, for which the German government set rates of compensation. They included loss of education, of a career, and of health. Loss of immovable property was mostly settled within the regular inheritance laws, not as a special agreement with victims of Nazism. It was done through assessment of the property value, and of inheritance rights, *via* a German judicial mechanism. It is therefore appropriate to divide the question into that of compensation for property loss, and that for personal suffering.

Property loss: The German model cannot be followed in the Palestinian-Israeli case, for several reasons.

A decision in each individual case will require trust by Palestinians in the good will of Israelis. This is improbable, so one can think, as an alternative, of an international court.

Even such a court can hardly carry out its mission: Land registration is not full, the number of potential claimants to each piece of property is huge, and in many cases no formal deed is available. All of this will require an immense amount of time to process the claims. In more recent examples of re-privatisation of property by previously communist countries, there is overwhelming evidence that the process is very slow, both because the passage of time makes it very difficult to establish who has the right to claim compensation, and because of the difficulty of assessing the value of property in the frequent cases in which it changed its character.

A major consideration is the budget constraint. An international court, deciding case by case, means that there is no budget constraint. In the German case, the funding of compensation for property loss was not large, because in a considerable number of cases title, rather than money, was transferred. In the Israeli case, this is impossible. Dearth of funds is also a major obstacle in re-privatisation in the formerly communist countries. Therefore, in the majority of cases, following the German example is not recommended. However, as will be suggested later, some of its elements could be incorporated, for a small number of cases.

Human suffering: In this matter the German example may be followed in principle, i.e. a list of compensation rates can be pre-determined, where the administrator will be either a refugee elected, or an international body. This is possible, because a prior rough estimate of the total budget required will be possible.

It seems to the author, that pre-determined rates should be used not only for compensating for suffering, but, for all of the aforementioned reasons, also for much of the loss of property. Recently it was suggested that compensation be multi-tiered. A flat rate will be given *per capita* as a compensation for suffering; then a list of rates for small property loss with varying strength of evidence of title should be established. Refugees may choose between two modes of compensation for property losses: (1) a “fast track” in which they will be compensated at the preset scale, and (2) a full judicial procedure, which may take a long time. Scales should be constructed so that the majority of refugees will find the fast track advantageous.

c. Should compensation depend on one’s country of residence?

German compensation was paid out regardless of the claimant’s country of residence (but reparations were given only to the government of Israel). It seems that in the Arab case personal compensation should be given to refugees regardless of their country of residence. Differential treatment in particular countries may consist of different rules for withdrawing the money.

Arrangements for Resolving Claims

End of Exile: Practical Solutions to the Palestinian Refugee Question

*Arthur C. Helton**

I. The Value of Comparisons

A sustainable peace in the Middle East will require a solution to the problem of Palestinian refugees. Indeed, this is why so much has been written about this issue in the context of peace negotiations. But this article takes a different approach, offering comparative historical perspectives on the organisation, procedures, and criteria for implementing the right of return and compensation for lost property. It is a technical and not a political treatment.

The objective of this article is to add new information and analytical insights to the debate; namely, research about how refugee and compensation solutions have been implemented in other situations. Practical implementation options are examined from a variety of comparative experiences. Examining these options could help soften the political absolutism that characterises the current impasse on the refugee issue. But there is value in any event in understanding the international system context, and mapping realistic scenarios for such matters as an institutional framework to implement a settlement, the criteria and procedures for relocating refugees, and techniques and methods to award adequate compensation. It is, in effect, a tutorial on what has worked in other settings, assuming a settlement of the conflict.

Arrangements relating to Palestinian refugees are in certain ways distinct from generic refugee responses. Research and analysis relating to these topics are similarly divergent. A comparative approach can pro-

---

* Senior Fellow, Council on Foreign Relations.

vide insights into the workability of a prospective settlement, the broad parameters of which are discernible from recent negotiations. But as recognised by the current head of UNRWA, "No one is working on this."

II. Situating the Palestinian Refugee Issue

The recently-published Roadmap to Peace in the Middle East is but the most recent reminder that the Palestinian refugee issue will be a key aspect of any settlement of the Palestinian-Israeli conflict. The Roadmap, authored by the Quartet (the European Union, United Nations, Russia, and the United States), and promoted now by US President George W. Bush, addresses at the outset a variety of issues ranging from security to settlements. Plans for the humanitarian rehabilitation of the West Bank and Gaza in this first phase, of course, would indirectly affect many of the 1.5 million Palestinian refugees registered there. But it is the last phase relating to a final settlement, where the refugee issue is explicitly featured.

After an international conference convened by the Quartet in early 2004, there is to be "an agreed, just, fair, and realistic solution to the refugee issue." This is an ambitious objective for many reasons, including sheer numerosity. Currently, there are some six million Palestinian exiles, nearly four million of whom are registered as refugees under the mandate of the United Nations Relief Works Agency for Palestine Refugees in the Near East (UNRWA) which operates in the region.

Indeed, the refugee issue has surfaced periodically as negotiations to settle the Israeli-Palestinian conflict have waxed and waned. Refugees were profiled recently in efforts by US President Bill Clinton, who convened in July 2000 a summit meeting at Camp David, Maryland, in an audacious bid to resolve the conflict. The issue emerged centrally in the course of the settlement gambit at Camp David, and follow-on exchanges at Taba in Egypt. In these settings, they became a deal-blocker, with both sides taking maximalist positions. Israeli negotiators, concerned about the demographic dimension, insisted on alternatives to an absolute right of return. Palestinian negotiators have long insisted on a categorical right of return, arguing that refugees should be given the maximum feasible choice in terms of where to live in the future.

In an attempt to finesse the return issue, a proposal was tabled in these recent discussions for the relocation of refugees to Israeli territory, which would then be transferred to a Palestinian state. In addition, the US proposed a financial package, reportedly of US$ ten billion, designed to break the impasse and help buttress a peace agreement, and was prepared to solicit donations from other countries to compensate Palestinian refugees. Palestinian negotiators have suggested that a figure of scores or even hundreds of billions of dollars would be necessary to constitute fair compensation.

Debates about the right of refugees to return to their homes in what is now Israel will permeate political commentary as well as settlement negotiations. Yet, the absorption of refugees into Israel will be highly controversial and likely be severely limited, with Israeli negotiators never having agreed to accept back more than 100,000 individuals annually even when the conflict was fresh. But the affirmation in principle of the right to return, and the reception of refugees into Israeli territory that is then transferred to Palestinian sovereignty, as well as continued family reunification admissions to Israel, may be feasible. In fact, questions over family reunification have been raised repeatedly in refugee negotiations, even though the issue is analytically distinct, with Israel agreeing in the past to admit 2,000 family reunification cases annually (6,000 persons). Actual practice has been more difficult to discern.

In envisioning a resolution of the problem, the nearly 400,000 Palestinian refugees who are registered in Lebanon have been prioritised in discussions as they are considered among the most needy and likely to be pressured to leave after a settlement. Also, both sides have discussed the establishment of an international commission and fund to deal with compensation issues. Both have suggested that relatively small sums of compensation could be paid on a *per capita* basis to refugees in fast track procedures. But there is no meeting of the minds relating to the method by which to calculate compensation, nor is there agreement on the amount that would be contributed to an international fund. Both sides have discussed UNRWA being phased-out, with the Palestinian side more favourable than the Israeli side to a continuing role for the agency.

III. The Early International Response: UNRWA

Historically, the principal international humanitarian response to Palestinian refugees has been UNRWA, which was established in 1949 by the UN General Assembly. When the agency began operations in 1951, it sought to address the humanitarian needs of some 900,000 refugees, 268,000 of whom resided in 60 different camps in the region. Because the General Assembly did not define who was a Palestinian refugee, agency officials developed their own registration criteria. Initially, UNRWA policy documents defined a refugee as a person who, as a result of the Palestinian conflict, had lost his home and means of livelihood. Subsequently this definition was further refined, and UNRWA has come to consider a refugee to be a person whose normal place of residence was Palestine during the period 1 June 1946 to 15 May 1948, and who, as a result, had lost both a home and means of livelihood, and the descendants of such a person.

In the early years, UNRWA began addressing the immediate needs of Palestinian refugees in terms of shelter, education, food and health services. When the prospect for more enduring arrangements seemed feasible, public works projects and small-scale integration projects were initiated by the agency, sometimes in the face of a highly suspicious refugee clientele who feared the extinguishment of their right to return and the liquidation of their cause through the promotion of assimilation and resettlement schemes. In practice, refugee status was perpetuated for political and economic reasons, and repatriation was considered infeasible. This left the UN with a lasting humanitarian assistance commitment institutionalised in the form of UNRWA.

The large sums needed for physical development were not forthcoming and the agency reverted to a routine of aiding refugees meet their survival needs. Education, a traditional generator of national identity, became a primary and sometimes controversial focus of UNRWA programming. The sensitivities were reflected by the fact that the contents of textbooks describing the origins and incidents of the conflict which underlay UNRWA's work had to be carefully negotiated.

The conflict waxed and waned over the decades, repeatedly interrupting the humanitarian and social agenda of UNRWA, including in 1956 in Gaza and 1958 in Lebanon. In 1967, war uprooted some refugees once again, and resulted in further Palestinian politicisation and militancy. Shelters became tent cities once more, and the UNRWA's work was reoriented to emergency relief over the next two decades.

The Palestinian *Intifada* fundamentally affected the agency. As this conflict of national aspirations evolved in the midst of the Israeli occupation, UNRWA added programmes and staff, and developed an innovative protection mandate. The agency utilised publicity and the deployment of special staff (Refugee Affairs Officers and Legal Officers) in an effort to provide some measure of redress for the abuse of refugees. UNRWA became an advocate for refugee rights, and a mechanism to report on and publicise Israeli treatment of Palestinians in the occupied territories under the terms of the Fourth Geneva Convention. "Protection by publicity" became a key agency strategy.

Once post-1967 emergency donations began diminishing, the agency fell into financial crisis, which persisted until 1983 when budget reforms were introduced. Improved stability and modernised planning and budgetary techniques once again encouraged donors to contribute funds. The notoriety associated with the *Intifada* stimulated contributions, but as the emergency became routine, budgetary shortfalls returned.

The relations of the agency with the parties to the conflict were often strained, including the Palestinian Liberation Organization. Politically, UNRWA balances between collaboration with the occupying authority, and cooptation by the refugees and their political organisations. The agency's local employees, many of whom are refugees, have sought to pressure UNRWA to take stands on behalf of refugee causes. The agency has often had difficulties with host governments, as well as the Israeli army, over its prerogatives as an international organisation, a source of continuous and intense negotiations. Rumours about whether or not humanitarian facilities and aid were being diverted to support the *Intifada* were frequently in the air in the midst of the conflict. But the agency's experience in Lebanon taught it that the existence of government, any government, was preferable to anarchy in terms of a working environment.

UNRWA has become enmeshed in the Arab/Palestinian-Israeli conflict. The killing of a senior UNRWA official by an Israeli soldier in a gun battle with Palestinian militants in 2002 is only the most recent manifestation of a highly polarised situation in which neutrals are not allowed. At this juncture, UNRWA is institutionally synonymous with the conflict. These circumstances will inevitably shape UNRWA's role after a resolution of the conflict.

IV. Refugee Solutions: New and Old Homes – Return, Local Integration, and Third-Country Resettlement

Resolution of the Palestinian refugee question will necessarily involve some combination of three possible place-based outcomes: (1) some measure of voluntary return, (2) a good deal of integration in current places of asylum, and (3) perhaps a significant degree of resettlement in third countries abroad. Indeed, the Canadian Prime Minister has reportedly mentioned that Canada may accept as many as 15,000 Palestinian refugees living in other Arab states. While this report is disputed, the notion of such an offer has resonated in speculations about a settlement. Of course, the precise dimension of each of these place-based outcomes, and their interrelationships, will be grist for the negotiators' mill.

The generic international regime relating to refugees provides a starting point for considering a realistic framework for practical solutions to the Palestinian refugee question. The generic refugee regime is treaty-based and concerns itself with the legal *status* of individuals who fear persecution upon return to their home country. Various civil and economic rights are to be respected by the country of asylum in the protection of refugees. In practice, this often means the provision of basic humanitarian assistance, and a firm rule, sometimes violated, not to force refugees back to a place of persecution.

The centrepiece of the generic regime is the 1951 Convention relating to the Status of Refugees, as amplified by its 1967 Protocol to deal with refugees around the world. Today, 145 states have signed one of these two UN refugee treaties and undertaken to provide protection and assistance for individuals who have left their home countries, and who meet the treaty definition of the term "refugee." That is, a person who, "owing to a well-founded fear of being persecuted for reasons of race, religion, nationality, membership of a particular social group or political opinion, is outside the country of his nationality and is unable or, owing to such fear, is unwilling to avail himself of the protection of that country." This contrasts with the operational construct for Palestinian refugees – residence at the specified place and time, coupled with loss of home and livelihood, and the descendants of such persons.

The implementing institution under the generic regime is the United Nations High Commissioner for Refugees (UNHCR). When UNHCR began operations in January 1951, it had a staff of 34 people based mainly in Geneva with a budget of about US$ 300,000. Over the course of the next five decades, the agency grew into a global institution with 268 offices in 114 countries, a staff of more than 5,500 people and a budget of just over US$ one billion. UNHCR currently helps approximately 20 million people around the world.

Under the generic regime, each state treaty party has the discretion to determine whether an individual's situation satisfies the refugee definition, resulting inevitably in some measure of differential treatment of like cases.

The status-oriented generic regime largely begs the question of providing a solution to the situation of international homelessness inherent in the refugee character. There is, nevertheless, an often-articulated policy preference, at least by states, for the voluntary repatriation of refugees – except in those instances, of course, when a different preference predominates. Such was the case after World War II when repatriation from the democratic West to the socialist East became ideologically disfavoured during the Cold War and resettlement became the norm. A more recent instance involved arrangements in the 1980s and 1990s to resettle Vietnamese and other Indochinese refugees.

Nevertheless, conceptually, repatriation is the most congruent solution to refugee flight. What could be more harmonious than the return home of an exile? Indeed, discussion of this outcome has been featured through the Palestinian-Israeli conflict. The reality, of course, is often quite different. Circumstances may have changed, and the community may no longer exist. Indeed, there may be nothing to which to return. New homes may beckon, or indeed, may have already been found.

1. Repatriation

The largest recent repatriation programme concerns Afghans returning to Afghanistan from Iran and Pakistan. Some two million Afghans have repatriated since the US-led military campaign ended in 2002. UNHCR has requested US$ 195 million to assist return to Afghanistan for 2003, including transportation and a rather meagre reintegration package for individuals comprising between US$ five to 30 to cover transportation costs, as well as plastic sheeting, flour, and hygiene materials.

Other significant repatriation efforts over the recent past have included Cambodia where between March 1992 and April 1993, UNHCR repatriated an estimated 370,000 refugees at the cost of over US$ 128 million. In Mozambique some 1.7 million refugees (from six neighbouring countries) returned home from 1992 to 1996, costing around US$ 150 million. In the case of Namibia, over 40,000 refugees were repatriated by UNHCR at a cost of US$ 36 million.

In the 1980s, more than two million people fled their homes from civil conflict in Central America. During the early nineties most of the 72,000 Nicaraguan refugees were repatriated, along with 350,000 internally displaced people, and 30,000 former combatants. By the mid-1990s, an estimated 32,000 Salvadoran refugees had been repatriated. And by the late 1990s, 42,000 Guatemalan refugees were repatriated from Mexico, with an additional 22,000 choosing to settle permanently in Mexico.

Refugee repatriation schemes normally involve UNHCR, which seeks to ensure the voluntariness of return and to provide transportation and some measure of reintegration assistance. International NGOs are often the logistical implementers of return programmes.

The repatriation operations in Central America, Cambodia and Mozambique reflected a somewhat broader approach to repatriation. Unlike the small-scale and short-term operations that UNHCR had previously engaged in, these new operations sought to include a longer-term approach which aimed at reconstruction, peace building, and reintegration. The results of this holistic approach have been difficult to measure.

Unlike generic repatriations, questions of voluntariness may not feature very prominently in the return of Palestinian refugees, since this is, indeed, the declared aim of Palestinian advocates. There will be logistical needs, but, depending on the dimension of repatriation, they may be relatively modest. Should return be limited to family unity cases, then there will be a need for the assessment of family ties, at least once agreement is reached on the definition of the family concept as it relates to extended members. UNHCR has had some experience with family-related adjudications for Indochinese and Haitians. But it is not a mainstream activity of the agency, and a variety of NGOs could be called upon to undertake this work as well.

2. Resettlement

A large-scale Palestinian refugee third-country resettlement programme, on the other hand, would require a new international framework. Currently, eight countries: Australia, Canada, Denmark, Finland, New Zealand, Norway, Sweden and the United States, accept most of the 100,000 or so refugees who are resettled world-wide each year, with the US, Canada, and Australia in the lead. Increasingly, UNHCR operates as a referral mechanism for cases of third-country resettlement, which the agency considers a remedy of "last resort" to address individuals with specific needs for protection. The International Organization for Migration, governed by a council of 98 member states and 33 observer states, typically provides practical and logistical support for the movement of resettling refugees. National resettlement groups ordinarily provide integration assistance.

While each country uses the generic refugee definition to determine eligibility, this is a necessary but not a sufficient condition for admission, and each country applies somewhat distinctive additional criteria for resettlement. Nordic countries, for example, have relatively small resettlement programmes, which give priority to minors or traumatised and disabled refugees.

Insights into the nature of the special institutional arrangements that would have to be made for a significant resettlement programme for Palestinian refugees can be garnered from other mass resettlement experiences. A case in point is the efforts to resolve the immense displacements caused by World War II. Upwards of 30 million persons were uprooted in Europe from 1939 to 1945. At the end of the conflict, over ten million individuals found themselves outside of their home countries and in need of assistance and protection.

In 1946, the International Refugee Organization (IRO) was established to coordinate resettlement. The IRO, which existed from December 1946 to January 1952, was founded to focus on the needs for new permanent homes for a residual population of individuals who had fled (refugees) and been dislocated (displaced persons) by reason of World War II. Initially, this uprooted population was ministered to by a predecessor UN Relief and Rehabilitation Administration (UNRRA), which focused on both societal recovery as well as humanitarian relief in the context of devastated post-war Europe in the 1940s. Unlike UNRRA, the IRO focused specifically on the refugee question, giving it a coherent organisational mission.

The IRO was the first major UN humanitarian operation. During its existence, the agency resettled 1,038,750 refugees to 65 different countries, including nearly 300,000 persons to the United States. IRO's annual budget was in excess of US$ 150 million with an administrative budget of nearly US$ five million. At the height of its operations, the agency had 5,600 staff, and arrangements with 120 humanitarian groups, in which it invested nearly US$ 40 million to provide ancillary social services to refugees and displaced persons. Overall, the IRO expended over US$ 400 million.

The IRO was established as the first UN "specialised agency," although its founders gave relatively little attention to what this form of organisation actually meant. In practice, the agency was granted considerable operational independence, as its programmes were not subject to supervision by the General Assembly.

The predominant mission of the IRO was resettlement in Western Europe and beyond. In the early years of the agency's operations, there was a small measure of refugee repatriation, with the IRO organising the return of 72,834 refugees to their home country.

But increasingly unwilling to repatriate, the residue of this displaced population became an object of international attention as the ideological confrontation of the Cold War worsened. Return to Communist-dominated homelands became unpalatable to Western governments, most notably the United States. The IRO, which was funded and thus governed by Western governments, faced early denunciations by the Soviet bloc as being dedicated primarily to promoting labour migration for political purposes. In this connection, it is interesting to note the difficulty the IRO faced in attempting to resettle refugees with high educational and professional attainments. Manual labourers were preferred in the labour-starved work places of post-war Europe.

Another illustrative mass resettlement scheme was prompted three decades later by a humanitarian crisis in Southeast Asia. As countries in the region refused to allow asylum seekers to land, thousands of Vietnamese perished in the South China Sea. A terrifying spectre emerged, of small, ramshackle boats containing thousands of desperate refugees roaming the seas of Southeast Asia, before they either drowned or starved. A group of countries led by the US intervened, creating programmes to relocate some two million individuals at a cost of US$ one billion plus associated integration costs over a 15-year period.

To begin the effort, in July 1979, the UN convened an international conference of 65 governments, along with international organisations and NGOs. The Secretary-General opened the conference by emphasising the need for all countries to realise the obligations and responsibilities of the countries of origin, asylum and final settlement. The countries of origin had an obligation to respect the right of emigration and family reunification, while avoiding any action leading to the departure of their nationals under dangerous conditions. They also had a responsibility to cooperate with UNHCR to ensure an orderly outflow. Since the countries of asylum were themselves developing countries with their own social and economic problems, it was considered essential that countries outside the area be primarily responsible for eventual resettlement.

Pledges were made at the conference by developed countries to expand greatly the number of refugees they would be willing to resettle. Funding was also pledged to finance the refugee support and relief operations. In order to reduce the size of the build-up of asylum seekers, Vietnam agreed to enforce a moratorium on illegal departures from its shores.

An initial decline in the number of boat people was not, however, permanent. In January 1986, Vietnam suspended its programme of orderly departures to the United States, the country that had accepted most of those legally departing. This development, coupled with increased arrivals and diminished third-country resettlement, presented another looming refugee crisis. Representatives of 76 governments met in Geneva in June 1989 at a second international conference on Indochinese refugees to establish procedures to screen on a region-wide basis those asylum seekers who arrived after a cut-off date in order to determine which among them deserved resettlement as refugees. Those rejected were subject to return, including mandatory deportation, to Vietnam in order to discourage clandestine departures and establish legal emigration as the eventual sole method of departure.

This new Comprehensive Plan of Action (CPA) was adopted at the conference under which countries in the region agreed to continue to provide first asylum in return for a promise of resettlement abroad of both the "long stayer" population as well as more recent arrivals determined to be "refugees," as defined under UN criteria. Status adjudication procedures were developed on a region-wide basis. Decisions were made to be taken by the national authorities in accordance with the generic criteria. UNHCR was to be a trainer and technical advisor to governments, as well as a monitor of the proceedings, and source of counselling resource for applicants. A Steering Committee of governments was established to implement the CPA.

What are the implications of these mass resettlement experiences for a Palestinian refugee resettlement programme? The IRO and CPA experiences suggest Palestinian resettlement could be effectuated by UNHCR and IOM, although UNHCR's refugee mandate is qualitatively different, and founded on the generic refugee concept of a person in flight from persecution. Agency culture certainly could complicate matters. Many UNHCR staff became disenchanted with the concept of resettlement particularly after involvement with resettling refugees from Southeast Asia. "There was not a detailed discussion of who was and was not a refugee," explained a UNHCR resettlement official, "the refugee camps were a problem that demanded a resolution." But many in the agency resented being pressured to resettle these refugees by the United States, UNHCR's largest single donor government. Agency staff saw themselves as unwilling participants in the creation of an "automatic resettlement machine."

But when asked, UNHCR engaged and implemented the broad resettlement objectives of the Indochinese operation, albeit with a bit of grumbling. A finite effort relating to Palestinian refugees should be workable, even in an era when resettlement procedures have become enmeshed in national security considerations.

Indeed, for a variety of reasons, security issues would likely permeate any arrangement for Palestinian resettlement. Security measures implemented after the horrific terrorist attacks in the US in September 2001 have radically reduced refugee admissions. New background checks have slowed the process and made it more expensive. Some of this delay is caused by the sequence of processing. Refugees are adjudicated as eligible and appropriate for admission before investigations are requested. In the case of Palestinian refugees, given the group nature of the determination, those desiring to avail themselves of resettlement abroad should be allowed to request a security check up front. Such a procedure would permit applicants to learn early on whether they may have an entry problem. For those who do not, the process could be expedited. A speedy and reliable third-country resettlement solution would help build confidence on all sides.

A more serious impediment to a significant resettlement effort concerns the difference between the Palestinian definition of refugee and the generic concepts. The immigration and refugee laws of the main resettlement countries generally incorporate the UN refugee standard. If Palestinian refugees are to be resettled in significant numbers, then adjustments would likely have to be made in numerous national legal systems. Potential resettling governments will thus have to review their laws and make any necessary amendments in order to establish new or expanded humanitarian admissions authorities that would cover Palestinians.

3. Local Integration

A local integration strategy will undoubtedly be the predominant solution for Palestinian refugees. This approach will require a comprehensive assistance and development strategy to address the well-being of Palestinian refugees as well as the host communities into which they would more fully assimilate. This would involve political, legal, social and economic initiatives designed to root refugees in their new communities. UNRWA could, of course, play an important role in this endeavour. Indeed, this is what UNRWA has done for much of its existence – provide assistance verging on development. The UN Development Group and World Bank would also play major roles in developing country and regional integration strategies as they did in Cambodia, Mozambique, and Central America in relation to past refugee repatriations.

Integration assistance, of course, can facilitate resettlement, local integration, or repatriation. Such assistance can cover matters such as language instruction, micro-credit lending, reviving agricultural production, and according citizenship. Development aid relating to Palestinian refugees, of course, has always been a sensitive question. Refugee advocates have resisted assistance such as housing aid, which might be construed as choosing integration and forfeiting the return option. Extending benefits to the host community is a conventional wisdom relating to promoting repatriation and local integration. It is also an accepted method of dealing with Palestinian refugees camps, which is necessitated by practical and logistical reasons, albeit without addressing the formal juridical status of the camps. Generic refugee repatriation efforts over the past few decades have sought to integrate repatriation and development assistance, with mixed success. Indeed, the difficulty of transitioning from humanitarian to development assistance modalities remains one of the principal challenges of humanitarian action in our era.

Integration assistance, moreover, can involve substantial sums. The annual budget of the European Commission's Humanitarian Office has been running at about € 500 million over the past several years, with about one-third each going to refugee reception and integration activities, and about half that amount used to facilitate voluntary repatriation around the world. In the region, Israel has been a leading practitioner of integration assistance. Since 1989, 1.1 million persons have emigrated to Israel, and, in recent years, the budget of the Israeli Ministry of Immigration Absorption has been operating at the equivalent of US$ 400 million. UNRWA's recent annual expenditures, some portion of which can be attributed to integration-like assistance for matters such as education and health, have amounted to approximately US$ 300 million.

V. Compensation/Restitution Comparisons

Another feature of a settlement of the Arab/Palestinian-Israeli conflict is likely to be the payment of some form of monetary compensation relating to Palestinian refugees. UN General Assembly Resolution 194, passed in 1948, explicitly contemplates compensation for property lost by non-returning Palestinian refugees as a result of the situation in Palestine in 1948. Subsequent discussions of compensation have also included the claims of Palestinians who were displaced, some a second time, by war in 1967, and of Jews from various Arab countries who moved to Israel during and after 1948 and were forced to leave behind their property. Negotiators have yet to agree upon the precise subjects of compensation in resolving the Israeli-Palestinian conflict.

Compensation for property loss is only one aspect of the possibility for financial resource transfers that may be included in a political settlement. Recent discussions about a settlement have identified additional payment modalities relating to the situation of Palestinians who departed from their homes, in effect, a notion of being "compensated" for the condition of international homelessness associated with refugeehood. Raised as well in discussions are the prospects of payments designed to help re-establish voluntarily repatriating refugees, facilitate their local integration in places of current residence, or their resettlement abroad in new home countries. Such different payment purposes would likely require quite divergent financial schemes.

For those desiring to return to long-lost lands and houses, confirmation of title may be crucial, particularly if currently occupied by others. For this purpose, a restitution mechanism could be used to award possession to returning refugees, like the Bosnian Commission for Real Property Claims of Displaced Persons and Refugees (CRPC) established under Annex 7 of the 1995 Dayton Peace Agreement. The Bosnian property commission is a mixed body of international and national commissioners, with three international members appointed by the President of the European Court of Human Rights, and six national members, of which four are appointed by the Federation of Bosnia and Herzegovina and two by the Republika Srpska. The commissioners have been supported by some 400 local staff, and 12 regional field offices. As of March 2003, CRPC had resolved 81 per cent of the 318,780 claims submitted for decision. This has required deep investigation of the complicated amalgam of historical legal traditions relating to the registration of property ownership, ranging from the methods used under the Austrian-Hungarian system to more recent socialist law enactments, in order to confirm title. But the investigation of title relating to Palestinian and Israeli property would be just as complicated. The CRPC is to complete its work in 2003.

A similar, but somewhat less well known mechanism, the Housing and Property Directorate to mediate disputed claims, and the Housing and Property Claims Commission, were established by the UN in 1999 in Kosovo to adjudicate rights disputes arising during Kosovo's post-autonomy period (1989-1999). The Kosovo mechanisms seek to regularise informal property trades and restore rights to those whose homes have been illegally occupied. Officials expect to process an estimated 100,000 residential claims.

In Kosovo, as of June 2003, 26,788 claims have been filed, and by April 2003, 3,580 cases had been decided. If mediation fails, then the claim is decided by a three-member panel of commissioners, one local and two international, and may be reviewed in limited circumstances by a second panel. The commission decisions are final and, unlike the Bosnian commission, may not be reviewed by any other judicial authority, including local courts.

Refugee return became a political imperative in the efforts of the United States and Western European powers to end the armed conflicts in Bosnia and Kosovo that were spawned after the disintegration over the past decade of Socialist Federal Republic of Yugoslavia. The bundle of human rights violations designed to displace people, commonly known as "ethnic cleansing," were reflected in property law arrangements which the Bosnian and Kosovo mechanisms were designed to unravel. But while considerable progress has been made at the formal level, both the Bosnian and Kosovo efforts have confronted difficulties in implementation by resistant local authorities, reflecting the tenuous nature of the peace. In Kosovo, for example, as of December 2002, only 681 forced evictions had been executed.

Palestinian refugee advocates have urged as an acknowledgement of accountability for past injustices a restitution-based approach to restore property to absent refugees and simultaneously protect the rights of current occupants as tenants. This is tantamount to ownership with no right to oust the current occupying tenant. But care should be taken not to introduce conflictual elements in an already tense situation. Such inconclusive arrangements could precipitate disputes along the line of those experienced in Bosnia and Kosovo.

The objectives of a compensation scheme, moreover, can be decisive. The Bosnian property commission and the more recent effort in Kosovo are designed to confirm property ownership in order to permit persons to regain possession. Local authorities have resisted compliance. As a lawyer familiar with claims and restitution mechanisms put it, "It is easier to dish out money than implementing solutions on the ground."

But even monetary compensation for lost Palestinian refugee and Israeli property will present several challenges. Such compensation arrangements will require the establishment of a special institution for the duration of the scheme. While there are unique features in the situation, there are other experiences which may provide useful insights for the development of such mechanisms.

In fact, there is a long history of using international claims tribunals to settle disputes, many dealing with alien property. From the Jay Treaty of 1794 between the United States and Britain, until World War II, claims tribunals were often used to effectuate war reparations. Such tribunals, however, came to be considered too slow and overly expensive, leading increasingly to the use of lump sum agreements. These involved state-to-state payments, with the claimant state expected to distribute funds to individuals, and the paying state obtaining a categorical release of its obligations.

A new generation of compensation mechanisms emerged with the advent of the Iran-United States Claims Tribunal, established by the two states in 1981 as part of the settlement of the crisis which began with the seizure of the US Embassy in Tehran and the freezing of Iranian assets in the US. While the Iran-United States Claims Tribunal proved relatively effective in resolving commercial disputes involving US government agencies and private firms, it was less effective in relation to the claims of private US citizens who had left Iran. Awards, mainly to US claimants, were paid out of frozen bank assets.

More recently, the United Nations Compensation Commission (UNCC), was set up in 1991 by the UN Security Council to process claims and pay compensation for direct losses resulting from Iraq's 1990 invasion and subsequent occupation of Kuwait. The UNCC is governed by a council comprising the 15 members of the UN Security Council, which declared Iraq liable under international law for these losses. In terms of its programme, the UNCC has a supporting secretariat of some 200 persons, and uses 18 three-member panels of commissioners who act as quasi-judges in the examination of claims. Under UNCC procedures, individual claims are presented by governments, and payments to claimants are made through governments.

The UNCC has become the epitome of a mass claims exercise. Since its inception, the UNCC has adjudicated approximately 2.6 million claims, 99 per cent of which have been resolved, with nearly US$ 44 billion in compensation being awarded (US$ 18 billion of which has actually been paid). Since 1996, UNCC awards have been funded by the UN Oil-for-Food programme established by the Security Council in 1996 to mitigate the adverse effects of economic sanctions on the people of Iraq. Both the UNCC and Oil-for-Food will end in 2003.

In recent years, the quest to right historical wrongs has led to the proliferation of new claims mechanisms which came about under the pressure of US class action court litigation. Notable among the efforts is the German foundation (Remembrance, Responsibility and the Future) which was established in 2000, and funded by the German State and a consortium of private companies to compensate individuals for Nazi abuses such as slave and forced labour, as well as property loss. Approximately two million claims have been brought by or on behalf of Jewish and non-Jewish former slave and forced labourers.

The German foundation is governed by a board of trustees, staffed by a management group, and operates through a complex system utilising a group of seven partner organisations which process claims from different categories of eligible claimants and which make payments to those claimants. The International Organization for Migration, for example, is one of the partner entities which, in its German Forced Labour Compensation Programme, has received approximately 330,000 slave and forced labour claims on a global basis for non-Jewish claimants. IOM has set up a separate Property Claims Commission to address more than 27,500 property claims. However, as of May 2003, only 3,182 have been resolved (703 positively and 2,479 negatively). These activities have preoccupied a substantial portion of IOM's staff in Geneva.

A similar compensation scheme was established under a Swiss Banks Settlement, reached in US class action litigation in 2001. The Settlement Agreement provided US$ 1.25 billion to settle claims by members of five represented classes of Nazi victims and their heirs who had deposited assets in Swiss banks. Significantly, the Swiss Banks Settlement mechanism includes an innovative "refugee" class of claimants – persons who attempted to flee Nazi persecution and who were refused entry into Switzerland and were abused thereafter. Approximately 6,380 claims were made under the refugee class category, and, as of May 2003, the Jewish Claims Conference has recommended that 1,180 of the claimants, mostly holocaust survivors, be awarded a total of US$ two million. The remaining refugee class claimants are mostly heirs and have yet to be reviewed.

These recent mass claims facilities ordinarily have three functional organs: one that sets and oversees policy, another that adjudicates the claims, and one that supports the process administratively. Rules are ordinarily developed during the process, and the participation of the parties is limited. Evidentiary standards are more relaxed than in more formal court proceedings, and claimants are often assisted in the efforts to present and substantiate their claims. Processing methodologies and techniques in the various claims programmes are similar. Monetary awards or restitution are generally enforced within the specially-established system.

A compensation scheme for lost Palestinian refugee property would introduce complications relating to the identification of refugee properties and choosing from among a range of methods of valuation. While much documentation has been collected on this question, these controversies have yet to be authoritatively resolved. In furtherance of a settlement, it would be necessary to map out the universe of refugee property, and assign values to the individual properties. In addition, compensation may be limited by the overall level of funds provided for this purpose, introducing yet another series of complexities.

Perhaps the most authoritative statistics assembled to date on the scope and value of Arab property was produced by the technical programme of the United Nations Conciliation Commission for Palestine (UNCCP), which began its work in 1952, and which reported initially in 1964. This report was amended in certain respects by the computerisation of the underlying data in 2000. The UNCCP Property database contains some 453,000 records documenting about 1.5 million individual holdings. The project calculated the scope of Arab land at 4,851,613.98 dunums (one dunum equals 1,000 square metres), with a value of 224,815,931 Palestinian pounds (one Palestinian pound in 1948 was the equivalent of US$ 4.03). Nevertheless, the fact that the exact scope and value of Palestinian refugee land continues to be debated by scholars and officials prompted the author of a forthcoming book on the question to include the abstracts of sixteen different studies of the question in the book's appendix.

In organising a programme of work, a compensation facility relating to Palestinian refugees would have to issue procedural rules, including a deadline for submission of claims, and design a claims form that requests all relevant information. Experience with other efforts teaches that close attention should be paid at the outset to the design of such a form in order to ensure both comprehensiveness and understandability. This will be particularly important as many claimants will be unfamiliar with such forms. As has been used with the German foundation and Bosnian property commission, a helpline and proactive efforts to facilitate the filing of claims will be needed.

In a Palestinian refugee claims mechanism, UNRWA would be an obvious resource in terms of notifying potential refugee claimants of the procedures and deadline for the filing of claims. But it cannot be the exclusive mechanism, because many refugees have no contact with the agency. A special outreach effort would be needed, particularly for claimants outside of the region of UNRWA's mandate.

Compensating refugee property claims would be more complicated and take longer than paying out departure claims, probably requiring a decade or so to complete the task given the experience of other property claims efforts. But relatively quick closure on this contentious issue could help to build confidence between the parties and avert renewed tensions.

A variety of measures could be used to expedite payments. Individual property values can be assessed using standardised methodologies. Claims that present common features can be grouped and sampling techniques can be used to check the accuracy of groupings. As was done in the case of the German foundation, a relaxed evidentiary standard, demanding that claims be supported by only plausible proof, could be used to take into account the loss of documentation and memory that typically accompanies the passage of time.

Determining the adequacy of compensation will be a key issue. Methods and techniques exist to determine the value of refugee property, either by individual valuation or through estimates. An overarching issue will be whether the funds available are sufficient to satisfy the claims, and, if not, whether the financial resources available are sufficient to provide adequate compensation.

For example, funding limitations might require that only a *pro rata* portion of property claims be paid. But it would be necessary even in this event to identify the claims and assign them values for purposes of equity. Whether based on departure or property loss, threshold estimates are likely to be inexact to some extent. One method of dealing with the resulting uncertainty is to pay fixed claims in instalments, say the first 60 per cent of the claim, until all claims are paid and an upward bound resource obligation is calculated. This could be followed by payment of the last instalment of 40 per cent, or a lesser remainder. Such a procedure has been used for German foundation claims.

Information and evidence contained in claims forms will have to be verified by using sources such as the UNCCP database or UNRWA records. As UNRWA evolved over five decades, it registered a growing and shifting refugee population and collected millions of records. The agency received records from the International Committee of the Red Cross and the American Friends Service Committee, which in 1948 the UN requested to provide relief to Palestinian refugees in the region before the establishment of UNRWA. Archives of records exist in Lebanon and Syria as well as in a Unified Registration System created in 1995.

Details about current UNRWA recipients of relief and social services, some 225,000 individuals, are contained in a computer database. Records relating to another 800,000 families exist, but are not computerised. A US$ six million proposal by UNRWA to scan the family files into a database, if funded, might take upwards of three years or more to implement, according to UNRWA staff.

The special institution to arrange compensation for Palestinian refugees will require a policy body comprising the principal stakeholders, commissioners to decide claims, and a supporting secretariat. Disputes over property claims could be resolved by an independent appeals board, as provided for in the German foundation claims procedure. A specific waiver of judicial remedies could avoid complicated institutional disputes which have vexed the Bosnian property commission.

A different set of technical issues would be raised in the organisation of a refugee fund. In particular, once a fund is established to defray the social costs associated with refugee return, integration and resettlement, it could be replenished through periodic financial contributions by donor governments for these purposes. Funds would be dispersed, as is normally the case, upon the preparation of needs assessments relating to the refugees and their communities and specific project proposals. Implementation could be evaluated for effectiveness.

Another approach still would likely be needed in order to organise payments for the departure of individuals. In this instance, in order to fix appropriate payment amounts, funds would have to be committed by governments at the outset. In addition, the number of eligible refugee claimants would have to be identified in order to calculate the level of compensation. This would raise contentious questions concerning *who* is a refugee, and *how many* refugees would be eligible to claim, including descendants of those who originally left Palestine.

Threshold definitional issues will concern such matters as the notion of refugee descendants, raising issues such as how many generations and what degree of relationship. How will loss of livelihood be evaluated? What about individuals who remained inside Israel? Or those uprooted in 1976 from the West Bank and Gaza who are sometimes referred to as "displaced persons." Once numbers have been identified, and once the amount of funds available is fixed, then lump sum payments for individuals and families could be calculated and paid to the individuals.

These claims would be similar in some respects to the departure claims that were paid under category "A" of the UNCC category. "A" claims are those of individuals who had to leave Kuwait or Iraq between the date of the invasion of Kuwait by Iraqi forces on 2 August 1990, and the date on which the Iraqi occupation came to an end on 2 March 1991. Compensation for successful claimants in this category was fixed at US$ 2,500 for individuals and US$ 5,000 for families (US$ 4,000 and 8,000, respectively, if claims were not lodged in other categories). In the case of the UNCC, payments to individuals were made by the governments that presented the claims.

The new generation of compensation mechanisms have proven workable, in part, because of the application of modern information technology and sampling methods. A lawyer who worked with the Iran-US claims tribunal, and who was deeply involved with the operations of the UNCC, emphasised the importance of computerisation in organising claims for processing. This requires an investment of resources up front but is "critical to the success" of any compensation effort.

The failure by governments to provide money at the outset, for example, slowed the work of the Bosnian property commission substantially. The entire enterprise was "a last minute thought" in peace negotiations, according to an official with the commission. Like the restitution mechanism in Kosovo, the Bosnian commission was starved for funds from the outset and only began to have an impact when it began to produce decisions and build the confidence of claimants.

However, the basic formula for a successful claims effort can be discerned from the experience of the past decade. As a lawyer familiar with the German foundation claims programme and UNCC noted, to be effective a claims scheme had to have both a "human face," referring to outreach and facilitates activities, as well as a "cold technical" capacity in the form of sophisticated information technology and computerisation.

VI. In Anticipation of Settlement

A settlement of the Palestinian refugee question would require a number of interrelated programme components relating to repatriation, local integration, and resettlement. In addition to these place-based options, there would also need to be mechanisms for compensation arrangements. It will be necessary to meld these components together in order to fashion a coherent international response.

An assemblage of new and old tasks would be necessary for dealing with the Palestinian refugee question. This might mean the creation of a new time-limited unified entity, like the IRO, in effect a Palestinian Refugee Organisation, or a situation-based solutions programme, like the Indochinese Comprehensive Plan of Action, in this instance a CPA for Palestinian refugees. While coherence of effort would be promoted by a unified entity, there is an understandable reluctance by donor governments to create new international organisations, particularly to deal with time-bound problems. This is often a criticism levelled against UNRWA.

UNRWA itself is too bound up with the underlying conflict to be the aegis for these multifaceted activities, and build confidence among parties which are likely to be wary even after a political settlement. While UNRWA has many important continuing roles to play, something new would be needed. This includes a discrete compensation mechanism, which could be either a programme component of an existing organisation, like IOM's property commission, or a free-standing but related organisation, like the Bosnian property commission.

The IRO experience provides the case for a separate, time-limited new agency in order to focus the mission. And while implementation would likely take many years, as did the work of the IRO, a separate dedicated agency could go out of existence at a future time when the problem it was mandated to address has been resolved. While compensation activities would require different sets of skills and tasks, a degree of comprehensiveness would be achieved by having one institutional rubric that included these activities as well, particularly if compensation were envisioned to help defray the costs of return, integration, and resettlement abroad.

Many issues relating to institutional framework and implementing procedures would have to await a settlement. But negotiations could address some critical matters which would facilitate resolution, such as was done in the property annex to the 1995 Dayton Peace Accord that ended the Bosnian conflict. For example:

(1). The terms "Palestinian refugee" and "family" should be defined in the settlement. This could give settlement implementers guidance on issues of what type of property loss is subject to compensation (loss of home and livelihood). It will also give donors and others a sense of the potential numbers of claimants, including descendants, as well as those in need of new homes or old homes;

(2). The best evidence of refugee property ownership should be identified, such as the UNCC records. While there may be lingering disputes at the margins that will have to be resolved, a consensus on this issue will enable claims work to begin so that refugees can see the benefits of a settlement quickly and begin to gain confidence in the process; and

(3). If a new unified organisation with a designated inter-governmental management structure is not established, then a steering group of interested governments should be created to oversee and provide policy guidance to the array of international organisations and NGOs that would be responsible for implementing a multi-faceted set of initiatives designed to resolve the refugee question. This body could also oversee the revision of national laws that would be necessary to implement a third-country resettlement programme. A similar approach was taken in the Comprehensive Plan of Action for Indochinese refugees.

Generic refugee solutions have evolved over the past century, and institutional mechanisms have been refined to implement these solutions. Similarly, mass compensation claims techniques and frameworks have evolved. While arrangements for Palestinian refugees will be complex, there is ample experience out of which to fashion the institutional framework, procedures, and criteria to implement a plausible settlement. All that remains is for the parties to make peace.

The Search for Durable Solutions for Palestinian Refugees: A Role for UNRWA?

*Lex Takkenberg**

I. Introduction

Whereas until fairly recently, the need to address the plight of the four million or so Palestinian refugees was often seen as a politically marginal, humanitarian subject, today there are few who do not acknowledge the centrality of the refugee issue within the overall search for a political settlement. In line with this development, the refugee issue has received increasing attention from both academia and politicians, especially since the mid 1990s. During the 2000 Camp David summit and subsequent Taba negotiations in early 2001, the issue was for the first time substantively addressed by Israeli and Palestinian negotiators.

In his book *The Status of Palestinian Refugees in International Law,*[1] the present author elaborates in the ninth chapter in quite some detail on the concept of permanent solutions for refugee problems, on the applicability of these solutions to the Palestinian case, on the relevance of international law to the search for solutions, and on some of the issues

---

* Deputy Director, UNRWA Affairs, and Chief, Field Relief & Social Services Programme, Syria. The views detailed in this article are these of the author, and they have sometimes been formulated in deliberately provocative terms in order to stimulate discussion. In no way do these opinions represent policies and views of UNRWA.

The author wishes to thank Rene Aquarone, Scott Custer, Karen Koning, James Lindsay and Terry Rempel for their constructive comments on an earlier version of the article.

1 L. Takkenberg, *The Status of Palestinian Refugees in International Law*, 1998.

that, in his view, need to be addressed during both bilateral and multilateral stages of future negotiations on the refugee issue, for an agreement to be minimally sustainable, including the role of UNRWA. As the observations therein remain as valid today as they were when the book was first published, this article will begin by highlighting some of these earlier conclusions and then, for the remainder, elaborate on whether UNRWA should have a part in the search for durable solutions and, subsequently, what likely role the Agency would play, once an agreement has been reached.

II. The Search for Durable Solutions: Guiding Principles

Although the Palestinian refugees have largely been left outside the general international refugee regime, durable solutions for Palestinian refugees should nevertheless be approached with the framework for permanent solutions to other refugee problems: voluntary repatriation; local integration; and third country resettlement.[2] And whereas the international community and the refugees themselves have always advocated voluntary repatriation as the desirable solution in the Palestinian case, the key General Assembly Resolution on durable solutions for Palestinian refugees – Resolution 194 (III) of 11 December 1948 – itself makes reference to alternative solutions, in addition to voluntary repatriation, and emphasises refugee choice.[3] Flexibility in combining the different options into a comprehensive settlement is likely to be in the interest of all parties concerned, not least the refugees.

The search for durable solutions should take relevant principles and rules of international law into consideration.[4] An agreement on the refugee issue that is not "rights-based" will have little chance of finding public acceptance and therefore of being sustainable in the long term.

---

[2] Ibid., ch. IX, section 2.

[3] Para. 11 of A/RES/194 (III) of 11 December 1948 reads as follows: "[The General Assembly] [r]esolves that the refugees wishing to return to their homes and live at peace with their neighbours should be permitted to do so at the earliest practicable date, and that compensation should be paid for the property *of those choosing not to return* and for loss of or damage to property which, under principles of international law or equity, should be made good by the Governments or authorities responsible." Emphasis supplied.

[4] Takkenberg, see note 1, ch. IX, sub-section 2.4.

There is a whole edifice of rules – under various branches of international law – that may serve as the legal foundation for any negotiated settlement on the refugee issue.[5] Equal application of these rules to both sides of the conflict will guarantee that the interests of both Israelis and Palestinians are protected. There is a word of caution, though. As most legal commentators on the Arab-Israeli conflict agree, the application of legal principles cannot in itself settle the underlying issues. Only a political solution imposing painful compromises on both sides may be able to create the conditions under which international law can be applied effectively.

The Oslo Agreement essentially formulated the need to find durable solutions for Palestinian refugees as a bilateral issue.[6] In this respect, the Road Map has taken a considerable leap forward, in clearly recognising the multilateral dimension of the refugee issue, to be addressed in one or more international conferences.[7] The majority of the four million Palestine refugees registered with UNRWA live in Jordan, Lebanon and Syria and by not addressing their plight, these refugees felt marginalised and accordingly were extremely sceptical about the Oslo process. An "agreed, just, fair, and realistic" solution to the refugee issue – to quote the Road Map – does not depend exclusively on Israeli-Palestinian agreement, but requires the involvement of many other parties, including the host countries, other Arab states, donor countries with a vested interest in stability in the region, the United Nations and other concerned international organisations. For this reason it will be essential for the negotiations on the refugee issue to be conducted in two stages.[8] During the first, bilateral, stage, the PLO and the Israeli government are to agree on the principles that would govern a comprehensive solution to the plight of the refugees. Subsequently, an international conference would be convened – as foreseen in the Road Map – to agree upon an integrated approach towards the political, legal, humanitarian and developmental dimensions of the refugee issue, consolidating an overall settlement.

---

5 For an overview, see ibid., chs. III – VIII.

6 Israel-PLO Declaration of Principles on Interim Self-Government Arrangements, 13 September 1993, re-printed in *ILM* 32 (1993), 1525 et seq.

7 A Performance-Based Road Map to a Permanent Two-State Solution to the Israeli-Palestinian Conflict, 30 April 2003. The Road Map was drafted and presented to the parties by the so-called Quartet: the United States, European Union, United Nations and Russia.

8 Takkenberg, see note 1, 333.

Without pretending to be exhaustive, the remainder of this section will briefly discuss some of the issues that need to be addressed during the refugee negotiations, either at the bilateral or at the multilateral level, or some even at both levels. The first of these issues is the question of *responsibility* for the cause and continued existence of the Palestinian refugee problem.[9] Some commentators have argued that this issue should not be raised at all.[10] Others, including this author, are of the view that the issue of responsibility is so central to the national narrative and the self-view of the Palestinian people that it must be adequately addressed.[11] There are a number of reasons why this is so important. First, real healing, real conciliation between the two people can only commence when such steps are taken. Secondly, it is clear that the exercise of the right of return unavoidably clashes with the practical obstacles to its implementation in the current circumstances. This being the case, it is all the more essential that the existential harm that was done to the Palestinian people be acknowledged by those who did that harm, or their successors in power. Some refer to this as "moral compensation."[12] Finally, the issue of responsibility should be addressed as it affects other aspects of the refugee issue, such as compensation and the right of return, and cuts across most other aspects of the conflict.

Acknowledgement of at least partial Israeli responsibility for the cause and continued existence of the Palestinian refugee problem does not need to undermine the legitimacy of the State of Israel. It should today not be too difficult for the Israeli government to acknowledge that for whatever good reasons there were for the establishment of the State of Israel in 1948, in view of the horrors of the World War II – and one only needs to visit Yad Vashem to be reminded of these reasons – it went at the expense of another people. If such a message would be delivered plainly, in the framework of a political settlement, the present author is convinced, having worked closely for almost 15 years with

---

9 Ibid., 334.

10 For example, Donna Arzt in D. Arzt, *Refugees into Citizens: Palestinians and the End of the Arab-Israeli Conflict*, 1997, 7, suggests that "Discussion of the refugee question must be forward, not backward-looking, so that age-old battles over fault and causes of dislocation will not be relitigated."

11 See also R. Khalidi, "Toward a Solution", in: CPAP (ed.), *Palestinian Refugees: Their Problem and Future – A Special Report*, 1994, 21 et seq.

12 See, for example, R. Khoury, *The importance of moral compensation for resolving the refugee issue*, paper presented during Stocktaking II Conference on Palestinian Refugee Research, Ottawa, 17-20 June 2003.

thousands of Palestinian refugees throughout the region, that it will go a long way towards addressing their deep-rooted grievance *vis-à-vis* the State of Israel.

Acknowledgement of responsibility also has an Arab and international dimension. The exodus of Palestinian refugees took place in the aftermath of Arab rejection of the United Nations Partition Plan and the subsequent outbreak of full-scale armed conflict when a number of Arab states declared war on the newly proclaimed State of Israel. Accordingly, these Arab states bear part of the moral and legal responsibility as well and so do states that actively supported the establishment of the State of Israel, especially the United Kingdom as former holder of the mandate over Palestine.[13] It would, therefore, be appropriate for this issue to be addressed during the multilateral phase of negotiations. This is an issue in need of further research, as it has not been substantively addressed heretofore in any literature on the conflict known to the author.

The *right of return* is at least as contentious an issue as the question of responsibility, and the two are closely interrelated. In the author's view, an individual right of Palestinian refugees to return to their homes of origin inside what is now Israel is firmly established in international law.[14] There is another side to the coin, though, as far as implementation of the right of return is concerned. In 1988, the PLO made the historic decision to accept a two-state solution to the conflict over Palestine. Five years later followed the mutual recognition of Israel and the PLO. By having recognised the State of Israel, the PLO implicitly recognised Israel as a Jewish state, although one may argue that it has recognised

---

[13] Similarly: *Report of the Joint Parliamentary Middle East Councils Commission of Enquiry on Palestinian Refugees and the Right of Return*, published by the Labour Middle East Council, Conservative Middle East Council, Liberal Middle East Council, London, March 2001. On p. 51 the Commission recommends that "The British Government might consider it particularly appropriate, at this time, to make some verbal gesture of acknowledgement of the historical responsibility that Britain bears for the creation of the refugee crisis that continues today."

[14] The right of return is anchored in several areas of international law: the law of nationality as applied upon state succession; humanitarian law; human rights law; and refugee law. For a clear and well-argued discussion of the right of return in relation to these four areas of international law, see G.J. Boling, *The 1948 Palestinian Refugees and the Individual Right of Return: An International Law Analysis*, 2001. See also the sources quoted in Takkenberg, see note 1, 231, note 9.

Israel as the Jewish state referred to in the United Nations Partition Plan rather than as a state with a necessarily Jewish majority.[15] Whatever the force of this argument, in pursuit of a two-state solution, it will be difficult for Palestinian negotiators to press for a large-scale return of Palestinians to their former towns and villages. Similarly, individual Palestinian refugees will somehow be expected to waive exercising their right of return – not to be confused with giving up the right – as their compromise in achieving a lasting settlement between the two peoples. Combined with the "moral compensation" referred to above, with Palestinian citizenship and with financial compensation, this is what eventually may constitute the "just" solution that all sides recognise is essential. No absolute but rather "attainable" justice. As stated earlier, for a settlement to be achieved, painful compromises will be required from both sides.

This does not imply that there should not be any return of refugees to what is now Israel. In recognition of its shared responsibility for the refugee issue, a peaceful and prosperous Israel could be expected to admit a significant number of Palestinians, especially those whose home villages still exist and who have family members living there. This, in fact, was under serious discussion at the 2001 Taba negotiations.[16]

The next issue to be addressed during the negotiations is that of compensation and property restitution. This subject has received considerable attention during the past five years with very significant research still ongoing. Experiences elsewhere have shown that it is essential for an agreement on the refugee issue to include, in as detailed a manner as possible, an effective remedy for the housing, land and property rights violations the Palestinian refugees have suffered.

The international conference mentioned earlier, should *inter alia* deal with the *status of those unwilling to "return"* to the Palestinian state-to-

---

[15] Plan of Partition with Economic Union, annexed to A/RES/181 (II) of 29 November 1947. The Plan, especially its section on citizenship (Part I, C, ch. 3, section 1) does not stipulate a Jewish majority for the proposed Jewish state.

[16] In early 2002, the EU Special Representative to the Middle East Peace Process released a paper summarising the general content of the Taba negotiations and positions of both parties on the Palestinian refugee issue. The EU "non-paper" makes reference to Israeli suggestions of a "15 year absorption programme" to facilitate a limited return of Palestinian refugees to Israel. According to the non-paper, "absorption" numbers suggested by Israel ranged from 25,000 over three years to 40,000 over five years.

be.[17] Refugees in the Arab host countries[18] have an acquired right of continued residency, deriving from their exceptionally lengthy stay, *de facto* integration, marriage, business activity, and so forth. One would therefore expect that the conference obtain guarantees for the continued residency for those (former) refugees who for various reasons would prefer to stay rather than to return. To provide the refugees with a real choice, *to return or not to return*, not only reduces the pressure on the new state's absorptive capacity but also does justice to their prolonged exile. As indicated earlier, for any solution to ultimately be satisfactory, refugee choice, i.e. the ability of individual refugees to take an informed decision on their future, is essential. As an absolute minimum, one would expect the conference to seek from the host countries guarantees against mass expulsion and other forms of involuntary population transfers, as prompted by emerging international norms in this respect.[19]

Continued residency may be shaped in different forms, taking into consideration the various political concerns of the host countries. There are roughly three possibilities. First, the refugees may be given the option of obtaining or, in the case of Jordan, keeping the nationality of the host country, *without* the possibility of formally obtaining Palestinian citizenship. Second, there may be the option of *dual* citizenship, enabling the refugees to formally acknowledge their link with Palestine, while at the same time establishing, or, again in the case of Jordan, maintaining the bond of citizenship with the country in which they lived for all, or most of, their lives. The third option is Palestinian nationality combined with *permanent residency* status (without formal citizenship) in the host country, comparable to that of "green card" holders in the United States.

Dual citizenship for (former) Palestinian refugees – Palestinian nationality and that of the host country – would provide an appropriate mechanism to significantly strengthen their legal status. Most of the host countries as well as the Arab League do not favour this option.

---

17 Takkenberg, see note 1, 343.

18 In addition to Gaza and the West Bank, the vast majority of Palestinian refugees took refuge in Jordan, Lebanon and Syria, with smaller numbers having settled in other countries in the region.

19 Cf. A.M. De Zayas, "The Illegality of Population Transfers and the Application of Emerging International Norms in the Palestinian Context", *Palestine Yearbook of International Law* 6 (1990/1991), 17 et seq.

One could argue that although generally undesirable,[20] dual nationality would be appropriate in the case of (former) Palestinian refugees who have resided most or all of their lives in the host countries. The exceptionally long duration of their exile has fostered very strong ties with the host countries, whilst at the same time the refugees concerned have traditionally maintained an equally strong Palestinian identity. The appropriate response to this exceptionally powerful simultaneous bond with two countries would be to grant dual citizenship.

It is important that the international conference, mentioned above, reaches agreement on a harmonised approach to citizenship and residency for former Palestinian refugees. The OSCE/UNHCR effort on harmonisation of citizenship and residency standards in the countries of the CIS is one example that may be considered for guidance. Lack of harmonisation could engender continued forced migration across the region and could lead to instability and/or conflict where one state's citizenship or residency laws – in the context of unresolved displacement or new flows – could be regarded as a threat by another state.

Whichever option or combination of options eventually materialises, what is essential is that the Palestinian refugees finally have the opportunity to get rid of their statelessness. Over the past 50 years, the legal and political impairment of being stateless, not belonging to a state, not having a national passport, in other words not having "the right to have rights" has been at the very heart of the Palestinian refugee problem. One may even argue that the element of statelessness has been more significant than the refugee aspect in negatively affecting the position of the Palestinian people. It is therefore absolutely essential that guarantees be obtained to the effect that (former) Palestinian refugees will at least have the possibility of obtaining one nationality.

Although important steps are being taken to improve living conditions of the camp inhabitants, longer-term upgrading of refugee camps to

---

[20] Although generally beneficial to the individual, dual citizenship is considered undesirable by many states. Under traditional international law, state sovereignty implied that states are the sole subjects of international law, and individuals are its objects. Accordingly, an individual could exercise his international rights and duties only through and at the discretion of his state of nationality. As a corollary of this doctrine, it was assumed that an individual could have only one nationality and owe allegiance to only one sovereign. Dual nationality also poses problems in respect of taxation and the exercise of diplomatic protection, which has prompted the International Court of Justice to develop the rule of effective nationality.

municipal standards should be addressed during the international conference. Housing will also be required for most of the returning refugees, and, together with the rehousing of the refugees already in Gaza and the West Bank, this will be one of the most challenging tasks of the Palestinian state-to-be. While a number of Israeli settlements, vacated as a result of the permanent status agreement, may provide accommodation for some of the refugees, the bulk of the housing units required will have to be newly constructed. Financial resources for this purpose could include Israeli compensation payments in addition to donor funding. Related questions that will have to be addressed concern conflicts over ownership of land. Rehousing efforts will have to be complemented by expanded programmes aimed at promoting the economic rehabilitation of the refugees.

III. A Role for UNRWA?[21]

The first question to be addressed in this section is whether the United Nations, and more specifically UNRWA should be involved in the search for durable solutions for Palestinian refugees. The first observation that presents itself is that from its inception, when it took over the mandate over Palestine from the League of Nations, the UN has asserted a particular responsibility for Palestine and the Palestinian refugees. The Madrid and Oslo processes of the past decade have to a considerable extent marginalised the UN in its political role in the conflict.[22] One of the things the Oslo process showed, however, is that a bilateral peace process does not work where the parties concerned are as

---

[21] On the question of a role for UNRWA in the search for durable solutions for Palestinian refugees, see also J. Al Husseini, *The Future of UNRWA and of the Refugee Camps*, paper drafted for the Palestinian Centre for Policy and Survey Research, 2003; B. Bowker, *The Political Management of Change in UNRWA*, paper presented to PRRN Workshop on the Future of UNRWA, UK, 2000; R. Brynen, *The Future of UNRWA: An Agenda for Policy Research*, paper presented to PRRN Workshop on the Future of UNRWA, UK, 2000; T. Rempel, *The UN Relief and Works Agency (UNRWA) and a Durable Solution for Palestinian Refugees*, BADIL – Information & Discussion Brief, Issue No. 6, July 2000; B. Schiff, *UNRWA in Transition*, paper presented to PRRN Workshop on the Future of UNRWA, UK, 2000.

[22] Cf. V. Gowlland-Debbas, "United Nations Responsibility in Palestine", Crans-Montana Forum, Switzerland, June 2002.

unequal as is the case with Israel and the PLO. A strong UN role is therefore important and it is encouraging that the UN is currently one of the four sponsors of the latest peace initiative known as the Road Map. The recent experience *vis-à-vis* Iraq may turn out to work in the UN's favour. The US and UK may be less inclined to pursue unilateral action in relation to other international conflicts after the war in Iraq, and both have in effect recognised that the UN grants legitimacy, i.e. that its endorsement constitutes a kind of *Appellation Contrôlée* in respect of state action.

Responsibility for seeking durable solutions for other refugee problems rests with UNHCR. In respect of the Palestinian refugees, the General Assembly assigned this responsibility to UNCCP. Since UNCCP effectively became defunct from the early 1960s onwards, no international body has been responsible to pursue the search for durable solutions, nor for the international protection of the Palestinian refugees. As a result there is currently no body representing Palestinians on the international plane in respect of the search for durable solutions. In respect of other refugee situations, UNHCR is intervening at various levels, with the directly affected governments, with donor countries, with refugees themselves, etc. in order to facilitate the achievement of permanent solutions. Where the plight of refugees is discussed at the negotiating table, UNHCR is often making sure their interests get represented.

It could be argued that the pursuit of durable solutions for Palestinian refugees would be considerably enhanced should there also, again, be a body to represent them for this purpose. Although the PLO is undoubtedly the recognised representative of the Palestinian people, its focus is, necessarily, not exclusively geared towards the plight of the Palestinian refugees. It has done a commendable job over the past five years in preparing itself for negotiations on the refugee issue. However, this does not free the international community from its responsibility. UNRWA is well placed to fill this lacuna at this particular junction. It could build on the work done by the UNCCP and look for further guidance to UNHCR. Some would argue that this could dangerously politicise UNRWA's work, although UNHCR's case has shown that being involved in the search for durable solutions does not conflict with an essentially humanitarian mandate. On the other hand, getting UNRWA involved in the way proposed could open up new opportunities. UNRWA could work with the PLO and Palestinian NGOs to involve ordinary refugees more systematically in the peace process. This would address a main grievance on the part of the refugees in respect of feeling left out of the ongoing political process. Being involved in, or at least being close to the negotiations, would also enable UNRWA to provide feedback to the refugees about the process, contributing towards more realistic perceptions about possible outcomes. Finally, it would facilitate making UNRWA's regular programmes and activities more conducive to the search for durable solutions.

UNRWA is, in fact, already facilitating a future settlement in a number of important ways. First and foremost, through UNRWA's education, health and relief & social services programmes, the vast majority of the Palestine refugees under its mandate are today totally self-supporting. Only 5.7 per cent of the refugees are still in need of ongoing relief assistance – not including those currently receiving emergency assistance in Gaza and the West Bank in response to the ongoing crisis[23] – and less then one third still live in refugee camps. It is this "residual" caseload of camp-dwellers and families in special hardship that demands, correctly, most public attention. However, essentially UNRWA has been a success story in promoting refugee self-reliance.

UNRWA programmes relating to the provision of small loans and stimulation of small business enterprises have contributed to the empowerment of Palestine refugees and their "re-integration into economic life," as foreseen as one of the Agency's original missions. Early income-generation schemes included the establishment of the Jordan Development Bank. Initiated in the early 1990s, UNRWA's Microfinance and Micro-enterprise Programme is now the largest non-bank financial intermediary in the occupied Palestinian territories. Since its establishment, the programme has invested US$ 88.5 million in 84,000 small business and micro-enterprise loans. The programme was expanded recently to both Jordan and Syria, where it is hardly able to cope with demand. At the same time, the Agency is in the process of restructuring a second micro-credit and savings scheme attached to its Relief & Social Services Programme, targeted more towards refugees under the poverty line requiring financial services in combination with social intermediation.

In recognition of its responsibility for refugees in special hardship, especially those living in refugee camps, UNRWA started rehabilitation of refugee shelters on a systematic basis since the late 1980s. Tens of thousands of shelters have been repaired or reconstructed during the past 15 years in all five fields, making sure that each family has at least two to four rooms, a kitchen and sanitary facilities, depending on family size,

[23] Some 230,000 families are currently receiving emergency food aid in Gaza and the West Bank.

which meet prescribed minimal standards. In addition to individual shelter upgrading, UNRWA is also increasingly embarking on larger-scale housing and infrastructure development. A number of multi-sector camp development projects are currently being planned or implemented in Gaza, the West Bank, Lebanon and Syria. If the international community so desired, these various initiatives could form the basis for a comprehensive integrated and participatory camp development strategy, which could eventually bring all 59 Palestinian refugee camps up to municipal standards.

Preparing new generations for their role in an increasingly interdependant world, where they can hopefully, in the not too distant future, live in a Middle East at peace, is a major responsibility that UNRWA takes very seriously. The Agency has embraced "global education" as its educational strategy in response to globalisation. Working within the constraints of a challenging environment – two of the countries in which UNRWA operates are still technically at war with Israel and in the occupied Palestinian territory violent conflict between Palestinians and Israelis has been going on for three years – the Agency has adopted a comprehensive approach towards promoting tolerance, knowledge about universal human rights, awareness about different cultures, and conflict resolution skills, which help students to better shoulder their responsibilities as positive members of their communities.

UNRWA pursues maximum harmonisation of Agency services with those of the host governments in respect of its programmes of education, health, relief and social services. It has tentatively considered plans for hand-over and/or phasing out of traditional Agency services and the buildings and land housing them, should this be called for as part of a peace settlement.

Finally, through its *Palestine Refugee Records Project*, UNRWA has started to optimise its refugee registration records – including preservation of historical "family files" – to make them more relevant and facilitate their future use by researchers, policy makers, and others.

The next question to be addressed is what possible role UNRWA could play, once an agreement on the refugee issue has been reached. The discussion thus far has made it clear that a comprehensive solution of the Palestinian refugee issue will require the effective cooperation amongst many different actors in the Middle East peace process. For this purpose, appropriate organisational arrangements will need to be incorporated in an eventual peace agreement, enabling the parties and other stakeholders to determine priorities, raise funds, work out detailed implementation plans, and review progress. A complex institutional set-up, involving several new and existing institutions, will also be required to administer refugee movements, absorption and rehabilitation, compensation, etc. as will eventually be agreed.

In view of its more than 50-years' experience in providing assistance to the Palestinian refugees, UNRWA is in a unique position to act as a lead agency for the first five to seven years of this endeavour. While this would imply the Agency's involvement in coordinating and, probably also partially implementing, large-scale programmes for the absorption, rehousing and rehabilitation of refugees within its area of operations, at the same time UNRWA's traditional, quasi-governmental services would be gradually taken over by the governments concerned.

UNRWA would also be cooperating with UNHCR and/or IOM on "return" of refugees from outside the region, and on resettlement to third countries. Resettlement, such as it might be agreed as one of a number of options available to the refugees, is likely to be handled by these two organisations, with UNRWA in a facilitating role. Finally, compensation is expected to be the responsibility of a special institution, to be established in the peace agreement, once again, in cooperation with UNRWA.

Once the emphasis shifts from refugee rehabilitation to longer-term development, UNDP could take over those functions of UNRWA that still require continued United Nations involvement, finally bringing the Agency's mandate to an end.

For UNRWA to play an enhanced and/or modified role, as described above, its mandate would have to be amended. Unlike other UN bodies, UNRWA was not provided with a statute or charter. UNRWA's mandate and functioning during the early period was primarily guided by the report of the Economic Survey Mission, which recommended the establishment of the Agency.[24] Over time, the General Assembly has extended relatively little guidance as to the evolution of UNRWA's mandate: tacit endorsement of new initiatives described in the Agency's Annual Report, rather than proactive approaches to steer the Agency into a certain direction. It is obvious, however, that any significant change to the mandate of the organisation in response to an agreement

---

[24] United Nations Conciliation Commission for Palestine, Final Report of the United Nations Economic Survey Mission for the Middle East, Part I (The Final Report and Appendices) and Part II (The Technical Supplement), UN doc. A/AC25/6, 1949.

on the refugee issue could only be made by the General Assembly. Accordingly, such an agreement would require endorsement by the Assembly, for any proposed changes to UNRWA's mandate to take effect.

In conclusion, the question posed in the title of the paper can be firmly answered in the affirmative. The parties and the wider international community would be well advised to make good use of UNRWA, both in the search for durable solutions and once an agreement on the refugee issue has been reached. UNRWA's massive operational and informational assets can significantly contribute to the successful implementation of a settlement. No other agency has the combination of experience, connection to the refugees, credibility and resources.

Comparative Perspectives on the Repatriation and Resettlement of Palestinian Refugees: the Cases of Guatemala, Bosnia and Afghanistan

*Michael Dumper**

This paper argues that the study of the Palestinian refugee issue has been characterised by a degree of exceptionalism that has constrained debate on policy initiatives. There is orthodoxy that the Palestinian refugee situation is unique. Because of its genesis through the creation of the State of Israel, because of its very longevity and because of the evolution of relief structures outside the main UN agency dealing with refugees, the UN High Commissioner for Refugees (UNHCR), it is seen as a category *sui generis*.[1] Consequently, it is argued that the resolution of the issue should also be formulated from within its own context. One important result of this view is that the experience of UNHCR and other international NGOs has not been utilised which, in turn, has led to a restricted range of policy options. While there has been considerable success in demonstrating the applicability of international law on refugees to the Palestinian situation, operational and programmatic studies in the field of forced migration have not encompassed the Palestinian refugees to any significant extent. This paper intends to link discussion over the resolution of the Palestinian refugee issue to the broader debate concerning repatriation and resettlement within the UN agencies and other NGOs through an exploratory comparative study.

---

* Research for this paper was carried out during a British Academy and Leverhulme Trust Senior Research Fellowship year. The author would like to thank them for their generous support.

[1] See for example N. Masrieh-Hazboun, "Refugee Resettlement in the Gaza Strip: Israeli Policy Revisited", in: J. Ginat/E. Perkins (eds), *The Palestinian Refugees: Old Problems –New Solutions*, 2001, 179 et seq., 179.

I. Introduction

To some extent, the lacuna in the application of the wider refugee experience to the Palestinian context can be explained by the lack of a comparative framework in forced migration studies. Despite the publication of numerous single case studies,[2] the study of refugee repatriation as a part of forced migration studies is methodologically underdeveloped. It lacks the body of comparative research such as we have in other fields, for example, the literature on transitions to democracy.[3] On both the analytical level and on the programme planning and policy level, there has been a failure to build upon the existing body of literature and research and, consequently, a frequent reinventing of the wheel. This paper, therefore, will also suggest a research methodology that can be adopted in order to erect a framework for comparative studies which may provide the vehicle for the transfer of best practice to the Palestinian context.

A comparative approach has many benefits in the study of the Palestinian refugee issue. First, it can identify elements from the experience of other repatriation and resettlement programmes elsewhere in the world and evaluate their relevance and utility to the Palestinian context. For example, in the Guatemala case, seen as a relatively successful repatriation programme, trilateral coordination established in 1986 between the Guatemalan and Mexican governments and UNHCR provided much of the framework for planning and refugee participation. Second, in planning what preparatory work should be undertaken for a repatriation programme in terms of training, identification of gender and age requirements, an examination of other situations reveals many guidelines to be adopted and pitfalls to be avoided. In the Bosnian case, for example, duplication and varying levels of assistance from different NGOs and governments during the mid 1990s led to competition and feelings of dissatisfaction among the refugee population. Or, similarly, in the

---

[2] J. Crisp, *Rebuilding a War-torn Society: A review of UNHCR's Reintegration Programme for Mozambican Returnees*, 1996; G. Kibreab, *Ready and Willing but Still Waiting: Eritrean Refugees in Sudan and the Dilemmas of Return*, 1996.

[3] Exceptions to this generalisation include L. Zeager/J. Bascom, "Strategic Behaviour in Refugee Repatriation: A Game-Theoretic Analysis", *Journal of Conflict Resolution* 40 (1996), 460 et seq.; S. Takahashi, "The UNHCR Handbook on Voluntary Repatriation: The Emphasis of Return over Protection", *International Journal of Refugee Law* 9 (1997), 593 et seq.

Guatemalan case, the focus on involving women in the early stages of preparation led to many positive results. Because the role of women in maintaining family networks is well documented in the Palestinian case, an examination of the gender elements in repatriation and resettlement programmes elsewhere could be utilised in drawing up a similar programme for Palestinian refugees.

There are three further discrete and crucial aspects to the future of the Palestinian refugees that can be examined using the comparative approach. The first aspect concerns the kind of compensation to which the refugees are entitled and the mechanism for its distribution. An examination of compensation regimes from South Africa after the dissolution of apartheid, in Central and Eastern Europe after regime changes there, and after the Gulf War of 1991 can provide many indications of the kind of compensation regime that is workable and appropriate. The second aspect is the question of the lead agency to oversee the resettlement or repatriation of refugees. Much of the current debate centres on the future role of UNRWA, the UN agency that has had responsibility for most Palestinian refugees since 1950. Many external donor agencies prefer a new institution with a new mandate. Others point to the expertise residing in UNRWA and its legitimacy in the eyes of the refugee community as being over-riding factors in favour of its retention, albeit with additional tasks conferred upon it. A comparative approach would assist a thorough evaluation of this issue. The final aspect is over the question of future housing provision. There is a lively debate currently taking place among officials from the Palestinian Authority, the World Bank, the EU, donor agencies, and Israel as to how best to direct Palestinian refugee inflows to the West Bank. One school of thought argues that such inflows should be incremental and directed to the margins of existing urban areas. Another school contends they should be one-off and directed to newly-created cities. A comparative study of resettlement programmes would draw in the experience of other communities and societies that have had to deal with the integration of large numbers of refugees.

Finally, it should be noted that in the Palestinian-Israel context, the insights provided by comparative studies are double-edged. They provide comfort and concern in equal measure to both sides. It may be disconcerting to many Israeli citizens to learn that repatriation programmes have taken place which do not have cataclysmic effects upon the society that is expected to absorb the returnees, and indeed may offer many advantages to it. By the same token, many Palestinians will be alarmed to hear of the degree to which, despite the full backing of international law and the presence of external military forces, many repatriation programmes do not succeed in meeting the aspirations of the refugees and indeed fall considerably short of them.

The paper will be divided into four parts. The first section will suggest a research methodology that can be used to provide an analytical framework for studying refugee repatriation programmes in a comparative perspective. The comparison as such will then be made on two distinct levels – the macro and the micro. The second section will examine the macro-level of the regional political architecture and multilateral arrangements that are in place, drawing on examples from the three case studies: Guatemala, Bosnia and Afghanistan. The third section will look at the micro-level of programme planning and logistics taking examples again from the case studies. The final section will identify the lessons that can be learnt form these experiences and examine their relevance to the Palestinian context. The paper is exploratory and marks the initial phase of a broader comparative project where a greater depth in analysis will be used to substantiate some of the observations this paper raises. The intention is that the project will culminate in a workshop in 2004 that will pool more detailed case studies with the view of identifying relevant best practice for the Palestinian context.

II. Towards a Comparative Methodology of Repatriation Programmes

As already mentioned, the comparative study of forced migrations and post-conflict repatriation and resettlement is underdeveloped methodologically. Unlike the transitions to democracy literature which has built up a corpus of material and developed a rich set of data bases and analytical frameworks since the 1970s,[4] the research methodologies available to scholars of forced migration studies are in their infancy. In addition, the field is also driven by the quest for policy relevant research. One aspect of this quest is the search for "prerequisites" for a "successful" and "effective" programme. Clearly there are problems as-

4 S.M. Lipset, "Some Social Requisites for Democracy: Economic Development and Political Legitimacy", *The American Political Science Review* 53 (1959), 69 et seq.; G. O'Donnell/P.C. Schmitter, *Transitions from Authoritarian Rule: Tentative Conclusions about Uncertain Democracies*, 1986; D.A. Rustow, "Transitions to Democracy: towards a Dynamic Model", *Comparative Politics* 2 (1970), 337 et seq.

sociated with the definition of a successful programme. To some extent the numbers of returned or resettled refugees is one important element in a definition, but other elements such as consistency with human rights law and refugee conventions or durability of the programme are also crucial elements. Researchers have to make it clear from the outset what their definition is.

Another problem is one that is associated with the comparative method itself. How does one compare situations with such disparate features or such an attenuated process or with such a large number of variables? Post-conflict repatriation programmes come in many different forms and have different rates of completion, target groups, political, economic and environmental conditions that comparisons can be contrived and artificial. Indeed, there is a strong case for exceptionalism in virtually every example used. Indeed, scholars using the comparative method have also identified other shortcomings that need to be taken into account. These include amongst others: (1) the inference from a restricted number of cases, (2) establishing cross-cultural equivalence in the use of terms and values, (3) the danger of intentionality or bias in the choice of case studies in order to strengthen one's argument and, finally, the possibility of drift in the levels of analysis whereby elements from different levels are incorporated into the level of analysis under consideration without differentiation.

Nevertheless, despite these shortcomings, the comparative method still offers up opportunities for analytical insights that should not be overlooked. Before continuing, we should briefly restate the case for the comparative method. There are four main benefits to be derived from comparison. First, it contextualises the description of political phenomena in a given country or case study. Scholars can both avoid an ethnocentric bias and place events and patterns within a broader perspective. Second, comparison allows a degree of classification in which separate cases can be grouped together and characterised. This process both simplifies discussion and encourages a focus on distinctive features that can be held in common. Third, once cases have been contextualised and classified, comparativists are able to look for explanatory factors by a process of hypothesis-testing. Relationships between variables (key actors, environmental conditions, socioeconomic groupings etc.) can be posited and illustrated. Finally, an important objective in comparative studies is the ability to make predictions based upon the generalisations constructed and observed. Correlations can be extrapolated from certain proven patterns and sequences.

When comparing a number of different cases, researchers have adapted John Stuart Mill's methods of difference and agreement and devised two types of systems design: the Most Similar Systems Design (MSSD) and Most Different Systems Design (MDSD). The MSSD methodology takes cases with many similar features but which do not all have the same outcome. The cases are compared in order to identify those explanatory factors that are different and which, therefore, may account for the range of outcomes. Thus, in forced migration situations, post-conflict repatriation programmes with many similar features such as external intervention or demographic profile of the refugees may have led to different outcomes. The explanatory factor may be the nature of the political settlement or the role of the international community. Most Different Systems Design (MDSD), on the other hand, compares cases that do not share many common features but have a common outcome. The challenge is to identify the explanatory factors that may account for the similar outcome.[5]

This paper will adopt the MSSD approach and examine three forced migration situations where similar features of a repatriation programme are correlated to the results of the programmes. Two levels of analysis will be selected to identify independent variables so that a range of prerequisites (dependent variables) can be isolated as essential components in any repatriation programme. The two levels are the political architecture or regional and multilateral frameworks (e.g. UNHCR-government or host country agreements) that are in place before repatriation commences and, secondly, the options available to refugees, be it compensation, return to country of origin, or host or third country resettlement.

The case studies of Guatemala, Bosnia, and Afghanistan have been selected in the light of the following similarities: a political settlement involving the international community, a desire on the part of refugees to return to their places of origin, the close involvement of host countries, the role of external lead agencies and, finally, a similarity in demographic profile (predominantly peasant and rural based forced migration) rather than absolute numbers. (It is important to note that the accessibility of primary data either in the form of documentation or through interviews of key personnel can also be a critical factor in mak-

---

[5] T. Landman, *Issues and Methods in Comparative Politics: An Introduction*, 2003, 2nd ed., 29; D. Collier, "New Perspectives on the Comparative Method", in: D. Rustow/K. Erikson (eds), *Comparative Political Dynamics: Global Research Perspectives*, 1991, 7 et seq.

ing selections.) Clearly the cases of Guatemala, Bosnia and Afghanistan taken in their totality exhibit enormous differences in genesis, in historical and political trajectory and in their role in the international system. The focus of this methodology and analysis, however, is on the repatriation and resettlement process which exhibit much closer similarities in both the independent variables and the outcomes, as will be shown. In this way it will be possible to identify explanatory factors which can be used to construct a set of prerequisites for programme planning.

1. Level 1: The Macro-Level of the Regional Political Architecture

This section will examine the three case studies at the level of the regional political architecture and multilateral arrangements between countries of origin, host countries, international organisations such as UNHCR and other international NGOs. By focussing on similar features in each case – forced migration leading to political settlement leading to repatriation – which have had similar outcomes – the partial repatriation of refugees – it is hoped to identify the key explanatory factors involved, be it external intervention, refugee participation or political reconciliation.

a. Guatemala

In the 1970s, Guatemala, along with its Central American neighbours El Salvador and Nicaragua, was immersed in social and political upheaval, with state forces reacting oppressively to any attempts at political participation. The internal conflict in Guatemala stemmed from inequalities in the land-ownership system and access to political power. 72 per cent of the arable land was owned by 2.1 per cent of landowners, mostly from a non-indigenous minority. Power was consolidated in the hands of the conservative military and private sector interests leading to widespread armed resistance in the 1970s. As a consequence the military regimes between 1978 and 1985 conducted a series of counter-insurgency campaigns which drove the guerrillas into the mountains and the rural population were subjected to scorched earth tactics and indiscriminate killings. Over one million, or some 20 per cent of the country's total population, was estimated to have been displaced, including between 150,000 and 200,000 people forced into exile. By 1981, 46,000 had entered Mexico, mostly to the impoverished provincial state of Chiapas, where they were registered and in 1982, the UNHCR opened offices there. The Mexican government adopted a policy of dispersal and at least 17,000 were resettled in the states of Campeche and Quintana Roo, some distance from the border with Guatemala.

The process of return for the Guatemalan refugees started in 1985, when elections for the first civilian President since 1969 took place and the constitution was revised. International support was contingent upon an improvement in the human rights situation and one of the important measures for this was deemed to be the issue of refugee return. In 1987 a Tripartite Agreement was signed between UNHCR and the governments of Guatemala and Mexico which established structures and operating guidelines for UNHCR to organise assistance to the voluntary repatriation of refugees and displaced Guatemalans who had fled across the borders into Mexico. However, the agreement did not lead to the desired mass return of refugees. While political conditions in Guatemala had changed, the refugees showed a deep mistrust of the government and its governance of the areas to which they were returning.[6]

The refugees created a group of representatives, the Permanent Commissions (or CCPP – Comisiones Permantes de Representantes de los Refugiados Guatemaltecos en México) to negotiate the terms of their repatriation directly with their own government and which became a representative body for the majority of refugees. In 1989, UNHCR gave them logistical and other support and although the Guatemalan government initially tried to ignore them, it eventually agreed to direct dialogue. In October 1992, an agreement was signed between the different interest groups making it possible for a formal return programme to take place. In January 1993, the first large-scale organised return took place. By 1996, 22,000 refugees had returned and following a peace agreement with the rebel movement there were further returns in 1997. Some 27,000 refugees remained in Mexico, most of whom were offered the option of integration and a secure legal status.[7]

It is important to note the extensive involvement of the international community in this whole process and the establishment of a number of consultation fora and monitoring groups that ensured the early airing

---

[6] S. Riess, *"Return is struggle, not resignation": lessons from the repatriation of Guatemalan refugees from Mexico*, New Issues in Refugee Research, Working Paper No. 21, Geneva, UNHCR Evaluation and Policy Analysis Unit, 2000, 13.

[7] UNHCR, *The State of the World's Refugees: A Humanitarian Agenda*, 1997, 95.

of grievances by all parties and that the process retained the confidence of the refugees themselves. One such forum was the Conference on Central American Refugees (CIREFCA). This was a conference initiated by the UN General Assembly in 1989 and which led to a standing follow-up committee representing regional governments and international organisations. Later regional and international NGOs as well as representatives from the displaced population were given the opportunity to have a voice. Supported jointly by UNHCR and UNDP, it was designed to be an evolving mechanism for coordination. It was seen, however, as successful in opening the door to initial solutions, but less successful in implementation and funding.

Another forum was the Mediation Group set up by the CCPP in 1990, which invited the participation of UNHCR, the Catholic Church through its standing Bishop's Conference, the newly created Human Rights Ombudsman and a human rights organisation set up by Guatemalans in exile. In addition, an international support group known as GRICAR was set up to assist with the negotiating process between returnees and the Guatemalan government. It was made up of embassy representatives from Sweden, Canada, Mexico and France as well as the International Council for Voluntary Agencies (ICVA) and the World Council of Churches. It was deemed unique because of the combination of national and international entities involved. The undisputed credibility of some of the members (especially a particular Catholic Bishop) and the respect engendered by the presence of members of the diplomatic corps were regarded as key to getting certain actors to sit down at the negotiating table. In addition, it provided an indirect form of capacity building in terms of developing the negotiating skills of those involved.

A final body with a clearer monitoring role was CTEAR (Spanish acronym for the Technical Commission for the Implementation of the Accord for the Resettlement of Population Displaced by the Armed Conflict). Set up in 1994 as part of the implementation of the peace accords, CTEAR comprised a six-person body with four voting members and two observers from the international community. The voting members were two representatives from the government and two from the newly created organisation of several grassroots groups representing displaced persons, refugees and returnees. The international community was represented by a consultative group of donor countries and UN agencies, elected UNDP officials (stipulated by the accord to administer CTEAR's trust fund) and the European Commission as formal representatives. It provided an opportunity for inter-institutional coordination, holding subcommittees on health, education and regeneration and allowed UNHCR to plan strategically and ensure sustainability of its intervention.

The return of Guatemalan displaced persons took place during a time of continued conflict and a heavy military presence. UNHCR has a responsibility to ensure that a repatriation process is conducted in a "safe" environment and a "dignified" manner by establishing minimal norms for returning refugees that parties in conflict will agree to respect. In the case of Guatemala, by the time the final peace agreement was signed, 78 per cent of total returnees had already returned. It is generally felt that with the majority having returned to conflict areas, this stimulated the demilitarisation of these areas and preceded the formal cease-fire that followed.

b. Bosnia-Herzegovina

Bosnia-Herzegovina, with a population of 4.3 million, was one of six republics of the former Federal State of Yugoslavia. Following the collapse of the communist system in Eastern Europe, Yugoslavia disintegrated and war broke out between the ethnically mixed populations of Bosnia-Herzegovina. Serbian support for minority Serbs in Bosnia-Herzegovina led to the expulsion of Muslim and Croat Bosnians from those areas. There was also conflict between Muslim and Croat forces. By 1992, 95 per cent of Muslim and Croats in eastern Bosnia and Herzegovina had fled their homes and over one million were displaced.[8] In 1994, despite the signing of the Washington Agreement in which a Bosnian Muslim-Croat Federation was created, fighting between Serb and Bosnian forces continued. During the conflict the economy collapsed, most of the post-war housing was destroyed or damaged and the country became divided along ethnic lines, creating the biggest movement of refugees in Europe since World War II. By 1995, 4.4 million people were displaced of which over 1.2 million fled to Western Europe and neighbouring countries.

The General Framework Agreement for Peace in Bosnia and Herzegovina (also known as the Dayton Peace Agreement) was signed in December 1995 between the Republic of Bosnia and Herzegovina (comprising two entities – Republika Srpska and the Muslim-Croat Federa-

---

[8] UNHCR, *The State of the World's Refugees: Fifty years of Humanitarian Action*, 2000, 218.

tion), the Republic of Croatia and the Federal Republic of Yugoslavia. It was witnessed by the "Contact Group" comprising the US, the Russian Federation, Germany, UK and France. The agreement stipulated the cessation of hostilities, withdrawal of foreign forces, redeployment of forces, the replacement of the UN peace-keeping forces (UNPROFOR) with a Nato-led Implementation Forces (IFOR) and prisoner exchanges. It also created the Office of the High Representative to coordinate the activities of organisations involved in the civilian aspects of the agreement and to monitor its implementation. The OHR received political guidance from the Peace Implementation Council (PIC) comprising 55 countries and international organisations that support the peace process and fund the OHR (53 per cent by the EU and 22 per cent by the US). A Steering Board meets regularly and issues *communiqués* concerned with the implementation of the Framework Agreement with regard to civilian aspects. By May 1996, significant progress had been made on the military provisions of the agreement.[9] Aware that civil harmony and the repatriation of refugees would only take place under safe conditions, the Annex 6 of the Framework Agreement laid down stringent "benchmarks" for human rights and set up mechanisms such as the Commission on Human Rights and the Commission for Displaced Persons and Refugees. These benchmarks were slow to be met, which had a direct bearing upon the implementation of the provisions relating to the repatriation of refugees contained in Annex 7.

Annex 7 institutionalised the role of UNCHR in the return and repatriation process by calling on it to develop a repatriation plan that will allow for an "early, peaceful, orderly and phased return of refugees and displaced persons." However, while the peace agreement specified that all refugees had a right to return to their homes of origin, no provision was made to ensure that such returns could take place. Instead, it relied upon the signatories to cooperate in creating the conditions for safe returns. As a result, by 2000 only 10 per cent of the Serbs from Croatia, 5 per cent of Muslims and Croats from western Bosnia and Herzegovina and only 1 per cent of those expelled by Serbs from eastern Bosnia and Herzegovina (Republika Srpska) returned to their homes.[10] The Bosnia and Herzegovina crisis has been characterised by a high degree of ex-

---

[9] S. Bagshaw, "Benchmarks or Deutschmarks? Determining the Criteria for the Repatriation of Refugees to Bosnia and Herzegovina", *International Journal of Refugee Law* 9 (1997), 566 et seq.

[10] UNHCR, see note 8, 231.

ternal involvement. UNHCR was involved from the outset of the crisis in emergency humanitarian assistance and post-1995 has been given the role of lead agency in the return of refugees and displaced persons. The Office of High Representative, the Peace Implementation Council, IFOR, and the UN International Peace Task Force have created a virtual international protectorate of the state with increasing interventions in legislation concerning property and the appointment of officials and jurists. The EU has also attempted to create a regional framework for reconciliation, multi-ethnic democratic processes and reconstruction through the promotion in 1999 of the Stability Pact for South Eastern Europe. Nevertheless, despite, or even perhaps, because of this external involvement, the repatriation of refugees has not gone smoothly. Recent figures suggest that out of a total of 4.4 million, approximately only 425,000 refugees and 500,000 displaced persons have returned to their pre-war homes.[11]

c. Afghanistan

Including Afghanistan in this series of case studies causes some problems as the repatriation programme is in its very early stages and the authority of the central government is limited. Nevertheless, due to the large number of refugees involved and the close involvement of host countries, it is hoped that logistical similarities to the Palestinian case will reveal some useful insights.

The Afghanistan refugee issue began during the Soviet invasion in 1980 when two million refugees fled the country to neighbouring Pakistan and Iran. This number increased to approximately six million as fighting broke out between the Soviet-backed regime and a coalition of *mujahidin* and tribal leaders. The Geneva Agreements in 1988 led to the withdrawal of Soviet forces and the creation of an interim government that was eventually taken over by the *mujahidin*. Between 1992-1994, approximately three million refugees returned but the outbreak of civil war that erupted between the former coalition partners allowed the Taliban to exert control over the country. As a result, the return of refugees slowed considerably. Following the attack by al-Qaeda on the US on 11 September 2001, the United States invaded Afghanistan in or-

---

[11] P. Prettitore, *The Right to Housing and Property Restitution in Bosnia and Herzegovina: A Case Study*, Unpublished paper presented to the BADIL Expert Forum Seminar on the Role of International Law in Peacemaking and Crafting Durable Solutions for Refugees, University of Ghent, 5 May 2003.

der to root out al-Qaeda bases in the country and install a pro-US government. As a result of US military actions between October 2001 and January 2002, a further 200,000 Afghanis arrived in Pakistan and over 1.2 million were internally displaced.

The Bonn Agreements in December 2002 led to the formation of the Afghanistan Interim Administration (AIA) which was to facilitate the calling of a *loya jirga* to appoint members of the Afghanistan Transitional Authority (ATA). The ATA was mandated to run the country until elections could be held in 2004. Security in the country was put into the hand of the International Security Assistance Force based in and around Kabul with the intention to extend its jurisdiction to the 32 provincial capitals. International aid was to be coordinated by a new UN body, the UN Assistance Mission in Afghanistan (UNAMA).

In terms of refugee assistance, the AIA included representatives of representatives of refugee communities in Iran and Pakistan to ensure that their needs were incorporated into the planning of the new administration. The ATA comprised a cabinet advisor on refugees. At the signing of the Bonn Agreements in December 2002, it was estimated that five million Afghanis remained internally displaced or in exile. UNHCR began an assisted repatriation programme in March 2002 with a target of 800,000 but by the end of September, already twice that number had returned, the largest and most rapid assisted return movement to have been organised by the UNHCR since 1972. This caused huge strains on not only UNHCR's budget but also on the capacity of the ATA to absorb returnees with resultant disappointment and unplanned urban migration. The ATA has established a Ministry of Repatriation and hopes to reform the management of repatriation by establishing offices in host countries to coordinate and regulate refugee flows.

2. Level 2: The Micro-Level of Logistic and Programmatic Strategies

This section will compare the implementation of repatriation programmes in each of the case studies. The features that they have in common encompass the activities of a lead agency (in this case UNHCR), logistical aspects such as transportation, housing and cash assistance, and, overall programmatic elements such as preparation, training and consultation.

a. Guatemala

Following the progress in 1992 of discussions between the CCPP and the Guatemalan and Mexican governments, UNHCR established four field offices in Guatemala in order to prepare for the return of 30,000 refugees over a two-year period. In January 1993, the first large-scale organised return took place and by 1996, 22,000 refugees had returned. For this programme, UNHCR adopted a two-track approach. The first was to ensure the safe repatriation of those displaced persons and refugees from Guatemala who wanted to return to their homes. The second was to facilitate the integration of those not returning. Assistance with the repatriation process comprised the following four main components: First, assistance with immediate humanitarian relief including one-off cash assistance packages. Second, the introduction of Quick Impact Projects (QIPs) contracted out to organisations with greater experience of project design and implementation. This was a recognition that UNHCR was too large an organisation to provide the quick response required in this kind of work, and also contributed towards ensuring that reintegration projects were conceived in a longer term context. Third, UNHCR developed a strategy of linkage with local NGOs and planning for eventual handover. Finally, UNHCR recognised that it had a key role to play in mediating between refugee groups and the government. This took place on two levels: the formal level, such as in the Mediation Group mentioned in the previous section and on a community level centred around specific activities.

In accordance with standard practice in UNHCR repatriation programmes, the packages of assistance given to returnees consisted of cash grants, food aid, agricultural tools and housing materials. In addition, all returnees were provided with the same identity documents as nationals. Whilst time-consuming, bureaucratic and complex, addressing the issue of documentation enabled returnees to rapidly exercise their civil and political rights. Due to the long distances and the remoteness of most of the returnee homes, transportation was a major operation. UNHCR, therefore, set up reception centres to receive new arrivals and where their various documentations, health and other needs could be assessed. Cash grants for those under 14 years were handed over to the mother while other entitlements went to both the man and the woman of each couple. In this way, women returnees increasingly played an active part in the decision-making regarding the use of these funds.

The Guatemala case is characterised by a high degree of involvement of returnees in the peace process. This process was started in the camps and programmes to train leaders who would be able to help and represent the community in this process were established. In the same way, teachers and other professionals were trained to provide the education and leadership that would be needed after return. The creation of women's networks were particularly encouraged and UNHCR staff were provided with training on gender awareness and how to incorporate gender issues into the planning of the repatriation programme. The networks also helped to increase the confidence of women refugees and they developed skills to publicly articulate their needs and aspirations. While it is clear that refugees were closely involved in the preparation and planning elements of the repatriation process, there is also some research which shows that the concept of voluntary repatriation was applied too broadly and loosely. In many cases, the lack of suitable alternatives obliged the refugees to cooperate in their repatriation.[12]

b. Bosnia

The Bosnian repatriation programme took place mainly from the mid-to-late 90s and was one element in a set of durable solutions available. The largest was integration into the host country and the smallest was resettlement in a third country. Repatriation was the middle option. From the outset the Bosnian repatriation process was characterised by duplication and the lack of coordination. This was despite the mandate given to UNHCR to coordinate such repatriation efforts.[13] In part this was due to the lack of legal harmonisation amongst EU member states on asylum policy in general. In addition, each state had a different set of policies towards repatriation, often offering different assistance packages, and over the issue of *refoulement*, or its voluntary nature. This is partly explained by the difference in numbers accepted by each state. Those with large Bosnian populations tended to establish distinct return programmes, whereas those with smaller numbers included the Bosnians in their existing migration policies. For example, Germany, where there was a large Bosnian presence, set itself ambitious targets of return that included a large programme of involuntary return. In contrast, countries like the Netherlands and Austria resisted the forcible return of any Bosnian refugee.

---

12 Riess, see note 6, 9.

13 UNHCR, *Operational Plan for Durable Solutions within the Framework of Annex 7 of the General Framework Agreement for Peace in Bosnia and Herzegovina and Related Regional Return and Repatriation Movements*, 1996, cited in Bagshaw, note 9, 572.

Exacerbating this disparity was the presence of a wide variety of NGOs representing a number of different interests. Although their presence was legitimate, their specific individual remits became confusing both for recipients of assistance as well as non-refugee populations. The range of programmes provided for returnees offered different types of assistance. Some focussed mainly on physical return, others provided in addition reintegration assistance to returnees, while others sought to promote the reconstruction of areas to which people were returning. However, despite this disparity in implementation a common overall aim can be discerned in that all assistance programmes contained short term, immediate assistance in the form of cash and travel grants, housing assistance and employment.

Travel costs were met by the host country, with arrangements made directly through existing return programmes or by contracting out the operation to the International Organization for Migration (IOM) which was, however, more expensive. "Look and see" schemes were also set up whereby refugees could visit their homes for a few weeks to ascertain how safe or realistic it was for them to return. These schemes were generally appreciated by the returnees and regarded as a successful component of the return programme. Cash benefits were provided to cover returnees' immediate subsistence needs until they were settled. For example, under a Dutch government scheme, all those under 50 received assistance for three months while those over 50 were given it for the rest of their lifetime. However, these varied from state to state within the EU, and even within states. The inconsistency of the approach of member states in the EU led to confusion and resentment amongst the returnees and became an important issue.

Addressing the provision of accommodation was complex. First, there was a shortage of housing for the population as a whole. The size of the existing housing stock bore no relation to existing needs and the influx of returnees. Some programmes linked their aid to reconstruction, developing building skills and the regeneration of the construction industry. However, these seem to have been of limited success. Second, the internal displacement of large numbers of people that had occurred over several years and led to secondary occupations which if reversed would cause further displacement. Finally, continuing ethnic divisions created a difficult environment in which to settle returnees from a minority group. It was not until the adoption of the Property Law Implementation Plan by the OHR, UNHCR and the Organization for Security and

Cooperation in Europe that progress on property restitution and compensation issues commenced.[14]

There were a number of approaches to employment generation in the repatriation process. Schemes to attract professionals were designed to find appropriate employment for individuals and to top up salaries by a percentage of the level they had obtained in the host country for up to two years. A scheme known as the Return of Qualified nationals (RQN) scheme and implemented by IOM, offered assistance over a 36 month period. Travel costs, an instalment grant of 380 ECU, a guaranteed salary at local wages and a 3560 ECU grant for equipment for the employing institution were included in these schemes. In addition, considerable emphasis was placed upon providing opportunities to develop new and more appropriate skills or upgrade existing skills. A third type of scheme focused upon micro enterprise. There were a number of schemes that assisted returnees develop small enterprises, largely through systems of loans, training and support in running their own business. However, these schemes encountered criticism in that they were seen to lack cost effectiveness and were deficient in tackling community based problems. Their small-scale nature resulted in them benefiting a minority of returnees and not the community at large and the focus on returnees alone engendered hostility against them from the community.

c. Afghanistan

As mentioned in the previous section, at the signing of the Bonn Agreements in December 2002, it was estimated that five million Afghanis remained internally displaced or in exile. By September 2002, it has been estimated that approximately 1.7 million refugees returned to Afghanistan in one of the largest examples of spontaneous refugee returns recorded. This caught UNHCR and the ATA unprepared. UNHCR provided cash grants to cover immediate needs and travel costs but the budget for these were soon depleted. In addition, the very large numbers of returnees requiring such grants ate into its budget for longer-term reintegration and reconstruction schemes. At the same time, the ATA was not in a position to provide any nationally based assistance for reintegration and reconstruction of damaged property. Its area of jurisdiction barely exceeded the perimeter of Kabul and plans for its Min-

---

[14] Prettitore, see note 11, 14.

istry for Repatriation to set up reception and needs assessment centres in host countries were barely underway. The lack of coordination among the various agencies concerned with the reconstruction of Afghanistan and the absence of central administration with effective control over its provinces and the ongoing military operations against the Taliban and al-Qaeda supporters has rendered a coherent repatriation process impossible.[15]

As a result, there have been two significant developments. First, there is growing evidence that many returnees either returned to their camps or drifted to the nearest urban settlement, usually Kabul. This is supported by an earlier UNHCR survey that suggested that 52 per cent of returnees intended to settle in Kabul. Already over 500,000 returnees have arrived in the capital where almost 50 per cent of the housing infrastructure has been destroyed.[16] Second, because of the conditions of unresolved conflict and inadequate reconstruction activity, UNHCR has begun to distinguish between "facilitating" and "promoting" repatriation. Due to its legal responsibility to ensure a safe and dignified return for refugees, it recognises its inability to guarantee such conditions. The distinction allows it to retain a role without obvious contravention of its responsibilities.

III. Lessons to Be Learnt

Clearly, every refugee situation is comprised of both a number of unique features and a number of features held in common. Even the features held in common require a certain amount of abstraction to draw out their similarities. However, from the case studies even in an exploratory examination such as this paper, it is clear that there are number of elements or prerequisites that are essential for an effective and durable repatriation programme.

---

15 N. Stockton, *Strategic Coordination in Afghanistan*, Afghanistan Research and Evaluation Unit, 2002; D. Turton/P. Marsden, *Taking Refugees for a Ride? The Politics of refugee return to Afghanistan*, Afghanistan Research and Evaluation Unit, 2002.

16 S. Petrin, *Refugee Return and State Reconstruction: a comparative analysis*, New Issues in Refugee Research, Working Paper No. 66, Geneva, UNHCR Evaluation and Policy Analysis Unit, 2002, 14.

From Level 1 we can see how a centralised state administration operating within firm and defined borders is a minimal requirement for a durable repatriation process. The lack of effective governance and reconstruction activity is a major contribution to the slow pace of repatriation in both Bosnia and in Afghanistan. In Afghanistan in particular, the weakness of central government, the insecure political environment and the inadequate progress on reconstruction presents severe obstacles to a repatriation programme to the extent to oblige UNCHR to redefine the nature of its activities as facilitating rather than promoting return. A planned repatriation process does not exist in the accepted sense.

In addition, it is clear that there is a need for external intervention in the coordinating elements in a repatriation process. The lack of a coordinated and harmonised approach by EU states led to a variety of different assistance programmes being implemented for returnees in Bosnia, offering varying levels of assistance. This caused resentment and confusion both amongst Bosnian returnees as well as those who remained. In addition, a chaotic NGO sector emerged, in which numerous international NGOs were present, often implementing host government schemes with little local accountability. Coordination at an operational level can ensure more efficient dissemination of information and avoid duplication of services. The Guatemalan programme on the other hand was characterised by extensive inter-institutional coordination. There were a variety of forums set up to improve communication, ensure cooperation and joint planning. Much of this coordination prompted informal and mutually beneficial capacity building, particularly around negotiation and organisational skills. In Afghanistan, on the other hand, the multiplicity of mandates has caused paralysis and competition.

Furthermore, it is clear that external intervention in enforcement and monitoring is also essential. Repatriation does not take place at the end of a process of reconciliation and the healing of wounds, but, usually, at the beginning. Indeed, it is part of the process of reconciliation and healing. At the beginning, emotions are running high and enmities are still very fresh. The Bosnian experience has shown that international intervention to safeguard human rights had an important political effect, especially in the form of the PIC, in ensuring that the civilian aspects of the Dayton Peace Agreement were implemented. The involvement of the international community in the Guatemala process was also vital.

The host countries and the country of origin also play a crucially important part in an effective and durable repatriation programme. The level of state cooperation can determine how effective the programme can be implemented. This can be seen in the legislation needed to facilitate return programmes, the issue of documentation as well in providing logistical assistance. A repatriation programme without host and country of origin participation and cooperation would be very hard to achieve.

Finally, from the evidence of Level 1 we see that the role of the lead agency and its mandate must be clear. The duplication and competition between NGOs can be very wasteful of resources and destructive in the sense that in a fragile and divided society suffering from conflict, a level of parity and consistency needs to be demonstrated. In the case studies examined, UNHCR played a clear role with a mandate determined by international law and conventions. Further comparative studies will need to look into other refugee situations where another agency operates to examine the impact this may have on the repatriation process.

From Level 2 there are a number of useful lessons that can be used in the planning of a Palestinian repatriation programme. The first is the importance of planning and preparation. Ensuring that demographic information on returnees is acted upon in order to plan for particular needs such as single women, young single men, elderly, disabled and unaccompanied minors makes a significant contribution. Building in this preparation time ensures that the systems to coordinate the contribution of all stakeholders can be identified and put in place; that joint standards of best practice can be discussed and agreed, and a common understanding of aims, objectives and ways of working can be developed. It took two years of preparation before the Guatemalan programme finally started. In contrast, the Bosnian and especially the Afghanistan cases were marked by a high degree of spontaneous returns and fast-track repatriations precipitated by the host country governments before the country of origin was in a position to receive them, both in terms of infrastructure but also in terms of legislation.

As important is the availability of objective advice and information for the prospective returnees. This will greatly assist in the returnees' ability to settle. Information offered in a range of forms, from "Look and See" schemes, to the activity of local displaced persons associations (DPAs), to printed materials, to advice centres located in the main areas of settlement proved to be successful in Guatemala and Bosnia.

The case studies also point to the fact that the involvement of returnees themselves in the design and implementation of return programmes is an essential component in the successful repatriation programme. In addition, the programme will only be effective if there is some sense of ownership and trust. In the Guatemala case, the groundwork done at grassroots level with both men and women was critical in securing a high level of refugee participation and was central to the success of the repatriation programme. It encouraged refugees to return and their involvement in shaping the nature of the repatriation process can be said to have ensured the durability of assistance schemes. In contrast, mechanisms to consult with potential returnees themselves were conspicuously missing from the process of return in Bosnia. Government and agency programmes were based upon speculation as to how Bosnians would react to return schemes.

In terms of direct material assistance, the success of assistance packages is dependent on several factors. First, the degree of consistency in the level of benefit for each returnee is important. Second, the degree to which the support given to returnees is seen to benefit the community as a whole, thus counteracting resentment from the existing community not receiving benefits. Third, the provision of advice, training and ongoing support to individuals in the scheme is essential. Fourth, it is important to provide appropriate legislation to support the creation of micro enterprise and the avoidance of a situation where the market for small businesses becomes saturated. Fifth, programmes need to demonstrate a clear commitment to ensuring both men and women benefit from the programme and include a coherent and systematic gender component. Enabling systems for women need to be put in place and to ensure, among other things, that women professionals benefit and are equally attracted to return.

There can be no question that every refugee situation has its unique trajectory and context that cannot be replicated. Yet at the same time, it is also clear that in a repatriation process there are some structural and operational features that are held in common. The evolution of conventions and UNHCR guidelines and handbooks are a testament to this. Much of this knowledge and experience has not been utilised in discussing solutions and implementing mechanisms for the Palestinian case. This paper has sought to demonstrate how this can be done and sought to map out the parameters of a repatriation process which takes into account both the unique features of the Palestinian case and the patterns discernible in a broader context.

The Reconciliation Process

Beyond Recognition: Staggered Limited Return of Palestinians Into Israel

*Dan Rabinowitz**

Abstract

A comprehensive, just and viable settlement of the tragedy of Palestinian refugees that will enjoy wide support within the Palestinian and the Israeli publics is a *sine qua non* for a sustainable peace settlement. Most on both sides, however, perceive the issue as an existential zero sum game in which the losing side might have its entire national project in jeopardy. Involving tangible matters such as territorial rights, demographic majority and political control, the notion of Palestinian return also raises fundamental aspects of identity on both sides. A sensible solution will thus have to take on board a host of symbolic elements, including notions of justice, guilt, responsibility, redress and forgiveness.

But unlike notions of transitional justice, which tend to privilege symbolic elements at the expense of tangible redress, justice for Palestinian refugees will require concrete interventions that would transform the lives of hundreds of thousands.

Informed by these assumptions and sensibilities, this article presents a formula for comprehensive solution of the Palestinian refugees' problem which includes staggered limited return into Israel proper.

---

* Sociology and Anthropology, Tel-Aviv University.

I. Narrating National Return

The decisive victory of the nascent State of Israel in the war of 1948 led to its territorial consolidation in an area of roughly 20,000 square kilometers (8,000 square miles), formally delineated in 1949 by what became internationally recognised as the "Green Line" boundary with Lebanon, Syria, Jordan and Egypt. On the Palestinian side, the same war spelt disaster – "*Nakba*" – with the uprooting of some 726,000 persons[1] – nearly 85 per cent of the Palestinian population that had resided prior to the war in the territory now subsumed within the State of Israel.

Scattered in the West Bank, Gaza, Lebanon, Syria, Jordan, the Arab World and beyond, people defined as Palestinian refugees are now estimated by Palestinian sources to number up to 6.5 million.[2] Almost four million have been registered at some point with UNRWA, the UN agency established in 1950 to cater specifically for the Palestinian refugees. Of these, an estimated 1.3 million still live in camps and separate urban neighbourhoods in Lebanon (ca. 211,000[3]), Syria (between 200,000 and 370,000[4]) and the Occupied Territories (ca. 800,000) – three communities that are widely recognised as the most underprivileged in

---

[1] B. Morris, *The Birth of the Palestinian RefugeeProblem Revisited*, 2004; R. Sayigh, *Too many Enemies: The Palestinian Experience in Lebanon*, 1994.

[2] The figures for Palestinian refugees quoted in these paragraphs are from the Palestinian internet site established as part of the campaign for return of Palestinian refugees <http://Al-awda.org>.

[3] L. Khalili, "Commemorating Contested Lands", in: I. Lustick/A. Lesch (eds), *Exile and Return: Predicaments of Palestinians and Jews*, 2005, 19 et seq., 21 indicates that the total number of Palestinians registered with UNRWA in Lebanon is just under 400,000, and goes on to cite UNRWA June 2003 figures that suggest that the number of Palestinians living in refugee camps in Lebanon is 211,769 (ibid., Table 2.1).

[4] GAPAR, the Syrian based General Association for Palestinian Arab Refugees, estimates the number of Palestinian refugees in Syria to be more than 400,000, 370,304 of whom are registered refugees of 1948 and their descendants with records at UNRWA (D. Chatty/G. Lewando-Hundt (eds), *Children of Palestine: Experiencing Forced Migration in the Middle East*, 2005, 11). They mostly (but not exclusively) live in ten refugee camps and three additional sites, the largest of which is the Yarmouk camp with a population of 90,000 (*idem*).

terms of basic human rights, economic and employment status, welfare, education and life chances.[5]

Solving the tragic predicament of Palestinian refugees generally, and of particular communities within this group specifically, is imperative if a final settlement of the Israeli-Palestinian conflict is to be attained. Unless resolved in ways that are acceptable to mainstream majorities on both sides, the issue of Palestinian refugees will hamper all attempts to reach agreement and will have a destabilising effect on regional politics for a long time to come.

But the tragedy of Palestinian refugees and, not least, the demand that they should be allowed the option to return to their original locations including those within the Green Line borders, is a complicated, vexing conundrum. Featuring basic elements that are at the heart of ethno-territorial conflict everywhere, including territorial domination, demographic majority, political control, the privilege to shape one's collective destiny – the case of Palestinian refugees also raises formidable tensions associated with visions of collective destiny and, not least, identity.

The Palestinian claim to a right of return emanates from a consolidated meta-narrative of Palestinian history, of Zionism and of the Arab-Israeli conflict. A key element of this narrative is the perception of the Palestinian people as an ancient, rooted, peaceful people, whose territory was transgressed in the early 20th century by Western colonialism spearheaded by an opportunistic Jewish contingent. The outcome was the Palestinian dispossession and dispersal in 1948, still experienced daily as a moral aberration which exerts unacceptable individual and collective tolls. This sense of historical injustice is buttressed by a conviction that the majority of Palestinians, including most would-be refugees, had no control over the war that led to their demise, and were hardly involved in initiating or conducting it.

This narrative of history produces an intuitive, self evident moral sensibility which is closely related to the main elements of the Palestinian demands for justice and redress. Standard Palestinian positions on the desirable future of refugees thus tend to feature four main elements. (a)

---

5 B. Serhan/S. Tabari, "Palestinian Refugee Children and Caregivers in Lebanon", in: Chatty/Lewando-Hundt, see note 4, 35 et seq.; A. Abdul Rahim, "Palestinian Refugee Children and Caregivers in Syria", in: Chatty/Lewando-Hundt, see note 4, 58 et seq.; S. Alzaroo, "Palestinian Refugee Children and Caregivers in the West Bank", in: Chatty/Lewando-Hundt, see note 4, 122 et seq.; A.A. Thabet/H. Abuateya, "Palestinian Refugee Children and Caregivers in the Gaza Strip", in: Chatty/Lewando-Hundt, see note 4, 149 et seq.

Return is the only genuine rectification of the gross injustices of 1948, and the only acceptable redress for suffering incurred in exile since. (b) Those personally displaced in 1948 and their descendants make one homogenous, indivisible community of entitlement. (c) Palestinian refugees should be offered a spectrum of possible options which should include return to original communities and property, restitution, compensation, integration into current locations, and resettlement elsewhere. (d) Choice between these options should be left entirely to the discretion of Palestinian individuals.

This purist position, which treats actual return as the option of choice, tends to dwarf and overlook the consequences – real and imagined – it might have for Israel and Israelis. And while few Palestinians actually believe such a scenario could materialise and should be advanced politically, the moral premise it embodies is obviously powerful. In fact in the fragmented, polyphonic and often divided socio-national realm that has defined the Palestinians since well before the trauma of 1948,[6] the call for return became a singularly unifying note. Buttressed by rage and horror at the ongoing Israeli occupation of the West Bank, Gaza, the Golan heights and, between 1982 and 2000 of South Lebanon, this conviction unites refugees and non-refugees, peasants and urbanites, rich and poor, Christians and Muslims, protagonists of a united secular Palestine, preachers for an Islamist *shari'a* state and those still advocating an independent Palestine alongside Israel. It is a view which treats resistance to Israel and the quest for eventual return as inherent, interrelated and self explanatory duties, stemming directly from the injustices that robbed the Palestinians of their old existence and their rights.

For the Palestinians, in other words, return is linked to who and what they think they are: a community of suffering[7] and memory[8] – a group whose very sense of identity hinges on belief in return.[9] They are, as it were, a returning people.

---

6 R. Sayigh, *Peasants to Revolutionaries: The Palestinians in Lebanon*, 1979.

7 E. Said, *The Politics of Dispossession: The Struggle for Palestinian Self-Determination, 1969-1994*, 1994; D. Rabinowitz, The Common Memory of Loss: Political Mobilization.

8 S. Slyomovics, *The Object of Memory*, 1998, after M. Halbwachs, *The Collective Memory*, 1980.

9 Cf. E. Barkan, "Considerations Towards Accepting Historical Responsibility", in: Lustick/Lesch, see note 3, 85 et seq., 94.

The notion of Palestinian return is pertinent for Israeli identity too, although in a diametrically opposed way. To begin with, Zionism and the State of Israel itself are premised on an emotive, highly institutionalised notion of (Jewish) return. Potential Palestinian return, on the other hand, is examined by most Israelis through a highly opaque blanket of denial, complicated by unarticulated guilt.[10] Most Israelis accept that if the Israeli-Palestinian conflict is resolved through a two-state solution, Palestinians who will want to take up residence and citizenship in the Palestinian state will be free to do so. The notion that Palestinian refugees should also have the opportunity to return to their original locations *within* Israel, however, is and will continue to be anathema to an overwhelming, remarkably unshakable majority of Israelis. For them the notion of Palestinian return into Israel is linked to disturbing key-scenarios of Jewish and Israeli history, identity and culture, analysis of which I leave for another occasion.[11]

The grave significance which both communities assign to the refugees issue and to potential return, restitution or compensation breeds an existential zero sum game. Israelis and Palestinians alike strongly believe that when it comes to assigning responsibility for the plight of refugees and defining the obligation to redress it, should the balance tip against their side, their national project and possibly their physical survival could be in jeopardy. True, there are Palestinians who believe that the practical implications of letting go of maximalist demands are still compatible with national survival; just as there are Israelis who believe that granting Palestinian refugees an option to return to Israel will have but negligible realistic impact on Israel and Israelis. Nevertheless, the social facts of the matter – namely the view of most on both sides that giving in an inch is tantamount to suicide and treason – must not be overlooked or otherwise discarded.[12]

---

10 Cf. E. Podeh, "The Right of Return Versus the Law of Return: Contrasting Historical Narratives in Israeli and Palestinian School Textbooks", in: Lustick/Lesch, see note 3, 41 et seq.

11 There (D. Rabinowitz, *Demographic anxieties and the Palestinian right of return: an Israeli perspective*, forthcoming) I argue that a hypothetic Palestinian influx is articulated as a penetration of the female body-state by hostile, rapidly multiplying foreign agents, and is imagined as an apocalyptic reversal of collective time.

12 Cf. H. Kelman, "The Role of National Identity in Conflict Resolution, Experience from Israeli-Palestinian Problem Solving Workshops", in: R.D.

II. Debating Return: Between Political Bargaining and Academic Musing

The refugees issue has hovered over every stage of Israeli-Palestinian negotiations since the 1990s. It was first raised, however tentatively and hesitantly, by Palestinians involved in the Madrid conference of 1991 and in the negotiations that ensued as part of the Oslo process in the early 1990s. On both occasions, however, the matter was flatly rejected by the US and Israel, and was unceremoniously brushed off the negotiation table. Relegated to the multi-lateral committees established to tackle the more peripheral and technical issues associated with a potential accord, it was shelved till further notice in 1996, when the whole process became deflated and derailed. The plight of Palestinian refugees made a fleeting re-entry at Camp-David (July 2000) and Taba (January 2001) conferences, only to emerge as a major stumbling block of an accord which was doomed to failure on a variety of other scores as well.

This re-entry, however, had one positive effect. The teleological approach of the Palestinians to the right of return on the one hand, and the extreme Israeli objection to it on the other, which hitherto stifled public debate of the matter on both sides, were for the first time challenged. The debate on both sides was elevated from the dark abyss of the unthinkable to the slightly less problematic realm of the unspeakable.[13] Instead of two opposing *doxas*, to use Bourdieau's term, two orthodoxies emerged, facilitating debate within and between the two communities. The inconceivable was slowly becoming improbable and dangerous – but it was, for once, present. The refugees issue, including the notion of return, became part and parcel of the legitimate political debate.

Ashmore/L. Jussim/D. Wilder (eds), *Social Identity, Intergroup Conflict and Conflict Resolutions*, 2001, 187 et seq.

13 The incident that took place at pollster Khalil Shikaki's office in Ramallah in mid July 2003 is a clear indication of what is meant by the term "unspeakable". Shikaki convened a press conference to present the results of a survey he had conducted with 4,500 refugees which looked at their perceptions and practical intentions *vis-à-vis* return. His main finding was that Palestinian refugees are on the whole less interested in actual return than had been hitherto assumed and argued. The press conference was interrupted and eventually hijacked by a group of Palestinians who emphatically argued that the survey results were invalid, harmful for the Palestinian cause and hence must not be relayed. A similar atmosphere surrounds the issue in Israeli circles.

The *Intifada* which erupted in the autumn of 2000 and escalated since in a bloody cycle of re-occupation, suicide bombing, targeted killing with civilian casualties, a dramatic tightening of the Israeli occupation and, eventually, the separation wall, suspended direct formal talks between the sides, reducing whatever brokerage role the US may have had until 2000 to a charade. But the arrest of real-time political debate created a window of opportunity for unofficial representatives and academics to think the issue through more freely and play with new ideas.[14] A string of studies, work groups, conferences and public debates on the future of Palestinian refugees developed in 2001-2003 that dwarfed the cumulative effort produced until then. An earnest attempt was clearly under way on both sides to articulate the unimaginable and find ways to make it permissible, perhaps even acceptable. This is the political and intellectual context in which this paper was conceived.

Let me offer a brief review of three approaches to the issue, employed recently by social scientists, lawyers and moral philosophers.

Most social scientific work on the future of the refugees is positivist pragmatic in nature. Taking prevailing circumstances and future projections as their two main points of departures, these studies tend to focus on what might be called "expanding the art of the possible". Those looking at economic aspects thus discuss the capacity of the Palestinian economy to integrate investment and at the types of expenditure which should be covered by compensations,[15] comment on entitlements to remuneration and the feasibility of calculating and administering them[16] or dwell on the potential financial sources to fund compensation and rehabilitation projects.[17] Sociological studies likewise comment on the

---

[14] One outcome of this window of opportunities is the well known liaison between the Israeli ex-general Amy Ayalon and the Palestinian intellectual Seri Nuseiba. Another is the Geneva Accord, which grew out of the semi-official Beilin-Abi-Mazen formula.

[15] R. Klinov, *Reparations and Rehabilitation of Palestinian Refugees* mimeo, Institute of Social and Economic Policy in the Middle East, Harvard University, 1997; *idem*, "Reparations and Rehabilitation of Palestinian Refugees", in this volume, 323 et seq.

[16] S. Tamari, "Palestinian Refugee Property Claims: Compensation and Restitution", in: Lustick/Lesch, see note 3, 246 et seq.

[17] M. Efrat, *The Palestinian Refugees: The Dynamics of Economic Integration in their Host Countries*, Israeli International Institute for Applied Economic Policy Review, DP, September 1993; T. Abdel Jaber/R. Klinov, *The Impact of the Return of Refugees to Palestine on the Jordanian Economy,* mimeo,

capacity of the Palestinian state and Israel respectively to absorb various quantities of newcomers in a variety of scenarios[18] and analyse the relationship between Palestinian family structure and norms and the potential willingness to relocate.[19] Political scientists writing within this positivist-pragmatic orientation tend to look at the dynamics of the political negotiations that took place so far, in an attempt to facilitate more fruitful outcomes when negotiations are resumed.[20]

Somewhat technical in nature, these works mostly tend to steer away from an explicit deliberation of the moral assumptions that guide them. Instead, they are pragmatic – interpreting, discarding or defending earlier claims about feasibility, impossibility or improbability.

This pragmatic quest is anything but trivial, and the attempt to marry the desirable with the workable must not automatically be assumed to represent neutrality. Pragmatism, with its explicit, commonsensical emphasis on prevailing conditions as necessary points of departure, insists on constructive forward looking. Consequently, it often privileges those who, when the process gets off the ground, happen to be endowed. Only seldom can pragmatic logic revolutionise the circumstances of the disenfranchised or otherwise assist them in their struggle for redress. The Oslo process, complete with the incremental agreements between Israel and the Palestinians, is a classic example of such

---

Institute of Social and Economic Policy in the Middle East, Harvard University, 1997.

18 S. Hanafi, "The Sociology of Return: Palestinian Social Capital, Transnational Kinships and the Refugee Repatriation Process", in this volume, 3 et seq.; E. Zureik, "Palestinian Perceptions of the Israeli Position on the Refugee Issue", in this volume, 131 et seq.

19 Hanafi, *idem.*

20 R. Brynen, *Palestinian Refugees and the Middle East Peace Process*, paper prepared for the New Hampshire International Seminar/Yale-Maria Lecture in Middle East Studies, University of New Hampshire, 3 April 1998, <http://www.arts.mcgill.ca/mepp/mepp.html>; M. Klein, "Between Right and Realization the PLO Dialectics of 'The Right of Return'", *Journal of Refugee Studies* 11 (1998), 1 et seq.; *idem*, "From a Doctrine-Oriented to a Solution Oriented Policy, The PLO's 'Right of Return' 1964-2000", in: J. Ginat/E.J. Perkins (eds), *The Palestinian Refugees, Old Problems – New Solutions*, 2001, 46 et seq.; *idem*, "The Negotiations for the Settlement of the 1948 Refugees", in this volume, 465 et seq.; M. Dumper, "Comparative Perspectives on the Repatriation and Resettlement of Palestinian Refugees: The Cases of Guatemala, Bosnia and Afghanistan", in this volume, 387 et seq.; A. Helton, "End of Exile: Practical Solutions to the Palestinian Refugee Question", in this volume, 349 et seq.

pragmatism and its limitations.[21] Working from the here and now, the process attempted to settle whatever issue the parties could agree on, leave difficult issues for future deliberation, and, most importantly, forget about the past in the hope it would be taken care of by the rosy future. The same logic of pragmatism resurfaced in the summer of 2000, when Israel and the US came to the Camp David summit only to find the Palestinians unwilling to play along.

The tendency of pragmatism to privilege those currently endowed at the expense of those seeking redress, which is abundantly clear to Palestinians but conveniently invisible to Israelis and Americans, was undoubtedly a major factor in the failure at Camp-David and, soon after at the Taba conference (January 2001), to make progress on the refugees front.

The picture is not much brighter when it comes to the work by legal experts. Writers who explicitly support Palestinian assertions of a right to return such as Quigley,[22] Mallison and Mallison,[23] Lawand,[24] Wakim[25] and Boling,[26] as well as those clearly against such assertion such as Benvenisti and Zamir,[27] Zilbershatz,[28] Benvenisti[29] and, to a

---

[21] Cf. D. Rabinowitz/K. Abu Baker, *Coffins on our Shoulders: the Experience of the Palestinians in Israel*, 2005, 95-114.

[22] J. Quigley, "Displaced Palestinians and a Right to Return", *Harv. International Law Journal* 39 no. 1 (winter 1998), pp 171-229.

[23] W.T. Mallison/S. Mallison, *The Palestine Problem in International Law and World Order*, 1986.

[24] K. Lawand, "The Right to Return of Palestinians in International Law", *In'l J. of Refugee L.* 8 (1996), 532 et seq., 556.

[25] W. Wakim, "The Internally Displaced": Seeking Return within One's Own Land", *Journal of Palestine Studies* 31 (2001), 32 et seq.

[26] G. Boling, *The 1948 Palestinian Refugees and the Individual Right to Return, An International Law Analysis*, Badil Resource Center for Palestinian Residency & Refugee Rights, 2001.

[27] E. Benvenisti/E. Zamir, *Private Property and the Israeli-Palestinian Settlement*, The Jerusalem Institute for Israel Studies, 1998, in Hebrew.

[28] Y. Zilbershatz, "International Law and the Palestinian Right of Return to the State of Israel", in this volume, 191 et seq.

[29] E. Benvenisti, *Modalities for Processing Refugee Claims for Compensation*, paper presented at the Israel and the Palestinian Refugees conference, Max Planck Institute for Comparative Public Law and International Law, Heidelberg, 11-13 July 2003.

lesser extent, Arzt and Zughaib,[30] structure their inquiry as exercises in law finding. Combing precedents in international practices and declarations, treaties, norms and rulings, authors seem to be on a constant quest for the ultimate trump card – the all-decisive legal language that would "objectively" define "the international law perspective" on the issue.

It is a problematic quest. Given the fluidity of what counts as "law" in the international arena, definitive directives here are hard to come by. This is complicated further by the non-reflexive nature of the legal discourse, whereby writers consistently misrecognise (or leave implicit) the political logic and moral assumptions that persuade them to consider certain possibilities and ignore or dismiss others. Not surprisingly, this positivist pragmatic approach once again steers writers away from discussing moral issues. Even the debate on whether or not the language of rights, and in particular the discourse of human rights, should be employed for the case of Palestinian refugees – for example Gavison's[31] critique of Boling[32] – tends to focus more on the long-term efficacy of using such terminology than on the moral implications of accepting or rejecting it in principle. In the final analysis, the main contribution of legal studies in the present context seems to be a list of precedents suggesting that large scale repatriation (read: return) is almost non-existent in modern history.[33]

A third approach is the one guided by moral philosophy. The procedure here tends to begin with listing competing moral arguments for or against the phenomenon in question (in our case it could be for or against Zionist and Palestinian versions of history, for or against ethno-territoriality and the rights which it engenders, and so on). This is then followed by discussion and disclosure of the argument deemed most valid morally. Finally, an attempt is made to match the favoured moral claim with an operational plan and to hope it will prove workable.

---

30 D. Arzt/K. Zughaib, "Return to the Negotiated Land: The Likelihood and Legality of Population Transfer Between Israel and a Future Palestinian State", *Journal of International Law and Politics* 24 (1992), 1399 et seq.

31 R. Gavison, *The Palestinian refugees and the language of rights*, paper presented at the Israel and the Palestinian Refugees conference, Max Planck Institute for Comparative Public Law and International Law, Heidelberg, 11-13 July 2003.

32 Boling, see note 26.

33 Cf. Barkan, see note 9, 95-99; Benvenisti/Zamir, see note 27.

Following this line of arguing, Gans[34] examines the validity of the Palestinian demand to return in light of the moral validity of Zionism. Acceptance of the historical narrative espoused by mainstream Zionism, Gans argues, negates Palestinian claims, whereas full or even partial rejection of Zionism paints a considerably different picture. One can reject "Cultural nationalism" altogether, negate Zionism as the cultural nationalist expression of the Jews, or resist its implementation in the particular territory where it evolved. Each stance would have a different implication on the claims of Palestinian to return. For his part Gans accepts the legitimacy of Zionism, but restricts it to the borders of 1967. This leads him to conclude that the bulk of Palestinian returnees will have to go to the Palestinian state, with only a limited number returning into Israel.

Marmor's[35] guiding principle is the immorality of forceful possession of land. The only tracts acquired by Israel in a morally defensible manner, he implies, are those assigned to it as part of the 1947 UN Partition Plan. This of course collapses the distinction between territories Israel seized in 1948 beyond its share in the Partition Plan[36] and territories it seized in 1967. The immorality of the Israeli seizures of much of the territory where would-be Palestinian refugees were living prior to 1948 thus becomes Marmor's guiding light as he assesses Palestinian demands to return and, more specifically, where precisely such return might be exercised in.

---

[34] C. Gans, "The Palestinian Right of Return and the Justice of Zionism", in this volume, 255 et seq.

[35] A. Marmor, "Entitlement to Land and The Right of Return: An Embarrassing Challenge for Liberal Zionism", in: L. E. Mayer (ed.) *Justice in Time: Responding to Historical Injustice*, Baden-Baden: Nomos Verlagsgesellschaft, 2004.

[36] The UN Partition Plan of 1947 assigned the Jewish state with some 11,000 square kilometres (some 4,400 square miles). By the time the 1948 War was over, Israeli forces had occupied an additional 9,500 square kilometres of land designated in the UN Partition Plan as part of the Arab state in Palestine. The new positions of the Israeli forces were the basis of the green line border determined in a series of cease fire agreements between Israel and Lebanon, Syria, Jordan and Egypt in 1949, and recognised by the international community as the international borders of the State of Israel. Some 45 per cent of the territory of Israel within the green line is thus territory which in Marmor's terms, was as illegally seized as the territories that Israel took from Jordan, Syria and Egypt in 1967 or those it occupied between 1982 and 2000 in Lebanon.

Working from Walderon's forward looking supersession thesis – the notion that an immoral act can, in some circumstances, be superseded by moves that make redressing it practically (hence morally) untenable – Marmor comments on the significance of the passage of time; on the replacement of the original Palestinian refugees with new generations; on the changed circumstances due to Israeli development; on the role that the lost property had and still has in the lives of dispossessed Palestinians; on the manner in which they made their grievance known; and on the balance between accommodating them and displacing Israelis. His conclusion is that at least some Palestinians should be allowed to return to their old homes, in "uninhabited areas" within Israel's 1967 borders, which he does not specify geographically.

Attempts to seek solutions guided by a moral-philosophical approach such as those reviewed are often crippled by the transient nature of political opportunities created at fleeting moments of *detante.* Constrained by political time-lines and, not least, by power inequalities, such moments are not conducive to protracted moral reasoning, and are often subsumed and brushed aside by political bargaining.

But the difficulty is not only temporal. It also involves division of labour and partisanship. The inevitable cross-over from ostensibly objective moral arguments of the type identified by moral philosophers to the arena of stark political negotiation has a dynamic of its own. Anyone who was ever party to bargaining, however trivial, knows how moral principles heralded at the outset can become redundant when concrete workable solutions make their first appearances. The last section of Marmor's argument is in fact a vivid illustration of such dynamics. There a critical reading of the Zionist left's territorial logic is watered down by forward looking practical considerations that arrest the moral imperative from being driven to their logical practical conclusion.

Peled,[37] adopting what Crocker,[38] Kiss[39] and others call "transitional justice", takes the moral argument in a slightly different direction. Peled

---

[37] Y. Peled, *Liberalism and The Right of Return Controversy in Israel: Deconstructing the Gans-Marmor Debate*, paper presented at the Israel and the Palestinian Refugees conference, Max Planck Institute for Comparative Public Law and International Law, Heidelberg, 11-13 July 2003.

[38] D. Crocker, "Transitional Justice and International Civil Society: Toward a normative Framework", *Constellations* 5 (1999), 492-517.

[39] E. Kiss, "Moral ambition within and beyond political constraints", in: R.I. Rotberg/ D. Thompson (eds), *Truth v. Justice: The Morality of Truth and Reconciliation Commissions*, 2000, 68 et seq.

concurs with Bhargava[40] that in the aftermath of violent dispossession victims suffer the further indignity of being excluded from the public domains in which politically significant issues – including their grievance, their future and their demand for justice – are determined. "It is this situation that is most often in need of rectification" Peled states,[41] before turning to discuss a number of ideas which emphasise, this way or another, the Palestinian right to return and the need to accompany this right by active measures. Slyomovics, in a recent article on belated remuneration and compensation offered by the Moroccan state to oppressed political detainees, sees indemnities primarily as a spiritual process. While not necessarily leading to closure, the process marries the practical world of commodities with the all important realm of memory, mental reckoning and, ultimately, forgiveness.[42]

Slyomovics's argument, namely that whatever happens in the realm of financial and physical rectification is at the same time symbolic of spiritual processes, is echoed by Lustick and Lesch.[43] This said, it is quite obvious, not least to Lustick and Lesch themselves later in the same text[44] that recognition and spiritual measures, while obviously crucial to any healing, are not enough. Gratifying as it may be for liberal minded intellectuals and convenient as it is for Israeli interests, in and of itself recognition is of little use for poor and disenfranchised Palestinians who have spent the best part of their lives in exile.

The ideal scenario envisaged by some Israeli liberals, of replacing tangibility with recognition, is thus hardly an option. Nor am I suggesting to forgo moral principles as bases for political solutions. On the contrary. In the debate surrounding the fate of Palestinian refugees, as in many others, morality seeps into action taken (or avoided) in a variety of complex ways. Whichever intellectual inclination and national affiliation people bring to this debate, they will inevitably end up having to negotiate morality and realism, theory and practice, desirables and deliverables, principles and politics. Which is precisely what I am about to

---

40 R. Bhargava, "Restoring decency to barbaric societies", in: Rotberg/Thompson, see note 40, 45 et seq.

41 Peled, see note 38.

42 S. Slyomovics, "No Buying Off the Past: Moroccan Indemnities and the Opposition", MERIP/Middle East Report 229 (2003), 34 et seq.

43 I. Lustick/A. Lesch, "The Failure of Oslo and the Abiding Question of the Refugees, Introduction, in: Lustick/Lesch, see note 3, 3 et seq., 14.

44 *Idem.*

do in the following section, dedicated to a formula for a potential comprehensive solution for the predicament of Palestinian refugees.

III. Elements of a Formula for Solution

The outline which follows assumes an internationally sanctioned Comprehensive Peace Settlement (CPS) between the independent states of Israel and Palestine.[45] Regarding refugees, this CPS should have five main components: formal recognition on the part of Israel of its chief responsibility for the creation of the Palestinian refugee problem; a concomitant acceptance of the principal right of Palestinian refugees to return; unlimited license for Palestinian refugees to immigrate and become citizens of the Palestine state; compensation and damages to Palestinian refugees for property lost and for suffering;[46] and staggered

[45] The settlement is assumed to include the following arrangements;

Territory: Israeli withdrawal from all territories occupied in 1967 barring minimal border alterations;

Relations: Israel and Palestine forming one customs, commerce, labour, insurance and possibly currency zone; Each state has full sovereignty on its land sea and air borders;

The West Bank and Gaza are connected with two land corridors detached from Israeli infrastructure;

Jerusalem: West Jerusalem remains the capital of Israel while East Jerusalem will be established as the capital of Palestine; Municipally, Jerusalem will be managed by one unified urban administration, with no checkpoints between its Jewish neighbourhoods and its Palestinian neighbourhoods, although both states can establish checkpoints between the part of the city under their control and the remainder of their territory;

Holy places: Access to all holy places will be free for all, with key Jewish and Muslim sites (e.g. Wailing wall, Harram a-sharif) administered by Israeli and Palestinian authorities as applicable;

Security: Israel and Palestine mutually forgo the use of military force. They take upon themselves to alert each other of terrorist initiatives organizing in their respective territories against the other, and not to allow foreign armies in their territories. Unilateral breach of the latter clause will give the other full and automatic right to self-defence.

[46] Every refugee who has lost property will be entitled to remuneration. All refugees will be entitled to compensation for suffering incurred. Israel will carry a significant proportion of the financial load involved, calculated partly in accordance with its gains from Palestinian property since 1948. The distribution

limited return of some Palestinian refugees into Israel within the Green Line borders.

Let me develop the last – and most contentious – point in some detail.

The first element of the formula is an agreed numeric quota of refugees who will be allowed to return to Israel and to become full citizens. One can assume it will be smaller than what Palestinians seek and larger than what Israel has ever entertained.[47] It is important to note, however, that the actual size of the quota agreed is not the crucial aspect. It is the criteria for eligibility and the staggered sequence they determine that are the heart and soul of my proposal.

Let me elaborate. Since the CPS is likely to take years to negotiate, agree and implement, and since elderly refugees perish all the time, it is suggested that at the very beginning of the negotiation process refugees born prior to 1948 in parts of Mandatory Palestine which subsequently fell within the Green Line borders – people I label First Generation Refugees (FGR) – will be offered an unmitigated option of return to Israel. Coming early at the process, as a first unilateral step on the part of Israel before negotiations are in full swing, this could become a positive gesture of good will and an effective trust building measure.

---

mechanism, to be detailed in the CPS, could be based on claims by and dispensation to individuals; on a bilateral collective agreement and lump sum payment between governments; or on a combination of the two. A development and rehabilitation fund for Palestine could be established, with the task of ensuring a proportion of the funds is diverted to infrastructure and other public projects in the Palestinian state. Other mechanisms could be put in place to ensure a proportion of the funds go to personal and collective investment in education, vocational training, small businesses and similar growth generating activities.

47 The Clinton plan discussed at Camp David in the summer of 2000 is believed to have included the return of 'tens of thousands' of returning Palestinians into Israel (a poll assuming these figures was conducted by the Tami Steinitz Center for the Study of Peace in December 2000). In this vein, Israeli Prime Minister Ehud Barak was reported in the Israeli press as having implicitly agreed that up to 100,000 Palestinian refugees would be allowed to return to Israel during the first ten years of a comprehensive peace settlement. A quota of that magnitude or even double can form a point of reference for the present proposition.

Estimated today at between 180,000 and 230,000 people,[48] FGR will be entitled to full Israeli citizenship. A liberal time span will be made available to them in which they will be able to apply – perhaps until the end of the second year after the signing of the CPS. Once an FGR applies, Israel will be obliged to grant him or her citizenship, with no discretionary power to refuse. The rights entailed in citizenship will be identical to those extended to every other Israeli citizen, including rights of residency, social security, health insurance, a welfare package, the vote and so on.

This early offer to FGR will not be extended to members of their families born in exile. Admittedly, this will make it difficult for many FGR to take the offer: few persons over 58, wherever they are and of whichever culture, are likely to choose to relocate alone (or, at best, accompanied by a spouse or a sibling), leaving children and grandchildren behind. All the more so Palestinian refugees, who have considerable emotional, social and economic investment in their kin.[49] And while extended kinship networks also play a part in Palestinian culture and society and some refugees do have such family connections inside Israel, this cannot be expected to fundamentally change FGR's (un)willingness to relocate to Israel without members of their immediate families.

But this does not imply that such an early offer to FGR must necessarily be reduced to only a symbolic gesture. Significantly, FGR who cannot or will not relocate to Israel will have the option of having their citizenship decoupled from their residency. Put simply, to claim his citizenship and benefits, an FGR who does not wish to enter Israel (let alone settle there), will not be compelled to. Rather, it will be possible to apply for citizenship, enjoy all financial benefits and conduct the necessary liaison with Israeli state officials consulates and specialised

48 The assumption here is that the population of Palestinian refugees in 1948 had a normal demographic structure in terms of age set distribution. The majority of FGR still alive today, who are by definition aged 58 and upwards, were between the ages of 0 and 30 in 1948 – an age set that would have made roughly 40 per cent of the entire population of refugees. With ca. 730,000 refugees all told, this proportion yields ca. 290,000. Allowing for mortality (but not, of course, for additional births), the number of survivors today would be around 200,000.

49 Hanafi, see note 18; Chatty/Lowendo-Hundt, see note 4.

bureaus which Israel would establish near existing concentrations of Palestinian refugees.[50]

Most theories of citizenship stress residence of some description as a prerequisite for citizenship. Some states however acknowledge non-residents as a legitimate sub-category of affiliates, and go out of their way to cater for them. Israel, for example, extends entitlement to citizenship to every Jewish person, including ones who have never set foot in it. While exercising this potential right hinges on travelling to Israel, basal entitlement is quite detached from presence. Likewise, some European states are willing to have old age pensions, social security remittances and entitlement to educational rights extended to citizens abroad; there are states which have tax relief and other financial incentives extended to expatriates abroad. Some allow their citizens to vote abroad in consulates. Israel itself, for an interesting example, has had tens of thousands of its own citizens receiving monthly pensions from the German government as of the early 1950s, as part of the "*shilumim*" (indemnities) agreement for suffering and losses incurred by the Nazi regime.

The option of decoupled citizenship will be effective immediately, but not indefinitely. For reasons that will soon become apparent, an FGR who takes decoupled citizenship but does not relocate to Israel within a finite period – say five years after the signing of the CPS – will have his or her citizenship expire. Note however that if this option is made available to FGR immediately (that is, at the outset of negotiations), certain individuals could have it as a valid option for the best part of a decade.

As indicated, FGR will probably not rush back to Israel. Their unwillingness and inability to severe immediate family ties is one obvious reason, but there are others. Data collected in recent surveys suggest that compared to other segments of the Palestinian refugee community, refugees older than 60 (in other words FGR) are least enthusiastic about return to Israel, least willing to consider living under Israeli sovereignty, and more willing than others to substitute return for other options.[51]

---

50 Palestinian refugees who would prefer to avoid any direct contact whatsoever with Israel but still receive their benefits, options can be created to have liaison done in offices of interest attached to embassies or consulates of other countries.

51 A 2001 survey conducted by the Israel Palestine Center For Research and Information (*Palestinian Refugees and the Negotiations for Permanent Status*, Israel Palestine Center For Research and Information (IPCRI), August 2001)

The implication is that FGR will probably fill only a fraction of the quota offered to Palestinian returnees. A more substantial proportion amongst them may opt for decoupled citizenship, staying put where they currently reside while benefiting from Israeli old age pensions, support for medical care etc. Many, perhaps most FGR, disinclined to have any contact with Israel to begin with, will opt for neither of these offers.

This is meaningful for mitigating Israeli existential anxieties. While Palestinian commentators insist – realistically, I would argue – that even if return were offered indiscriminately only a small proportion of refugees would opt for it, Israelis stubbornly refuse to believe them. Most Israelis are in fact convinced that granting Palestinians the option to return will result in an immediate stampede. The outline I suggest here, which will offer every elderly Palestinian refugee an option to return to Israel proper, but which will demonstrate quite clearly that only a fraction of them actually do decide to come, will be an eye-opener for many Israelis and will put them at ease. Moreover, since FGR are men and women nearing old age and mostly past their reproductive phases, their potential presence would be less threatening to Israeli concerns with demographic balances. As a result, Israel could become more fa-

---

which had some 1600 respondents in 16 communities of Palestinian refugees in the West Bank and Gaza, found that only 11.7 per cent of those over 60 indicated a willingness to return to their original places if it meant living under Israeli sovereignty. In a similar vein, only 11.7 per cent of those over 60 indicated a willingness to return to their original places if it meant living under Israeli sovereignty. 29.7 per cent of respondents over 60 indicated they were undecided, and 58.6 per cent declared complete refusal to live under the sovereignty of Israel. In the general population the proportion of those willing to live under Israeli sovereignty was 85.2 per cent.

Likewise, almost 70 per cent of all respondents indicated willingness to return even if it involved relinquishing a right to monetary compensation. Amongst those over 60 less than 1 per cent were willing to do so. And 21.9 per cent of those above 60 were willing to accept integration into the communities where they currently reside, or resettlement (in a different place but not in Israel) instead of return. The proportion amongst all respondents who indicated similar propensity was only 3.6 per cent. These findings are corroborated by a similar survey conducted by Badil, which indicates for example that almost half of the original refugees refuse to go back to their old place if the original family house no longer stands. With the majority of structures long ruined, such an assertion is highly suggestive. A survey conducted by Khalil Shikaki published in mid July 2003 came up with similar results.

vourably inclined towards a larger quota, edging nearer the minimal number acceptable for Palestinians.

The next phase will begin with the signing of the CPS, when refugees who are not natives of Mandatory Palestine, such as spouses who married FGR in the diaspora and offsprings born there (hereafter labelled Subsequent Generation Refugees or SGR) will be able to apply for return. The number of vacancies that would become available for SGR at this point can be calculated, at least in principal: the original quota, minus the number of FGR who actually returned, minus those who took decoupled temporary citizenship and are still undecided about their own residency.

To use a concrete example: say the overall quota of Palestinians to return to Israel proper is 200,000. If by the time the CPS is signed 10,000 FGR have opted to return, and 65,000 additional FGR had opted for decoupled citizenship, the number of vacancies available for SGR will be 125,000, and could yield five annual instalments of 25,000 returnees. To this number will also be added the number of FGR with decoupled citizenship who in the mean time died in the diaspora, and whose entitlements will revert back to the general quota. Note that the quota does not have to be agreed before the initial gesture of allowing all FGR full return to Israel is made. Since it is quite clear that only a fraction of FGR will opt to return, the initial offer can go ahead without the Israelis fearing that the actual number of FGR returning would predetermine negotiations of the final quota.

Whereas the offer to FGR will be a blanket offer – hopefully a quota large enough to take in every FGR who chooses relocation into Israel – when it comes to SGR the process will become selective. Decision powers here will be granted to Palestinian representatives, who will of course be at liberty to give priority to refugee communities deemed most vulnerable. Amongst those are stateless refugees in Lebanon and Syria, and refugees from Gaza who had travelled to Kuwait since the 1950s using Egyptian travel documents,[52] fled to Jordan at the time of the Gulf War in 1991, were denied Jordanian citizenship then and are stuck stateless in Jordan since.

The option of SGR to take residence in Israel will be valid for a number of additional years – say five. As their quota is gradually filled, FGR holding decoupled temporary citizenship whose kin were now included

52 See A. Lesch, "No Refuge for Refugees: The Insecure Exile of Palestinians in Kuwait", in: Lustick/Lesch, see note 3, 161 et seq.

amongst those SGR offered return to Israel may decide to join them. Thus, five years after the signing of the CPS two processes will simultaneously mature. One: the proportion of the quota made available for SGR will have been filled. The other: FGR holding decoupled citizenship who have chosen not to return to Israel will have their citizenship expire. Their vacancies will revert back to the overall quota, enabling other SGR's to return in their stead.

In Israel, the process of return of both FGR and SGR will be regulated by a comprehensive set of immigration laws that will eclipse the existing laws of Return (1950) and Nationality (1952). The new legislation will be informed by the process of return sketched here, and will safeguard the principle that return of Palestinians cannot result in the displacement of Israelis from their current homes.

The international community, including Arab states and states in Europe, the Americas and more, will offer Palestinian refugees who prefer resettlement additional quotas of immigration visas. Offers could range from 2,000 to 50,000 visas per state, depending on population size, settlement policies and economic strength. The principal of decoupling citizenship and residency suggested for FGR returning to Israel could perhaps be duplicated in the case of refugees obtaining citizenships in other countries too.

The CPS will define the relationship between the independent states of Israel and Palestine in ways that will enable Palestinian and Israeli citizens to commute, visit, make pilgrimage and work in the respective states with ease and dignity. This element may prove pertinent as the process unfolds, when Palestinians will need to make individual and familial decisions about residence and citizenship.

IV. Conclusions

Some of the structuring principles of the formula described above are relevant to moral and identity related issues.

First, singling out FGR as the first group to be offered full return carries moral and symbolic significance. It is FGR, after all, whose lives were most dramatically disrupted by the war of 1948, and who best embody "the returning people". In terms of distributive justice, it offers those who were personally traumatised the widest range options. Emotionally, it offers some redress to the outrage and the sense of injustice at the initial dispossession, and solidarity with those whose lives best personify Palestinian identity.

A second principle upheld here has to do with universally recognised nativity rights – the link between a person's birth in a given territory and her entitlement to citizenship there. In the case in point, upholding the right of Palestinians born in Mandatory Palestine to Israeli citizenship redresses the injustice embodied in the Israeli Law of Absentee Property (1950). This law, designed primarily to transfer property of Palestinian refugees to Israeli control, defines "absentee" in such a way that Palestinians who were away from their domiciles for any length of time at any point since 29 November 1947 (a condition which applies to the overwhelming majority of Palestinians) are stripped of their inherent right to citizenship. Singling out FGR as a separate category goes some way to rectify this aberration.

Third is that Palestinian Refugees, particularly FGR, are offered a real choice between options, most of which entail conditions which are considerably better than those prevailing, at least in refugee communities in Lebanon, Syria, Jordan, the West Bank and Gaza. If nothing else, for FGR the principle of individual choice between a variety of options is upheld in full.

Fourth, decoupling citizenship from residence could enable FGR embedded in their current places, who prefer to stay put, to nevertheless receive substantial benefits associated with their Israeli citizenship for the best part of a decade. This is significant. Return may be idealised by Palestinians as a collective act, but when it comes to practice it suddenly becomes a very private – and sometimes lonely – enterprise. A complicated step under normal circumstances, it is often doubly problematic for the elderly and poor. The possibility of decoupled citizenship, complete with a tangible welfare package, could help individuals to willingly forgo their erstwhile vision of return but at the same time receive a tangible welfare package if they wanted to. The staggered time frame, and the fact that the entitlement of FGR not wishing to return reverts to the overall pool of vacancies. The Palestinian collective as a whole, in other words, does not miss out on either vacancies nor time.

The low probability that FGR will chose to take the option of return which they are offered is not necessarily a drawback. At the end of the day, the number of Palestinians who will eventually return to Israel will be the same as it would have been had the CPS simply included a numeric quota and a time frame.

A pressing need exists to engage the issues relating to the Palestinian refugees and their future in innovative ways. This paper moves away from "objective" solutions which ostensibly emanate from scientific procedure or purely moral tenets, seeks to address links between identity and return, and sketches a formula which is informed by these sensibilities and follows the political course which they engender.

The details of the formula are important in one sense and less so in another. They are important inasmuch as time has come for the debate on Palestinian refugees to move beyond abstractions and clichés and to become de-mystified and de-mythologized.[53] Hammering out details thus assumes both philosophical and tactical considerations. Since moral tenets and the practical considerations which they engender are fragile, and tend to be eclipsed and evaporate when politicians begin bargaining, practical details should be there as the flesh that holds the skeleton together, preventing its distortion.

In another sense, however, the practical details and principles presented here *per se* are less important. Attempting to combine a moral stand with attention to practical detail, prevailing legal tenets, political dynamics and, above all, sensibilities which emanate from issues of identity on both sides is a daunting task. It can only progress as a synergetic process. In this sense this paper, which has already benefited substantially from input by Palestinian, Israeli and other colleagues, is but a draft. Its analytical premises and the concomitant measures it suggests should and will be modified.

---

53 Cf. Lustick/Lesch, see note 44, 14.

Negotiations

The Arab States and the Refugee Issue: A Retrospective View

Jalal Al Husseini

I. Introduction

This chapter aims at defining the Arab states' position with regard to the Palestinian refugee question. It will focus on the states neighbouring Israel that are the Palestinian's main host states, namely: Jordan, Lebanon, and Syria.[1] In the past few years, several studies have been devoted to the living conditions and the legal status of the refugees in each of these states.[2] However, little attention has been paid to their possible roles within the framework of the permanent-status negotiations on the refugee issue. Yet, before implementation, any peace agreement will

---

1 According to the PLO Department of Refugee Affairs, in 1999 the total number of Palestinian refugees worldwide amounted to 5.2 million (1.8 million resided in Jordan, 0.38 million in Lebanon and 0.4 million in Syria). 3.6 million were registered with the United Nations Relief and Works Agency for Palestine Refugees in the Near East (UNRWA). *The Palestinian Refugees Factfile*. Department of Refugee Affairs (PLO), Jerusalem/Ramallah, April 2000. The number of refugees currently registered with UNRWA amounts to 4.2 million, 62.1 per cent of whom are registered in the Arab states, outside Palestine: 42 per cent in Jordan; 9 per cent in Lebanon and 10 per cent in Syria. See: UNRWA, *Figures as of 31 December 2004*, Public Information Office, UNRWA Headquarters (Gaza), April 2005.

2 See E. Zureik, *Palestinian Refugees and the Peace Process*, 1996; L. Takkenberg, *The Status of Palestinian Refugees in International Law*, 1998; *Constructing order: Palestinian Adaptations to Refugee Life*, (coll.), FAFO Report 236, 1997, 19 et seq.; and B. Kodmani-Darwish, *La diaspora palestinienne*, 1997. Most of these studies highlight the more or less unsatisfactory situation of the Palestinian refugees in the Arab host countries.

necessarily need to be agreed upon by these states, and, therefore take their political and socioeconomic interests into account.

However, Arab leaders, individually or under the aegis of the Arab League, have usually limited their declarations to public endorsements of the right of refugees to return to their homes, as formulated in Resolution 194 (III) of the United Nations General Assembly (UNGA), thus keeping in line with the refugees' creed since 1948.[3]

This chapter endeavours to show that in practice, specific state interests linked to the preservation of internal stability, from either political or socioeconomic perspectives, have been instrumental in guiding policy since 1948. This trend will prevail in the future, once the Arab states are included in, or impose themselves on the peace process.

II. The Roots of the Arab States' Position Regarding the Palestinian Refugee Question (1948-1950)

1. From Return to Resettlement[4]

Shortly after the signing of the first armistice agreements that put an end to the first Arab-Israeli war,[5] the United Nations Conciliation

---

3 Interpreted by the refugees as a legitimisation of their right of return, paragraph 11 of this resolution adopted in December 1948, resolves that: "... the refugees wishing to return to their homes and live at peace with their neighbours should be permitted to do so at the earliest practicable date, and that compensation should be paid for the property of those choosing not to return and for loss of or damage to property which, under principles of international law or in equity, should be made good by the governments or authorities responsible."

4 A/RES/393 (V) of 8 December 1950, para. 4 defined the UN's strategy regarding the refugee issue by promoting the "reintegration of the refugees in the economic life of the Near East either through repatriation of resettlement." The resettlement schemes conducted by UNRWA until the mid-1950s aimed at settling permanently the refugees in their first host state or at helping them emigrate to other states, be it in the Near East or elsewhere. In this report, I will use the word "resettlement" as meaning either permanent settlement in the first host state or in third states.

5 Israel signed armistice agreements with Egypt on 24 February 1949, with Lebanon on 23 March 1949, with Jordan on 3 April 1949 and with Syria on 20 July 1949.

Commission for Palestine (UNCCP) organised a peace conference in Lausanne, Switzerland. The major issues that were to be discussed at Lausanne between April and September 1949 sealed the fate of over 700,000 "Arab refugees from Palestine" who had left their homes – be it through direct or indirect use of force – and who have thus far not been allowed to return to their former homes.

The Lausanne Conference offers a clear example of the Arab states' ambiguous perceptions and positions towards the Palestinian refugee question. At an Arab League meeting held shortly before the beginning the Conference, Arab governments maintained a unified stance that reflected the opinion of the overwhelming majority of the refugees and of their own populations. Resolution 231 of the Arab League of 17 March 1949 stated that:

> "The Council considers that the lasting and just solution of the problem of the refugees would be their repatriation and the safeguarding of all their rights to their properties, lives and liberty, and that these should be guaranteed by the United Nations."

The Arab consensus on a quick repatriation of the refugees (prior to any Arab-Israeli peace agreement) was asserted again at the beginning of the Conference. In early May, the Arab delegations decided to shelve their political differences so as to appear as one single entity at the negotiations.[6] Their proposals regarding the refugee issue went beyond the mere reassertion of the right of return; several memoranda sent to the UNCCP from May to September 1949 also tackled the modalities of implementation.[7] Also broaching the issue of compensation for those

---

[6] This refers mainly to the differences between Jordan, which sought to annex the West Bank of the Jordan River and to secure access to the Mediterranean Sea, and Egypt, that opposed Jordan's designs. Following informal talks, the delegations agreed that Jordan would postpone its territorial claims, while Egypt committed itself to lend its support to the Jordanian claims at any appropriate time. See "E. Sasson (Lausanne) to M. Sharet", 8 May 1949, in: Israel State Archives (ISA), *Documents on the Foreign Policy of Israel*, May-December 1949, 1949 (companion volume), No. 12, 10 et seq.

[7] The Arab states suggested on 18 May that repatriation schemes should firstly benefit the main Arab economic actors in Palestine, namely the landowners and their personnel, the religious authorities and all those refugees eligible for family reunification schemes. A week later, they demanded the immediate repatriation of all those refugees who lived in the regions of Palestine attributed to the Arab State in the Partition Plan (A/RES/181 (II) of 29 November 1947, in addition to Israeli defense force withdrawal from these regions. See "Editorial note: Memorandum on the refugees by the Arab delegations and by the

refugees who would decide not to be repatriated (and who would thus be resettled), the Arab delegations suggested that compensation be paid in kind under the form of territorial transfer. The territories transferred were to be large enough to host the bulk of the refugees.[8]

However, behind these shared stands, each Arab delegation pursued individualistic strategies, defined by specific political and socioeconomic interests. These strategies undermined in many ways the relevance of the right of return in the eyes of some of the UNCCP members, namely: the United States, France and Turkey.

On 9 May 1949, the Syrian delegation secretly informed the French member of the UNCCP that it would accept to resettle up to 250,000 refugees, i.e. three times the estimated number of Palestinian refugees residing at that time in Syria.[9] It was also ready to conclude a separate peace treaty with Israel in exchange for territorial compensations in Galilee and international aid packages.[10]

King Abdallah of Jordan had from the outset expressed his utmost interest in the economic and political opportunities deriving from an agreement with Israel. Such an agreement would enable him to achieve his territorial designs, namely secure access to the Mediterranean and annex the West Bank of the River Jordan.[11] Resettlement schemes – and

Conciliation Commission", in: ISA 1949 (companion volume), No.26; and "W. Eytan to C. de Boisanger", 25 May 1949, in: ISA 1949 (companion volume), No. 35, 27; and "Third Progress Report [of the CCP]" (A/RES/927), 21 June 1949, para. 17.

[8] Proposal put forward on 15 August 1949. See "Fourth Progress Report [of the CCP]" (A/RES/992), 22 September 1949, para. 10.

[9] In September 1949, the Economic Survey Mission of the United Nations (ESM) estimated the refugee population in Syria at about 75,000. Gaza's refugee population was estimated at 200,000; Iraq's at 4,000; Jordan's at 70,000; Lebanon at 97,000; and the West Bank of the Jordan River at 280,000. See "First Interim Report of U.N. Survey Mission for Middle East" (A/RES/1106), 17 November 1949, 1 et seq.

[10] On the Syrian resettlement designs (as promoted by Zaïm, the French-speaking Syrian leader and France), see "Meeting: M. Fischer – R. Busson (Paris, 3 June 1949)", in: ISA 1949 (companion volume), No. 54, 91. On Syria's territorial and financial claims, see: "The Minister in Switzerland (Vincent) to the Secretary of State", 9 May 1949, in: *Foreign Relations of the United States (FRUS)* 1949, Vol. VI, 989; and "Sasson (Lausanne) to M. Sharett", 8 August 1949, in: ISA 1949 (companion volume), No. 188, 113 et seq.

[11] Jordan's territorial claims were presented throughout and after the Lausanne Conference by the Jordanian representatives; see for example: "The

the flow of financial and technical assistance that such schemes necessitated – were also likely to boost the state's rudimentary economy.[12] In July 1949, the Jordanian delegation informed the UNCCP and the Israelis of its intention to resettle about 200,000 refugees, provided substantial financial aid was obtained from the United Kingdom.[13]

Even Egypt, whose delegation had staunchly rejected any resettlement scheme on its territory on account of the limited absorption capacity of its economy, hinted that it could revise its position, provided there were border arrangements with Israel and international financial and technical assistance.[14]

Such Arab focus on resettlement did not only result from opportunistic calculations in terms of economic and territorial gains. It also stemmed from the assessment of their situation in the wake of the 1948 War. Israel, with whom most of them had already concluded armistice agreements, had – at least temporarily – imposed itself as a major actor in the Near East, and time was not ripe for revenge. Aware of their military state of inferiority and concerned by a possible future war of expansion by Israel, Jordan, Egypt and Syria even tried to prevent, as early as 1949, refugee infiltration into Israel.[15] Security concerns also stemmed

---

Minister in Lebanon (Pinkerton) to the Secretary of State", 1 October 1949, in: *FRUS* 1949, Vol. VI, 1416.

12 See "Memorandum by the Coordinator on Palestine Refugee Matters (Mc Ghee) to the Secretary of State", 22 April 1949, in: *FRUS* 1949, Vol. VI, 935 et seq. All the members of the Jordanian government did not share the King's views. Doubts were raised as to whether Jordan would be able to absorb, from an economic and political perspective, such a number of refugees. Besides, Jordan had no assurances that Israel would accept its territorial claims. See S. Mishal, *West Bank/East Bank – The Palestinians in Jordan, 1947-1967*, 1978, 27 et seq.

13 See "E. Sasson (Lausanne) to M. Sharett", 4 July 1949, in: ISA 1949 (companion volume), No. 121, 64.

14 See "Forth report [of the UNCCP] on the evolution of the situation" (A/RES/992), 22 September 1949, para. 10. The Egyptian territorial claims were very clearly put forward by the Egyptian delegate, Abdel Mu'min, to his Israeli counterpart, E. Sasson. They include the South of the Negev and the enlargement of the Gaza Strip until the Beersheba-Majdal (Ashqelon) line. See "E. Sasson (Lausanne) to M. Sharett", 4 August 1949, in: ISA 1949 (companion volume), No. 178, 106.

15 On that, see for instance A. Plascov, *The Palestinian Refugees in Jordan 1948-1957*, 1981, 73 et seq. and 87 et seq.; Y. Sayigh, *Armed Struggle and the*

from internal security matters. The mass arrival of hundred of thousands of refugees was viewed as likely to foster socioeconomic and political instability; all the more as the local regimes were already discredited by their military defeat and rumors of collaboration with Israel during the 1948 conflict. The United States added to the Arab host states' fears by waving the threat of a possible exploitation by the USSR of any situation of turmoil in the Near East.[16]

In private discussions, Arab leaders also questioned the refugees' claims for return. Thus, the Egyptian delegation at Lausanne confided to Western delegations that few refugees would agree to return in regions now under Israeli sovereignty, even if they were given the choice to do so. Resettlement was therefore the only solution, but preferably outside Egyptian territory.[17] Sociological explanations were also put forward by Arab delegations to explain the relevance of resettlement for the most destitute refugees, i.e. the (former) farmers. As W. Eytan, then a member of the Israeli delegation recounted after an informal meeting with the Jordanian Minister of Foreign Affairs, Fawzi al-Mulki:

> "Is preference to be given to town-dwellers or to state folk? On these questions Transjordan (or at any rate Mulki) has clear-cut notions. Preference should go to property owners. If a man owns land or a house, he has something to attach him to his place of origin ... On the other hand, a penniless peasant is the same everywhere; it makes no difference to him whether he ploughs a field in Israel or in Transjordan. For this reason, according to the Transjordan idea, property-owners have prior claim to repatriation, and Mulki added that he was sure they were also the most desirable and stable element from our point of view ... My impression was that Mulki

---

Search for State – The Palestinian National Movement, 1949-1993, 1997, 58 et seq.

16 For a US appraisal of the USSR's influence in the region, see "Policy Statement Prepared in the Office of Near Eastern Affairs", 28 December 1950, in: *FRUS* 1950, Vol.V, 272.

17 See "The Secretary of State to the Embassy in Egypt", 25 June 1949, in: *FRUS* 1949, Vol. VI, 1181. A few years later, in 1955, Nasser declared to American diplomats that most refugees would not wish to return to Israel, if they saw the living conditions of the Arabs who lived there. He also revealed that it would be very difficult for any Arab leader to take a stance that would deprive the refugees from their right of return; see: "Telegram From the Embassy in Egypt to the Department of State", in: *FRUS* 1955-1957, Vol. XIV, 807.

would be perfectly satisfied if nobody except the landowners were repatriated."[18]

The question as to whether Mulki's opinions were prevalent amongst the Jordanian or the Arab delegations present at the Lausanne Conference is a moot point. What is more important is the extent to which those opinions may have reinforced Israel's reluctance to deal with the issue of the return of the "Arab refugees."

2. Towards Controlled Resettlement

None of the proposals put forward by the Arab delegations bore fruit. Snubbing its own negotiators,[19] the Israeli government refused to make any territorial concessions or to abide by the terms of Resolution 194 (III). It put forward two "peace proposals" in May and July 1949 consisting first in the annexation of the Gaza Strip and the taking in charge of its 200,000 refugees, and second in the repatriation within Israel's borders of 100,000 refugees in accordance to the needs of the Israeli economy. Both proposals were rejected by the Arab delegations and by the UNCCP for not being in accordance with the provisions of Resolution 194 (III).[20]

Israel's intransigence placed Arab governments in a delicate position *vis-à-vis* the refugees and public opinion at large. Indeed, how to sell the principle of refugee resettlement, to which Arab opinion was violently opposed, without any Israeli compensation in exchange? Ulti-

---

[18] In: "W. Eytan to M. Sharett", 1 July 1949, in: ISA 1949 (companion volume), No. 113, 193.

[19] E. Sasson, the Israeli delegate in charge of the informal talks with the Arab delegations, ascribed the failure of the Lausanne Conference to the uncompromising stand adopted by the Israeli government: "Firstly, the Jews believe that it is possible to achieve peace without paying any price, maximal or minimal. They want to achieve a) Arab surrender of all the areas occupied today by Israel, b) Arab agreement to absorb all the refugees in the neighbouring states, c) Arab agreement to rectification of the present frontiers in the center, south and Jerusalem area in favour of Israel only;" see "E. Sasson (Lausanne) to S. Divon", 16 June 1949, in: ISA 1949 (companion volume), No. 81, 47 et seq.

[20] "Note by the Conciliation Commission to the Israeli Delegation in Lausanne", 12 September 1949, in: ISA 1949 (companion volume), No. 281, 456.

mately, as the US Ambassador to Lebanon reported, the Arab governments' legitimacy was at stake:

> "Opinion in Arab states remains so violently opposed to the abandonment of rights of refugees to repatriation in Palestine that contemplation by governments of settling them elsewhere would likely make governments shaky."[21]

In such a context, Arab strategy consisted in politicising the humanitarian assistance approach adopted by the UNCCP at the end of the Lausanne Conference.

By September 1949, the Commission had abandoned its efforts to find a solution based on Resolution 194 (III). Instead, it established the Economic Survey Mission (ESM) with a view to studying the means of enabling the host governments to overcome economic dislocations created by the presence of refugees.[22] The ESM's interim report (September 1949) recommended the following: rather than remaining objects of charity, idle refugees were to be given an opportunity to go to work where they were. The UN was thus to organise, simultaneously with relief aid, a programme of public works in cooperation with the local governments that would gradually absorb the refugees in the host economies. As the refugees were resettled, the relief assistance programme would be reduced, and the 60 camps that hosted about one third of the registered refugees dismantled.[23] In order to persuade the host states into accepting the ESM programme, the United States – the programme's main financial supporter – promised that the development schemes would benefit not only the refugee population, but also the host state's entire population.[24]

On the basis of the ESM's interim report, the United States, Great Britain, France and Turkey drafted a resolution that was presented before the UNGA Special Political Committee (UNSPC) in December 1949. The draft resolution aimed at creating a non-political temporary agency,

---

21 See "The Minister in Lebanon (Pinkerton) to the Secretary of State", 18 October 1949, in: *FRUS* 1949, Vol. VI, 1442 et seq.

22 See "First Interim Report of the U.N. Survey Mission for Middle East", see note 9.

23 The ESM was also supposed to facilitate repatriation. It did not do so, probably "because Israel will not admit them," *idem.*

24 Refer to the "Mc Ghee plan" in: "Memorandum by the Coordinator on Palestine Refugee Matters (Mc Ghee) to the Secretary of State", see note 12, 935 et seq.

the Near East Relief and Works Agency (NERWA), which would implement the recommended relief and public works programmes in collaboration with the host governments concerned, i.e. Egypt in the Gaza Strip, Jordan, Lebanon and Syria. It was also to consult with these governments concerning measures to be taken by them when international assistance was no longer available.[25]

During the discussions that preceded the adoption of the draft resolution, the Arab states, whose cooperation was a prerequisite for implementation, were able to impose their views concerning the new Agency's mandate. Their amendments to the draft resolution highlighted their political and socioeconomic concerns and interests with regard to the Palestinian refugee issue. The final, amended, resolution (General Assembly Resolution 302 (IV) of 8 December 1949) was to set the legal framework within which the debate around that issue would be dealt with in the following decades.

a. The Necessary Public Emphasis on UN Involvement

Arguing that they had not required any assistance, the Arab states suggested that the new Agency's affiliation with the United Nations be clearly mentioned. They thus proposed that the NERWA be renamed "United Nations Relief and Works Agency for Palestine Refugees in the Near East" (UNRWA).[26] This emphasis on the centrality of the UN's role, and in particular the Western powers, also reflected the Arab creed that the international community was responsible for the creation of the refugee problem given its direct involvement in the creation of the State of Israel in November 1947.

b. The Link between UNRWA's Mandate and Resolution 194 (III)

Whereas the draft resolution only mentioned Resolution 194 (III) in its preamble, the Egyptian amendment insisted that the final resolution

---

[25] See "United States of America, France, United Kingdom of Great Britain and Northern Ireland, and Turkey: draft resolution", 1 December 1949 (A/RES/AC.31/L.46/Rev.1), para. 7.

[26] See "Egypt: amendment to the draft resolution presented by the United States…" (A/RES/AC.31/L.48/Rev.1), 2 December 1949, para. 4; see also the discourse by the Iraqi delegate at the 4th session of the Special Political Committee (A/RES/1060, A/RES/1060/Add.1, A/RES/1106), para. 117.

stipulate that the new international assistance programme would not be prejudicial to the provisions of Resolution 194 (III) (para. 5 of Resolution 302 (IV)). It also insisted the resolution include a paragraph directing "*UNRWA to consult with the UNCCP in the best interests of their respective tasks, with particular reference to paragraph 11 of General Assembly resolution 194 (III) of 11 December 1948*" (para. 20 of Resolution 302 (IV)).[27] By adopting this resolution, the UN endorsed implicitly the principle that the refugee communities had been stressing since their exodus, namely that international assistance was not a mere temporary assistance venture, but a recognition of their status as refugees endowed with the right to return to their homes. This formal link established in Resolution 302 (IV) between Resolution 194 (III) and international assistance, has turned for the refugees the latter into a legal (temporary) entitlement.

c. Controlling the Modalities of UNRWA's Mandate's Implementation

The Egyptian amendment also sought to give the host states the opportunity to control UNRWA's activities. It provided that UNRWA's Director and Advisory Committee should consult with each Near Eastern Government concerned in the selection, planning and execution of the projects (para. 8 of Resolution 302 (IV)).[28]

d. Perpetuating the Temporary

The Egyptian proposal modified the draft resolution's stipulation that the direct relief programme should be terminated no later than 31 December 1950. In charge of such direct relief programmes until late 1948, the local host authorities had conspicuously failed to meet the operational and socioeconomic challenges posed by having to cater to hundreds of thousands of destitute refugees. In late 1948, the United Nations had taken over, setting up UN Relief for Palestine Refugees (UNRPR), whose task was to purchase relief and medical supplies and hand them over to three international voluntary agencies based in the

---

[27] Ibid., paras 1, 2 and 7.

[28] Ibid., para. 5. The Advisory Committee consisted of representatives of the United States, the United Kingdom, France, Turkey and three other western states. Its mission was to advise and assist UNRWA's Director (para. 8, Resolution 302 (IV)).

field. In turn, these agencies were in charge of distributing the humanitarian supplies to the refugees.[29] The host states' role became to help the voluntary agencies accomplish their mission by providing campsites, guaranteeing security in those camps, facilitating transportation of goods, etc. Clearly, they were not ready to assume the politically sensitive and financially burdening relief distribution scheme. The Egyptian amendment thus introduced a new clause mentioning that the termination of international relief assistance might occur "*unless otherwise determined by the General Assembly at its fifth regular session*" (para. 6 of Resolution 302 (IV)).[30] Therein lay the basis for possible extensions of the international relief programme. Until the late 1960s, relief and social services even remained the main item in UNRWA's budget, followed by education and health services.

Resolution 302 (IV) gave the Arab host states the opportunity to achieve two seemingly contradictory objectives. On the one hand, the international development assistance programmes conducted by UNRWA could possibly boost their deteriorated economies, thus reducing threats to the internal stability. At minimum, by taking responsibility for the refugees' basic needs, UNRWA's services would cushion the negative impact of the refugees' burden on the economy. This explains why even Lebanon, whose authorities kept warning against any resettlement option on its territory, voted in favour of UNRWA's mandate. On the other hand, Resolution 302 (IV) kept alive the right of return as embodied in UNGA Resolution 194 (III) on the UN agenda, despite the demise of the UNCCP.[31] This allowed the Arab states to

---

29 The three agencies were the International Committee of the Red Cross (in territories now covering Israel and the West Bank), the League of the Red Cross Societies (in Jordan, Syria and Lebanon) and the American Friends Service Committee (Quakers) in the Gaza Strip.

30 See "Egypt: amendment to the draft resolution presented by the United States...", see note 26, para. 6.

31 Following the Lausanne Conference, the Commission organised another round of inconclusive peace negotiations conferences in Paris (1951) and took a few other peace-making initiatives, such as the (failed) mediation mission of its "representative" Joseph Johnson in 1961. More significantly, it created an office which was given the responsibility of making such arrangements necessary for the assessment and payment of compensation in pursuance of paragraph 11 of UNGA Resolution 194 (III). From 1955 until 1964, the office studied and established the scope and value of Palestinian property losses and identified the owner(s) of every plot of Arab-owned land in that portion of Palestine that became Israel as of 14 May 1948. Yet, the 453,000 documents attesting to lost

appear as the genuine representatives of the socioeconomic and political interests of the refugees. Until the 1960s this role would be all the more easy to perform as the Palestinian political elite, as represented before 1948 by Hajj Amin al-Husseini's Higher Arab Committee and other competing political groups, was discredited and marginalised on the Arab political scene.

III. Managing the Return/Resettlement Dilemma (1950-1993)

1. Ambivalent Resettlement (1950-1955)

The strategy pursued by the Arab states in the years that followed the creation of UNRWA was shaped by three major dilemmas:

Internal stability dilemma: how to use international aid through UNRWA without giving the impression of giving up on the right of return and thus trigger political instability?

Development versus relief services dilemma: how to promote UNRWA's ambitious developmental schemes (except for Lebanon), while retaining access to its basic (or regular) services?

National sovereignty dilemma: how to benefit from UNRWA's development schemes without undermining the host states' national sovereignty? For Jordan, who was to annex the West Bank of the River Jordan and grant citizenship to the refugees, another dilemma lay ahead. However, the following question remained: how to turn refugees into fully-fledged Jordanian citizens while retaining their status as "UNRWA refugees?" In 1953, the Agency's Acting Director himself (L.J. Carver) highlighted the incongruity of the situation in Jordan:

> "There is something incongruous in the presence of an alien organization ... furnishing the basic necessities for a large proportion of the population of a state, particularly when – as in the commendable

Arab property were never put to use by the UNCCP or any other body as part of a compensation regime. Since 1964, the UNCCP has not accomplished any substantial work. Although its mandate was never terminated – it usually meets once a year – it has become the symbol of the UN's incapacity to resolve the Arab-Israeli dispute.

case of Jordan – the refugees have been made full citizens of the State."[32]

These dilemmas led the Arab states to strike a balance between their state-interests for economic development and political stability on the one hand, and their symbolic commitment to the refugees' rights to return on the other.

At the normative level, the first Arab League resolution on UNRWA, Resolution 325 of 12 June 1950, recommended ambiguously to the host states that they should cooperate with UNRWA provided "that every State should declare its reservations to the said Agency in respect of the final settlement of the Palestinian problem and the rights of the refugees to return to their homes and to be compensated for their funds and properties." A year later, the UNGA decided to expand UNRWA's development programme so as to include large-scale resettlement projects in the Jordan Valley and the Sinai involving the bulk of Jordan's and the Gaza Strip's camps residents, respectively.[33] The Arab League once again responded hesitantly by accepting in its Resolution 389 of 10 October 1951 this new reorientation of UNRWA's mandate on the condition that the refugees' vested rights to return and be compensated were respected, and that their living standards not be affected negatively. Additionally, the United Nation's responsibility towards the refugees should remain intact pending the implementation of return and compensation. Finally, on 23 September 1952, Resolution 462 of the Arab League defined the operational limits of UNRWA's developmental tasks, by stating that its projects should not embody any stipulation for permanent residence.

At the operational level, the Arab host states resisted UNRWA's pressures to get fully involved in the implementation of the resettlement programmes. Because of its negative implications on the right of return, the very concept of "resettlement" (*tawtin*) even became taboo in their

---

32 In: Report of the Director of the United Nations Relief and Works Agency for Palestinian Refugees in the Near East (Director of UNRWA), 1 July 1952-30 June 1953, Suppl. No. 13 (A/2470), para. 18.

33 The Jordan Valley/Yarmouk agricultural project, concluded by an agreement between UNRWA and Jordan in March 1953, was expected to lead to the resettlement of 100,000-150,000 refugees. The Sinai project, about which Egypt and UNRWA signed an agreement in June 1953, was expected to lead to the resettlement of about 70,000 refugees. See "UNRWA Experience with Works Projects and Self-Support Programmes: An historical Summary (1950-1962)", *UNRWA Reviews*, Information paper No. 5, Beirut, September 1962.

official discourse. Fear of internal instability is a key factor to consider in that respect. As the US ambassador to Egypt testified after an Arab League meeting in early 1951:

> "They are of course certain in their own mind that the refugees are not going to get back and that resettlement work must be started ... Politically they do not dare to admit such a possibility and the very word 'resettlement' would be ruinous to their careers."[34]

Refusing direct involvement in UNRWA's resettlement activities first meant resisting the Agency's and its Western supporters' pressures to "enlighten" the refugees, which rested on explaining the virtues of resettlement coupled with reassurances that it would be carried out without any prejudice to the right of return. As the Secretary-General of the Arab League, Azzam Pacha, put it: "As regards enlightening the refugees, he [Azzam Pacha] said that the Arab League could certainly not undertake any such propaganda: the League would be regarded as sold to the Jews and blown sky-high."[35]

The Arab states' lack of cooperation extended to the refusal to grant UNRWA enough physical resources for development; such as land for irrigation works purposes as happened in northern Syria (Jezireh area, between 1952-1954) and in Egypt in the Sinai (1955).[36] They also re-

---

[34] In: "The Ambassador in Egypt (Caffery) to the Department of State", 7 February 1951, in: *FRUS* 1951, Vol.V, 1982, 578. See also the research conducted by Avi Plascov on the basis of Jordan's police secret records: Plascov, see note 15. The study shows how the Jordanian authorities alternatively played the refugees against UNRWA and *vice versa*.

[35] See "Savingram from British Middle East Office (BMEO) to Foreign Office", 12 January 1951, in: *The Arab League: British Documentary Sources 1943-1963*, Vol. 7, 1951-1953, 34 et seq. The same concerns were aired in Syria (see "The Chargé in Lebanon (Bruins) to the Department of State", 31 August 1951, in: *FRUS* 1951, Vol. V, 847) and in Jordan (see "The Chargé in Jordan (Fritzlan) to the Department of State", 3 April 1952, in: *FRUS* 1952-1954, Vol. IX, part 1, 910 et seq.). Among the rare Arab policy-makers who advocated "enlightening the refugees" is Samir Rifa`i (Jordan) who declared to a UK delegation that the Arab League should reeducate the refugees to the idea that they would never be readmitted in Israel; see "Message from the delegation in Amman to the Foreign Office, 15 January 1951", in: *The Arab League: British Documentary Sources 1943-1963*, Vol. 7, 1951-1953, 36.

[36] As reported in UNRWA's annual reports: See Report of the Director of UNRWA, 1 July 1952–30 June 1953, Suppl. No. 12 (A/2470), para. 35; Report of the Director of UNRWA, 1 July 1953–30 June 1954, Suppl. No. 12 (A/2470), para. 35; Report of the Director of UNRWA, 1 July 1953–30 June 1954, Suppl.

frained from associating themselves with UNRWA's highly unpopular measures of thinning out its (inflated) ration lists,[37] and refused persistently to take responsibility for the Agency's regular services (education, health and relief and social services).[38]

The host states resorted to technical or socioeconomic reasons to justify their hands-off policy towards resettlement. However, as recognised by UNRWA itself, the protracted nature of the Arab-Israeli conflict (that was the immediate cause of the Jordan Valley resettlement scheme in 1955) and the refugees' steady opposition to resettlement schemes were the key factors.[39] Indeed, not only did refugee opposition undermine UNRWA's projects in the field, it also heavily influenced the host authorities' level of cooperation. For instance, Egypt's final decision to shelve the Sinai scheme on the ground that the natural resources were already earmarked for national projects, occurred in the wake of the 1955 anti-resettlement demonstration in the Gaza Strip. Likewise, Jordan announced that same year that it would ultimately not participate in a previously agreed to agreement with UNRWA for a massive ration list thinning out campaign after anti-Western demonstrations broke out in cities across the country. In both cases, the demonstrations were organised by opposition parties (the Muslim Brotherhood, the Communist and the Baath parties mainly) with the full involvement of the camp refugees.

By 1955-1956, it appeared clear that the refugees, the camps and UNRWA would remain permanent features of the Near East landscape. According to UNRWA, the number of refugees resettled as of June

---

No.12 (A/2470), para. 35; Report of the Director of UNRWA, 1 July 1954–30 June 1955, Suppl. No. 15 (A/2974), para. 34; Report of the Director of UNRWA, 1 July 1953–30 June 1954, Suppl. No. 12 (A/2470), para. 35; Report of the Director of UNRWA, 1 July 1955–30 June 1956, Suppl. No.14 (A/3212), para. 66.

[37] In August 1950, the number of refugees registered with UNRWA was at about 922,000, while the UN estimated the actual number of eligible refugees at about 748,000. The difference is due to the "false registrations," i.e. unreported deaths, duplication of registration cards, etc.

[38] See "The Chargé in Lebanon (Bruins) to the Department of State", 10 August 1951, in: *FRUS* 1951, Vol. V, 1982, 829 et seq.; "The Problem of the Rectification of the UNRWA Relief Rolls", *UNRWA Reviews*, Information paper No. 6, Beirut, September 1962, 9.

[39] See Report of the Director of UNRWA, 1 July 1954–30 June 1955, Suppl. No. 15 (A/2978), paras 34-35.

1957 – i.e. who had been thinned out of its ration lists following the improvement of their living conditions – stood at 24,000 whereas the number of people registered on its lists exceeded 933,000.[40] It was also clear that in future the Arab host states would not endorse any plan that could be interpreted as undermining the refugees' rights, thus threatening political stability. Devoid of any national leadership that could represent their interests, the refugees had nonetheless proven that their clout with national politics should not be underestimated. As the host authorities had feared from the outset, they could be instrumental – or instrumentalised by opposition parties – in nullifying policies and decisions that they considered at variance with their vested interests, and most particularly with their right of return.

2. No Resettlement/No Return (1959-1993)

By the late 1950s, the Arab host states' stances regarding the Palestinian refugee issue revolved around two main concerns: the preservation of the right of return on the one hand, and the adaptation of the refugees' legal status to the prevailing political and socioeconomic situation.

a. The Preservation of the "Right of Return Discourse"

The Arab official discourse kept in line with the refugees' claims, and centered around the implementation of the right of return and the preservation of UNRWA as a symbol of both the refugees' plight and of the international community's responsibility for implementing Resolution 194 (III). The resettlement programmes, once cautiously promoted, became the official symbol of betrayal for the refugee cause. However, the term "return" has continued to be aired as an empty slogan devoid of any clear reference to the modalities of implementation of return; either as regards the repatriation procedure, or the political regime that might prevail in a recovered Palestine. This contributed to transform the right of return from a concrete, practical procedure of repatriation into a matter of abstract principle of justice and, as is amply evidenced in Palestinian literature, into a myth featuring "return" as a triumphal march towards Palestine. Nevertheless, keeping the right of return alive en-

---

[40] See "UNRWA Experience with Works Projects and Self-Support Programmes: An Historical Summary (1950-1962)", see note 33, 8, 11.

abled the Arab host states to assuage the refugees' frustration and to maintain internal stability while preserving a negotiation chip for possible future negotiations with Israel. It also fit perfectly alongside the interests of a state like Lebanon who opposed the resettlement of the refugees on its soil for specific political and socioeconomic reasons, i.e. power balance between the various religious communities and limited absorptive capacity.

The preservation of the right of return also implied the institutionalisation of UNRWA, whose assistance programmes were increasingly of crucial importance. As UNRWA grew in proportion with the refugee population, it became a pillar of the economy of the host states, enabling them to save the bulk of the funds devoted every year to the refugees' basic needs. One must also take into account the fact that UNRWA became one of the main employers of the Near East, right behind the public sector.[41]

Lack of clarity also marked the Arab definition of resettlement. Whereas the Arab states managed to reach a consensus about the refusal of large-scale programmes, they found it more difficult to hold a unified position on small-scale, individual resettlement, especially when this meant emigration outside the Near East.[42] In January 1954, for instance, the Arab League postponed discussions regarding an offer of the US Congress that decided to admit 2,000 adult Palestinian refugees, before deciding three months later that it was up to the refugees to make up their own minds.[43] Likewise, in November 1954, the Arab League postponed indefinitely a debate around the resettlement of Palestinian refugees in Libya.[44] Finally, in 1959 the United Nations Secretary-General put forward proposals aimed *inter alia* at actively involving the refugees in the socioeconomic development of the Middle East at large and the

---

41 The current number of UNRWA employees is about 25,500; UNRWA, see note 1.

42 Since the early 1950s, the Arab states had informed the State Department of the United States that emigration within the Arab world would not be considered as resettlement (see "The Chargé in Lebanon (Bruins) to the Department of State", 10 August 1951, see note 38, 830). A Conference gathering the host states in September 1956 confirmed that approach; see *al-Difâ`*, 12 September 1956, 7.

43 See resolutions of the Arab League No. 708 of 27 January 1954 (R/708/20/8) and 760 of 5 April 1954 (R/760/4/21).

44 Resolution 824 (29 November 1954) of the Arab League (R/824/22/3).

wealthy Gulf states in particular.[45] The Arab League rejected these proposals for they saw them as an indirect means of depopulating the camps and burying the right of return. It also argued that the socioeconomic development of the region should not be linked to the settlement of the refugee issue.[46] On their part, the 45 representatives of nine refugee organisations based in Lebanon also rejected the proposals, although they warned that UNRWA had already started implementing them on a small scale.[47] However, these initial fears quickly subsided. Since the departure rate remained much lower than the birth rate, individual emigration did not threaten the existence of the camps. Even more, it became an important source of income. The remittances sent by the emigrants (mostly teachers and vocational workers) to their relatives in cash and in kind became a mainstay of the "refugee economy" and contributed to the consolidation of the camps.[48] The emigration process also benefited the PLO, whose funding would be largely secured by the Palestinian communities living in those states until the late eighties.[49]

With the emergence of the PLO as a fully-fledged actor on the international scene in the mid-1970s, the Arab host states' political role as promoters of the refugees' rights lost a great deal of its significance. The PLO, as the sole legitimate representative, managed to politicise the refugee question by turning it from an individual matter into the collec-

---

[45] The Secretary-General recommended that US$ 1.7 billion be gathered so as to employ up to 500,000 refugees by 1970. That plan was embedded within a larger US$ 12 billion Middle-East development programme targeting the Middle-East region at large. See "Proposals for the Continuation of United Nations Assistance to Palestine Refugees" (A/4121), 15 June 1959.

[46] See: Recommendations by the Committee of Arab Experts to the Proposals of the U.N. Secretary-General Regarding the Continuation of U.N. Assistance to the Palestine Refugees; M. Khalil (ed.), *The Arab States and the Arab League: A Documentary Record, Vol. II, International Affairs*, 1962, 654 et seq.

[47] See "The refugees of Lebanon reject the Hammarskjoeld recommendations", *al-Difâ`*, 13 July 1959, 1.

[48] See H. Elnajjar, "Planned Emigration: The Palestinian Case", *International Migration Review* 27 (1993), 34 et seq.

[49] For example, from the late 1960s to the late 1980s the Kuwaiti government collected 5 per cent of its Palestinian employees' salaries as a "liberation tax" which was then given to the Palestinian National Fund; similar taxes were also directly levied by the PLO where it was able to do so, such as in Lebanon in the 1970s.

tive, national right of the Palestinian people.[50] The UN arguably acknowledged this achievement when the General Assembly reaffirmed within Resolution 3236 (XXIX) of 22 November 1974, "*the inalienable rights of the Palestinians to return to their homes and property from which they have been uprooted, and calls for their return*" (para. 1 b). In the field, however, the emergence of the PLO has, at times, led the host states to tame or fight it (for instance in Jordan 1970-1971) and to tightly control the refugee communities.

The advent of the first *Intifada* enabled the PLO to establish for good its political preeminence on the Palestinian political scene. Cashing in on the severance of Jordan's administrative links with the West Bank in July 1988 and the Declaration by the Palestinian National Congress of a Palestinian State in the Occupied Territories in November 1988, it asserted its stature as a pre-state body. Since then, the Arab states have usually publicly supported the PLO's efforts to end occupation and achieve statehood. They have also called repeatedly for the implementation of Resolution 194 (III), though remaining unclear about the modalities of its implementation.

b. The Legal Status of the Refugees in the Host States

Ever since the early 1950s, the Arab League has tried to ensure, through numerous resolutions, that the Palestinian refugees would be given treatment on a par with the citizens of the host states in such socioeconomic fields as employment, residency, education and free movement. In 1965, these various legal instruments were synthesised in one document, the Casablanca Protocol, which was adopted by the Council of Foreign Ministers of the Arab League.[51] The Protocol however admitted that the Palestinians should retain their original nationality as a means of keeping the Palestinian's right of return alive. With the notable exception of Jordan, whose authorities granted them nationality,[52] the other Arab states have granted refugees special travel documents provided for by the Arab League (Refugee Documents (RDs)).

---

50 See the UNGA Resolution 3237 (XXIX) of 22 November 1974 as well as the Arab Summit Resolution adopted in Rabat on 29 October 1974.

51 See the text of the Protocol in Takkenberg, see note 2, annex 3, 374 et seq.; the book also includes a list of the relevant resolutions adopted by the Arab League since 1952 (370 et seq.).

52 See Article 3 para. 2 of the Jordanian Nationality Law of 1954.

No Arab state has ever fully or consistently implemented the Protocol. As a matter of fact, the Palestinian refugees have generally been subjected to discriminatory legal statuses. The most striking example is Lebanon where, except for a group of about 30,000 wealthy and/or skilled refugees who were offered nationality in the fifties, Palestinian refugees have been subject to laws pertaining to foreigners. Suspended after the conclusion of the "Cairo Accords" between the PLO and the Lebanese authorities in 1969, these discriminatory regulations have been fully enforced with respect to the Palestinians since the nullification of these accords in 1987. By contrast, Syria has been the most equitable towards its Palestinian refugee population, granting it the same rights as its own nationals in the fields of employment, trade and military service, while restricting access to land ownership (to prevent resettlement). Besides feelings of solidarity, Syria's generosity can also be ascribed to the fact that the refugees only amount to a little percentage of the total population. In Lebanon that percentage is higher (11.5 per cent) and its impact on the religious-based constitutional system is far more significant.[53]

The host states have resorted to various excuses to justify their discriminatory attitude, from the absolute necessity of preserving the right of return to the need to protect their fragile political and socioeconomic environments. Since the late 1950s, UNRWA has implicitly given credit to the host states' policies by acknowledging that the host states did not possess the absorptive capacity needed to integrate a refugee population of such magnitudes.[54] The Agency has also praised host states for the assistance they have delivered since the 1950s in terms of the provision of private or state-owned land for campsites, the enforcement of the rule of law in the camps, and the provision of supplementary medical, welfare and educational services (post-preparatory phase). Jordan, the main host state in terms of the number of refugees hosted, has also set up three official camps ("non-UNRWA camps"), where housing is free

[53] According to UNRWA's registration figures (which do not represent the total Palestinian refugee population): 2.7 per cent in Syria, 11.5 per cent in Lebanon, 32.6 per cent in Jordan; 84.5 per cent in the Gaza Strip, and 34.8 per cent in the West Bank (UNRWA, see note 1). The overwhelming majority of the Palestinian refugees are Muslim. For a comprehensive survey of the status of the Palestinian refugees in the Arab states, see Takkenberg, see note 2, ch. IV, 131 et seq.

[54] See: Report of the Commissioner-General of UNRWA, 1 July 1959–30 June 1960, Suppl. No. 14 (A/4478), paras 8-10.

of charge and which are serviced by Jordan.[55] According to official sources, the sums spent by Jordanian authorities on behalf of the refugees, in coordination with UNRWA or on its own, amounted to US$ 365 million in 1999 (US$ 237 per refugee). In comparison, UNRWA's budget for Jordan the same year stood at US$ 75 million (i.e. US$ 49 per refugee).[56]

In light of these developments, one may infer the kind of priorities that will emerge for the host states within the framework of a permanent settlement. The first priority will be to regularise the legal status of those refugees who will resettle permanently. The second priority will be to get compensated for the resettlement programme required and for the taking over of UNRWA's services.

IV. From Oslo to the Future

Given the format of the "Oslo peace process," the Arab host states have been excluded from formal talks on permanent-status issues that were restarted in 1999, including the "1948 refugees" issue. Hence, a strange situation has arisen, whereby decisions affecting host states directly – as regards resettlement for example – could be made at their expense and without their active cooperation. Nevertheless, these states have continued to follow the course of negotiations and to take initiatives so as to anticipate any possible outcome. Thus, their isolation from matters that affect them directly has resulted in a two-pronged response: the international level, i.e. in connection with the development of various

---

55 These governmental camps are the Al Hassan or Al Nasser camp in the Amman governorate; the Madaba camp in the Madaba governorate; and the Sukhneh Camp in the Zarqa governorate. The Jordanian authorities have set up camps for the 1967 displaced people. However, neither UNRWA nor the host authorities recognise administratively as camps several refugee-inhabited locations considered as such by the refugees, such as Bir Zeit, Silwad or Kaddura in the West Bank, Waqqas in Jordan and Yarmouk in Syria.

56 The Department of Palestinian Affairs, *Five Decades of Responsibility in the Refugee Camps of Jordan*, 2000, 62. The host authorities, including the PNA, also contribute little amounts to UNRWA's regular budget. Their contributions for the period 1 January 2000-31 December 2000 amounted to US$ 482,461 (out of a total of US$ 354,850,253). Report of the Commissioner-General of UNRWA, 1 July 2001–30 June 2002, Suppl. No. 13 (A/57/13), Table 10.

peace plans (A), and the internal level, in relation to the legal status of their refugee population (B).

1. The Arab States and the Permanent-Status Settlement

At the pan-Arab level, the Arab League has traditionally adopted resolutions in favour of the right of return. More specifically, it has tried to curb initiatives taken by the Western sponsors of the peace process, aimed at resuming the approach they had failed to implement in the early fifties through resettlement programmes and the reduction of UNRWA's regular programmes. In March 1997, for example, a resolution was adopted rejecting any attempt aimed at detaching that question from its political dimension (i.e. the right of return and to compensation). With that aim in view, it has also pressed for the active involvement of the United Nations in the permanent-status agreement process. The UNCCP and UNRWA were asked to prepare a peace proposal based on UNGA Resolution 194 (III).[57] Such recommendations have continued to be inscribed in various Arab Summit declarations or peace proposals.[58] By referring to Resolution 194 (III) without mentioning the "right of return" *per se*, the Arab League has rehabilitated the long-rejected options of compensation and resettlement as possible alternatives to return. However, this is not to be seen as a betrayal of the PLO's position. Since 1988, the organisation's position has been predicated on the political resolution adopted by the 19th Palestinian National Council (November 1988) that affirmed, without even referring to Resolution 194 (III), the necessity of resolving the refugee issue according to the relevant UN resolutions (para. 6). At the same time, the traditional slogan "the right of return is sacred" has continued to appear regularly in the Arab leaders' discourses, mainly for public-consumption purposes.

---

[57] The Arab press relayed the Arab League's declarations and condemned the "arabisation" of UNRWA that was taking place through the shelving of Resolution 194 (III) and the constant reductions of UNRWA's services. See for instance "The Arab leaders aware of the plot and refuse to 'arabize' the refugees issue….", *Al-Hayat* (Jordan), 29 March 1997, 1.

[58] By the same token, the "Beirut Declaration" concluding the Arab Summit in Beirut in March 2002 called for the "achievement of a just solution to the Palestinian refugee problem to be agreed upon in accordance with UN General Assembly resolution 194."

The timorous evolution in rhetoric has had no impact on the Arab parties' practical vision of how return and compensation could be implemented. The revival of the Palestinian state project in the occupied territories following the outbreak of the first *Intifada* (1987-1994), blurred these concepts even more. Increasingly, moderate voices within the PLO itself have advocated a "realistic" implementation of the right of return, limiting itself to repatriation to the future Palestinian State.[59]

Simultaneously, the host states have responded determinedly to the Western-sponsored mass refugee resettlement plans that surfaced informally in the late nineties parallel to the Israeli-Palestinian talks. According to these plans, most of the refugees would be resettled permanently in their current place of residence or in Europe and North America. Jordan and the PNA and Iraq were to receive extra-refugees from Lebanon, the latter being asked to absorb a reduced refugee population. Israel, on its part, could be asked to repatriate about 100,000 refugees on a humanitarian basis (family reunification schemes).[60]

Despite the large international aid package involved in these plans, the Arab states have refused to back them in public, by advocating instead various political and socioeconomic agendas, including the right of the refugees to return to their homeland.[61] For Jordan, however, its stance does not entail outright rejection of resettlement. Convinced that a regional peace would soon prevail, its leadership has clearly addressed it

---

59 The idea that the right of return should be implemented with flexibility, and mostly as a repatriation process limited to a Palestinian state was first publicly endorsed at the level of the PLO by Salah Khalaf (Abu Iyad), in: S. Khalaf, "Lowering the Sword", *Foreign Policy* 78 (1990), 92 et seq.; and the supplement of this article in the form of an interview by Foreign Policy with Abu Iyad, "Questions and Answers with Abu Iyad", 102 et seq.

60 See for instance D. Arzt, *From Refugees to Citizens: Palestinians at the End of the Arab-Israeli Conflict*, Council of Foreign Relations, 1997; or for a summary of US plans: "American Proposals to Tranfer Lebanon's Palestinians", *Middle East Intelligence Bulletin* 2 (2000); and L. Drake, "The Future of Palestinian Refugees in Lebanon", in: J. Ginat/E.J. Perkins (eds), *The Palestinian Refugees: Old Problems-New Solutions*, 2001, 203 et seq.

61 See for instance "Jordan rejects resettlement of Palestinians", *Jordan Times*, 10 February 2001; or "The Lebanese President: We refused an international offer of US$ 20 billion in exchange for the resettlement of the refugees", *Al-Quds*, 16 August 2000. During the Camp David talks of Summer 2000, compensation funds for host states were articulated, whereby Jordan and the PNA would receive US$ 40 billion each, Syria and Lebanon over US$ 10 billion each.

as a relevant option in the "Wadi Araba" peace treaty with Israel in October 1994. That treaty provided *inter alia* for the implementation of agreed United Nations programmes and other agreed international economic programmes concerning refugees and displaced persons, *including assistance for their settlement* (Article 8 para. 2).[62]

Over the years, Jordan's hopes have been shattered by the many snags in the Israeli-Palestinian peace process; and by the late 1990s, its representatives had joined Syria and Lebanon in condemning any plan aimed at giving away the refugees' rights. Jordanian officials became wary of a scenario where Israeli and the Palestinian negotiators would decide tacitly to keep the refugee issue off the negotiating table, thus imposing unfair and uncompensated resettlement plans on them. Accordingly, they have tried to draw the international community's attention towards their own concerns, thereby claiming their right to represent the Palestinian refugees living on Jordan's soil. As the Prime Minister put in August 2000, referring to the Israeli-Palestinian talks: "We are supporting the Palestinians, but we have Jordanian interests to safeguard, especially [when it comes to] the Palestinians' right to return and to be compensated."[63]

More precisely, Jordan has clearly hinted that, in due time, they would demand compensation for the refugees who would not return, as well as for the State of Jordan. The latter claim would be predicated on three main grounds: the implementation of rehabilitation/resettlement schemes, the taking over of UNRWA's regular services, and in return

---

[62] Emphasis added. Resolving the human problems caused by the conflict in the Middle East was at the core of the peace treaty concluded between Jordan and Israel in October 1994. Among the other means of reaching this end – provided for in the treaty – were action through the Multilateral Working Group on Refugees and bilateral negotiations. One notices that Resolution 194 (III) and the issues of return and compensation are not even mentioned. The opposition political parties have repeatedly denounced the government's projects as resettlement schemes undermining the right of return.

[63] See for instance Jordan's former Prime Minister's statements in "Abou Ragheb: Jordan 'pillar of peace'", *Jordan Times*, 28 August 2000, 1. In future, one may expect a showdown to take place between the Jordanian government and the PLO over the political representation of the refugees residing in Jordan. These refugees are *de jure* Jordanian citizens.

for having hosted refugees and helped UNRWA in its humanitarian duties since 1950.[64]

In future, the Arab states will try to maintain internal stability while securing economic benefits within the framework of a permanent-status peace agreement. However, by adding to his acceptance of the roadmap declaration denying unilaterally the right of return,[65] the Sharon government has reinforced the Arab states' fears of a *de facto* resettlement process. On the more positive side, this threat may in turn foster Arab unity and encourage pan-Arab initiatives aimed at enhancing both the refugees' rights and their own political and socioeconomic state interests.

2. The Arab States and the Legal Status of the Refugees

The Arab League has seemingly abandoned its efforts to guarantee minimal legal protection for the Palestinian refugees in the Arab host states. Its Resolution 5093 of 12 September 1991 has subjected Palestinians to the rules and laws in force in each state. While it is not clear whether that resolution has formally revoked the Casablanca Protocol or not, it has unquestionably weakened the legal obligations embodied in it.[66]

Following the signing of the "Oslo Agreements," the situation of the refugees in the Arab host states deteriorated. Resorting to various excuses, from the preservation of the "right of return" to the maintaining of the Taef Agreements of 1989, the Lebanese policy-makers of all political colours have openly expressed their rejection of any future regu-

---

64 See for instance extracts of Mr. Abu al-Ragheb's statements in *al-Ra'i*, 11 January 2001, 1. Regarding UNRWA, its general fund budget as of 31 December 2004 devoted US$ 76 million for Jordan, US$ 55 million for Lebanon, US$ 28 million for Syria and US$ 164 million for the occupied territories (US$ 57 million in the West Bank and US$ 107 million in Gaza). UNRWA, Figures as of 31 December 2004, Public Information Office, UNRWA Headquarters (Gaza), April 2005, see above note 1.

65 The peace plan devised by the Quartet (the EU, Russia, the UN and the USA) aims at achieving a long-standing peace to the Middle-East conflict by 2005.

66 While A. Shiblak argues that this resolution has officially revoked the Protocol, other analysts, such as L. Takkenberg, have taken the position that an international agreement cannot be nullified by a mere recommendation.

larisation of the Palestinian refugees. In 1994, the Minister of Foreign Affairs even advocated pushing them to emigrate permanently.[67] Meanwhile, the successive Lebanese governments have kept enforcing the legal restrictions against the Palestinian community (discriminating regulations on the job market (over 70 jobs banned), rising university fees, systematic obstruction for the renewal of *laissez-passes*, etc.).[68] The impact of these discriminatory measures has been compounded since the early 1990s by the reduction the PLO's social infrastructure, as well as by UNRWA's austerity measures.

In Jordan, two different trends have occurred. On the one hand, the authorities have decided to improve the camps' infrastructure under the banner of rehabilitation (*ta'hîl*), insisting that this would not prejudice in any way the refugees' right of return. As such, the developmental approach has done nothing but institutionalise an informal phenomenon observable in all the Arab world; since the late 1960s, camp refugees have restored and extended their housing units, while getting better access to water and electricity. The move towards *de facto* "normalisation" of the camps was reinforced by the gradual integration of the refugees in the regional economy of the Arab Middle East. The PLO may have also encouraged self-supporting initiatives by stressing the necessary transformation of the Palestinians' representation: from a destitute collectivity dependent on "international charity" to an active and self-determined people. Although that phenomenon has remained uneven, depending chiefly on the legal status of the refugees in each host state, it has reflected a gradual acceptance of development among the camp-dwellers, provided that the camps preserve their temporary status.

On the other hand, Jordanian nationalist circles, while questioning the refugees' double-identity as "Jordanians-Palestinians," triggered in the

---

[67] See the Lebanese Minister of Foreign Affairs' interview in *al-Safir* (Lebanon) in 1994, as mentioned in: P. Mattar (ed.), *Encyclopedia of Palestine*, 2000, 261. As various sources have it, whereas the number of refugees registered with UNRWA amounts to about 400,000 people (UNRWA, see note 53), the actual number still residing in the state is estimated by various informal sources at around 200,000-300,000.

[68] See H. Khashan, "Palestinian Resettlement in Lebanon: Behind the Debate", Palestinian Refugees (Background Papers), Centre d'études pour le développement (Canada), Alternatives, March 1995, 56 et seq.; and A. Shiblak, "Palestinians in Lebanon and the PLO", *Journal of Refugee Studies* 10 (1997), 270 et seq.

mid-late 1990s an "anti-Palestinianism" or "Jordanian first" campaign.[69] For the camp refugees, however, their major concern stemmed from rumours that the camps would be dismantled, either as a result of unilateral governmental policies or of legal action taken by the original owners of the camp land wanting to restore their rights.[70] Fearing that evacuation of camp refugees would stir up discontent state wide, Jordanian and Palestinian authorities have managed to preserve the *status quo*. Yet, they have so far failed to provide conclusive clarifications regarding the future status of disputed camp land.

The *Intifada al-aksa* has somehow reunited the Jordanians, whatever their origin, in support of the Palestinians' struggle against occupation, and, more particularly, against the possibility of new *en masse* deportations. In late 2002, the Jordanian authorities tried to reinforce this trend by launching a national nation-wide campaign dubbed "Jordan First." One of its main goals was to "*deepen the sense of national identity among citizens and spread a culture of respect and tolerance to integrate and fortify a diverse, but united, national and social fabric that thrives in an atmosphere of justice, democracy...*"[71] The "Jordan First" message also addressed regional powers. By insisting that the state's priorities should emphasise "*the preeminence of Jordan's interests above all other considerations,*"[72] the Jordanian authorities made it clear that under no circumstances would they accept to absorb another wave of refugees, be it from Iraq or from the Palestinian Occupied Territories.

However, it remains to be seen whether the host Arab states will be able to promote their specific internal interests in the face of the pressures that are exerted on them by the international community. For an Israeli-Palestinian agreement on refugees might well include massive resettlement.

---

69 See A. Abu Odeh, *Jordanians, Palestinians & the Hashemite Kingdom in the Middle East Peace Process*, 1999, 235 et seq.

70 The initiatives taken by the owners of the Wihdat and the Hussein camps' land in 1996 and 1998 were brought up in the press; see newspaper *Al-Quds*, 11 February 1998.

71 See "Jordan First national campaign aims to prepare society for a better future", *The Daily Star* (57th Anniversary of Independence Feature Supplement), 27 May 2003, 4.

72 *Idem.*

V. Conclusion

The Israeli governments have regularly accused the Arab host states of using the refugee issue as a political tool against Israel. However, as the chapter has shown, since 1948 host state strategies have reflected various internal concerns regarding political and socioeconomic stability. Accordingly, there has been a discrepancy between the Arabs' discourse, staunchly bent on the strict implementation of Resolution 194 (III), and their practice, which has at times indicated readiness, (in the early 1950s particularly), to compromise on the right of return.

However, due to the protracted nature of the Arab-Israeli conflict, such readiness has never bore fruit. UNRWA's small and large-scale resettlement programmes, which were supposed to durably solve the refugee issue in its humanitarian aspects – and the issue altogether from an Israeli and Western perspective – were shelved as a viable option as of the mid-late fifties. The refugees' refusal of any collective resettlement process, lest that lead to the burial of their hopes of return to their homes, was key in shaping the Arabs states' stances on the issue.

This prompted a two-pronged policy as regards the refugees. On the one hand, Arab host states have tried to keep the right of return alive by numberless public declarations declaring that right is sacred. On the other hand, each one of them has submitted the refugees to a specific legal status that befittingly mirror the interests of their respective economies and political systems. More than anything else, UNRWA embodies the *status quo*. On the one hand, its regular activities have been interpreted by the Arab world as a symbol of the international commitment to solve the refugee issue and the symbol of their plight. On the other, the Agency has played a crucial role as a stabiliser by cushioning the socioeconomic impact of the refugees' presence.

However, the minimal *status quo* that the host states have managed to preserve on the "refugee front" has eroded since the start of the Oslo process. Arabs have been unable to prevent UNRWA's main donors (the United States and Europe) from decreasing their contributions to below an adequate level. Also, excluded from the Israeli-Palestinian permanent-status talks, the Arab states have had to counter numerous formal and informal initiatives aimed at resettling the refugees on their territory with little consideration for their own priorities and aspirations.

The Arab states' weakness stems partly from their inability to display a cogent vision of the core concepts of return, compensation or resettlement. Today, the Arab position boils down to common slogans that seek to reassert the relevance of Resolution 194 (III) and the need to preserve UNRWA. Putting aside the need to solve the refugee issue, one must also take stock of the fact that neither Arab, nor Palestinian detailed settlement plans exist. This may be due to a lack of explicit Palestinian doctrine on the subject; thus, the nature of the future relations that will develop between the refugees (who will remain in the Arab host states) and the State of Palestine remains unclear. Should the refugees be granted, as has been the case in Jordan since the early 1950s, the nationality of the host state? Should they be given a double nationality? Whatever their formal citizenship is, the question still remains as to how to guarantee that the basic human rights of the Palestinians, including full access to education, social services and employment, will be ensured whatever their future place of residence is. These questions are all the more important to consider as they tackle the making of a future Palestinian diaspora, and of the Middle East at large.

The negotiating stance displayed recently by Israel's government that envisages the right of return as a non-starter, or even more insidiously, as a claim to drop in exchange for a Palestinian State, should prompt the Arab states, including the PNA, to coordinate on any matter related to the refugee issue. The relevance of such a "coordinated approach" first stems from the fact that any Israeli-Palestinian accord will need to be agreed upon by the host states before it is implemented. A unified Arab position would also strengthen the Arab parties within the framework of both the interim and post-agreement periods.

Such a "coordinated approach" should be supported by technical discussions aimed at documenting and underpinning the Arabs' claims *vis-à-vis* Israel and the international community. It may also lead the Arab states and the Palestinians to tackle thorny issues that have so far been overlooked for the sake of Arab unity, such as the exact role of the Arab states in the forthcoming Israeli-Palestinian negotiations and, more significantly, the future legal status of the refugees.

The Negotiations for the Settlement of the 1948 Refugees

Menachem Klein

I. Introduction

The following article deals with the PLO and Israeli attempt to solve the question of the Palestinian refugees, an issue that dates back to 1948. In the 1993 Oslo Agreement, both parties agreed to postpone any discussion on this subject until final status negotiations were in sight. To that end, the negotiations that took place in 1999-2001 are key to understanding the refugee issue and shall be analysed herein accordingly.

The article though does not deal with the definition of a refugee. That issue, although highly significant, is replete with economic, legal, social, ideological and political considerations. In other words, who is a refugee, how many refugees are there, what were their losses since 1948 and what may be the cost of these shall not be dealt with herein. It also goes beyond the premise of this work to delve into the financing of the refugees in their present host countries, the manner in which they are settled, their social patterns and whether they are entitled to sue the Israeli government collectively or personally. These issues have to be treated separately, as do concerns over the crystallisation of the refugee consciousness, especially since such issues are burdened by their own considerations, both mythical and political. One cannot, nonetheless, ignore the manner in which these questions have been raised, if in fact they have, during the Israeli-Palestinian final status negotiations. In other words, these questions shall not be addressed herein *per se*, although one cannot entirely ignore the manner in which they have been dealt with in the permanent settlement negotiations.

To that end, this article is not a comparative study of the Israeli-Palestinian peace negotiations juxtaposed alongside similar cases in modern history. Certain issues such as the "package-deal" and any trade-offs between the 1948 Palestinian refugee question and other topics discussed between Israel and the PLO in their final status talks shall not be dealt with herein either. True, these issues must be dealt with in final status talks, as they are interrelated. Yet, in order to comprehensively understand the subject one must bear in mind the whole picture of the negotiations, which explains in part why some topics exceed the boundaries of the following article. Finally, track two talks on the refugee problem, an unofficial form of talks between involved citizens, professionals, activists, public opinion shapers and the like, might well form the basis of a future article. For these perspectives also have a significant impact on the official negotiations.

In any event, only the following questions shall be addressed herein: who are the typical conversing sides at the negotiating tables and who do these people represent; what problematic aspects have been addressed thus far and how were they discussed? What has not been dealt with and what are the limits of past negotiations? What are the tools often employed by negotiators? In what areas has there been progress and in what areas, and to what extent, do irreconcilable differences exist; and why do such differences exist?

II. The Multilateral Talks

The formal question of who on the Arab side will negotiate over the refugee problem remains no less important than the substantive issues themselves. In general, Arab participants in the conflict have long demanded "comprehensive" and "international" peace negotiations, which involve a multilateral negotiating framework (thus enabling Arab parties to pool their collective negotiating resources), that includes participants such as the United Nations, Europeans and former USSR, who are often seen as more sympathetic to Arab aspirations than the United States. Israel, for its part, has long preferred a bilateral negotiating dynamic; as such an approach enables Israel to maintain a position of strength given an accompanying ability to exploit inter-Arab divisions. Israel, of course, has opposed all external involvement other than that of the US.[1]

---

[1] R. Brynen, *Palestinian Refugees and the Middle East Peace Process*, paper prepared for the New Hampshire International Seminar/Yale-Maria Lecture in

Due to its refusal to recognise the PLO as the sole representative of the Palestinian people and its denial of the very existence of the Palestinian national collective, Israel could not implement its bilateral negotiation preference on the refugee issue at the Madrid conference; this 1991 conference structured a multilateral forum to discuss the issue. The multilateral forum, however, suited Israel's standpoint from another perspective. Israel has all long claimed that the refugee problem is about individuals who belong to and fled from various Arab nations during the 1948 War. This Israeli perspective is diametrically opposed to that of the refugees who view themselves as a nation seeking self-determination, a nation that was uprooted by Israel.

However, at the Madrid conference, while Israel agreed to negotiate on the refugee issue, the Arab states no longer patronised the Palestinian case. From an Arab perspective the groundwork had been laid for Israeli-Palestinian bilateral talks. Therefore, Arabs helped the PLO bypass an Israeli veto over the PLO's participation through a Jordanian-Palestinian delegation that did not include official PLO members. The conference established multilateral "working groups" on issues that are common to the region and that "can best be addressed by the concerted effort of the regional parties together with the support of the international community and the resources and expertise that it can provide."[2] The refugee issue was among these issues.

The Refugee Working Group (RWG) was formally initiated in Moscow in January 1992. The RWG focused on seven main themes, each of which was directed by a leading country or "shepherd." The themes were: Data Bases, Family Reunification, Human Resources Development, Job Creation and Vocational Training, Public Health, Child Welfare and Economic and Social Infrastructure. In cooperation with the regional parties, the shepherds were responsible for defining needs, developing responses and mobilising required resources. During the plenary session, each shepherd made a report on the progress achieved under its theme since the last plenary.[3]

Middle East Studies, University of New Hampshire, 3 April 1998, <http://www.arts.mcgill.ca/mepp/mepp.html>.

2 J. Baker, "Opening Comments", opening session of the multilateral track of the peace process, Moscow, 28 January , quoted in Brynen, *idem.*

3 Brynen, *idem.*

From January 1992 to December 1995, there were eight plenary sessions of the RWG. Most of the debates with Israel were on the participants list and on the agenda of the RWG.

Israel boycotted the first full session of the RWG in Ottawa in May 1992. It protested the participation of Palestinian delegation members from outside the West Bank and Gaza Strip. The boycott, however, had little effect. The meeting was held anyway, and in Israel's absence the RWG included family reunification in its agenda. For Israel, "family reunification" seems to touch upon Palestinian demands for a "right of return" – something that Israel has consistently opposed.[4]

With a new Labour government in power, Israel had agreed to participate in the second Ottawa meeting in November 1992. But its participation was delayed by a dispute over participation of the head of the Palestinian delegation, first represented by Elias Sanbar from "outside" Palestine and then by Muhammad Hallaj, who was a member of the Palestine National Council, the PLO's parliamentary body. This difficulty was overcome by a face-saving formula in which Hallaj publicly stated that he was not a member of the PNC at that time.[5] The question of PLO representation was no longer an issue, at least since the third plenary meeting of RWG in May 1993, which witnessed an increased pace of Palestinian-Israeli bilateral negotiation, and which in turn led to the signing of the Oslo Agreement. As a result of the Oslo Agreement, signed in September 1993, the Palestinian delegation has been able to separate itself officially from its Jordanian partner; for example, it was represented by PLO members in the RWG meeting in Tunis, October 1993.[6]

Thus, the remaining impediment was the "family reunification" issue. Jordanians and the Palestinians claim that tens of thousands of Palestinian families have long remained divided because Israel has not approved their application for reunification in the West Bank and Gaza Strip. Moreover, those who did not renew their travelling permit on time in the past, were often refused entry into Israel. Although the debate itself is now over 1967 displaced persons, the discussions on the issue were always shadowed by the debate over principles regarding 1948 refugees.

---

[4] *Idem*; S. Cahana, "Differing and Converging Views on Solving the Palestinian Refugees' Problems", *Davis Papers on Israel's Foreign Policy* 51 (1996), 7 et seq.; and see below.

[5] Cahana, ibid., 9 et seq.

[6] Brynen, see note 1; Cahana, ibid., 13 et seq.

Israel has perpetually insisted on the "resettlement" and "rehabilitation" of refugees in host countries, while its counterparts (Jordan and Egypt) have emphasised the Palestinians' right to compensation and return. Israel eventually recognised the theme of "family reunification," but only as a humanitarian need in the context of discussing practical initiatives for ameliorating the refugees' need in areas such as public health, child welfare, vocational training and job creation.[7] Israel did make a commitment to increase the number of persons permitted to return to the West Bank and Gaza Strip for humanitarian purposes – not exceeding a quota of 6,000 persons, and it reduced the period for processing applications to less than three months as well as to regularise the status of spouses and children whose visitor's permit has expired.[8] Yet, in practice, family reunification continues to encounter serious stumbling blocks.[9]

Another issue in this debate has been Israel's demand to add to the agenda the Jewish refugees from Arab countries. From an Israeli viewpoint, the 1948 War brought about a population exchange. Palestinian refugees have been replaced by the influx of Jewish refugees from North Africa, Yemen, Iraq and other Arab countries. Israel has stated that it will demand compensation for all the havoc, destruction, the loss of life and properties of the Jews who were forced to leave Arab lands due to the Arab-Israeli wars. The Palestinians have responded by suggesting that Israel should raise the issue bilaterally with the respective states just as Palestinians raise the issue while negotiating with Israel.[10] Unfortunately, the May 1996 election of hard-line Israeli Prime Minister Benjamin Netanyahu brought about the consequent deterioration of Palestinian-Israeli negotiations. This fact coupled with increased Israeli settlement activity in the occupied territories led to an Arab League vote in March 1997 that suspended Arab participation in the multilateral talks.[11]

In conclusion, the Madrid peace conference established the multilateral track as a track for professionals who aim to solve technical and practi-

---

7 Brynen, idem; Cahana, ibid., 9, 11 et seq.

8 Cahana, ibid., 19; S. Tamari, *Return Resettlement Repatriation The Future of Palestinian Refugees in the Peace Negotiations*, Final Status Strategic Studies, The Institute for Palestine Studies, 1996.

9 Brynen, see note 1.

10 Cahana, see note 4, 10; Tamari, see note 8.

11 Brynen, see note 1.

cal problems alongside other international actors. However, this track soon became political and left the technical and professional problems unsolved. The multilateral forum nurtured this political debate up until the Oslo 1 Agreement. Since then, the multilateral forum arguably no longer serves either the PLO or Israel, but, rather, serves the interests of several international actors who desire to maintain their involvement in the issues.

III. The 1967 Refugee Problem

The negotiation on the 1967 refugees originated in the 1978 Israeli-Egyptian Camp David accord, which provided for the construction of a quadripartite committee of the parties involved in the 1967 refugee problem, namely: Egypt, Jordan, Israel, and the Palestinians. The denouncement and rejection of the Camp David accords by the Arab world prevented the implementation of such an approach.[12] In the peace process following the Madrid conference, however, the issue was reintroduced into the RWG agenda under the title of "family reunification." The obstacles in achieving substantial progress on this issue brought it into the Israeli-PLO Oslo talks, where it was approved as part of an overall deal that also included the 1948 refugee problems. In 1993, Israel and the PLO agreed to postpone the discussion of the 1948 refugee problem to the permanent status agreement. As for the displaced persons from the West Bank and Gaza Strip in 1967, it was agreed that in principle they should be allowed to return. According to the DOP, a standing committee of the Palestinian Authority, Israel, Egypt and Jordan will be formed in order to decide "on the modalities of admission of persons displaced from the West Bank and Gaza Strip in 1967, together with necessary measures to prevent disruption and disorder."[13]

The Quadripartite Committee first met in Amman in March 1995. In this and other meetings, it soon became apparent that if any progress was to take place at all, it would be slow. Israel had held out for a minimalist definition of a "displaced person" (namely those actually displaced by the fighting in 1967), limiting the term to 200,000-300,000

12 Cahana, see note 4, 3 et seq.

13 See the Palestinian-Israeli Declaration of Principles on Interim Self-Government Authority, reprinted in: M.A. Hadi (ed.), *Documents on Palestine, Vol. 2*, 1997, 145 et seq., 146.

persons. The Arab parties held on to a broader definition (i.e. those who had been registered as West Bank and Gaza Strip residents in 1967, but who were trapped outside these territories when the war broke out, in addition to those who had left the territories after 1967 but who had later been refused readmission by Israel, including deportees, and their descendants), totalling 800,000-1.1 million.[14]

The PLO and the governments of Egypt and Jordan have agreed to conduct a regional registration of the 1967 displaced inhabitants. Such a population census has not been carried out. However, the bilateral Jordanian-Palestinian committee agreed to define as displaced anyone who on 4 June 1967 was officially registered as resident in the West Bank or their descendants.[15] Furthermore, Palestinian leaders have expressed their awareness of the need to coordinate between the return of 1967 displaced persons and the building of infrastructure within areas administrated by the Palestinian Authority, lest systems and public services such as education, health and housing collapse.[16]

IV. The Parties Official Standpoints Before the Official Negotiations

1. Israel

Israel has used two sets of arguments to justify its position. One set is oriented towards the past, while the other leans towards the future. Israel has always maintained that the dispute itself was created as a result of the Arab and Palestinian rejection of the 1947 UN Partition Plan and the subsequent decision by these parties to declare war on the nascent Jewish state. During the war, the Arab states called on the Palestinians to temporarily leave the country and to "return with the victorious

---

14 Brynen, see note 1; Tamari, see note 8; Cahana, see note 4, 23 et seq.

15 *Saut al-Sha`ab*, 27 January 1994.

16 Abu-Mazin, *al-Quds*, 7 January 1994; the political report presented by Abu-Mazin to the 21st PNC, Gaza, April 1996, *al-Quds*, 24 April 1996; E. Sanbar, *Filastin al-Thawra*, 1 May 1994; *al-Sharq al-Awsat*, 8 February 1994; *al-Dustur*, 27 January 1994; *Saut al-Sha`ab*, 27 January 1994. No further step has been taken by the PLO leaders, nor has any policy of absorption been suggested by them (*al-Quds*, 1 January 1997; *Ha'aretz*, 5 March 1995; ibid., 8 March 1995).

Arab armies." Moreover, both Arab states and the Palestinians, according to Israel, are responsible for failing to resolve the issue by absorbing the 1948 refugees in the host countries. Therefore, Israel rejects categorically the right of the refugees to return. Shlomo Gazit puts the Israeli position as following:

> "Israel denies the legality of the Palestinian claim. If it recognises the 'right' of return it would also be admitting responsibility, and perhaps even culpability for creating the problem. But Israel categorically denies any responsibility for the War of 1948. On the contrary, the guilt and responsibility are all Arab-Palestinian ... Israel would deny any responsibility even if there were no practical demands for a 'return' of the refugees; even more so when recognition of such a right would deny Israel the right to control and veto the number of returnees."[17]

Israel argues that UNRWA (the United Nations Relief and Works Agency) statistics on the number of the Palestinian refugees are grossly exaggerated, reflecting interests of local people who desire access to the Agency's services. Considering the 1948 War and its aftermath, one cannot help but notice that the Israeli government uses the case of Jewish refugees from Arab Middle East countries fleeing to Israel in order to take the Arab and Palestinian claims off the table. Israel has continually argued that refugee movements and exchanges of populations are common phenomena in world history, and that Israel itself absorbed nearly 600,000 Jews from Arab countries. Israel expects the Arab states to deal with their 1948 war refugees in the same manner. Israel often points to the period between 1949 and 1967, at which time Israel allowed family reunification, where around 40,000-50,000 refugees returned to Israel, and where several additional thousands returned after 1967; especially since the foundation of the Palestinian Authority in 1994 thousands of PLO political and security apparatus members of 1948 refugee families have returned to PA ruling areas that are part of Historical Palestine. Israel argues that if viewed from this perspective, it is clear that it has fulfilled its 1949 agreement to absorb 100,000 refugees.

In evaluating the option of 1948 refugees' right to return, Israel has argued that the entry of masses of refugees on to its territory would pose a very real existential threat to security, law and order; this says nothing of the fact that Israel's social fabric itself worships the demographic vi-

---

17 Shlomo Gazit qouted in Cahana, see note 4, 60 et seq.

ability of Israel as the world's only Jewish state. Return will create a motivation for a Palestinian irredentism, as the argument goes, in addition to ownership problems over homes, land and villages. The fact is that villages that the refugees left behind in 1948 were destroyed, which also means that homes and properties have long been occupied by Israelis. Therefore, Israel argues that any return is impossible. Israeli "hawks" argue that a mass return to a neighbouring Palestinian state could create a geopolitical threat to Israel. A small Palestinian state with its current massive population and limited resources could not absorb hundreds of thousands of refugees. The fear here is that refugees will gather along the Palestinian border with Israel in order to create a public outcry that would enable them to cross the border and return to their homes. The fear is that allowing a return of masses of 1948 refugees to a Palestinian state limited only to 1967 territories creates a source of destabilisation.

In short, according to Israel's arguments there is no basis for negotiation. The idea of reaching a compromise on the 1948 Palestinian refugee case remains a taboo topic of discussion for the vast majority of the Israelis. Because the 1948 War is perceived as an event of foundation and liberation. The Israelis are afraid that once they admit any responsibility for Palestinian expulsion in 1948, they then lose their moral justification and the right of their state to exist. Many Israelis have trouble even accepting the term "the right of return," as they fear that it is a Palestinian symbol that will prevent the parties from bringing about an end to the conflict. Instead of a permanent agreement that would bring to an end the case of the 1967 refugees, it would open up the case of the 1948 refugees, which was a formative experience for both sides. Furthermore, acceptance of the term "right" grants the right to demand the full realisation of that right, now and in the future. Thus, Israel has not initiated any political tools whatsoever to deal with the refugee problem. Despite Palestinian demands to open up the debate, Israel has sought to close the file altogether. Therefore, the state machinery has not traditionally prepared itself to negotiate on this sensitive issue. However, gradually Israel has agreed to put the issue on the table. Israeli negotiation positions, however, were and still are combined of its remaining taboos.[18]

---

[18] See Brynen, see note 1; J. Alpher/K. Shikaki with the participation of the additional members of the joint working group on Israeli Palestinian relations, "The Palestinian Refugee Problem and the Right of Return", *Middle East Policy* 6 (1998/1999), 167 et seq.

2. The PLO

For Palestinians, the displacement of half of their population from Palestine in 1948 was a defining national moment. For the refugees were forcibly driven from Palestine by the conscious and deliberate policy of a Zionist movement that was explicitly committed to the establishment of a *Jewish* state. Once Palestinians had fled, their lands were seized, and most refugees were prevented from returning. In this view, Israel has been, and continues to be responsible for the process through which the refugee problem was crafted; a process that exerted violence against civilian populations in times of war, followed by expropriation of their lands and homes after it. Therefore, from this flows the belief that Israel must unilaterally acknowledge moral culpability for the injustice of the refugees' expulsion; that is, of course, if Israel truly seeks a reconciliation with the Arabs and if it in turn recognises their coexistence. The basis for a just solution thus lies in the implementation of UN General Assembly Resolution 194. Based on this resolution, the Palestinians insist on the right of the refugees to return to their homes and properties, or, for those who choose not to do so, to accept compensation. Compensation, however, can not replace the recognition of the right of return of all those, and their descendants, who were expelled, forced to leave their homes, displaced, lost land and property during the 1948 and 1967 Wars, and who were not allowed to return to their homes thereafter. All schemes of resettlements in host countries or immigration have thus far been rejected. The resettlement and absorption in a Palestinian state, whose sovereignty is limited to 1967 territories only, cannot be seen as an exercise of the right to return.[19] The PLO though did not hold this stand from the start. In its formative years (1964-1974) the PLO was occupied with rebuilding its national institutions and ideology, and return was defined as a national collective task rather than an individual right. For the PLO the idea of return was not separated from the notion of "liberation." The PLO initially sought to realise the return of refugees after liberating Palestine either by regular Arab armies, as the PLO hoped between 1964-1968, or by its own armed struggle; as eventually the PLO became a vanguard of the Arab armies, a position it has advocated since 1968.[20]

---

[19] Cahana, see note 4, 8; Brynen, *idem*; Alpher/Shikaki, *idem*.

[20] M. Klein, "Between Right and Realisation the PLO Dialectics of 'The Right of Return'", *Journal of Refugee Studies* 11 (1998), 1 et seq.; *idem*, "From a Doctrine-Oriented to a Solution Oriented Policy, The PLO's 'Right of Re-

The first significant change in the PLO's doctrine of liberation occurred in 1974 when the 12th PNC adopted a political programme, which implied that the liberation of Palestine be divided into two consecutive phases.[21] In the first paragraph of its platform, the PLO declared its rejection of UN Security Council Resolution 242, as "it obliterates the patriotic (*wataniyah*) and national (*qawmiyah*) rights of our people and deals with our people's cause as a refugee problem."[22] The programme used the idiom "the right of return" (*Haq al-`Awda*) and put it at the forefront of the PLO's political-ideological "trinity" of "national rights" or "inalienable rights," notably: the rights of return, of self-determination and of establishing an independent state.[23]

Thus, the PLO changed the ideological status of the right of return from an undefined outcome of complete liberation to a necessary means which would assure the liberation. Yet the PLO's 1974 programme was aimed implicitly at Israel's destruction, although later it became the first step in making peace with it. While Resolution 194 conditioned return with living at peace under Israeli sovereignty, the PLO used it as a means of fighting. By demanding to fulfil the right of return, the PLO reaffirmed its commitment to the total liberation of Palestine.[24] Thus, the right of return became an important factor in the PLO's call for recognition given that the Palestinians view themselves as a nation against which an injustice has been inflicted. According to this formula, any rejection of the right of return is tantamount to a denial of Palestinian collective identity, which constitutes yet another form of deportation and expulsion. Contrary to Resolution 194, by advocating the return of individual refugees who wish "to live in peace with their neighbours," the PLO has stood for a national-collective return. More-

---

turn'1964-2000", in: J. Ginat/E.J. Perkins (eds), *The Palestinian Refugees, Old Problems – New Solutions*, 2001, 46 et seq.

21 Y. Lukacs (ed.), *Documents on the Israeli-Palestinian Conflict 1967-1983*, 1984, 157.

22 *Idem.*

23 M. Steinberg, "The PLO's Solution: The Meaning of a Triangular Formula", in: A. Hareven (ed.), *Is There a Solution to the Palestinian Problem? Israeli Positions*, 1982, 151 et seq., in Hebrew; Lukacs, see note 21, 156 et seq.; "The Declaration of Independence of the State of Palestine", *Journal of Palestine Studies* 18 (1989), 214, and *al-Dustur*, 16 November 1988.

24 Klein, "Between Right and Realisation the PLO Dialectics of the 'The Right of Return'", see note 20; *idem*, "From a Doctrine-Oriented to a Solution Oriented Policy, The PLO's 'Right of Return' 1964-2000", see note 20.

over, by declaring that national rights may not be forfeited, the PLO has stood against the option that Resolution 194 gives to 1948 Palestinian refugees to choose between return and compensation.[25] Inasmuch as the PLO's mainstream has reconciled itself with Israel and distinguished between Palestinian self-determination and Israel's right to exist, doubt among its ranks has arisen regarding the relevance of the right of return.[26] During the aforementioned period, PLO leaders displayed four attitudes towards the relevance of the right of return in the context of a political settlement with Israel, namely: utter disregard of the concept, acceptance of Resolution 194 word for word, calling for full realisation of the right of return in a Palestinian state whose borders correspond to those before 1967, and a differential realisation aiming to implement a collective return with the foundation of the Palestinian state over 1967 territories, while the individual one to 1948 borders remains either unfulfilled or as a right to be exercised voluntarily. Each of these options had limits and costs *vis-à-vis* the tension between the classic formula of the right of return, and maximising any chance to achieve acceptance for Palestinians to implement this right. Often PLO leaders expressed more than one of those four attitudes, as well as declaring their commitment to the old 1974 conservative formulation, thereby attempting to establish and maintain a purposely ambiguous stance.[27]

Of the four approaches to the right of return, it should be noted that between disregard and literal acceptance of Resolution 194, literal acceptance became the official attitude expressed by the PLO in its formal documents. The other two options, full realisation of the right of return within a 1967-border-styled Palestinian state and differential realisation, are still informal attitudes expressed privately by senior PLO officials. By emphasising Resolution 194, the PLO leaders can stress their commitment to international legitimacy, the common ground on which they strive to operate politically.

---

25 *Idem.*

26 Sh`un Filastiniyya, 1986, 108-109, 82 et seq.; Klein, "Between Right and Realisation the PLO Dialectics of the 'The Right of Return'", see note 20; *idem*, "From a Doctrine-Oriented to a Solution Oriented Policy, The PLO's 'Right of Return' 1964-2000",see note 20.

27 Klein, *idem.*

a. Utter Disregard and Acceptance of Resolution 194 – the Official References

The right of return is absent from some of the most important statements made by senior PLO officials. It does not appear in Basam Abu-Sharif's June 1988 article about the prospects of a Palestinian-Israeli settlement.[28] Nor did Arafat mention it in his speech to the UN General Assembly in December 1988. Contrary to the documents from the 18th PNC calling for the right of return, where Arafat noted he will inform the UN General Assembly accordingly, Arafat chose to speak only of "the implementation of the Palestinian-Arab people's right to self-determination, political independence and sovereignty on their soil." Arafat's comments ignored the third wing of 1974 formula.[29] Since its inception, the PLO has rejected Resolution 194, which proclaimed the right of each individual Palestinian refugee to choose between return or compensation. The organisation has always claimed that the Palestinian problem is to be treated as a national one, and that therefore a collective return should be realised. Even when the PLO moved forward on its political track, it did not accept Resolution 194 expressly. Thus, the political statement of the 18th PNC expressly invoked the right of return four times in its conservative approach and only then hinted at Resolution 194 by calling for "the question of the Palestinian refugees [to be settled] in accordance with the relevant UN resolutions."[30] Clearly, acceptance of Resolution 194 was declared by the 20th PNC in September 1991, the session in which the PNC confirmed Palestinian participation in the Madrid peace conference.[31] In their efforts to regain international recognition and legitimacy, stemming from Palestinian support for Saddam Hussein's invasion of Kuwait and for Iraq during the 1991 Gulf War, the PLO accepted the invitation to participate in the Madrid conference, and accepted Resolution 194. It should be noted that by allowing the refugees to choose between return and compensation, the PLO situated itself as a mediator, if not as the patron of the way the problem should be solved. Moreover, in choosing to materialise this option, the

---

[28] B. Abu-Sharif, "Prospects of a Palestinian-Israeli Settlement", *Journal of Palestine Studies* 18 (1988), 272 et seq., and in the *Middle East Mirror*, 2 June 1988; *Ha'aretz*, 8 July 1988.

[29] *Journal of Palestine Studies* 18 (1989), 167; *Ha'aretz* 14 December 1988.

[30] *Idem.*

[31] *Journal of Palestine Studies* 21 (1992), 152; *al-Quds*, 29 September 1991.

PLO sees itself as responsible for bringing Israel to accept Resolution 194, which it had totally rejected since 1948.

b. Full Realisation, but only in 1967 Territories and Differential Realisation – the Informal Stance

This policy has two meanings. First, achievement of national independence in the 1967 territories by a fully sovereign Palestinian state may be considered a realisation of the right of return. Secondly, the Palestinians may establish this small entity as the state of all the Palestinians wherever they may be, granting them the automatic right to return.[32] In other words, the complete collective return demanded by the PLO in its formative period is no longer a matter of the whole of Palestine but rather that of total independence.

Contrary to the preceding option, in the differential realisation method the PLO spokespersons distinguished between the collective fulfilment of the right of return and the individual one. The collective realisation lies in the establishment of the Palestinian state according to 1967 borders, while the right to return to 1948 territories remains as an unfulfilled right or as a right to be exercised individually by each Palestinian refugee who chooses to do so.[33]

Until 1998, various opposition groups failed in politically mobilising the dissatisfied refugees as a pressure group upon the PA leadership. Thus, the PA leaders were free to decide upon their own agenda. The opposition's inability to gather support among the refugees was caused by the growing fragmentation among the refugees after the 1993 Oslo Agreement. In addition to former geographical and economic divisions between different refugee communities, the DOP created new subdivisions: 1948 refugees whose status will be discussed only later, and 1967 displaced persons whom Israel would allow to return; those in the West

---

[32] Interview with Faisal al-Husaini, *Journal of Palestine Studies* 18 (1989), 7 et seq.; see also N. Sh'ath, "Challenges of 1992 – The Palestinian Situation", *Middle East Policy* (1992), 39 et seq.

[33] Arafat in his February 1990 letter to the International Conference of World Jewish Leaders, *Journal of Palestine Studies* 19 (1990), 160, and in *Filastin al-Thaura*, 11 March 1990; E. Sanbar, *Filastin al-Thaura*, 1 May 1994; Faisal al-Husseini, a member of the PLO's Executive Committee, and Radwan Abu-A`yyash, head of the Palestinian Broadcasting Authority and himself a 1948 refugee, in F. al-Husseini/R. Abu-A`yyash, *Ha'aretz*, 25 July 1994,; *idem*, *Ha'aretz*, 5 August 1992.

Bank and Gaza Strip who hope to enjoy the investments promised by several foreign countries and international organisations; and those outside Palestine who must continue to rely on the limited support of UNRWA; and finally, among the refugees staying abroad, the older generation that will find great difficulties in immigrating back "inside" Palestine due to deprivation in terms of education, occupation, economic class and social status, and the younger generation which is more capable of adjusting itself to new environments and career alternatives.

In conclusion, for years the PLO had claimed that the Palestinian problem was not a refugee problem, but rather a problem of self-determination and national liberation. The return was not perceived as the return of individuals but rather as a collective return.[34] The establishment's return ethos was collective, while the memories of the refugees and their descendants were personal and concrete. Yet, as long as the moment of decision had not come, there was no contradiction between the two and they could exist in parallel. Unrest in the refugee camps and the growth of a new opposition, and the fact that the Palestinian Authority neglected the rehabilitation of the refugee camps under its control, created a problem for the Palestinian leadership.

With the emergence of the new opposition in the PA territories in the years 1998-2000, on the eve of the final status negotiations, and given its power-base in PA refugee camps,[35] the PLO/PA changed its stand and moved closer to its fundamental positions. It had difficulty accepting the Israeli demand that it wash its hands of any right to return to the State of Israel itself, a proposal that sought to transfer at least part of the burden of deciding this to the individuals themselves. The PA leadership proposed a framework in which there would be various options. It would indicate its preference and try to channel individuals in that direction, but the decision would be that of every individual or family on its own (see below).

To conclude, Israel faced a dilemma: due to the formation of a wide Arab coalition, Israel found it difficult to run a multilateral negotiation along the Madrid process, 1991, while managing a bilateral track with the PLO, which was impossible anyways at that time because of the PLO's high national aspirations, which Israel opposed. Following the

---

34 Klein, "From a Doctrine-Oriented to a Solution Oriented Policy, The PLO's 'Right of Return' 1964-2000", see note 20, 1 et seq.

35 *Idem*, "By Conviction, Not by Infliction: The Debate over Reforming the Palestinian Authority", *Middle East Journal* 57 (2003), 194 et seq.; *idem*, *The Jerusalem Problem: The Struggle for Permanent Status*, 2003.

1991 Madrid conference, Israel was pulled into multilateral discussions over the refugee issue, in which it conducted fierce debates. Israel chiefly argued about its partner's identity – opposing any PLO representative. Secondly, it debated the negotiations official agenda (limiting family reunification and raising the issue of Jewish refugees from Arab countries) as well as the hidden agenda (essentially opposing the return of Palestinian refugees and instead suggesting their resettlement in third or hosting countries and compensating them). At the multilateral level, no fundamental achievement has been made. However, multilateral talks (between the PLO and Israel *via* the Oslo track, 1993) have reached the point that Israel's partner with respect to the refugee issue is the PLO; likewise, the manner in which the 1967 refugee issue is to be solved has increasingly become more clear.

V. The Official Negotiations

1. Stage One: Stockholm Secret Talks

The "Stockholm track" is the name of a secret channel of discussions between Israel and the PLO from April to June 2000. In all there were seventeen sessions that culminated in meetings in Stockholm under the auspices of the Swedish government. Both sides tried to conclude a draft framework for a permanent status agreement in order to prepare their leaders for a summit.[36] The dispute over the refugee issue was not resolved during these talks. For Israel refused to mention UN General Assembly Resolution 194, approved in 1948, which mandated the return of individual refugees to Israel under certain conditions. Furthermore, Israel refused to accept responsibility for the creation of the 1948 refugee problem, fearing that such an acknowledgement would open a flood of lawsuits over property. In the end, however, Israel did express a willingness to take in 10,000-15,000 Palestinian refugees in a multi-year process, but not under the rubric of the right of return as the Palestinian delegation demanded.

However, the sides agreed to the establishment of two bodies, one of which would register the refugees and the other of which would deal with compensation. Registration of refugees would be based on data

[36] The analysis below, on the final status talks is essentially referred to from *idem*, *The Jerusalem Problem: The Struggle for Permanent Status*, *idem*.

from UNRWA, the UN refugee agency with responsibility for the Palestinian refugee camps. The body that would oversee the financial compensation of refugees, the rehabilitation of the refugee camps themselves, and the resettlement of the refugees, would have as members the states hosting the refugees and the countries that would contribute funds for this purpose. The projects would be carried out by a professional fund and not by the states involved. It was also agreed that each family could submit a single claim to property.[37]

2. Stage Two: The Camp David Summit

Instead of the refugee issue taking centre stage, Jerusalem became the focal point of the second Camp David summit held between 11 and 24 July 2000. The Israeli, Palestinian and American participants did address the 1948 Palestinian refugee problem, but they did not go beyond Stockholm track discussions. The debate in Camp David on the principles of this problem, unlike in Stockholm track, was both emotional and sharp. Israel was not willing to admit any responsibility for the creation of the refugee problem in 1948, it refused to recognise the principle of the right of the 1948 Palestinian refugees to return, and it categorically rejected Resolution 194. Israel also rejected the Palestinian proposal of establishing a mechanism that would channel the refugees towards more attractive possibilities than return to the State of Israel once the principle of the right of return was accepted. According to the Palestinian offer, the return of Palestinian refugees from Lebanon would serve as a pilot programme for examining how the system would work and where the refugees would prefer to realise their right of return. As in the Stockholm track, Israel expressed a willingness to absorb a maximum of 2,000 refugees per year over a five-to-six-year period. This meant a total of 10,000-12,000 refugees within the framework of family reunification, which, of course, was purely a humanitarian gesture.

Israel felt that it should neither bear sole responsibility for the 1948 refugees' lost property nor be made to compensate these refugees for the great suffering they underwent. Israel agreed only to participate in the establishment of an international fund that would raise the money

---

[37] A. Shavit, "The Day Peace Died", *Ha'aretz weekly magazine*, 14 September 2001; S. Gilad, *Just Beyond Reach – The Israeli-Palestinian Peace Negotiations 1999-2001*, 2001, 95, 99, 102, 107 et seq., 221, 225, in Hebrew.

for compensation. Furthermore, Israel claimed that compensation should also be paid to the Jews who left their homes in Arab countries as a result of the 1948 War, and that Israel would thus share the compensation funds with the Palestinians. Israel proposed dismantling UNWRA within a ten-year period and to establish in its place a new body that would oversee the rehabilitation and resettlement of the refugees.[38]

The gap between the two sides was so great that, for all practical purposes, no negotiations on the 1948 refugee issue took place at Camp David. At most encounters when the subject was raised, there were only exchanges of accusations and myths and unproductive arguments.[39] Real negotiations on the refugees took place only at Taba, where the two sides picked up where they had left off in the Stockholm channel.

3. Stage Three: President Clinton Parameters and Taba Talks

The Taba talks (January 2001) achieved great progress in the subcommittee that dealt with the issue of the 1948 refugees. In practical terms, this was the first time since the Stockholm talks that the two sides had conducted serious negotiations over the issue. This was due in no small part to the fact that Yossi Beilin and Nabil Sha'ath were placed at the head of the subcommittee. Beilin and Sha'ath bore no scars from Camp David and the subsequent talks. The negotiators at Taba in January 2001 grappled with these problems on the basis of President Clinton's ideas and those produced in the Stockholm talks. However, no understanding was reached on the foundation of 1948 refugee issue. The Palestinians demanded an Israeli recognition of its moral and legal responsibility for displacing civilian populations during the 1948 War, in addition to preventing their return thereafter; as well as the acceptance of the right of each 1948 refugee and his descendants and spouse to return to his home in Israel according to the United Nations General Assembly Resolution 194. According to Resolution 194, the right of return of

[38] U. Benziman, "The Dairies of Dan Meridor", *Ha'aretz*, 28 September 2001; Gilad, ibid., 199, 213 et seq., 216; Abu Mazen, *al-Ayyam*, 29 July 2001.

[39] Gilad, ibid., 216; A. Haniyyeh, "Camp David Papers", *al-Ayyam*, 29 July 2000-10 August 2000.

each refugee shall not expire until he/she has exercised it according to the agreement within an unlimited time frame.[40]

Israel, in its response to the Palestinian proposal, used the term "the right of return" only once, but put it in quotation marks, suggesting it was nothing more than a Palestinian yearning. The Israeli paper did not contain acceptance of Resolution 194, which by definition deals with the return of 1948 refugees to their homes on an individual and voluntary base. Rather, it related to the implementation of this resolution in a manner consistent with the existence of the State of Israel as the homeland of Jewish people. The two Palestinian principles of the right of return and Resolution 194 were put in the Israeli paper in connection with issues it already accepted: the establishment of an independent Palestinian state and Security Council Resolution 242. Israel suggested a joint narrative in which it was ready to accept limited responsibility for the creation of the refugee problem, i.e. Israel was prepared to express its regret for it, but was not willing to accept legal responsibility.

Therefore, the two sides agreed that each side would retain the right to maintain its own narrative about the circumstances under which the problem of the 1948 refugees came into being. They also ratified their commitment to a solution based on two national ethnic states, so that the refugee problem would not upset Israel's existence as the state of the Jewish nation. Israel suggested a "return basket" that includes five options: rehabilitation and citizenship in the refugee's current location; absorption in the Palestinian state; settlement in territories that Israel would transfer into Palestinian sovereignty in the framework of territorial exchange; emigration to a country outside the region; and emigration to Israel. Preferences in all five options would be given to Palestinian refugees in Lebanon. The options, however, would not have equal status. Further, incentives and financial aid would be used to encourage refugees to waive their right to return to Israel. Whereas, the Palestinians stressed that these options shall be subject to the individual refugee's free choice and shall not prejudice their right to return to their homes.[41]

---

[40] See the "Palestinian Proposal on Palestinian Refugees, 22 January 2001, Taba", *Journal of Palestine Studies* 31 (2002), 145 et seq.; "Israeli Privet Response to the Palestinian Refugee Proposal of 22 January 2001, Non-Paper, Draft 2, 23 January 2001, Taba", *Journal of Palestine Studies* 31 (2002), 148 et seq.; A. Eldar, "The Peace that Nearly Was at Taba", *Ha'aretz*, 15 February 2002.

[41] *Idem.*

In keeping with President Clinton's ideas from December 2000, it was understood that Israel's immigration quotas would be low relative to the quotas for immigration from other destinations. No numbers were agreed upon, but, unofficially, Israel referred to 25,000 in the first three years of a 15 years absorption programme and 40,000 in the first five years; while the Palestinian paper enabled all refugees resident in Lebanon to return, plus an unfixed number from other countries.[42] Both sides concluded that Israel would also have the sovereign right to decide which refugees had the right to return to its territory and which did not, subject to criteria agreed on by both sides.

Another agreement reached at Taba was that each refugee would have to give up his refugee status and accept full and equal citizenship in his new place of residence. His choice of residence would be his final location as a refugee. Israel stressed that in accepting this he/she would also give up all property claims against Israel. Further, a refugee who did not give notice within five years of which option he preferred would lose both his status and rights as a refugee. Both parties agreed that during this five-year period an international commission and international fund would be established as a mechanism for dealing with compensation to replace UNRWA in order to administer the rehabilitation of refugees. The two international bodies, therefore, would raise money for the rehabilitation of the refugees and would grant compensation for private real estate expropriated from the refugees. The question of public property remained in dispute, as did the level of compensation that Israel would grant. These issues were thus tabled for discussion, whereby Israel would play a central role in raising financial resources for the new body's operations.

The Taba talks also established the procedure for submitting a claim for compensation. It was agreed that there would be two channels for such claims: a fast track that would grant compensation on the basis of a general estimation of property, whose criteria were to be agreed upon by Israel and the PLO. Any estimates would be based on fixed and unitary measures for each refugee. The slow track, on the other hand, would allow each refugee interested in doing so to submit a detailed claim against Israel for his property. Unfortunately, no understanding was reached on the calculation of compensation for material losses, land and

---

[42] *Idem.*

assets expropriated nor was there agreement on the amount of restitution for lost refugee property.[43]

VI. Conclusion

In a nutshell, the PLO wanted to open the official talks on the permanent settlement with a fundamental decision from which pragmatic solutions would be derived. Israel dissented and disagreed with the PLO's fundamental principles. Instead, Israel suggested several practical arrangements in an attempt to solve the Palestinian refugee issue. The negotiations in the Stockholm talks and at the Camp David summit (Spring and Summer 2000, respectively) were overshadowed by disagreements as to what was fundamental in resolving the 1948 refugee issue. Thus, no breakthrough was made during those talks. Actual progress, however, did take place in Taba (Winter 2001) based on President Clinton's parameters, where the two delegations negotiated the finalisation of refugee status, reaching consensus as to each side's claims. The issues were negotiated in Taba on a pragmatic level, but not as expressions of the core debate. As a result, progress commenced and the actual aspects of return that were only slightly dealt with at Stockholm and Camp David talks were shaped, so that: the different parameters of where to return and by who, the mechanisms needed for managing the return, as well as an administration that would deal with compensations; types of compensation, the right to claim and get it, and on what calculation.

The negotiations, however, failed to reach an agreement with respect to the historical narrative: who is responsible for the creation of the refugee problem, what is the extent of such responsibility and on which international principles should the agreement be based upon. The wish to reach such an inclusive agreement originated not only from the standards both sides set for themselves, namely, to reach an end of the historic conflict and to conclude simultaneous legal claims; but also their wish to agree on their respective foundation for a legitimate narrative.

The Israeli 1948 War of Independence was the Palestinian *Nakba*, which led to the displacement of about half of the Palestinian nation.

---

[43] *Idem*; A. Eldar, "The Monster of the Right of the Return", *Ha'aretz*, 31 May 2001; Y. Beilin, *Guide for A Wounded Dove*, 2001, 204 et seq., 214 et seq., in Hebrew.

By means of an agreement on this narrative, the elite negotiating groups wished to signal to their people the road to historical reconciliation. A pragmatic agreement that would simply weaken the fire was considered insufficient. Both sides were seeking a way to treat the root of the problem in order reach a historic peace. Their lack of success forced the use of another strategy: to promote a pragmatic – technical – legal agreement and leave the understanding on history to both people's social forces and civil society organisations. The question as to which model is preferred and more attainable remains an open question.

The 1948 refugee question is thus ultimately tied to self-identity for each side. As Herbert Kelman has expressed,[44] the change of identity is not a result of a peace process, although it is part and parcel of dialogue. It is in this sense that an identity change makes negotiation possible. Whereas, the peace-talks themselves serve to further push the process forward. Moreover, it is possible to negotiate over identity issues when the sides involved move from a zero-sum game to coexistence coupled with the non-rejection of the other's identity. Such a move happens primarily when a change of identity occurs by moving from being exclusive and monolithic to an inclusive identity. Secondly, it happens when a transcendental identity develops – not in place of a particular identity, but alongside it. The agents of identity change represent the necessity and ability to make the change happen.

Change is done informally and *via* the accommodating of one identity with another. Kelman identified the following stages in the identity changing process: removing the negation of the other; identifying shared elements; identifying different identity bounders, that is to say seeing the different frameworks to differing identity fragments; altering priorities in the identity ranges; developing multi-dimensional dialogue between the sides and the handling not only of the symbolic area but also in practical issues and their implementations. Simply put, both sides must go through a public process of identity deconstruction and reconstruction to reach improvements in their interaction.

Herbert Kelman based his conclusions on the experience he acquired in running the track two talks (unofficial talks between Israeli and Palestinian academics with accessibility to their media, public and decision makers) on the refugee issue. As I hope to show in a different research,

[44] H. Kelman, "The Role of National Identity in Conflict Resolution, Experience from Israeli-Palestinian Problem Solving Workshops", in: R.D. Ashmore/L. Jussim/D. Wilder (eds), *Social Identity, Intergroup Conflict and Conflict Resolutions*, 2001, 187 et seq.

his track was the most fruitful one of those dealing with the 1948 refugee issue. Track two talks in general, and Kelman's in particular, contributed several important working tools to the official track. But their influence was limited and did not help much to improve the interaction in the formal talks.

Analysis of the official talks on the final status of the 1948 refugee issue shows that both sides have only just begun their negotiations. Most of Herbert Kelman's process stages lie ahead. Even if the sides will go through the whole process, it is better to recall that change in self-identity cannot be carried out by means of social engineering, but as a result of partly invisible social procedures and partly as a result of overt dialogue, both managed before and parallel to the official track. The absent public debate on the different aspects of the 1948 refugee question has been a key element in the failure of final status negotiations.

VII. Appendix

1. Clinton Parameters on Refugees[45]

I sense that the differences are more relating to formulations and less to what will happen on a practical level.

I believe that Israel is prepared to acknowledge the moral and material suffering caused to the Palestinian People as a result of the 1948 war and the need to assist the international community in addressing the problem.

An international commission should be established to implement all the aspects that flow from your agreement: compensation, resettlement, rehabilitation, etc. The US is prepared to lead an international effort to help the refugees.

The fundamental gap is on how to handle the concept of the right of return. I know the history of the issue and how hard it will be for the Palestinian Leadership to appear to be abandoning this principle.

The Israeli side could not accept any reference to a right of return that would imply a right to immigrate to Israel in defiance of Israel's sovereign policies and admission or that would threaten the Jewish character of the state.

---

45 Clinton proposal, <http//www.jmcc.org/documents/clintonprop.htm>.

Any solution must address both needs.

The solution will have to be consistent with the two-state approach that both sides have accepted as a way to end the Palestinian Israeli conflict: the state of Palestine as the homeland of the Palestinian people and the state of Israel as the homeland of the Jewish people

Under the two-State solution, the guiding principle should be that the Palestinian State would be the focal point for Palestinians who choose to return to the area without ruling out that Israel will accept some of these refugees.

I believe that we need to adopt a formulation on the right of return that will make clear that there is no specific right of return to Israel itself but that does not negate the aspiration of the Palestinian people to return to the area.

In light of the above, I propose two alternatives:

1- Both sides recognize the right of Palestinian refugees to return to Historic Palestine, Or,

2- Both sides recognize the right of Palestinian refugees to return to their homeland.

The agreement will define the implementation of this general right in a way that is consistent with the two-state solution. It would list the five possible homes for the refugees:

1- The state of Palestine.

2- Areas in Israel being transferred to Palestine in the land swap.

3- Rehabilitation in host country.

4- Resettlement in third country.

5- Admission to Israel.

In listing these options, the agreement will make clear that the return to the West Bank, Gaza Strip, and areas acquired in the land swap would be right to all Palestinian Refugees.

While rehabilitation in host countries, resettlement in third countries and absorption into Israel will depend upon the policies of those countries.

Israel could indicate in the agreement that it intends to establish a policy so that some of the refugees would be absorbed into Israel consistent with Israel's sovereign decision.

I believe that priority should be given to the refugee population in Lebanon. The parties would agree that this is implement resolution 194.

2. Taba Non-Paper[46]

Refugees

Non-papers were exchanged, which were regarded as a good basis for the talks. Both sides stated that the issue of the Palestinian refugees is central to the Israeli-Palestinian relations and that a comprehensive and just solution is essential to creating a lasting and morally scrupulous peace. Both sides agreed to adopt the principles and references which could facilitate the adoption of an agreement.

Both sides suggested, as a basis, that the parties should agree that a just settlement of the refugee problem in accordance with the UN Security Council Resolution 242 must lead to the implementation of UN General Assembly Resolution 194.

3.1 Narrative

The Israeli side put forward a suggested joint narrative for the tragedy of the Palestinian refugees. The Palestinian side discussed the proposed narrative and there was much progress, although no agreement was reached in an attempt to develop an historical narrative in the general text.

3.2 Return, Repatriation and Relocation and Rehabilitation

Both sides engaged in a discussion of the practicalities of resolving the refugee issue. The Palestinian side reiterated that the Palestinian refugees should have the right of return to their homes in accordance with the interpretation of UNGAR 194. The Israeli side expressed its understanding that the wish to return as per wording of UNGAR 194 shall be implemented within the framework of one of the following programs:

A. Return and repatriation
  1. to Israel
  2. to Israel swapped territory
  3. to the Palestine state.

---

[46] Eldar, see note 40.

B. Rehabilitation and relocation

1. Rehabilitation in host country.
2. Relocation to third country.

Preference in all these programs shall be accorded to the Palestinian refugee population in Lebanon. The Palestinian side stressed that the above shall be subject to the individual free choice of the refugees, and shall not prejudice their right to their homes in accordance with its interpretation of UNGAR 194.

The Israeli side, informally, suggested a three-track 15-year absorption program, which was discussed but not agreed upon. The first track referred to the absorption to Israel. No numbers were agreed upon, but with a non-paper referring to 25,000 in the first three years of this program (40,000 in the first five years of this program did not appear in the non-paper but was raised verbally). The second track referred to the absorption of Palestinian refugees into the Israeli territory, that shall be transferred to Palestinian sovereignty and the third track referring to the absorption of refugees in the context of family reunification scheme.

The Palestinian side did not present a number, but stated that the negotiations could not start without an Israeli opening position. It maintained that Israel's acceptance of the return of refugees should not prejudice existing programs within Israel such as family reunification.

3.3 Compensation

Both sides agreed to the establishment of an International Commission and an International Fund as a mechanism for dealing with compensation in all its aspects. Both sides agreed that "small-sum" compensation shall be paid to the refugees in the "fast-track" procedure, claims of compensation for property losses below a certain amount shall be subject to "fast-track" procedures.

There was also progress on Israeli compensation for material losses, land and assets expropriated, including agreement on a payment from an Israeli lump sum or proper amount to be agreed upon that would feed into the International Fund. According to the Israeli side the calculation of this payment would be based on a macro-economic survey to evaluate the assets in order to reach a fair value. The Palestinian side, however, said that this sum would be calculated on the records of the UNCCP, the Custodian for Absentee Property and other relevant data with a multiplier to reach a fair value.

3.4 UNRWA

Both sides agreed that UNRWA should be phased out in accordance with an agreed timetable of five years, as a targeted period. The Palestinian side added a possible adjustment of that period to make sure that this will be subject to the implementation of the other aspects of the agreement dealing with refugees, and with termination of Palestinian refugee status in the various locations.

3.5 Former Jewish Refugees

The Israeli side requested that the issue of compensation to former Jewish refugees from Arab countries be recognised, while accepting that it was not a Palestinian responsibility or a bilateral issue. The Palestinian side maintained that this is not a subject for a bilateral Palestinian-Israeli agreement.

3.6 Restitution

The Palestinian side raised the issue of restitution of refugee property. The Israeli side rejected this.

3.7 End of Claims

The issue of the end of claims was discussed, and it was suggested that the implementation of the agreement shall constitute a complete and final implementation of UNGAR 194 and therefore ends all claims.

The Palestinian Refugee Problem and Its Historical Origins and Developments: Should These Issues Be Part of the Political Agreement? A New Approach to a Possible Solution

Shelly L. Fried

"The stream is shrunk, the pool is dry,
And we be comrades, thou and I;"
Rudyard Kipling[1]

I. Introduction

The main argument of this paper is that the historical information about the birth of the Palestinian refugee problem, and the question of responsibility for the problem, should not be a part of the political agreement. This paper will argue that history proves that whenever these questions were dealt with in the framework of a political agreement, these issues were one of the main causes of its failure. Ironically, I, as a historian, am suggesting that a political agreement cannot be finalised without putting history aside.

It is not my intention to argue, however, that these questions are not important. On the contrary – this paper will illustrate that since the questions of the origin, responsibility, and guilt for the Palestinian refugee problem are so important, that it is vital to exclude them from the political agreement.

The point here is that the refugee issue – and the question of peace between the Israelis and the Palestinians – should be dealt with on more

---

1 R. Kipling, "How Fear Came", *The Jungle Books*, 173.

than one level and in various fora. A political agreement should give a form of stabilisation to both peoples. Other levels of the peace process, such as emotional and educational issues for example, should be part of an overall process. It is in these latter areas where history should play a role.

II. A Historical Account of the Israeli Foreign Policy Toward the Palestinian Refugee Problem

When examining past attempts to achieve a political agreement to the refugee issue, it is clear that questions of responsibility and guilt were amongst the main obstacles. Shortly after the 1947-1949 War, both sides – the Arab world, with no real Palestinian representative, and Israel – clearly stood at opposite ends of the spectrum: the Arab world demanded the full return of the refugees to their place of origin; whereas Israel refused to allow any refugees to return to their homes.

This adamant Israeli position was initially determined by its own government on 16 June 1948. It was the Israeli foreign minister, Moshe Sharett – probably after consultation with the Israeli Prime Minister, David Ben-Gurion – who declared that "they [i.e. the Palestinian Refugees] are not coming back." In short, the Israeli policy was based on three principles:

(1). Preventing the return of the 700,000 refugees into Israel.

(2). The solution to the refugees should be their rehabilitation in their current place, i.e. mainly the Arab states.

(3). An Israeli willingness to pay compensation for refugee lost property, and that the payment will be implemented collectively through a representative body of the refugees, and not on an individual basis.

Beyond these three policy principles, an additional three points influenced Israeli thinking. Israel argued that the Palestinians would be "a fifth column" in Israel, and therefore could not return. Nevertheless, Israel did permit some repatriation, under the reunification of families. It seems that recently, around 2,000-4,000 Palestinian were allowed to return to Israel under this label every year. The third principle was the taking over of Palestinian lost property – which included agricultural lands (cultivated and uncultivated), orange groves, rural homes, urban lands, city houses, movable property of all sorts, and deposits left in Israeli banks – by governmental institutions, mainly in order to settle new Jewish immigrants.

Thus, it is essential to emphasise three points:

(a). Although a large demographic change of population did take place, and large scale taking over of property occurred, it was not a case of a deliberate transfer of population. In fact, Israeli policy was not a pre-planned policy, but a realisation of the outcomes of war according to basic ideals of the Zionist movement.

(b). The mediator bodies, which were mainly the UN and the USA, accepted the Israeli arguments, although they still insisted on some partial return of some refugees to Israel.

(c.) Most importantly, from June 1948 onwards, Israel dealt with the Palestinian refugee problem within the framework of its foreign policy, which was determined in June 1948. This last point is one of the keys to the future political agreement, and it is this point that will be elaborated on herein.

III. Putting History Aside

After realising the historical basis of the Israeli policy towards the Palestinian refugee problem,[2] it is important to note two points concerning the difficulties of dealing with the 1947-1949 War narrative; and, therefore, why it is more advisable to leave this narrative aside.

First, the war of 1947-1949, like any war, produced many narratives. In my view, dealing with the 1947-1949 War narrative will never end. Therefore, it should not be the focus of the debate on narratives. Moreover, the 1947-1949 War is where both sides feel especially "strong" in their narratives. The Palestinians were victims. That is their narrative. The Israelis were under threat. That is their narrative. Thus, the debate about narratives should take place were both sides are less "strong;"

---

[2] For a more detailed analysis of the Israeli policy towards the Palestinian refugee problem, see S.L. Fried, *"They Are Not Coming Back" – The crystallisation of Israeli foreign policy toward possible solutions of the Palestinian refugee problem, 1947-1956: From the UN Partition Resolution to the Suez Campaign*, in Hebrew, Thesis submitted for the degree Doctor of Philosophy, Submitted to the Senate of Tel-Aviv University, May 2003 (in review); and also *idem*, *Precious Land - Israel's Policy on Compensation for Abandoned Palestinian Property, 1947-1951: From the UN Partition Resolution to the Paris Conference*, in Hebrew, Thesis submitted for the M.A. Degree in History at Tel-Aviv University, October 1998.

that means that the debate about the narratives should take place in the substance of both sides national ideals. Viewed in this manner, Israelis would have to deal with the concept of a Jewish state which discriminates against others. The Palestinians for their part should deal with their failure to accept Zionists as neighbours with rights, especially since Jews were victims of European anti-Semitism in the first half of the 20th century.

The other point that should be noted is that history is being re-written all the time according to political needs (this is done mainly by the general public, and its political leaders, although this tends to happen less so amongst professional historians). For years, many Israelis told me that nothing wrong happened in the 1947-1949 War. I argued differently, that there was not a pre-planned transfer, but that atrocities were made, and that after the 1947-1949 War, there was a planned taking over of Arab lands, and that there was a complete denial of any right of return. Since the new outbreak of violence in October 2000, I am now told that Israel should do to the Palestinians what was done in the 1947-1949 War. That means that Palestinians should be removed from Israel. Again, one must note that in 1947-1949 there was not such a pre-planned transfer. History, therefore, is being re-written according to political needs. This is yet another reason why narratives are so difficult to tackle, especially in the framework of a political agreement.

IV. The Historical Experience and its Relevance to a Possible Solution

When examining the diplomatic negotiations between Israel and the Arab world, it is very evident that whenever the questions of narrative, guilt, and responsibility were involved, negotiations failed. Therefore, the issue of the refugees is usually postponed during negotiations, and other practical issues often take centre stage during negotiations. This fact is demonstrated very clearly in three events:

November 1948 – separation of armistice talks and agreements on the refugee issue led to the failure of the Lausanne conference.

September 1978 – the refugee issue was taken out of the Israeli-Egyptian Camp David agreement.

August-September 1993 – the refugee problem was not dealt with, but rather postponed in the Oslo Accords, leading to final status talks.[3]

This author posits that yet another separation is in order, but this time the parties should make a separation between two components of the refugee issue. First, the parties should resolve the practical issue of compensation; and, subsequently, the parties should deal with their respective narratives in order to address questions of responsibility and guilt.

In a way, this is somewhat similar to what was tried in the past with the establishment of the "Integration Fund" in 2 December 1950 by United Nations General Assembly Resolution 393 (V).

In the early 1950s, Israel's Foreign Minister Moshe Sharett considered an initiative that included the paying of compensation prior to any peace negotiations. Indeed, Sharett feared future international pressure on Israel, and believed that such an initiative would be an appropriate tool in reducing any burden laid upon Israel. Yet, one should also note that Sharett realised that such an initiative could have other advantages too. Sharett came to the conclusion – from his past experience with the negotiations of 1949 – that the Israeli public and political arenas would not accept any return of the refugees. Therefore, he believed the Israelis might accept compensation. When refugees are allowed to return, he argued:

> "One should live with them, work with them, integrate them in the economic life, and here [in Israel] the general public is not ready to accept this, and this is without mentioning the difficulties such as housing, and national and personal security. This [a large scale return of the refugees] will be hell."

Therefore, Sharett argued that a compensation-based solution would be much more practical, as it would not involve the daily involvement of the Israeli public, which meant that the Israeli public would not fight the idea.[4]

In the summer of 1950, Sharett advanced his concept of paying compensation prior to the Israeli Government entering any new peace ne-

---

3 For a detailed analysis of these events, see S.L. Fried, "The Refugee Issue at the Peace Conferences, 1949-2000", *Palestine-Israel Journal* 9 (2002), 24 et seq.

4 "Consultation at the Ministry of Foreign Office", 31 January 1950, in: State of Israel, *Documents on the Foreign Policy of Israel, 1950, Vol. 5*, Do 62, 82 et seq, in Hebrew.

gotiations. For now, Sharett had additional arguments. He believed that such negotiations and payments would help to alleviate the human suffering of the refugees, thereby disarming the issue as a weapon in the Arab-Israeli conflict. He also believed that such payments could lead to a peace agreement on all other matters. Although Sharett argued that his idea was consistent with Israeli policy as it was determined in 16 June 1948, the Israeli Government, nevertheless, under the leadership of Ben-Gurion rejected the idea.[5] However, a few months later, in the autumn of 1950, the government was compelled to revisit the idea again, but this time as a UN-USA initiative. As a result, in December 1950, Israel agreed to join the UN Integration Fund.[6]

The UN resolution concluded that

> "The General Assembly: ...
>
> 4. Considers that, without prejudice to the provisions of paragraph 11 of General Assembly resolution 194(III) of 11 December 1948, the reintegration of the refugees into the economic life of the Near East, either by repatriation or resettlement, is essential in preparation for the time when international assistance is no longer available, and for the realisation of conditions of peace and stability in the area.
>
> Instructs the Agency [UNRWA] to establish a reintegration fund which shall be utilised for projects requested by any government in the Near East and approved by the Agency [UNRWA] for the permanent re-establishment of refugees and their removal from relief [of UNRWA];"[7]

At first, the Arab countries supported the Fund, but after a short period they ceased to do so, and the Fund failed to solve the Palestinian refu-

---

5 "Stenograms of the Israeli Government", 3 August 1950, Israel State Archives (ISA), 40 et seq.; 21 August 1950, 3 et seq.; "File of Classified Government Decisions 1949-1954", A10/7484, 21 August 1950; Documents 5, "M. Sharett to A. Eban", 27 August 1950, Do 356, 502; "A. Eban to M. Sharett", 31 August 1950, Do 365, 513; G. Sheffer, *Moshe Sharett - Biography of a Political Moderate*, 1996, 551.

6 "Stenograms of the Israeli Government", 30 October 1950, ISA, 8 et seq.; Documents 5, "W. Eytan to the Israeli Missions Abroad", 31 October 1950, Do 435, 611.

7 Documents 5, appendix a, 737 et seq.

gee problem, and as a result did not achieve its purpose.[8] Nevertheless, it is still a model that can be used in a future political agreement.

V. Conclusion and Recommendations

This author posits that in article 1 of any future agreement, both sides should agree that they disagree on the questions of narratives, guilt and responsibility. In article 2, both sides should declare that they are not giving up their basic positions on these questions. In article 3 both sides should agree that a period of years – five to ten years for example – will be set aside for the establishment of dialogue groups, truth and reconciliation committees, and modalities to create democratic dialogue within the refugees in order to make them part of the process.[9]

Article 4 should state that meanwhile, and "without prejudice" to the right of return, money will be paid to the refugees, integration will take place, so on and so forth.

It should again be emphasised that from June 1948 onwards, compensation has always been within the framework of the Israeli foreign policy.

Any agreement must also involve a new approach by both sides. Up until now Israel has said: "take the money, but do not return!" Now, the Israelis should show empathy and concern. Israel should say: "take the money, improve your life, and once you do that, we can open dialogue on your right of return that I [Israel] might accept." On the other hand, the Israelis should stress that they shall not just listen to the Palestinians' demands – for they too need to tell their narrative, and in return they might expect a modicum of empathy.

However, one should consider the advantages and disadvantages of this proposed model given the political dynamic that exists today. On the Israeli side, it may very well be that its political leadership will not accept this model because it does not bring "an end to the conflict." The Israelis will fear that such a model will keep the Palestinian demand of

---

[8] J. Al Husseini, "The Arab States and the Refugee Issue: A Retrospective View", in this volume, 435 et seq.; Fried, see note 2.

[9] See for example K. Nabulsi, *Participatory Models of Democracy and the Refugee Issue*, working paper presented in the conference the Stocktaking II Conference on Palestinian Refugee Research, IDRC (International Development Research Centre), Canada, 17-20 June 2003.

their right of return alive, despite the fact that compensation payments were given to them.

The Palestinians, on the other hand, are very likely to reject this model as well, because it might appear to them as mere Israeli manipulation. It is often argued that Israel tries to achieve practical solutions because such solutions serve its political stance on the refugee issue: no return, and integration in other countries in exchange for compensation. Thus, this model could be seen as yet another Israeli attempt to achieve a solution without accepting the Palestinian right of return.

Without neglecting these political difficulties, the model proposed here has its advantages. As mentioned before, this model will put aside the questions of responsibility and guilt that both sides cannot agree upon at the moment. Therefore, under this model, the peace process can proceed.

Once the economic situation of many of the inhabitants of the Middle East – including the refugees – improves, it might be easier to discuss the political settlement of the questions of responsibility and guilt. This is not to say that money will solve everything. It is rather to suggest, that under better economic and living conditions, both sides will be able to discuss the roots of the conflict with less fear of their immediate interests being in danger. Therefore, better economic conditions will lessen fear, and might even provide more scope for trust and hope, which will be of course backed up by political declarations and commitments that deal with the question of the right of return. Therefore, it could very well be that under better economic conditions the refugees will agree to an Israeli declaration that does not include a return to their original homes; it could also be that that under better economic conditions the refugees would seem less eager to return to their original places, and thus the Israelis would not be too afraid to accept their right of return; it could also be, that because of future developments within the Israeli society, the terms of the Zionist ideology and practice will change in such ways that the Israelis will have a different vision of their state, and the place of the Palestinians in it. As mentioned before, history is being re-written according to political needs – although this fact can be, under the proposed model, an advantage.

This author further posits that a political agreement should form a model that would not neglect the questions of responsibility and guilt, but only because it shall deal with them in other fora, albeit not political ones. It seems that no political agreement can be achieved in any other way. For once a practical political agreement is achieved, then it shall be very much possible to solve the historical questions of the Palestinian refugee problem.[10]

[10] An interesting case study for such a model can be the German-Israeli experience after World War II. For that, see R.W. Zweig, "Restitution of Property and Refugee Rehabilitation: Two Case Studies", *Journal of Refugee Studies* 6 (1993), 56 et seq.

Max-Planck-Institut für ausländisches öffentliches Recht und Völkerrecht

Beiträge zum ausländischen öffentlichen Recht und Völkerrecht

Hrsg.: A. von Bogdandy, R. Wolfrum

Bde. 27–59 erschienen im Carl Heymanns Verlag KG Köln, Berlin (Bestellung an: Max-Planck-Institut für Völkerrecht, Im Neuenheimer Feld 535, 69120 Heidelberg); ab Band 60 im Springer Berlin, Heidelberg, New York, London, Paris, Tokyo, Hong Kong, Barcelona

---

189 Eyal *Benvenisti*, Chaim *Gans*, Sari *Hanafi* (eds.): **Israel and the Palestinian Refugees.** 2007. VIII, 502 Seiten. Geb. € 94,95 zzgl. landesüblicher MwSt.

188 Eibe *Riedel*, Rüdiger *Wolfrum* (eds.): **Recent Trends in German and European Constitutional Law.** 2006. VII, 289 Seiten. Geb. € 74,95 zzgl. landesüblicher MwSt.

186 Philipp *Dann*, Michał *Rynkowski* (eds.): **The Unity of the European Constitution.** 2006. IX, 394 Seiten. Geb. € 79,95 zzgl. landesüblicher MwSt.

184 Jürgen *Bast:* **Grundbegriffe der Handlungsformen der EU.** 2006. XXI, 485 Seiten. Geb. € 94,95

183 Uwe *Säuberlich:* **Die außervertragliche Haftung im Gemeinschaftsrecht.** 2005. XV, 314 Seiten. Geb. € 74,95

182 Florian *von Alemann:* **Die Handlungsform der interinstitutionellen Vereinbarung.** 2006. XVI, 518 Seiten. Geb. € 94,95

181 Susanne *Förster*: **Internationale Haftungsregeln für schädliche Folgewirkungen gentechnisch veränderter Organismen.** 2007. XXXIV, 421 Seiten. Geb. € 84,95

180 Jeanine *Bucherer:* **Die Vereinbarkeit von Militärgerichten mit dem Recht auf ein faires Verfahren gemäß Art. 6 Abs. 1 EMRK, Art. 8 Abs. 1 AMRK und Art. 14 Abs. 1 des UN-Paktes über bürgerliche und politische Rechte.** 2005. XVIII, 307 Seiten. Geb. € 74,95

179 Annette *Simon:* **UN-Schutzzonen – Ein Schutzinstrument für verfolgte Personen?** 2005. XXI, 322 Seiten. Geb. € 74,95

178 Petra *Minnerop:* **Paria-Staaten im Völkerrecht?** 2004. XXIII, 579 Seiten. Geb. € 99,95

177 Rüdiger *Wolfrum,* Volker *Röben* (eds.): **Developments of International Law in Treaty Making.** 2005. VIII, 632 Seiten. Geb. € 99,95 zzgl. landesüblicher MwSt.

176 Christiane *Höhn:* **Zwischen Menschenrechten und Konfliktprävention. Der Minderheitenschutz im Rahmen der Organisation für Sicherheit und Zusammenarbeit in Europa (OSZE).** 2005. XX, 418 Seiten. Geb. € 84,95

175 Nele *Matz:* **Wege zur Koordinierung völkerrechtlicher Verträge. Völkervertragsrechtliche und institutionelle Ansätze.** 2005. XXIV, 423 Seiten. Geb. € 84,95

174 Jochen Abr. *Frowein:* **Völkerrecht – Menschenrechte – Verfassungsfragen Deutschlands und Europas. Ausgewählte Schriften.** Hrsg. von Matthias *Hartwig*, Georg *Nolte*, Stefan *Oeter*, Christian *Walter*. 2004. VIII, 732 Seiten. Geb. € 119,95

173 Oliver *Dörr* (Hrsg.): **Ein Rechtslehrer in Berlin. Symposium für Albrecht Randelzhofer.** 2004. VII, 117 Seiten. Geb. € 54,95

172 Lars-Jörgen *Geburtig:* **Konkurrentenrechtsschutz aus Art. 88 Abs. 3 Satz 3 EGV. Am Beispiel von Steuervergünstigungen.** 2004. XVII, 412 Seiten (4 Seiten English Summary). Geb. € 84,95

171 Markus *Böckenförde:* **Grüne Gentechnik und Welthandel. Das Biosafety-Protokoll und seine Auswirkungen auf das Regime der WTO.** 2004. XXIX, 620 Seiten. Geb. € 99,95

170 Anja *v. Hahn:* **Traditionelles Wissen indigener und lokaler Gemeinschaften zwischen geistigen Eigentumsrechten und der *public domain*.** 2004. XXV, 415 Seiten. Geb. 84,95

169 Christian *Walter*, Silja *Vöneky*, Volker *Röben,* Frank *Schorkopf* (eds.): **Terrorism as a Challenge for National and International Law: Security versus Liberty?** 2004. XI, 1484 Seiten. Geb. € 169,95 zzgl. landesüblicher MwSt.

168 Kathrin *Osteneck:* **Die Umsetzung von UN-Wirtschaftssanktionen durch die Europäische Gemeinschaft.** 2004. XXXIX, 579 Seiten. Geb. € 99,95

167 Stephan *Sina:* **Der völkerrechtliche Status des Westjordanlandes und des Gaza-Streifens nach den Osloer Verträgen.** 2004. XXI, 410 Seiten. Geb. € 84,95

166 Philipp *Dann:* **Parlamente im Exekutivföderalismus.** 2004. XXIII, 474 Seiten. Geb. € 89,95

165 Rüdiger *Wolfrum* (Hrsg.): **Gleichheit und Nichtdiskriminierung im nationalen und internationalen Menschenrechtsschutz.** 2003. VIII, 299 Seiten. Geb. € 74,95

164 *Rüdiger Wolfrum, Nele Matz:* **Conflicts in International Environmental Law.** 2003. XI, 213 Seiten. Geb. € 64,95 zzgl. landesüblicher MwSt.

163 Adam *Bodnar,* Michał *Kowalski,* Karen *Raible,* Frank *Schorkopf* (eds.): **The Emerging Constitutional Law of the European Union.** 2003. IX, 595 Seiten. Geb. € 99,95 zzgl. landesüblicher MwSt.

162 Jochen Abr. *Frowein,* Klaus *Scharioth,* Ingo *Winkelmann,* Rüdiger *Wolfrum* (Hrsg.): **Verhandeln für den Frieden/Negotiating for Peace. Liber Amicorum Tono Eitel.** 2003. XIII, 866 Seiten. Geb. € 129,95

161 Michaela *Fries:* **Die Bedeutung von Artikel 5 (f) der Rassendiskriminierungskonvention im deutschen Recht.** 2003. XIX, 429 Seiten. Geb. € 84,95

160 Helen *Keller:* **Rezeption des Völkerrechts.** 2003. XXXV, 855 Seiten. Geb. € 129,95

159 Cordula *Dröge:* **Positive Verpflichtungen der Staaten in der Europäischen Menschenrechtskonvention.** 2003. XX, 432 Seiten. Geb. € 89,95

158 Dagmar *Richter:* **Sprachenordnung und Minderheitenschutz im schweizerischen Bundesstaat.** 2005. LIV, 1315 Seiten. Geb. € 179,95

157 Thomas *Giegerich:* **Europäische Verfassung und deutsche Verfassung im transnationalen Konstitutionalisierungsprozeß: Wechselseitige Rezeption, konstitutionelle Evolution und föderale Verflechtung.** 2003. LXV, 1534 Seiten. Geb. € 199,95

156 Julia *Sommer:* **Verwaltungskooperation am Beispiel administrativer Informationsverfahren im Europäischen Umweltrecht.** 2003. XXX, 891 Seiten. Geb. € 129,95

155 Frank *Schorkopf:* **Die Maßnahmen der XIV EU-Mitgliedstaaten gegen Österreich – Möglichkeiten und Grenzen einer „streitbaren Demokratie" auf europäischer Ebene.** 2002. XIII, 217 Seiten. Geb. € 64,95

154 *Hanri Mostert:* **The Constitutional Protection and Regulation of Property and its Influence on the Reform of Private Law and Landownership in South Africa and Germany.** 2002. XXV, 643 Seiten. Geb. € 99,95 zzgl. landesüblicher MwSt.

153 Stefan *Ohlhoff:* **Methoden der Konfliktbewältigung bei grenzüberschreitenden Umweltproblemen im Wandel.** 2003. XXX, 651 Seiten. Geb. € 99,95

152 Hans-Joachim *Cremer,* Thomas *Giegerich,* Dagmar *Richter,* Andreas *Zimmermann* (Hrsg.): **Tradition und Weltoffenheit des Rechts. Festschrift für Helmut Steinberger.** 2002. XVI, 1483 Seiten. Geb. € 199,–

151 Nico *Krisch:* **Selbstverteidigung und kollektive Sicherheit.** 2001. VIII, 449 Seiten. Geb. € 84,95

150 Beate *Schulte zu Sodingen:* **Der völkerrechtliche Schutz der Wälder: nationale Souveränität, multilaterale Schutzkonzepte und unilaterale Regelungsansätze.** 2002. XXXI, 575 Seiten. Geb. € 99,95

149 Mahendra *Singh:* **German Administrative Law in Common Law Perspective.** 2001. XXXI, 377 Seiten. Geb. € 79,95 zzgl. landesüblicher MwSt.

148 Utz *Remlinger:* **Die Einwirkung des Gemeinschaftsrechts auf die Rückabwicklung rechtswidriger Beihilfeverhältnisse.** 2001. XXVI, 393 Seiten. Geb. € 84,95

147 *Dagmar Patricia Stroh:* **Die nationale Zusammenarbeit mit den Internationalen Straftribunalen für das ehemalige Jugoslawien und für Ruanda.** 2002. XXVII, 395 Seiten. Geb. € 84,95

146 Rainer *Grote,* Thilo *Marauhn* (Hrsg.): **Religionsfreiheit zwischen individueller Selbstbestimmung, Minderheitenschutz und Staatskirchenrecht – Völker- und verfassungsrechtliche Perspektiven.** 2001. VIII, 632 Seiten. Geb. € 99,95

MIX
Papier aus verantwortungsvollen Quellen
Paper from responsible sources
FSC® C105338

If you have any concerns about our products,
you can contact us on
ProductSafety@springernature.com

In case Publisher is established outside the EU,
the EU authorized representative is:
Springer Nature Customer Service Center GmbH
Europaplatz 3, 69115 Heidelberg, Germany

Printed by Libri Plureos GmbH
in Hamburg, Germany